Yahwism under the Achaemenid Empire

Beihefte zur Zeitschrift für die alttestamentliche Wissenschaft

Volume 548

Yahwism under the Achaemenid Empire

Professor Shaul Shaked in Memoriam

Edited by
Gad Barnea and Reinhard G. Kratz

DE GRUYTER

ISBN 978-3-11-101609-2
e-ISBN (PDF) 978-3-11-101863-8
e-ISBN (EPUB) 978-3-11-101913-0
ISSN 0934-2575
DOI https://doi.org/10.1515/9783111018638

Library of Congress Control Number: 2024937145

Bibliographic information published by the Deutsche Nationalbibliothek
The Deutsche Nationalbibliothek lists this publication in the Deutsche Nationalbibliografie; detailed bibliographic data are available on the internet at http://dnb.dnb.de.

The book is published open access at www.degruyter.com.
Typesetting: Meta Systems Publishing & Printservices GmbH, Wustermark
Printing and binding: CPI books GmbH, Leck

www.degruyter.com

FSC www.fsc.org MIX Papier | Fördert gute Waldnutzung FSC® C083411

Prof. Shaul Shaked (1933–2021)

Preface

This book contains the fruit of a three-day international symposium – held in memory of the late Prof. Shaul Shaked – in Dec. 2022 at the university of Haifa. Prof. Shaked (05 March 1933–27 October 2021) was born in Debrecen, Hungary in 1933 and migrated with his family to Palestine one year later. His studies in secondary school in Haifa under the renowned Islamicist scholar Meir J. Kister led to him pursuing academic studies in Arabic Language and Literature and Semitic Philology at the Hebrew University in Jerusalem where he earned his BA in 1955 and his MA in Arabic Language and Literature and Comparative Religion in 1960. He continued and pursued his PhD in the School of Oriental and African Studies (SOAS) in London – first under Walter Bruno Henning and then with Mary Boyce – which he completed in 1964. Following his PhD, Shaked returned to the Hebrew University in Jeruslaem and taught there until his retirement in 2001. His memory lives on in the minds of his many students, colleagues, and friends remember him as a ground-breaking and generous scholar, an out-of-the-box thinker and a permanently curious and productive mind. He has been a member of the Israel Academy of Sciences and Humanities since 1986.

The field of Iranian studies in general and of Jewish-Iranian connections in antiquity in particular owes a tremendeous debt to Prof. Shaked's scholarship over his erudite articles covering every period – from the Achaemenid era through Elephantine, Qumran, and Persepolis, to the Parthian and Sassanian empires and from ostraca and papyri to amulets and magic bowls. Shaked published a series of volumes from 1982 to 2019 under the title *Irano-Judaica: Studies Relating to Jewish Contacts with Persian Culture Throughout the Ages* and organized a series of conferences on this topic. His final *magnum opus*, which unfortunately he did not live to see through, is the Middle Persian Dictionary Project (MPDP) – a pioneering Digital Humanities project marrying a vast corpus on textual data with sophisticated technology. It is in the spirit of Prof. Shaked's scholarship, his vision and his collaborative and innovative approach that the 2022 conference as well as this book were concieved. May they be a worthy contribution to his memory.

The contributions to this book study the touchpoints between Yahwistic communities throughout the Achaemenid empire and the Iranian attributes of the empire that ruled over them for about two centuries. This is arguably the most formative period in the development, redaction and composition of some of the most central texts within the Jewish canon. However, there has historically been too little dialogue between scholars of Achaemenid history and Iranian linguistics and those of Jewish history, the Bible and archeology. To respond to these lacunae, both the conference and the present book take a fundamentally interdisciplinary

https://doi.org/10.1515/9783111018638-202

approach. They bring together scholars of Achaemenid history, literature and religion, Iranian linguistics, historians of the Ancient Near East, archeologists, biblical scholars and Semiticists – and encourage dialogue and cross-fertilization between these fields. The goal is to better understand the interchange of ideas, expressions and concepts as well as the experience of historical events between Yahwists and the empire that ruled over them for over two centuries. All the lectures from the conference were video-recorded and streamed live during conference and are available at the conference's YouTube channel (https://www.youtube.com/@yahwistichistory) which makes for an excellent companion to the present book.

The Yahwistic colony on the island of Elephantine at the Nile's first cataract, facing modern-day Aswan (ancient Syene) during the Achaemenid period, is central in one way or another to almost all of the studies presented in this book. This community has left us the most extensive and varied corpus of documents documenting Yahwistic daily life from that period. It is from these documents that we can learn about cultic practices, administration, language and forms of expression, historical events, communication with Yehud and Samaria as well as with imperial authorities and the many ethnic groups that lived in close proximity to them.

Since many of the articles are, by design, interdisciplinary, and combine several fields together, this book is not organized according to subject matter, but alphabetically. The first contribution, by Gad Barnea, offers a new and detailed analysis of P. Berlin 13464 which is famously known as the "Passover papyrus." Barnea presents a detailed epigraphic study of the papyrus, including the history of its previous publications and suggests that since there is no hint of a Passover or a feast of Maṣṣot being known and observed prior to the Hellenistic period, another cultic observance could fit the description better. This, according to Barnea, is the Zoroastrian *yasna* – specifically, the Haoma-drinking ritual intended to purify those who partake in it. Unlike the Passover or the Maṣṣot festival, this ritual is well documented in the Achaemenid period and the cultic assimilation of the Yahwists with Achaemenid-Zoroastrianism was so strong that they had an *'atrwdn* – a Zoroastrian fire-altar – in their temple to Yhw.

Moving from Elephantine to Samaria, Diana Edelman presents a comprehensive study of the archeology and cultic profile of the sacred structures in that Achaemenid Province – both at the city of Samaria and at Mt. Gerizim – the development of which she traces from a possible Iron Age IIC date to Hellenistic times. She offers two options for which character of the deity Yhwh was honored in Samaria: Yhwh Shomron, with or without his Asherah, and Yhwh Elohim and notes that both have implications for the composition of the Pentateuch. Finally, she makes the suggestion that the governor of Samaria in the Achaemenid period, Sanballat the Harranite, may have been directly involved in the commissioning of Pentateuch. His epithet refers to the city of Harran, which figures multiple times in the patriarchal origin stories of Abraham and Jacob but only three times elsewhere in the Hebrew Bible.

Back at Elephantine, Margaretha Folmer's contribution studies words of Persian and Egyptian origin (classified either as loanwords or as context switching) in documents written by Yahwists who lived on Elephantine or who were writing from other places in Egypt to family members in Elephantine. In both cases, she shows an accelerating use of the adopted terms from the second half of the fifth century BCE towards the end of that century. It is not surprising that loanwords tend to be more commonly found in official correspondence but are practically absent from the private letters and ostraca. Her conclusion is that the variety of Aramaic spoken by the Elephantine Yahwists was not deeply influenced by Old Persian vocabulary. Greater language familiarity can be detected with regards to Egyptian language "code-switching." the scribes of the Yahwistic community were familiar enough with the Egyptian terms used to analyse the them grammatically and syntactically – which can probably serve as an indication that they possessed an intimate familiarity with the Egyptian language.

In the fourth contribution, Benedikt Hensel looks at Yahwism in Idumea during the Persian Period. He looks at archeological, epigraphic and biblical sources and shows that, much like other parts of the Achaemenid empire, Idumea during that period hosted a variety of ethnicities. However, the Yahwists living there formed the second largest group. That said, Hensel underlines the existence of multiple Yahwisms in the Persian period from which, according to Hensel, early Judaism emerged.

Moving from the Idumeans to the Samarian diaspora in Egypt, Tawny Holm presents her work on Samarians in P. Amherst 63. Only one passage in this papyrus mentions Samaria and Samarians explicitly (the Samarian-Judean arrival poem in xvii 1–6), however, clear northern traits are found in some of the hymns in this document dedicated to the Yahwistic deity Yahō/Adonay. Several of these hymns demonstrate that Yahō may be identified with the Aramean deity Bethel while retaining his superior position relative to all the gods, including Baʕal. The papyrus also serves as a witness to the close – even familial – relations between Judeans and Samarians and possibly hints at both groups seeking refuge in a foreign land. Probably in Egypt.

Itamar Kislev delves into the Hebrew Bible – specifically the so-called "Priestly Source" (P), in a quest to find evidence for influence of the Achaemenid Zoroastrian cultic fire. Kislev noted six interpolations of differing levels of certainty relating to the sanctity of the fire in these sources such as the commandment to maintain a perpetual fire on the altar, the first being seen as coming from Yhwh and, as such, being viewed as "divine," as opposed to "alien fire," which is strictly prohibited. His analysis points to these text being Persian-period interpolations and he also suggests that they occurred very late in that period – consistent with the assumed dating of the development of the Achaemenid fire temples.

Staying in the realm of cultic practices, Ingo Kottsieper investigates the changes in the nomenclature of the divine name *Yhh* (יהה) and *Yhw* (יהו) at Elephantineas well as the use of the terms *Ṣb't* (צבאת) and *Mr' Hšmy'* (מרא השמיא). Through this evolution, he posits that the community initially maintained the traditions it brought with it from Palestine, but started developing other naming conventions in the second half of the fifth century BCE. Within this latter period, he sees the designation of the community as *Ḥyl' Yhwdy'* (חילא יהודיא) – first recorded in 420–419 BCE – and its aftermath, as a significant event leading to a new terminology and ethnic characteristics.

Returning to biblical traditions, Reinhard Kratz ponders the place of "biblical" Yahwism in the Persian period comparing it with Yahwism found in epigraphic sources of the time. The point is mainly methodological and conceptual – calling for a more critical approach to the study of Yahwism during that period, underlining the importance of giving precedence to the archaeological and epigraphic findings for the historical reconstruction of the history of Judaism and Yahwism in Achaemenid times and using the results as a foundation for everything else, subordinating the biblical sources to this blueprint. Specifically, he notes that the particular brand and characteristics of Yahwism found in the Hebrew Bible are found nowhere in the epigraphic sources of the period and thus must have been very limited in their adoption. The "biblical" brand only became popularized in later periods – especially under the Hasmoneans.

Archeologist Oded Lipschits looks at life among the ruins of Jerusalem in the Persian period and its interpretation. The ruins served as a "landscape of memory" wherein the people lived surrounded by vestiges of past glories that are to be reanimated. Two schools of thought emerged in this situation: those who wanted to rebuild at the earliest opportunity and those who waited for a divine signal prior to doing so. This can, for example, be detected in the prophecy of Ezekiel (36:10, 33–38) who considers the ruins as evidence of Yhwh's power and their potential restoration as dependent on the purification of sins, the deity's forgiveness, and the rebuilding of the land that will come only at the appointed time. Thus the ruins among which the small populace of Jerusalem lived, served also as a backdrop for theological contemplation.

James D. Moore, focuses on the administration of cult at Elephantine and specifically on the role of its temple. His analysis of the data shows that the temple of Yhw seems to have been more than a cultic center. It was also center of administration – as was the case across the ancient Near East, and as was expected by the Achaemenid overseers. It thus would have served principally as an economic hub for the community – which, according to Moore, was, in fact, its primary role, over and above the cultic. It would also have served in a judicial capacity as a community court.

Offering an Iranist perspective, Antonio Panaino proposes a new study of Cyrus as a Messiah – seen in its ancient Iranian context and viewing its representation in the Hebrew Bible and the New Testament as a "Theology of Power." This is supported through various later traditions that reflect the connection between Cyrus and Jesus as *personae sacrae*: the legendary view of Cyrus serving as a model for representing Jesus of Nazareth as the Christ; traditions that present the prediction, made by Zoroaster himself, about the birth of Jesus; the miraculous birth of the three posthumous sons of the Iranian prophet, the last of whom, i.e., the *Saošiiaṇt-* (in Pahlavi *Sōšyans*) was expected to resurrect the dead. Panaino shows that late antiquity Jews and Christians had used the image of Cyrus in sometimes opposing ways.

Laurie Pearce treats the question of Ezra's ban on marriages with foreign wives from the perspective of Babylonia in the Achaemenid period. She provides a review of examples from that region and shows that concerns regarding the administration of marriage both in Ezra's account and in Babylonia share a background of considerations of regulating marriage, divorce, and inheritance. She concludes that the specifically Jewish marriage ban promulgated by Ezra can best be understood not as a unique event in the region at the time, but as one example out of many cases of reacting to political and economic change in the early to mid-fifth century BCE.

Bezalel Porten traces the evolution of variants of Yawhistic names across different communities and focuses specifically on the form *Yama* found in the Babylonian sources as compared to the more expected forms found at Elephantine and the Bible. He concludes that the names served as identity markers for the Yahwistic communities, which maintained these names from generation to generation.

Returning to the archeological perspective, Michael Shenkar looks at the origin of the Fire-Temples and the phenomenon of the "ever burning fire" within a closed structure in the Achaemenid empire. While fire played a central role in Iranian cult for generations prior to the that period, the evidence for a constantly sustained fire at that time is limited – although it cannot be excluded. Shenkar posits that the closed temple model developed in the Iranian world only after the Macedonian conquest.

Konrad Schmid brings us back to the Hebrew Bible and studies the theory of the Persian imperial authorization of local regulations and the Torah as a force that contributed to its formation from D and P sources. The Pentateuch, according to Schmid, reflects reactions to Achaemenid rule that are hard to reconcile – on one hand it implicitly represents that era as the "end of history," while simultaneously contesting this characterization, showing that history itself could very well lead to other conclusions.

Remaining in the Pentateuch, Stefan Schorch looks at its transmission in the Persian period – specifically in its Samaritan variant. He notes that it is this version which clearly reflects the elaboration of the Pentateuchal text both as a closed text and as an open text (specifically with regards to Deuteronomy). Thus, the transmission of the text in the Achaemenid period should primarily be understood as that of a "cluster text" rather than that of a unified text.

Jason Silverman examines Yahwism as a "religious field" during the Achaemenid era by using Bourdieu's theoretical system. He analyzes such concepts as religious capital and supernatural social capital, which prove useful in understanding internal evolution within a cultic system (e.g., the introduction of a new feast).

Karel van der Toorn looks at the expressions *dātu* (or *dātu ša šarri*) in the Achaemenid period – expressions which refer to a written compendium containing royal decisions that must be followed without alteration. This concept, he shows, is fundamentally different from that found in the Torah. He points out the evolution in the sense of the word Torah – from "instruction, teaching" to, in the Persian period, something more similar to a law code, which is the way in which it was understood by the leadership of the province Yehud.

Finally, Ran Zadok's contribution, which closes the book looks at evidence for Israelites (in the broad sense of the term) in the Iranian sphere. While evidence is scarce to non-existent prior to the Achaemenid period, the area surrounding Babylon at the time became the hotbed of a Judeo-Iranian interaction. Zadok complements his scholarship with a look at the the Iranian "Age of Empies" in general, including the Parthian and Sasanian eras and a vast amount of supporting data. The article is accompanied by an alphabetical list and a lengthy appendix meticulously analyzing the names found in the various sources across this long period.

We wish to thank the sponsors of the original conference for their support which made the entire venture possible: The Sir Isaac Wolfson Chair of Jewish Thought, University of Haifa, the faculty of Humanities at the University of Haifa, the Joseph & Racheline Barda Chair for the Study and Research of Jewish Heritage in Egypt, the Israeli Association for the Study of Religions (IASR), and the Haifa Laboratory for Religious Studies. Above all, we wish to thank the Theological Faculty of the Georg-August-University of Göttingen for its generosity in sponsoring the Open Access availability of this book.

A special thankful recognition goes to the contributors for their important studies which they share in this volume. Moreover, we wish to thank Yoel Halevi and Moshe Diengott for their support during the conference and to the Hadarim center for hosting it.

Haifa and Göttingen, March 2024 Gad Barnea and Reinhard G. Kratz

Table of Contents

Gad Barnea

P. Berlin 13464, Yahwism and Achaemenid Zoroastrianism at Elephantine

1 The Cultic Profile of the Elephantine Yahwists

The island of Elephantine, facing modern-day Aswan (historical Syene) on the first cataract of the Nile, hosted a remarkable settlement of migrants from the Levant during the late-Saite and Achaemenid periods. The founders of this community had originally arrived at the Syene area from Palestine, most probably in the middle of the sixth century BCE, still under the rule of the Egyptian twenty-sixth dynasty.[1] Their chief ethnic deity was *Yhw(h)* – a deity known also from the Hebrew Bible and a number of ancient inscriptions.[2] According to their own account, prior to the conquest of Egypt by Persian king Cambyses in 526 BCE,[3] their forefathers had already built a full-fledged temple to this deity on this important and already millennia-old Egyptian cultic center. The temple was complete with priests (and priestesses),[4] sacrificial offerings, and an altar. Some of the leaders of this temple-based community were referred to as "priests of *Yhw*" (כהניא זי יהו).[5] They expended significant resources and a lot of effort building a temple for their deity,[6] claimed that he dwells therein,[7] referred to leading members of the community – both male and female – as "servant of *Yhw*" (לחן/ה זי יהו),[8] had theophoric names based on his and raised funds for his service.[9] One of the most striking aspects of the Elephantine Yahwists' cult is its active syncretism,[10]

1 Barnea, "Migration of the Elephantine Yahwists." For different views on the arrival of the Yahwists to the island, see Kahn, "The Date of the Arrival," and Kottsieper, "From יהה צבאת to יהו מרא שמיא: Aspects of religious development on Elephantine," in this volume.
2 For recent studies on early records of the deity *Yhwh*, see van Oorschot and Witte, *Origins of Yahwism*.
3 Quack, "persischen Eroberung Ägyptens."
4 Barnea, "Justice at the House of Yhw(h)."
5 TAD A4 3: 1.
6 TAD A4.7: 9–11.
7 TAD B3.12: 2.
8 E.g., TAD B3.12.
9 TAD C3.15; See analysis in Barnea, "*Interpretatio Ivdaica*," esp. pp. 369–372.
10 The term "syncretism" is admittedly problematic, but no satisfactory alternative has been offered. In the context of this article, I use it broadly and non-polemically with no negative implications to merely indicate a symbiosis of cultic ideas, practices and expressions. See discus-

Gad Barnea, University of Haifa, Israel

https://doi.org/10.1515/9783111018638-001

showing a dynamic dialogue with Egyptian, Levantine and Achaemenid Zoroastrian (AZ) features.[11] The footprint of AZ within this community has been relatively little studied, but its impact on its cultic life is palpable through its textual sources – including the famous P. Berlin 13464, also known as the "Passover papyrus."

2 AZ Features at Elephantine: An Overview

It is important to underline at the outset, that the Achaemenid empire was, by far, the largest the world has ever seen up to that point and the first that can objectively be defined as a super-power. Through the Achaemenid royal inscriptions, copies of which were sent to all corners of the empire and were widely read,[12] imperial ideology – including its conceptions of the divine, aspects such as the proper forms of worship and even ethics – was disseminated far and wide, with long-lasting effects.[13] The promulgation of Achaemenid concepts are known to have impacted pretty much all cultures that came into contact with its sphere of influence. Its impact on the Hellenic civilization was profound,[14] as was its influence on Egyptian law[15] and the Hebrew Bible.[16] I have devoted an article elsewhere to an in-depth analysis of AZ cultic features among the Yahwists at Elephantine,[17] which I will presently summarize in order to provide the contextual setting for the study of P. Berlin 13464.

---

sion in Jones, *Encyclopedia of Religion*, 8926–8938 (esp. see the entry entitled "Syncretism [Further Considerations]," pp. 8934–8938).

11 Barnea, "*Interpretatio Ivdaica.*" See also Granerød, "YHW the God of Heaven," and Kratz, "Where to put 'Biblical' Yahwism in Achaemenid Times?," in this volume. For a broader perspective regarding the general contours of Zoroastrianism in the Achaemenid period from an archeological perspective, see Shenkar. "The 'Eternal Fire', Achaemenid Zoroastrianism and the Origin of the Fire-Temples," in this volume.

12 A copy of the Behistun inscription (DB) was found at Elephantine. See Greenfield and Porten, *Bisitun inscription.* In the Behistun inscription itself Darius I claims that "[a]fterwards, this inscription was sent by me everywhere among the provinces; the people universally were pleased." (DB §70).

13 For example, a paraphrase of a passage from the Behistun inscription with a court-legend constructed around it was also found in Qumran, see Barnea, *4Q550*. See also Kratz, "Aḥiqar and Bisitun," 301–22.

14 See Duchesne-Guillemin, "Greece iii."

15 Lippert, "codes de lois en Égypte."

16 See several treatments in this volume: Kislev, "The Cultic Fire in the Priestly Source," Kratz, "Where to put 'Biblical' Yahwism in Achaemenid Times?," and Schmid, "The End of History and the Ends of History: Assessing the Political-Theological Status of the Achaemenid Empire in Persian Period Judaism." See also Kratz, "Isaiah and the Persians."

17 Barnea, "Achaemenid Zoroastrian Echoes."

2.1 The Aswan Stele

A damaged middle-part of a larger red sandstone stele was found in Aswan. It was dedicated on June, 458 BCE[18] and contained the following text:

> This *brzmdn'*, ○○*d/rn*[ ] commander of the garrison of Syene built in the month of Siwan, that is Meḥir, in year seven year of Artaxerxes the King. ○○*wrnḥty* [the/to/of] God, peace.[19]

For the sake of this paper, I will focus solely on the term *brzmdn'* found in this inscription.[20] This Indo-Aryan term – found here transliterated into Aramaic – is almost certainly related to the term *ạrtāčā bạrzmaniy* found in Xerxes I's XPh inscription – i.e., *bạrzman* with a suffix of place (-*dan*).[21] The term *ạrtāčā bạrzmaniy* is complex but its basic meaning is: "(and) the Order[YAZATA] characterized by the exaltation[RITE]."[22] This syntagm, as it is found in XPh, is governed by the verb *yad-* "to worship" and defines the character by which A^h*uramazdā* and *Artā* (the Order[YAZATA]) are to be worshipped – which was now the imperially sanctioned form of worship according to AZ principles. The stele is dated to June 6–13, 458 BCE – i.e., the seventh year of Artaxerxes I,[23] Xerxes I's son. Since this

---

18 First published by de Vogüé, "Inscription araméenne." Some scholars, starting with Lemaire ("Recherches d'épigraphie araméenne"), have suggested a much later dating on the assumption that the broken text before "god" אלהא must refer to a deity, which was interpreted as an Egyptian god, and therefore associated with a period immediately after the end of the first Achaemenid occupation of Egypt. I presented elsewhere a detailed analysis of why this cannot be a Divine Name (DN) and why this theory should be disregarded, see Barnea, "*ṛtāčā brzmniy*."
19 My translation. See detailed analysis in Barnea, "Achaemenid Zoroastrian Echoes."
20 Walter Hinz (*ASN*, 67) follows Bogoliubov ("An Aramaic inscription") in understanding this term as a "house of rites, temple," as does Tavernier (*Iranica*, 438), which is certainly correct. The etymological connection with *brazmaniya* (or *barzm-*), referring to the *barǝsman-*, the bundle of twigs used by the Zoroastrian priests in their liturgy, proposed by Kent ("Old Persian artāčā brazmaniya"), is compelling. However, Hinz rightly observes that the Aswan stele clearly states that it refers to a building that was "built" – defining its use. Hence its interpretation as a "house of rites, temple," and not merely a "Barsom-Behälter," should be preferred. These are not mutually exclusive, however, and the reference is probably a "place of Barsom rites (=*yasna*)." The Barsom was "an essential requisite in the liturgical service of the Yasna," cf. Kanga, "BARSOM."
21 Barnea, "*ạrtāčā bạrzmaniy*."
22 For a detailed analysis of this expression and translation, see Barnea, "*ạrtāčā bạrzmaniy*." This term, spelled a-r-θ-a-c-a : b-r-z-m-n-i-y was recently published in a newly discovered Old Persian version of Artaxerxes II's A²se inscription, showing that this concept was still promulgated during his reign (ca. 404–358 BCE). See Fattori. "Miscellanea Epigraphica Susiana."
23 This inscription is dated to the months of Sivan/Meḥir (Babylonian and Egyptian calendars respectively) of the seventh year of Artaxerxes. This must refer to Artaxerxes I, since by the seventh year of Artaxerxes II, Elephantine – and, indeed, all of Egypt was already back under Egyptian rule. Therefore, this inscription is to be dated to 458 BCE and the overlapping of the

brzmdn' is described as having been "built," it indicates that a cultic structure, set up according to the AZ concept of *bạrzman* was functioning at Syene already at the middle of the fifth century BCE. Such a place would presumably include the presence of *Maguš*-priests,[24] possibly also a fire-altar and provisions for the sacred drink *haoma* and other necessities.

2.2 Magi

The presence of Magi – in contact with the Yahwists at Elephantine – is, in fact, documented on a legal papyrus from Oct. 30, 434 BCE,[25] in which a house is bequeathed to a certain woman and where a previous real-estate transaction between Caspians with Iranian names and a Yahwistic family is recorded. These Magi serve as witnesses to the transaction. They have names that reflect Mazdean/Indo-Iranian cultic roots – Mithrasarah and Tāta.[26] They lived in proximity to the Yahwists and seem to have been intimate enough with them to serve as witnesses for a relatively mundane property transaction. Several additional names with similar cultic features appear in the Elephantine onomasticon, in various forms of association with Yahwists.[27] These names are important as they reflect AZ concepts that were central in Achaemenid times and show that they were known in Egypt at the time. They include *Artā* (Av. Aša "(cosmic) truth/order"); *Āter* (also *Āçi*): the Sacred Fire; *Baga*: "The god(s)"; *Fravarti*: a Zoroastrian term for the spirit of protection, the abode of an individual's soul; *Haoma*: *Yazd* Haoma or the AZ ritual drink; *(A^hura)Mazdā*: "(Lord) Wisdom" Head of the pantheon; *Miθra*: one of the chief deities; *Spənta*, "bountiful, holy," used to describe the *Aməša Spəṇta* divinities – one of which, *Ārmaiti*, is also used in a theophoric personal name (PN) at Elephantine; *(A)yaza-*: *yaza-*, the Avestan concept of god-worship and sacrifices to the gods; *Artābarzana*: recorded here only as a patronymic. This last PN is probably a *Zitatname* of the concept behind

Babylonian and Egyptian calendars allows to narrow it down even further to June 6–13, 458 BCE. See explanation in TAD, vol 4, 234.

24 It is interesting to note that Magi are documented to have had administrative (but not cultic) oversight over temples in the Achaemenid period. See Dandamayev, "The Ebabbar Temple."

25 "25th of Tishri, that is the 25th day of the month of Epiph, year 31 of King Artaxerxes." TAD B3.5:1.

26 I analyze these names in Barnea, "Achaemenid Zoroastrian Echoes."

27 These names and their connection with Yahwists are analyzed in Barnea, "Achaemenid Zoroastrian Echoes."

ạrtācā bạrzmaniy found in XPh (!),[28] which also featured on the Aswan Stele, as discussed above.[29]

2.3 The *ʾtrwdn*: Fire-Altar

However, the most striking sign of assimilation of AZ ritual elements documented among the Yahwists at Elephantine is the "fire altar," which they themselves describe as being associated with their temple. In one of the papyri documenting the events surrounding the destruction of the Yahwistic temple at Elephantine, offerings made to *Yhw* in the temple are mentioned with the loanword *ʾtrwdn* אתרודן – from the Persian *ātar*, "fire." This papyrus is dated to ca. 410 BCE.[30] This is often translated simplistically as "brazier."[31] However, there can be little doubt that this is an AZ technical cultic loanword into Aramaic – rooted in the Avestan *Atār* – the holy fire. There would be no need to resort to a technical Mazdean cultic term – especially when addressing what was probably an Iranian official – if the intent was to simply refer to a common fire container. If the Yahwists wanted to describe a fire-container without Mazdean connotations, they could have easily expressed this through something along the lines of the purely Aramaic *dwdʾ dnwrʾ* דודא דנורא or similar. The term *ʾtrwdn* is precisely the term used to this day for the Zoroastrian fire-altar – *Ātašdān*, except with in the older Avestan form, *Atār*, which is the expected Achaemenid usage.[32] The term appears in one of the accounts of the violence perpetrated against the Yahwistic temple during one of the incidents related to the Egyptian revolt. It is written on a single column on the verso and is badly preserved. Nevertheless, the key terms: offering *mnḥh*

28 As far as I could find, all known occurrences of this PN occur either after the reign of Xerxes, or in that of his father Darius I – but not earlier. The concept of *ạrtācā bạrzmaniy* – though first documented in XPh – might very well have originated already under Darius I. The PN is documented in ART §29 (misread as *Artā-bar-vana*) dated to Artaxerxes I and in Elamite in PF 1463, 2052, and PFNN 2200 as *Ir-da-bìr-za-na* (see Tavernier, *Iranica*, 293–294).

29 While some of these terms (e.g., *Baga*, *Ārmaiti* and *Miθra*) have a broader Indo-Iranian usage, several key terms are exclusively Avestan (i.e., Zoroastrian), such as *Mazdā*, *Spənta*, *Fravarti*, both parts of the name *Artābarzana* (artā + *bạrzman*), and the verb *yaza-*. In any case, the concepts behind these names – whether broadly shared among Iranic peoples or ristrictively among AZ practitioners – must have been familiar to the Elephantine Yahwists.

30 TAD 4.5:17, where it is translated simply as "brazier".

31 DNWSI, s. v. *ʾtrwdn*. Tavernier, *Iranica*, 461. DAÉ, 404 note o.

32 Note the "*-dan*" suffix here (denoting a "container," see Kent, *Old Persian*, 189) which is identical to the term used by the Elephantine Yahwists, as by modern Zoroastrians (آتشدان). For more information, see Boyce, "ĀTAŠDĀN." In any event, the use of this highly specialized term cannot be arbitrary, but points to a very specific AZ cultic term.

מנחה, *yhw* יהו the god, and the *ʾtrwdn* אתרודן. the fire-altar, are all mentioned within the same immediate context. I provide only the relevant text.

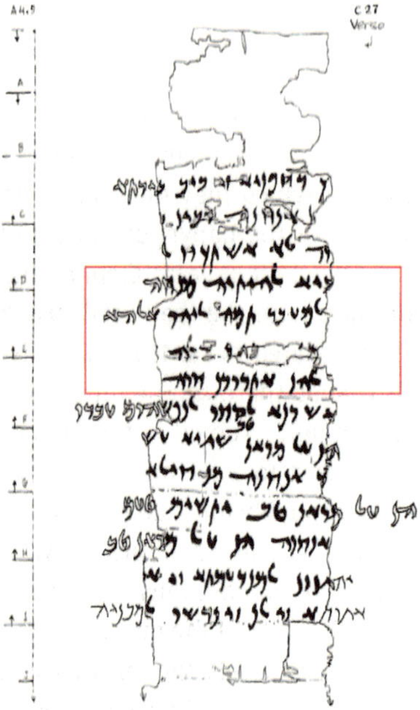

[........] יא להיתיה מנח]ה
[........] למעבד תמה ליהו א]להא
[........]מ.[...]בגו [.]לה
[........] להן אתרודן חדה

Fig. 1: © Porten and Yardeni. Used with permission. Image cropped with red rectangle added by the author.

Translation:
[........] to bring *mnḥ*[*h*
[........] to offer there to yhw the g[od
[........] in which ... [
[........] except for a/one fire-altar [...

The fact that this cultic technical term, *ʾtrwdn* אתרודן, is mentioned in the context of the damage wrought on the Yahwistic temple, an offering and the deity *Yhw* – makes it practically certain that this is a fire-container serving for ritual – i.e., a fire-altar – associated with the Yahwistic temple. It thus seems that the Yahwists at Elephantine maintained a Mazdean-inspired fire-altar that was linked with their temple and, as the text seems to suggest, with an offering – *mnḥh*[33] – made

33 As tempting as it is to consider the *ʾtrwdn* and the *mnḥh* offering as related – with the *ʾtrwdn* possibly being an "incense altar" (e.g., Lev 2:1–16), this is unlikely. As mentioned, the deliberate

to their ethnic deity, *Yhw*. Since this text deals with the damages inflicted upon the Yahwistic temple, the mention of a fire-altar within what appears to be a list of items damaged in the attack, would indicate that the fire-altar was physically within the *Yhw*-temple compound, which would also suggest that the temple to *Yhw* most probably had other features assimilated from AZ customs. Fire altars can be seen pictographically in several Achaemenid-era sources, such as a seal impression found at Persepolis showing a priest holding the barsom twigs in front of a fire altar,[34] as well as reliefs from Daskyleion in western Anatolia and Bünyan, which show officiants holding a barsom-twig in an AZ ritual.[35] The presence of a fire-altar in the *Yhw*-temple does not denote conversion and did not make the Yahwists Zoroastrian. Nothing of the sort would be required of them. It merely shows their allegiance to the imperial paradigm of purity and moral accountability, and demonstrates their loyalty to the king – being part of the "good creation." In the context of the then-reigning cultic worldview, there was no problem whatsoever for *Yhw* to be assimilated with *A*^{h}*uramazdā* – a process which is also reflected in the biblical text, especially in Deutro-Isaiah and Ezra.[36] Worship of a non-assimilated *A*^{h}*uramazdā* was expected only of Mazdeans – at least nominally.[37] Among other cults, however, as Philip Kreyenbroek explains, "Zoroastrianism may have been perceived as a progressive Iranian tradition, whose coexistence with local traditions was accepted as a matter of course."[38]

choice made by the Yahwists to use the cultic term *'trwdn* – whose AZ underpinnings could not have escaped their attention – rather than a purely Aramaic alternative such as *dwd' dnwr'* דודא דנורא (or simply *mdbḥ'* מדבחא) is significant. The AZ term *'trwdn* is not a common or intuitive choice and TAD 4.5 is actually its earliest documented instance. In fact, around the same time TAD 4.5 was written (using *'trwdn*), other documents mention a *mdbḥ'* in the temple of *Yhw* (TAD A4.7:26, 4.8:25) and another document mentions *mnḥh* with an altar on which it is specifically to be offered, but the term *mdbḥ'* (TAD A4.9:9–10) was used for this case. Moreover, an AZ fire-altar (*'trwdn*) is not an altar in the sense this term is generally understood. It is a fire holder for the purposes of veneration – nothing is offered on it or consumed by its fire. It must be kept pure – it cannot be used to "consume" an offering and cannot be confused with an incense altar. Using this pregnant cultic term for such a case would be entirely inappropriate. Regarding *mnḥh*, see Fabry and Weinfeld, "מִנְחָה" and on the topic of fire altars, see Garrison, "FIRE ALTARS."

34 Razmjou, "The Lan Ceremony."

35 Boyce, *A History of Zoroastrianism*, 200–209; Wiesehöfer, *Das antike Persien*, 32. On the cult of fire and fire altars in the Achaemenid period from an archeological perspective, see Shenkar "The 'Eternal Fire'," in this volume.

36 See Kratz, "Isaiah and the Persians," and Blenkinsopp, "Deutero-Isaiah and the Creator God," 20–25.

37 Kreyenbroek, "Zoroastrianism under the Achaemenians," 105.

38 Id. loc.

3 P. Berlin 13464

The papyrus catalogued as P. Berlin 13464 is better known as the "Passover letter." It was associated with this biblical feast and/or the feast of the unleavened bread (henceforth *maṣṣot*), since its *editio princeps* in 1911.[39] Sachau, who was the first to publish it, characterized this papyrus as "Sendschreiben betreffend das Passah-Fest" ("letter concerning the Passover festival"). He confesses to have relied upon Deut 16 and Exod 12 throughout his analysis and proposed restoration of the text, as does Ungnad, following in his footsteps.[40] Meyer, about a year later, considered it, more cautiously, to be related to the "Mazzenfest,"[41] while Anneler, that same year, insightfully took the more guarded route claiming that it "*wahrscheinlich* vom Mazzothfest handelt, da durchaus nichts auf das Passafest hindeutet."[42] These options, as I will discuss in more detail below, have often seemed to be a "Procrustean bed" of sorts since the contents of the text do not correspond to either one of these feasts beyond the date-range of Nisan 15–21 and the mention of yeast. Therefore, this highly important document, which has significant implications for the history of Yahwism in general and the biblical text in particular – requires an extra-careful study, and in so doing, it is critical to keep preconceptions based on the biblical text in check. The complex context in which the Yahwists lived – especially their documented intimate interactions with AZ cult and ideology – outlined above – must be taken into account.

3.1 Preconceptions in the Interpretation of P. Berlin 13464

It is important to underscore that, if this text did, in fact, deal with the biblical feasts of *psḥ* or *maṣṣot*, it would be the earliest extra-biblical and the only datable document to do so. These facts alone require extra caution to be taken in its analysis, since the nature of these feasts, their associated biblical references – or even their existence *as such* in the fifth century BCE, cannot be assumed *a priori*. As I will show below, the few mentions of *psḥʾ* as they are found at Elephantine accentuate this point since they do not correspond to any biblical version of the *psḥ*, but seem to refer to relatively minor, intimate, and stressful events – and

39 Sachau, *Aramäische Papyrus*, 36; Ungnad and Sachau, *Aramaische Papyrus aus Elephantine*, 13. Cf. also Cowley, *Aramaic papyri*, 60.
40 Ungnad and Sachau, *Aramaische Papyrus aus Elephantine*, 13.
41 Meyer, *Der Papyrusfund von Elephantine*, 91–97.
42 Anneler, *Geschichte der Juden*, 93 (emphasis added).

probably served in an apotropaic capacity.[43] The status of the *maṣṣot* feast at that point in time is even more nebulous since, unlike the *psḥ'*, it is recorded nowhere and the very word defining it – *mẓh* מצה– might even be of Greek origin (μάζα).[44] Therefore, the following analysis proposes a *tabula rasa* re-examination that preconceives of nothing regarding the level of adherence of this papyrus to the biblical text. In his discussion of the restoration of this text, Porten made the frank admission that "[i]f the papyrus has been restored with any degree of success it is only because its contents parallel several Biblical prescriptions."[45] I must, however, take issue with this premise which has very little in terms of scientific methodology to support it. Rather, I concur with Erasmus Gaß, who in 1999 asserted that "Methodisch erscheint es deshalb unstatthaft, die Lücken mit subjektiv beliebigen Sätzen aus dem Pentateuch oder den Targumen aufzufüllen," to which he later adds a maxim that should be adhered to not only in the case of P. Berlin 13464 but when one comes to analyze ancient texts in general: "Besser ein Text mit vielen Fragezeichen, als ein subjektiv gewonnener Text ohne erkennbaren Rückhalt an der Tradition, die den Text hervorgebracht hat."[46] As will be shown, the approach relying on Exodus and Deuteronomy has led to serious misreadings, to say the least, at the epigraphic level, even at the hands of cautious scholars who are otherwise consummate professionals and for whose work I have nothing but the highest respect. In parallel, since I have already declared that I will be reading P. Berlin 13464 in the context of AZ features, the same principles must be applied to the analysis that will be followed later in this paper. Care must be taken to define what can be proven via datable evidence to be known about AZ cult at the time this papyrus was authored. All features known from later Zoroastrian practice must be relegated to the realm of hypothesis.

As mentioned, preconceptions regarding this text already overshadowed its interpretation as dealing with the *psḥ* and/or *maṣṣot* festivals. It is, of course, to be

43 See Barnea, "Reading Berlin P. 10679".

44 The first to suggest this were Beer and Holtzmann, *Die Mischna*. For a detailed recent discussionsupporting this interpretation, see Kellermann, "מַצָּה." The general view in biblical scholarship deduces that the feast of *maṣṣot* reflects an older tradition (Exod 23:15 and Deut 16:16), based on certain terms used in its description (esp. the month of *abib*) and its agricultural features. However, this view relies exclusively on inference from the biblical text itself. There is simply no extra-biblical support for such a cultic tradition. No observance related to unleavened – or even *flat* – bread is known in the region and practically all cognate languages lack a specialized term for such a bread, which seems to be the reason why the Hebrew had to borrow a Greek term. Given this total lack of external support, the added use of *abib* may very well be an archaizing feature inserted by the redactor.

45 Porten, *Archives from Elephantine*, 128.

46 Gaß, "Der Passa-Papyrus," 56.

expected that for anyone raised in Jewish or Christian *milieux*, the date-range 15–21 of Nisan immediately connects to theses biblical feasts, especially given the fact that leaven is also mentioned in the context. This was certainly my initial intuition as well. In fact, this papyrus has never been read differently and the confidence in its general contours was, and still is, unshakable.[47] Cowley asserted that this document "is an edict of Darius ordering an observance of the feast of Unleavened Bread, and, if the proposed restoration is right, the Passover," continuing to claim that "[t]his can only mean either that the festivals in question were unknown in the colony, or that they had fallen into desuetude."[48] Vincent is just as adamant, stating that this papyrus "nous apporte la preuve qu'ils connaissaient également la fête de Pâque et qu'ils observaient les Azymes."[49] Rohermoser is rightly more reserved noting that "Bei TAD A4.1 handelt es sich mit größter Wahrscheinlichkeit um Vorschriften zur Begehung des Mazzotfestes, denn die angegebenen 7 Tage des Festes und die Erwähnung von Gesäuertem weisen darauf hin."[50] In any event, for all scholars thus far, the question is not *if* the ritual(s) prescribed in P. Berlin 13464 is the *psḥ* and/or *maṣṣot* feasts – but whether both are intended or just the *maṣṣot* feast, and by extension determining the date in which these feasts become "canonized." The assumption is either that they became standard around the promulgation of this "decree" or prior to it. The question of a different cultic context for this text – namely the possible AZ features found in it, never came up – not only because of Western Jewish or Christian preconceptions based on the bible, but also because the scholars studying it had no (or very limited) knowledge of Indo-Iranian cult, rites and scriptures.

3.2 Misalignments with the Biblical Passover or the Feast of Maṣṣot

Serious difficulties have often been recognized as standing in the way of the Passover / Maṣṣot interpretation of P. Berlin 13464. There are, in fact, important misalignments between the contents of this papyrus – as it is preserved in the text that has come down to us – and the biblical *psḥ* and/or *maṣṣot*:

47 For example, the recent Museum edition of this papyrus (from the ERC-Project ELEPHANTINE), still retains the these conjectural reconstructions: https://elephantine.smb.museum/objects/object.php?o=100463.

48 Cowley, *Aramaic papyri*, xxiv.

49 Vincent, *La religion des Judeo-Arameens*, 234.

50 Rohrmoser, *Götter, Tempel und Kult*, 258.

- The key term: *Psḥ'*, is not mentioned in P. Berlin 13464.
- There is nothing related to בין הערביים ("between the evenings," Exod 12:6), but rather a מערב שמשא ("setting of the sun") – which is not synonymous.
- The context does not fit any known biblical description of the feast: there are no sacrifices, no gathering of the people, no communal consumption of the sacrifice, etc.
- The type of food *to be eaten* is nowhere mentioned. There is no מצה – or its Aramaic cognate פטיר(א). In contrast, the biblical feast of the Maṣṣot stresses a commandment: שִׁבְעַת יָמִים מַצּוֹת תֹּאכֵלוּ ("Seven days you shall eat unleavened bread," Exod 12:15). It would thus be a misnomer to refer to this observance as a "Feast of Maṣṣot".
- As will be demonstrated paleographically below, the document contains *no clear prohibition of any kind* – neither regarding the drink to be consumed nor regarding yeast/leaven.
- Significantly, there is *no hint of this observation repeating annually* and there is no record of this ceremony taking place ever again. This is therefore probably not an annually recurring event and thus does not fit the definition of a *festival.* Nothing like a לְדֹרֹתֵיכֶם חֻקַּת עוֹלָם ("throughout your generations, a statute forever," Exod 12:14) is intimated in the text.

Realizing the problems posed by the succinctness of the document and that the Elephantine Yahwists seem to be already familiar with at least some of its stipulations (such as "purity"), several scholars have suggested that this document might have served as a response to the Yahwists seeking instructions regarding the calendrical organization of time[51] or how to observe the biblical rites.[52] These notions should also be discarded since there is no hint in the preserved text that it is a response to a previous question nor to any other Yahwistic community or central authority with which a calendar is to be synchronized – and, as noted, there is no hint of this ever having to be repeated again. Thus, the only elements of which we can be certain that the ceremony described in P. Berlin 13464 shares with the feast of *maṣṣot* are the date range: 15–21 Nisan, and the mention (but *no clear prohibition!*) of yeast/leaven. Is this enough to judge that we are dealing with the feasts of *psḥ* and/or *maṣṣot*?

---

51 Becking, *Identity in Persian Egypt*, 28. See also Granerød, *Dimensions of Yahwism*, 177. However, there are no calendrical references (i.e. recurrences) as such in the document. There is only a very specific day range: 15–21 Nisan. There are also no references to other Yahwistic communities with whom to synchronize a calendar, no mention of a central authority and no other dates.

52 Korpel, "Disillusion among Jews," 148.

3.3 Description (with Images)

P. Berlin 13464 was originally about 28 cm wide by 10.5 cm high with twelve lines for text, three of which are left empty.[53] Six lines are perpendicular to the fibers on the recto, parallel to the joins; on the verso, there are three lines of text (see explanation below) followed by two *vacat* lines and one line containing the external address parallel to the fibers.[54]

Fig. 2: P. Berlin 13464 recto (CC-BY-NC-SA).

53 For more on the restoration of the precise dimensions of the papyrus, see Porten, "The Aramaic 'Passover Papyrus'."
54 Information taken from Porten, *The Elephantine Papyri in English*, 125. I was unable to verify this from the images I had access to.

Fig. 3: P. Berlin 13464 verso (CC-BY-NC-SA).

3.4 Text

RECTO

upper margin

1. [אל אחי י]דניה וכנותה ח[ילא]יהודיא אחוכמ חננ[י]ה שלמ אחי אלהיא[ישאלו . .]

2. [בכל עדנ]וכעת שנתא זא שנת /VV/ דריוהוש מלכא מנ מלכא שליח על ארש[מ. . .]

3. [. . . . .]יא כעת אנתמ כנ מנו ארבׄ[. . .]

4. [. . . . .]דו ומנ יומר/VV/ עד יומד\ ל[. . . . . .]

5. [. . . . .]דכינ הוו ואזדהרו עבידה א[. . . . .]

6. [. . . . .]ל תשתו וכל מנדעמ זי חמיר א[. . .]

VERSO

upper margin

7. [. . . . .]מערב שמשא עד יומ ד\ לניס[נ . . .]

8. [. . . . .]עלו בתוניכמ וחתמו בינ יומיא[. .]

9. [. . . . . .ד]יא [

10.

11.

12. [. . . . .] אחי ידניה וכנותה חילא יהודיא אחוכמ חנניה בׄ[. . . . .]

3.5 Translation

The following is an entirely new translation of P. Berlin 13464. It is made according to the results of the analysis provided below and aims to offer as precise a translation as possible. The terms *ḥyl'* and *Yhwdy'* require a discussion that goes beyond the scope of this paper and are therefore not translated, but are transliterated "as is."

3.5.1 Translation Conventions

- [text within square brackets] = reconstructed text with high degree of certainty.
- superscript = facilitates reading in English (not part of the text).
- *text in italics* = transliterated word.
- TEXT IN SMALL CAPS = parts of words whose reconstruction is uncertain.
- ⌜text within quarter-brackets . . .⌝ = probable text, but not certain.
- PN's are transliterated.

In situations where there can be more than one possible translation, I chose the one that is most likely. The choice logic will be explained in context in the philological notes below.

3.5.2 Translated Text

1. [To my brothers] *Ydnyh* and his colleagues, *ḥyl' Yhwdy'*, your brother *Ḥnnyh*. The peace of my brothers may the gods [seek after].
2. [at all times.] And now, this year, year 5 of King *Drywhwš*, something/someone has been sent from the king to *Ạršā*[ma . . .].
3. [. . . . .]Y'. Now, you, so shall you appoint, fou⌜r . . .⌝
4. [. . . . .]DW. And from day 15 to day 21 of [. . . .]
5. [. . . . .] pure you shall be and beware. Work [. . .]
6. [. . . . .]L you shall drink, and anything of leaven ⌜. . . ⌝
7. [. . . . .] sun-set until day 21 of Nisa⌜n . . .⌝
8. [. . . . .]LW in your chambers and seal between the days [. .]
9. [. . . . .]DY'

10.–11. Empty

12. [. . . To] my brothers *Ydnyh* and his colleagues, *ḥyl' Yhwdy'*, your brother *Ḥnnyh* B[. .]

3.6 Epigraphic and Philological Notes

Line 0: *vacat* = margin (containing an ink smudge).[55]

Line 1: The first part of this PRAESCRIPTIO[56] is entirely reconstructible because it parallels the OUTSIDE ADDRESS. It is followed by the ubiquitous INITIAL GREETING commonly found in these letters, which in all probability flowed to beginning of the next line.

Line 2: After a LACUNA of about 8 characters, the legible part of this line begins with *wkˁt*, an epistolary topical marker whose etymology and function are debated.[57] It possibly introduced the body of the message or continued the SALUTATION.[58] The emphasis is clearly on the year. The clause "this year, year 5 of Darius the king," is noteworthy. The key temporal expression *šnt' z'* שנתא זא "this year" is a *casus adverbialis*, as noted by Sachau[59] – and puts the stress on the current year. On one hand, it is not a date and on the other, it does not contribute any new information unknown to the addresses. Therefore, it would be unnecessary, unless intended to put the spotlight on the year itself, which was special in the eyes of the epistle's author – almost certainly a commemorative year.[60] The fact that no date is given in the document is irregular. The line continues with a mention of something or someone, sent to Ạršāma.

Line 3: The line beings with a long LACUNA of about 38–40 characters. The legible area of the line begins with what is probably the end of a *pl. emph. subs.* – possibly or even probably *Yhwdy'* again,[61] but this cannot be ascertained. This is followed by a second epistolary topical marker, *kˁt*, introducing the inner MESSAGE BODY which contains an order to *appoint* (root: *mny*, D-stem)[62] someone, but it could also mean *assign* an inanimate object[63] – of course, to *count* something (as has been suggested since Sachau) is also possible. The only clearly legible letters of the object of this appointment, assignment or enumeration are an *'alep* followed by a *dalet* or a *reš*, possibly referring to four, fourteen or forty units of

55 Porten, "The Aramaic 'Passover Papyrus'," 41.
56 Lindenberger, *Ancient Aramaic and Hebrew letters*, 7–8.
57 Elitzur A. Bar-Asher Siegal, "The Epistolary Terms k't, k'nt."
58 The use of the term *kˁt* in the middle of a salutation is documented. It is ostensibly used to draw attention to a portion of its contents – and might not be directly related to the BODY of the letter. See TAD A.6.7:1–2.
For a discussion with more examples, see Tuplin, "The Bodleian Letters," 111.
59 Sachau, *Aramaische Papyrus*, 38.
60 See TAD vol. 3, 59.
61 Arnold, "The Passover Papyrus," 6.
62 This is its meaning in all other documented cases of this root. See TAD A4.5:9, A6.7:5, C1.1:37.
63 Cf. Tg. Ps.-J. Isa 9:9: וְדְטָבִין מִנְהוֹן נְמַנֵי נִכסַיָא אִתבְזִיזוּ וְדְשַׁפִּירִין מִנְהוֹן נִקְנֵי.

something (men, days, ?) that need to be appointed/assigned/counted. Most scholars preferred to see ארב[עת עשר] here i.e., the fourteenth (of Nisan), but as insightfully noted by Grelot, counting is not part of the biblical *psḥ*.[64] In addition, nowhere else in this text are numbers spelled-out, but are instead written using numerals. This might be due to the difference between ordinal and cardinal numbers, though quantities are regularly expressed with numerals in letters.[65] Dershowitz's reading the month name אדר[66] here instead of ארבׄ and seeing the text as an instruction to keep a second Adar is intriguing and paleographically possible, but it goes against the content of the document, which deals with a specified period of seven days *within* the month of Nisan. A reading of אדרון ("room") i.e., "assign a room" is paleographically as well as contextually possible since rooms/chambers are mentioned again in the text (line 8), though with the lexeme תון. A number, probably *four*, is still the best option.

Line 4: After another long LACUNA of about 35 characters, it seems that a plural verb ending with a *dalet* or a *reš*, *דו or *רו, is legible. This could be the verb עבד ("to do/make") but it could also be any number of other verbs ending with *dalet* or possibly a *reš*, context permitting. The remainder of the line contains only a date-range with ordinal numbers: the 15th day to the 21st day of some month – certainly Nisan, based on line 7.

Line 5: The line begins with a long LACUNA of about 35 characters, following which the directive to be collectively pure and to "take heed" is given. This is followed by the word עבידה ("work"). Ever since Sachau, the interpretation was that this lexeme is followed by some kind of prohibition (fig. 4).[67] However, there can be no certainty that the *'alep* following the substantive "work" is the first letter of a prohibitive *'l* – especially given the observations regarding prohibitions (or lack thereof) in the next line.

Fig. 4: End of line 5. © Staatliche Museen zu Berlin – Ägyptisches Museum und Papyrussammlung. PhotoGad Barnea.

64 Grelot, "Etudes sur le 'Papyrus Pascal'," 357.

65 For one example out of dozens, see TAD A4.2 where both dates and enumerated objects are expressed through numerals.

66 Dershowitz, "The Elephantine Passover Papyrus."

67 Sachau, *Aramaische Papyrus*, 38. He specifically notes that this interpretation is based on Exod 12:16 and Deut 16:8, but does not add the prohibitive *'l* in his Aramaic restoration.

Line 6: Another long *lacuna* opens the line – also of about 35 characters long. The legible text starts with a final *lamed*. The traces of the letter before it do not allow for its definite reconstruction. Like its predecessor, it has been read as the prohibitive particle *ʾl* אל, which Sachau notes is a "guess."[68] However, it should also be noted that – even though this phoneme is composed of just two consonants – no prohibitive *ʾl* can be said to exist with any degree of certainty in the *entire* document. As can be seen by comparing figs. 5 and 6 below, Ada Yardeni, in her reconstruction, *added* a tiny left leg of an *ʾalep* (fig. 6) which is simply not there in the actual papyrus! (fig. 5). The reading of an *ʾalep* in the trace before the *lamed*, is unlikely since a typical *ʾalep* in the fifth-fourth centuries BCE – and *any other ʾalep* in the document, has its left leg extend farther to the left (e.g., fig. 8) past the left head of the letter[69] – a feature which Grelot excused (fig. 7) in his reconstruction in spite of having correctly copied it (with the extended left leg) everywhere else.[70] It should be noted that a *lamed* always aligns with the ceiling of the row (fig. 17).[71]

Fig. 5: Trace before lamed. © Staatliche Museen zu Berlin – Ägyptisches Museum und Papyrussammlung. Photo Gad Barnea.

Fig. 6: Yardeni's 1986; reconstruction (TAD). @ Porten and Yardeni, used with permission; red circle added by the author.

68 Sachau, *Aramaische Papyrus*, 38.

69 See Yardeni's own epigraphic analysis of the diachronic development of *ʾalep* in Yardeni, *Osef teʿudot Aramiyot*, vol. B, 168 (in English). This *ʾalep* would correspond to type ב.7 in her classification. Whether this is a textbook or a bona fide edition, these "adaptations" cannot be written off as "nothing but representations of Porten's and Yardeni's interpretations," *pace* Ingo Kottsieper, "Review: Das religiöse Leben," 305. No scholar should add to or alter the data represented in the document to conform to their interpretations. Rather, the scholar's interpretation must be governed by the reality of text.

70 Grelot, "Etudes sur le 'Papyrus Pascal' d'Elephantine," 370.

71 Naveh, *The Development of the Aramaic Script*, 20.

Fig. 7: – Grelot's reconstruction.

Fig. 8: A "typical" *'alep*. © Staatliche Museen zu Berlin – Ägyptisches Museum und Papyrussammlung. Photo Gad Barnea.

I propose, cautiously, that what precedes the *lamed* might be a *yod* (fig. 9)[72] of the word *ṣlyl* ("pure") or something to that effect,[73] signifying that this beverage should be consumed pure paralleling the preceding line of the text ("be pure and take heed").

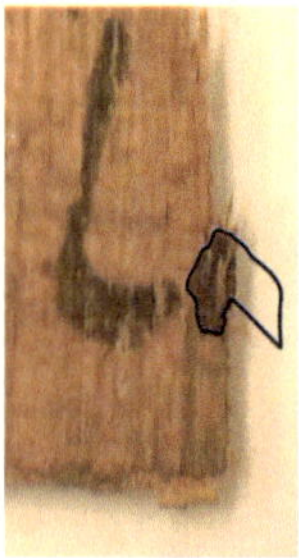

Fig. 9: Proposed restoration of the Yod. © Staatliche Museen zu Berlin – Ägyptisches Museum und Papyrussammlung. Photo Gad Barnea.

It should be noted that the emphasis in this text, as we have it, is on the beverage to be consumed. This is not only the first, but also the *sole* verb of consumption preserved in the text. To this is added, via a *conjunction-waw*, כל מנדעם זי חמיר ("anything of *ḥmyr*," i.e., yeast/leaven).[74] This is followed by another *'alep* at the edge of the document. However, the trace after this *'alep* does not correspond to a *lamed* and the space between them is too wide. A *lamed* is always aligned to the ceiling line (fig. 15, 17) and the remaining trace is far too low – even below the left leg of the *'alep*. Seeing this, Sachau "recommended" to read איתי בה here,[75] rather than אל תאכלו – a proposal that was also adopted by Arnold and Cowley.

72 Restoration based on the outline of the 2nd *yod* on line 4 of P. Berlin 13464.
73 Cf. Tg. Ps.-J. Exod 7:24: וחפרו מצראי חזרנות נהרא מוי למישתי ולא אשכחו צלילן.
74 See also Gaß, "Der Passa-Papyrus," 58, note 18.
75 Sachau, *Aramaische Papyrus*, 38.

Vincent supplied the non-Aramaic אל ימצא.[76] Yardeni, in her reconstruction, "raised" the trace and placed it closer to the *ʾalep*. Interestingly, her version as published in Porten's 1979 article the trace of her restored *lamed* was still "hollowed out." (fig. 13)[77] Grelot, in 1954, saw an upward-pointing trace of a *lamed* (fig. 12), but reverted to Sachau's original איתי בה in 1967.[78] In any case, the trace of the letter following the *ʾalep*, seems to "hug" the tear in the papyrus, as can be seen clearly in the IR version of the image (fig. 16). This makes it probable that this is the trace of a *samek* (fig. 11).[79] The first reconstruction in which the prohibitive *ʾḻs* are represented as certain seems to be Porten and Yardeni's 1986 TAD edition.

Fig. 10: Original end of line. © Staatliche Museen zu Berlin – Ägyptisches Museum und Papyrussammlung. Photo Gad Barnea.

Fig. 11: Restoration with samek. © Staatliche Museen zu Berlin – Ägyptisches Museum und Papyrussammlung. Photo Gad Barnea.

Fig. 12: Grelot's reconstruction.

Fig. 13: Yardeni's 1979 reconstruction. © Porten and Yardeni, used with permission.

Fig. 14: Yardeni's 1986 reconstruction (TAD). © Porten and Yardeni, used with permission.

Instead, what follows the *ʾalep* could very well be the verb *ʾsp* ("gather," in the pl. *ʾspw* – i.e., "gather up/collect anything of leaven/yeast") among several other options, such as the *yod* proposed by Sachau. In any case, no prohibition is preserved in the text whether regarding work, the drink to be consumed or yeast.

76 Vincent, *La religion*, 246. However, the verb *mṣʾ* is not Aramaic, which would use *škḥ*.
77 Porten, "Aramaic 'Passover Papyrus'," 43. See also a similar "hollowed out" version in Porten, "Aramaic Papyri and Parchments." 89.
78 Grelot, "Le papyrus pascal d'Éléphantine," 204.
79 Restoration based on the outline of the samek of line 7 of P. Berlin 13464.

Fig. 15: Ceiling line (red line added by author). © Staatliche Museen zu Berlin – Ägyptisches Museum und Papyrussammlung. Photo Gad Barnea.

Fig. 16: IR view. © Staatliche Museen zu Berlin – Ägyptisches Museum und Papyrussammlung. Photo Gad Barnea.

Fig. 17: 'Normal' lamed alignment (as part of 'lhy' [אלהיא]). © Staatliche Museen zu Berlin – Ägyptisches Museum und Papyrussammlung. Photo Gad Barnea.

Line 7: The first line of the VERSO also begins with a long LACUNA of about 35 characters after which the words *mʿrb šmšʾ* מערב שמשא ("setting of the sun") are clearly legible, even though the initial *mem* is damaged. The remainder of the line continues with a temporal clause "to the 21st of Nisan." A *possible* reconstruction would be to repeat the date range in line 4: "the 15th to the 21st of Nisan". However, only this final day is certain – the start date of this date-range can technically be any date prior to the 21st of Nisan. Even though the full month name is never fully legible, there can be no doubt about this lexeme.

Line 8: A LACUNA of approximately 35 characters opens up this line as well. The first partially legible lexeme on this line ends with *ʿlw* עלו*. This has been understood to represent the imperative [ה]נעלו "to bring", which is technically possible, deriving from *ʿll* עלל. However, this verb usually takes the preposition *l*- -ל rather than *b*- -ב, making this reconstruction somewhat less likely.[80] Since only *ʿlw* is certain, it could also be a number of other verbs ending with *ʿl* על*, such as פעל. Whatever this verb may be, its object is to be performed and sealed (the reading of a *ḥet* in *ḥtmw* חתמו is virtually certain here)[81] in their rooms/cells/chambers between said days.

Line 9: line 9 held some text of which only minute traces are currently detectable. The final letter on this line – and thus of the entire body of text of this papyrus – is an *ʾalep*. The trace preceding the *ʾalep*, is almost certainly a *yod* – as can be seen when compared to a clearly preserved *yod*+*ʾalep* combination from line 3 (figs. 18, 19).

Fig. 18: Yod + ʾalep from line 3. © Staatliche Museen zu Berlin – Ägyptisches Museum und Papyrussammlung. Photo Gad Barnea.

Fig. 19: Yod + ʾalep from line 9. © Staatliche Museen zu Berlin – Ägyptisches Museum und Papyrussammlung. Photo Gad Barnea.

Lines 10–11: (*vacat*).

Line 12: Beginning with a LACUNA of about 10 characters, this OUTSIDE ADDRESS repeats the first part of the first line but adds something after the PN *Ḥnnyh* which might be the back part of a *bet*. This has been interpreted as possibly being the *gender-conjunction* of the patronymic of *Ḥnnyh*, i.e., *br* ("son of"). But given that *Ḥnnyh* seems to be "well-known" and is never mentioned with a patronymic in other instances where he is recorded, this is most probably not the case. In addition, had this been the case, it would have been expected to be used already in *Ḥnnyh*'s initial identification on line 1. I would instead suggest that it might rather be the *bet* of *bʿl tʿm* בעל טעם but this cannot be ascertained.

80 But see Folmer, *The Aramaic Language*, 608 (excursus ii).
81 Cowley, *Aramaic Papyri*, 65, suggested that this might be a *samek* instead of a *ḥet*, the meaning would still remain the same, but to me, the reading of a *ḥet* is pretty clear.

3.7 Commentary

Following the standard salutations in the INTERNAL ADDRESS, the HEADER[82] of this letter puts a clear stress on the current year as a special year – in all probability, the centenary of the unveiling of the Behistun inscription. It is year five of Darius II. This is not a date and is not expressed as such. Porten notes: "[i]t is strange that no month and day date were given. Since the New Year began in Nisan, we may imagine that the rescript was issued at the end of year 5 (before April 15, 418 BCE), with an eye to the Passover of year 6." However, it seems clear that the goal was to introduce the *current year* as significant and the importance of the month of Nisan is simply that it is the first month of the year, after Nō Rōz/ Navasarda.[83] It is undoubtedly a well-known fact to all involved that they are in the fifth regnal of the king. Since *Ḥnnyh* calls this fifth year *šnt' z'* שנתא זא ("this year") and writes with regards to the fifteenth of the month of Nisan of that same year, the letter must have been written close to the beginning of that month – a maximum of two weeks prior to the beginning of the seven-day observance. In all likelihood it was written and dispatched in the first days of Nisan – late-March or early-April 419.[84] This would also indicate that Ḥananiah was in Egypt when he wrote this letter since it had to have made its way up the Nile to Elephantine rather quickly. Since it seems that a copy of the (modified) Behistun inscription was made around the same time-frame, some scholars have rightly suggested that the copy was made as an anniversary of something relating to Darius I – probably the centenary of the unveiling of the Behistun inscription.[85] The year of the unveiling of this inscription was argued for convincingly by Heinz Luschey, who dated its final form, its "unveiling" so to speak, archeologically, to 519 BCE.[86]

82 This section is tagged INSTRUCTIONS I in Porten, *Elephantine Papyri*. However, my interpretation is that it does not contain instructions, neither to Ảršāma nor to the *Yhwdy'*, but is a statement regarding the arrival of Ḥananiah in Egypt intended to give context to the instructions following it. I therefore classified this as a header instead.

83 On the question of what Nō Rōz / Navasarda may have been in the Achaemenid period and its calendar reform, see Boyce, "NOWRUZ I."

84 According to Leo Depuydt, Darius II acceded to the throne on April 10th 423 BCE, one day before the 1st of Nisan that year, see Depuydt, "Regnal Years," 170, note b. The fifth year of Darius II (i.e. Nisan 1st) began on March 27th 419 BCE. See Parker and Dubberstein, *Babylonian Chronology*, 31.

85 TAD, vol.3, 59. See also Tavernier, "An Achaemenid Royal Inscription," 161, and more recently Granerød, "By the Favour of Ahuramazda."

86 Heinz Luschey convincingly dates the work on the inscription between 522–519 BCE, with it being finished "shortly after 519 BCE" based on archeological analysis, see Luschey, "Studien zu dem Darius-Relief," 80, 92–94.

Greenfield and Porten explain that "[t]he recopying of the inscription celebrating the triumphs of Darius I during the days of Darius II would have been a reaffirmation of the loyalty of the Elephantine Jews to the Persian crown."[87] The ceremony to be observed should thus be viewed in the context of an imperial commemoration – and more broadly as part of Darius II's push to restore and enhance his namesake's legacy – in other words, as propaganda. This document is significant in one more aspect. This is the first documented instance in which the Elephantine Yahwists are called a *ḥyl'*. Sachau read this as *exercitus Iudaeus*,[88] which is how it has been understood ever-since. However, in the Old-Persian sense of the word, it had both the meaning of a military unit and an *ethnos* – cognate to the OP *kāra*.[89] Thus, it would seem that Ḥananiah either informs the Elephantine Yahwists of their imperial recognition as a "free" ethnic group, or – as is more probable – follows up on a recent official imperial announcement to that effect. In order to now become an *ethnos* in the Persian empire and thus part of the *good creation*,[90] they must become ritually pure and realign themselves with AZ ideals of purity.

---

87 Greenfield and Porten, *Bisitun Inscription*, 3.

88 Sachau, *Aramaische Papyrus*, 36.

89 The OP *kāra*, featuring prominently in Darius' Behistun inscription, is ambiguous in that it designated both "army" and "people" as, unfortunately, do the terms *ūqu* and *taššup* that translate it in Babylonian and Elamite respectively. This lexeme only appears in the singular with the verbs and adjectives agreeing. However, its referent assumes a plurality, as indicated by the use co-referent plural enclitic pronouns, e.g., gen. *-šām* (DB/OP II:20) or accusative *-diš* (DB/OP I:65). See especially Filippone, "Political Discourse," 109. It is found exclusively, yet frequently, in Darius I's inscriptions (DB, DPd, DPe) and thus seems to have had a special meaning in the context of that monarch's propaganda and to define his policy toward a select group of peoples. In DB, this term is exclusively attached to people-groups that are a core part of the twenty-three *dahyāva* enumerated in it: the Persians, the Elamites and the Babylonians. As summarized by Ela Filippone in her extensive study, "The Persian *kāra*-probably represented the ethno-classe dominante during the whole history of the Achaemenid state, as the royal texts and iconography let think; however, in no time the royal chancellery stressed this concept as straightforwardly as in the time of King Darius" (Filippone, "Political Discourse," 117). The Aramaic term *ḥyl'* in the Achaemenid period should be seen as having this additional meaning – a cognate of *kāra*, as Chul-Hyun Bae noted in his thorough study of the Behistun inscription (Bae, "Comparative Studies," 370, 80). P. Berlin 13464 was composed under the reign of Darius II, who chose this throne-name to present himself as a *Darius redivivus*. He restored several of his namesake's policies (ostensibly including the *kāra* "ethno-classe dominante") and had an amplified version of DB promulgated at that time – the centenary of the unveiling of the original inscription (Luschey, "Studien zu dem Darius-Relief," 80, 92–94) – a copy of which was found among the documents of the Elephantine Yahwists. For further context, see Granerød, "Favour of Ahuramazda," 471–478 and Briant, "Ethno-classe dominante."

90 Boyce, *History of Zoroastrianism*, vol. 2, 189–90.

3.7.1 Excursus: On the Existence of the *Psḥ* and *Maṣṣot* Feasts in the Fifth Century BCE

Before moving forward with the analysis of P. Berlin 13464, it is important to consider the possibility of the existence of the *psḥ* and/or *maṣṣot* festivals in the fifth century BCE.[91] For many scholars (myself included at the beginning of my study), the existence of these feasts – in more-or-less the form in which they were known from the Hebrew Bible – was almost taken for granted and P. Berlin 13464 seemed to prove this beyond doubt. The reigning scholarly position is summed up neatly by Lester Grabbe in his discussion of the Torah at Elephantine:

> Scholars generally agree that [the Passover] has a history with roots long before the Persian period, though Passover and Unleavened Bread may have originally been distinctive festivals. Although the main source prior to the Elephantine documents is the biblical text, it still seems possible to deduce some of the history of the festival from it. This is confirmed by the Elephantine letters that suggest the Passover is a part of ordinary Jewish life and not something new.[92]

P. Berlin 13464, which is often referred to as the "Passover papyrus," would indeed be the sole extra-biblical anchor for these feasts – *if* it could be proven to refer to that feast. However, the analysis presented above must call this into question. Objectively, there can be no certainty that P. Berlin 13464 has anything to do with the biblical *psḥ* or *maṣṣot* feasts – at least not directly. It possibly reflects a *precursor* to the *maṣṣot* feast, as I will postulate below, but contains no clear knowledge of these feasts. The argument that these feasts – and specifically the feast of *maṣṣot* – existed when P. Berlin 13464 was written cannot, of course, rest on the circular logic that make this very same document the sole extra-biblical witness to the existence of the feast!

I have already noted, in passing, the fact that the *psḥ'* at Elephantine seems to have been an intimate, probably communal, and most likely apotropaic[93] event related to highly stressful situations[94] and was evidently nothing like its biblical

---

91 See discussion in footnote 43 above.

92 Grabbe, "Elephantine and the Torah," 130. More recently, see Kratz, "Centralization of Festivals."

93 The apotropaic nature of *psḥ'* seems to be preserved in the biblical Text (Exod 12:23), where it is connected to a practice meant to ward off the "Destroyer": "For YHWH will pass through to strike the Egyptians, and when he sees the blood on the lintel and on the two doorposts, YHWH will pass over the door and will not allow the destroyer to enter your houses to strike you" (וְעָבַר יהוה לִנְגֹּף אֶת־מִצְרַיִם וְרָאָה אֶת־הַדָּם עַל־הַמַּשְׁקוֹף וְעַל שְׁתֵּי הַמְּזוּזֹת וּפָסַח יהוה עַל־הַפֶּתַח וְלֹא יִתֵּן הַמַּשְׁחִית לָבֹא אֶל־בָּתֵּיכֶם לִנְגֹּף׃). See Barnea, "The meaning of psḥ'" 16–18. See also Kratz, "Centralization of Festivals," 240, 245.

94 Both of the clear mentions of *psḥ'* at Elephantine fit this description: TAD D7.6 deals with an exceedingly stressful situation concerning toddlers who are to be kept in close watch and not to

image. It is, however, clear that the term *psḥ'* was known at Elephantine. It is recorded at a much earlier date than P. Berlin 13464,[95] yet this papyrus does not make use of this term – at least in the form that we currently have. It is also safe to assume, at least on etymological grounds, that the Aramaic *psḥ'* held some connection to the biblical *psḥ*. In proceeding to examine this document, the question invariably turns to the question of precedence: i.e., whether something like a *biblical* form of *psḥ* existed and/or was known to the Elephantine Yahwists or is the *psḥ'* recorded at Elephantine a precursor to what will become the biblical *psḥ* – i.e., the observance documented at Elephantine was somehow related to the process which will eventually culminate in the institution of the *psḥ* and *maṣṣot* festivals. Bob Becking recently summed this question up nicely: "[o]ne can speculate whether this seasonal festival had been an older tradition of the Yehudites that needed some revision, or whether the troublesome times at the end of the fifth century BCE invited them to start this festival."[96] It therefore seems that since P. Berlin 13464 cannot be taken as sure confirmation of the pre-existence of the *psḥ* and/or *maṣṣot* festivals – and, based on the epigraphical analysis above is probably not (directly) related to these feasts – the text must be analyzed on its own merits without pre-conceptions and projections from the biblical text. Since we cannot be sure that the feast existed yet in the fifth century BCE – in *Yhwd* or at Elephantine – we are required to look elsewhere. This involves a reconsideration of the general devotional and political climate at Elephantine at the time and rereading the text with these in mind. Might assimilation with Achaemenid and/or Egyptian ideology/devotional patterns provide a more suitable context for P. Berlin 13464?

3.7.2 The Observance Prescribed in P. Berlin 13464

What are the known elements of the observance prescribed in P. Berlin 13464? First of all, the context: this epistle is sent in the context of an important event –

be entrusted to anyone. TAD D7.24 (P. Berlin 10679) likewise deals with a situation of significant anxiety caused by difficulties in the interpretation of an important letter. See Barnea "Reading Berlin P. 10679".

95 TAD D7.6 and D7.24 are both dated paleographically to the first quarter of the fifth century BCE. Even though paleographic dating is highly problematic, see Moore, *New Aramaic Papyri*, 219–221. These specific ostraca are probably on a more secure footing regarding their dating since they were probably written by the same scribe, who is responsible for about 32 different ostraca, which allow us to also use circumstantial evidence and not just rely on paleography. See Naveh, *development of the Aramaic script*, 37–39.

96 Becking, *Identity in Persian Egypt*, 28.

a commemorative year and/or a special recognition of the *Yhwdy*ʾ.[97] In any case, the context is one of a momentous occasion of which Ḥananiah is author, administrator or both. In addition:

- People need to be appointed (or something is to be assigned or counted).
- The ceremony encompasses a heptad, a 7-day period, from the 15th to the 21st of Nisan.
- There is a solemn injunction to maintain purity and to beware.
- Some sort of drink *should be consumed* and something relating to "anything of yeast/leaven" *ḥmyr* is mentioned – possibly gathering it.
- Something should be done and sealed in the chambers of the community between two dates.

Historically, the date-range and the word *ḥmyr* have received the bulk of scholarly attention, because of the assumed connection to the *psḥ*/*maṣṣot*. However, the cultic focus here is on ritual purity and the consumption of some drink. All that can be said regarding the date-range is that it is a heptad – a seven-day period – after the first full-moon of the year. The full-moon was a significant time across the ANE and a *daθušō aiiarə*, "day of the creator"[98] in the AZ worldview and the seventh day after the full-moon was called *vī šaptaθa*.[99]

3.8 Traces of a AZ-inspired Cult in P. Berlin 13464?

Before examining the question posed in the title of this chapter – which might seem radical at first – it is important to reiterate what is known about AZ practice at Elephantine in the second half of the fifth century BCE. As shown above, there was a *brzmdn*ʾ place of worship, set up according to the AZ concept of *bạrzman* at Syene around 450 BCE. *Maguš*-priests serve as witnesses to the transaction of Yahwists around 430 BCE. Names with Avestan elements are documented to be in various forms of association with Yahwists across the time period. Most significantly, the Yahwists themselves mention a "fire altar" (using the Mazdean cultic loanword *ʾtrwdn*) as being associated with offerings made to *Yhw* in their temple. These features – especially the presence of an *ʾtrwdn* in the temple to *Yhw* – point

97 The idea that P. Berlin 13464 reflects a watershed moment in the history of the Elephantine Yahwists has been suggested by van der Toorn, *Becoming Diaspora Jews* and from a different angle, previously, by Kottsieper, "Die Religionspolitik."

98 Malandra, "DAY."

99 Y 1.8, 2.8, 3.10, 4.13, 6.7, 7.10, 17.7, 22.10, Yt 7.42, Ny 3.6.

to a deeply intimate cultic association between the Yahwists and AZ, that should allow for additional points of contact between the two.

The term *yasna*[100] literally means "sacrifice" and designates the central ritual in the Indo-Iranian cultic practice. Its ultimate goal is "the maintenance of the cosmic integrity of the good creation of Ahura Mazdā"[101] specifically preformed "to recreate the world of light after a period of darkness."[102] A *yasna* is a ritual. It is not a festival and does not occur on fixed dates – rather, festivals include *yasna* ceremonies, but these ceremonies can be performed independently of any festival. The *yasna* "reproduces Ahura Mazdâ's primeval sacrifice, by which he established the Ordered Cosmos, and its purpose is the revitalization of this cosmos, now constantly under attack by the forces of darkness and destruction."[103] Typical elements of a *yasna* are the ceremony of the sacred drink, *haoma* (*hōm*) and the offering of the "sacred share", *drōn*, which often was – and still is – unleavened-bread.[104]

3.8.1 Haoma

The term *haoma* designates a number of interrelated concepts: a *yazata*-deity, a special plant (whose identification is contested) and a sacred drink (mixed with pomegranate, water and milk) extracted from this plant, known as *soma* in the Rigveda and Indian traditions.[105] The word itself carries the meaning "that which is pressed, extract" from Av. *hu-*, Skt. *su-*, "press, pound"[106] or "crushed" with a mortar, from the action – physically and symbolically – taken to produce the juice from the plant. The *Haoma* ceremony is one of the most ancient elements in the Indo-Iranian cult. This drink and its centrality in the life of worship are well documented in pre-Achaemenid and Achaemenid times. Imperial inscriptions, covering the entire timeline of the Achaemenid empire, mention the Sakā *haumavargā* ("the *hauma/haoma*-drinking or -preparing Scythians")[107] – as separate from the Saka *tigraxaudā* ("pointy-hat Scythians"), the theophoric PN *Haoma-dāta*

---

100 I will use the lower-case *yasna* to refer to the ceremony, while references to the textual corpus with the same name will have the first letter capitalized: *Yasna*.

101 Malandra, "YASNA."

102 Skjærvø, *The spirit of Zoroastrianism*, 34.

103 Skjærvø, *Introduction to Zoroastrianism*, 58.

104 Choksy, "DRŌN."

105 In fact, most of the hymns of the Rigveda were composed for the soma ritual. See Jamison and Brereton, *The Rigveda*, 30.

106 Taillieu, "HAOMA i."

107 DNa 25, DSe 24–25, XPh 26 and A?P 14 (Artaxerxes II or III).

הומדת ("given by Haoma") is recorded at Elephantine,[108] at Persepolis,[109] where inscribed implements for the preparation of *haoma* were found,[110] and the Hebrew Bible.[111] The drink was seen as *life-giving* and *life-preserving*. It is drunk unfermented since "there is not enough time during the ritual preparation of haoma/soma for fermentation to take place,"[112] and the intoxication derived from it is viewed as highly positive and is "the only one that has the effect of re-establishing cosmic Order."[113] Plutarch notes this drink as part of the Achaemenid imperial rite observed by Artaxerxes II upon accession – a ritual which, according to him, goes back to Cyrus "the elder" (i.e. Cyrus II).[114] It is also fitting to the context of this papyrus that "the preliminary stage of the ceremony involves a careful purification of the *officiating priests* and of the *implements* and *materials essential to the ritual.*"[115] The *haoma*-ceremony was part of a sevenfold ceremony of re-creation representing the doctrine of the seven great *Aməša Spəntas* and the seven creations. Every element in the liturgy had a symbolic role representing one of these creations.[116] Given the emphasis on keeping purity in P. Berlin 13464 – with the only clear command to consume anything as part of the observance being to a certain drink (but not to any kind of food), the correspondence with the *Haoma* ceremony is striking. This could be dismissed as mere coincidence if we did not have clearly documented AZ cultic elements adopted by the Yahwists at Elephantine, but these cannot be ignored.

3.8.2 Drōn

While the *drōn* (< Av. *draonah-* "portion of food") is mentioned in the *Yasna* and was clearly a requisite offering for the performance of the *yasna* even in pre-Achaemenid times. It is described as the portion of an animal sacrificed and presented to Haoma (as a yazata, a divine being).[117] Unless new sources are found to shed more light on AZ cult, it will be impossible to know precisely what the *drōn* consisted of in the Achaemenid period. However, we do know that at some

108 TAD B2.3: 1–2, 2.4: 1–2.
109 Aramaic Texts from Persepolis 14:2, 15:3.
110 See Barnea, "Arachosian Tribute."
111 Esther 3:1 הַמְּדָתָא.
112 Taillieu, "HAOMA i."
113 Skjærvø, "Smashing Urine," 264.
114 Plutarch, Artaxerxes, 3.1–3a.
115 ART, 10 (emphasis added).
116 Boyce, *history of Zoroastrianism*, vol. 1, 219–20.
117 Y 11.4.

point in time it came to consist of a flat, round unleavened wheat bread, as described in the Pahlavi sources[118] – practically identical to the *maṣṣa* used in the biblical Passover traditions. Did this evolution begin already in Achaemenid times? We cannot know for sure, but it stands to reason that this development started early on in imperial times – if only for practical and economic reasons. For a ceremony that occurs daily, sacrificing an animal is prohibitively expensive and might not be possible in many parts of the empire. It would have been significantly more effective – especially in imperial times – to use a barley offering instead.

4 Conclusions

This paper surveyed the links that are documented to have existed between the Yahwistic community at Elephantine and AZ and suggested that P. Berlin 13464 can be read within the context of an AZ *yasna*, rather than the biblical Passover or *maṣṣot* festivals, as scholars with Jewish or Christian backgrounds have read it thus far. Yet the question arises: am I merely replacing the problematics of the *psḥ* (Passover) with those of AZ? Some speculation is evidently required in both cases, but the fact is that the *yasna* – and specifically the centrality of the *Haoma* drink purification ceremony – are abundantly documented in Achaemenid times (and even earlier) whereas the Passover or the *massot* festival are entirely undocumented extra-biblically. Moreover, the clear evidence of an *ʾtrwdan* (fire-altar) in the Yahwistic temple in the same general time-frame of P. Berlin 13464 (to within a decade), provides a complementary point of evidence to the very high level of intimate syncretistic association with AZ being practiced by the Elephantine Yahwists. While we cannot be absolutely certain that P. Berlin 13464 represents a *yasna* (or a *yasna*-inspired) observance, it is undoubtedly more probable that it does do so, than the *psh*ʾ / *massot*. Significantly, the only cultic practices to involve an intoxicating drink (specifically, one based on pressing and crushing) and unleavened bread are the *yasna* and the *psḥ*/*maṣṣot* feasts. There is nothing in the Egyptian or Levantine traditions that parallels this. Ultimately, these observations can support the hypothesis that the biblical Passover evolved over time, from these AZ-inspired cultic features in the fifth century BCE to the form known to us from the Hebrew Bible – which would make P. Berlin 13464 a possible *precursor* to the *maṣṣot* feast.

---

118 Choksy, "DRŌN."

Bibliography

Anneler, Hedwig, *Zur Geschichte der Juden von Elephantine*, Bern: Drechsel, 1912.

Arnold, William R., "The Passover Papyrus from Elephantine," *JBL* 31, no. 1 (1912): 1–33.

Bae, Chul-Hyun, "Comparative Studies of King Darius's Bisitun Inscription," PhD; Harvard University, 2001.

Bar-Asher Siegal, Elitzur A., "The Epistolary Terms k't, k'nt in Official Aramaic, the Feminine Endings in Aramaic Dialects and Other Dialectal Features in the History of Aramaic," *ANES* 48 (2011): 199–231.

Barnea, Gad, "Deciphering Arachosian Tribute at Persepolis: Orthopraxy and the Achaemenid 'Regulated Gift' Economy," 2024 forthcoming.

Barnea, Gad, "The meaning of psḥ' in Achaemenid Aramaic sources," (2024 forthcoming).

Barnea, Gad, "Reading P. Berlin 10679 (TADAE D7.24) Inside Out," Tel Aviv, 2024 forthcoming.

Barnea, Gad, *4Q550 – A New Edition, Translation and Commentary*, DSSE. Leiden: Brill, forthcoming.

Barnea, Gad, "Some Achaemenid Zoroastrian Echoes in Early Yahwistic Sources," *Iran: Journal of the British Institute of Persian Studies* (2024 forthcoming).

Barnea, Gad, "The Significance of *ṛtācā brzmniy* in Xerxes' Cultic Reform," *Iran and the Caucasus* (forthcoming).

Barnea, Gad, "Justice at the House of Yhw(h): An Early Yahwistic *Defixio in Furem*," *Religions* 14.10 (2023), 1324. https://doi.org/10.3390/rel14101324.

Barnea, Gad, "*Interpretatio Ivdaica* in the Achaemenid Period," *Journal of Ancient Judaism* 14 (2023): 355–391.

Barnea, Gad, "The Migration of the Elephantine Yahwists under Amasis II," *Journal of Near Eastern Studies* 82, no. 1 (2023): 103–18.

Becking, Bob, *Identity in Persian Egypt: the fate of the Yehudite community of Elephantine*, University Park: The Pennsylvania State University Press, 2020.

Berner, Christoph, "How Pesaḥ and Maṣṣot Became Connected with the Exodus: The Development of the Festival Etiologies in Exod. 12:1–13:16," *Religions* 14 (5), 2023: 605. https://doi.org/10.3390/rel14050605.

Beer, Georg, and Holtzmann, Oscar, *Die Mischna: text, Ubersetzung und ausfuhrliche Erklarung. mit eingehenden geschichtlichen und sprachlichen Einleitungen*, Giessen: A. Topelmann, 1912.

Bogoliubov, Mikhail N., "An Aramaic inscription from Aswan," *Palestinski Sbornik* 15 (78) (1966): 40–46 (in Russian).

Bowman, Raymond A., *Aramaic Ritual Texts from Persepolis*, University of Chicago Oriental Institute publications. Chicago: University of Chicago Press, 1970.

Boyce, Mary, *A history of Zoroastrianism*, Leiden: E. J. Brill, 1996.

Briant, Pierre, "Ethno-classe dominante et populations soumises dans l'Empire Achemenide: Le cas d'Egypte," pages 137–73 in *Achaemenid History* III (Leiden: Nederlands Instituut voor het Nabije Oosten, 1988).

Choksy, Jamsheed K., "DRŌN," Pages 554–55 in *Encyclopædia Iranica*. Vol. VII, Fasc. 5. New York: Encyclopædia Iranica Foundation, 1995.

Cowley, Arthur E., *Aramaic papyri of the fifth century B.C edited, with translation and notes*, Oxford: Clarendon Press, 1923.

Dandamayev, Muhammad A., "The Ebabbar Temple and Iranian Magi," *Altorientalische Forschungen*, 22, no. 1 (1995): 34–36.

Depuydt, Leo, "Regnal Years and Civil Calendar in Achaemenid Egypt," *The Journal of Egyptian Archaeology* 81 (1995): 151–73.

Duchesne-Guillemin, Jacques, "Greece iii. Persian Influence on Greek Thought," pages 319–21 in *Encyclopædia Iranica*. New York: Encyclopædia Iranica Foundation, 2002.

Fabry, Heinz-Josef, and Weinfeld, Moshe "מִנְחָה," In *Theological Dictionary of the Old Testament*, edited by G. Johannes Botterweck and Helmer Ringgren, translated by Douglas W. Stott, VIII: 407–21, Grand Rapids, MI; Cambridge, U.K.: William B. Eerdmans Publishing Company, 1997.

Fattori, Marco, "Miscellanea Epigraphica Susiana: Textual Observations on some Achaemenid Inscriptions from Susa," *Arta* 2023, no. 003 (2023): 1–26.

Filippone, Ela. "DPd/DPe and the Political Discourse of King Darius," pages 101–19 in *DARIOSH STUDIES II: Persepolis and its settlements: territorial system and ideology in the Achaemenid state*. Edited by Gian Pietro Basello and Adriano V. Rossi. Napoli: Università degli Studi di Napoli "L'Orientale", 2012.

Folmer, Margaretha L., *The Aramaic language in the Achaemenid period: a study in linguistic variation*, Leuven: Peeters, 1995.

Gaß, Erasmus, "Der Passa-Papyrus (Cowl 21) – Mythos oder Realität?," *BN* 99 (1999): 55–68.

Grabbe, Lester L., "Elephantine and the Torah," pages 125–35 in *In the Shadow of Bezalel: Aramaic, Biblical and Ancient Near Eastern Studies in Honor of Bezalel Porten*, edited by A. F. Botta. Leiden: Brill, 2013.

Granerød, Gard, "YHW the God of Heaven: An interpretatio persica et aegyptiaca of YHW in Elephantine," *JSJ* 52, no. 1 (2020): 1–26.

Granerød, Gard, *Dimensions of Yahwism in the Persian period: studies in the religion and society of the Judaean community at Elephantine*, Berlin: De Gruyter, 2016.

Granerød, Gard, "'By the Favour of Ahuramazda I Am King': On the Promulgation of a Persian Propaganda Text among Babylonians and Judaeans," *JSJ* 44 (2013): 455–80.

Greenfield, Jonas C., and Porten, Bezalel, *The Bisitun inscription of Darius the Great, Aramaic version*, London: Lund Humphries, 1982.

Grelot, Pierre, *Documents araméens d'Égypte*, Paris: Éditions du Cerf, 1972.

Grelot, Pierre, "Le papyrus pascal d'Éléphantine: Essai de Restauration," *VT* 17, no. 2 (1967): 201–07.

Grelot, Pierre, "Etudes sur le "Papyrus Pascal" d'Elephantine," *VT* 4, no. 4 (1954): 349–84.

Hinz, Walther, *Altiranisches Sprachgut der Nebenüberlieferungen.* Wiesbaden: Harrassowitz, 1975.

Hoftijzer, Jacob, et al., *Dictionary of the North-west Semitic inscriptions*, 2 vols. Leiden: Brill, 1995.

Jamison, Stephanie W., and Brereton, Joel P., *The Rigveda: the earliest religious poetry of India*, South Asia research. New York: Oxford University Press, 2014.

Jones, Lindsay, *Encyclopedia of Religion*, 2nd ed. 15 vols, Gale Virtual Reference Library. Detroit: Macmillan Reference USA, 2005.

Kahn, Dan'el, "The Date of the Arrival of the Judeans at Elephantine and the Foundation of Their Colony," *Journal of Near Eastern Studies* 81.1 (2022): 139–164.

Kanga, Maneck F., "BARSOM," pages 825–27 in *Encyclopædia Iranica*,. New York: Encyclopædia Iranica Foundation, 1988.

Kent, Roland G., "Old Persian artācā brazmaniya." *Language* 21, no. 4 (1945): 223–29.

Kellermann, Diether, "מַצָּה." In *Theological Dictionary of the Old Testament*, edited by G. Johannes Botterweck, Helmer Ringgren, and Heinz-Josef Fabry, translated by Douglas W. Stott, VIII: 494–501. Grand Rapids, MI; Cambridge, U.K.: William B. Eerdmans Publishing Company, 1997.

Kislev, Itamar, "The Cultic Fire in the Priestly Source," pages 225–244 in *Yahwism under the Achaemenid Empire, Prof. Shaul Shaked in memoriam*. Gad Barnea and Reinhard Kratz, eds. (BZAW; Berlin: de Gruyter, 2024).

Korpel, Marjo C. A., "Disillusion among Jews in the Postexilic Period," pages 135–57 in *The Old Testament in Its World Papers Read at the Winter Meeting, January 2003 The Society for Old Testament Study and at the Joint Meeting, July 2003 The Society for Old Testament Study and Het*

Oudtestamentisch Werkgezelschap in Nederland en België, edited by Robert P. Gordon & Johannes C. de Moor. Leiden: Brill, 2005.

Kottsieper, Ingo, "Review: Das religiöse Leben der Juden von Elephantine in der Achämenidenzeit by Joisten-Pruschke," *JNES* 72, no. 2 (2013): 299–306.

Kottsieper, Ingo, "From יהה צבאת to יהו מרא שמיא: Aspects of religious development on Elephantine," Pages 245–266 in *Yahwism under the Achaemenid Empire, Prof. Shaul Shaked in memoriam*. Gad Barnea and Reinhard Kratz, eds. (BZAW; Berlin: de Gruyter, 2024)

Kottsieper, Ingo, "Die Religionspolitik der Achämeniden und die Juden von Elephantine." Pages 150–78 in *Religion und Religionskontakte im Zeitalter der Achämeniden*. Edited by Reinhard G. Kratz. Vol. Bd 22 of Gütersloh: Kaiser/Gütersloher Verlagshaus, 2002.

Kratz, Reinhard G., "Where to put 'Biblical' Yahwism in Achaemenid Times?," Pages 267–278 in *Yahwism under the Achaemenid Empire, Prof. Shaul Shaked in memoriam*. Gad Barnea and Reinhard Kratz, eds. (BZAW; Berlin: de Gruyter, 2024).

Kratz, Reinhard G., "The Centralization of Festivals in Deuteronomy 16:1–17," pages 213–45 in *Kritische Schriftgelehrsamkeit in priesterlichen und prophetischen Diskursen: Festschrift für Reinhard Achenbach zum 65. Geburtstag*. Edited by Lars Maskow and Jonathan Robker. Vol. 27 of *BZAR*. Wiesbaden: Harrassowitz, 2022

Kratz, Reinhard G., "Aḥiqar and Bisitun: The Literature of the Judeans at Elephantine," pages 301–22 in *Elephantine in Context*. edited by Bernd U. and Kratz Schipper, Reinhard Gregor. Edited by Bernd U. Schipper. Tübingen: Mohr Siebeck, 2022.

Kratz, Reinhard G., "Isaiah and the Persians," pages 155–68 in *Imperial Visions. The Prophet and the Book of Isaiah in an Age of Empires*, edited by Reinhard G. Kratz and Joachim Schaper. Vol. 277 of *FRLANT*. Göttingen: Vandenhoeck & Ruprecht, 2020.

Kreyenbroek, Philip G., "Zoroastrianism under the Achaemenians: A Non-Essentialist Approach," pages 103–10 in *The world of Achaemenid Persia*. Edited by John Curtis and St John Simpson. London: I.B.Tauris, 2010.

Lemaire, André, "Recherches d'épigraphie araméenne en Asie Mineure et en Égypte et le probleme de l'acculturation," pages 199–206 in *Asia Minor and Egypt: proceedings of the Groningen*, edited by Heleen Sancisi-Weerdenburg and Amélie Kuhrt. Achaemenid history. Leiden: Nederlands Instituut voor het Nabije Oosten, 1991.

Lindenberger, James M., *Ancient Aramaic and Hebrew letters*, Atlanta: SBL, 2003.

Lippert, Sandra, "Les codes de lois en Égypte à l'époque perse," pages 78–98 in *Writing Laws in Antiquity / L'écriture du droit dans l'Antiquité*, edited by Dominique Jaillard and Christophe Nihan. Beihefte ZABR. Wiesbaden: Harrassowitz, 2017.

Malandra, William W., "DAY," pages 163–64 in *Encyclopædia Iranica*. Vol. VII, Fasc. 2. New York: Encyclopædia Iranica Foundation, 1994.

Malandra, William W., "YASNA," *Encyclopædia Iranica* (online edition). New York: Encyclopædia Iranica Foundation, 2006.

Meyer, Eduard, *Der Papyrusfund von Elephantine, Dokumente einer jüdischen Gemeinde aus der Perserzeit und das älteste erhaltene Buch der Weltliteratur, von Eduard Meyer.* Leipzig: J. C. Hinrichs, 1912.

Moore, James D., *New Aramaic Papyri from Elephantine in Berlin*, Leiden: Brill, 2022.

Naveh, Joseph, *The development of the Aramaic script*, Jerusalem: Israel Academy of Sciences and Humanities, 1970.

Oorschot, Jürgen van, and Witte, Markus, eds., *The Origins of Yahwism*: De Gruyter, 2017.

Parker, Richard Anthony, and Dubberstein, Waldo H., *Babylonian chronology 626 B.C.–45*, Chicago: The University of Chicago press, 1942.

Porten, Bezalel. “The Aramaic ‘Passover Papyrus’: Physical Format and Textual Reconstruction,” *Actes du XVe Congres international de papyrologie, Bruxelles–Louvain, 29 août–3 septembre 1977 / edites par Jean Bingen et Georges Nachtergael* 3 (1978–1979): 39–45.

Porten, Bezalel, “Aramaic Papyri and Parchments: A New Look,” *BA* 42, no. 2 (1979): 74–104.

Porten, Bezalel, *Archives from Elephantine: the life of an ancient Jewish military colony*, Berkeley: University of California Press, 1968.

Porten, Bezalel, *The Elephantine papyri in English: three millennia of cross-cultural continuity and change*, Studies in Near Eastern archaeology and civilization, 2nd rev. ed. Atlanta: Society of Biblical Literature, 2011.

Porten, Bezalel and Yardeni, Ada, *Textbook of Aramaic Documents from Ancient Egypt*, 4 vols. Jerusalem: The Hebrew University, 1986–1999.

Quack, Joachim F., “Zum Datum der persischen Eroberung Ägyptens unter Kambyses,” *Journal of Egyptian History* 4 (2011): 228–46.

Razmjou, Shahrokh, “The Lan Ceremony and Other Ritual Ceremonies in the Achaemenid Period: The Persepolis Fortification Tablets,” *Iran* 42 (2004): 103–17.

Rohrmoser, Angela, *Götter, Tempel und Kult der Judäo-Aramäer von Elephantine*, Münster: Ugarit-Verlag, 2014.

Sachau, Eduard, *Aramäische Papyrus und Ostraka aus einer judischen Militar-Kolonie zu Elephantine: altorientalische Sprachdenkmaler des 5. Jahrhunderts vor Chr*, Leipzig: J. C. Hinrichs, 1911.

Shenkar, Michael, “The ‘Eternal Fire’, Achaemenid Zoroastrianism and the Origin of the Fire-Temples,” Pages 379–390 in *Yahwism under the Achaemenid Empire, Prof. Shaul Shaked in memoriam*. Gad Barnea and Reinhard Kratz, eds. (BZAW; Berlin: de Gruyter, 2024).

Schmid, Konrad, “The End of History and the Ends of History: Assessing the Political-Theological Status of the Achaemenid Empire in Persian Period Judaism,” Pages 391–412 in *Yahwism under the Achaemenid Empire, Prof. Shaul Shaked in memoriam*, Gad Barnea and Reinhard Kratz, eds. (BZAW; Berlin: de Gruyter, 2024).

Skjærvø, Prods O., *Introduction to Zoroastrianism*, Self-published, 2005.

Skjærvø, Prods O., “Smashing Urine: on Yasna 48.10,” In *Zoroastrian rituals in context*, edited by Michael Stausberg. Leiden: Brill, 2004, 253–81.

Skjærvø, Prods O., *The spirit of Zoroastrianism*, New Haven: Yale University Press, 2011.

Taillieu, Dieter, “HAOMA i. BOTANY,” pages 659–62 in *Encyclopædia Iranica*. Vol. XI, Fasc. 6. New York: Encyclopædia Iranica Foundation, 2003.

Tavernier, Jan, “An Achaemenid Royal Inscription: The Text of Paragraph 13 of the Aramaic Version of the Bisitun Inscription,” *JNES* 60, no. 3 (2001): 161–76.

Tavernier, Jan, *Iranica in the Achaemenid period (ca. 550–330 B.C.): lexicon of old Iranian proper names and loanwords, attested in non-Iranian texts*, Orientalia Lovaniensia analecta. Leuven: Peeters, 2007.

Toorn, Karel van der, *Becoming Diaspora Jews: Behind the Story of Elephantine*, New Haven: Yale University Press, 2019.

Tuplin, Christopher J., “The Bodleian Letters: Commentary,” In *Aršāma and his World: The Bodleian Letters in Context*, edited by Christopher J. Tuplin and John Ma. Oxford: Oxford University Press, 2020, 61–283.

Ungnad, Arthur, and Sachau, Eduard, *Aramaische Papyrus aus Elephantine*, Kleine Ausg. ed. Leipzig: J. C. Hinrichs, 1911.

Vincent, Albert, *La religion des Judeo-Arameens d'Elephantine*, Paris: Librairie Orientaliste Paul Geuthner, 1937.

Vogüé, Melchior de, “Inscription araméenne trouvée en Égypte,” *CRAI* 47, no. 4 (1903): 269–76.

Wiesehöfer, Josef, *Das antike Persien : von 550 V. Chr. bis 650 N. Chr*, Zurich: Artemis & Winkler, 1993.

Yardeni, Ada, *Osef te'udot Aramiyot, 'Ivriyot ṿe-Nabaṭiyot mi-Midbar Yehudah ṿe-ḥomer ḳarov*, 2 vols. Yerushalayim: ha-Universiṭah ha-'Ivrit bi-Yerushalayim, ha-Merkaz le-ḥeḳer toldot Yiśra'el 'a. sh. Ben-Tsiyon Dinur, 2000.

Diana V. Edelman

Yhwh Shomron and Yhwh Elohim in the Achaemenid Province of Samaria

1 Introduction

The discovery of what is commonly considered the earliest phase of the Samarian temple dedicated to Yhwh on Mt. Gerizim, dated by the excavators to the first half of the fifth century BCE, prompts the question, "Which form of Yhwh was worshipped there via a sacrificial cult?" Was this a satellite sanctuary for the main deity of the city of Samaria, Yhwh Shomron, or was it dedicated to Yhwh Elohim, a newly emergent concept of divinity that embraced a henotheistic philosophy? The latter is known from the Pentateuch, which appears to have served or came to serve as a set of authoritative, sacred writings for those associated with the cult of the deity located on Mt. Gerizim but not, apparently, for the deity in Samaria, as far as we know. As such, it appears the Gerizim temple community shared the Pentateuch with the contemporaneous, rebuilt temple community in Jerusalem in the adjoining province of Yehud. Therefore, it might have honored the same manifestation of deity as the one favored in Jerusalem in the Persian period and later.

The ensuing investigation will take place in three sections. In the first I will establish the existence of discrete forms of conceptualization for the deity Yhwh in Israel/Samaria and Judah/Yehud. In the second I will review the archaeological findings from excavations conducted at Mt. Gerizim in the Persian period and consider if the temple on Gerizim had already been built in the Iron Age, as has been suggested to account for some of the material finds. Finally, I will discuss some of the historical implications that arise from the assessment of the date and nature of the first sacred complex at Mt. Gerizim.

2 Forms of Yhwh

Both the Hebrew Bible and archaeological evidence have confirmed that the deity known as Yhwh had different conceptual and manifest forms in different regions and cities. In the former, there is *yhwh ṣəbāʾôt*, *yhwh (hā)ʾĕlōhîm*, *yhwh ʾĕlōhê*

Diana V. Edelman, University of Oslo, Norway

https://doi.org/10.1515/9783111018638-002

yisrā'el, and *yhwh 'ĕlōhê ṣəbā'ôt*. In the kingdom of Israel, this deity was represented at the sanctuaries of Dan and Bethel by its attribute animal, the bull, which could represent either an *'ēl*-type deity or a *ba'al*-type deity. In the south, or at least in Jerusalem, Yhwh was represented by an enthroned male figure, indicated by the epithet, cherubim-sitter (1Sam 4:4; 2Sam 6:2; 2Kgs 19:15; Isa 37:16; Ps 80:2, 99:1) and the two prophetic visions in Isaiah (6:1–7) and Ezekiel (1:2–28, 10:1–22), which also feature the same seated figure. This is a typical representation for an *'el*-type figure.

Inscriptional evidence adds additional forms, titles, and attributes of Yhwh. At Kuntillet 'Ajrud, located in the Wadi Quraiyeh in northeastern Sinai, Yhwh Shomron and Yhwh of the South (*yhwh tmn*) are called upon for blessings and protection, alongside their respective female partners, Asherah. An inscribed large stone basin there bears an inscription indicating it belonged to Obadyo son of Adnah; it mentions blessings to or from the deity *yhw*, without the final *heh*. The relative dating provided by the pottery and ^{14}C dates, in conjunction with paleographic considerations, has been set ca. 830–750 BCE.[1]

Crude graffiti in a cave at Khirbet Beit Lei in the Judean Shephelah have been read to refer to Yhwh, the divinity of all the earth (*yhwh 'lhy kl h'rṣ*) and to designate this specific deity as *'lhy yršlm*, "the divinity of Jerusalem." The god appears to be invoked as *yh 'l ḥnn*, "Yah, a gracious god," and *yh yhwh*, "Yah, Yhwh." Another inscription in the same cave states, "I am Yhwh your Elohim," a common phrase found in Deuteronomy. There is a three-chambered tomb with a central room inside the cave that likely was hewn sometime in the eighth-seventh centuries BCE and reused in the Persian period, so the inscriptions could date from either period and may not be connected to the funerary context. No pottery was found *in situ*, but Persian-era pottery was found broken outside this and a nearby second cave, suggesting ancient or recent tomb-robbing is likely to have taken place.[2]

Two additional inscriptions from the southern Judean regions are relevant. An inscription from a two-chambered cave in the Judean desert near 'En Gedi, dated on paleographic grounds to ca. 700 BCE, invokes Yhwh and a few lines later, seems to refer to this same deity by the title, *'dny*.[3] Then, one Idumean ostracon from the late Persian period mentions a *bet yhw* in a list of lands likely

---

1 For a detailed discussion, see Zevit, *Religions*, 370–405. The alternate spelling of the divine name *yhw* appears in #8.

2 For a discussion and alternate readings of the graffiti, see Zevit, *Religions*, 405–38. He argues that paleographically, the graffiti exhibit letter forms that are consistent with those used in the late eighth-early seventh century BCE.

3 Zevit, *Religions*, 351–59, with alternate possibilities.

exempted from planting, alongside a *bêt ʿUzzaʾ*.[4] It is not clear if the temple was still functioning or was a ruined landmark at the time, and no further information concerning possible epithets of this form of Yhw have surfaced.[5]

In the surviving Aramaic papyri excavated in the Judean military colony of Yeb on the island of Elephantine just north of the first cataract on the Nile, the divine name, when used independently, appears as *yhw* (*TAD* A3.2:1; A4.8:21; B2.2.6; B3.3:2; C3.15:126; D4.9:1) or *yh* (*TAD* B3.4:25), never *yhwh*, as in the HB. Similarly, when found with the qualifier, "the god" after it, it is spelled *yhw* in all but two cases: *yhw ʾlhʾ* (*TAD* A3.2:2; A4.3:1; A4.7:6, 24, 26; A4.8:5, 24; A4.10:8; B2.2.4; B2.10:6; B3.2:2; B3.4:3; B3.5:2, 10; B3.7:2; B3.10:2, 23; B3.11:2, 17; B3.12:2; B7.1:4; C3.15:1). Once, however, the spelling is *yhh ʾlh* (B2.7.14) and in another is *yhh ʾlhʾ* (B3.3:2). In ostraca found at the site, the deity name is consistently written *yhh* (D7.16:3, 7; D7.18:2–3; D7.21:2), as in the previous two exceptions. The expression *yhh ṣbʾt* occurs on three ostraca (CG 167, 175, 186; *TAD* D7.35:1–2 [reconstructed, = CG 186]). The expression *yhw mrʾ šmyʾ*, "Yhw, lord of heaven," appears twice in the papyri (A4.7:15; A4.8:14), paralleling the Hebrew epithet *ʾdny* found in the cave near ʿEn Gedi. The expression *ʾlh šmyʾ*, "the god of heaven," appears multiple times (*TAD* A.3.6:1 (likely); A4.3:2 [likely], 3, 5; A4.7:2; A4.8:2; A4.9:3–4), though in only two instances is it directly preceded by *yhw* (*TAD* A4.7:27–28; A4.8: 26–27). Finally, the phrase "Yhw the god in the fortress of Yeb" occurs at least once (*TAD* B2.2:4), as does the variant, "Yhh the god in the fortress of Yeb" (*TAD* B3.3:2).[6]

Numerous fragments of dedicatory inscribed stones have been found scattered around Mt. Gerizim and its slopes and associated with the temple complex in existence during the first half of the second century BCE (Phase 2). Yitzhak Magen has proposed they may have been part of a retaining wall of the temple that separated it from other buildings in the sacred complex and formed a barrier to those excluded from entrance into the temple proper.[7] Anne Katrine de Hemmer Gudme, on the other hand, notes the possibility that all the stones once were blocks belonging to a wall somewhere in the sacred complex whose construction either was funded by private donations or was meant to display the names of private, wealthy donors of sacrifices or money.[8] The two views are not mutually exclusive.

---

4 For further discussion of this ostracon see Hensel "Reconsidering Yahwism in Persian Period Idumea in Light of the Current Material Findings," in this volume.

5 For this revised reading of ostracon #283, which has abandoned an earlier proposed reference to a third temple, for Nabu, see Lemaire, *Levantine Epigraphy*, 118–19, with fig. 3.25.

6 Porten, *Archives from Elephantine*, 105–6, 109. For various forms of Yhwh at Elephantine and the spellings of the deity name, see in this volume the articles by Kottsieper, Folmer and Porten.

7 Magen, "Mount Gerizim," 105.

8 de Hemmer Gudme, "Permanent and passing words," 47, 50–52.

The inscriptions refer generically, in Aramaic, to the god (*'lh'*) (for example, ##149, 172, 190, 191, 200, 213) or "the god in this place" (*'lh' b'tr' dnh*) (for example, ##152, 154, 155, 162). Two (##150, 151) use the Hebrew title "lord" (*'dny*)[9] but are written in cursive Aramaic script. It can be noted that these uses overlap with those at Yeb in three ways: both employ the singular vs. plural form, *'elo^{a}h*; each uses *'adonay/mar'a* to refer to the deity; and both associate the deity with a particular location.

The proper name Yhwh appears on only one preserved fragment (#383) at Gerizim. Uncharacteristically, it is written in Hebrew, as are words on eight other fragments (##150 but in cursive Aramaic script, 382, 384–388. Four share with #383 the same use of carved horizontal ruling lines and vertical lines at the left and probably also the right margin (##382, 384, 385, and 387). It seems likely they all once comprised a single dedicatory inscription; they were all recovered from "Area S, between the east wall of the church enclosure and the east wall of the sacred precinct, south of the east gate."[10]

In addition to the tetragrammaton (#383), the fragments with ruling lines contain references to the title priest (##382, 388), the proper name Pinḥas and the adjective *gdwl*, which might have designated him as high priest, together with three letters of a proper name, *yšʿ*, which might have read [Abi]shua (#384).[11] This inscription is generally considered to have been contemporaneous with the recovered Aramaic and Greek inscriptions from Phase 2 but also might have been earlier.[12]

3 Was Yhwh of Samaria a City God or a Regional Deity?

Was the Yhwh Shomron invoked in the inscription at Kuntillet ʿAjrud being conceived of as the god of the city of Samaria or the god of the territorial kingdom

9 Magen, Misgav, and Tsafania, *Mount Gerizim Excavations 1*, 141–43; de Hemmer Gudme, "Permanent and passing words," 47.

10 Magen, Misgav, and Tsafania, *Mount Gerizim Excavations 1*, 253.

11 The title priest occurs as well in Aramaic in ##24, 25, 389, while Pinḥas appears elsewhere in Aramaic inscriptions ##24, 25, 61. The latter may not necessarily all refer to the same person, however.

12 E.g. Dušek, *Aramaic and Hebrew Inscriptions*, 58. The dedicatory inscription might have been composed at the time the Persian-era complex was inaugurated instead, similar to the one found at the temple of Patgaia or Pdry in Ekron from the Iron IIB period or the trilingual Xanthus inscription from the Persian period. In this case, the governor or sponsoring patron of the facility would have commissioned its carving rather than the king of the city. If the analogies hold, it

of Israel? In extrabiblical texts, the three latest references to Israel or Israelite occur in the ninth century BCE (Kurkh Monolith, 853 BCE; Mesha inscription, ca. 840–830 BCE, and the Tel Dan inscription). New designations, the land of Omri/ son of Omri/House or Dynasty of Omri, begin to appear in 840 BCE and continue in use until 715 BCE or so, at which point they are describing the newly established province under Sargon II. During the eighth century, the terms Samaria and Samarian also began to appear in extra-biblical texts, overlapping in use with the Omride terminology. But it is only in two inscriptions written ca. 690 BCE that the relatively new Assyrian province comes to be designated by its main administrative city, Samerina, which was the former seat of the Omrides and their successors (Nimrud Prisms D and E [2.118D]).[13]

The available extra-biblical evidence suggests that in the eighth century, the Assyrians tended to describe the kingdom in the central hill-country of Cisjordan as though it were an Aramean kingdom named after its dynastic founder, Omri, but they also were aware that the main seat of the kingdom was located in the city of Samaria.[14] The small "Summary" Inscription of Sargon II (2.118F) talks of the plundering of Samerina and the entire land of Beth Omri, while his Pavement Inscription 4 (2.118G), dated to 729 BCE, mentions the conquest of Samaria and the entire land of Beth Omri.[15] Summary inscription 13 (2.117G) in particular states that only the city of Samaria was spared in [the land of Beth Omri]. In all these cases, Samaria/Samerina designated the city. Fairly soon after the territory of the former kingdom was converted to provincial status, however, without a local dynastic family in control, the name of the former capital was chosen to designate the entire unit. The city continued to function as the administrative seat of the Assyrian province and remained the provincial seat under the Neo-Babylonian, Achaemenid, and Hellenistic empires.

Thus, it is safe to conclude that in the inscription at Kuntillet 'Ajrud, which dates somewhere ca. 830–750 BCE, Shomron is designating the city, not the kingdom of Israel or the land of the Omrides.[16] This in turn also implies that the city

---

would tend to suggest a temple building had been included in the complex, dedicated to Yhwh. For the Ekron inscription, see e.g., Gitin, Dothan, and Naveh, "A Royal Dedicatory Inscription," 8–13. For its symbolic power, see Smoak, "Inscribing Temple Space," 328. For the name of the deity, see e.g. Berlant, "Mysterious Ekron Goddess," 15–21. For the Xanthus or Letoon trilingual text, see e.g. Teixidor, "Tringual Stele," 181–85; Lemaire, "Xanthos Trilingual," 423–32. For the deity, see Vernet, "Letoon Trilingual," 81–100.

13 For the texts, see Hallo, *The Context of Scripture* 2, 295–96; Tappy, *Archaeology of Israelite Samaria*, Vol. 2, 609–11.

14 So also, e.g. Cogan, *The Raging Torrent*, 26.

15 For the text of all three inscriptions, see Hallo, *Context of Scripture 2*, 292, 297–98.

16 For the argument that Samaria is a regional term here and that the main cult center of Yhwh of Samaria was at Bethel, not Samaria, see Na'aman, "In Search of," 78–82.

hosted a temple dedicated to this deity at that point in time. It is unclear if there would have been a separate temple honoring Asherah, who also is invoked in the inscription, or whether the divine pair would have been housed in a single cultic complex located somewhere inside the city walls of the city of Samaria, if not on the acropolis proper.

Logically, a temple for Yhwh Shomron would have been constructed when the city was first founded by the Omrides, in addition to the palace complex. The excavations conducted at Sebaste have uncovered the royal acropolis complex, built upon an artificially constructed platform above the uneven bedrock. It contained a palace, a large open courtyard, and various freestanding royal buildings, and casemate storerooms, all of which are poorly preserved. The substantial rebuilding of city by Herod the Great (ca. 72–4 BCE) included the siting of a monumental temple dedicated to Sebaste, the Greek name of Emperor Augustus, on the site of the former royal complex on the acropolis. Large portions of the preceding levels were cleared away to place the new foundations on bedrock. There was sufficient space for a temple to have been situated within the royal complex in the Iron Age, although no traces of it remain *in situ*. A temple could have been built elsewhere on the acropolis, however, in its own compound. The likely contents of a possible Iron-Age shrine or temple were uncovered ca. 900 meters east of the royal compound. Lots of potsherds and animal and human figurines dating to the eighth century BCE were found in a trench measuring 4–6 meters wide by 2–5 meters deep in Area E 207.[17]

What we know about deity cults is that cities like Samaria, a royal seat, would have had a city god or divine couple that often doubled as the deity/ies of the royal family in power. That deity or pair of deities would have legitimated the ruling dynasty through an established set of rituals. In an ancient city-state, this pair would have been supreme over clan and family gods of the inhabitants. In the case of ancient territorial states or empires, a "national" divine couple would have emerged as the top of the pantheon comprising all the deities honored within the boundaries of the polity, as it grew or shrank.

Logically, then, the main temple for Yhwh Shomron in the city of Samaria should have remained in use through the conversion of the kingdom to an Assyrian and then Neo-Babylonian and Persian province. As the long-established native god of the city, it would have been imprudent to forcefully close down its cult in favor of one honoring the gods of the new rulers or a new ethnic majority. No such policy has been detected to have been enacted by the Achaemenid administration within its Empire or by its predecessors. At most, the Yahwistic temple in

---

17 For the plan and a brief description, see for example, Herzog, "Settlement and Fortification," 249–50. Avigad, "Samaria (City)," 1,300–10 (1,306 for the possible cultic site).

Samaria could have lost any tax-exempt status it might have enjoyed under the Assyrians or Neo-Babylonians when the Persians became the new imperial rulers, requiring a segment of the local population that had remained in place to assume the cost of maintaining the cult.

Under Achaemenid administration, Samaria bore the status of a *bîrâ,* a walled site that contained a military garrison alongside administrators and facilities.[18] It is so described in Wadi Daliyeh papyri ##1.1 and 4.1.[19] The same term was applied to the sites of Syene and Yeb (Elephantine) near the First Cataract of the Nile. It also is used to describe Jerusalem under the Achaemenids in the book of Nehemiah (1:1; 2:8; 7:2), but because this book is likely written in the Hellenistic period, it is unclear whether it is accurately describing the historical reality of the Persian period or only of the Hellenistic period.[20] Since it is probably a loan-word from Aramaic or Akkadian used in Achaemenid administration, however, it is logical to think the term had already been applied in the Persian period and continued in use in the Hellenistic period.

The situations at both Xanthus in southern Turkey and Yeb in Egypt indicate that in the context of contingents of ethnically cohesive mercenaries posted to fortresses outside their homeland, permission had been granted by the ruling Achaemenid authorities to establish or continue maintaining a temple for the native god or main divine couple of the newcomers alongside the one of the native local male and/or female deity, as long as it was self-funded. The trilingual inscription from Xanthus makes this clear in its wording. "The land-owners of Arnna have instituted a cult to worship the Lord god of *kbydšy* (Greek reads "king of Kaunios") and they made Simias son of Koddorasi priest.[21] And there is a *bg* [a group of fields belonging to several owners] that the landowners gave to the Lord God. Year after year the sum of a mina and a half will be given by the region. The aforesaid priest will sacrifice a sheep every new moon to the Lord God and to [...], and an ox every year (lines 6–17).[22]

Yeb was established before Achaemenid imperial rule began in Egypt, but the correspondence relating to efforts to rebuild the temple to Yhw after it is destroyed suggests it was self-funded, and the list of silver collected for the various cults (*TAD* C3.15) specifically points in that direction, whether it was for new

18 For the definition, see Lemaire and Lozachmeur, "*Birah/birta'*," 261–66; Will, "Qu-est ce qu'une *Baris*?," 253–59.

19 Gropp *et al.*, *Wadi Daliyeh II*, 34–35, 65–66.

20 For details, see Finkelstein, *Hasmonean Realities*.

21 The Greek and Lycian texts specify that the priesthood would be hereditary within the same family. So Teixidor, "Aramaic Text," 183.

22 Teixidor, "Aramaic Text," 181–82. See also Lemaire, "Xanthos Trilingual," 423–32.

deity statues or for operating expenses.[23] Thus, it is quite possible that post 722 BCE, under the Assyrians, Neo-Babylonians, and Achaemenids, new temples or shrines were constructed both in the city of Samaria and elsewhere in the territory of the province by transferred population groups and administrators, but not at the expense of the long-standing cult of Yhwh Shomron in the provincial seat, Samaria.[24]

With Alexander's destruction of the site of Samaria for insurrection in 331 BCE, the long-standing cult of Yhwh Shomron would have been terminated; the site lay abandoned for some decades. The Ptolemies eventually rebuilt the city as a garrison for troops, and a temple to Serapis and Isis was established on site for those stationed there. An inscription dating to the third century BCE reads, "Hegesandros, Xenarchis and the children, to Serapis [and] Isis." Then, under the Seleucids in the second century BCE, this cult was replaced by one dedicated to Kore.[25] Thus, after 331, those seeking to continue to worship Yhwh would have needed to relocate to the vicinity of a temple dedicated to a form of this deity. There may have been others in the province, but we know for sure that the one on Gerizim would have been well-established for over a century by this time. Even though most, if not all, of the fragmentary Aramaic and Greek dedicatory stones at Gerizim derive from the Hellenistic period, they indicate that Yhw was honored at that site as "the god" and "lord" of Mt. Gerizim, which likely would have been the case in the preceding Persian period as well.

---

23 For the suggestion the silver was intended for deity statues rather than the annual endowment to fund the cults, see Cornell, "Cult Statuary," 298–305.

24 Hanan Eshel suggested that a Samarian coin dating to the fourth century BCE bears the image of a temple and equates it with the temple to Yhwh in the city of Samaria ("Prayer of Joseph," 131–32 [Hebrew]). Seth Schwartz, with due caution, points out, "a central provincial temple would have been located in the provincial capital, Samaria. [...] It is entirely reasonable to posit the existence of temple at Samaria; why should it have lacked one?" ("John Hyrcanus I's Destruction," 23, n. 27). Similarly, Nadav Na'aman notes, "the absence of a reference to a cult place in the capital city does not indicate none existed" ("In Search of," 82). Thomas Römer concurs; he suggests that late redactors might have changed a reference to such a Yahwistic temple in 1Kgs 16:32 into a temple dedicated to Ba'al instead, to give the impression that the sanctuary in the northern capital was baalistic and so illegitimate. He also thinks there would have been other temples in the kingdom beyond those few mentioned by the biblical writers ("Des temples yahvistes," 40).

25 For the dating and possible locations, see Magness, "Cults of Isis and Kore," 157–77.

4 Regional Manifestations of Yhwh in the Kingdom of Israel and Province of Samerina

Turning to the Iron Age kingdom of Israel, how many temples for the national divine couple, Yhwh Shomron and his Asherah, would have been established and maintained outside the capital, and what would have warranted the construction of additional temples or sanctuaries over time? From the scant available evidence, the cult of the territorial or imperial god or gods was not typically imposed on existing settlements, where the established city/town god(s), clan, and family gods continued to be honored as before. However, their cult would have been able to have been implemented in newly founded settlements built by royal directive, like trade centers, administrative towns, and military forts, or in rebuilt abandoned or destroyed sites, had the ruler wanted that to happen.

The scribes responsible for the books of Kings and Amos claim that King Jeroboam established national temples for Yhwh at Dan and Bethel (1Kgs 12:25–33; also e.g. Amos 7:13 for Bethel) and yet never mention the existence of a temple to Yhwh in the capital city, Samaria. Dan and Bethel are commonly understood to have been border sanctuaries; however, no other historical examples of this assumed practice have been cited from the ancient Near East.[26] Typically, borders are fluid and meant to be temporary, since the goal of most rulers of an ancient territorial state or empire was to expand them.

There seems to be a definite pro-Judean (Judahite), anti-Samarian (Israelite) strategy at work in the book of Kings, meaning caution is needed in evaluating the historicity of the portrayed events. The failure to acknowledge that a separate form of Yhwh had existed in the capital of the kingdom of Israel would be one of two complementary strategies used in the books of Kings to express the view that the Israelite kingdom had broken away illegitimately from the divinely chosen Davidic dynasty and its deity, Yhwh Ṣəbāôt. It uses silence to deny the exis-

26 As noted by Nadav Na'aman, by analogy, the same concept of temples near borders might be associated in Judah with the phrase, "from Geba to Beersheba" in 2Kgs 23:8. Although he admitted no traditions have been preserved about a sanctuary at Geba, there are a number associated with Beersheba (Gen 21:27, 31–33; 26:24–25, 31; Amos 8:14) ("In Search of," 87–90). There is, however, a deliberate equation of Gibeah, Geba, and Gibeon in Samuel and Kings, so perhaps the memory of a sanctuary at Gibeon, which the Chronicler characterizes as having been like a sanctuary of the kingdom, where Solomon allegedly underwent dream incubation, is being deliberately altered in those books. Be that as it may, we should doubt the validity of the concept of "border sanctuaries" and think instead of royal sanctuaries established at points along important trade routes, often at crossroads.

tence of another official form of Yhwh in the northern capital but then attacks the two cults seemingly associated with the same manifestation of this deity established by royal order in other towns or on nearby heights in the Israelite countryside.

In 2Kgs 17, the scribe has caricatured the monarchic-era Israelites as having built *bāmôt* (open-air sanctuaries with sacrificial altars that could contain outbuildings) in all their towns, from watchtower to fortified city (v. 9), to have set up *maṣṣēbôt* and *'ăšērîm* on every high hill and under every green tree (v. 10), and to have served idols (v. 12), including two golden calves and Asherah (v. 16). They also worshipped all the host of heaven and served Ba'al (v. 16). This is given as the reason for their defeat and exile by the Assyrians and the creation of province of Samerina. He has also condemned the new immigrants transplanted into Samaria for having converted existing Israelite *bāmôt* to the worship of their native gods (vv. 29–31) in addition to having adopted the cult of Yhwh at established Israelite *bāmôt*, setting up new priesthoods in each case (v. 32).

While clearly intended to be polemical in a context where Yahwistic henotheism was being developed and espoused, the text assumes a worldview that was a believable and acceptable worldview during the preceding Iron Age. Native inhabitants related to the divine world via many forms of deities, from the family ancestors and clan deities to local town deities, to regional deities, which might or might not have been the "national," royally sponsored divine couple. Relocated groups would have wanted to relate to the familiar, lower-level divine entities and family gods from their homeland and possibly also higher- level ones but also would have wanted to honor the native weather god(s) of the new land, thought to control its fertility. Thus, it is likely that in addition to household shrines, there would have been shrines or cultic places founded on virgin soil or on abandoned sacred spots by immigrant populations after 722 BCE, dedicated to home deities or to some form of Yahweh, which could have continued to be frequented by their descendants into the Persian period.

5 The Sacred Precinct and Adjoining Settlement on Mt. Gerizim in the Persian Period

Excavations were conducted atop Mt Gerizim/Çebel eṭ-Ṭōr by Yitzhak Magen beginning in 1982 and intermittently until 2009, with additional salvage operations on the northern slope conducted in 2019–2021. The excavators have uncovered a walled sacred precinct measuring some 96 meters from north to south and 98 meters from east to west, including one preserved gate, built on bedrock.[27] It contained an open-air altar, whose location and physical structure has not been preserved. Evidence of its existence is provided, however, by a thick layer of bones of sheep, goats, cows, and pigeons and ash in a square building on the northeastern side of the precinct near the north gate. Similar deposits also were found in the southwestern corner of the fortified enclosure near the western staircase and in the inner southwestern side of the enclosure.[28]

The courtyard of the ash-filled, square building near the northern gate contained a cistern that would have been functioning during this first phase of the complex's use.[29] It is unclear if any of the other six or seven large cisterns excavated on the eastern side of the temple precincts were also in use in this phase, rather than being constructed in the Hellenistic or Byzantine period.[30] Thus, the sacred complex had at least one source of water during the Persian period.

Based on the ceramics and the earliest coin found on the summit but outside the walled sacred enclosure, Magen has argued it is likely that the sacred area was built in the first half or mid part of the fifth century BCE. The pottery retrieved from the Persian occupation in Phase I includes storage jars, juglets, flasks, basins, cooking pots, kraters that frequently were ornamented with wedge decoration, bowls, some of which were red-slipped and burnished, and lamps with a flat base.[31]

5.1 Was There a Temple in the Sacred Complex on Gerizim in Phase 1?

Whether this complex contained a temple building from the beginning or at any point during the Persian period is a matter of current debate. Magen argues the feature he has called the "Twelve Stones" provides likely evidence of a temple dating to the Persian period. The base layer of a wall or platform made of dressed stones measures 6.5 × 18 m. A second layer seems to be *in situ*, most of which are

27 Magen, *Mount Gerizim 2*, 143.
28 Magen, *Mount Gerizim 2*, 148, 160.
29 Magen, *Mount Gerizim 2*, 17.
30 Magen gives the total number of large cisterns as both seven and eight (*Mount Gerizim 2*, 149, 159, respectively). He suspects many date (already) from the Hellenistic period (149).
31 Magen, *Mount Gerizim 2*, 168; for the pottery and coin plates, see 182–99. Eran Arie notes, however, that coins can only provide evidence of periods of use, not of founding. Since it was not until the Persian period that coinage became adopted in the southern Levant, one should not expect to find coins from the Iron IIC period in any structure already in existence on the summit at that time ("Revisiting Mt. Gerizim," 54*–55*).

not dressed in the photograph. In his view, this stone feature could be the remains of the western wall of the original "holy of holies" of the first temple building. It stood inside the western enclosing wall of the sacred complex in Phase 1 and in his view, was built before the precinct's western wall.[32] He states this row of stones remains sacred to the Samaritan community to this day, even though it was only recently excavated. He also says they no longer believe a temple (ever) existed on Gerizim, in which case, it is unlikely the Samaritans would have had a native tradition that considered the feature part of their first, Persian-era temple.[33] Magen's argument would have been more persuasive had the feature been incorporated into the Hellenistic temple structure, which would have better marked and preserved its sanctity. The location of this latter building remains uncertain, however, so this could have been the case if the building corner lying slightly northeast of the feature was not part of the Hellenistic temple, as he has surmised.[34] The clustering of cisterns at the edges of the sacred complex could be seen to indicate that a building had occupied the more central area in both Phase 1 and Phase 2.

Others doubt the existence of a temple during the Persian period. In 1991, while the excavations were still underway, Robert T. Anderson argued a lack of financial and labor resources would have limited the sacred precinct to containing an altar only.[35] Etienne Nodet has cited the large quantities of animal bones as proof that one or more altars had existed in the early complex, but the lack

---

32 Magen, *Mount Gerizim 2*, 113–14. He is not specific about the evidence he is relying upon to support this sequence of construction.

33 Magen, *Mount Gerizim 2*, 151–52. Reinhard Pummer concurs that the Samaritans deny that a temple building ever existed on Mt. Gerizim ("Was There an Altar," 3, 10, 14). He seems to provide an independent assessment of various sources and does not refer to Magen's prior discussion. Elsewhere he notes that the Byzantine historian "Procopius' official denial that the Samaritans ever had a sanctuary where the church was built is tendentious and unreliable." This comment seems to relate to the issue of whether a synagogue succeeded the destroyed temple, not to the earlier temple itself, however ("Samaritan Synagogues," 132).

34 To Magen's mind, the reason the Hellenistic builders would have left only it intact when they built the new temple, a corner of whose foundations he thinks he has identified adjacent to the northern side of the "Twelve Stones," would have been special sanctity (*Mount Gerizim 2*, 114, 152). If he is correct, they dismantled the rest of the temple, including its foundations, when they built the new temple of ashlar masonry during the reign of Antiochus III (223–187 BCE) (114, 143, 153–54). Another option to consider is that the Byzantine builders chose to leave this feature and the adjacent but non-contiguous building corner when they cleared the area to construct their church. They might have understood that both related to earlier temple structures and kept them as memorials *in situ* but outside their own new structure, which was dedicated to the Christian god, not the Samaritan one.

35 Anderson, "Elusive Samaritan Temple."

of any physical evidence of a free-standing architectural structure indicates there was no *cella* in the Persian period. He argues the temple was eventually added after the one in Jerusalem was up and running, with Persian authorization.[36] Jürgen K. Zangenberg has suggested the "twelve stones" might have marked the site of the original altar rather than the rear wall of a temple; he doubts this open-air sanctuary had included a temple in the Persian period.[37]

A stone inscribed with Greek from a Samarian synagogue on the island of Delos might indicate a temple existed at Gerizim by ca. 250 BCE, which was still during Phase 1 of the complex according to Magen's stratigraphy, even though it was after the end of Persian imperial rule. "The Israelites who make first-fruit offerings to the holy temple/sanctuary (*'hieron*) on Mt. Gerizim honor Menippos, son of Artemidorus of Herakleion, both himself and his descendants, for constructing and dedicating his own funds for the synagogue of God [...] and crown him with a gold crown [...]." On paleographic grounds, the Greek inscription has been dated ca. 250–175 BCE, which includes the end of Phase 1 and the first 25 years of Phase 2 on Mt. Gerizim.

The key issue is what Hebrew or Aramaic term might underlie the word *'hieron* in this inscription, assuming it is a noun, as argued by Reinhard Pummer, rather than an adjective.[38] Is it *bêt*, which would clearly represent a temple, *'gwr* or *miqdāš*, which could include a temple building, as at Elephantine,[39] or an open-air sacred space with altar only? Recognizing the ambiguous nature of the term in Greek, where the same two meanings are possible, Pummer opts for "temple" because of the reference to "contributions" being made.[40] Jan Dušek opts for "sanctuary," which would equate it with more with *miqdāš*, the term that occurs in the third line of inscription #150 from Mt. Gerizim, although this term does not exclude a temple building as an option.[41] The mentions of a house of sacrifice (*bbyt dbḥ'*) (#199, line 2) and likely of the temple (*[h]klh*) (#211, line 2) on personal dedicatory Aramaic inscriptions from Gerizim probably refer to the Hellenistic-era temple of Phase 2.[42]

---

36 Nodet, "Israelites, Samaritans," 122, 141.

37 Zangenberg, "Sanctuary on Mount Gerizim," 409.

38 Pummer, "ΑΡΓΑΡΙΖΙΝ," 20, n. 7.

39 The complex at Elephantine, which definitely included a temple building, is referred to in the papyri as *'gwr'/'gwr zy yhw 'lh'* (*TAD* A4.7:6; A4.8:6; A4.10:8; B2.7:14; B2.10:6; B3.4:9–10) and once as *byt mdbḥ' zy 'lh šmy'byb byrt'* (A4.9.3–4).

40 Pummer, "Was There an Altar," 16.

41 Dušek, *Aramaic and Hebrew Inscriptions*, 78. This is the only inscription in the collection that uses Hebrew written in "proto-Jewish" script rather than "neo-Hebrew" script. See Magen, Misgav, and Tsafania, *Mount Gerizim 1*, 141–42. Dušek prefers to describe the former as cursive Aramaic (5).

42 See Dušek, *Aramaic and Hebrew Inscriptions*, 84; Benedikt Hensel, *Juda und Samaria*, 54–58.

If the approximated date range for the Delos inscription is reliable, it could indicate a temple existed already before the end of the first phase on Gerizim. Even so, it would not confirm if it would have been built when the sacred enclosure was first established or added secondarily as another feature of what had previously been an open-air sanctuary housing only an altar. Either way, the temple would have been constructed in Phase 1, before the expansion of the site ca. 200 BCE, even if its location is no longer traceable.[43]

However, in trying to narrow the date range, Jan Dušek has argued that the adjective "holy," found in this inscription from Delos but not in a subsequent one referring to the same sanctuary on Har Gerizim dated ca. 150–50 BCE, may designate a tax-exempt status instituted by the Seleucids for both the temple on Gerizim and the one in Jerusalem.[44] If he is correct, then the reference could be to the temple on Gerizim constructed in Phase 2, ca. 200 BCE. Its location is no longer certain either, due to the extensive clearing done to construct the Byzantine church complex. In the latter case, then, this inscription could no longer be used as potential evidence for a Persian-era temple building.

Another factor influencing this debate over the existence of a temple already in the Persian period is the date when residential areas were established outside the walls of the sacred complex. Jürgen K. Zangenberg, for example, states,

> The fact that no houses were found around the first sacred precinct suggests to me that no permanent cult was performed there, but that worshippers and perhaps also parts of the cult personnel came to the sanctuary only at particular moments. Mount Gerizim VII clearly was a pilgrimage center [...].[45]

His conclusions rely on Yitzhak Magen's claim that the first houses were built only in the Hellenistic period late in Phase 1.

Contrary to the initial publication that stated there were no pre-Hellenistic residences outside the sacred complex in the Persian era, the now-published coin report and the results of further excavations have demonstrated that a residential quarter existed on the summit already in Phase 1 in the fifth century BCE. Dalit and Uzi Greenfeld have noted that Persian-era coins were found *in situ* in Residential Building 37 in Area S north of the Phase 2 grand staircase leading to the eastern gate of the sacred complex, in Mansion Complex 23 that included dwelling space, an oil press, and shops, and in Public Building 25. The latter two are in

---

43 Reinhard Pummer has noted that the presence of a roofed temple building in Phase 2 is corroborated by Aramaic inscription #199, which, though fragmentary, reads, "bulls in all [... sacrifi]ced in the house of sacrifice [*byt dbḥ'*] [...]" ("Was there an Altar," 8.)

44 Dušek, *Aramaic and Hebrew Inscriptions*, 78–79, 84–85.

45 Zangenberg, "Sanctuary on Mt. Gerizim," 407.

Area P west of the western enclosing wall of the sacred complex.[46] Fragments of at least two black-glazed Attic vessels also were found in Areas S and P, both of which lay outside the walls of the sacred precinct in the same areas where the earliest Persian-era coins were recovered.[47] Black glazed ware tended to succeed red figured ware toward the end of the fifth century BCE, indicating the residential areas were already in use in the first half of Phase 1.[48]

Renewed salvage excavations conducted in 2019–2021 on the northern slopes uncovered additional residential structures in Field 37 and Areas B, C, and D of Field 42 that date to the Persian period. They were constructed more or less on terraces, whose retaining walls allowed fill to be added behind them to create a level surface for the buildings.[49] Thus, it appears there were residential and storage areas on the summit outside the walls of the sacred complex already in the Persian era. This, in turn, might point to the presence of a temple building during the Persian period, requiring full-time cultic personnel living adjacent to it to staff it and source its needs.

The precinct continued in use, no doubt with modifications, until ca. 200 BCE according to Yitzhak Magen, when its layout was extensively altered, representing Phase 2, which lasted only some 100 years. The temple precinct was extensively expanded to measure 212 meters from north to south and 136 meters east to west,

---

46 Regev and Greenfeld, "Persian Pottery." They cite Bijovsky, "Coins from the Excavations," 12, 130. Bijovsky erroneously has described all of Area S as "the sacred precinct" (84). Thus, they fall outside of or are mistakenly included in the 72 Persian-period coins Magen claims were uncovered inside the precinct (*Mount Gerizim 2*, 168).

47 Magen, *Mount Gerizim 2*, 168, 182–92.

48 The earliest coin found so far is a drachma from Cyprus (Soli?), roughly dated to 480 BCE (cat. #7), from locus 4122 in Area P. In addition, two other bronze coins, one minted at Idyma in Caria (cat. #2) from locus 498 in Area S (ca. 450–400 BCE) and another of uncertain origin but possibly Lydian, (cat. #3) from locus 801 in Area S, date to the fifth century BCE. A Philistine silver drachma from Gaza found in locus 4106 in Area P dates from 450–400 BCE (cat. #8). A Tyrian silver stater from locus 408 in Area S might date from the end of the fifth century (cat. #73), and some of the 13 Sidonian silver 1/16 shekels minted under Baʿal-Shillem II might derive from the closing years of the fifth century and if not, from the first quarter of the fourth century (cat. ##35–47) (Magen, *Mount Gerizim 2*, 168). They were uncovered in five loci in Area P: 4176, 4178, 4278 (x 2), 4287 (x 5), 4289; in loci 499 and 799 in Area S, in locus 31 in Area N, and in locus 915 in Area E. All these fifth century or early fourth century coins were from buildings outside the sacred precinct. Overall, 90 silver and bronze coins of various denominations and diverse minting authorities datable to the Persian period were recovered during Magen's excavations, and 7 early Hellenistic ones. These 97 all have been assigned to Phase 1, which ended about 200 BCE. Those in loci outside the enclosing walls of the sacred precinct likely were from residents of a neighborhood already built around the complex and occupied in the Persian period.

49 Regev and Greenfeld, "Persian Pottery," 67–71, 85.

and the interior layout was also altered, only to be destroyed by John Hyrcanus (ruled 134–104 BCE) and his forces in 111–110 BCE.[50]

6 A Possible Iron Age Sacred Complex on Mt. Gerizim?

Recently, Eran Arie has reassessed the material finds presented in the site report publications to date and has suggested that a sanctuary complex was first built on Mt. Gerizim in the Iron IIC period, not initially in the mid-fifth century BCE. If he is correct, there are important implications that would follow concerning the possible identity of the deity worshipped there; it need not have been Yhwh Shomron or another form of Yhwh at all but could have been dedicated to one or more deities introduced by new immigrants forcefully settled in the area by the Assyrian or Neo-Babylonian imperial rulers.

6.1 The Evidence for an Iron Age Presence

Four main arguments have been offered in support of the presence of an Iron-Age sanctuary. First is the three-chambered gate giving access to the complex on its northern side; this style of gate is not known to have been used in the southern Levant after the Iron IIB period. After assessing the evidence, Arie suggests that its use logically needs to be extended into the Iron IIC period because of the presence of Iron IIC pottery on site.[51]

Second is the recovery of three "proto-Ionic" or volute carved stone blocks. The two that are almost complete are made of *nāri*, a form of limestone that is "almost unique on Mount Gerizim,"[52] while the third one consisting of part of the right volute only is made of hard limestone but apparently was found in the same debris. *Nāri* was not found locally on Mt. Gerizim. According to Magen,

> The upper level [of rock] was hard and brittle, unsuitable for the production of ashlars. [...] During the Persian period, the upper layer of rock was removed, producing unworkable fieldstones. In the Hellenistic period, the same technique was used for rocks from lower

50 Magen, *Mount Gerizim 2*, 103, 152.

51 Arie, "Revisiting Mt. Gerizim," 42*, 56*. It is noteworthy that in the 2008 preliminary report on the Persian-era complex, all three reconstructed gates are drawn as four or eight-chambered, not three or six-chambered in fig. 185.

52 Stern and Magen, "Archaeological Evidence," 50*.

levels and the quarried stones were more skillfully hewn, producing workable field stones.[53]

It is worth noting, however, that *nāri* was the preferred material for ashlars and for stone volutes in the ancient southern Levant.[54] Of the seventeen volutes in collections in modern Israel that were able to be studied in 1967, sixteen were made of *nāri*; they were from Megiddo, Hazor, Samaria, and Ramat Raḥel. The remaining one from Jerusalem was made of hard *mizzi ḥelū*.[55]

The two almost complete stones are described to have been part of "a large concentration of fallen stones, which contained pillar sections and some inscriptions," on the eastern slope "below the flight of steps that led visitors into the temple."[56] Apparently the third fragment was in the same debris "on the eastern staircase ascending to the sacred precinct."[57] This staircase was in use throughout Phase 2 (ca. 200–110 BCE).

One of the two almost complete blocks (#10025) was found in locus 7019, which was above the staircase itself, and the other (#10540) was found to the right of the southern side of the entry gate to the staircase, in locus 7035. Arie has mistakenly understood them to have lain in the fill under the staircase.[58] Clearly, there are important implications for dating depending on a location above or below the stairs. Their final use, then, was in the Hellenistic period, but they could have been in secondary use already at that point. Comparative data suggests the volutes either should be dated to the seventh-sixth centuries BCE or to the Hellenistic period, although all the examples otherwise known from the Northern Kingdom date from the ninth-eighth centuries BCE, which is certainly not the case with these.[59]

Norma Franklin notes that the three carved volute blocks are unique among exemplars from the territory of Israel in that "their volutes protrude beyond their narrow bases, making them – in effect hanging volutes."[60] Ephraim Stern and Yitzhak Magen note likely evidence of the reshaping of both. They propose that

53 Magen, *Mount Gerizim 2*, 4.

54 So e.g. Shiloh and Horowitz, "Ashlar Quarries"; Itkin *et al.*, "*Nāri* in the Levant," 211, map, which is not, however, exhaustive.

55 Kenyon, *Jerusalem*, pl. 20, cited by Shiloh and Horowitz, "Ashlar Quarries," 39 (8 years later).

56 Stern and Magen, "Archaeological Evidence," 49*–50*.

57 Magen, *Mount Gerizim 2*, 152.

58 I thank Norma Franklin for drawing my attention to this discrepancy in private conversation at the EABS Conference in Siracusa, Sicily, 10–13 July, 2023.

59 E.g., Lipschits, "Origin and Date," 207; Arie, "Revisiting Mt. Gerizim," 43*–49*. For a survey and the dates of known examples, see Franklin, "Stone Volutes," 156–69.

60 Franklin, "Stone Volutes," 163.

the three-step feature on what is now recognized to be the base of stone volute 10549 "may have run along the entire width of the capital, and probably had been cut away on both ends, perhaps when the stone was prepared for secondary use."[61] Then, stone volute 10025 might have the heads of seven uraei cut away; "this capital too had been fitted for secondary use and only their bodies remained intact."[62] Franklin concurs that the two more complete examples likely had been reworked, without relying on their specific proposals: "all [three were] roughly refashioned, apparently for secondary use [...]."[63] Eran Arie, on the other hand, specifically rejects both proposals of secondary re-shaping made by Stern and Magen.[64]

Like many others, Magen notes the Phoenician origin of stone volutes and their likely symbolism of rebirth in that culture and others that adopted their use. He proposes that they originated either in the Iron Age or the Persian period, when the tradition seems to have disappeared otherwise from Samaria and Yehud but continued in use along the Phoenician coast and in Phoenician and Punic settlements. He believes strongly that they "unquestionably adorned the façade of the Samaritan temple at Mt. Gerizim from its first phase."[65] Magen suggests they either originated in an unlocated Iron Age temple in Shechem and were reused to build the temple on Gerizim in Phase 1, which he ultimately rejects, or that they were created in the Persian period as imitations of Phoenician volutes or "of similar capitals that stood at the gates of the Jerusalem Temple in the Return to Zion period."[66] He rejects out of hand their origin in Phase 2, assuming that by the Hellenistic period, the aniconic tradition would have been fully in effect but in the Persian period, it was not scrupulously observed, evidenced by the uraei on the one volute stone and Samaritan and Jewish coinage. He also asserts that "a different type of capital inspired by the contemporary architecture" replaced this type in the Hellenistic period.[67]

---

61 Stern and Magen, "Archaeological Evidence," 52. For its publication upside down, see Arie, "Revisiting Mt. Gerizim," 44*.

62 Stern and Magen, "Archaeological Evidence," 54.

63 Franklin, "Stone Volutes," 164.

64 Arie, "Revisiting Mt. Gerizim," 47*.

65 Magen, *Mount Gerizim 2*, 152–53.

66 Stern and Magen, "Archaeological Evidence," 55–56; Magen, *Mount Gerizim 2*, 153, including the quote. For the Phoenician origin of this motif as a decorative element and its symbolism, see e.g., Betancourt, *The Aeolic Style*," 46–47; Shiloh, "The Proto-Aeolic Capital"; Stern and Magen, "Archaeological Evidence," 50–55; Franklin, "Megiddo to Tamassos," 132–34; Kahwagi-Janho, "chapiteaux à volutes"; and Faegersten and López-Ruiz, "Beyond 'Volute Capital'." I thank the last two authors for sharing this unpublished material with me and allowing me to cite it.

67 Magen, *Mount Gerizim 2*, 153.

In her detailed study of the volute motif carved on stone blocks of various sizes, Norma Franklin has noted the two complete and partial third exemplars from Mt. Gerizim are carved on one face only and relative to their size, are extremely thin, only 21 cm thick. Comparably thin examples have been found in the reliefs on pilasters of the tombs at Tamassos, dating to the seventh-sixth centuries BCE. However, the latter are carved into rectangular blocks of about the same depth but have the volutes raised in relief against a solid stone background.[68] The ones at Gerizim protrude as free-standing elements.

The carved volute stones could not have been load-bearing structural components, like orthostats, nor free-standing elements, given their relatively narrow base elements and carving on one face only. They are not likely to have been components in a balustrade either. They are not carved on all sides, like the ones found more recently at Armon ha-Natziv, south of Jerusalem, and are larger than those smaller examples.[69] The larger, comparable examples, also carved on all sides, together with a similar example from Ramat Raḥel, further south in Yehud, are thought to have topped free-standing square columns. The later, Hellenistic-era ones from Umm el-Amed, a Phoenician site in Lebanon with two temples, are parts of capitals atop round stone columns. The Mt. Gerizim examples were meant to be seen from only one side; following the leads of Franklin and Arie,[70] to my mind, the most logical functional explanation would be that they were secured to a solid façade, possible to top relatively thin, engaged columns that either had been carved to protrude from a stone façade or had been attached secondarily to a stone facade of a building. Perhaps they had been integral elements of the façade of the wall into which the votive inscriptions had been embedded.[71]

---

68 Walcher, "Royal Tomb 5," 78–85.

69 Billig, Freud, and Bocher, "Luxurious Royal Estate," 14–16, 22–26.

70 Franklin, "Stone Volutes," 163–64; Arie, "Revisiting Mt. Gerizim," 47*.

71 The reconstruction proposed by Magen (*Mount Gerizim 2*, 272), where they would have topped a square column serving as the side uprights of a thick doorway or entryway is inaccurate in having the volutes protrude beyond the width of the column, which would have required that portion of the back to be finished and carved since it would have been visible. Similarly, the one depicted on the righthand side topping a free-standing column is contra-indicated, since only one side was finished. After restoration, the two more complete exemplars now also feature a narrowing under the volutes as well as above them; so Arie, "Revisiting Mt. Gerizim," 45*–47*. The closest examples I have found are the stylized trees that form part of the glazed brick decoration depicted on the south wall of the main courtyard leading to the throne room in the south palace of Nebuchadnezzar II in Babylon from the late seventh-early sixth centuries BCE. Three stacked volutes top a thin palm tree trunk punctuated at intervals with groups of three bandings that resemble the three bands that extend below stone volute f See conveniently, https://www.lingfil.uu.se/forskning/assyriologi/babylon/#Downloads. I am not claiming, however, that they must date from this same period.

The accumulating evidence would allow the stone volutes to have originated in either the late Iron Age, the Persian period, or the Hellenistic era, which also means they could have been in secondary or even tertiary use when they were discarded, probably at the time the Phase 2 temple was destroyed ca. 111 BCE. Even so, this does not mean that they must have belonged to a temple in all three periods; they were used in palaces and elite residences as well.[72]

Third, fifteen pottery forms excavated within the sacred precinct have Iron IIC parallels from Phoenician sites in the coastal plain not included by Magen in his analysis.[73] Referring to the published pottery assemblage from Phase 1, Arie states, "I have traced several pottery vessels that can be exclusively dated to the Late Iron Age. The dating is mainly based on complete vessels that were uncovered in secure contexts."[74] After presenting the relevant forms with Iron IIB or IIC parallels, he concludes, "In fact, almost 20 % (15 of 89 sherds and vessels) of the local pottery published by Magen should be re-dated to Iron IIC [...]."[75] The pottery, then, provides clear proof that some sort of occupation or event(s) took place on Mt. Gerizim, possibly but not necessarily involving a permanent structure, initially already in the Iron Age II.

Finally, Arie has noted that two of the eleven ^{14}C samples have dates that are significantly earlier than the other nine; sample 1 has a calibrated date of 760–390 BCE and sample 2 from 810–540 BCE. Since the majority of the samples were from charcoal, one cannot discount the possibility of their coming from "old wood," but in light of the other evidence, they might belong to an Iron Age phase of use.[76]

6.2 A New Sanctuary Built ca. 650 BCE?

With a proposed new date between ca. 650–550 BCE for the building of an Iron Age complex atop Mt. Gerizim, Arie assumes that its function would have been cultic, as it was in the recognized two succeeding phases, and sets out three possible contexts for its construction. The earliest would have taken place

72 For the use of such volutes in non-sacred architecture, see Reich, "Palaces and Residences," 212–13; Lipschits, "Origin and Date," 203–25, who offers a chronological development and spread via Assyrian influence. His proposal is critiqued and rejected by Kletter, "A Clay Model Shrine," 55–64. Kletter concludes the volutes from Gerizim were probably post-Iron Age (73), citing Zangenberg, "Sanctuary on Mt. Gerizim," 402–4.

73 Arie, "Revisiting Mt. Gerizim," 49*–54*, contra Magen, *Mount Gerizim 2*, 168.

74 Arie, "Revisiting Mt. Gerizim," 50*.

75 Arie, "Revisiting Mt. Gerizim," 54*.

76 Arie, "Revisiting Mt. Gerizim," 55*.

ca. 650 BCE "as an independent center for the new population brought in by the Assyrians."[77] In addition to the common citation of 2Kgs 17:24–34,[78] a possible reflex of this scenario might be found in Ezra 4:1–3, where the Samarians are presented as claiming, "We worship your god as you do, and we have been sacrificing to him since the days of Osnappar (Ashurbanipal? who ruled 669–631 BCE), King of Assyria, who let us go up here."[79] If there is any sort of historical kernel present, the sanctuary could have been dedicated to a form of Yhwh. But equally, setting the quote in Ezra 4:1–3 aside as late and unreliable, the sanctuary could have been dedicated to the native deity of a group newly settled in Shechem or the surrounding area.

The last survey of the Shechem valley was conducted by the Drew McCormick team in 1968; the Manasseh Hill Country Survey has not yet published results from a newer survey in this area among the 8 volumes currently in print in English. The following observations must remain preliminary, then, based on currently available data.

There were 54 sites visited by the Drew McCormick team, with 29 additional sites identified in the region by previous surveys that were not revisited by the team. Of this total of 83 sites, 41, almost half, were settled in the Iron II period (ca. 1000–600 BCE), while only 11 contained Persian-era pottery (550–331 BCE). Of these, "most" also showed Iron II, but a systematic distinction between Iron IIB, IIC and IID was made only at 12 of the 54 sites, based on comparable forms in stratified contexts at Shechem. In these cases, four, Kh. Tânâ et Taḥtâ (#18), Kh. Ṣur (#42), Tell Ṣofar (#52), and Kûmeh (#54) remained occupied throughout the Iron IIA–D; one was settled during the Iron IIB–D (#26 Kh. el-ʿUrmeh); another during the Iron IIB–C (#11 Diʿâra). Two long-time settlements disappeared before the Neo-Babylonian period (#33 Kh. en-Nebi, Iron IIA–C and #7 Kh. Kefr Kûz, probably Iron IIA–C also), and one appears to have been a single-period Iron IIA site, not relevant to our investigation (#12 Sâlim).

The remaining three are the strongest candidates for immigrant settlers: #17 Kh. Tânâ el-Fôqâ, a one-period Iron IIC site; #24 Kh. Ḥaiya, also first established in the Iron IIC and possibly continuing into the Iron IID, and #13 Kh. esh-Sheikh Naṣrallah, set up in the Iron IID after a possible occupational gap from the Iron

77 Arie, "Revisiting Mt. Gerizim," 56*.

78 See e.g. Hensel, "Das JHWH-Heiligtum," who argues on linguistic and polemical grounds that 2Kgs 17:24–41 is a later addition dating from the Hellenistic period (82–88).

79 Etienne Nodet adds to this passage the curious one in Ezra 6:22 that mentions the king of Assyria instead of the king of Persia. He suggests this is "a coded message that now the Jerusalem temple is the only one for all of Israel, including ancient returnees," making it like Solomon's temple ("Israelites," 124–25).

I period. However, of the remaining nine, eight could have had continuous settlement after 722 BCE or could have had a change in population, with immigrants assigned settlements that had been cleared of their native residents, who had been sent into exile.

Of these same twelve sites, in addition to #1 Shechem, five or six continued to be used in the Persian period with no established gap (#13 Kh. esh-Sheikh Naṣrallah, #26 Kh. el-ʿUmmeh, #27 Kh. Shurrâb, #52 Tell Ṣofar, #54 Kûmeh, and possibly #32 Kh. eṭ-Ṭirah).[80] That means roughly half. The implication of the general data is a significant decline in population over time, with the Persian period hitting a low. The Hellenistic period marks expansion again, to 35 sites.[81] Would a new sanctuary have been established on Mt. Gerizim to meet the needs of three recently established immigrant settlements in the Shechem Valley, but possibly more, if existing settlements were repopulated?

All three of Arie's proposed scenarios for the building of an Iron Age sacred space on Mt. Gerizim prior to the Persian-era complex are predicated on this sanctuary space serving a regional population, not just the inhabitants of nearby Shechem. How large a radius "regional" would entail is unclear. To properly assess this suggestion, it would be necessary to establish the location of new immigrant settlements post-722 BCE (and later) throughout Samerina at large and then see where they cluster and if there might have been other such potential sanctuaries established around the same time in other sectors, in order to integrate the newcomers into the worship of the territorial deity, Yhwh (Shomron?). Such an undertaking goes beyond the scope of the present chapter. Sites identified in the Manasseh Hill Country survey as Iron III that had been founded on virgin soil or in locations that had not been occupied since the Iron IIA would provide a starting point for such an undertaking. However, there would be no way to identify immigrant resettlement at sites that may have had their Israelite populations exiled and then replaced by new groups. On the ground, this would look either like continuous occupation or immediate reoccupation after destruction, without being able to ascertain if it was resettled by survivors of the original population or a new group.

In the Manasseh Hill Country Survey, what distinguishes a site as Iron III, which covers the province under Assyrian and Neo-Babylonian rule (721–586 BCE in one statement but 721–535 BCE in another),[82] is the wedge-decorated bowl, very

80 Campbell, *Shechem II*, 9–10.

81 Campbell, *Shechem II*, 96–97.

82 Zertal, *Manasseh Survey 1*, 43–44, 56–57. These dates use political events- the fall of Samaria and creation of the Assyrian province of Samerina, on the one hand, and either the fall of Jerusalem and likely creation of the Neo-Babylonian province of Yehud or three years after the Achaemenids became the new imperial rulers of the Levant, on the other. The 586 date is not

angular hole-mouth jars with a broad ledge rim protruding inward and outward, strongly angled, ridged jars, and a style of cooking pot whose ridge moves up to the middle of the thin, round rim.[83] While the wedge-decorated bowls are thought possibly to reflect a new population group of Babylonian origin,[84] it is unclear if any of the remaining three diagnostic forms might have resulted from immigrants adapting local forms to be closer to the pottery in their homeland(s) or are the result of the local evolution of forms over time. If the latter, Iron II sites without any of these diagnostics might have continued in use into the Iron III. We do not know if entire regions in Samerina were forcefully exiled, leaving none of the older population intact, to be resettled by one or more entirely new groups, or if only selected areas within a region were vacated, with new groups interspersed among the remaining Israelites.

6.3 A New Sanctuary Built ca. 600 BCE?

The second date for the proposed Iron IIC sanctuary would be ca. 600, after King Josiah's reform and the alleged dismantling of the temple at Bethel/Beitin, a site possibly already in decline according to a fresh examination of the pottery.[85] Such a proposal might posit as a correlate the transfer of the names of Bethel and Luz

---

directly relevant for the history of Samerina unless one wants to argue that a number of Judahite refugees fled north. Since local pottery does not change immediately in response to a change in rulership, using political dates for archaeological periods is problematic in any event, but has been a convenient and long-standing tradition.

83 Zertal, *Manasseh Survey 1*, 44.

84 Zertal, "Bowls Decorated"; Zertal, "Wedge-Shaped Decorated Bowl"; Itach, Aster, and Ben Shlomo, "Wedge-Impressed Bowl." This might corroborate the claim in 2Kgs 17:24 that the king of Assyria settled people from Babylon and Cuthah (Tal Ibrāhīm, Iraq) in Samerina. But it is likely this biblical passage was used as a clue for where to search for precedents for the new ware in the first place. It is unclear if Zertal and others have systematically ruled out the region of Hamath in Syria or the more enigmatic Havva and Sepharvaim, also mentioned in the same verse, as the homelands of other deportees. Itach, Aster, and Ben Shlomo have found no parallels in the Assyrian heartland in the middle or Neo-Assyrian periods (84), but it does not appear Syria has been examined as a possible source.

85 Arie ("Revisiting Mt. Gerizim," 56*) cites as the source of this possibility Finkelstein and Singer Avitz, "Reevaluating Bethel," 45. They do not propose it directly, however, in their fresh look at the pottery remains from the excavations and their new chronology for the history of settlement at the site. He proposes it based on their revised chronology. For a critique of their historical reconstructions of the history of occupation at the site that is based on both the limited areas excavated around the site and the limited remains still available from the excavations, where the majority of plain sherds were discarded on site and never counted, see Lipschits, "Bethel Revisited," 238–41.

to Gerizim that is only documented in much later Hellenistic sources. One has to weigh the possibility that in Phase 2, an attempt was made to transfer the Pentateuchal Jacob cycle as a foundational story to the temple on Gerizim, if it had not already served this function in Phase 1. Yet, such a transfer would only make sense if Mt. Gerizim had served as a regional temple site within the province. With the sanctuary in the provincial seat still likely in operation at this time, 12 km. away, would it have been deemed necessary? We do not know if the Assyrian imperial administration would have fiscally supported any temple in operation at or near Beitin after 722 BCE or, like the Achaemenids, would have expected locals to finance it.[86]

6.4 A New Sanctuary Built post-586 BCE?

The third possible date of establishment in Arie's view would be after the Babylonian destruction of Jerusalem in 586 BCE, in order to fill the cultic gap following the annihilation of the Jerusalemite temple.[87] Though not cited as a potential source of this idea, Oded Lipschits already had proposed that some Judeans might have "sought alternative places of worship and worked to establish them," naming Shechem, Bethel, Mizpah, and Gibeon as possibilities.[88] But why would Yehudites have needed to travel to the neighboring province to worship a different form of Yhwh and, in the case of Shechem (Mt. Gerizim), possibly contribute to construction costs, when they probably could have frequented existing sanctuaries to local forms of Yhwh within their own newly created province, like those at Gibeon, Mizpah, possibly Bethel/Beitin, and others, no doubt?

6.5 Evaluation of Eran Arie's Theory about an Iron-Age Sanctuary on Mt. Gerizim

Eran Arie rejects the third, post-586 context as improbable because it does not explain why such a complex would be erected at a new site with no prior cultic

86 For the excavation of an open-air cultic site dating to the ninth-eighth centuries BCE (Iron IIA and B) atop a hill 900 northeast of Beitin at Elevation Point 419 in 2016, see Tagvar, "'And He Called." He proposes that this was the sanctuary of Bethel. Based on Tagvar's initial 2015 discussion in Hebrew ("E.P. 914 East of Beitin") Oded Lipschits proposed the same understanding ("Bethel Revisited," 242–43).

87 Arie, "Revisiting Mt. Gerizim," 56*.

88 Lipschits, *The Fall and Rise of Jerusalem*, 113.

connection.[89] That same objection would apply to the second option, ca. 600, as well, however, even though he does not state it. On the other hand, his observation would be logical in the context of the first post-722 option, particularly if the new temple would have been dedicated to one or more non-native deities of a new population group. A virgin site makes sense in that context, and the sanctuary of the oak of Moreh, referenced as outside Shechem but seemingly in the valley and not on Mt. Ebal or Mt. Gerizim (Gen 12:6, Josh 24:26), might have been a long-standing Shechemite or Israelite sacred place dedicated to a form of Yhwh (and Asherah?). Yet, it is equally possible that the "oak of Moreh" is a cipher meant to point to the Gerizim sanctuary, especially the second element, which refers to "teaching" or a "teacher" and could implicitly link the sanctuary site to the giving of Torah (i.e. "teaching, instruction") or the commemoration of this event.

In Arie's thought, the second and third options presume that cultic centralization had gone into effect in both Samerina and Judah/Yehud in the late Iron Age, which is questionable. As already noted, part of his reason for favoring the interpretation of the Iron Age complex as a sacred precinct is what he perceives to be an inability to understand "where the main cultic center of Samaria was during the Babylonian period, and why the Persian Empire granted permission to build a temple in a new place with almost no cultic tradition as opposed to their ordinary religious policy."[90] He and others have overlooked the strong historical likelihood that a Yahwistic temple would have existed in the capital city, Samaria, during the time of the Israelite kings and would have continued in operation under the Assyrians, the Neo-Babylonians, as well as the Persians. There is no reason to assume that there had only been three temples to Yhwh in the kingdom of Israel during its existence (Samaria, Bethel, and Dan); others probably continued in use as well after 722, now supported by local initiatives.[91] The temple in Samaria would have had a long-standing hereditary priesthood supported by prebends no doubt, as would any other ones with a long pedigree.

---

89 Arie, "Revisiting Mt. Gerizim," 56*–57*.

90 Arie, "Revisiting Mt. Gerizim," 56*. Similarly, Pummer surmises one explanation for the failure of the Elephantine community to address their petition to any high priest in Samaria as they had in their letters to Jerusalem but only to the sons of Sanballat might have been because, in the city of Samaria, "there was no Yahwistic temple as far as we know at the present" ("Was There an Altar," 16). Zangenberg, "Sanctuary on Mt. Gerizim," 406–7, also seems to assume the same.

91 The observations I have made concerning potential changes to religion in Yehud among those who remained in the land after 586 BCE apply equally to the native Israelite population in the province of Samerina after 722 BCE. See Edelman, "Early Forms of Judaism," 267–68.

The Iron IIC pottery with coastal connections is irrefutable evidence that some sort of activity took place atop Mt. Gerizim in that period, unless they provide new evidence for the continuation of some of those styles thought to cease in the Iron IIC into the early Persian period.[92] The stone volutes can be placed in Phase 1 or Phase 2 of the sacred complex instead of in a new proposed Phase 0, contemporaneous with the Phoenician Iron IIC pottery. The three (or rather, six)-chambered northern gate could have imitated such a layout still in existence in the regional seat in Samaria, possibly one giving entrance to the temple there. If so, it could have been built as part of the Persian-era sacred complex in spite of being "anachronistic." Thus, it does not provide incontrovertible proof relating to the Iron IIC usage of the site. The two ^{14}C wood samples might be from "old wood." None of samples were analyzed to determine their taxon source as of 2008, so one cannot try to determine their possible function in the Iron IIC period.

7 Options for the Iron II Presence on Mt. Gerizim

The relevant remains consist of Iron IIC undecorated Phoenician pottery bowls and cooking pots, some that are thought to date exclusively to the late Iron Age, and two of five charcoal samples from Area S, locus 256. The others cluster in the Persian to mid-Hellenistic period. Arie is careful to note both that "Theoretically, this pottery could be residual in its context and may predate the precinct" and that the charcoal could reflect "old wood."[93]

What options would make sense for the location of some sort of inferred sacred or building complex atop Mt Gerizim in the Iron IIC period? Its advantages would have been height, with good visibility of the surrounding landscape and roads, protection, given the steep slopes, making attack less attractive, access to breezes, and closeness to the divine realm. It disadvantages would have included no water source on-site and the need to haul food, building supplies, furnishings, and possible sacrificial offerings, including live animals, up and down the steep slopes. There also would have been more intense exposure to the natural elements in windy and stormy or snowy weather, even with shelter available.

92 The lifespan of a ceramic form is determined by examples found in excavated site layers and judgment calls about when a shape has either disappeared from the repertoire altogether or changed sufficiently that it no longer is considered a continuation of the prior form.
93 Arie, "Revisiting Mt. Gerizim," 54*–55*.

7.1 A Sacred Complex, as Proposed By Eran Arie?

There is no need to revisit the arguments sketched above, which involve four potential types of evidence. It is worthwhile to explore their implications, however. If the pottery is coastal plain Phoenician and the stone volutes imitate a Phoenician style, then were the workmen Phoenicians employed by the local imperial authorities of Samerina to build the complex for a form of Yhwh of Samaria and possibly his Asherah? Since the top layer of rock on Mt. Gerizim could not produce ashlars but only irregularly shaped field stones, there would not necessarily have been a need to seek out foreign masons skilled in ashlar masonry. Local masons accustomed to building with unworked stones would have sufficed, unless the lower layer that was workable was able to be exposed in some areas. Perhaps Phoenician carpenters and artists could have been employed, however, for interior finishing work and decoration.

Or, were Phoenicians among the groups resettled in the Shechem Valley post-722 BCE, who built the complex for one of their native deities? In light of the proposed occupational gap of some 100 years at Shechem between the end of Persian-era Stratum V (ca. 425 BCE) and the beginning Hellenistic-era Stratum IV ca. 335 BCE,[94] the references in Josephus to the Shechemites allegedly telling both Alexander and Antiochus IV they were Sidonians (*Ant.* 11.340–47; 12.257–64), creatively elaborating on 2Macc 6:1–2, cannot be used to argue that a Phoenician presence at Shechem traces back uninterrupted to the Iron IIC period.[95]

Alternatively, as they moved their goods from the coast to their intended inland destinations, did Phoenician traders stop *en route* to make offerings to a or the local god honored at an existing *bāmâ*, an open-air sacred complex with an altar and sometimes some outbuildings, that had been built atop Gerizim, enjoying a meal after sacrificing an animal? In all these scenarios, it is hard to separate the pots from physical Phoenicians or coastal groups; analysis of the potential clay source(s) used to make this everyday ware for cooking and eating would be most helpful, allowing an assessment of whether they are made locally or imported from the coast.

---

94 Campbell, *Shechem III 1*, 8.

95 For an evaluation of this claim, see e.g. Isaac, "A Seleucid Inscription," 143; Hjelm, *Samaritans and Early Judaism*, 207–12; Dušek, *Aramaic and Hebrew Inscriptions*, 101–16; Kartveit, "Josephus on the Samaritans," 111–12, 116–18; Pummer, "Samaritan Ethnicity," 55–56. For the proposal that a Sidonian settlement had been established in Shechem in the second century BCE, like the one at Marisa in the Judean Shephelah, see e.g. Alt, "Geschichte der Grenze," 398, n. 2; M. Delcor, "Vom Sichem," 35–38; Kippenberg, *Garizim und Synagoge*, 79; Bickerman, "document relatif," 118–23; Pummer, "Genesis 34," 185; Egger, *Josephus Flavius und die Samaritaner*, 264–68.

7.2 A Possible Watchtower or Fire Relay Station?

Bearing in mind the plusses and minuses of the location atop Mt Gerizim, a logical type of structure that might have been positioned there could have been a watchtower or a fire relay station. Within an Assyrian or Neo-Babylonian imperial context, a small patrol could have been assigned to use a watchtower built there to monitor the local road systems for commercial activity and invading armies entering from the coast or from the highlands to the north or south. In this case, the water cistern near the northern gate in operation in the Persian period could already have been cut to collect and store water for this outpost. The three or six-chambered gate could have been part of a defensive wall enclosing the watchtower and a courtyard area where wood was stacked to be able to be lit as a fire signal in case of trouble and the need for reinforcements. The charcoal could have been from wooden beams supporting floors inside the watchtower, from doors giving access through the gate, or from fires used to signal or cook food. Patrol members could have taken food supplies with them that would suffice for the length of their assigned duty.

Given the presence of coastal plain Phoenician bowls and cooking pots, one might need to propose that a contingent of Phoenicians had been posted there; it seems less likely that a caravan passed by and some enterprising members hiked up the mountainside to sell or barter such items with the few men on duty there. Since it seems it would have been a waste of skill and manpower to use sailors for such inland military duty, perhaps instead we could propose that a non-seafaring group from the coastal region would have been deployed. It also seems improbable that the stone volutes would have been part of the architecture used in such a basic military outpost or that Phoenician craftsmen would have been needed to construct it.

7.3 A Possible Summer Palace or Villa for an Assyrian or Neo-Babylonian Official?

Jürgen K. Zangenberg notes in theory that the earliest complex on Mt. Gerizim could have been a large public building rather than a sacred complex, based on the use of the volute stone blocks and the excavated northern, three-chambered gate.[96] He ultimately rejects this possibility, however, and prefers to accept both as anachronistic building features used in the Persian period, as Magen did in

96 Zangenberg, "Sanctuary on Mt. Gerizim," 402–4.

his preliminary report. He goes on to talk about the foundation of the Persian-period open-air sanctuary in the walled space instead.[97]

The possibility needs to be considered that the evidence cited for a possible Iron II structure on Mt. Gerizim could have come from the summer residence of an Assyrian or Neo-Babylonian governor or official, built using skilled Phoenician craftsmen. The summer breezes and higher altitude would have made it a great retreat for a governor or other high official during the hot summer months, although the acropolis of Samaria would already have afforded those same advantages to a large degree. Escape from constant scrutiny and demands in the capital for some "down time" or change of venue would have been incentive enough, however.

It also is possible that such an individual had been granted estate lands in and around Gerizim by the Assyrian or Neo-Babylonian imperial regime in power at the time, which had resulted in the building of a villa atop Gerizim for the views and breezes, on the one hand, and visibility from the valley floor as a display of conspicuous status, on the other. It might also have served as a retreat where the governor of Samerina could have met with the governor of Yehud or other provincial and visiting Babylonian officials from the heartland to discuss business more privately, away from the eyes and ears at the regional seat.

Engaged columns crowned by attached volute blocks could have flanked one or more external or internal entryways or could have been spaced at intervals around the main façade or internally in the main reception hall. They were not limited to temples, as indicated by their use at Ramat Raḥel in Judah, and in this case, may have been non-religious or even copied royal symbols of abundance and wealth, depending where the occupant of the home might have been from.[98] However, the stone for such engaged columns, like that of the two volutes made of *nāri*, would have had to have been imported, unless it was able to have been quarried from the layer below the top layer of bedrock on site.

The three-chambered gate could have been in place at this time, giving access into the walled complex that housed a residence, a courtyard, and potentially a few outbuildings. If slightly anachronistic, it might have been copied from an older building complex in the regional seat in Samaria. Otherwise, the terminal date for the use of this style of gate in Cisjordan needs to be adjusted to include the Iron IIC period, based on this exemplar, as Arie has noted. The two outlying ^{14}C wood dates could belong to wood employed in this earliest phase for doors, paneling, columns, or cooking. Since the pottery with Phoenician coastal parallels in the Iron IIC is domestic in nature and coarse rather than fine ware, it cannot

---

97 Zangenberg, "Sanctuary on Mt. Gerizim," 407.

98 Recognized already by Reich, "Palaces and Residences," 212–13.

reflect an elite predilection for exotic "foreign" objects of beauty. Rather, it would suggest either that some of the finish work had been completed by Phoenicians or that that some of the staff employed there might have been Phoenician. It should be noted in passing that any governor's residence probably would have had a chamber set aside for use as a shrine, for the performance of household cult and perhaps, for the propitiation of more powerful deities.

Once again, at least one cistern would have needed to be cut in this period. Phoenician stone masons would not have been needed really, unless the upper layer of friable rock was relatively thin and was exhausted relatively quickly in the production of field stones, allowing skilled masons to extract block segments from the next layer below. On the other hand, Phoenician carpenters and artists might well have been employed for interior finishing and ornamentation.

The villa's eventual possible abandonment could have had something to do with that official or as his successor falling out of favor or dying with no heir, or with the change-over in imperial regimes from the Assyrians to the Neo-Babylonians or the latter to the Achaemenids. Or, under the Achaemenids, a decision could have been made that it would have been an excellent location for a new sanctuary dedicated to Yhwh (Elohim?), being located along the main N-S route that provided direct access between Jerusalem and Mt. Gerizim.[99] At this point, the existing structure(s) inside the walls entered through one or possibly more three/six-chambered gates would have been torn down and its stones reused in constructing the new sacred facility.

As noted above, the McCormick survey shows that settlements in the Shechem Valley had declined by the end of the Iron Age and reached a nadir in the Persian period. This might have resulted in a similar abandonment of the monumental residence atop Mt. Gerizim for a new favored spot for such a residence under the new Achaemenid regime. Such a scenario would leave a clear path for the complex to be repurposed as a sanctuary for the first time in the early Persian period. Any structure could well have been dismantled and its stone blocks reused to build a temple structure.

8 Reflections and Tentative Proposals

Dedicatory stones from Mt. Gerizim confirm that Yhw(h) was the patron deity of the sanctuary; no references to his Asherah or other deities have been found to date. The male deity was also referred to as god *'eloah* and lord (*'adonay)* of Har

99 See Dorsey, *Roads and Highways*, 132–36, Map 7, route N 1.

Gerizim. Since the sanctuary was in continuous use from the mid-fifth century to its destruction ca. 111–110 BCE, with possible periods of limited use during the rebuilding and expansion in Phase 2, it probably is safe to assume the same male deity was worshipped there during that entire period.

8.1 Eran Arie's Evidence in an Early Persian Context

None of the three options explored in the preceding section is particularly convincing in its ability to account for the presence of ordinary coastal bowls and cooking pots on Mt. Gerizim that date to the Iron IIC period, although a possible local sanctuary or a possible elite residence cannot be ruled out. The watchtower seems much less likely. This leads me to ask if the recovered pottery forms might have continued in use into the early Persian period, which would extend their life cycles some 100 years in some cases. All profiles for the life cycle of a given pottery form are built from exemplars recovered from controlled excavations, which allows the creation of a relative timeline. The beginning and end points are adjusted over time as new evidence emerges that requires such redefinition. Might Gerizim provide new evidence? If so, the recovered pottery could have been used by Phoenician carpenters and masons who had been hired to help build the Persian-era sacred complex, to prepare their daily meals using familiar cooking pots and tableware.

The remaining three types of evidence can be explained in an early Persian context. The two samples of charcoal that might reflect an Iron Age context could have originated from "old wood." The six-chambered gate could have been modelled on one or more entrances to the temple to Yhwh Shomron and his Asherah in the city of Samaria, which likely was still functioning. This need not imply, however, that the Mt. Gerizim complex was being dedicated to the same form of Yhwh found in Samaria or that it was a satellite of that facility. It could have been dedicated to Yhwh Elohim and yet still borrowed or copied elements from the other, long-standing temple in the provincial seat, if only for the sake of familiarity in the hopes of enticing cross-over worshippers. Alternatively, it may have been selected for use by the head builder for reasons only he knew. A search in the Phoenician-Punic world for six-chambered gates might reveal that this tradition continued in use there longer than in the interior areas of Cisjordan.

The unique stone volutes, on the other hand, if Persian and not Hellenistic in date, could have been the contribution of at least one Phoenician mason, who was instructed to include such decorative flourishes and their symbolism atop engaged, segmented engaged columns on one or more external or internal entryways or walls of a temple building proper or in some other location within the complex. Perhaps already in the Persian period, some areas of the friable upper level of limestone had been able to be stripped away sufficiently to produce field stone to construct the sacred complex and the initial domestic areas to allow more experienced and skilled Phoenician masons to begin to remove smaller blocks of workable stone from the next layer of rock.

Further excavation may turn up more examples of stone volutes, allowing a more accurate assessment of their potential use in Phase 1. They might have been a repeating element along a stretch of wall, perhaps, or might have been limited in number to perhaps two trees of life flanking the entrance into a temple, which might have had two or three such stones stacked above one another as crowns to the trunk of a slender palm tree. They would have employed the then-current options being practiced in the Phoenician world, probably getting a design approved by the master builder before proceeding.

We should not overlook the recent confirmation that private housing existed on artificially constructed terraces along the slopes, outside the sacred precinct proper, already in fifth century BCE. The Phoenician craftsmen could also have been commissioned to build and decorate some of these private dwellings. The larger ones could have contained the lighter-weight decorative stone volutes crowning engaged columns or pillars in some capacity equally well.

In the fifth century BCE, there appear to have been ties between the Samarian governor, Sanballat, and the contemporary King of Sidon, evidenced by the use of Sidonian imagery on coinage issued by Sanballat.[100] He probably was governor at the time the sacred complex on Gerizim in Phase 1 was either first built or possibly when a temple building and accompanying residential quarter was added to a previously existing Iron IIC open-air *bāmâ* on the mountain top. Thus, Sanballat could easily have commissioned Phoenician builders and craftsmen for this project.

8.2 The God of Mount Gerizim and the Formation of the Pentateuch

Let us now explore the options for which form of Yhwh might have been honored when the sacred complex was dedicated in the Persian period and the accompanying implications. We will begin with Yhwh Shomron, with or without his Asherah. If initially built with Asherah, we would have to postulate that at some subsequent point in the Persian period in Phase 1 or in the renovations of Phase 2, the

100 See Meshorer and Qedar, *Samarian Coinage*; Edelman, *Origins*, 40–50.

cult of the goddess was eliminated, along with any of her symbols. This could have stemmed from a cultic reform enacted in Samaria and extended to this outlying sanctuary as well, or only initiated locally. But at this point in time, we have no firm evidence pointing to her presence at any point.[101]

Implications follow concerning the production of the Pentateuch. We could assume the Pentateuch was a joint venture between the scribes of the provincial seat in Samaria and scribes of the provincial seat in Jerusalem and that modifications had been implemented in the long-standing temple to Yhwh Shomron in Samaria to align with the concept of Yhwh Elohim as expressed, in its fullest, in the book of Deuteronomy. This would have involved, in particular, the elimination the cult of Asherah and the worship of other lesser gods in both Samaria and Gerizim, had the Gerizim sacred precinct already existed. If it were built after a possible reform in Samaria, on the other hand, the complex on Mt. Gerizim could have been built to honor Yhwh Shomron alone, who now, essentially, would have been made into Yhwh Elohim, as Yhwh Ṣebaot would be in Jerusalem. Eventually, this deity would come to be known as the god of Har Gerizim. But was there a need for a new complex for worshipping Yhwh Shomron-turned-Elohim only 12 km. away? Perhaps, but only if Shechem had been a sub-regional administrative center in the Persian province, alongside other such district seats, all of which had built a Yahwistic sanctuary nearby.[102]

Alternatively, we could assume instead that the new sacred complex was established because it was dedicated to a form of Yhwh that differed from Yhwh Shomron and his Asherah, whose long-established temple lay 12 km. away. In this scenario, we could assume either that the Pentateuch had been written by scribes in Jerusalem and made its way to the Mt. Gerizim temple community at some point or that it was a joint venture between scribes in Jerusalem and scribes

101 It is worth noting that Silvia Schroer has suggested that small Iron Age shrine models in the Levant and Cyprus that have palm trees flanking the entrance were associated primarily with goddesses and their cult, although she allows for some being used for male deities ("Iconography of the Shrine Models," 137, 150, 153). Examples have been found at e.g. Amathos, Tell Jawa, Tell el- Far'a North, and Tell el-Umayri. The symbolism associated with palm trees and trees of life seems not to be limited to a specific category of female goddess, so it is not likely these stone volutes has been intended to symbolize Asherah in some way, especially when they remained in use until the destruction of the temple ca. 111–110 BCE.

102 It has been recognized that, after the construction of the sanctuary on Mt. Gerizim, not all the inhabitants of the province of Samaria would have affiliated with the new cult. So, e.g., Kippenberg, *Garizim und Synagoge*, 34; Freyne, "Behind the Names," 122–23. Freyne is referring specifically to possible Sidonian traders who might have settled at Shechem in the second century BCE, but he considers it a wider applicable principle, adding that not all in Jerusalem would have followed the views of Jason and his followers.

who were moved to or moved voluntarily to Mt Gerizim, who shared the newer, henotheistic concept of Yhwh Elohim and hoped to make it a reality in both functioning cults.[103] In fact, it could have been written ultimately by scribes of Judean origin, even if it was written exclusively on Mt. Gerizim without further collaboration with scribes back in Jerusalem.

8.3 Sanballat as Patron of the Gerizim Temple and the Pentateuch?

The location of the new temple at Gerizim would have been determined by the circumstances of its sponsor(s) or founder(s). Had a *bāmâ* already existed on site, the addition of a full-time priesthood in charge of a new temple built within the confines of the existing former enclosure, now dedicated to Yhwh Elohim, would have allowed a prebendary system to be instituted for the increased staff who lived beside the complex in houses built on terraces. Had some sort of elite villa been there, or if ceramicists decide Gerizim provides new evidence that certain Phoenician forms stayed in use longer than previously thought, into the early Persian Period, then the sacred complex, likely with a temple and housing for priests and scribes from the beginning, would first have been built in Phase 1.

Both alternatives would have been possible under the governorship of Sanballat, but the latter corresponds better with Josephus' account of the founding of this temple (*Ant.* 11.302–12, 321–25). Even with its clear historical inaccuracies about the founding date just before Alexander's invasion and the attempt of the author to portray the Samaritans as opportunistic, in contrast to the Jews,[104] it provides a better motive for his building of this new complex. Josephus claims that Sanballat built the temple for his Yehudite son-in-law, Manasseh, the grandson of the high priest of the temple in Jerusalem. Sanballat would have had to have secured imperial permission to establish the new facility and would have had to have guaranteed local funding. Even so, the big draw would have been

---

103 Gary N. Knoppers argued it is much more likely that the religious or at least scribal communities of Samaria and Yehud both possessed and valued the Pentateuch than that one borrowed it from the other wholesale. The relatively few sectarian changes are thought to date to the late second or first century BCE, while the bulk is shared in common ("Parallel Torahs," 510–514, 528).

104 For an assessment of Josephus' underlying motivations in his portrayal of the Samaritans who worshipped at Gerizim and the likely historical accuracy of his various claims about this religious group, see e.g. Kartveit, *The Origins of the Samaritans*; Pummer, *The Samaritans in Flavius Josephus*. For a claim he should not be termed "anti-Samaritan," see Egger, *Josephus Flavius*.

his ability to appoint its priesthood. This might have included one or both of his own sons as well as his priestly son-in-law.

The circumstantial evidence available from the book of Nehemiah, the Wadi Daliyeh papyri, and the Elephantine papyri about when Sanballat lived, serving as governor of Samerina, and by when he had died places him within the fifth century.[105] If the Mt. Gerizim complex had been founded by him, then a date in the mid-fifth century is indicated. This is within the ballpark for Magen's founding date, though probably at least a decade or two later than the earliest Cypriote coin dated to 480–475 BCE. Such a coin could have been kept as an heirloom that arrived on site with either a Phoenician mason or carpenter or with the person whose house it was found in outside the sacred complex. It shows little wear (plates, #7 under Persian period), but coinage was a newer phenomenon in the Achaemenid Empire. As a novel, foreign coin, it could have been kept in a residence on Gerizim as a special piece to show off.

The question has to be asked, though, whether Josephus had any sources beyond Nehemiah for his story or whether he drew inferences from it and concluded the marriage of Sanballat's daughter to a grandson of the Jerusalemite high priest would naturally have led to the construction of a temple for him so he could employ his birthright and training. Giving him the name of the most vilified king of Judah, Manasseh, could have been meant to imply guilt by association, and assuming other Yehudites would have "defected" with him to staff the new facility would have been logical. The discrepancy in dating might have been motivated by a desire to post-date the founding of the Gerizim temple well after the rebuilt, Persian-era temple in Jerusalem, to make it seem illegitimate in the light of Deuteronomy's implied single chosen site where the divine name or reputation will be set.

But even if this is the case, might Josephus have been right about the inference that Sanballat would have founded a new cultic site where his son-in-law and future grandchildren could become hereditary, prebendary priests? This would not have been possible in an existing, functioning temple in the provincial seat, Samaria, or elsewhere in the province, which would account nicely for the decision to found a new one, probably on virgin ground but possibly at an existing *bamah*.[106] In this case, it is likely Judean priestly and scribal traditions would have been transferred and instituted with the influx of Judean professional per-

105 E.g. Edelman, *Origins*, 38–53; Dušek, *Les manuscrits araméens*, 514–48.

106 Magnar Kartveit is one of the few scholars who has acknowledged that a sanctuary already would have existed in the city of Samaria in the fifth century when the Gerizim temple was built. He notes that Sanballat Horonite "may have endorsed a new project inside his jurisdiction" (*Origins*, 358).

sonnel. The Pentateuch might have been produced in the wake of the founding of the new sacred complex with adjoining residential quarters, to provide a common Israelite identity for both communities by combining older northern and southern traditions. Whether this would have been done in a deliberate move to exclude the conceptualization of Yhwh associated with the temple in the city of Samaria needs more consideration in another study.[107]

Circumstantial evidence could point to the possibility that Sanballat was "a" or "the" patron who sponsored the creation of the Pentateuch.[108] The epithet applied to him in the Hebrew Bible, which seems to indicate a place of origin, has been variously understood. Those who accept the MT pointing Horonite tend to associate him either with Upper or Lower Beth Horon (mod. Beit Ur el Fauqa and Beit Ur el Taḥta) in the southwestern Ephraimite hill country on the road from Jerusalem to Joppa, or with the site of Kh. el-Huwara 4.52 miles south of Shechem on the road to Ramallah and Jerusalem.[109] Those who opt instead to revocalize tend to consider his place of origin the Syrian city of Harran, where the cult of Sin was prominent, explaining the deity invoked in his name.[110] Had he been born in the province of Samerina, his ancestry might have traced back to settlers introduced after 722 BCE via forced migrations from a region honoring the deity Sin, who had remained an influential family god for some 175 years.

Is it coincidental that the city of Harran in Syria features prominently in the origin stories of Abraham and Jacob (Gen 11:26–29, 31–32; 12:4–5; 27:43; 28:10; 29:4)? The current MT vowel pointing may be an attempt to disassociate the vilified figure of Sanballat from the two illustrious patriarchs. However, if such a link had once been intentional, then it opens a number of intriguing avenues to explore.

---

107 The possibility that Ezra was a late Jerusalemite composition meant to provide a new counter-narrative for the origins of the Pentateuch to this older one should be considered. As part of the desire to obscure or "forget" the earlier tradition that indirectly associated Sanballat with the origins of Torah through allusions to two patriarchs, here the character of Ezra possibly was created as a replacement, with strictly Judean diasporic and Jerusalemite connections.

108 For a detailed development of the ideas that are briefly sketched below, see my forthcoming article, "Sanballat, Abraham, And Jacob," in a Festschrift honoring Thomas Römer, edited by Christoph Nihan and Jean-Daniel Macchi, to be published in 2025.

109 For the first, e.g. Ran Zadok, "Samarian Notes," *BO* 42 (1985): 567–72 (569–70); for the second, Yitzhak Magen, "The Dating of the First Phase of the Samaritan Temple on Mt Gerizim in Light of Archaeological Evidence," in *Judah and the Judeans in the Fourth Century B.C.E.*, Oded Lipschitz, Gary N. Knoppers, and Rainer Albertz (Winona Lake, IN: Eisenbrauns, 2007), 157–211 (188).

110 So, e.g. Samuel Feigin, "Etymological Notes," *AJSL* 43 (1926): 53–60 (58, n. 2); Kurt Galling, "Assyrische und persische Präfekten in Gezer," *PJ* 31 (1935): 75–93 (87); Meshorer and Qedar, *Samarian Coinage*, 27; André Lemaire, "Épigraphie et religion en Palestine à l'époque achéménide," *Transeu* 22 (2001): 97–113 (104); Edelman, *Origins*, 38–39.

In canonical Genesis, Abraham comes to represent both the Judean diaspora community via his origin in Ur of the Chaldees and the Israelite/Samarian diaspora community via his temporary new home in Harran. However, there is ambiguity in the location of Abraham's first encounter with Yhwh, where he is told to leave behind the place of his birth, his immediate family, and his clan. While the initial impression is that it took place in Harran, logic leads one ultimately to conclude it took place in Ur. As a result, Terah's leaving Ur with Abram and Sarai and taking his grandson Lot as well, as though he were responsible for family decisions, and his subsequent decision to put down roots in Harran and not continue on to Canaan, leads to Abram's first failure to obey a divine command.

Yet, as noted by others, Harran is not *en route* to Canaan but well over 100 km. north of the Euphrates River. From Ur in Chaldea (modern modern Tell el-Muqayyar in southern Iraq),[111] one would have followed the west bank of the Euphrates until Ḫindānu, where one would have traveled west to the Tadmar oasis. Alternatively, a somewhat longer route would have involved proceeding further north along the western riverbank past the mouth of the Ḫabur tributary to the road that cut in just west of the mouth of the Balikh tributary. One then would have turned south to Raṣappa and from there proceeded to the Tadmar oasis.[112] Harran lay some 170 km. north of the road junction to Raṣappa. Thus, with the confusion over where the initial divine call to Abram took place and the illogical route followed, it is natural to wonder if Harran had even been involved in the earliest story line relating to Abraham or whether it might have been introduced in order to interweave an older version of the Jacob cycle with an older version of the Abraham cycle. It might have been an integral part of the early Jacob cycle, or it could have been introduced when the patriarchal sequence was being constructed because it was Sanballat's place of origin, and the scribe responsible wanted to honor this individual through this oblique reference.[113]

111 In an attempt to smooth over this inconsistency, Gary Rendsburg has sought a location for Ur north of Harran, around Urfa, so that the family would have passed Harran *en route* to Canaan ("Ur Kasdim"). However, the group of Chaldeans Xenophon (ca. 431–354 BCE) mentions as warring neighbors of the Armenians in *Cyropaedia* 3.1.34 were located east of Harran and north of the royal Assyrian road that ran from Nineveh westward through Gozan and Harran, not to the north. For the road, see Parpola and Porter, *Atlas of the Near East*, 3–4.

112 So e.g. Rendsburg, "Ur Kasdim"; Adamczewski, "Abraham and Sanballat," 17.

113 Both Ur and Haran had historically been cult centers for the worship of moon deities, so a case can be made that these two cities were not randomly chosen. Since neither appears elsewhere in the HB as a site where Israelites or Judeans had been forcefully resettled, there is not a conscious attempt being made to create intertextual allusions. At the same time, however, both could represent symbolically the *golah*-communities of each former kingdom. For a discussion of features in the Abraham narrative that seem to allude to the historical figure, Sanballat, see Adamczewski, "Abraham and Sanballat."

The references to Abram building an altar outside Shechem (Gen 12:6–7), Jacob buying land from the sons of Hamor, Shechem's father, outside the city and building there an altar he called El-elohe-Israel together with his burying the "foreign gods" under the terebrinth near Shechem (Gen 35:1–4) before building a new altar at Luz called El-Bethel (Gen 35:5–7) all provide ancestral roots for one or more Israelite altars in the vicinity of Shechem. Then, Deut 11:29; 27:12 call more specifically for a ceremony of covenant renewal or completion relating to the event portrayed to have taken place in the plains of Moab, to take place between Mt. Ebal and Mt. Gerizim, with the blessing on Mt. Gerizim and the curse on Mt. Ebal (with follow-up in Josh 8:33 outside the Pentateuch.) This latter text would provide a reason for locating a sanctuary on Mt. Gerizim that would relate to what emerged as a Pentateuchal tradition, even if this were meant to be a one-time event in the story world. It grounds any sanctuary eventually located there within the foundational Mosaic covenant and its accompanying concept of Yhwh, particularly Yhwh Elohim as expressed in the book of Deuteronomy.

This brief sketch highlights a number of intriguing connections between Sanballat, Harran, the Shechem area, and the patriarchal figures, Abraham and Jacob. They may be intentional rather than coincidental, in which case, the informed ancient reader may have been expected to have connected the dots and seen an allusion to Sanballat. Since the stories tend to be positive in tone, such a linkage would have been intended to honor the governor, not to denigrate him in some way. Whether they are original or secondary remains open for further investigation.

The consistent pointing of Sanballat's epithet as Horonite is found in Judean texts, which suggests a deliberate attempt by southern scribes to erase any intentional connection of this individual with Harran in Genesis at some point after the creation of the Pentateuch. In his place Ezra, the priest and scribe, is lifted up as the one responsible for bringing the Torah of Moses from Babylon to Jerusalem (Ezra 7:6, 10; Neh 8:2). Perhaps not coincidentally, he is given a lineage tracing back to Moses' brother Aaron via his son Eleazar, his grandson Pinḥas, and his great grandson Abishua (Ezra 7:5). As noted earlier, one of the fragments of the ruled Hebrew inscription recovered from Gerizim mentions Pinḥas, probably as a high priest, and an [Abi]shua (#384). In addition, one can note that the name Eleazar appears in Neo-Hebrew script on a ring (#390) found in Area J outside the sacred complex. It likely belonged to a priest or scribe.[114] The genealogy pro-

114 Magen, Misgav and Tsafania, *Mount Gerizim 1*, 260. Two other stones, carved in lapidary Aramaic, name an Eleazar (#32) (#1) and an Eleazar whose patronym is no longer legible, who has made offerings on behalf of his wife Imma and his sons (#1) (73, 49–50). These might well have been lay individuals.

vided in Ezra 7:5 might have been designed to trace Ezra's pedigree to the same roots as those of the priestly line at Gerizim, to preempt their claims of association with the Torah, via its potential patron, Sanballat, in favor of a fictitious character with strictly southern roots and an origin for Torah in Babylon among Judean exiles.[115]

Finally, why Mt. Gerizim in the Persian period? The possibility should be considered that Sanballat had been given a landed estate in the immediate area by the Achaemenid administration as a perk associated with his governorship. Whether it was located within Shechem itself, where an official Persian bulla turned up in fill,[116] or nearby, somewhere on the valley floor or on an adjoining slope, even on Mt Gerizim itself, is indeterminable in light of the current data. The private stamps on wine jars found in Shechem[117] could have been associated with such an estate. Similar estates have been identified in Yehud at Ramat Raḥel and possibly Nebi Samwil and Lachish under the Achaemenids.[118] More thought and scrutiny needs to be given in the future to whether any or all of the Shechemite traditions in Genesis and especially those in Deuteronomy existed and were known in written or oral form before the establishment of the Persian-era sacred complex on Mt Gerizim or were developed afterwards.[119] It would have been a savvy move for those involved in the new Yhwh Elohim movement to have taken up some of the foundational myths and stories from the older Iron Age cults of Yhwh Ṣebaot and Yhwh Shomron and his Asherah and to have repurposed them to reflect their new understanding, giving the impression of continuity even where there was a break for purposes of gaining adherents more easily.[120]

---

115 This is part of a wider strategy apparent in both Ezra and Nehemiah to separate out "foreign" elements within Israel. The prohibition of intermarriage is another, where "foreign" may well be a cipher for Samarian Yahwists and the example of the marriage of Sanballat's daughter to a son of the high priest in Jerusalem being a specific object lesson (Neh 13:28). For this strategy, especially in terms of intermarriage, see e.g. Hensel, "Ethnic Fiction," 141–45.

116 Campbell, *Shechem III*, 307–9.

117 Campbell, *Shechem III*, 309.

118 Edelman, "Different Sources, Different Views," 421–30. Avi Faust would add to this list a number of square structures thought to be forts but not located on road systems: Kh. 'Eres, Har Adar, Kh. Qeiyafa, Pisgat Zeev D, Tel 'Eton, Tel Halif, Kh. Er-Rasm, and Kh. Luzifar ("Forts or agricultural estates?," 48, 51).

119 For Magnar Kartveit, even if the building happened during the governorship of Sanballat, the choice of Gerizim was based on the role Gerizim plays in Deut 24:7, to conform to Mosaic command, "against the arguments in favour of Samaria (strategy), or Shechem (Abraham), and it would even beat David's choice of Jerusalem on the basic question of the most ancient authority"; it was not to please a son-in-law (*Origins*, 356).

120 For a model of the life cycle of an identity movement, which includes various strategies used to grow the movement over time or confine it to an insular group, see Lebel, "The Survival of Identity Groups." This is one such specific strategy.

9 Tentative Conclusions

In the Iron IIC period, there may already have been a *bāmâ* (open-air) sanctuary built atop Mt. Gerizim. If so, it could have been dedicated to a form of Yhwh Samaria and his Asherah, another unattested northern conception of Yhwh, or to a deity whose worship was introduced by an immigrant group settled in the Shechem Valley. Phoenician traders could have worshipped there *en route* inland. Equally, there might have been an elite villa built atop Mt. Gerizim instead, built using Phoenician tradesmen. Both would have required at least one water cistern to have been cut into the bedrock as a much-needed source of water. The volute stones in theory might have originated in either the Iron IIC, the Persian period, or the Hellenistic period.

Assuming the coastal Phoenician pottery was Iron IIC in date, in the first half of the fifth century BCE, probably during the governorship of Sanballat, either the villa was dismantled and a sacred enclosure, likely with a temple, an altar, and at least one water cistern, was constructed. Or, an existing open air structure was expanded by adding a temple building, and residences for a permanent staff were built outside the enclosure on terraces built on the slope, to man it in rotation, receiving prebends in return. More cisterns may have been added at this point.

Two options for which conception of Yhwh was honored there have been explored: Yhwh Shomron, with or without his Asherah, and Yhwh Elohim, as depicted particularly in the book of Deuteronomy. Both have implications for the composition of the Pentateuch. In the first case, scribes in the provincial seat of Samaria could have worked with scribes in Jerusalem, with Gerizim built as a satellite facility to the temple in Samaria. In the second instance, scribes at Gerizim instead of Samaria could have worked with those in Jerusalem. Or, admitting the tendentious nature of Josephus' account of the building of the temple on Gerizim, some scribes still could have moved to Gerizim from Jerusalem. In such a case, the writing of the Pentateuch could have reflected southern ideas, in fact, even if it might have been physically written on Gerizim. It is also possible, however, that these relocated southern scribes would have had contact with scribes in Samaria, or that some scribes from Samaria were also moved to Gerizim, where an exchange took place of religious traditions that were modified and repurposed to fit the newly inaugurated cult of Yhwh Elohim. In any event, the new temple would have been built as a rival to the one honoring Yhwh Shomron in the city of Samaria and would have been aligned conceptually with the emergent concept of Yhwh Elohim, which was also implemented in the Persian-era temple in Jerusalem in place of Yhwh Ṣebaot.

Finally, the suggestion has been made that Sanballat was directly involved in the commissioning of the production of the Pentateuch, evidenced by his epithet, the Harranite, referring to the Syrian city of Harran, which figures multiple times in the patriarchal origin stories of Abraham and Jacob but only three times elsewhere in the collection of texts forming the Hebrew Bible (2Kgs 19:12 and Isa 37:12 alongside Gozan and as a trading partner of Tyre In Ezek 27:23). The subsequent re-vocalization of the epithet as Horonite would have been done to obscure this allusion that had been meant to honor him originally. He may have been assigned an estate in the vicinity of Mt. Gerizim, accounting for the selection of that location for the new temple, which would have been overseen by his son-in-law and future blood descendants borne by his daughter.

Bibliography

Adamczewski, Bartosz, "Abraham and Sanballat," *OTE* 34 (2021): 14–26.

Alt, Albrecht, "Zur Geschichte der Grenze zwischen Judäa und Samaria," pages 346–62 in *Kleine Schriften zur Geschichte des Volkes Israel: Zweiter Band.* Munich: C. H. Beck'sche Verlagbuchhandlung, 1953.

Anderson, Robert T., "The Elusive Samaritan Temple," *BA* 54 (1991): 104–7.

Arie, Eran, "Revisiting Mt. Gerizim: The Foundation of the Sacred Precinct and the Proto-Ionic Capitals," pages 39*–63* in *New Studies in the Archaeology of Jerusalem and Its Region*, edited by Yehiel Zelinger, Orit Peleg-Barkat, Joseph Uziel, and Yuval Gadot. Collected Papers 14. Jerusalem: The Israel Antiquities Authority, 2021.

Avigad, Nahman, "Samaria (City)," pages 1,300–10 in *The New Encyclopedia of Archaeological Excavations in the Holy Land*, vol. 4, edited by Ephraim Stern, Ayelet Lewinson-Gilboa, and Joseph Aviram. Jerusalem: The Israel Exploration Society and Carta, 1993.

Berlant, Stephen R., "The Mysterious Ekron Goddess Revisited," *JANES* 31 (2009): 15–21.

Betancourt, Philip P., *The Aeolic Style in Architecture: A Survey of Its Development in Palestine, the Halikarnassos Peninsula, and Greece, 1000–500 B.C.*, Princeton: Princeton University Press, 1977.

Bickerman, Elias J., "Un document relatif à la persécution d'Antiochus IV Épipane," pages 105–35 in *Studies in Jewish and Christian History II*, AGAJU 9. Leiden: Brill, 1980.

Bijovsky, Gabriela, "The Coins from the Excavations at Mount Gerizim," pages 81–203 in *Mount Gerizim Excavations*, Vol. 3, *The Coins*, edited by Yitzhak Magen, Gabriela Bijovsky, and Yoav Tzionit, JSP 3. Jerusalem: Israel Antiquities Authority, 2022.

Billig, Ya 'akov, Freud, Liora and Bocher, Efrat "Luxurious Royal Estate from the First Temple Period in Armon ha-Natziv, Jerusalem," *TA* 49 (2022): 8–31.

Campbell, Edward F., Jr., *Shechem II: Portrait of a Hill Country Vale: The Shechem Regional Survey*, ASOR Archaeological Reports 2. Atlanta: Scholars Press, 1991.

Campbell, Edward F., *Shechem III: The Stratigraphy and Architecture of Shechem/Tell Balâṭah*, Vol. 1, *Text*, ASOR Archaeological Reports 6. Boston: ASOR, 2002.

Cogan, Mordechai, *The Raging Torrent: Historical Inscriptions from Assyria and Babylonia Relating to Ancient Israel.* Jerusalem: Carta, 2008.

Cornell, Collin, "Cult Statuary in the Judean Temple in Yeb," *JSJ* 47 (2016): 291–309.

Delcor, M[athias]. "Vom Sichem der hellenistichen Epoche zum Sychar des Neuen Testamentes," *ZDPV* 78 (1962): 34–48.

Dorsey, David A., *The Roads and Highways of Ancient Israel*. Baltimore: The Johns Hopkins Press, 1991.

Dušek, Jan, *Aramaic and Hebrew Inscriptions from Mt. Gerizim and Samaria between Antiochus III and Antiochus IV Epiphanes*, CHANE 54. Leiden: Brill, 2012.

Dušek, Jan, *Les manuscrits araméens du Wadi Daliyeh et la Samarie vers 450–332 av. J.-C.*, CHANE 30. Leiden: Brill, 2007.

Edelman, Diana V., "Different Sources, Different Views: Snapshots of Persian-Era Yehud Based on Texts and on Archaeological Data," *EstBib* 76 (2018): 411–51.

Edelman, Diana V., "Early Forms of Judaism as a Mixture of Strategies of Cultural Heterogeneity and the Re-embedding of Local Culture in Archaic Globalization," pages 242–92 in *Levantine Entanglements: Local Dynamics of Globalization in a Contested Region*, edited by Terje Stordalen and Øystein LaBianca. Sheffield: Equinox, 2021.

Edelman, Diana V., *The Origins of the 'Second' Temple: Persian Imperial Policy and the Rebuilding of Jerusalem.* Sheffield: Equinox, 2005.

Edelman. Diana V., "Sanballat, Abraham, And Jacob," in a Festschrift for Thomas Römer, edited by Christoph Nihan and Jean-Daniel Macchi, BZAW. Berlin: de Gruyter, forthcoming, 2025.

Egger, Rita, *Josephus Flavius und die Samaritaner: Eine terminologische Untersuchung zur Identitätsklärung der Samaritaner*, NTOA 4. Freiburg: University Press and Göttingen: Vandenhoeck & Ruprecht, 1986.

Eshel, Hanan, "The Prayer of Joseph from Qumran, a Papyrus from Masada and the Temple on ΑΡΓΑΡΙΖΙΝ," *Zion* 56 (1991): 125–36 (Hebrew).

Faegersten, Fanni and López-Ruiz, Carolina, "Beyond 'Volute Capital': Materials, Meaning, and Adaptations of a Phoenician Motif," *JEMAHS*, forthcoming.

Faust, Avi, "Forts or agricultural estates? Persian period settlement in the territories of the former kingdom of Judah," *PEQ* 150 [2018]: 34–59.

Feigin, Samuel, "Etymological Notes," *AJSL* 43 (1926): 53–60.

Finkelstein, Israel, *Hasmonean realities behind Ezra, Nehemiah, and Chronicles: archaeological and historical perspectives*, AIAL 34. Atlanta: SBL Press, 2018.

Finkelstein, Israel and Singer Avitz, Lily, "Reevaluating Bethel," *ZDPV* 125 (2009): 33–48.

Franklin, Norma, "From Megiddo to Tamassos and Back: Putting the 'Proto-Ionic Capital' in its Place," pages 129–40 in *The Fire Signals of Lachish: Studies in the Archaeology and History of Israel in the Late Bronze Age, Iron Age, and Persian Period in Honor of David Ussishkin*, edited by Israel Finkelstein and Nadav Na'aman. Winona Lake, IN: Eisenbrauns, 2011.

Franklin, Norma, "Stone Volutes: United by a Common Motif not by a Common Function," pages 156–74 in *The Ancient Israelite World*, edited by Kyle H. Keimer and George A. Pierce. London: Routledge, 2022.

Freyne, Sean, "Behind the Names: Galileans, Samaritans, *Ioudaioi*," pages 114–31 in *Galilee and Gospels: Collected Essays*, WUNT 125. Tübingen: Mohr Siebeck, 2000.

Galling, Kurt, "Assyrische und persische Präfekten in Gezer," *PJ* 31 (1935): 75–93.

Gitin, Seymour, Dothan, Trude, and Naveh, Joseph, "A Royal Dedicatory Inscription from Ekron," *IEJ* 47 (1997): 1–16.

Gropp, Douglas M., et al., *Wadi Daliyeh II: The Samarian Papyri from Wadi Daliyeh; and Qumran Cave 4 XXVIII Miscellanea, Part 2*, DJD 28. Oxford: Clarendon, 2001.

Hallo, William W., *The Context of Scripture: Canonical Compositions, Monumental Inscriptions, and Archival Documents from the Biblical World*, Vol. 2, *Monumental Inscriptions from the Biblical World.* Leiden: Brill, 2000.

Hemmer Gudme, Anne Katrine de. "Permanent and passing words: Addressing the divine in the sanctuary on Mount Gerizim," pages 44–60 in *Divine Names on the Spot: Towards a Dynamic Approach of Divine Denominations in Greek and Semitic Contexts*, edited by Thomas Galoppin and Corinne Bonnet, OBO 293, Leuven: Peeters, 2021.

Hensel, Benedikt, "Ethnic Fiction and Identity-Formation: A New Explanation for the Background of the Question of intermarriage in Ezra-Nehemiah," pages 133–48 in *The Bible, Qumran, and the Samaritans*, edited by Magnar Kartveit and Gary N. Knoppers, SJ 104, Studia Samaritana 10. Berlin: de Gruyter, 2018.

Hensel, Benedikt, "Das JHWH-Heiligtum am Garizim: eine archäologischer Befund und seine literar- und theologiegeschichltiche Einordnung," *VT* 68 (2018): 73–93.

Hensel, Benedikt, *Juda und Samaria: Zum Verhältnis zweier nach-exilischer Jahwismen*, FAT 1.110. Tübingen: Mohr, 2016.

Herzog, Zeev, "Settlement and Fortification Planning in the Iron Age," pages 231–74 in *The Architecture of Ancient Israel: From the Prehistoric to the Persian Periods*, edited by Aharon Kempinski and Ronny Reich. Jerusalem: Israel Exploration Society, 1992.

Hjelm, Ingrid, *The Samaritans and Early Judaism: A Literary Analysis*, JSOTSup 303. Sheffield: Sheffield Academic, 2000.

Isaac, Benjamin H., "A Seleucid Inscription from Jamnia-on-the-Sea: Antiochus V Eupator and the Sidonians," *IEJ* 41 (1991): 132–44.

Itach, Gilad, Zelig Aster, Shawn and Ben Shlomo, David, "The Wedge-Impressed Bowl and the Assyrian Deportation," *TA* 44 (2017): 72–97.

Itkin, Danny, et al., "*Nāri* in the Levant: Historical and Etymological Aspects of a Specific Calcrete Formation," *Earth Sciences History* 31 (2012): 210–28.

Kahwagi-Janho, Hany, "Les chapiteaux à volutes verticals de Liban," *Chronos* 29 (2014): 95–125.

Kartveit, Magnar, *The Origins of the Samaritans*, VTSup 128. Leiden: Brill, 2009.

Kartveit, Magnar, "Josephus on the Samaritans – his Tendenz and Purpose," pages 109–20 in *Samaria, Samarians, Samaritans: Studies on Bible, History and Linguistics*, edited by József Zsengellér, SJ 66, Studia Samaritana 6. Berlin: de Gruyter, 2011.

Kenyon, Kathleen, *Jerusalem: Excavating 3000 Years of History.* London: Thames and Hudson, 1967.

Kippenberg, Hans G., *Garizim und Synagoge: Traditionsgeschichtliche Untersuchungen zur samaritanischen Religion der aramäischen Periode*, RVV 30. Berlin: W. de Gruyter, 1971.

Kletter, Raz, "A Clay Model Shrine," pages 28–84 in *Yavneh II: The 'Temple Hill' Repository Pit*, edited by Raz Kletter, Irit Ziffer, and Wolfgang Zwickel, OBO Series Archaeologica 30. Fribourg: Academic Press and Göttingen: Vandenhoeck & Ruprecht, 2015.

Knoppers, Gary N., "Parallel Torahs and Inner-Scriptural Interpretation: The Jewish and Samaritan Pentateuchs in Historical Perspective," pages 507–31 in *The Bible, Qumran, and the Samaritans*, edited by Magnar Kartveit and Gary N. Knoppers, Studia Samaritana 10, Studia Judaica 104. Berlin: de Gruyter, 2011.

Lebel, Efi, "The Survival of Identity Groups: A Case Study of the Jewish People's Survival during the Second Temple Period," PhD dissertation, University of Haifa, 2022.

Lemaire, André, "Épigraphie et religion en Palestine à l'époque achéménide," *Transeu* 22 (2001): 97–113.

Lemaire, André, *Levantine Epigraphy and History in the Achaemenid Period (539–333 BCE).* Oxford: Oxford University Press, 2015.

Lemaire, André, "The Xanthos Trilingual Revisited," pages 423–32 in *Solving Riddles and Untying Knots: Biblical, Epigraphic, and Semitic Studies in Honor of Jonas C. Greenfield*, edited by Ziony Zevit, Seymour Gitin, and Michael Sokoloff. Winona Lake, IN: Eisenbrauns, 1995.

Lemaire, André and Lozachmeur, Hélène, "*Birah/birta'* en araméen," *Syria* 64 (1987): 261–66.

Lipschits, Oded, "Bethel Revisited," pages 233–46 in *Rethinking Israel: Studies in the History and Archaeology of Ancient Israel in Honor of Israel Finkelstein*, edited by Oded Lipschits, Yuval Gadot, and Matthew J. Adams. Winona Lake, IN: Eisenbraus, 2017.

Lipschits, Oded, *The Fall and Rise of Jerusalem: Judah under Babylonian Rule*. Winona Lake, IN: Eisenbrauns, 2005.

Lipschits, Oded, "The Origin and Date of the Volute Capitals from the Levant," pages 203–25 in *The Fire Signals of Lachish: Studies in the Archaeology and History of Israel in the Late Bronze Age, Iron Age, and Persian Period in Honor of David Ussishkin*, edited by Israel Finkelstein and Nadav Na'aman. Winona Lake, IN: Eisenbrauns, 2011.

Magen, Yitzhak, "The Dating of the First Phase of the Samaritan Temple on Mt Gerizim in Light of Archaeological Evidence," pages 157–211 in *Judah and the Judeans in the Fourth Century B.C.E.*, edited by Oded Lipschitz, Gary N. Knoppers, and Rainer Albertz. Winona Lake, IN: Eisenbrauns, 2007.

Magen, Yitzhak, "Mount Gerizim and the Samaritans," pages 91–148 in *Early Christianity in Context – Monuments and Documents*, edited by Frédéric Manns and Eugenio Alliata (Jerusalem: Franciscan Printing Press, 1993).

Magen, Yitzhak, *Mount Gerizim Excavations*, Vol. 2, *A Temple City*, JSP 8. Jerusalem: Israel Antiquities Authority, 2008.

Magen, Yitzhak, Misgav, Haggai and Tsafania, Levana *Mount Gerizim Excavations*, Vol. 1, *The Aramaic, Hebrew and Greek Inscriptions*, JSP 2. Jerusalem: Israel Antiquities Authority, 2004.

Magness, Jodi. "The Cults of Isis and Kore in Samaria-Sebastiye in the Hellenistic and Roman Periods," *HTR* 94 (2001): 157–77.

Meshorer, Yaakov and Qedar, Shraga, *Samarian Coinage*, NSR 9. Jerusalem: Israel Numismatic Society, 1999.

Na'aman, Nadav, "In Search of the Temples of YHWH of Samaria and YHWH of Teman," *JANER* 17 (2017): 76–95.

Nodet, Etienne, "Israelites, Samaritans, Temples, Jews," pages 121–71 in *Samaria, Samarians, Samaritans: Studies on Bible, History and Linguistics*, edited by József Zsengellér, SJ 66, Studia Samaritana 6. Berlin: de Gruyter, 2011.

Parpola, Simo and Porter, Michael, eds., *The Helsinki Atlas of the Near East in the Neo-Assyrian Period*. Helsinki: The Casco Bay Assyriological Institute and the Neo-Assyrian Text Corpus Project, 2001.

Porten, Bezalel. *Archives from Elephantine: Life of an Ancient Military Colony*. Berkeley: University of California Press, 1969.

Pummer, Reinhard, "ΑΡΓΑΡΙΖΙΝ: A Criterion for Samaritan Provenance?," *JSJ* 18 (1987): 18–25.

Pummer, Reinhard, "Genesis 34 in Jewish Writings of the Hellenistic and Roman Periods," *HTR* 75 (1982): 177–88.

Pummer, Reinhard, "Samaritan Ethnicity in Josephus: Rhetoric and Historicity," *JAAJ* 7 (2019): 45–73.

Pummer, Reinhard, *The Samaritans in Flavius Josephus*, TSAJ 129. Tübingen: Mohr Siebeck, 2009.

Pummer, Reinhard, "Samaritan Synagogues and Jewish Synagogues: Similarities and Differences," pages 118–60 in *Jews, Christians, and Polytheists in the Ancient Synagogue: Cultural Interaction during the Greco-Roman Period*, edited by Steven Fine. Baltimore Studies in the History of Judaism. New York: Routledge, 1999.

Pummer, Reinhard, "Was There an Altar or a Temple in the Sacred Precinct on Mt. Gerizim?," *JSJ* 47 (2016): 1–21.

Regev, Dalit and Greenfeld, Uzi, "The Persian Pottery from the Salvage Excavations at Har Gerizim (2019–2021): Preliminary Findings," pages 65–88 in Social Groups behind Biblical Traditions: Identity Perspectives from Egypt, Transjordan, Mesopotamia, and Israel in the Second Temple

Period, edited by Benedikt Hensel, Bartosz Adamczewski, and Dany Noquet, FAT 167. Tübingen: Mohr Siebeck, 2023.

Reich, Ronny, "Palaces and Residences in the Iron Age," pages 202–22 in *The Architecture of Ancient Israel: From the Prehistoric to the Persian Periods*, edited by Aharon Kempinski and Ronny Reich. Jerusalem: Israel Exploration Society, 1992.

Rendsburg, Gary, "Ur Kasdim: Where is Abraham's Birthplace?," *TheTorah.com* (2006). https://thetorah.com/article/ur-kadim-where-is-Abrahams-birthplace

Römer, Thomas, "Des temples yahvistes au Temple unique," *MdB* 233 (2020): 38–41.

Schwartz, Seth, "John Hyrcanus I's Destruction of the Gerizim Temple and Judaean-Samaritan Relations," *Jewish History* 7 (1993): 9–25.

Schroer, Silvia, "The Iconography of the Shrine Models of Khirbet Qeiyafa," pages 137–58 in *Khirbet Qeyeifa in the Shephelah: Papers Presented at a Colloquium of the Swiss Society for Ancient Near Eastern Studies Held at the University of Berlin, 2014*, edited by Silvia Schroer and Stefan Münger, OBO 282. Fribourg: Academic Press and Göttingen: Vandenhoeck & Ruprecht, 2017.

Shiloh, Yigal, "The Proto-Aeolic Capital – The Israelite 'Timorah' (Palmette)," *PEQ* 109 (1977): 39–52.

Shiloh, Yigal and Horowitz, Aharon, "Ashlar Quarries of the Iron Age in the Hill Country of Israel," *BASOR* 217 (1975): 37–48.

Smoak, Jeremy D., "Inscribing Temple Space: The Ekron Dedication as Monumental Text," *JNES* 76 (2017): 319–36.

Stern, Ephraim and Magen, Yitzhak, "Archaeological Evidence for the First Phase of the Samaritan Temple on Mount Gerizim," *IEJ* 52 (2002): 49*–57*.

Tappy, Ron E., *The Archaeology of Israelite Samaria*. Volume 2: *The Eighth Century BCE*, HSS 50. Atlanta: Scholars Press, 2001.

Tavgar, Aharon, "'And He Called the Name of that Place Bethel' (Gen 28:19): Historical-Geography and Archaeology of the Sanctuary of Bethel," pages 201–2 in *The History of the Jacob Cycle (Genesis 25–35): Recent Research on the Compilation, the Redaction, and the Reception of the Biblical Narrative and Its Historical and Cultural Contexts*, edited by Bendikt Hensel. Tübingen: Mohr Siebeck, 2021.

Tavgar, Aharon, "E.P. 914 East of Beitin and the Location of the Ancient Cult Site of Bethel," *In the Highland's Depth: Ephraim Range and Binyamin Research Studies* 5 (2015): 49–69 (Hebrew).

Teixidor, Javier, "The Aramaic Text in the Tringual Stele from Xanthus," *JNES* 37 (1978): 181–85.

Vernet, Mariona, "The Letoon Trilingual revisited: Some notes on the 'King of Kaunos'," pages 81–100 in *Studies in the languages and language contact in Pre-Hellenistic Anatolia*, edited by Federico Giusfredi and Zsolt Simon, Barcino Monographica Orientalia 17, Series Anatolica et Indogermanica 2. Barcelona: Institut del Pròxim Orient Antic, 2021.

Walcher, Katja, "Royal Tomb 5 of Thamossos: an analysis of its decoration with regard to religious or representative prototypes," pages 77–89 in *Cyprus: Religion and Society from the Late Bronze Age to the End of the Archaic Period: Proceedings of an International Symposium on Cypriote Archaeology, Erlangen, 23–24 July* 2004, edited by Vassos Karageorghis, Hartmut Matthäus, and Sabine Rogge. Möhnesee: Bibliopolis, 2005.

Will, Ernest. "Qu-est ce qu'une *Baris*?," *Syria* 64 (1987): 253–59.

Zadok, Ran, "Samarian Notes," *BO* 42 (1985): 567–72.

Zangenberg, Jürgen K., "The Sanctuary on Mount Gerizim: Observations on the Result of 20 Years of Excavation," pages 399–418 in *Temple Building and Temple Cult Architecture and Cultic Paraphernalia of Temples in the Levant (2.–1. Mill. B.C.E.): Proceedings of a Conference on the Occasion of the 50th Anniversary of the Institute of Biblical Archaeology at the University of Tübingen*, edited by Jens Kamlah, ADPV 41. Wiesbaden: University of Tübingen Press, 2012.

Zertal, Adam, "Bowls Decorated with Wedges and the Origins of the Cutheans," *EI* 20 (1988): 181–87 (Hebrew).
Zertal, Adam, *The Manasseh Hill Country Survey*, Vol. 1, *The Shechem Syncline*, CHANE 21.1. Leiden: Brill, 2004.
Zertal, Adam, "The Wedge-Shaped Decorated Bowl and the Origin of the Samaritans," *BASOR* 276 (1989): 77–84.
Zevit, Ziony, *The Religions of Ancient Israel: A Synthesis of Parallactic Approaches*. New York: Continuum, 2001.

Margaretha Folmer

The Linguistic Milieu of Elephantine Aramaic: Persian Loanwords and Examples of Egyptian Code-switching

Preliminary Remarks

This contribution[1] is devoted to several lexical aspects of the Aramaic documents from Elephantine written by the island's Judean population. It examines the distribution and integration of lexical materials from languages other than Aramaic in these documents, with a focus on Old Persian loanwords[2] and instances of Egyptian code-switching (rather than loanwords). It represents an attempt to better our understanding of the linguistic milieu of Elephantine Aramaic.[3]

1 Aramaic in the Persian Period

Aramaic in the Persian Period was not a uniform language and many varieties of Aramaic flourished across the vast area ruled by the Persian Empire between ca. 550–330 BCE. Aramaic was the *lingua franca* (also 'vehicular language' or 'link language') of the Persian Empire and an official variety of Aramaic functioned as the language of the Persian administration. This official variety had a more or less standardised form, with a uniform orthography, and included many stock phrases. Both its lexicon and its (morpho)syntax were heavily influenced by Old Persian, while the influence of native local languages is also often noticeable, particularly in the case of texts produced by local scribes who spoke these local languages. This official variety of Aramaic was more or less immune to change over time, as evidenced by official letters from ancient Bactria that date to the middle of the 4th century BCE.

---

1 I am thankful to Daniel Waller for the correction of the English.
2 I have chosen to focus on this aspect of the Elephantine texts in honour of the highly esteemed late Prof. Shaul Shaked.
3 In this contribution, I use the translations of the Elephantine documents in *TAD* with only minor adjustments. Where I have made larger changes, these are always indicated.

Margaretha Folmer, Leiden University, The Netherlands

https://doi.org/10.1515/9783111018638-003

In addition to this official variety of Aramaic, local varieties of Aramaic were also used across the Persian Empire. In some cases, these local varieties reflect a spoken variant of Aramaic. This is most clearly the case in the so-called Hermopolis letters, but it is also evident in several texts from Elephantine written by local Judeans. From certain morphological characteristics of the Aramaic used in the Hermopolis letters, it is clear that the Arameans who wrote these letters spoke and wrote a variant of Aramaic that resembles later Western Aramaic, whereas the Judean population of Elephantine probably spoke and wrote a variety of Aramaic that is typologically closer to the official variant of Aramaic.

Elephantine Aramaic is not uniform either and the term 'Elephantine Aramaic' is only of partial use. The texts found on the island belong to different textual genres, while not all of the texts found at Elephantine were actually written there.[4] Moreover, the texts found on the island were written by people from different backgrounds. The inhabitants of Elephantine lived on an island but not in perfect isolation: the onomasticon attested in the rich Aramaic documentation from Elephantine shows that this small corner of the world represented a flourishing multicultural and multilingual society. Though the Elephantine documents primarily reflect a local variant of Aramaic that was used principally by the island's Judean population, it is clear that these Judeans had substantial contacts with other *ethnoi*, including intermarriage (with Egyptians), daily contact with their neighbours on the island and in the twin town of Syene on the opposite bank of the mainland, and through their military activities (since the military units to which they belonged also included other *ethnoi*). The Elephantine Judeans also communicated with family members in other parts of Egypt and with the authorities in Palestine, as evidenced by the letters that concern the destruction and rebuilding of the Yhw temple at Elephantine (part of the Yedanyah correspondence). This local form of Aramaic used by the Judeans on Elephantine was not immune to change, and this is clearly visible in dated legal documents from across the length of the 5th century BCE. It also reveals certain idiosyncrasies and clear traces of a vernacular form of Aramaic.

2 Elephantine Aramaic and Its Linguistic Milieu

A picture of a complex and multilingual society emerges from the Aramaic documents found at Elephantine. Most of the Aramaic documents from the island were produced by its Judean population. Elsewhere I have shown that the Elephantine

4 This is particularly true of letters.

Judeans were speakers of Aramaic,[5] though their ancestral language was undoubtedly Hebrew; there is no compelling evidence in the Elephantine documents, however, that Hebrew was still a spoken language.[6] Elephantine Aramaic not only bears traces of language contact with Hebrew, but also with Akkadian (the administrative language of the earlier Neo-Assyrian and Neo-Babylonian empires), Old Persian (the native language of the Achaemenid rulers),[7] and Egyptian, the native language of the Judeans' direct neighbours.[8]

Linguistic borrowing – in the widest sense of the word – is the result of a contact situation between speakers of different languages.[9] The sociolinguistic position of the borrowers is of prime importance when it comes to distinguishing the two main types of linguistic borrowing: adoption and imposition. This distinction depends on whether the borrower is a native speaker of the receiving language or a non-native speaker.[10] In the first situation, native speakers of the receiving language adopt linguistic elements from a donor language into their native language (native speaker agentivity; called 'adoption'), whereas in the second situation, non-native speakers – usually speakers of the donor language – impose linguistic items on the receiving language (non-native speaker agentivity; called 'imposition').[11]

Generally speaking, structural borrowings into Aramaic are mostly found in texts with a clear background in the Achaemenid administration.[12] In most cases of structural borrowing, (morpho)syntactic properties of Old Persian are involved.

5 Folmer, *Aramaic Language*, 745. The clearest evidence for this is the presence of pronunciation spellings in the Elephantine texts, the most important examples being *ylty* for *yldty* (*TAD* B3.6:8) and *ʾdbr* for *ʾldbr* (*TAD* B5.3:3) in two legal documents, and *ʾznh* for *ʾd znh* in the letter *TAD* A4.7:20, with the supralinear addition of *d*.

6 See Folmer, "Contribution," 136–37, especially 137. On Hebrew loanwords, see also van der Iest, "Judean Cultural Identity."

7 Many scholars today are in agreement that the Old Persian of the Achaemenid royal inscriptions was a rather artificial court language, whereas the vernacular Persian of the Achaemenids was developing toward Middle Persian. As an administrative language Old Persian is principally known from indirect sources, such as Aramaic, Babylonian, and Elamite. On this, see Tavernier, "Old Persian," 638–57, esp. 639, 651–52.

8 There may have been contact with other languages as well, but this has not left visible traces in the Aramaic documents from Elephantine.

9 In what follows, I adopt the terminology used by Haspelmath, "Lexical Borrowing," 35–54.

10 Thomason and Kaufman use the term 'borrowing' for adoption and 'substratum interference' for imposition. See Thomason and Kaufman, *Language Contact*, 20–21. They argue that "in borrowing proper many words will be borrowed before any structural interference at all occurs; but in substratum interference [...] structural interference comes first." (21).

11 See Haspelmath, "Lexical Borrowing."

12 On structural borrowings versus material borrowings, see Haspelmath, "Lexical Borrowing," 38–39. Structural borrowings involve the copying of syntactic, morphological, and semantic patterns. Loanwords are material borrowings.

This observation is particularly true of the Aršama and Akhvamazda letters and the Bisitun inscription.[13] These cases clearly reflect the structural borrowing or imposition of syntactic features by non-native speakers. Some of these same syntactic features are also found in legal documents from Elephantine written by non-Judean scribes, that is, scribes with Persian, Akkadian, and Aramean names.[14]

Elephantine Judeans adopted linguistic elements from several donor languages into Aramaic.[15] Most such borrowings in the Elephantine documents are lexical: loanwords from Akkadian, the language of the Neo-Assyrian and Neo-Babylonian administrations; loanwords from Old Persian, the native language of the Achaemenid rulers and the official language of the Achaemenid administration (see n. 7); lexical items from Egyptian,[16] the language spoken by the immediate neighbours of the Elephantine Judeans; and loanwords from Hebrew, the ancestral language of the Judeans.[17]

In the following, I do not discuss loanwords from Akkadian. Contact between Aramaic and Akkadian stretches back to the time of the Neo-Assyrian Empire when Aramaic was adopted by its rulers as a *lingua franca* and the language of the central administration.[18] Neither do I discuss Hebrew loanwords, as I have dealt with such loanwords elsewhere.[19] Most Hebrew loanwords belong to the semantic domain of religion. Instead, I focus on Old Persian loanwords (3) and Egyptian words (which probably reflect code-switching) (4).[20]

---

13 See Folmer, "Aramaic of the Akhvamazdā letters," 325–53.

14 See Folmer, *Aramaic Language*, 718–22. These features are not discussed in the present contribution.

15 On the spoken language of the Elephantine Judeans, see above n. 5.

16 I avoid the term loanwords with respect to Egyptian, because, as I will demonstrate, Egyptian words in Aramaic more closely resemble code-switching than loanwords.

17 Loan translations ('calques') are not considered in the present study. These are structural borrowings, as they copy a pattern (see Haspelmath, "Lexical Borrowing," 39). An example of a loan translation from Old Persian is the use of *ʾḥr* at the beginning of the main clause (apodosis) of a conditional sentence; this reflects Old Persian *pasāva* (see Folmer, *Aramaic Language*, 417–418; on *pasāva* see Schmitt, *Wörterbuch*, 229). An example from Hebrew is *khnʾ rbʾ* which reflects Biblical Hebrew *hkhn hgdwl* (see Mizrahi, "History and Linguistic Background").

18 Akkadian lexical items were borrowed into Aramaic during the period of the Neo-Assyrian and Neo-Babylonian Empires. The semantic domains to which these borrowings belong principally involve communication and administration. Akkadian loanwords in Aramaic have been extensively discussed in *AIA*, 30–115. See also Abraham and Sokoloff, "Aramaic Loanwords," 59.

19 On this, see Folmer, "Contribution," 136–37. Hebrew and Aramaic resemble each other to the extent that Hebrew loanwords in Aramaic are very difficult to recognise, unless the spelling points to a specific Hebrew reflex of a Proto-Semitic consonant. On the criteria used to recognise such loanwords, see Stadel, *Hebraismen*, 7–9.

20 I have excluded accounts from a systematic treatment in the following discussion, as they do not contribute substantially to our understanding of the distribution and use of Persian and

3 Old Persian Loanwords

Aramaic texts that evidence Old Persian loanwords have been found across the area of what was the Persian Empire. Almost all Old Persian loanwords in Persian Period Aramaic are nouns and adjectives. Only occasionally is an adverb attested.[21] This agrees with cross-linguistic evidence, which shows that nouns are the easiest and usually the first lexical items to be borrowed.[22]

The nature of the linguistic contact is clear from the semantic domains in which the loanwords occur. In the Persian Period, Aramaic was the official language of communication and administration and, accordingly, one can expect loanwords within semantic domains pertaining to communication and administration. Many loanwords concern lexemes that denote the functions of employees of the Persian administration, lexemes that refer to documents produced by them, and specific legal terminology.

An important methodological problem within the study of the Old Persian lexicon is the fact that Old Persian texts are basically all royal inscriptions, whether funerary inscriptions or other texts for public display. This relatively small but steadily expanding corpus is highly formulaic and its vocabulary is not very extensive. This leads to an odd situation, such that Aramaic is an important yet indirect source for the Old Persian lexicon. For the etymology and semantics of Old Persian lexical items in Aramaic, scholars often need to search for parallels

---

Egyptian words in Elephantine documents written by Judeans. However, several Egyptian words in accounts that are of interest to the discussion here will be discussed in section 4.

21 Although there are no examples of verbs borrowed from Old Persian, there is evidence in some Aramaic texts for so-called 'light verbs' (also 'dummy verbs'), where the Aramaic verb *ʿbd* 'to do' is complemented by a direct object that is an Old Persian loanword. These direct objects are always preposed (as in Old Persian). Examples are: *ʾwpšr* 'repairs' (*TAD* A6.2:3.9 f.) and *ʾwpkrt* 'calculation' (*TAD* A6.2:5, an Aršama letter found at Elephantine); *hndrz* 'instruction' (*TAD* A6.13:3; A6.14:3, Aršama correspondence); *hndrz* 'instruction' (A4:1; A5:2; A6:6.8) and *wprkn* 'ditch' (A4:1.6, in this combination 'to build') (Akhvamazda correspondence); *ʾwdys* 'statement' (*TAD* A4.10:12) and *dwškrt* 'evil act' (*TAD* A4.5:3) (Yedanyah correspondence). In addition, there are several examples of Old Persian loanwords that are the subject of a passive construction with *ʿbd*: *ʾwpšr* 'repair' (*TAD* A6.2:6, Aršama letter found at Elephantine); *gst ptgm* 'a harsh word' (*TAD* A6.8:3 f.; A6.10:9, Aršama correspondence); *hndrz* 'instruction' (A2:1, Akhvamazda correspondence). There is another possible example in l. 7 of the Xanthos inscription from Asia Minor (see *DNWSI*, 537, s. v. krp 'cult' or 'sanctuary' [uncertain meaning]); see also Tavernier, *Iranica*, 522). On light verbs, see *Trask's Revised Historical Linguistics*, 31; Matras, *Language Contact*, 182.

22 See *Trask's Revised Historical Linguistics*, 27, where this is explained by the fact that nouns are easier to adapt to the grammatical system of the borrowing language. According to Matras (*Language Contact*, 168, 172, and also 134), this 'high borrowability' is best explained by their specific referentiality.

in other contemporary and later Iranian languages. An invaluable handbook for the Old Persian vocabulary in Aramaic is Jan Tavernier's work on Old Iranian proper names and loanwords in non-Iranian languages.[23]

Not all of the Persian loanwords that will be discussed in what follows are known from Old Persian inscriptions, though they are all known from one or more Iranian languages, whether Old Persian, an Iranian language contemporary with Old Persian, or a later Iranian language. The oldest transmitted Iranian languages are Old Persian and Old Avestan. The earliest Old Persian texts date to the Persian Period.[24]

3.1 Aramaic Corpora with Old Persian Loanwords

Old Persian loanwords are not evenly distributed among the different genres of Elephantine Aramaic texts. In Persian Period Aramaic, Old Persian loanwords are most frequently found in official documents that were issued by the chancelleries of the central authorities. The best-known examples are the letters and the letter orders sent by and to the Satrap of Egypt Aršama (end 5th century BCE) (*TAD* A6.1–6.16), including the letter order sent by Aršama (*TAD* A6.2) and the letter to Aršama (*TAD* A6.1) that were both found among the Elephantine papyri, although – as far as can be concluded from the remains of the letter – no Judean official was involved in the drafting of *TAD* A6.1. The Akhvamazda letter orders from ancient Bactria (northern Afghanistan, 4th century BCE) also belong to the same genre. In addition, the central authorities appear to have circulated Aramaic copies of the Bisitun inscription that Darius the Great had cut into stone around 520 BCE. One such copy was found among the Elephantine documents (*TAD* C2.1, copied ca. 420 BCE). It is likely that the Old Persian loanwords in these texts were imported by speakers of Old Persian, as the Aramaic of these texts also bear clear signs of strong influence from Old Persian on its (morpho)syntax. This influence can only be explained on the basis of interference from the spoken language of the people who drafted these texts (non-native speaker agentivity, imposition). The Yedanyah correspondence also includes a considerable number of Old Persian loanwords, though not nearly as many as the Aršama and Akhvamazda letters.[25] The Yedanyah letters were drafted by members of the Elephantine commu-

---

23 Tavernier, *Iranica.* Unfortunately, Tavernier's work antedates the final publication of the Aramaic texts from ancient Bactria, which abound with lexical items that derive from Iranian languages (see Naveh and Shaked, *Aramaic Documents*).

24 Skjærvo, "Old Iranian," 43.

25 The Yedanyah correspondence is often referred to as an 'archive'. On the notion 'archive', see Granerød, "Canon and Archive."

nity and reflect an obvious attempt to replicate the official style of the Aramaic letters issued by the Persian administration. In addition, legal documents from Elephantine contain a good number of Old Persian loanwords.

Several corpora among the surviving Elephantine texts contain very few or are completely devoid of Old Persian loanwords. This is true of two literary compositions, the Proverbs of Aḥiqar and the Story of Aḥiqar (which were combined into one composition on the papyrus sheets found at Elephantine). The absence of loanwords presumably indicates that the two works were composed before the Persian Period. The proverbs are often believed to have their origin in the late 8th or early 7th century BCE.[26] We have a *post quem* date of 669 BCE for the Story of Aḥiqar, as its text mentions both Sennacherib (r. 704–681) and his son Esarhaddon (r. 680–669). Both works may have been copied at Elephantine. In addition to these literary texts, private letters on papyrus from Elephantine contain relatively few Old Persian loanwords, while letter ostraca from Elephantine are also devoid of Old Persian loanwords to a large degree (based on *TAD* D7.1–54). Letter ostraca consist of short messages sent between persons who knew one other. The absence of Old Persian loanwords in these private communications suggests a speech situation among the Judeans whereby contact with speakers of Old Persian was not part and parcel of their daily life.[27]

In what follows, I begin my investigation of Old Persian loanwords in the legal documents from Elephantine, followed by the Yedanyah correspondence, and then private letters on papyrus and ostraca.

3.2 Old Persian Loanwords in Legal Documents

Elephantine legal documents are an invaluable source of information for lexical items derived from other languages. This is because the texts are dated at the beginning of the document and incorporate scribal formulae that include the scribe's name: *ktb* PN *b.* PN *spr' znh b*LN (with variations).[28] The scribes are often named using both their given and paternal name. In my previous research, these dates and names proved helpful when it came to uncovering linguistic and orthographic changes, as well as the linguistic and orthographic peculiarities specific to individual scribes. For this reason, legal documents represent the starting-point for my investigation of Old Persian loanwords.

26 For this date, see Kottsieper, "Aḥiqar and the Bible," 88.

27 On the presence of Old Persian loanwords in the Clermont-Ganneau letter ostraca, see n. 124.

28 See Table 1, col. 6.

3.2.1 Classes of Old Persian Loanwords in Legal Documents

Only Old Persian nouns and adjectives are attested with certainty in the Elephantine legal documents, though an adverb (*ʾpm*) of disputed origin also appears in these texts. Tavernier and others before him have suggested an Iranian (Avestan) etymology for this word (*apam 'from now on, henceforth').[29] While it is very plausible that an Old Persian adverbial ending *-m* would appear in Persian Period Aramaic from the 4th century BCE,[30] it is equally possible that the *-m* in *ʾpm* in the Elephantine legal documents is linked to the common Northwest Semitic adverbial *-m*.[31] In my opinion, an Iranian etymology for *ʾpm* is suspect: apart from the fact that nouns are more easily borrowed than adverbs, there is also the fact that the earliest Elephantine legal document in which this word occurs is dated to 471 BCE; this antedates the legal documents in which undisputed Old Persian loanwords appear by some twenty years (measures of weight and capacity excepted; for a detailed discussion, see below 3.2.7). Further to this, three of the documents in which the word *ʾpm* appears do not contain any other Old Persian loanwords (*TAD* B2.1, 471 BCE; *TAD* B2.2, 464 BCE; *TAD* B2.3, 460/459 BCE), *krš* excepted (see Table 1, col. 4).

3.2.2 Semantic Domains of Old Persian Loanwords in Legal Documents

The semantic domains covered by the Old Persian loanwords in the Elephantine legal documents include:

Measures

krš 'karsh' (< Old Persian *kạrša-; Tavernier, *Iranica*, 81[32]) (passim)

ʾrdb 'ardab' (< Old Persian *ṛdba-; Tavernier, *Iranica*, 449) (*TAD* B4.3:4.5.6.8; B4.5:4.5.7.8)

---

29 See Tavernier, *Iranica*, 411.

30 This ending appears in Aramaic texts from ancient Bactria in the adverbs *knm* (A6:5), *kʿnm* (A6:3), and *qdmnm* (A1:1; 5:2; 6:6). For an edition of these texts, see Naveh and Shaked, *Aramaic Documents*.

31 For the two possible interpretations, see *DNWSI*, 96. A Northwest Semitic origin is also assumed in *GEA*, §90b (cf. also §22a, n. 428). The adverb *ʾpm* 'furthermore' is found in several Elephantine legal documents from 471 BCE onwards (*TAD* B2.1, 471 BCE; *TAD* B2.2, 464 BCE; *TAD* B2.3, 460/459 BCE; *TAD* B3.5, 434 BCE; *TAD* B2.9, 420 BCE; *TAD* B2.10, 416 BCE; *TAD* B3.9, 416 BCE; *TAD* B3.13, 402 BCE). A variant form *ʾm* (with the same meaning and function) is found in documents produced by the scribe Ḥaggai b. Šemaʿyah (*TAD* B2.7; B3.4; B3.10; B3.11; thus also in *GEA*, §90c). It has the same function and meaning as the adverb *twb* 'furthermore' in the oldest document from Elephantine (*TAD* B5.1:7) (cf. also *twb* in *TAD* B2.4:12).

32 *DNWSI*, 537: 'certain type of weight, coin'.

g (abbreviation for *gryw* or *gryb* 'griv') (< Old Persian *grīva-; Tavernier, *Iranica*, 448[33])

Official Titles and Epithets

prtrk 'garrison commander', lit. 'superior' (< Old Persian *frataraka-; Tavernier, *Iranica*, 421) (*TAD* B2.9:14)
hptḥpt 'guardian of the seventh (part of the world/kingdom)' (< Old Persian *haptaxvapātā; Tavernier, *Iranica*, 425) (*TAD* B3.9:2)
prypt 'chief of the beloved'[34] (< Old Persian *frya-pati-; Tavernier, *Iranica*, 422) (*TAD* B3.12:11)
mgš 'magian' (< Old Persian *magus; Tavernier, *Iranica*, 79) (*TAD* B3.5:24 2x)

Administration

Military (Administrative) Domain

hndz 'garrisoned' (adjective), lit. 'co-inhabitant of the fortress' (< Old Persian *handaiza-; Tavernier, *Iranica*, 451[35]) (*TAD* B2.7:4)
ptp 'ration' (< Old Persian *piθfa-; Tavernier, *Iranica*, 410) (*TAD* B3.13:4.5.8.10)

Legal (Administrative) Domain

hngyt 'partner in chattel' (< Old Persian *hangaiθa-; Tavernier, *Iranica*, 425) (*TAD* B3.6:5; B3.10:18; B3.11:12; B3.12:27; B5.5:9); always in combination with *hnbg*, which follows *hngyt*.
hnbg 'partner in realty' (< Old Persian *hanbaga-; Tavernier, *Iranica*, 425) (*TAD* B3.6:5; B3.10:18; B3.11:12; B3.12:27; B5.5:9); always in combination with *hngyt*, which precedes *hnbg*.
ʾdrng (< Old Persian *ādranga- 'guarantor'; Tavernier, *Iranica*, 442) (*TAD* B3.10:18; B3.11:12; B3.12:27; B3.13:9)

33 *DNWSI*, 235, s. v. gryw.
34 Porten and Yardeni translate 'preferred'.
35 This word has been the subject of much discussion. For a brief overview, see Tavernier, *Iranica*, 451; see also Driver, *Aramaic Documents*, 53–54. The word is usually understood as an adjective (see, e.g., *DNWSI*, 288, s. v. hndz 'being held [in the fortress], confined'). According to Tavernier, it derives from *handaiza- (known from Median), the literal meaning of which is presumably 'co-inhabitant of the fortress' (from **hama-* 'co-, alike' and **daiza* 'fortress'). The word is invariable in Persian period Aramaic. Apart from its appearance in the legal document *TAD* B2.7:4, the word also occurs in one of the Yedanyah letters (*TAD* A4.5:7) and in one of the Aršama letters (*TAD* A6.7:6). In these two instances, the inflectional element *-n* is absent where it is expected. See 3.3.7 (b).

ʾb(y)grn (< Old Persian *abigarana- 'fine'; Tavernier, *Iranica*, 442) (*TAD* B2.9:14; B2.10:15; B2.11:10; B3.6:14; B3.7:17; B3.8:31; B3.9:7; B3.10:20; B3.11:10; B3.12:30; B3.13:6.7; B5.5:6)
nprt (< Old Persian *niparta- 'litigation'; Tavernier, *Iranica*, 448) (*TAD* B2.8:3[36])
ʾzt 'free' (< Old Persian *āzāta- [adjective]; Tavernier, *Iranica*, 404) (*TAD* B3.6:4)
psšdt (< Old Persian *pasčadāta- 'after-gift'; Tavernier, *Iranica*, 409) (*TAD* B3.11:7.9; B3.12:9.18[37])

Constructions and Furnishing/Equipment
hnpn 'protecting (wall)' or 'roofed passage'[38] (< Old Persian *hanpāna-; Tavernier, *Iranica*, 439[39]) (*TAD* B3.10:9; B3.11:4)
ʾšrn 'furniture, equipment' (< Old Persian *āčarna-; Tavernier, *Iranica*, 437) (*TAD* B3.4:23)

The etymology of several presumed Old Persian loanwords is uncertain. Both the word *hyrʾ*[40] (*TAD* B3.2:3.6.9, 451 BCE) and the word *npʾ*[41] (*TAD* B2.9:4, 420 BCE; *TAD*

36 The word also appears in *TAD* B8.9:5, a court record from Saqqarah: *mwmʾ nprt* 'oath of litigation'.
37 Read in *TAD* B as *psšrt*.
38 Porten and Yardeni translate *ʾgrʾ zy hnpnʾ* (*TAD* B3.10:8 f.) as 'the protecting wall' (*TAD* B, 98) and *hnpnʾ* (*TAD* B3.11:4) as 'the protecting (wall)' (*TAD* B, 93). In Elephantine Aramaic, *ʾgr* certainly has the meaning 'wall' (as in Akkadian) (see also *DNWSI*, 12). In later Aramaic, there is a semantic change to 'roof'. It is theoretically possible that *ʾgr* in Elephantine Aramaic had both meanings.
39 From **han-pāna-* (Avestan *pāna* 'protection').
40 The text reads: *bdmy hyrʾ zylk* 'as a payment of the *hyrʾ* of yours' (*TAD* B3.2:3); *bšm hyrʾ znh* 'in the name of [= regarding] this *hyrʾ* (*TAD* B3.2:6.9). A Persian etymology is suggested by the fact that the noun is probably combined with the emphatic state morpheme, which in general is not the case with Egyptian words (see 4.3). The word *hyrʾ*, with a value of five shekels, is usually believed to have an Egyptian origin. Traditional explanations include 'wooden tool', 'metal vase', 'street', 'house' (see *DNWSI*, 279) and 'abandoned property' (see Porten and Szubin, "Litigation," 281); see also *GEA*, 345, no. 7 (without translation). The word is also attested in *TAD* D 1.26:4 (to be consulted with Moore, *New Aramaic Papyri*, 47–48), but the latter text does not substantially contribute to the understanding of the word. Moore (*New Aramaic Papyri*, 48) is of the opinion that the word refers to property and its expected yield (either a monetary payment or a commodity exchange), but "[t]he meaning of *Hyr* remains unclear."
41 See also *DNWSI*, s. v. npʾ 2: "word of unknown meaning, indicating type of tribunal or process?" A noun of Egyptian origin is unlikely since there are no further parallels in Aramaic for an Egyptian word that belongs to the semantic domain of law. Theoretically, both an interpretation as a noun or as a placename are possible. The text of *TAD* B2.9:4 reads *ʾn[ḥ]nh ršynkm bdyn npʾ qdm rmndyn prtrk wydrng rb ḥylʾ* 'We brought suit of npʾ against you before Ramnadaina (the) Chief (and) Vidranga the garrison commander' (thus *TAD* B, 43; more literally: 'we sued you in the court of *npʾ*' or 'we sued you in the process of *npʾ*'). In most cases, however, the verb *ršy* governs a double direct object, one being *dyn wdbb* or simply *dyn* (for references to texts,

B7.2:4, 401 BCE) may have a Persian origin, though an Egyptian origin cannot be completely excluded. *TAD* B3.2 was written by Bunni b. Mannuki (with a non-Judean name); the scribe of *TAD* B7.2 is unknown.

3.2.3 Comments on Specific Semantic Domains

In the following, I discuss the loanwords that pertain to the administrative domain (both the legal and military subdomains). It is in this domain that most Old Persian loanwords are found in the Elephantine documents.

3.2.4 Old Persian Legal Terms in Specific Legal Formulae

Several Old Persian loanwords in the Elephantine legal documents appear in specific legal clauses: the penalty clause (*ʾb(y)grn* 'penalty') and the waiver of suit (*hnbg* 'partner in realty', *hngyt* 'partner in chattel', and *ʾdrng* 'guarantor').

(a) Penalty Clause

The word *ʾb(y)grn* appears in all legal documents drawn up from 427 BCE (*TAD* B3.6) onwards in which a fine is stipulated: *TAD* B3.6:14, 427 BCE; *TAD* B3.8:31, 420 BCE; *TAD* B2.9:14 f., 420 BCE; *TAD* B3.7:17, 420 BCE; *TAD* B2.10:15, 416 BCE; *TAD* B3.9:7, 416 BCE; *TAD* B2.11:10, 410 BCE; *TAD* B3.10:20, 404 BCE; *TAD* B3.11:10, 402 BCE; *TAD* B3.12:30, 402 BCE; *TAD* B3.13:6.7, 402 BCE; *TAD* B5.5:6, 420 or 400 BCE). It is found in construct noun phrases (*ʾbygrn ksp* 'a fine of silver'), as in the legal documents written by Ḥaggai b. Šemaʿyah (*TAD* B3.6; B3.10; B3.11; B3.12), in the documents by the unknown scribes of *TAD* B3.7 and *TAD* B5.5, and in the single document written by Rauxšana b. Nergalušezib (*TAD* B3.9); in *zy*-phrases (*ʾb(y)grnʾ zy ksp* 'the fine of silver'), as in the documents by Maʿuziyah b. Natan (*TAD* B2.9; B3.8; B2.10); and in single word noun phrases, as in the document by Nabutukulti b. Nabuzeribni (*TAD* B2.11) and the document by Šaweram b. Ešemram b. Ešemšezib (*TAD* B3.13) (see Table 1, cols. 2 and 4). In older documents, there is no specific word used to indicate a fine. In those documents, the Aramaic simply says *yntn l*X *ksp* krš(n) Y 'he will/must give to X in silver Y karsh'

---

see *DNWSI*, 1086–87). In legal documents, *bdyn* is only found in combination with the verb *hwk* 'to go in court' (*TAD* B2.3:22; B3.1:19; B3.11:15). The text of *TAD* B7.2:4 reads [ʾ]*nt qb*[*lt ʿly*] *bnpʾ* '[Y]ou com[plained against me] in np''. According to Porten (*EPE*, 193, n. 9), no place with this name is known.

(Y = amount) (and the like). This is already the case in the oldest dated document from Elephantine, *TAD* B5.1:6–7 (495 BCE):[42]

wzy ygrnky ... yntn lky ksp kršn 5 'and whoever shall institute (suit) against you ... shall give you silver 5 karsh'

(b) Enumeration of Potential Litigants in the Waiver of Suit

The enumeration of potential litigants or claimants in Aramaic legal documents in the 'waiver of suit' (*TAD* B)[43] developed over the course of the 5th century BCE and reflects quite some variation among individual scribes and their documents.[44] The clause begins with the alienor(s)' affirmation (in the first person sg. or pl.) not to be able to start a suit on account of the alienated property. This is followed by an enumeration of persons that likewise are not able to initiate a suit. In most cases, this begins with kinship terms, son or daughter, followed by brother or sister, and ends with different terms that indicate a relationship to the alienor(s) that is not based on kinship. The Old Persian loanwords *hngyt* 'partner in chattel', *hnbg* 'partner in realty', and *ʾdrng* 'guarantor' were the final additions made to this formula. The words *hngyt* and *hnbg* probably filled a void in the Aramaic lexicon, though this is less clear-cut for *ʾdrng*, as there may have been an Aramaic alternative (see below in this section).

Hngyt 'partner in chattel' and *hnbg* 'partner in realty'

The words *hngyt* and *hnbg* appear – always as a pair – in the legal documents *TAD* B3.6 (427 BCE), *TAD* B3.10 (404 BCE), *TAD* B3.11 (402 BCE), and *TAD* B3.12 (402 BCE), all of which were written by the scribe Ḥaggai b. Šemaʿyah between 427 and 402 BCE.[45] The word pair is not attested in documents written by other scribes, with the exception of *TAD* B5.5, whose scribe is unfortunately unknown,[46]

---

42 Sometimes the verb *ntn* is preceded by the verb *ḥwb* 'to be liable'. In two instances, only the verb *ḥwb* is used in the penalty clause, followed by the sum to be paid (*TAD* B3.6:14; 4.4:15).

43 Porten and Szubin use the term 'promise of non suit' ("Litigants").

44 The three Persian loanwords discussed here do not appear in the enumeration of protected parties. On the enumeration of potential litigants and protected parties, see Porten andte Szubin, "Litigants," 45–67. Porten and Szubin's main argument is that the list of potential litigants develops in order to better protect the alienee and their heirs against suit from the alienor (and their heirs, beneficiaries, and representatives) ("Litigants," 47). The three Persian loanwords discussed here belong to the latest stage of this development.

45 The word pair does not appear in the oldest document written by this scribe (*TAD* B3.4, 437 BCE).

46 The document was certainly not written by Ḥaggai b. Šemaʿyah, as he always employed *ʾd(y)n* 'then' without a subsequent placename in the first line of his documents, whereas the scribe of *TAD* B5.5 has *ʾdyn byb* 'then in Yeb'.

as is its precise date (420 or 400 BCE). In the last three documents written by Ḥaggai b. Šemaʿyah, the waiver of suit is expanded with *ʾdrng* (see below in this section).

Several documents written after 427 BCE (the year of the first attestation of the word pair *hngyt whnbg*) do not feature this word pair in the waiver of suit. This is the case with *TAD* B2.9 (420 BCE) and *TAD* B2.10 (416 BCE), both written by Maʿuziyah b. Natan, and *TAD* B2.11 (410 BCE), written by Nabutukulti b. Nabuzerbini. The scribes of these documents use a non-specific term instead: *wʾnth wʾyš ly* 'and wife or man of mine' (*TAD* B2.10:9) and *wʾnš zyly* 'or an individual of mine' (*TAD* B2.11:8; *TAD* B, 51: 'or an individual who is mine').[47] The word pair *hngyt whnbg* clearly reflects the need for more specific terminology and was first used by Ḥaggai b. Šemaʿyah.[48]

An interesting case is the fragmentary document *TAD* B5.5, interpreted in *TAD* B (also in *EPE*, 258) as a mutual quitclaim by two sisters – Mibṭaḥyah and Eswere (daughters of Gemaryah). It contains two waivers of suit (both damaged), each pronounced by one of the two sisters, and, as far as can be concluded from the remains of the text, they differ significantly as far as the last element in the list of potential claimants is concerned.[49] Whereas the first waiver (pronounced by Mibṭaḥyah) reads *br wbrh ly ʾḥ wʾḥh ly qryb wrḥyq* (l. 4) 'son or daughter of mine, brother or sister of mine, someone near or far' and only concerns heirs,[50] the second (pronounced by Eswere) reads *br] ly wbrh ly hngyt whnbgʾ zy l[y.* According to Porten and Szubin, the two clauses cover two separate transactions, though they do not explain the difference between the two transactions, seemingly because of the fragmentary state of the document.[51]

ʾDrng 'guarantor'

The term *ʾdrng* is added to the waiver of suit in the last three documents written by Ḥaggai b. Šemaʿyah (*TAD* B3.10, 404 BCE; *TAD* B3.11, 402 BCE; *TAD* B3.12,

47 In *TAD* B2.9, *ʾyš zyln* 'man of us' is not the last element in the waiver of suit. Another example is *wʾyš ly* in *TAD* B3.9 (written by Rauxšana b. Nergalušezib in 416 BCE). In that document, it does not appear in a waiver of suit but in an affirmation of non-enslavement. In *TAD* B5.2 (last quarter of the 5th century BCE), the last element of the otherwise damaged waiver of suit is *w]ʾyš ly.*

48 See also Porten and Szubin, "Litigants," 67.

49 The two waivers and two promise-penalty clauses reflect two different transactions (thus Porten and Szubin, "Litigants," 65).

50 According to *EPE*, 259, n. 14. On the interpretational problems around *qr(y)b wrḥ(y)q*, esp. 'related or not related' or 'close or distant relative', see *DNWSI*, 1031, s. v. qrb_9.

51 Porten and Szubin, "Litigants," 65. This is reflected in the two waivers and promise-penalty clauses. The same interpretation is found in Botta, *Aramaic and Egyptian Legal Traditions*, 116–17.

402 BCE). The term *ʾdrng* is also found in another document from the same period, *TAD* B3.13 (402 BCE), written by the scribe Šaweram b. Ešemram b. Ešemšezib, though it does not appear within the waiver of suit but in a clause stipulating that the obligation for the repayment of the debt in case of the death of the creditor rests with the heirs or with the guarantor(s) of the debtor; it appears a second time in the following clause, which stipulates the right of the creditor to seize the security in case of a failure by the heirs or guarantor(s) to make repayment. It is noteworthy that the name of the debtor is Hebrew and that the name of the creditor is Egyptian. The name of the scribe, on the other hand, is Aramean (Šaweram b. Ešemram b. Ešemšezib) and the document was drawn up in Syene.[52] This document is the latest loan contract from Elephantine in which the term *ʾdrng* appears.[53]

Persian Period Aramaic is familiar with the Aramaic word *ʿrb* 'guarantor'.[54] This legal term appears in one of the Hermopolis letters from the end of the 6th century BCE (*TAD* A2.9:9).[55] It is also found in later legal documents from Wadi Murabbaʿat and Naḥal Ṣeelim.[56] There is also another Aramaic word for a guarantor, namely *ʾḥry*. This is found in legal documents from the same region, where it even appears in hendiadys with *ʿrb*.[57] According to literary and documentary sources, both legal terms appear in later marriage documents written in Jewish Palestinian Aramaic.[58] As a legal term, the word *ʾḥry* 'responsible' now has a precursor not only in a fragmentary Aramaic legal document from the Hellenistic period (possibly Edfu, 3rd century)[59] but also in a document from the Persian Period. In one of the Akhvamazda letters from 4th-century BCE Bactria, the term is found in coordination with *ʾdrng* in the following clause: *ʾdrng ʾḥry*

52 Already noted in Porten and Greenfield, "The Guarantor," 154.

53 The term does not appear in the only other loans from Elephantine, both of which stem from the first half of the century: *TAD* B4.2 from 487 BCE and *TAD* B3.1 from 456 BCE (both are loans of silver). The first of these two documents lacks a clause defining the obligation of the heirs of the loanee, though the second does possess such a clause, but without an extension to the guarantor: *whn mytt wlʾ šlmtk bkspʾ znh wmrbyth bny hmw yšlmwn lk kspʾ znh wmrbyth* (*TAD* B3.1:14–15) 'And if I die and have not paid you this silver and its interest, it will be my children (who) shall pay you this silver and its interest'.

54 Note that the latest two loan documents from Elephantine both include the related noun *ʿrbn* 'security' (*TAD* B3.1:13.17; B3.13:10); this security could be taken by the creditor if repayment by the heirs or guarantor(s) failed.

55 Porten and Greenfield point out that the two nouns are synonymous. See Porten and Greenfield, "The Guarantor," 154.

56 See *DJA*, 72.

57 See *DJA*, 30: 1. 'later'; 2. 'responsible'.

58 *DJPA*³, 20, s. v. **ʾḥryy* 2. 'responsible, guarantor'; *DJPA*³, 471–72, s. v. *ʿrb* #2 'guarantor'.

59 *TAD* D1.17:7 *ʾḥryʾ* 'the responsible' (as in *TAD* D, 36).

bgwnt ʿl dtšprn 'liable and responsible is Bagavanta to Dathushafarna' (A10:1–2).[60] According to Naveh and Shaked, *ʾdrng ʾḥry* is the semantic equivalent of *ʾḥry wʿrb* in the documents from the Judean desert. The word *ʾdrng* also appears in Akhvamazda letter A6:4. In these two cases, Naveh and Shaked translate *ʾdrng* as 'obliged, indebted' (A6:4) and as 'liable' (A10:1), pointing to the similar semantic range of the Semitic root *ḥwb*, with reflects notions of both guilt and obligation in Aramaic.

3.2.5 Other Old Persian Legal Terms: *nprt*, *ʾzt* and *psšdt*

In addition to the legal terms *hnbg*, *hngyt*, *ʾdrng*, and *ʾbygrn*, several other words belonging to the legal domain appear in the Elephantine legal documents: *nprt* 'litigation' (*TAD* B2.8:3, 440), *ʾzt* 'free' (*TAD* B3.6:4, 427 BCE) (with reference to the release of female slaves), and *psšdt* 'after-gift' (*TAD* B3.11:7.9; B3.12:9.18, both 402 BCE).[61] These represent very specific terminology, and a specific Aramaic word was in all likelihood not available in these three cases.

3.2.6 Old Persian Military Terms: *hndz* and *ptp*

The word *hndz* 'garrisoned' (literally 'co-inhabitant of the fortress'[62]) (*TAD* B2.7:4, 446 BCE) appears in the oldest document that contains an Old Persian loanword (apart from words for measures; see 3.2.7). This is interesting, as *hndz* represents an elementary feature of the Judean presence on the island during Persian rule over Egypt. The word *ptp* 'ration (in kind)' (*TAD* B3.13:4.5.8.10, 402 BCE) is another word deeply rooted in the Persian administration.[63]

3.2.7 Distribution of Old Persian Loanwords in Legal Documents

Without exception, Old Persian loanwords from the first half of the 5th century BCE concern measures of weight and capacity: *krš*, which is almost omnipresent

---

60 Naveh and Shaked, *Aramaic Documents*, 128.
61 Read in *TAD* B as *psšrt*.
62 See Tavernier, *Iranica*, 451.
63 Briant, *Cyrus to Alexander*, 451.

in legal documents,[64] *ʾrdb*,[65] and the abbreviation *g* (for *gryw* or *gryb*).[66] The earliest attestation of the word *krš* is found in a legal document written by an unknown scribe in 495 BCE (*TAD* B5.1:7). This is the oldest legal document from Elephantine, and the word is found here in a penalty clause: *yntn lky ksp kršn* 5 (ll. 6–7). The word *ʾrdb* also appears in two documents written by Hošeaʿ b. Hodavyah (*TAD* B4.4; B4.3, both from 483 BCE), while the abbreviation *g* appears in the first of these two documents (*TAD* B4.4:7).

Measures are also the sole Persian borrowings in documents written by the scribes Pelaṭyah b. Aḥio (*TAD* B2.1, 471 BCE), Itu b. Abah (*TAD* B2.2, 464 BCE), and Attaršuri b. Nabuzeribni (*TAD* B2.3; 2.4, 460/59 BCE), all of whom were active in the first half of the 5th century BCE. Old Persian loanwords are completely absent from *TAD* B4.2 (488/87 BCE), a document written by Gemaryah b. Aḥio (see also n. 64).

Apart from measures, Old Persian loanwords only appear in the Elephantine legal documents in the second part of the 5th century BCE (see Table 1, col. 4). These loanwords are found in documents by scribes from different backgrounds: Natan b. Anani (*TAD* B2.7, 446 BCE), Peṭeese b. Nabunatan (*TAD* B2.8, 440 BCE),[67] Maʿuziyah b. Natan b. Ananyah (*TAD* B3.5, 434 BCE; *TAD* B2.9, 420 BCE; *TAD* B3.8, 420 BCE; *TAD* B2.10, 416 BCE),[68] Ḥaggai b. Šemaʿyah (*TAD* B3.4, 437 BCE; *TAD* B3.6, 427 BCE; *TAD* B3.10, 404 BCE; *TAD* B3.11, 402 BCE; *TAD* B3.12, 402 BCE),[69] Rauxšana b. Nergalušezib (*TAD* B3.9, 416 BCE),[70] Nabutukulti b. Nabuzerbini (*TAD* B2.11, 410 BCE),[71] Šaweram b. Ešemram b. Ešemšezib (*TAD* B3.13, 402 BCE).[72] These loanwords appear in documents written by scribes with Hebrew/Judean, Egyptian,

64 The *krš* equals 10 shekels. It does not appear in documents which do not define a fine in silver, such as *TAD* B4.2 (loan of silver, written by Gemaryah b. Aḥio, 487 BCE), *TAD* B3.1 (loan of silver, written by Natan b. Anani, 456 BCE), *TAD* B7.1 (obligation to take a judicial oath, 413 BCE), written in *swn* (scribal name restored in l. 9 as [Maʿuziyah b. Natan b.] Anani, better known as Maʿuziyah b. Natan), or documents that are damaged.

65 A measure of capacity (26 liters).

66 A dry measure of capacity (for grain; 9.7 litres). The abbreviation also appears in an account from Elephantine (*TAD* C3.14:37.40).

67 The given name is Egyptian and the paternal name is Aramean/Aramaic.

68 Both the given name and the paternal name are Hebrew/Judean. Old Persian loanwords are found in all of the documents known to have been written by this scribe.

69 Both the given name and the paternal name are Hebrew/Judean. Old Persian loanwords are found in all of the documents known to have been written by this scribe.

70 The given name is Persian and the paternal name is Akkadian.

71 Both the given name and the paternal name are Akkadian.

72 Both the given name and the paternal name are Aramean/Aramaic.

Persian, Akkadian, and Aramean/Aramaic given names and Hebrew/Judean, Akkadian, Persian, and Aramaic/Aramean paternal names.[73]

As Table 1, col. 4 shows, the earliest certain Old Persian borrowing (apart from lexemes indicating measures of weight and capacity) appears in what is possibly the latest legal document written by the Judean scribe Natan b. Ananyah (*TAD* B2.7). This document is dated to 446 BCE. The loanword in question, *hndz* 'garrisoned', pertains to the military administrative domain. In this document, the Judean Maḥseyah b. Yedanyah (of the *dgl* 'detachment' of Varyazata) gives his daughter a house in exchange for the goods that she gave him during the time he was garrisoned in the fortress: *kzy hndz hwyt bbyrt* (*TAD* B2.7:4) 'when I was garrisoned in the fortress'.

The absence of loanwords pertaining to semantic domains other than measures in the first half of the 5th century BCE may of course be accidental, but it is equally possible that the reason for the relatively early borrowing of exactly these words reflects the fact that the prime interest of the Persian administration was financial, namely, the levying and collection of taxes in conquered areas. The distribution of the loanwords seems to reflect the fact that, in Upper Egypt, the influence of the native language of the Persian administrators on legal and military matters became stronger in the second half of the 5th century BCE. This may have been the result of intensified contact between the Judeans and their Persian overlords, possibly the outcome of a (gradual?) change in administrative structures which led in turn to an increase in the influence of the Persian administrative apparatus on the local population of Elephantine/Syene. The cause of this intensified contact requires further investigation by historians of the Persian Period.

Over time, Old Persian loanwords increase in number in individual documents. If we exclude measures of weight and capacity (*krš*, *ʾrdb*, and the abbreviation *g*), this increase is reflected in the growth from one Old Persian loanword in *TAD* B2.7 (446 BCE) to six loanwords in two documents from the end of the 5th century BCE (*TAD* B3.11; B3.12). These two legal documents are among the latest dated legal documents from Elephantine and were written by the Judean scribe Ḥaggai b. Šemaʿyah in 402 BCE.

---

73 Apart from the use of the word *krš*, documents of wifehood contain very few Old Persian loanwords. Old Persian loanwords are absent in the documents of wifehood *TAD* B2.6 and *TAD* B3.3 (*krš* again excepted; the same holds for the fragmentary documents *TAD* B6.1, B6.2, and B6.3). In addition to *krš*, the document of wifehood *TAD* B3.8 contains the Old Persian loanword *ʾbygrn* 'penalty'.

3.2.8 Morphological Integration of Old Persian Loanwords in Legal Documents

Most Old Persian loanwords were adapted to Aramaic morphology. There is evidence for singular masculine and plural masculine inflectional endings. These will be discussed in what follows.

(a) Masculine Inflectional Endings

Singular masculine emphatic state -ʾ
Ample evidence (not referred to).

Plural masculine absolute state *-n*
kršn (passim)
ʾrdbn (*TAD* B4.3:5; B4.4:5.7.8)[74]

Loanwords were also combined with a pron. sf. (*ʾdrngy* 'my guarantors' in *TAD* B3.13:9 [twice]; with a pron. sf. sg. 1c.)

There is no evidence for the emphatic state plural masculine *-yʾ* in legal documents, but this is accidental: there is evidence for this in other Elephantine texts, as well as in Aramaic texts from other places.

Evidence for Aramaic inflectional endings attached to borrowings from Old Persian is also lacking for the Aramaic construct plural masculine (*-y*). This is in concord with evidence from other Aramaic texts from Elephantine, as well as other Aramaic texts from the Persian Period. Elsewhere I have shown that there may have been a constraint on the use of plural masculine construct forms of words borrowed from Old Persian.[75]

(b) Feminine Inflectional Endings

There is no positive evidence for Aramaic feminine inflectional endings attached to nouns or adjectives borrowed from Old Persian (sg. abs. *-h*; sg. emphatic *-tʾ*; pl. abs. *-n*; pl. emphatic – *tʾ*). Feminine endings are absent in the words *prypt* and *ʾzt* in the following two texts:

ʾzt šbqtky bmwty wšbqt lyhyšmʿ šmh brtky (*TAD* B3.6:4, 427 BCE)
'I release you as a free person upon my death and I release Yehoyišmaʿ your daughter' (*TAD* A, 73: 'I released')

74 For a possible case of reanalysis, see the discussion of *ʾšrn* (*TAD* B3.4:23) in 3.2.10.
75 Folmer, "Aramaic of the Akhvamazdā Letters," 350.

nšn tpmt ʾntth prypt zy mšlm br zkr (*TAD* B3.12:11, 402 BCE)
'lady Tapamet his wife, (the) main beloved of Meshullam son of Zakkur'

The word *ʾzt* in *TAD* B3.6:4 is agreed to be an adjective.[76] In view of its function in *TAD* B3.12:11, one would expect the feminine ending *-h* (of the absolute state). It is also possible to view the word as an adverbial noun, however: 'I release you as a free person'. The noun *prypt* 'chief of the beloved' in *TAD* B3.12 is an apposition to (*nšn*) *tpmt ʾntth*. An emphatic ending *-tʾ* is expected here (see also below 3.2.9 [d]). In both cases, the final *t* is certainly part of the reconstructed Old Persian word (see above 3.2.2). Evidence for Aramaic feminine inflectional endings attached to Old Persian loanwords is completely lacking from other Aramaic texts from the Persian Period. Whether this is accidental or not cannot be known.

It is possible that the scribe who wrote these two documents (Ḥaggai b. Šemaʿyah) somehow associated the final *t* of the two words with a feminine ending. If that is the case, the two instances should be regarded as a form of reanalysis (for a more certain case of reanalysis, see below 3.2.10).

3.2.9 Morphosyntactic Integration of Old Persian Loanwords

Old Persian loanwords occur in the following noun phrases:[77] construct noun phrases (a), *zy* phrases (b), *zyl-* phrases (c), and appositions (d).[78] These noun phrases are discussed below.

(a) Old Persian Loanwords in Construct Noun Phrases

First Term of the Construct Noun Phrase Is a Loanword

ʾbygrn ksp 'a penalty of silver'

Only singular forms are attested in the first term. The construct noun phrase *ʾbygrn ksp* is found in documents written by Ḥaggai b. Šemaʿyah (*TAD* B3.6:14, 427 BCE; B3.10:20, 404 BCE; B3.11:10, 402 BCE; B3.12:30, 402 BCE), in the document written by Rauxšana b. Nergalušezib (*TAD* B3.9:7, 416 BCE), and in two documents written by an unknown scribe (*TAD* B3.7:17, 420 BCE, and *TAD* B5.5:6, 420 or 400 BCE).[79] See also above (3.2.4 [a]).

---

76 *DNWSI*, 28; Tavernier, *Iranica*, 404.

77 Single word noun phrases are not included in this overview of noun phrases.

78 There is no evidence for attributive noun phrases.

79 Note that in *TAD* B3.13:6 (402 BCE), *ʾbgrn krš ḥd 1 ksp ṣryp* 'a fine, one 1 karsh, in pure silver' is not a construct noun phrase. Cf. *ʾbygrnʾ ksp ṣryp kršn ʿšrh bmtqlt mlkʾ* 'the fine, in pure silver, ten karsh by the weight of the king' in *TAD* B2.11:10–11 (410 BCE).

Second Term of the Construct Noun Phrase Is a Loanword

There may be another example of a construct noun phrase in the Elephantine legal documents with a possible loanword in the second term (*bdyn np'* in *TAD* B2.9:4, 420 BCE) but the etymology of the noun (?) *np'* is unknown; a placename is also possible.[80] If *np'* is indeed a noun (possibly in the emphatic state), it is likely of Persian origin given its immediate context (a lawsuit conducted in the presence of two Persian high officials):

'n[ḥ]nh ršynkm bdyn np' qdm rmndyn prtrk wydrng rb ḥyl'
'We brought suit of np' against you before Ramnadaina (the) Chief (and) Vidranga the garrison commander' (article added in *TAD* B, 43) (*TAD* B2.9:4)

(b) Old Persian Loanwords in zy Phrases

First Term is a Loanword

'b(y)grn' zy ksp 'the penalty of silver' (*TAD* B3.8:31; B2.9:14 f.; B2.10:15)

All of the instances of *'b(y)grn' zy ksp* are found in documents written by Maʿuziyah b. Natan. The noun indicates the materialised form of the penalty.

Second Term is a Loanword

'gr' zy hnpn' 'the protecting wall'; literally 'the wall of the protection' (see n. 38) (*TAD* B3.10:8 f.)

(c) Old Persian Loanwords in zyl- Phrases

In legal documents, Old Persian loanwords only occur in *zyl-* phrases that are a final extension of lists of potential litigants (parallel to *br wbrh ly*, etc.). In most cases, the modified noun is in the absolute state; in one case, however, the modified noun is in the emphatic state (third example):

hngyt zyly whnbg w'drng zyly (*TAD* B3.10:18, 404 BCE)
'partner-in-chattel of mine, or partner-in-land or guarantor of mine' (*TAD* B, 89: 'who is mine' instead of 'of mine')
hngyt whnbg w'drng zyln (TAD B3.12:27, 402 BCE)
'partner-in-chattel or partner-in-land or guarantor of mine' (*TAD* B, 97: 'who is mine')

---

80 On *np'*, see above n. 41 for more detail.

hngyt whnbgʾ zy l[y[81] (*TAD* B5.5:9, 420 or 400 BCE)
'partner-in-chattel or partner-in-land of mi[ne' (*TAD* B, 127: 'who is mi[ne')

In the first example (*TAD* B3.10), the scribe probably made an error. The intention may have been to write *hngyt whnbg zyly wʾdrng zyly* (with *zyly* modifying the two preceding nouns, which always appear as a word pair). Alternatively, the scribe may have intended to write *hngyt whnbg wʾdrng zyly* (in similar fashion to *TAD* B3.12).

The emphatic ending of *hnbg* in the last example (*TAD* B5.5) is notable. The construction with *zyl-* occurs more often in later additions to lists of potential claimants in waivers of suit (*TAD* 2.7:8 *wzrʿ zyly*; B2.9:10 *ʾyš zyln*; B2.11:8 *wʾnš zyly*) but the modified noun is always in the absolute state in these cases, not only in the examples quoted above but also when other nouns are concerned (*br wbrh ly* and *ʾḥ wʾḥh ly* and the like[82]). It is possible that the scribe's intention was for *zy l[y* to modify both *hngbʾ* and the preceding *hngyt*, as the two always appear as a word pair, though the difference in the state of the nouns continues to remain awkward.

(d) Old Persian Loanwords in Appositions

The Noun in Apposition Has the Emphatic State Morpheme

qdm wydrng hptḥptʾ rb ḥylʾ zy swn
'before Vidranga the Guardian of the Seventh, the garrison commander of Syene' (*TAD* B3.9:2, 416 BCE)
mtrsrh mgšyʾ tt mgšyʾ
'Mithrasarah the Magian'; 'Tata the Magian' (*TAD* B3.5:24, 434 BCE)

The noun in Apposition Does Not Have the Emphatic State Morpheme

qdm rmndyn prtrk wydrng rb ḥylʾ zy swn
'before Ramnadaina (the) Chief (and) Vidranga the garrison commander' (article added in *TAD* B, 43) (*TAD* B2.9:4–5, 420 BCE)
nšn tpmt ʾntth prypt zy mšlm br zkr 'lady Tapamet his wife, (the) main beloved of Meshullam son of Zaccur' (article added in *TAD* B, 97) (*TAD* B3.12:11, 402 BCE)

In several cases in the Elephantine legal documents, inflectional endings were not attached to Old Persian loanwords in apposition. In the examples above, this occurs now and then in appositions to a personal name which refer to a function

81 written as two separate words in *TAD* B5.5.
82 Where a noun in the absolute state is followed by the preposition *l* with a pron. sf. On the waiver of suit, see also 3.2.4 (b).

or indicate an appellative of the person named (these normally occur in the emphatic state form).

The scribes of the two documents in which the emphatic ending is lacking have Judean names: *TAD* B2.9 was written by Maʿuziyah b. Natan and *TAD* B3.12 by Ḥaggai b. Šemaʿyah. In *TAD* B2.9, there is a contrast between *rmndyn prtrk* 'Ramnadaina (the) Chief' and the following definite apposition (construct noun phrase) in *wydrng rb ḥylʾ* 'Vidranga the garrison commander'. In *TAD* B3.12, the word *prypt* lacks the singular feminine emphatic ending (on this word, see also 3.2.8 [b]). These two scribes apparently had problems handling an Old Persian loatenword in apposition.

There are also two cases of apposition in the Elephantine legal documents in which the noun is combined with an emphatic state morpheme (*TAD* B3.9:2 *hptḥptʾ*; *TAD* B3.5:24 *mgšyʾ*, which appears twice). In *TAD* B3.5, the word *mgšyʾ* 'the magian' (with the gentilic ending *-y* in the emphatic) is twice appended to the name of a witness with a Persian name. It is noteworthy that the scribe who wrote *TAD* B3.9 has a Persian given name and an Akkadian paternal name: Rauxšana b. Nergalušezib. Rauxšana clearly knew how to handle a Persian noun in apposition in Aramaic. The two witnesses of *TAD* B3.5 apparently also knew the correct Aramaic emphatic form of their function, though the scribe who wrote that document, the Judean Maʿuziyah b. Natan, made an error.

3.2.10 A Case of Reanalysis in the Elephantine Legal Documents

There may be a case of reanalysis of the Old Persian word *ʾšrn* in *TAD* B3.4:23 (437 BCE), which reads:

wkl ʾšrn zy yhkn ʿl bytʾ zk (l. 23) 'and all fittings that will have gone in that house'

It seems that the noun *ʾšrn* was treated by the Judean scribe of this text as a plural (it is the subject of a plural verb form *yhkn*), which is unique for Persian Period Aramaic.[83] In Elephantine Aramaic, construct noun phrases construed with *kl* in the first term and a plural noun in the second term are followed by a noun in the absolute state instead of a noun in the emphatic state.[84] For this

83 In *TAD* A6.2:9.21 (Aršama letter found at Elephantine), the noun is treated as a sg.: as *znh ʾšrnʾ* and *ʾšrnʾ znh* respectively (no conclusions can be drawn from its occurrence in l. 5). The noun is also treated as a singular in two letters belonging to the Yedanyah correspondence (*TAD* A4.5:18; *TAD* A4.7:11), where we find *ʾšrnʾ* (with the emphatic sg. m. ending -ʾ).

84 I have excluded noun phrases that are followed by a number, as nouns followed by a number are always in the absolute state. The evidence for *kl* + noun in the plural absolute state in letters and legal documents from Elephantine is: *kl nwnyn ʾw dmyhm* 'all fish or their value' (*TAD*

reason, we must consider the possibility that we are dealing in *TAD* B3.4 with a case of reanalysis. This might indicate that the scribe who wrote this document, Ḥaggai b. Šemaʿyah, worked from a written model or other written document and misinterpreted the final *-n* in the word *ʾšrn* as the Aramaic plural m. ending of the absolute state.[85] It is also worth noting that the sellers of the property detailed in the document are a Caspian couple with Iranian names. They may have indicated to the scribe that the word *ʾšrn* should be included in the defension clause. This is the only case in which *ʾšrn* appears in a legal document from Elephantine (on *ʾšrn* in letters, see 3.3.5 [a] and 3.3.6 [b]). On two further possible cases of reanalysis in two documents written by the same scribe (*ʾzt TAD* B3.6 and *prypt* in *TAD* B3.12), see 3.2.8 (b).

3.2.11 Glosses on Old Persian Loanwords in Legal Documents

There is a possible one-to-one Egyptian gloss on the Old Persian loanword *hnpn* in one of the documents written by the scribe Ḥaggai b. Šemaʿyah. Glosses can be recognised by the use of *hw* 'that is':[86]

ʾgrʾ 9. *zy hnpnʾ zy bnhw mṣryʾ hw tmwʾnty* 'the protection wall which the Egyptians built, that is the way of the god' (*TAD* B3.10:9, 404 BCE)

B7.1:6); *kl yrḥn wšnn* 'all months and years' (*TAD* B7.1:8) (*DNWSI*, 505 translates 'every month'); *kl nksn wqnyn* 'all goods and property' (*TAD* B2.8:4); *bkl nksn zy yhwwn byn ʿnny wtmt* 'to all goods which will be between Anani and Tamet' (*TAD* B3.3:11; cf. also l. 12); *wkl nksyn zy qnh ʾbdw wkl gbryn zy bʿw bʾyš lʾgwrʾ zk kl qṭylw* 'and all goods which he had acquired were lost and all persons who sought evil for that Temple, all (of them), were killed' (*TAD* A4.7:16–17). (Note that in *TAD* the article has sometimes been added in the translation; it is omitted in the translations given here). It should be mentioned that *kl spyntʾ* 'all the ships' is attested in the Customs Account (from an unknown harbour in Egypt) (*TAD* C3.7 Fv iii:18). The plural noun is also attested in the emphatic state in similar cases in Old Aramaic and in Biblical Aramaic (for Old Aramaic, see *DNWSI*, 505, s. v. kl_1 meaning 4). This remarkable feature of Elephantine Aramaic, which is also reflected in several legal documents from Naḥal Ḥever and Wadi Murabbaʿat from the period of Middle Aramaic (for references, see *DJA*, 56, s. v. כֹּל, and *DNWSI*, 505, s. v. kl_1 meaning 4), deserves further investigation.

85 Alexander Schütze concludes from the relative homogeneity of the legal clauses in Aramaic legal documents from Elephantine that the Aramaic scribes may have used sample forms, just as Egyptian scribes used Demotic sample forms, as is apparent from the Codex Hermopolis, a legal handbook from the 3rd century BCE (Schütze, "The Legal Context").

86 Cf. also the original gloss in Ezra 4:9 (דהוא), which was later misunderstood (see the *qere*). Not every occurrence of *hw* points to a one-to-one gloss; the word can also have a wider explicative function (see also *GEA*, §39b).

In this line, the Egyptian word *tmwʾnty* glosses the emphatic form of the Old Persian loanword *hnpn* (which is known from *TAD* B3.11, written by the same scribe in 402 BCE, a little more than one year later).

The document *TAD* B3.10 also contains a more explicit gloss in line 4:

wplg trbṣʾ hw plg tḥyt mṣryt
'and half the courtyard that is half the *ḫyt* (as it is called) in Egyptian' (*TAD* B3.10:4)

In this passage, the Egyptian word *tḥyt*[87] glosses the emphatic form of the Aramaic word *trbṣ* 'courtyard' (which is of Akkadian origin).[88] The word *mṣryt* 'in Egyptian' (an adverbial adjective) clarifies that *tḥyt* is the Egyptian equivalent of *trbṣ*. A comparable way of glossing is probably found in the damaged document *TAD* B3.7, written by an unknown scribe in 420 BCE. Line 5 of this text reads *ʾmrn lh mṣryt* 'they say to it in Egyptian'. Although both the gloss and the glossed word are lacking (due to the fragmentary state of the document) it is very probable that, in this case, the words *tḥyt* and *trbṣ* were also concerned (see 5.5).

For other Egyptian equivalents to Aramaic words in *TAD* B3.10 and in *TAD* B3.11, and their implications for the language situation at Elephantine, see below 4.5 and 5.

3.3 Old Persian Loanwords in Letters

In official letters from Elephantine, Old Persian loanwords are found in the Yedanyah correspondence, in (semi-)official letter *TAD* A5.2 (not connected with the Yedanyah correspondence), and in the two letters that are connected with the figure of Aršama the Satrap of Egypt (see 3.3.1). In private letters, Old Persian loanwords are very rare.

3.3.1 Distinction between Official Letters and Private Letters

The distinction in *TAD* A between (semi-)official and private letters is made principally on the basis of their contents and the 'parties' involved.[89] Script, writing material, and letter formulae also play an important role in making this distinc-

87 With the sg. f. article *tꜣ-* (see 4.2).

88 On the word *trbṣ* in *TAD* B3.4, written by the same scribe in 437 BCE, see n. 155.

89 *TAD* A, 81. By 'parties', Porten and Yardeni probably mean to indicate that the names of the 'correspondents' are not sufficient to conclude whether a letter is (semi-)official or private.

tion; likewise, the presence of Old Persian loanwords in a given letter can be another important factor.[90]

The Yedanyah letters deal with important communal matters and include, among other things, copies of an official correspondence with the authorities in Palestine (*TAD* A4.7; A.4.8). Two letters found among the Elephantine papyri (*TAD* A6.1, 427 BCE; *TAD* A6.2, 411 BCE) are connected with the figure of Aršama the Satrap of Egypt and resemble the Aršama letter orders written on leather (from the late 5th century BCE). Aršama is the sender of one of these letters (*TAD* A6.2) and the addressee of the other (*TAD* A6.1). For this reason, these two letters can be labelled official. (The two letters are, however, not discussed in the following because they emanated from the Achaemenid administration and the interest of this contribution is the presence of loanwords in documents written by Judeans.)

The communication in private letters is often between family members, and these letters usually deal with family matters. From Elephantine we have private letters written on papyrus, used for long distance communication, and private letters written on potsherds (ostraca), used for short distance communication, in particular with Syene on the mainland.[91]

3.3.2 Old Persian Loanwords in the Yedanyah Correspondence

Old Persian loanwords are found in four letters belonging to the Yedanyah correspondence that were sent to external addressees (*TAD* A4.5; A4.7; A4.8; A4.10) and in a letter that was sent to Elephantine (*TAD* A4.2).[92] The remaining documents in this collection, both letters (*TAD* A4.1; A4.3; A4.4; A4.6) and the famous memorandum giving permission for the reconstruction of the Elephantine temple (*TAD* A4.9), are devoid of Old Persian loanwords.

The letters *TAD* A4.5, *TAD* A4.7, *TAD* A4.8, and *TAD* A4.10 all concern the destruction of the Judean temple and/or its rebuilding and the resumption of sacrifices therein. The letters *TAD* A4.7 and *TAD* A4.8 are drafts of a letter that was sent to Palestine (*TAD* A4.8 *may* be a copy of the letter that was actually sent to Palestine). In these two versions of the petition, the Judeans address the Persian governor of Judea, Bagohi. The draft version and copy of this letter were kept in the local chancellery.

---

90 On letter formulae, see Schwiderski, *Handbuch*.

91 See Folmer, "'Hi Aḥuṭab'."

92 Letter *TAD* A5.2 (not connected with the Yedanyah correspondence) is also included in the following overview (see 3.3 and 3.3.6 [b]).

Even though the names of the correspondents of *TAD* A4.5 are not preserved and the letter is fragmentary, the letter clearly relates to the subject matter of *TAD* A4.7 and *TAD* A4.8. It may be a draft or perhaps a copy of a letter written by Judean leaders that was kept in the Elephantine administrative centre. The letter was possibly addressed to a Persian official who was authorised to start an investigation into a series of crimes the Egyptians were accused of by the Judeans (including the destruction of the Judean temple).[93] The letter contains many elements that are also present in *TAD* A4.7, especially in the following lines:

bšnt 14 *dryhwš* [*ml*]*kʾ kzy ʾršm ʾzl ʿl mlkʾ znh dwškrtʾ zy kmryʾ zy ḥnwb ʾlhʾ* [*ʿbd*]*w byb byrtʾ hmwnyt ʿm wydrng zy prtrk tnh hwh* 'In year 14 of [Ki]ng Darius, when our lord Arsames went to the king, this is the evil act which the priests of Khnub the god [di]d in Elephantine the fortress in agreement with Vidranga who was Chief there' (*TAD* A4.5:2–4; see also *TAD* A4.7:4–6[94])
ʾgwr]*ʾ zy ln zy ndšw l*[*mbnyh*] 'to [build] our [Temp]le which they demolished' (*TAD* A4.5:24; see also *TAD* A4.7:9)
ʾšrnʾ lqḥw lnpš[*hwm ʿbdw*] 'the fittings they took (and) [made (them) their] own' (*TAD* A4.5:18; see also *TAD* A4.7:13[95])

The letter also contains a characteristic stock phrase that is found in other official correspondences as well: *hn ʿl*] *mrʾn ṭb* ... '[if it] pleases our lord' (*TAD* A4.5:19.21.22 [?]).[96]

Letter *TAD* A4.10 lacks the address and starts with *ʿbdyk* followed by the names of the senders (five Judean leaders of the Elephantine community). For that reason, it is probably a draft version.[97] Granerød thinks that the letter was perhaps addressed to Aršama.[98] In the list of the senders that follows the word *ʿbdyk*, each name is followed by *šmh* and the senders refer to themselves as Syenians, while using a form with a Persian morpheme (see 3.3.5 [a]): *swnknn zy*

93 Granerød, *Dimensions of Yahwism*, 86.

94 Note that *znh dwškrtʾ* is phrased in *TAD* A4.7:17 as *zʾ bʾyštʾ*. On *dwškrt*, see 3.3.4. Note that *hmwnyt ʿm* is also found in *TAD* A4.7:5 (but not in *TAD* A4.8:5; this version just mentions that Vidranga was bribed by the Egyptians, as in *TAD* A4.5).

95 See also *TAD* A6.15:6 (Aršama correspondence); A1:11 (Akhvamazda correspondence). Cf. also *TAD* B7.2:6.

96 For parallels to *hn ʿl*] *mrʾn ṭb*, see *TAD* A4.7:23; A4.8:22 (Yedanyah correspondence; letter to the authorities in Palestine); *TAD* A6.3:5; A6.7:8; A6.13:2 (Aršama correspondence); A1:9 (Akhvamazda correspondence); for parallels to *ʾšrnʾ lqḥw lnpš*[*hwm ʿbdw*], see *TAD* A4.7:13 (Yedanyah correspondence); *TAD* A6.15:6 (Aršama correspondence); A1:11 (Akhvamazda correspondence).

97 Granerød, *Dimensions of Jahwism*, 222.

98 *Dimensions of Jahwism*, 44, 87, 219; cf. the use of *mrʾn* in l. 12 (ibidem, 222).

byb byrt' 'Syenians who are in Elephantine the fortress' (l. 6). Several phrases are typical for official letter writing.[99]

The letter *TAD* A4.2 is addressed to Yedanyah, Maʿuziyah, Uriyah, and the garrison. The formula used in the letter is that of a subordinate addressing his superiors: *ʾl mʾry ... ʿbdk* (l. 1; cf. also the remains of the external address in l. 17). The name of the sender is not preserved. The tone of the letter is official, as it describes several problems and contains a request for help, but it does not contain any of the stock phrases that we know from the official correspondences that emanated from the Achaemenid chancelleries (the Aršama and Akhvamazda correspondences).[100] The address formula also differs somewhat from the Aršama letters: *ʾl mʾry ... ʿbdk* instead of *mn ʾršm ʿl* PN.[101] As such, it seems likely that the sender was a Judean from Elephantine (cf., for instance, *TAD* A4.3, which contains the same address formula; in that document the sender is Maʿuziyah, probably the same Maʿuziyah addressed in *TAD* A4.2). There are references in *TAD* A4.2 to Aršama (ll. 5.8.9), the Egyptians (ll. 4.5), Memphis (l. 11), the province of Thebes (l. 6), and the letters also contain references to persons with Egyptian and Persian personal names (as well as Akkadian patronyms).

3.3.3 Classes of Old Persian Loanwords in the Yedanyah Correspondence

As with the legal documents, most of the Old Persian loanwords in the Elephantine letters are nouns and adjectives. The interpretation of several Old Persian loanwords in the letters belonging to the Yedanyah correspondence is somewhat problematic (on *hnd(y)z* and *ʾzd*, see 3.2.2 and 3.3.4 respectively).

An adverb possibly appears in the Yedanyah correspondence in the form of the word *hmwnyt* (*hamaunitā 'in agreement with' [Tavernier, *Iranica*, 411]; *TAD* A4.5:4; A4.7:5). The word is based on an Iranian abstract noun, but the etymology of the *-t* in particular, is disputed. Tavernier lists the word under adverbs and prepositions, but does not specify which word class it belongs to.[102] One wonders

99 *kn ʾmrn hn mrʾn* '(they) say thus: I If our lord ...' (*TAD* A4.10:7); *wmrʾn ʾwdys yʿbd* and 'should our lord make a statement' (*TAD* A4.10:12). On the use of a light verb (*ʿbd*) in the latter example, see n. 21.

100 See the phrases quoted above in this section.

101 The latter in *TAD* A6.2–A6.13 (*TAD* A6.2 is from Elephantine); see also *mn wrwhy ʿl* PN (*TAD* 6.14); *mn wrpš ʿl* PN (*TAD* 6.15); *mn ʾrtḥy ʿl* PN (*TAD* 6.16). Cf. also *TAD* 6.1:5 (letter to Aršama found at Elephantine): *ʿl*] *mrʾn ʾršm* [external address]. On the distribution of these address formulae, see Folmer, "Bactria and Egypt," 419–22; Schwiderski, *Handbuch*, 102–11, 195–206.

102 Tavernier, *Iranica*, 411. In *DNWSI*, 284, the word is translated as 'in agreement, in league with' and labelled as an adverb.

if the preposition *ʿm* which follows the Old Persian loanword *hmwnyt* might be a gloss on *hmwnyt*. If this is the case, *hmwnyt* was glossed by the scribes of these two letters as a preposition, regardless of the function the word may have had in Old Persian.[103] On glosses, see below 3.3.8.

3.3.4 Semantic Domains of Old Persian Loanwords in the Yedanyah Correspondence

The Old Persian loanwords (nouns and adjectives) that appear in the Yedanyah archive belong to the following semantic domains.

Measures

krš (*TAD* A4.4:9) (on the etymology, see above 3.2.2)
ʾrdb (*TAD* A4.10:14) (on the etymology, see above 3.2.2)

Official Titles and Epithets

gwšk 'informer, spy' (< Old Persian *gaušaka; Tavernier, *Iranica*, 423) (*TAD* A4.5:9)
prtk 'foremost' (< Old Persian *frataka-; Tavernier, *Iranica*, 421) (*TAD* 5.2:7)
prtrk 'governor' (on the etymology, see above 3.2.2) (*TAD* A4.5:4; A4.7:5; A4.8:5)
ptprs 'investigator, interrogator' (Old Persian *patifrāsa; Tavernier, *Iranica*, 428) (*TAD* A4.2:3)
typt 'supervisor, chief of the guards' (< Old Persian *tipati-; Tavernier, *Iranica*, 431) (*TAD* A4.5:9)

The word *d/rḥpnyʾ* (TAD A4.5:17) is possibly another Old Persian loanword which refers to officials.[104]

Administration

Military (Administrative) Domain

hndyz 'garrisoned' (literally 'co-inhabitant of the fortress') (on the etymology, see above 3.2.2) (*TAD* A4.5:7)

---

103 It is important to keep in mind that loanwords are usually unanalysable units for the speakers of the recipient language (see Haspelmath, "Lexical Borrowing," 37).
104 The word is unclear but it is unlikely that it is of Semitic origin.

Legal (Administrative) Domain
ʾwdys 'statement, investigation report' (Old Persian *avadaisa-; Tavernier, *Iranica*, 447) (*TAD* A4.10:12)
ʾzd 'known' (< Old Persian *azdā; Tavernier, *Iranica*, 411 [adverbial use of adjective *azda*][105]) (*TAD* A4.5:8–9)
dwškṛt 'crime' (< Old Persian *duškṛta-; Tavernier, *Iranica*, 448) (*TAD* A4.5:3)

Constructions and Furnishing/Equipment
ʾšrn 'furniture, equipment' (on the etymology, see above 3.2.2) (*TAD* A4.5:18; A4.7:11)
ywdn 'grain house' (< Old Persian *yaudāna- or *yavadāna-; Tavernier, *Iranica*, 441) (*TAD* A4.5:5)

Religious Domain
ʾtrwdn 'brazier, fan to fan the fire'[106] (< Old Persian *ātṛvadana-; Tavernier, *Iranica*, 461) (*TAD* A4.5:17)

Some of these loanwords also appear in legal documents: *krš*, *ʾrdb*, *prtrk*, *hnd(y)z*, and *ʾšrn*.

3.3.5 Morphological Integration of Old Persian Loanwords in the Yedanyah Correspondence

(a) Masculine Inflectional Endings
Singular masculine emphatic state -ʾ
ywdnʾ (*TAD* A4.5:5); *ʾšrnʾ* (*TAD* A4.5:18; A4.7:11)

105 In Tavernier, *Iranica*, 411, the word is listed under adverbs and prepositions. On the etymology of this word, see also Schmitt, *Wörterbuch*, 148. According to Schmitt, the word *azdā* 'bekannt, bewußt' is an adverb. In Old Persian, the word appears in the phrases *azdteā bav* 'bekannt/bewußt werden' and *azdā kar* 'sich bewußt machen' (medial). An active construction *azdā kar* 'bekannt machen' is only known from indirect and later sources (Schmitt, ibidem). This results in *TAD* A4.5:8–9 in the translation 'If it will be established (will be made clear/known) by the judges, police and spies who are appointed in the province of Tshetres, it will be kn[own] to our lord' (*hn ʾzd ytʿbd mn dynyʾ typtyʾ gwskyʾ yty*[*dʿ*] *lmrʾn*) (translation mine). The older interpretation of *azdā* as a noun ('announcement, news') is still reflected in the translation in *TAD* A4.5:8–9 by Porten and Yardeni: *hn ʾzd ytʿbd mn dynyʾ typtyʾ gwškyʾ zy mmnyn bmdynt tšṭrs* 'If inquiry be made of the judges, police and hearers who are appointed in the province of Tshetres' (*TAD* A, 62; also in *EPE*, 138); see *DNWSI*, 25, s. v. ʾzd 'inquiry'. The word *ʾzd* also appears in a court record from Saqqarah (*TAD* B8.11:4 *ʾzd ʿbdw*) and in one of the letters from ancient Bactria (B1:3 *ʿb*]*d ʾnt ʾzd zy* 'you make known the fact that') (Naveh and Shaked, *Aramaic Documents*, 135). Cf. מִלְּתָא מִנִּי אַזְדָּא in Dan 2:5.
106 For the interpretation 'fire altar', see now Barnea, "Achaemenid Zoroastrian Echoes."

***Plural masculine absolute state* -n**
ʾrdbn (*TAD* A4.10:14)

There is also a notable instance where the Aramaic ending *-n* (pl. m. absolute state) is used. In this instance, it was added to the placename *swn* (Syene) to which a borrowed Old Persian affix *-ka-* or *-aka-* was attached:[107]

swnknn 'Syenians' (*TAD* A4.10:6)

The noun *swnknn* is preceded by a list of names which concludes with *kl gbrn 5* 'all (told) 5 persons'.[108]

The same affix *-ka-* also appears in a legal document from the end of the 5th century BCE (*swnkn* 'a Syenian').[109] In this case, the Persian affix was also added to the placename *swn*. (The *-n* following *-k-* is inexplicable, as in the preceding example). The affix *-k-* is also found in Biblical Aramaic in שׁוּשַׁנְכָיֵא 'the people of Susa' (Ezra 4:9).[110]

From this evidence, it seems that, near the close of the 5th century BCE, it was not unusual to use this morphological borrowing from Old Persian when referring to people stationed in (the military fortress) of Syene, in the singular as well as in the plural (with the Aramaic ending *-n*).[111]

***Plural masculine emphatic state* -yʾ**[112]
dynyʾ typtyʾ gwškyʾ (*TAD* A4.5:9)

***Plural masculine construct state* -y**

There is no evidence for this.

---

107 Old Persian has many affixes that produce nouns and adjectives. Among them are *-ka-* / *-aka-* (see Skjærvo, "Old Iranian," 167). Note, however, that there is also an affix *-i-* / *-iya-* in Old Persian which denotes all kinds of appurtenances, including ethnic affiliation (e.g., Bāxtriya- 'Bactrian' and Aθuriya 'Assyrian'; for examples, see ibidem, 167, and Schmitt, *Wörterbuch*, 142, 153). The *nun* following the affix *-k-* in *swnkn* and *swnknn* is at present unexplainable but probably cometees from Old Persian as well. There is also an affix *-na* / *-ana* that is used for verbal derivation (Skjærvo, "Old Iranian," 167).

108 This list of names also contains a *possible* loan translation from Old Persian (*šmh* 'his name'). On the use of this word in Persian Period Aramaic, see Folmer, *Aramaic Language*, chapter 5.13.

109 The text reads *mtn br yšbyh ʾrmy swnkn ldgl* [...] 'Mattan son of Yašobyah an Aramean, a Syenian of the detachment of [PN]' (*TAD* B5.2:2).

110 *HALOT*, vol. 5, 1789. On the gloss that follows, see n. 86.

111 Note that the Aramaic gentilic ending *-y* (sg. m. absolute state) and *-yn* (pl. m. absolute state) is never combined with the placename *swn* or *yb* in Persian Period Aramaic. It is, however, found in *yhwdy* 'Judean', *ʾrmy* 'Aramean' (as in *TAD* B5.2; see n. 109), and the like.

112 Another likely case is]*k d/rḥpnyʾ zy byb b*[*yrt*] 'the ... which are in Elephantine' (*TAD* A4.5:17). The noun probably refers to some sort of official.

(b) Feminine Inflectional Endings

There is no positive evidence for feminine inflectional endings in the letters under discussion. On the absence of the singular feminine absolute ending *-h* in *ʾtrwdn ḥdh* 'a brazier' (*TAD* A4.5:17), see 3.3.7 (a).

3.3.6 Morphosyntactic Integration of Old Persian Loanwords in the Yedanyah Correspondence

Single word noun phrases are not included in the following overview.[113]

(a) Old Persian Loanwords in Construct Noun Phrases

First Term of the Construct Noun Phrase is an Old Persian Loanword

There is no evidence for this.

Second Term of the Construct Noun Phrase is an Old Persian Loanword

ʿm šyryt ʾšrnʾ 'with the rest of the fittings' (*TAD* A4.7:11)

In this case, the noun is clearly a singular form in the emphatic state (in contrast with legal document *TAD* B3.4:23, where the noun *ʾšrn* is treated as a plural form; on this case of reanalysis, see 3.2.10.[114]

(b) Old Persian Loanwords in zy Phrases

The First Term is an Old Persian Loanword

qṣt mn ywdnʾ zy mlkʾ 'part of the royal barley house' (*TAD* A4.5:5)

Another example is found in an official letter that does not belong to the Yedanyah correspondence (see 3.3, with n. 92):

prtkyʾ zy npyn rb ḥylʾ zy swn 'the foremost (aides) of Naphaina, garrison commander of Syene' (*TAD* A5.2:7)

The loanword *prtkyʾ* (with the pl. m. emphatic state morpheme) is found in the first term of a complex *zy* phrase.

The Second Term is an Old Persian Loanword

There is no evidence for this in the Yedanyah correspondence.

---

113 As in 3.2.9 (discussion of legal documents).

114 Another instance of *ʾšrnʾ* occurs in *TAD* A4.5:18 (broken context).

(c) Old Persian Loanwords in zyl- *Phrases*

There is no evidence for this in the Yedanyah correspondence.

(d) Old Persian Loanwords in Appositions

lwydrng prtrkʾ zy tnh hwh 'to Vidranga, the Chief, who was there' (*TAD* A4.8:5)

This is a change of *hmwnyt ʿm wydrng zy prtrk tnh hwh* 'in agreement with Vidranga who was Chief here', which occurs in *TAD* A4.7:5 (the first draft of the petition) and also in *TAD* A4.5:4:

hmwnyt ʿm wydrng zy prtrk tnh hwh (*TAD* A4.7:5)
hmwnyt ʿm wydrng zy prtrk tnh hwh (*TAD* A4.5:4)

In these two texts, *prtrk* functions as the subject in a dependent clause.[115] The change to *prtrkʾ* in *TAD* A4.8 is a well-informed change, in agreement with the more general construction of a noun in apposition to a PN (see 3.2.9 [d]). This is in contrast with appositions in the absolute state in the legal documents discussed above (see 3.2.9 [d]).

(e) Old Persian Loanwords in Attributive Noun Phrases

ʾtrwdn ḥdh 'a brazier' (*TAD A*4.5:17)

The head word is not combined with a feminine ending (see also 3.3.7 [a]).

3.3.7 Peculiarities in the Yedanyah Correspondence

(a) Singular Feminine Absolute State Ending -h

As seen above (3.3.5 [b]), there is no positive evidence for any feminine morphological ending. Moreover, there is evidence that the singular feminine absolute state morpheme *-h* was not used:

ʾtrwdn ḥdh 'a brazier' (*TAD* A4.5:17)

The feminine form *ḥdh* 'one' clearly suggests that the noun is feminine.[116]

(b) The Word hndyz

In *TAD* A 6.7:6, the word *hndyz* is not combined with a plural masculine absolute state morpheme *-n*, so there is no agreement with the pref. conj. plural 3 masculine *yhwwn*:

115 For another subject in the absolute state, see *TAD* A4:7: *npyn brh zy rbḥyl hwh bswn byrtʾ*.
116 Cf. also *DNWSI*, 137.

kzy hn hndyz yhwwn bbr' [z]*k my' šṭyn* (*TAD* A4.5:7)
'so that when they would be garrisoned they would drink water from that well'[117]

It is noteworthy that, in the Aršama correspondence, the same word lacks inflection as well:

kzy mṣryn mrdt wḥyl' hndyz hww (*TAD* A6.7:6)
'when Egypt rebelled and the troop was garrisoned'

In this case, agreement with a plural verb form (*hww* is a sf. conj. pl. 3m. of the verb *hwy*) is also absent. In general, Old Persian loanwords were well adapted to the Aramaic morphological system of nouns, as in the Aršama correspondence. This raises doubts about the use of this borrowing in Aramaic. Regardless of its etymology, it is possible that the word was used as an adverb in the Aramaic texts.

(c) Old Persian Loanwords Preceded by a Preposition

There are two notable cases in an official letter (*TAD* A4.2) in which the scribe did not use the expected preposition *l* in combination with the verb *qbl l* 'to complain to'. The person who is being complained to happens to be indicated by an Old Persian loanword:

hw qbl ptyprsn 'he complained to investigators'[118] (*TAD* A4.2:3)
ḥd zywk hw qbl ptyprs 'one Zivaka, he complained to an investigator' (*TAD* A4.2:3)

The preposition is omitted twice in this letter; as such, this does not seem to be an occasional error.[119] Apparently the unknown scribe had difficulties with handling a preposition before an Old Persian loanword. The letter stands out in that it is part of an exchange of letters between the Judean leaders of Elephantine and an unknown sender who refers to the addressees of his letter as his superiors; the sender probably reports from Aršama's court in Memphis and it is possible that he was a Judean from Elephantine. In that case, an exchange of letters among Elephantine Judeans would be concerned. The production of this letter presumably did not involve a scribe with training in the Achaemenid chancellery, as it is highly unlikely that such a scribe would have made this mistake.

---

117 *TAD* A, 62: 'so that whenever they would be garrisoned (there) they would drink the water in [th]at well'.

118 The translation 'the investigators' in *TAD* A, 56 is unjustified.

119 In the same letter, a third occurrence of the word *ptyprs* (emphatic form *ptyprs'*) is without a clear context (*TAD* A4.5:12).

There is plenty of evidence in Persian Period Aramaic that 'to complain to X about (or: against) Y' is expressed by *qbl l* X *ʿl* Y, for example, in the following texts (all by the scribe Ḥaggai b. Šemaʿyah):

wzy yqbl ʿlyk lsgn wmrʾ wdyn 'or whoever will complain about you to prefect, lord or judge' (*TAD* B3.12:28)
lʾ ykhl ... wyqbl ʿlyky lsgn wmrʾ wʿl bnyky ʾḥryky 'he will not be able to ... or to complain about you and about your children after you to prefect or lord' (*TAD* B3.10:18–19; also in l. 20)
zy ... wyqbl ʿlyk wʿl bnyky lsgn wmrʾ 'whoever ... or will complain about you and about your children to prefect or lord' (*TAD* B3.11:12–13)

Evidence for this is also found in the official Aršama and Akhvamazda correspondences.[120]

3.3.8 Glosses on Old Persian Loanwords in the Yedanyah Correspondence

There are two instances of a possible Aramaic gloss on an Old Persian loanword in *TAD* A4.5:4 (ca. 410 BCE) and *TAD* A4.7:5 (407 BCE). It is possible in these two instances that the word *ʿm* 'with' is an Aramaic gloss on the Old Persian loanword *hmwnyt* (*hamaunita 'in agreement with') (Tavernier, *Iranica*, 411):[121]

znh dwškrtʾ zy kmryʾ zy ḥnwb ʾlhʾ[ʿbd]w byb byrtʾ hmwnyt ʿm wydrng zy prtrk tnh hwh 'this is the evil act which the priests of Khnub the god [di]d in Elephantine the fortress in agreement with Vidranga who was Chief there' (*TAD* A4.5:4–5)
kmryʾ zy ḥnwb ʾlhʾ zy byb byrtʾ hmwnyt ʿm wydrng zy prtrk tnh hwh 'the priests of Khnub the god who are in Elephantine the fortress, in agreement with Vidranga who was Chief there' (*TAD* A4.7:5)

Another gloss on a Persian loanword (*hnpn*) is attested in one of the legal documents from Elephantine (see above 3.2.11). There, the gloss is Egyptian (*tmwʾnty*) and is preceded by an explicative use of *hw* (*TAD* B3.10). This is not the

120 E.g., in *TAD* A6.14:1, a letter belonging to the Aršama correspondence. In the legal document *TAD* B2.2:5, the person who is being complained to is not expressed (the text has *qbl ʿl* 'to complain about, to lodge a complaint against'). In one of the Akhvamazda letters (from Bactria), the name of the person to whom the complaint is lodged is preceded by the preposition *l* (A1:1.4.6); the person being complained about is expressed by *mn* (*mn bgwnt* 'about Bagavanta'in A1:1) (on this use of the preposition *mn* see also *qblt mnk* 'a complaint about you' in *TAD* A6.8:3, one of the Aršama letters). In lines 4 and 6 of the same document, the person who is being complained about is not mentioned.
121 On the word class of this lexeme, see 3.3.3.

case in the two examples in the Yedanyah correspondence (*TAD* A4.5 and *TAD* A4.7). As such, the interpretation as a gloss in these two texts is doubtful.

3.3.9 Persian Loanwords in Private Letters

Apart from the measure of weight *krš* and the measure of capacity *ʾrdb* (abbreviated as *ʾ*), private letters on papyrus (*TAD* A3.1–11) and letter ostraca (*TAD* D7.1–54) are in general devoid of Persian loanwords:[122]

krš (on the etymology, see above 3.2.2) (*TAD* A3.2:10; A3.8:2.3.4; A3.10:4.5)
ʾ (abbreviation for *ʾrdb*) (on the etymology, see above 3.2.2) (*TAD* D7.8:15; D7.50:3)

The only other certain loanword in private letters is the word *ptgm* in ostracon *TAD* D7.39:

šlḥ ly ptgm ‘send me word’ or ‘he sent me word’ (*TAD* D7.39:8)

Note that, in line 10 of this ostracon, the Persian name *prndt* appears, giving the ostracon an official Persian colouring. In ostraca, the verb *šlḥ* ‘to send’ is often used without an explicit direct object. In some cases, a direct object is expressed (*spr* ‘letter’, *ʾgrh* ‘letter’, or *mlh* ‘word’).[123]

There are no other certain instances of Persian loanwords in private letters on papyrus or in the collection of Aramaic letter ostraca in *TAD* D7.1–54.[124]

4 Egyptian Words

At Elephantine, Egyptian words (nouns and adjectives) appear in legal documents and letters written by Judeans. These words are discussed in what follows.[125]

122 This holds for the letter ostraca that were published by Porten and Yardeni in *TAD* D7.1–54. On the ostraca in the Clermont-Ganneau collection, see n. 124.

123 Folmer, *Aramaic Language*, 655 (with n. 292).

124 There may be several Old Persian loanwords in the Clermont-Ganneau Collection published in Lozachmeur, *La collection Clermont-Ganneau*. The index to the edition of the Elephantine ostraca in Lozachmeur’s study lists several lexical items that are known from other sources as lexical borrowings from Old Persian (*ʾbygrʾ*; *ʾzd*; *ʾpyty*; *ʾšrn*; *krš*; *ptkr*; *stwn*). However, the reading and context of most of these words is uncertain. For this reason they are not discussed in the present contribution. Note, however, that the best pieces from this collection are also included in *TAD* D7.

125 Most of the following Egyptian words are attested in Demotic, the language and script that was used, among other things, for documentary texts and letters. Demotic is contemporary with Aramaic legal documents and letters from Elephantine. In all likelihood Egyptian words in Ele-

There are also many Egyptian words in the letter order by Aršama that was found among the Aramaic papyri from Elephantine (*TAD* A6.2). In this letter, Aršama gives instructions for the disbursement of materials needed for a boat repair. In every aspect, this is a typical letter order issued by the Achaemenid chancelleries, with the difference that many Egyptian words are used in this letter order which refer to materials and the parts of the boat under repair. This letter is of great interest because it shows that, in the official Achaemenid administration, Egyptian words were also used in communication with local individuals whenever this was deemed necessary or appropriate. The addressee of this letter order was an individual with an Egyptian name, Waḥpremakhi, who was probably in charge of the warehouse at Elephantine from which the materials were distributed. The Egyptian words in this letter are not discussed in what follows because the document emanated from the Achaemenid administration and the primary interest of this contribution is the presence of Egyptian words in documents written by Judeans. It is nevertheless of great value here because the text mentions two persons who were actively involved in the production of this letter order, namely Nabuʿaqab (an Aramean name) who wrote the letter (*nbwʿqb ktb*) and the Judean scribe Anani who is said to have acted as a chancellor (*ʿnny sprʾ bʿl ṭʿm*) in this case (l. 23). Anani is also known from other Elephantine documents and was in all likelihood from the scribal family of Natan b. Ananyah and Maʿuziyah b. Natan.[126] It is possible that Anani was involved in the production of this specific letter because of his expert knowledge not only of Aramaic but also of Egyptian.[127] His precise role in the production of this document, however, is disputed.[128] Egyptian words in the semantic domain of shipping (including words for the cargo in question and a word related to taxation) also abound in the Customs Account (*TAD* C3.7). This administrative text was not written at Elephantine, but the erased papyrus was reused for the Elephantine copy of the Aḥiqar story and proverbs. The Customs Account is not discussed here, as it has nothing to do with the Elephantine Judeans.[129] Other Aramaic texts that contain Egyptian words are a

---

phantine Aramaic derive from Demotic or a contemporary spoken variety. In most cases, however, there are also parallels for these words in older or later phases of the Egyptian language. I refer to all these lexical items in Aramaic as 'Egyptian'. For references to parallels in older phases of Egyptian, see CDD. If there is no parallel in CDD, I refer to dictionaries of earlier and/ or later phases of Egyptian.

126 On his possible identity, see Folmer, "Bactria and Egypt," 426–27.

127 An Egyptian scribe (Sabosek) added an administrative note in Demotic.

128 For recent discussions of the problems involved, see Folmer, "Bactria and Egypt," 424–27; Tavernier, "The Use of Languages," 367–77; Schütze, "Local Administrations," 505–6; Moore, "The Persian Administrative Process."

129 For some remarks on this text, see 4.4 (c) and 4.6.

list of wine disbursements (*TAD* C3.12), a votive inscription (*TAD* D20.1), two funerary stelae (*TAD* D20.5; D20.6), all of unknown origin, and Aramaic documents from the Saqqarah/Memphis region. These texts are not discussed in detail here.

4.1 Egyptian Words in Legal Documents

Egyptian words are found in legal documents from Elephantine from the middle of the 5th century BCE onwards. Two groups of words can be distinguished. The first group consists of lexical items that appear in the dowry lists in documents of wifehood (*spr ʾntw*). These list the personal belongings of the wife (*TAD* B2.6, 458 or 445 BCE; *TAD* B3.3, 449 BCE; *TAD* B3.8, 420 BCE; *TAD* D3.16, middle of the 5th century BCE). Several words in these dowry lists are presumably of Egyptian origin, though their etymology has not been identified (see n. 148). These words are not discussed in the main text of this contribution. Another group of Egyptian words is found in documents that belong to the archive of Ananyah b. Azaryah who was married to an Egyptian slave. Several documents in this archive concern the transfer of real estate and contain several Egyptian words that refer to constructions used for religious or domestic purposes (*TAD* B3.4, 437 BCE; *TAD* B3.5, 434 BCE; *TAD* B3.7, 420 BCE; *TAD* B3.10, 404 BCE; *TAD* B3.11, 402 BCE; *TAD* B3.12, 402 BCE). There are no examples of titles or epithets, though such examples are known from other sources, including funerary stelae from Egypt (*TAD* D20.5 and D20.6) and a court record from North Saqqarah (*TAD* B8.12:4).[130] There are no certain Egyptian terms in the documents under discussion that belong to the semantic domain of administration (on the word *hyrʾ* in *TAD* B3.2, see n. 40).[131]

4.2 Semantic Domains of the Egyptian Words in Legal Documents

Nouns of Egyptian origin in legal documents belong to the following semantic domains:

130 *tmnḥʾ* 'excellent one' (f.) (*TAD* D20.5) and *mnḥh* 'excellent one' (m.) (*TAD* D20.6) (on these two words, see n. 147); *psḥmṣnwty* 'the scribe of the book of god' (< Egyptian *pꜣ sẖ-mḏꜣ.t-nṯr*, with sg. m. article *pꜣ*) (*TAD* B8.12:4) (*GEA*, 346, no. 20; *DNWSI*, 922; CDD S (13.1), s. v. (sẖ) 'scribe'; CDD M (10.1), 299, s. v. mḏ(ꜣy).t 'bookroll'); CDD N (04.1), 144, s. v. nṯr 'god'.

131 See, however, the Demotic administrative note in the earliest legal document in Aramaic from Egypt (*TAD* B1.1, 515 BCE; lease between a Philistine settler and an Egyptian farmer; the document is not from Elephantine). On this note, see Quack, "Ein demotischer Ausdruck." See also *GEA*, 347, no. 33.

Measures of weight and capacity

qb 'qab' (< Egyptian *qb.t*[132]) (*TAD* B7.1:8)

Flora

gm' 'reed' (< Egyptian *qmꜣ*[133]) (*TAD* B2.6:15; B3.8:17; D3.16:11)

Clothing

šnṭ' 'linen robe' (< Egyptian *šnt*[134]) (*TAD* B3.8:11)

Household Utensils

p(y)q 'tray' (< Egyptian *pq*[135]) (*TAD* B2.6:16; B3.3:6; B3.8:18)

Products

tqm 'castor oil' (< Egyptian *tgm*[136]) (*TAD* B2.6:16; B3.3:6; B3.8:20)

---

132 According to Benjamin Noonan, the word is of Egyptian origin (Noonan, *Non-Semitic Loanwords*, 190). See also *GEA*, 346, no. 25; CDD Q (04.1), 19, s. v. qb(ꜣ)(.t) 'jug, pitcher' (f.); CDD refers to *qb* and to *tqbh* / *tqbt* in the Hermopolis papyri; according to CDD the meaning of the word was extended. See, however, the question mark in *DNWSI*, 977, s. v. qb_1. In my view, the fact that the word is f. in Egyptian and m. in Aramaic is remarkable and raises questions about an Egyptian etymology. The word *qb* in Aramaic is clearly m. (see section 4.6 on *bqb' rb'* in *TAD* D7.46:2). See also the plene form *qbyn* (pl. m.) in a legal document from Wadi Murabba'at (*DJA*, 76, s. v. קַב).

133 *GEA*, 345, no. 4; *DNWSI*, 225, s. v. gm'; CDD Q (04.1), 33, s. v. qmꜣ 'reed'. On the occasional use of *g* for Egyptian *q* (instead of the more frequent *q*), see Noonan, *Non-Semitic Loanwords*, 274 (Table 5.1) and 275.

134 *GEA*, 347, no. 34; *DNWSI*, 1175, s. v. šnṭ' 'some type of garment, dress'; cf. *DAE*, 234, n. 1; CDD Š (10.1), 183, s. v. šnt 'kilt; cloak; piece of linen' (f.). Apparently, the -' in *šnṭ'* is what remains of the f. ending in Egyptian (see also *tmnḥ'* in *TAD* D 20.5:1, mentioned in n. 130 and n. 147).

135 *GEA*, 346, no. 23; *DNWSI*, 931, s. v. pq; *DAE*, 194, n. m; CDD P (10.1), 168, s. v. pq (m.) 'thin sheet, strip' (variant of pk 'fragment').

136 See *DNWSI*, 1228; *GEA*, 347, no. 44; CDD T (12.1), 323, s. v. tgm (m.) 'castor plant, castor seed, castor oil' (also ibidem, 308, s. v. tkm 'castor plant, castor seed, castor oil').

Materials

šš 'alabaster' (< Egyptian *šś*[137]) (*TAD* B3.8:18; D3.16:12)

Religious Constructions

tmy and *tm'* 'the way, the road' (< Egyptian *tꜣ my.t*; with sg. f. article *tꜣ*[138]) (*TAD* B3.4:8 *tmy*; *TAD* B3.5:10 *tm'*)
tmw'nty 'divine road', lit. 'the road of god' (< Egyptian *tꜣ my.t-nṯr*; with sg. f. article *tꜣ*[139]) (*TAD* B3.10:9)
qnḥnty 'divine shrine', lit. 'the shrine of god' (< Egyptian *qnẖ.t-nṯr*[140]) (*TAD* B3.10:9)

Domestic Constructions

try rsy 'the southern room':

try 'room' (< Egyptian *tꜣ-ry.t*; with sg. f. article *tꜣ*[141]) (*TAD* B3.11:3; B3.5:3.6; B3.10:4; written with *d* in *TAD* B3.10:3: *dryrsy*[142])

rsy 'southern' (only in combination with *try*) (< Egyptian *rsy.t*; adjective with f. ending -*t*[143]) (*TAD* B3.10:3; B3.11:3)

---

137 *GEA* 347, no. 36; CDD S (13.1), 449, s. v. sš 'alabaster' (< *šś*). See also *DNWSI*, 1196, s. v. $šš_1$ 'alabaster, marble' (the origin of the word is not discussed).

138 *DNWSI*, 1220, s. v. tmy_2; for *tm'*, see the cross-reference under tm'; *GEA*, 347, no. 38; *DAE*, 217, n. e; CDD M (10.1), 45, s. v. mi͗.t 'road' (f.). The possibility has also been raised that the word reflects Egyptian *dmy* 'town' (see the suggestion by Günther Vittmann in *EPE*, 214, n. 18; see also CDD T (12.1), 200, s. v. tmy 'town, village', with a reference to Aramaic); against this interpretation, however, see von Pilgrim, "Archaeological Background," 12.

139 *GEA*, 347, no. 39 (possibly an erroneous rendering of *my.t*); *DNWSI*, 1220, s. v. tmw'nty 'the road of the god'; CDD M (10.1), 45, s. v. mi͗.t 'road' (f.); CDD N (04.1), 144, s. v. nṯr 'god'.

140 *GEA*, 346, no. 30; *DNWSI*, 1014, s. v. qnḥnty; CDD Q (04.1), 48, s. v. qnḥ.t 'shrine, chapel' (f.); CDD N (04.1), 144, s. v. nṯr 'god'. On the loss of the final approximant -*r*, see Müller, "Egyptian," 113.

141 See also *EPE*, 237, n. 8; *GEA*, 347, no. 45; *DNWSI*, 1230, s. v. try^1; *DAE*, 221; CDD R (01.1), 11, s. v. ry.t 'side, part', 'room', and also 'gate, portico'; *CD*, 287b-286a, s. v. ⲣⲓ 'cell, room' (f. noun).

142 Perhaps this is a pronunciation spelling. For the progressive neutralisation of *d* and *t* in Egyptian, see Noonan, *Non-Semitic Loanwords*, 274.

143 *DNWSI*, 1078; *GEA*, 347, no. 32; CDD R (01.1), 65, s. v. rs 'south'; adj. 'southern'. On the dropping of final -*t*, see Müller, "Egyptian,", 113; ibidem, 117 on the adjectival ending -*y* (m.) and -*y.t* (f.).

tḥyt 'the courtyard' (< Egyptian *tꜢ ḥyt*; with sg. f. article *tꜢ*[144]) (*TAD* B3.7:5.10.13; B3.10:4.13.15)

The dowry lists in particular contain a number of as yet unidentified but presumably Egyptian words that refer to certain household items.[145] The word *tms'* in the dowry list in *TAD* B3.8:13 is probably not of Egyptian origin.[146]

4.3 Morphological Integration of Egyptian Words

Egyptian words were not adapted to Aramaic morphology: no Aramaic inflectional endings were added to the nouns of Egyptian origin in the documents under discussion. On the possible exception of the word *qb* 'qab', see 4.6; on *ntr* 'natron' in the Customs Account (*TAD* C3.7, not from Elephantine), see n. 175; on *qlby* and *qlwl* in account *TAD* C3.12 (of unknown origin), see n. 163.

4.4 Morphosyntactic Integration of Egyptian Words

Egyptian words are found in construct noun phrases (a), *zy* phrases ([b] and [c]), *zyl-* phrases (d), attributive noun phrases (e), and single word noun phrases (f).

(a) Egyptian Words in Construct Noun Phrases

There are only examples of Egyptian words in the second term of a construct noun phrase in legal documents from Elephantine:

---

144 *GEA*, 347, no. 37; *DNWSI*, 1206, s.v tḥyt 'porch'; CDD Ḥ (01.1), 19, s. v. ḥyt 'entrance hall, vestibule, gatehouse' (m.), with a variant form ḥyt.t (f.).

145 *prks* 'box' (*TAD* B2.6:16; D3.16:14; an object made of *ḥṣn* 'palm leaves'), *qp* 'chest' (*TAD* B3.8:19; an object made of wood) and, possibly related, *qpp* 'chest' (*TAD* B3.8:17; an object made of *ḥwṣn* 'palm leaves'; for garments), *zlwṣ* (*TAD* D3.16:11; an object made of *gm'* 'reed'). The word *slq* (*TAD* B2.6:16; B3.8:18 [2x]) indicates the material of which a *pyq* is made. According to Grelot, *slq* may reflect the Coptic word *σιλουκι* which refers to a kind of plant 'osier' (*DAE*, 194, n. m). *CD* 330b indicates that the meaning of this word is unknown but that it "grows near a swamp." These words are not included in the list of Egyptian loanwords in *GEA* and their meaning is marked as uncertain in *TAD* (the meaning given there is contextually based).

146 In *tms' 1 zy nḥš* '1 bowl of bronze'. See *DAE*, 194, n. j (reference to Akkadian *nemsētu* 'wash-basin'); on this word, see Black, George, and Postgate (eds.), *A Concise Dictionary of Akkadian*, 249. See also *DNWSI*, 1222, s. v. tms 'bowl, dish' (the origin of the word is not discussed). The word is not included in the list of Egyptian loanwords in *GEA*.

plg try rbt' 'half the large room' (*TAD* B3.5:3.6)
plg tḥyt 'half the *ḫyt*' (*TAD* B3.10:4)
byt qnḥnty 'the house of the shrine of the god' (*qnḥnty* is a compound noun) (*TAD* B3.11:5)
nʿṣbn zy ʾbn šš 'vessels of alabaster stone' (*TAD* B3.8:18)

The example *plg tḥyt* is interesting because it glosses *plg trbṣ'* (*wplg trbṣ' hw plg tḥyt mṣryt*). In this case, the scribe (Ḥaggai b. Šemaʿyah) clearly gave an exact equivalent and was conscious of the definite article in Egyptian. On this gloss, see below 4.5. On *try rbt'* in *plg try rbt'*, see below (e).

The noun phrase *byt qnḥnty* is remarkable. The Egyptian word does not have an Egyptian definite article, whereas determination is expected in this noun phrase.

On the indefinite construct noun phrase *ʾbn šš*, see below (c).

(b) Egyptian Words in *zy* Phrases (Denoting Ownership)

First Term is an Egyptian Word

tmy zy ḥnwm ʾlh' 'the way of Khnum the god' (*TAD* B3.4:8)
tm' zy ḥnwm ʾlh' 'the way of Khnum the god' (*TAD* B3.5:10)

In theory, *tm'* can be interpreted as a noun in the emphatic state, but given the overwhelming evidence for the absence of Aramaic inflection on Egyptian words, *tmy* and *tm'* are probably variant spellings of the same word. Both *tmy* and *tm'* reflect the Egyptian feminine article *tꜣ* at the beginning of the word.[147]

Second Term is an Egyptian Word

btrʿ zy tḥyt 'through (the) gateway of the *ḫyt*' (article added in *TAD* B, 89) (*TAD* B3.10:15)

Note that the state of the Aramaic word *trʿ* is unexpected, as one would expect the emphatic state in this context.

147 Additional evidence for Egyptian words in the first term of *zy* phrases is found in two funerary stelae made for an Egyptian individual (of unknown origin and from the first half of the 5th century BCE): *tmnḥ' zy ʾwsry ʾlh'* 'the excellent (one) of Osiris the god' (*TAD* D20.5:1) (apposition to a f. Egyptian PN) and *mnḥh zy ʾwsry ʾlh'* '(the) excellent (one) of Osiris the god' (*TAD* D20.6:1) (apposition to a m. Egyptian PN; *-h* in this apparent sg. m. form is problematic; it is unlikely but not impossible that this represents an Aramaic sg. m. emphatic state morpheme; a proleptic pron. sf. sg. 3m. is highly unlikely). See *DNWSI*, 659, s. v. mnḥh$_3$; *GEA*, 345, no. 14 and 347, no. 41; CDD M (10.1), 111, s. v. mnḫ 'excellent, beneficent' (adj.). See also *KAI* ii, 319 (no. 269), 325 (no. 272).

(c) *zy* Phrases (Denoting Materials)

First Term (Egyptian Word) Denotes the Object that Is Made of the Material Indicated by the Second Term[148]

šnṭ' 1 zy ktn ḥdt '1 skirt/robe of new linen'[149] (*TAD* B3.8:11)
pq 1 zy slq '1 tray of *slq*' (*TAD* B2.6:16[150])
pyq zy slq 2 '2 trays of *slq*' (*TAD* B3.8:18)

The first term of these items is expected to be in the absolute state. This is evident in those cases in which the noun in the first term is of Aramaic origin: *lbš 1 zy qmr ḥdt* '1 garment of new wool' (*TAD* B3.8:6); *gmydh 1 zy qmr ḥdt* '1 garment of new wool' (*TAD* B3.8:7); *nʿṣbn zy ʾbn 4* '4 vessels of stone' (*TAD* B2.6:5); *nʿṣbn zy ʾbn šš* 'vessels of alabaster stone' (*TAD* B3.8:18).[151] None of the presumably Egyptian words above have a prefixed Egyptian article. On the basis of words like *pyq* (without either the Egyptian or the Aramaic article) in the dowry lists, it seems safe to assume that the final -*ʾ* in *šnṭʾ* is part of the Egyptian word. If this is correct, *ḥdt* probably modifies *ktn* to give 'new linen', just as in *TAD* B3.8:7 one needs to assume that *ḥdt* modifies the masculine noun *qmr*: *gmydh 1 zy qmr ḥdt* '1 garment of new wool' as quoted above.[152]

The absolute state is also the norm for nouns in the Customs Account, which stems from an unknown location in Egypt (*TAD* C3.7), and in the Aršama letter found at Elephantine (*TAD* A6.2), both of which are rich in Egyptian words. Most of the Egyptian words found in these two documents appear in a list of materials to be shipped (*TAD* C3.7) or in a list of materials that are needed for the repair of a boat (*TAD* 6.2). These Egyptian words do not have an article (Egyptian or Aramaic). However, as will be shown in 4.6, there are several cases where the Egyptian word does have an article. In all of these cases, the noun is followed by the number 'one' (either written out or written with a stroke; see 4.6).

148 Several examples in the dowry lists probably belong to this category as well, but the Egyptian etymology of these words has not always been identified (*prks*, *qp*, *qpp*, *zlwṣ*). The words appear in the following phrases: *prks 1 zy ḥṣn ḥdt* '1 new palm-leaf box' (*TAD* B2.6:16); *qp zy ʿq 1 tḥt ḥmdyh* '1 wooden chest for her jewels' (*TAD* B3.8:19); *qpp 1 zy ḥwṣn tḥt lbšyh* '1 palm-leaf chest for her garments' (*TAD* B3.8:17); *zlwṣ zy gmʾ ḥdt 1* '1 new *zlwṣ* of papyrus-reed' (*TAD* D3.16:11). The word *tmsʾ* in *tmsʾ 1 zy nḥš* '1 bowl of bronze' (*TAD* B3.8:13) is probably of Semitic origin (see n. 146).
149 On this interpretation, see below in this section.
150 Without the addition of *zy slq* in the dowry list in *TAD* B3.3 (l. 6 *pyq 1*).
151 For this interpretation of *nʿṣbn*, see *EPE*, 181, n. 32.
152 The word *gmydh* derives from the Akkadian word *gamidatu* (f.) and must be f. See *AIA*, 51. Porten and Yardeni's translations should thus be corrected to 'new wool' and 'new linen'. Whether this is also the case for items made of *gmʾ* 'reed' cannot be decided on the basis of the evidence at hand.

Second Term Indicates the Material of which the First Term Is Made

t.[.] *zy gm' 1 ḥdt* '1 new [bas]ket of papyrus reed' (*TAD* B3.8:17)
šwy 1 zy gm' '1 papyrus-reed bed' (*TAD* B2.6:15)
zlwṣ zy gm' ḥdt 1 '1 new*zlwṣ* of reed' (*TAD* D3.16:11)
pq 1 zy slq '1 tray of *slq*' (*TAD* B2.6:16)
pyq zy slq 2 '2 trays of *slq*' (*TAD* B3.8:18[153])
n'ṣbn zy 'bn šš 'vessels of alabaster stone' (*TAD* B3.8:18.
... *zy 'bn šš* '... of alabaster stone ...' (*TAD* D3.16:12))

In the last two examples the second term is an indefinite construct noun phrase.

***(d) Egyptian Words in Constructions with* zyl-**

try rbt' zyly 'the large room of mine' (*TAD* B3.10:4; B3.11:6)

(e) Egyptian Words in Attributive Noun Phrases

Egyptian Head Noun; Aramaic Modifying Adjective

try rbt' zyly 'the large room of mine' (*TAD* B3.10:4; B3.11:6)
plg try rbt' 'half the large room' (*TAD* B3.5:3.6)

The Egyptian word *try* has a prefixed Egyptian feminine article and the Egyptian noun underlying the form is feminine. This is also reflected in the feminine emphatic form of the Aramaic adjective (*rbt'*). Also in this case the scribe of the document (Ḥaggai b. Šema'yah) was conscious of the definite article in Egyptian.

Egyptian Head Noun; Egyptian Modifying Adjective

try rsy 'the southern room' (*TAD* B3.11:3; in the variant spelling *dryrsy* in *TAD* B3.10:3)

(f) Egyptian Words in Single Word Noun Phrases

tmw'nty 'the way of the god' (*TAD* B3.10:9)
tqm ḥpnn 5 'castor oil, 5 handfuls' (*TAD* B3.3:6; B3.8:20 f.; D3.16:9)
pyq 1 '1 tray' (*TAD* B3.3:6)

Single word noun phrases are of interest here because the last two examples do not have an article, as is usually the case with nouns followed by a number or a volume (however, see 4.6).

---

153 Cf. the instance of *zy slq* at the end of the same line: *rmn* / *dmn zy slq 1* '1 *d*/*rmn* of *slq*'.

4.5 Egyptian Glosses

A possible Egyptian gloss on an Old Persian loanword (*hnpn*) was discussed in 3.2.11 above, together with two more explicit glosses. In this section, I discuss the Egyptian glosses in more detail. Egyptian glosses occur in two late legal documents written by the scribe Ḥaggai b. Šemaʿyah (*TAD* B3.10, 404 BCE, and *TAD* B3.11, 402 BCE), and in an earlier, related document from the same archive written by an unknown scribe (*TAD* B3.7, 420 BCE). The same property is concerned in all three of these documents, which the Judean Ananyah b. Azaryah had written for his daughter Yehoyišmaʿ.

The possible Egyptian gloss *hw tmwʾnty* on the Old Persian loanword *hnpn* (in *ʾgrʾ zy hnpnʾ zy bnhw mṣryʾ hw tmwʾnty* 'the protection wall which the Egyptians built, that is the way of the god', *TAD* B3.10:8–9) shows the need in this document to provide an Egyptian equivalent to a Persian word. Apparently, the wall in question (built by the Egyptians) was better known to the local population by its Egyptian word. Since the word *hnpn* only appears here and in *TAD* B3.11:4 (*hnpnʾ zy bnw mṣryʾ*), it is quite possible that it was a nonce borrowing (a non-conventionalised borrowing) and not an established borrowing (a regular or conventionalised borrowing) in Official Aramaic, but this is impossible to tell and may well be true for many other loanwords.[154]

An explicit Egyptian gloss is found in two of the three documents mentioned above (*TAD* B3.7 and *TAD* B3.10). The latter of the two is an explicit gloss on the emphatic form of the word *trbṣ* 'courtyard' (of Akkadian origin[155]):

wplg trbṣʾ hw plg tḫyt mṣryt 'and half the courtyard that is half the *ḫyt* (as it is called) in Egyptian' (*TAD* B3.10:4)

Interestingly, following this Egyptian gloss on an Aramaic word, the following two clauses proceed to define the daughter's right to half the courtyard and her right to exit through the courtyard, but this time the Aramaic word glosses the Egyptian word:

ʾp šlyṭʾ ʾnty btḫyt hw trbṣʾ 'moreover, you have right to the *ḫyt*, that is the courtyard' (*TAD* B3.10:13–14)
ʾp šlyṭʾ ʾnt lmnpq btrʿ zy tḫyt hw trbṣʾ 'moreover you have right to go out through (the) gateway of the *ḫyt*, that is the courtyard' (*TAD* B3.10:14–15)

---

154 On the traditional idea of nonce borrowings (and the drawbacks of the term), see Haspelmath, "Lexical Borrowing," 41.
155 On this Assyrian loanword, see *AIA*, 107, with n. 381.

The scribe glossed the word *trbṣ* upon its first mention in the text (l. 4) and this should guide its interpretation. Apparently, after the initial Egyptian gloss on the Aramaic word *trbṣ*, the scribe felt obliged to give the Egyptian word with the Aramaic word (*trbṣ*) as well. The distribution gives the impression that, after the scribe wrote down the gloss and continued with the Egyptian word, he gave the Aramaic equivalent in those cases where the property rights of the new owner were defined. This agrees with the absence of a gloss on the word *trbṣ* in line 7 of this document, where the transferred property is described (*TAD* B3.10:7; also in *TAD* B3.11:3; on this text, see below in this section). Moreover, the word *trbṣ* also appears in *TAD* B3.4:4 (437 BCE), the earliest known document written by Ḥaggai b. Šemaʿyah, where there is no gloss on the word *trbṣ* either; as in *TAD* B3.10, the word appears in the description of the transferred property.

A second explicit gloss is found in *TAD* B3.7:

ʾmrn lh mṣryt 'they call it in Egyptian'[156] (*TAD* B3.7:5, 420 BCE)

Both the glossed word and its Egyptian equivalent are missing. Since the three documents concern the same property and the following (fragmentary) lines of *TAD* B3.7 refer twice to *tḥyt* (*TAD* B 3.7:10.13) we may safely assume that we have another Egyptian gloss on the word *trbṣ* here, just as in *TAD* B3.10.

Not every instance of explicative *hw* indicates a gloss (see also n. 86). Several examples of a wider explicative function can be found in *TAD* B3.10 and *TAD* B3.11.[157]

Apparently at least part of the Judean population of Elephantine had knowledge of the Egyptian language by the last quarter of the 5th century BCE. This certainly must have been the case for the family of Ananyah b. Azaryah, who was married to an Egyptian woman from 449 BCE (*TAD* B3.3). He had the three

---

156 *TAD* B, 77: '(which) they call (in) Egyptian'. After this, the line breaks off.

157 One example is *drgh wtrbṣh hw bbh lmnpq* 'its stairway and its courtyard, that is its gate (through which) to go out' (*TAD* B3.11:3). Here, explicative *hw* does not introduce a gloss; instead, *hw* in *bbh* 'its gate' refers to the whole complex of *drgh wtrbṣh* 'its stairway and its courtyard'. Two other examples include *hw* in *hw try rsy* 'that is the southern room' (*TAD* B3.11:3), which refers to *by tḥty ʾḥd gšwrn wdššn 3* 'a lower house containing beams and 3 doors' (*TAD* B3.11:2–3) and *yhbt^{h} lky dryrsy hw* 'I gave ^{it} to you – that is the southern room' (*TAD* B3.10:3). In the last example, *hw* refers to the supralinear pron. sf. (which refers to *qṣt mn byty* in l. 2). The word order in the latter case requires some explanation. The most plausible interpretation is that the scribe originally wrote 'I gave you the southern room (*dryrsy*)', which he changed into *yhbt^{h}* 'I gave it to you'. It was the scribe's intention to change the following text into *hw dryrsy* (as he also did in the later document *TAD* B3.11:3), but as he had already written *dryrsy*, he wrote *hw* immediately following *dryrsy*. In *hw try rbt' zyly* 'that is my large room' (*TAD* B3.11:6), *hw* is also clearly not a gloss.

related documents *TAD* B3.7 (420 BCE), *TAD* B3.10 (404 BCE) and *TAD* B3.11 (402 BCE) written for his acknowledged daughter Yehoyišmaʿ, who was raised by an Aramaic speaking father (Ananyah b. Azaryah) and an Egyptian speaking mother (Tapmet).

4.6 Egyptian Words in Letters

There are no Egyptian words in the Yedanyah correspondence. This does not come as much of a surprise if one takes into account the subject matter of these letters and the semantic domains covered by the Egyptian words that appear in the Elephantine legal documents.

Apart from several unknown vocabulary items,[158] the private letter *TAD* A3.8 contains the following presumably Egyptian word:

pʿqs 1 '1 leather belt' (< Egyptian *pꜣ ʿgs*; with sg. m. article *pꜣ*[159]) (*TAD* A3.8:9)

The word is found in an enumeration of goods that are to be brought to Memphis. The article *pꜣ* in this word is notable, as one would expect an undetermined noun (see 4.4[c]).

Mention should be made here of the private letters on papyrus found at Hermopolis (addressed to Aramean family members in Syene). These letters are written in a type of Aramaic that differs from the Aramaic written by the Judeans living on Elephantine. In these letters some vocabulary items with an Egyptian origin are found:

tqm 'castor oil' (on the etymology, see above 4.2) (*TAD* A2.2:13; A2.4:12; A2.5:5)
tqbt / *tqbh* 'the vessel' (< Egyptian *tꜣ qb.t*; with sg. f. article[160]) (*TAD* A2.1:5 *btqbh 1*; *TAD* A2.2:11 *tqbt 1 špyrt*)

The two different spellings of the word *tqbt* / *tqbh* present some difficulties. If the proposed etymology is correct, then the *-t* probably represents the original feminine ending of the Egyptian noun, even though an Aramaic ending cannot be excluded. The ending *-h* is *possibly* a variant spelling of the Egyptian ending *-t* (though I do not know of any further examples that support this reading). The

158 Some of which may be of Egyptian origin, such as *wʾsh* in l. 8 and *srḥlṣ* in l. 9.

159 *GEA*, 346, no. 21; CDD ʿ (03.1), 149, s. v. ʿgs 'a type of cloth or belt' (m.) (with a question mark); a different reading and interpretation is offered in *DNWSI*, 929, s. v. pʿps.

160 *GEA*, 347, no. 43; *DNWSI*, 1227: 'substantive of unknown meaning'; *DAE*, 155 (n. e); CDD Q (04.1), 19, s. v. qb(ꜣ).t 'jug, pitcher' (f.); CDD Q (04.1), 19 also lists qb(ꜣ).t 'large cloth' (two different lexemes).

ending *-t* / *-h* may also reflect an Aramaic singular feminine absolute ending.[161] Aramaic inflectional endings attached to Egyptian words are unprecedented, not only in the texts from Elephantine discussed above (with the only exception of the measure *qb*) but also in the Aršama letter found at Elephantine (*TAD* A6.2). Elsewhere the attachment of Aramaic inflectional endings to Egyptian words appears as a rare phenomenon in accounts (*ntr* in the Customs Account [*TAD* C3.7]; the measures *qlby* and *qlwl* in account *TAD* C3.12, both of unknown origin). See n. 163 and n. 175.

Further to this, the prefixed Egyptian feminine article *tꜣ-* in the word *tqbh* / *tqbt* also stands out, as the word is followed in both cases by a number ('one'). The parallel in letter *TAD* A3.8:9 (*pʿqs* 1) shows that this happens now and then in other texts as well. A further example of this possibly appears in the Aršama letter from Elephantine: *pḥṭmwny lpʿrʿr ḥd* 'one mooring post for the prow' (*TAD* A6.2:12).[162] It is notable that, in all of the instances where this phenomenon is found, the noun is followed by the number 'one' (either written out or written with a stroke).

The measure of capacity *qb* occurs several times in letter ostraca from Elephantine (*qb* in *TAD* D7.6:7; D7.43:5.8; D7.45:8; D7.49:3; *qbʾ* in *TAD* D7.46:2 and *qbn* in *TAD* D7.7:2). According to Noonan and others the word is of Egyptian origin but this is not undisputed (see n. 132). The discussion is further complicated by the fact that in the Elephantine Aramaic texts under discussion the word *qb* would be the only Egyptian word with Aramaic inflectional endings:[163]

---

161 The interpretation is further problematised by the ending *-t* of *špyrt* (and other Aramaic forms). See Folmer, *Aramaic Language*, 252–55.

162 On the assumed etymology of the counted noun *pḥṭmwny* (with the Egyptian sg. m. article *pꜣ*), see *EPE*, 120, n. 45; *DAE*, 290 n. d; see also *GEA*, 346, no. 18. *TAD* A, 99 translates 'mooring post for prow ... 1', but if *p* in *lpʿrʿr* represents the Egyptian sg. m. article, this is less accurate. In all other instances in this text, counted nouns are not combined with an Egyptian article. There is evidence for the following nouns with Egyptian etymologies: *tp* (*EPE*, 119, n. 30), *sʿbl* (*EPE*, 119, n. 37; *GEA*, 346, no. 17), *ḥl* (*EPE*, 120, n. 43; *GEA*, 345, no. 8), *ʾpsy* (*EPE*, 120, n. 47; *GEA*, 345, no. 1), *tmys* (*EPE*, 120, n. 50; *GEA*, 347, no. 40) where the numbers/volumes that are given are higher than one.

163 Two Egyptian words that indicate measures for liquids are found in an account of wine disbursements of unknown origin, probably not from Elephanine (*TAD* C3.12; dated to 420 or 411 BCE): *qlby* and *qlwl*. Both terms are combined with the Aramaic plural ending *-n* (the text has instances of *qlby 1*, *qlbyn 2*, *qlwl 1*, and *qlwln 2*). On *qlby*, see *DNWSI*, 1011, s. v. qlby; *DAE*, 99, n. a; CDD Q (04.1), 75–76, s. v. qlby 'a jar for drinking wine or beer; a liquid measure the size of such a jar'; on the possibly related word *qlwl*, see *DAE*, 99, n. b; see also CDD K (01.1), 31, s. v. krl. Most of the persons that receive a quantity of wine have Egyptian names, but there is also one person with a Persian name (l. 24), and one person with an Akkadian name (l. 31; the same name is also found in 1Chron 4:2 [Ahumai]; cf. *HALOT*, vol. 1, 31). On *ntr* in the Customs Account (*TAD* C3.7; not from Elephantine), see n. 175.

TAD D7.7:2 *mlḥ qbn 2* 'salt, 2 *qabs*'
TAD D7.46:2 *bqbʾ rbʾ*['in the big *qab*'

The first example is clear but in the second example the lacuna between *kʿn hwšr* in line 1 and *bqbʾ rbʾ* at the beginning of line 2 prevents an unambiguous interpretation of the latter.

According to Noonan the word was borrowed into Northwest Semitic before ca. 700 BCE (cf. also 2Kgs 6:25). It is possible that, unlike the examples of code-switching, the word *qb* is an established borrowing in Persian Period Aramaic.

There are no further certain instances of Egyptian words in private letters on papyrus and in the collection of Aramaic letter ostraca in *TAD* D7.1–54 from Elephantine.[164]

5 Conclusions

The Elephantine legal documents and official and private letters (especially those on papyrus and a limited number on potsherds [*TAD* D7.1–54]) offer a unique window onto language contact in 5th-century BCE Egypt. In the preceding, I investigated words of Persian and Egyptian origin in those documents written by Judeans who lived on Elephantine or who were writing from other places in Egypt to family members in Elephantine.

Persian Loanwords

The distribution, use, and integration of Old Persian loanwords in Aramaic texts written by Elephantine Judeans are more or less the same for legal documents (mostly dated) as they are for letters (especially official letters). As far as the morphological and morphosyntactic integration of these loanwords is concerned, the evidence largely concurs with the evidence in the Official Aršama and Akhvamazda correspondences.[165]

164 The index to the edition of the Elephantine ostraca from the Clermont-Ganneau collection published by Lozachmeur, *La collection Clermont-Ganneau*, vol. 1 lists several Egyptian words: *gmʾ*, *dyw*, *šnṭʾ*, *tqm* (unfortunately, with the exception of *šnṭʾ*, these are not labelled as such). As mentioned above (n. 124), the reading and context of most of these words is uncertain (and Lozachmeur's philological commentary is limited to a minimum). For this reason, these words are not discussed in this contribution.

165 Discussed in Folmer, "Characteristics," 327–40, 349–50.

In dated legal documents from the first half of the 5th century BCE, the only Old Persian loanwords are words that indicate measures of weight and capacity (*krš* 'karsh', *ʾrdb* 'ardab', and the abbreviation *g* for *gryw* or *gryb*). Regardless of the background of the scribe, most loanwords in legal documents appear in the second half of the 5th century BCE and increase in number up to a total of six loanwords in some legal documents at the end of the 5th century BCE. It may be of interest to note that the first judge known by name from the Elephantine documents has a Persian name (*TAD* B2.2:6 *dmyt wknwth dynyʾ* 'Damidata and his colleagues the judges'). In fact, with only one exception, all of the Elephantine judges referred to by name have Persian names.[166] These judges were responsible for the settlement of disputes in the local court, and settled disputes for Egyptians and foreigners alike.[167] The adoption in Aramaic of Persian legal terms like *ʾzt*, *nprt*, *ʾbygrn*, *hngyt*, *hnbg*, and *ʾdrng* can be understood against the background of Persian interference with local jurisprudence. These words probably filled a void in the Aramaic lexicon, *ʾdrng* excepted (see 3.2.4).

Nouns and adjectives are the most commonly borrowed words, though there is perhaps some evidence for the borrowing of Old Persian adverbs (see the discussions in 3.2.4, 3.3.3 [*hmwnyt*], and 3.3.4 [*ʾzd*]; cf. also the discussions on *hndyz* in 3.3.7 [b] and *ʾpm* in 3.2.1). Other word classes are not represented in these documents (although there is some evidence for the borrowing of so-called 'light verbs' in the Yedanyah correspondence; see n. 21). These loanwords belong primarily to the administrative domain, and legal terms are particularly well represented, though there are also several words that belong to the military sub-domain. A large number of loanwords denote various officials in a clear reflection of the bureaucratic character of the Persian administration. Only occasionally do Old Persian loanwords fall into other semantic domains (*hnpn* and *ywdn* refer to constructions, *ʾšrn* to furnishing or equipment, and *ʾtrwdn* to the religious domain).

There is evidence only for Aramaic masculine inflection on Old Persian loanwords. There is evidence for the following endings: the singular masculine emphatic state -*ʾ*, the plural masculine absolute state -*n*, and the plural masculine emphatic state -*yʾ*. The Aramaic gentilic ending -*n* (pl. m. absolute state) was even added to the placename *swn* in cases where it was expanded with the Persian affix -*k*- (*swnkn*, *swnknn*; see 3.3.5 [a]).

No feminine inflection on Old Persian loanwords is attested (3.2.8 [b]; 3.3.5 [b]). There is some evidence for the absence of feminine inflection on Old Persian

166 Schütze, "Local Administration," 498.

167 Schütze, "Local Administration," 497–98; Botta, *Aramaic and Egyptian Legal Traditions*, 60–61.

loanwords in appositions where an emphatic form is usual (*prypt* in *TAD* B3.12:11). The word *ʾzt* in *TAD* B3.6:4 also lacks feminine inflection (see 3.2.8 [b]). Feminine inflection on Old Persian loanwords was also avoided in one of the Yedanyah letters (*ʾtrwdn ḥdh* in *TAD* A4.5:17; see 3.3.7 [a]).

Old Persian loanwords could be combined with a poss. pron. sf. The sole piece of evidence for this comes from a legal document (*ʾdrngy* in *TAD* B3.13:9 [twice]).

Old Persian loanwords were used in all types of noun phrases. There is evidence for Old Persian loanwords in construct noun phrases (both in the first and in the second term), *zy* phrases (both indicating ownership and the material of which an object is made), *zyl-* phrases, appositions, and attributive noun phrases (though the only evidence for an attributive noun phrase is from a letter [*TAD* A4.5]).

There is no evidence for the attachment of a proleptic pron. sf. to Old Persian loanwords in the first term of a *zy* phrase, though there are several examples of this in the Aršama correspondence.[168]

There is also no evidence for the use of an Old Persian loanword in the plural construct form in legal documents and letters written by the Elephantine Judeans. This agrees with the evidence from both the official Aršama and the official Akhvamazda correspondences, where the evidence points to avoidance of the plural construct form. In fact, there may have been a constraint on the use of the plural construct ending *-y* in combination with Old Persian loanwords.[169] The singular masculine noun, on the other hand, does occur in the first term of a construct noun phrase, in the Elephantine documents as well.

Despite the successful adaptation of Old Persian loanwords to the Aramaic system of declension of nouns and the generally correct use of the loanwords in noun phrases, the Judean scribes sometimes had difficulties with Old Persian loanwords. One of the legal documents contains a probable case of reanalysis (*ʾšrn* in *TAD* B3.4:23; see 3.2.10). The form was misinterpreted by its scribe (Ḥaggai b. Šemaʿyah) as a plural form. This may imply that the scribe was working from a model or another type of document in which the word appeared. It is also possible that *ʾzt* (*TAD* B3.6:4) and *prypt* (*TAD* B3.12:11) should be interpreted in this way (see 3.2.8 [b]). Some unexpected determinations of Old Persian loanwords are found (*whnbgʾ zy l*[*y* in *TAD* B5.5:9; see 3.2.9 [c]), and determination is now and then omitted in appositions (see 3.2.9 [d]). It is noteworthy that Rauxšana b. Nergalušezib, a scribe with a Persian given name, knew how to handle Old Persian loanwords in appositions (*TAD* B3.9:2 PN *hptḥptʾ*), as did the Persian witness-

168 See Folmer, "Characteristics," 336.
169 See Folmer, "Characteristics," 335, 337, 350.

es who wrote their name and function in another document (*TAD* B3.5:24 PN *mgšy*ʾ 2x), whereas the scribe of that document (Maʿuziyah b. Natan) did not correctly handle an Old Persian loanword in apposition in one of his other documents (*TAD* B2.9:4–5 PN *prtrk*). In another document by Ḥaggai b. Šemaʿyah, an Old Persian loanword in apposition lacks the expected emphatic state ending (*prypt* in *nšn tpmt ʾntth prypt zy mšlm br zkr* [*TAD* B3.12:11]). By contrast, the scribe of official letter *TAD* A4.8 (Yedanyah correspondence) had no problems handling an Old Persian loanword in apposition (PN *prtrkʾ* in l. 4; see 3.3.6 [d]).

In one of the letters belonging to the Yedanyah correspondence (*TAD* A4.2), its scribe erred several times with the preposition *l*. This preposition is required before a noun or name (in this case, a Persian loanword) that indicates the person to whom one may lodge a complaint (*qbl l*). In short, it is clear that Old Persian loanwords now and then caused the Judean scribes difficulties.

An Egyptian gloss (*hw tmwʾnty*) on an Old Persian loanword (*hnpnʾ* in *ʾgrʾ zy hnpnʾ*) in a document from the end of the 5th century BCE (*TAD* B3.10:9) is of special interest (see 3.2.11). It shows that the construction that is referred to (*hnpn*) was better known to the local population of the time by its Egyptian equivalent (and not an Aramaic equivalent). The Aramaic word *ʿm* is possibly used in another gloss on an Old Persian loanword, namely *hmwnyt* (*TAD* A4.5:4; A4.7:5; see 3.3.3). Whether this interpretation is correct remains uncertain, as this supposed gloss is not preceded by *hw*, as is the case in other glosses.

In official letters written by Judean scribes, Old Persian loanwords are not uncommon. This lines up with the general impression that, in these letters, an effort was made to copy the syntax, style, spelling, and vocabulary of the official letters issued by the Achaemenid chancelleries. By contrast, Old Persian loanwords are almost absent from the private letters that were found at Elephantine, both in letters on papyrus and in letter ostraca (*TAD* D7.1–54) (see 3.3.9). The same is true of the Hermopolis letters (*TAD* A2.1–2.7) from the end of the 6th century, which were written by persons from an unknown place in Egypt (possibly Memphis) to their Aramean family members in Syene and Ofi (they include many Aramean personal and divine names). Though the time gap between the Elephantine letters (written by Judeans) and the Hermopolis letters (written by Arameans) is considerable, both corpora suggest that Old Persian lexical influence on the spoken language of the Judeans and the Arameans was minimal (and perhaps even completely absent in the Hermopolis letters). It is admittedly hard to gauge the extent to which the written language of these texts mirrors the spoken language of the people who wrote them, but given the evidence from the Elephantine letter ostraca in particular (*TAD* D7.1–54, which in all likelihood reflect the spoken language more closely than any other textual genre), one may assume that the variety of Aramaic spoken by the Elephantine Judeans was not deeply influenced by Old Persian vocabulary.

Egyptian Code-switching

Only some legal documents from Elephantine contain Egyptian lexical items (*TAD* B2.6, 458 or 445 BCE; *TAD* B3.3, 449 BCE; *TAD* B3.4, 437 BCE; *TAD* B3.5, 434 BCE; *TAD* B3.7, 420 BCE; *TAD* B3.8, 420 BCE; *TAD* B3.10, 404 BCE; *TAD* B3.11, 402 BCE; *TAD* B3.12, 402 BCE; *TAD* D3.16, middle of the 5th century BCE [fragmentarily preserved dowry list]). The earliest Egyptian words in legal documents from Elephantine appear in the middle of the 5th century BCE in the dowry lists included in documents of wifehood, either 458 BCE (*TAD* B2.6) or 449 BCE (*TAD* B3.3), depending on the date of *TAD* B2.6 (458 or 445 BCE). It is remarkable that all of these documents were written by scribes with Judean names: Natan b. Ananyah (*TAD* B2.6; B3.3), Maʿuziyah b. Natan (*TAD* B3.5; B3.8), Ḥaggai b. Šemaʿyah (*TAD* B3.4; B3.10; B3.11; B3.12). (Only the names of the scribes who wrote *TAD* B3.7 and *TAD* D3.16 are unknown.) This can be explained in part by the fact that only Judean scribes appear to have written documents of wifehood for Judeans.

The amount of Egyptian lexical items in letters is surprisingly low: they are totally absent from the official Yedanyah letters and there are only a few examples in private letters on papyrus and ostraca letters (see below).

The lexical domains covered by the Egyptian words in the Elephantine legal documents predominantly embrace flora, clothing, household utensils, products, materials, and religious and domestic constructions. A considerable number of the loanwords are found in the dowry lists included in documents of wifehood (*TAD* B2.6, 458 or 445 BCE; *TAD* B3.3, 449 BCE; *TAD* B3.8, 420 BCE; *TAD* D3.16, middle of the 5th century). There is no (certain) administrative terminology of Egyptian origin within the documents studied, which is remarkable when one considers that Aramaic legal formulae were probably heavily influenced by the legal formulae in Demotic documents.[170] Apparently, Aramaic legal language was open to influence from Demotic formulae, while at the same time resisting the inclusion of legal terms (see above on Old Persian legal terms). The only Egyptian administrative term that I know of is found in the Customs Account (*TAD* C3.7) from ca. 470 BCE; it concerns a local tax, *tšy* 'the customs duty'.[171] This text was written in a local Egyptian bureau and is devoid of Persian loanwords (with the

170 See Schütze, "Local Administration," 499–500.
171 With sg. f. article *tꜣ* (< Egyptian *tꜣ-šꜣy.t*). See *GEA*, 347, no. 46; Erman and Grapow, *Ägyptisches Handwörterbuch*, 187, s. v. *šꜣy.t* 'Abgabe, Steuer'; Faulkner, *A Concise Dictionary of Middle Egyptian*, 261, s. v. *šꜣyt* 'dues, taxes'; Lesko and Switalski Lesko, *A Dictionary of Late Egyptian*, vol. 3, s. v. *šꜣyt* 'taxes, dues'.

exception of *krš* and the abbreviation *g*). The Egyptian word is embedded in a recurring Aramaic taxation formula that is difficult to understand.[172]

The Egyptian words that were included are typically culture words that will to a large extent have filled lexical gaps in Aramaic: words for realia (certain types of clothing, plants, vessels, oils, stones, and specific constructions, both religious and domestic) that were new to the Judeans who had settled in Egypt, far from the homeland of their ancestors. It is illuminating to find that, in other corpora from the Persian Period (undiscussed in the present contribution), one sees extensive shipping and shipbuilding terminology derived from Egyptian (in *TAD* C3.7, the Customs Account [not from Elephantine], and in *TAD* A6.2, the Aršama letter that was sent to Elephantine). The remarkably low number of Egyptian words in private letters may be purely accidental and probably has to do with the subject matter of these letters.[173] In letters where there is a demand for certain special articles, one can expect Egyptian words (private letter *TAD* A3.8; see also the Hermopolis papyri, addressed to members of the Aramean community in Syene). This is true for letters on papyrus as well as for letter ostraca.

Egyptian words in Elephantine Aramaic are always nouns and adjectives. In general, they were not adapted to the Aramaic inflection of nouns, which is also true of other texts that are rich in Egyptian terminology, more specifically the Customs Account (*TAD* C3.7) and the Aršama letter found at Elephantine (*TAD* A6.2). Instead, some Egyptian words were included in Aramaic texts with their Egyptian nominal inflection (although the singular feminine ending in particular is not always recognizable as such, since Egyptian lost many of its endings in the course of its history,[174] for instance, in the adjective *rsy* 'southern'). Apart from that, many Egyptian loanwords were written with the Egyptian article: the singular feminine definite article *tꜣ* is particularly well represented. The singular masculine definite article *pꜣ* is also found, but there are no attestations of the Egyptian plural definite article *n-* in legal documents and letters; neither is there evidence for this in other Aramaic texts from the Persian Period.

A possible exception to the aforementioned behaviour of Egyptian words in Elephantine Aramaic is the word *qb* (see 4.2 [with n. 132] and 4.6]). This word

---

172 See Folmer, "Taxation of Ships," 268. At that time, I assumed that the Egyptian term was an apposition to the preceding *ksp*ʾ and headed a double construct noun phrase. At present, I would only suggest an apposition to the word *kspʾ*: *kspʾ tšy dmy ntrʾ zy hnpqw lymʾ bh* / *bhm ksp kršn X* 'the silver, the tax, (on) the value of the natron that they brought out to the sea in it/them, is X karsh in silver' (see, e.g., *TAD* C3.7 Kv iii). The interpretation of the line remains problematic.

173 One should also keep in mind that the corpus of ostraca in *TAD* D7 is relatively small.

174 See Müller, "Egyptian," 116.

occurs with Aramaic inflection in several letter ostraca. The word should perhaps be regarded as an established loanword.[175]

Egyptian words occur in the same types of noun phrases as Old Persian loanwords: construct noun phrases, *zy* phrases, phrases with *zyl-*, attributive phrases, and single word noun phrases (see 4.4).

It is noteworthy that, in most of the instances where the emphatic state ending is missing (but expected according the rules of Aramaic syntax), the Egyptian word is imported with its prefixed article. This observation applies to words with both the masculine and the feminine article. It is only by chance that the feminine article *tꜣ* is dominant.

In contrast to Old Persian loanwords, Egyptian words are never combined with a poss. pron. sf. in the surviving materials. This is not surprising, as other Aramaic inflectional endings were also avoided. Instead of a noun with a possessive pron. sf., the analytical construction with *zyl-* was used in combination Egyptian words (see 4.4 [d] above). There is also no evidence for an Egyptian word in the first term of a construct noun phrase; *zy* phrases were used instead (*tmy*[*ʾ*] *zy ḥnwm ʾlh*ʾ).[176] This may point to a constraint on the use of an Egyptian noun in the first term of a construct noun phrase, as with Persian loanwords in the plural (see above and 3.2.8 [a]). In addition, we find attributive phrases in which an Aramaic adjective agrees with a preceding Egyptian word (*rbtʾ* in *try rbtʾ zyly* 'the large room of mine' *TAD* B3.10:4, and *plg try rbtʾ* 'half the large room' *TAD* B3.5:3.6).

As with Old Persian, mistakes were sometimes made in noun phrases with Egyptian words. These omissions involve Egyptian as well as Aramaic words. In one *zy* phrase, the Aramaic first term does not have the emphatic state (*btrʿ zy tḥyt* in *TAD* B3.10:15; see 4.4 [b]), and in one construct noun phrase the Egyptian word does not have an Egyptian definite article (*byt qnḥnty* in *TAD* B3.11; see 4.4 [a]). Both documents were written by the same scribe (Ḥaggai b. Šemaʿyah).

Overall, the evidence shows that the Judean scribes who wrote the documents under discussion were able to analyse the Egyptian words that they used. This probably indicates an intimate familiarity on the part of these Judeans with the Egyptian language. It is often difficult to decide whether words that are not integrated into the recipient language are lexical borrowings or examples of code-switching among bilingual individuals. In our case, we are probably dealing with

175 Also the words *qlby* and *qlwl* in *TAD* C3.12 (of unknown origin) are an exception (see above n. 163). It is of interest that both *qlby* and *qlwl* are words that indicate measures. The word *ntr* 'natron' in the Customs Account (*TAD* C3.7; not from Elephantine) is another exception. It occurs several times in the emphatic state form in the taxation formula quoted in n. 172 above.

176 Additional evidence for this comes from two funerary stelae (see n. 147).

code-switching. Apart from the fact that Egyptian words were not integrated into the Aramaic morphological system, there are several additional arguments in support of this. First, definite articles that are copied from one language to another are usually not productive but they are in Elephantine Aramaic.[177] Second, the documents include several Egyptian glosses, one on a Persian word and several glosses on Aramaic words. These glosses are found in documents from 420 BCE onwards, while most of them appear in two late documents by the scribe Ḥaggai b. Šemaʿyah (*TAD* B3.10 [404 BCE] and *TAD* B3.11 [402 BCE]). Two of these glosses are explicit:]*ʾmrn lh mṣryt* 'they call it in Egyptian'[178] (*TAD* B3.5:5, 420 BCE) and *hw plg tḫyt mṣryt* 'that is half the ẖyt (as it is called) in Egyptian' (*TAD* B3.10:4).[179]

On the basis of these arguments, one can conclude that Egyptian was a spoken language for (at least some) Judeans at Elephantine from 420 BCE onwards. This does not come as a surprise, as many Judeans were connected with Egyptians through marriage. This also explains why almost all of the Egyptian words in legal documents appear in dowry lists and in documents that belong to the Ananyah archive (see 4.1 and 4.2). Ananyah was a temple servant who married an Egyptian woman named Tapamet in 449 BCE. His archive contains several documents that include Egyptian words: two documents of wifehood (Tapamet's document of wifehood [*TAD* B3.3] and her daughter Yehoyišmaʿ's document of wifehood [*TAD* B3.8]) and several documents that concern the transfer of property from Ananyah to Tapamet or his acknowledged daughter Yehoyišmaʿ (*TAD* B3.5; B3.7; B3.10; B3.11). These documents are particularly rich in Egyptian words.

177 See Matras, *Language Contact*, 174. Matras also notes that articles that are borrowed with nouns are frequently 'doubled' by a native article (in the case of Aramaic, the emphatic state morpheme). I have argued above that the Egyptian article is productive in the Aramaic texts reviewed here.

178 It is also possible to translate this phrase with 'as *we* call it in Egyptian'. The word that precedes the active participle *ʾmrn* at the end of the previous line is missing and, instead of *hmw* 'they', it is equally possible to restore *ʾnḥn* 'we' at this point.

179 Further to this, the variant spelling *dryrsy* (for *try rsy*) in *TAD* B3.10:3 may in fact be a pronunciation spelling. This requires further investigation by specialists.

Tab. 1: Old Persian Loanwords in Legal Documents from Elephantine.

Col. 1: Document and date (in chronological order)	**Col. 2: Scribal name (included in scribal formula[180])**	**Col. 3: Emic label**	**Col. 4: Persian loanwords[181]**	**Col. 5: Context**	**Col. 6: Place where document was written 1. *ʾdyn b*LN 'then in LN' 2. scribal formula**
TAD B5.1 (C 1) 495 BCE	scribe unknown (document does not include the scribal formula)	endorsement missing[182]	*krš* 'karsh'	*yntn lky ksp **kršn** 5* (ll. 6–7) (fine in penalty clause)	1. – 2. scribal formula not included in document (unique)

180 Scribal formula: *ktb* PN *b.* PN *sprʾ znh b*LN *byrtʾ* 'PN son of PN wrote this document in LN the fortress' (with variations).
181 Several instances of *krš* are found in fragmentary documents: *TAD* B4.5:5.6 (obligation), *TAD* B5.3:1 (conveyance), *TAD* B5.4:6 (gift of house), and *TAD* B6.1:5.6 (document of wifehood). The word *krš* does not appear in documents which do not define a fine in silver: *TAD* B4.2 (loan of silver, written by Gemaryah b. Aḥio, 487 BCE); *TAD* B3.1 (loan of silver, written by Natan b. Anani, 456 BCE); *TAD* B7.1 (obligation to take a judicial oath, 413 BCE); *TAD* B7.3 (oath). The word *krš* does also not appear in several documents that are too fragmentary: *TAD* B4.3 in the table above (obligation); *TAD* B7.2 (obligation to make judicial declaration; 401 BCE); *TAD* B5.2, B6.2, B6.3 and B6.4 (documents of wifehood). In several documents the amount due is too small to be expressed in *krš* (e.g. in *TAD* B4.6 [obligation]). No other Persian loanwords are found in the aforementioned documents.
182 *TAD* B, 119: "exchange of inherited shares."

TAD B4.3 (C 3) 483 BCE (fragmentary)	Hošeaʿ (b. Hodavyah)[183]	endorsement missing[184]	*ʾrdb* ‘ardab’	*ṭlpḥn* ***ʾrdbn*** *20*[(l. 5; measure of capacity in receipt of grain) *ṭlpḥn* ***ʾrdb*** *1* (l. 8; the same)	1. lacuna 2. –
TAD B4.4 (C 2) 483 BCE (copy of B4.3)	Hošeaʿ (b. Hodavyah)[185]	label not included in endorsement[186]	*g*[187] ‘griv’ *ʾrdb* ‘ardab’ *krš* ‘karsh’	***g*** *2* (l. 7; measure of capacity in a receipt of grain) ***ʾrdbn*** *2* (l. 7; the same) *ʾnḥnh nḥwb lk ksp* ***kršn*** *100* (l. 15; fine penalty clause)	1. lacuna 2. –
TAD B2.1 (C 5) 471 BCE	Pelaṭyah b. Aḥio	*spr ʾgrʾ zy bnh* ‘document of the wall which is built’[188]	*krš* ‘karsh’	*ʾntn lk ksp* ***kršn*** *5 bʾbny mlkʾ ksp ṣryp* (l. 7) (fine in penalty clause)	1. – 2. –
TAD B2.2 (C 6) 464 BCE	Itu b. Abah	*spr mrḥq*[189]	*krš* ‘karsh’	*yntn lk ksp* ***kršn*** *20 hw ʿšrn bʾbny mlkʾ ksp r 2 lʿšrtʾ* (l. 14–15; fine in penalty clause)	1. – 2. *ktb … bswn byrtʾ*

183 Hošeaʿ is both the scribe and one of the parties of the agreement. The scribal line is different from the standard scribal formula (see n. 180): *ktb hwšʿ bkpy n*[*pšh* ‘Hošeaʿ wrote with [his] o[wn] hands[…’ (l. 21). The paternal name is known from the line in which the parties of the legal transaction are identified (ll. 1–2).

184 *TAD* B, 108: “Obligation to Deliver Grain (Fragmentary).”

185 See also n. 183. The scribal line differs from the standard scribal formula (see n. 180): *ktb hwšʿ ʿl pm ʾḥyʾb* ‘Hošeaʿ wrote upon the instruction of Aḥiʾab’ (l. 18). The paternal name is known from the line in which the parties of the legal transaction are identified (ll. 1–2).

186 *TAD* B, 111: “Obligation to Deliver Grain (Fragmentary)” (second copy). The endorsement reads *ktb hwšʿ wʾḥ*[*y*ʾ]*b lʾsp*[*mt* ‘Hošeaʿ and Aḥ[iʾa]b wrote for Espe[met’ (l. 22).

187 Abbreviation for *gryb* or *gryw*.

188 *TAD* B, 18: “Grant of a Built Wall.”

189 *TAD* B, 21: “Withdrawal from Land.”

Tab. 1 (continued)

Col. 1: Document and date (in chronological order)	**Col. 2: Scribal name (included in scribal formula[180])**	**Col. 3: Emic label**	**Col. 4: Persian loanwords[181]**	**Col. 5: Context**	**Col. 6: Place where document was written 1. *ʾdyn b*LN 'then in LN' 2. scribal formula**
TAD B2.3 (C 8) 460/459 BCE	Attaršuri b. Nabuzeribni	*spr by*	*krš* 'karsh'	*yntn lky … ksp* ***kršn*** *10 hw ʿšrh bʾbny mlkʾ ksp r 2 lʿšrtʾ* (ll. 13–14; fine in penalty clause) *ʾnh ʾntn lky ksp* ***kršn*** *10 bʾbny mlkʾ ksp r 2 lʿšrtʾ* (l. 21; fine in penalty clause)	1. – 2. *ktb … bswn byrtʾ*
TAD B2.4 (C 9) 460/459 BCE	Attaršuri b. Nabuzeribni	endorsement missing[190]	*krš* 'karsh'	*ʾnh ʾntn lk ksp* ***kršn*** *10 bʾbny mlkʾ ksp r 2 lʿšrtʾ* (ll. 14–15; fine in penalty clause)	1. – 2. *ktb … bswn*
TAD B3.2 (K 1) 451 BCE	Bunni b. Mannuki	endorsement missing[191]	*krš* 'karsh' *hyrʾ* (?)	*bdmy* ***hyrʾ*** *zylk* (l. 3; value of the object of complaint) *bšm* ***hyrʾ*** *znh* (ll. 6.9; the object of complaint in penalty clause [l. 6] and in defension clause [l. 9]) *ʾntn lk ksp* ***kršn*** *5* (l. 8; fine in penalty clause)	

190 Initial *s* excepted (first letter of *spr*).
191 *TAD* B, 59: "Withdrawal from *hyrʾ*."

TAD B2.6 (C 15) 458 or 445 BCE	Natan b. Ananyah	endorsement missing[192]	*krš* ‘karsh’	***krš*** *1 … bʾbny mlkʾ* (ll. 6–7; cash money brought in by the bride [part of the dowry]) *ksp* ***kršn*** *2 … bʾbny mlkʾ* (ll. 8–9; value of dowry item) *ksp* ***kršn*** *6 … ksp r 2 lšrtʾ bʾbny mlkʾ* (l. 14; value of dowry) *ʾntn l*PN *ksp* ***kršn*** *20 bʾbny mlkʾ* (ll. 34.36; fine in penalty clause)	1. – (lacuna, but no space for LN) 2. – (lacuna, but no space for LN)
TAD B2.7 (C 13) 446 BCE	Natan b. Ananyah	*spr by*[193]	*hndz* ‘garrisoned’ *krš* ‘karsh’	*kzy* ***hndz*** *hwyt bbyrt* (l. 4; military term describing previous circumstances of one of the parties) *yntn lky ksp* ***kršn*** *10* (l. 11; fine in penalty clause)	1. – 2. –
TAD B2.8 (= C 14) 440 BCE	Peṭeese b. Nabunatan	*spr mrḥq*[194]	*nprt* (legal term) *krš* ‘karsh’	*ʿl dynʾ zy ʿbdn bswn* ***nprt*** *ʿl ksp wʿbwr wlbwš wnḥš wprzl* (l. 3; legal term specifying kind of lawsuit [?]) *ʾnh … ʾntn l*PN *ksp* ***kršn*** *5 bʾbny mlkʾ* (ll. 9–10; fine in penalty clause)	1. – 2. *ktb … bswn*

192 *TAD* B, 33: “Document of Wifehood.”
193 *TAD* B, 37: “Grant of House to Daughter.”
194 *TAD* B, 39: “Withdrawal from Goods.”

Tab. 1 (continued)

Col. 1: Document and date (in chronological order)	**Col. 2: Scribal name (included in scribal formula[180])**	**Col. 3: Emic label**	**Col. 4: Persian loanwords[181]**	**Col. 5: Context**	**Col. 6: Place where document was written 1. *ʾdyn b*LN 'then in LN' 2. scribal formula**
TAD B3.3 (K 2) 434 BCE	Natan b. Ananyah	*spr ʾ[ntw]*	*krš* 'karsh'	*hnʿlt tmt bydh lʿnny ksp* ***krš*** *1 šqln 5* (l. 16; amount of dowry addition)	1. – 2. –
TAD B3.4 (K 3) 437 BCE	Ḥaggai b. Šemaʿyah[195]	*spr by*[196]	*ʾšrn* 'equipment' *krš* 'karsh'	*wkl* ***ʾšrn*** *zy yhkn ʿl bytʾ zk* (l. 23; equipment added to transferred property) *wyhbt ln dmwhy* ***krš*** *1 šqln 5 … bʾ bny mlkʾ ksp zwz l****krš*** *1* (ll. 5–6; price of transferred property) *ʾnḥn nntn lk ksp* ***kršn*** *20 ksp zwz lʿšrtʾ* (ll. 15–16; fine in penalty clause 1) *ytntn lk* ***kršn*** *20 ksp zwz l10* (l. 18; fine in penalty clause 2)	1. – 2. –

195 Scribal formula supralinearly added.
196 *TAD* B, 67: "Sale of Abandoned Property."

TAD B3.5 (K 4) 434 BCE	Maʿuziyah b. Natan	*spr by*[197]	*mgš* 'magian' *krš* 'karsh'	PN ***mgšy'*** (2x in l. 24; PN + title in list of witnesses) *'nh 'ḥwb w'ntn lky ksp* ***kršn*** *5 hw ḥmšh b'bny mlk' ksp r 2* ***lkrš*** *1* (ll. 14–15; fine in penalty clause 1) *yntn lhm ksp* ***kršn*** *10 b'bny mlk' ksp r 2* ***lkrš*** *1* (ll. 21–22; fine in penalty clause 2)	1. – 2. –
TAD B3.6 (K 5) 427 BCE	Ḥaggai b. Šemaʿyah	[*spr*] *mrḥq*[198]	*'zt* 'free' *hngyt* 'partner in chattel' *hnbg* 'partner in realty' *'bgrn* 'fine' *krš* 'karsh'	*'nh 'štt lky bḥyy'* ***'zt*** (ll. 3–4; legal term in manumission clause) ***hngyt whnbg*** (l. 5; claimants in affirmation of non-reenslavement) *yntn lk* ***'bgrn*** *ksp* ***kršn*** *50 b'bny mlk'* (l. 8; fine in penalty clause 1) *'nḥn nḥwb lk … ksp* ***kršn*** *50 b'bny mlk' ksp ṣryp* (ll. 14–15; fine in penalty clause 2)	1. – (*'dn*) 2. *ktb … byb*
TAD B3.7 (K 6) 420 BCE	Unknown	endorsement missing[199]	*'bygrn* 'fine' *krš* 'karsh'	[*yntn l*PN…] … ***'bygrn*** *ksp* ***kršn*** *10*[… (ll. 16–17; fine in penalty clause)	1. *'dyn* [*byb by*]*rt'* (lacuna) 2. lacuna

197 *TAD* B, 71: "Bequest of Apartment to Wife."
198 *TAD* B, 73: "Testamentary Manumission."
199 *TAD* B, 77: "A Life Estate of Usufruct."

Tab. 1 (continued)

Col. 1: **Document and date (in chronological order)**	**Col. 2:** **Scribal name (included in scribal formula[180])**	**Col. 3:** **Emic label**	**Col. 4:** **Persian loanwords[181]**	**Col. 5:** **Context**	**Col. 6:** **Place where document was written** **1. *ʾdyn b*LN ‘then in LN’** **2. scribal formula**
TAD B2.9 (C 20) 420 BCE	Maʿuziyah b. Natan	*spr [mrḥq]*[200]	*prtrk* ‘garrison commander’ *npʾ* (legal term) *ʾbygrn* ‘fine’ *krš* ‘karsh’	PN ***prtrk*** (l. 4; title of Persian official in court) *ršynkm bdyn* ***npʾ*** (l. 4; legal term specifying kind of lawsuit [?]) *yntn lkm …**ʾbygrnʾ** zy ksp **kršn** ʿšrh hw **kršn** 10 bʾbny mlkʾ ksp rbʿ 2 l**krš** 1* (ll. 14–15; fine in penalty clause)	1. *ʾdyn byb byrtʾ* 2. –
TAD B3.8 (K 7) 420 BCE	Maʿuziyah b. Natan b. Ananyah	*spr ʾntw*[201]	*ʾbygrn* ‘fine’ *krš* ‘karsh’	*yn]tn l[hʾ]**bygrnʾ** zy ksp **kršn** ʿšrn bʾbny mlkʾ ksp r 2 l10* (ll. 31–32; fine in penalty clause) *ksp **kršn** šbʿh hw[…] … bʾbny mlkʾ ksp zwz lʿšrtʾ* (l. 16; value in silver of dowry and mohar)	1. *ʾdyn] byb byrtʾ* 2. –
TAD B2.10 (C 25) 416 BCE	Maʿuziyah b. Natan	*spr mrḥq*[202]	*ʾbygrn* ‘fine’ *krš* ‘karsh’	*yntn lkm **ʾbygrnʾ** zy ksp **kršn** ʿšrh hw **kršn** 10 ksp rbʿ 2 l**krš** 1 bʾbny mlkʾ* (ll. 15–16; fine in penalty clause)	1. *ʾdyn byb* 2. –

200 *TAD* B, 43: “Withdrawal from Goods.”
201 *TAD* B, 83: “Document of Wifehood.”
202 *TAD* B, 47: “Withdrawal from House.”

TAD B3.9 (K 8) 416 BCE	Rauxšana b. Nergalušezib	endorsement missing[203]	*hptḥpt* 'guardian of the 7th' *ʾbygrn* 'fine' *krš* 'karsh'	*qdm wydrng* ***hptḥpt'*** *rb ḥyl' zy swn* (ll. 2.3; title of Persian official in court) *yntn lk ʾ**bygrn** ksp **kršn** tltyn bmtqlt mlkʾ ksp zwz lʿšrtʾ* (ll. 7–8; fine in penalty clause)	1. *ʾdyn bswn* 2. –
TAD B2.11 (C 28) 410 BCE	Nabutukulti b. Nabuzeribni	*spr plgn*[204]	*ʾbygrn* 'fine' *krš* 'karsh'	*nntn lk ʾ**bygrn**ʾ ksp ṣryp **kršn** ʿšrh bmtqlt mlkʾ* (ll. 10–11; fine in penalty clause)	1. *byb byrtʾ* 2. *ktb ... byb byrtʾ*
TAD B3.10 (K 9) 404 BCE	Ḥaggai b. Šemaʿyah	*spr by*[205]	*hnpn* 'protecting (wall)' *hngyt* 'partner in chattel' *hnbg* 'partner in realty' *ʾdrng* 'guarantor' *ʾbygrn* 'fine' *krš* 'karsh'	*mwʿh šmš lh ʾgrʾ zy **hnpn**ʾ zy bnw mṣryʾ* (ll. 8–9; in description of location of transferred property) ***hngyt*** *zyly w**hnbg** wʾ**drng** zyly* (l. 18; claimants in waiver of suit) *yntn lky ʾ**bygrn** ksp **kršn** 30 bʾbny mlkʾ ksp ṣryp* (l. 20; fine in penalty clause)	1. – (*ʾdyn*) 2. *ktb ... byb byrtʾ*

203 *TAD* B, 85: "Adoption."
204 *TAD* B, 51: "Apportionment of Slaves."
205 *TAD* B, 89: "Bequest in Contemplation of Death."

Tab. 1 (continued)

Col. 1: Document and date (in chronological order)	**Col. 2: Scribal name (included in scribal formula[180])**	**Col. 3: Emic label**	**Col. 4: Persian loanwords[181]**	**Col. 5: Context**	**Col. 6: Place where document was written 1. *ʾdyn b*LN 'then in LN' 2. scribal formula**
TAD B3.11 (K 10) 402 BCE	Ḥaggai b. Šemaʿyah	*spr by*[206]	*hnpn* 'protecting (wall)' *psšdt* 'after-gift' *hngyt* 'partner in chattel' *hnbg* 'partner in realty' *ʾdrng* 'guarantor' *ʾbygrn* 'fine' *krš* 'karsh'	*mwʿh šmš lh ʾwṣr mlkʾ dbq ʾgr bʾgr* ***lhnpn***ʾ *zy bnw mṣryʾ* (ll. 3–4; in description of location of transferred property) *ʾnh* PN *yhbth lk* ***psšdt*** *qbl zy lʾ* [*ktb ʿl spr ʾnttky*] *ʿm* PN (ll. 7–8; legal term referring to addition of earlier transferred property to marriage contract [*TAD* B3.10]) *byth zy yhbt lk brḥmn* ***psšdt*** *ʿl spr ʾnttky* (l. 9; legal term referring to addition of earlier transferred property to marriage contract [*TAD* B 3.10]) ***hngyt hnbg*** *wʾ****drng*** (l. 12; claimants in waiver of suit) *ʾḥwb wʾntn l*PN ***ʾbygrn*** *ksp* ***kršn*** *30 ksp ṣrp bʾbny mlkʾ* (ll. 10–11; fine in penalty clause) *yḥwb wyntn lky wʿl bnyky* ***ʾbygrn*** *ksp* ***kršn*** *30 bʾbny mlkʾ* (ll. 13–14; fine in penalty clause)	1. – (*ʾdyn*) 2. *ktb … byb*

206 *TAD* B, 93: "Dowry Addendum."

TAD B3.13 (K 11) 402 BCE	Šaweram b. Ešemram b. Ešemšezib	*spr* [ʿ]*bwr*[207]	*ptp* ‘ration’ *ʾdrng* ‘guarantor’ *ʾbgrn* ‘fine’ *krš* ‘karsh’	*mn* ***ptp****ʾ zy ytntn ly mn ʾwṣr mlkʾ* (l. 4; ration from which repayment of loan will be made) *kzy ytntn ly* ***ptp****ʾ mn byt mlkʾ* (ll. 5–6; ration from which repayment will be made [in penalty clause]) *bny wʾ****drngy*** (ll. 8–9; in obligation of heirs) *bny wʾ****drngy*** (l. 8; in clause stipulating seizure of security when heirs are in default) *ʾḥr ʾnh* PN *ʾḥwb wʾntn lk ksp* ***ʾbgrn krš*** *ḥd 1 ksp ṣryp* (l. 7; fine in penalty clause) *ʾḥr ʾnh* PN *ʾšlm wʾntn lk* ***ʾbgrn****ʾ zy mnʿl ktyb* (l. 7; fine in penalty clause)	1. *ʾdyn bswn byrtʾ* 2. *ktb … bswn byrtʾ*
TAD B3.12 (K 12) 402 BCE	Ḥaggai b. Šemaʿyah	*spr by*[208]	*prypt* ‘chief of the beloved’ *psšdt* ‘after-gift’ *hngyt* ‘partner in chattel’ *hnbg* ‘partner in realty’	*tpmt ʾntth* ***prypt*** *zy mšlm br zkr* (l. 11; title of one of the parties) *byth zy yhbt lk* ***psšdt*** (l. 9; legal term referring to addition of earlier transferred property to marriage contract [*TAD* B3.10])	1. – (*ʾdyn*) 2. *ktb … byb byrtʾ*

207 *TAD* B, 100: “Loan of Grain.”
208 *TAD* B, 97: “Sale of Apartment to Son-in-Law.”

Tab. 1 (continued)

Col. 1: Document and date (in chronological order)	**Col. 2: Scribal name (included in scribal formula[180])**	**Col. 3: Emic label**	**Col. 4: Persian loanwords[181]**	**Col. 5: Context**	**Col. 6: Place where document was written 1. *ʾdyn b*LN 'then in LN' 2. scribal formula**
			ʾdrng 'guarantor' *ʾbygrn* 'fine' *krš* 'karsh'	*bytk … zy yhbn l*PN *brtn* ***psšdt*** (ll. 17–18; legal term referring to addition of earlier transferred property to marriage contract [*TAD* B3.10]) ***hngyt whnbg*** *w*ʾ***drng*** *zyln* (l. 27; in waiver of suit) *wyhbt ln dmy bytn ksp* ***krš*** *ḥd hw 1 … ksp ywn sttry 6 …* (l. 5; in payment of transferred property) *wyhbt ln dmwhy ksp* ***krš*** *ḥd … ksp ywn sttry 6 …* (ll. 13–14; in payment of transferred property) *yḥwb wyntn lk wlbnyk* ***ʾbygrn*** *ksp* ***kršn*** *20 bʾbny mlkʾ ksp ṣrp* (ll. 29–30; in penalty clause)	

TAD B5.5 (C 43) 420 or 400 BCE	unknown	label missing[209]	*ptp* 'ration' *hngyt* 'partner in chattel' *hnbg* 'partner in realty' *ʾbygrn* 'fine' *krš* 'karsh'	***wptp**ʾ zy hw ly mn byt mlkʾ* (l. 8; reference in withdrawal to transferred ration) ***wptp**[ʾ zy] ktyb mnʿl* (l. 10; reference in penalty clause 2 to the transferred ration) ***hngyt whnbg**ʾ zy ly* (l. 9; claimants in waiver of suit) *ʾnh yhbt lky ksp šqln 6 hw šth bʿbny mlkʾ ksp zwz **lkrš** 1* (l. 3; in payment for service) *yntn lky ʾ**bygrn** ksp **kršn** 2* (l. 6; in penalty clause 1)	1. *ʾdyn byb* 2. –

209 *TAD* B, 127: "Mutual Quitclaim."

Bibliography

Abraham, Kathleen, and Sokoloff, Michael, "Aramaic Loanwords in Akkadian – A Reassessment of the Proposals," *AfO* 52 (2012): 1–92.

Barnea, Gad, "Some Achaemenid Zoroastrian Echoes in Early Yahwistic Sources," *Iran: Journal of the British Institute of Persian Studies* (2024, forthcoming).

Black, Jeremy, George, Andrew and Postgate, Nicholas (eds.), *A Concise Dictionary of Akkadian*, Wiesbaden, Harrassowitz, 2000.

Botta, Alejandro, *The Aramaic and Egyptian Legal Traditions at Elephantine: An Egyptological Approach*, London: T & T Clark, 2009.

Briant, Pierre, *From Cyrus to Alexander: A History of the Persian Empire*, trans. Peter T. Daniels. Winona Lake: Eisenbrauns, 2002.

Cowley, Arthur E., *Aramaic Papyri of the Fifth Century B.C.*, Oxford: Clarendon Press, 1923.

Driver, Godfrey R., *Aramaic Documents of the Fifth Century B.C.*, Oxford: Clarendon, 1957.

Erman, Adolf, and Grapow, Hermann, *Ägyptisches Handwörterbuch*, Darmstadt: Wissenschaftliche Buchgesellschaft, 1961.

Faulkner, Raymond O., *A Concise Dictionary of Middle Egyptian*, Oxford: Griffith Institute, 2002.

Folmer, Margaretha, *The Aramaic Language in the Achaemenid Period: A Study in Linguistic Variation*, OLA 68. Leuven: Peeters, 1995.

Folmer, Margaretha, "Bactria and Egypt: Administration as Mirrored by the Aramaic Sources," pages 413–54 in *Die Verwaltung im Achämenidenreich: Imperiale Muster und Strukturen. Akten des 6. Internationalen Kolloquiums zum Thema »Vorderasien im Spannungsfeld klassischer und altorientalischer Überlieferungen« aus Anlass der 80-Jahr-Feier der Entdeckung des Festungsarchivs von Persepolis, Landgut Castelen bei Basel, 14.–17. Mai 2013*, edited by Bruno Jacobs, Wouter F. M. Henkelman, and Matthew W. Stolper. Classica et Orientalia 17. Wiesbaden: Harrassowitz, 2017.

Folmer, Margaretha, "'Hi Aḥuṭab': Ostraca from Elephantine with Letters in Aramaic (5th c. BCE and Beyond)," pages 145–64 in: *Using Ostraca in the Ancient World: New Discoveries and Methodologies*, eds. Clementina Caputo and Julia Lougoyova. Materiale Textkulturen 32. Berlin: Walter de Gruyter, 2020.

Folmer, Margaretha, "Aramaic as *Lingua Franca*," pages 373–99 in *A Companion to Near Eastern Languages*, edited by Rebecca Hasselbach-Andee. Hoboken, NJ: John Wiley & Sons, 2020.

Folmer, Margaretha, "Taxation of Ships and Their Cargo in an Aramaic Papyrus from Egypt (*TAD* C3.7)," pages 261–300 in *Taxation in the Achaemenid Empire*, edited by Kristin Kleber. Classica et Orientalia 26. Wiesbaden: Harrassowitz, 2021.

Folmer, Margaretha (ed.), *Elephantine Revisited: New Insights into the Judean Community and Its Neighbors*, University Park, PA: Eisenbrauns, 2022.

Folmer, Margaretha, "The Contribution of Elephantine to the Study of Aramaic," pages 124–41 in *Elephantine Revisited: New Insights into the Judean Community and its Neighbors*, edited by Margaretha Folmer. University Park, PA: Eisenbrauns, 2022.

Folmer, Margaretha, "Characteristics of the Aramaic of the Akhvamazdā letters from Ancient Bactria," pages 325–53 in *The Persian World and Beyond. Achaemenid and Arsacid Studies in Honour of Bruno Jacobs*, edited by Mark B. Garrison and Wouter F. M. Henkelman. Melammu Workshops and Monographs 6. Münster: Zaphon, 2023.

Granerød, Gard, *Dimensions of Yahwism in the Persian Period: Studies in the Religion and Society of the Judaean Community at Elephantine*, Berlin: Walter de Gruyter, 2016.

Granerød, Gard, "Canon and Archive: Yahwism in Elephantine and Āl-Yāḫūdu as a Challenge to the Canonical History of Judean Religion in the Persian Period," *JBL* 138 (2019): 345–64.

Haspelmath, Martin, "Lexical Borrowing: Concepts and Issues," pages 35–54 in *Loanwords in the World's Languages: A Comparative Handbook*, edited by Martin Haspelmath and Uri Tadmor. Berlin: Mouton de Gruyter, 2009.

Iest, Ruwan N. van der, "A Study on Judean Cultural Identity in Egypt During the Fifth Century BCE: Characterizing Judean Cultural Identity Using Elements of Judean Matrimonial Law Attested in the Aramaic Matrimonial Property Arrangements from Elephantine Island," Ph.D. diss., Groningen 2023.

Kottsieper, Ingo, "On Aḥiqar and the Bible," pages 86–105 in Margaretha Folmer, *Elephantine Revisited: New Insights into the Judean Community and Its Neighbors*. University Park, PA: Eisenbrauns, 2022.

Kraeling, Emil G., *The Brooklyn Museum Aramaic Papyri: New Documents of the Fifth Century B.C. from the Jewish Colony at Elephantine*, New Haven: Yale University Press, 1953.

Lesko, Leonard H., and Switalski Lesko, Barbara, *A Dictionary of Late Egyptian*, 5 vols. Providence: B. C. Scribe Publications, 1982–90.

Lozachmeur, Hélène, *La collection Clermont-Ganneau: ostraca, épigraphes sur jarre, étiquettes de bois*, 2 vols. MAIBL 35. Paris: de Boccard, 2006.

Matras, Yaron, *Language Contact*, Cambridge: Cambridge University Press, 2009.

McColl Millar, Robert (ed.), *Trask's Revised Historical Linguistics*, London: Routledge 2013.

Mizrahi, Noam, "The History and Linguistic Background of Two Hebrew Titles for the High Priest," *JBL* 130 (2011): 687–705.

Moore, James D., "The Persian Administrative Process in View of an Elephantine Aršāma Decree (*TAD* A6.2)," *Semitica et Classica* 13 (2020): 49–62.

Moore, James D., *New Aramaic Papyri from Elephantine in Berlin*, Leiden: Brill, 2022.

Müller, Matthias, "Egyptian," pages 107–28 in *A Companion to Ancient Near Eastern Languages*, edited by Rebekka Hasselbach-Andee. Hoboken NJ: John Wiley & Sons, 2020.

Naveh, Joseph, and Shaked, Shaul, *Aramaic Documents from Ancient Bactria (Fourth Century BCE) from the Khalili Collections*, London: The Khalili Family Trust, 2012.

Noonan, Benjamin J., *Non-Semitic Loanwords in the Hebrew Bible: A Lexicon of Language Contact*, University Park, PA: Eisenbrauns, 2019.

Pilgrim, Cornelius von., "On the Archaeological Background of the Aramaic Papyri from Elephantine in the Light of Recent Fieldwork," pages 1–16 in *Elephantine Revisited: New Insights into the Judean Community and its Neighbors*, edited by Margaretha Folmer. University Park, PA: Eisenbrauns, 2022.

Porten, Bezalel, and Greenfield, Jonas C., "The Guarantor at Elephantine-Syene," *JAOS* 89 (1969): 153–57.

Porten, Bezalel, and Szubin, Henri Z., "Litigation Concerning Abandoned Property at Elephantine (Kraeling 1)," *JNES* 42 (1983): 279–84.

Porten, Bezalel, and Szubin, Henri Z., "Litigants in the Elephantine Contracts: The Development of Legal Terminology," *Maarav* 4 (1987): 45–67.

Quack, Joachim F., "Ein demotischer Ausdruck in aramäischer Transkription," *Die Welt des Orients* 23 (1992): 15–20.

Schmitt, Rüdiger, *Wörterbuch der Altpersischen Inschriften*. Wiesbaden: Reichert Verlag, 2014.

Schütze, Alexander, "Local Administrations in Persian Period Egypt," pages 489–515 in *Die Verwaltung im Achämenidenreich: Imperiale Muster und Strukturen. Akten des 6. Internationalen Kolloquiums zum Thema »Vorderasien im Spannungsfeld klassischer und altorientalischer Überlieferungen« aus Anlass der 80-Jahr-Feier der Entdeckung des Festungsarchivs von Persepolis, Landgut Castelen bei Basel, 14.–17. Mai 2013*, edited by Bruno Jacobs, Wouter F. M. Henkelman, and Matthew W. Stolper. Classica et Orientalia 17. Wiesbaden: Harrassowitz, 2017.

Schütze, Alexander, "The Legal Context of the Aramaic Legal Tradition at Elephantine Reconsidered," pages 55–73 in *Elephantine in Context*, edited by Reinhard G. Kratz and Bernd Schipper. Tübingen: Mohr Siebeck, 2022.

Skjærvo, Prods O., "Old Iranian," In *The Iranian Languages*, edited by Gernot Windfuhr, 43–195. London and New York: Routledge, 2009.

Stadel, Christian, *Hebräismen in den aramäischen Texten vom Toten Meer*, Schriften der Hochschule für Jüdische Studien Heidelberg 11. Heidelberg: Universitätsverlag Winter, 2008.

Schwiderski, Dirk, *Handbuch des nordwestsemitischen* Briefformulars, Berlin: Walter de Gruyter, 2000.

Tavernier, Jan. *Iranica in the Achaemenid Period (ca. 550–330 B.C.)*. Leuven: Peeters, 2007.

Tavernier, Jan, "Old Persian," pages 638–57 in *The Oxford Handbook of Ancient Iran*, edited by Daniel T. Potts. Oxford: Oxford University Press, 2013.

Tavernier, Jan, "The Use of Languages on the Various Levels of Administration in the Achaemenid Empire," pages 337–412 in *Die Verwaltung im Achämenidenreich: Imperiale Muster und Strukturen. Akten des 6. Internationalen Kolloquiums zum Thema »Vorderasien im Spannungsfeld klassischer und altorientalischer Überlieferungen« aus Anlass der 80-Jahr-Feier der Entdeckung des Festungsarchivs von Persepolis, Landgut Castelen bei Basel, 14.–17. Mai 2013*, edited by Bruno Jacobs, Wouter F. M. Henkelman, and Matthew W. Stolper. Classica et Orientalia 17. Wiesbaden: Harrassowitz, 2017.

Thomason, Sarah G., and Terrence Kaufman, *Language Contact, Creolization, and Genetic Linguistics*. Berkeley: University of California Press, 1991.

Benedikt Hensel

Reconsidering Yahwism in Persian Period Idumea in Light of the Current Material Findings

An Orientation: Yahwism and Emerging Judaism in the Persian and Hellenistic Periods

This chapter discusses and re-evaluates all the available material evidence in the Idumean region and province that may be indicators of a practiced Yahwism in Persian times in this region (sections 1–6). In this context, certain biblical, namely late Persian, traditions of the Hebrew Bible also need to be taken into account: the focus at the end of the paper will be on the genealogical vestibule of Chronicles with its dominant Judean genealogy, in which "Edomite," i.e., "non-Israelite" cultural traits are "made" into Judean ones. Likewise, a look at the post-P narrative Genesis 23 will have to be taken in this context (section 7).

The question of Yahwism is seen as part of the overall phenomenon of "Yahwism in the Persian Period." According to the latest research, this phenomenon is characterized by a high degree of regional diversification and cultural-religious-social plurality. Yahwism in Idumea is accordingly classified in this system of coordination. This article represents the first study dealing with Yahwism in Idumea – in research it is either not mentioned at all (in favor of a focus on the imagined "norm group" of Judaism in Jerusalem – see below) or it is left with a short reference to the famous Idumea Ostracon from the 4th century BCE, which mentions a "Yaho temple" – apparently in Idumea.

In order to carefully grasp the phenomenon of "Yahwism in Idumea," some terminological and conceptual clarifications are necessary. I would like to highlight three central aspects in the following:

1. As I understand it, the study of the phenomenon of "Yahwism in the Persian period" is part of the research on ancient Judaism.[1] The term "early Judaism" or "emerging Judaism" typically refers to the formation of Judaism in the

1 See on Yahwism in the Persian period and Emerging Judaism my overview of research, with the detailed outline of my own approach in Hensel, "Yahwistic Diversity and the Hebrew Bible" and most recently Hensel, "Who Wrote the Bible."

Benedikt Hensel, University of Oldenburg, Germany

https://doi.org/10.1515/9783111018638-004

early Persian period.[2] The key aspect in this is the fact that this phase of the formation of Identity begins in the early Persian period. In contrast to the established research, however, I have already shown many times[3] that this process is not limited to the early Persian period, but extends at least until the late 2nd/early 1st century BCE and is to be regarded as a long-term process. It is only from this time on[4] that Judaism begins to develop those identity markers (especially the practice and understanding of the Torah, circumcision, food and purity laws,[5] and monotheism). As recently shown by Yonatan Adler in his study on the "Origins of Judaism,"[6] the archaeological evidence for the dissemination and observance of the Tora does not begin until the late 2nd century BCE; the same is the case with the epigraphic sources found at Qumran as has been convincingly argued by Reinhard G. Kratz in several studies now.[7]

2. In addition, there is the crucial circumstance that this emerging/early Judaism constitutes only one aspect of the far more extensive phenomenon of "Yahwism in Antiquity." I understand this to mean that Judaism emerged over time and in a long-term process from the various forms of Yahwism of the time before. Therefore, I consistently prefer the term "Yahwism" as a neutral term in religious studies to the traditional termini such as "Judaism" or "Judaisms."[8] As has become clear in the meantime and in recent years through various small-scale studies, this Yahwism is characterized by a high degree of regional diversification and cultural as well as religious-sociological

2 See, most recently Schmid and Schröter, *The Making of the Bible*, 105–139 (the chapter on the Persian Period: "Emerging Judaism").

3 See in the latest article Hensel, "Who Wrote the Bible," 12–13.

4 Cohen, *The Beginning of Jewishness*.

5 Especially for this aspect of the Diaspora, see now Schöpf, *Purity without Borders?*.

6 Adler, *The Origins of Judaism*, 197–208, 223–236.

7 See especially his article *in this volume*.

8 Frevel has, with good argument, supported the designation "Judaism" (in current publications) as a larger entity or "Judaisms." ("Judentümer") (see Frevel, "Alte Stücke – Späte Brücke?"); Edelman has also used the term "Judaisms" in recent publications: Edelman, "Introduction," 1–5. In my opinion, the phenomenon should, from the approach of religious studies, be viewed as neutrally as possible: the different groupings exist alongside each other in these periods, even if they display differences in detail regarding religious practice and the sociology of religion. So, for example, monotheism is a *possible* option during the Persian period (Judah and Samaria) but not an *exclusive* option for faith in the God of Israel (so, e.g., Elephantine and Idumea). Moreover, "Judaism" is only one single development within a wider entity. The "Samaritans" for example, would never call themselves (nor would they have in antiquity) "Jews." See also a very recent article by Barnea ("Yahwistic Identity") who suggests based on archeological and onomastic evidence, that the identifier *Yhwdy* was adopted by all Yahwists (incl. Samari(t)ans) in the 6th c. BCE.

plurality. The established coordinated system of an imagined Jerusalem Orthodoxy in Persian times and other deviant groups outside the country (be it Samaria, Elephantine or Babylon, to name only the best known) can no longer be effective here. For the present contribution, this means that I use the term "Yahwistic" or "Yahwistic individuals" etc. to describe – in general terms – that group or particular individuals, who become tangible in the material findings, are cultically oriented to Yaho. I refrain, where possible, from using other ethnic or national markers or labels that are too presuppositional (such as "Jewish names," "Judahites," or "Judeans," etc.; for a detailed discussion in this regard see section 6).

3. The Persian and – in my understanding, as outlined above and in more detail elsewhere.[9] also – the early Hellenistic periods are widely recognized as the so-called formative period for the Hebrew scriptures and emerging Judaism.[10] Yet, there is very much still a decisive desideratum in research, namely there is still a lack of detailed studies that "bridge the gap," so to speak, between redaction history and the historically tangible groupings. There has been a long tradition in research of identifying biblical redactors and redactor groups as well as the groups of biblical tradents of this period with the social groups of Judea (and especially those of Jerusalem). This is also still the case for the majority of the biblical texts: the Hebrew Bible seems to be, in the end, clearly a Judean-dominated tradition. However, this is not true for all texts. It seems clear that, even if most of the traditions at the surface of the text were shaped from a Judean perspective, this diversity is still reflected in certain biblical traditions or redactional material. In this regard, another question arises: which social groups or redactor groups (Judean as well as "non-Judean") stand *behind* the Hebrew Bible's productional processes? This crucial question has – for the first time – been addressed in a holistic approach with a series of articles in the 2023 volume "Social Groups behind Biblical Traditions."[11] In any case, the observations of the most recent research in this regard allow for the conclusion that diverse redactor groups of the period in question were aware of the multifaceted nature of the Yahwistic groups. This is why the present article will also ask the question if – against the backdrop of the material evidence from Idumea – there might be traces or reflection of the representation of this group in certain biblical traditions.

9 See most recently Hensel, "Who Wrote the Bible," 11–23, esp. 15–19.
10 See Schmid, "Textual, Historical, Sociological"; Römer, "Zwischen Urkunden, Fragmenten und Ergänzungen," 2–24; Kratz, "The Analysis of the Pentateuch"; Gertz, Levinson, Rom-Shiloni, and Schmid, *The Formation of the Pentateuch*.
11 Hensel, Adamczewski, and Nocquet, *Social Groups behind Biblical Traditions*.

Edom, Idumea and Edomite, Idumeans: Terminological Limitations

A final terminological remark is necessary before reviewing the evidence. The distinction in terminology between "Edom" as referring to the Iron-Age kingdom centered east of the Wadi ʿArabah and "Idumea" as referring to the region south of Judah in the Hellenistic Period is a totally modern one, existing in neither ancient Hebrew nor Greek. I will detail the several aspects involved in the course of the article when the evidence is reviewed. The effect of this distinction is further blurred by the fact that the Edomite heartland was originally located in Transjordan (on the Edomite plateau) and later gradually evolved into the Southern Negev (but not later than the 8th century BCE). What we see in some scholarly literature, therefore, is a rather artificial distinction between "Edom" in Transjordan and "Idumea" in Cis-Jordan. But this distinction overlooks the fact that the Jordan was never understood in antiquity as a border – both "Edoms" (Cis- and Transjordanian) are a crucial part of one cultural contact zone. That being said, the cultural traits evident in the material need to be labelled somehow. And thirdly, the terminological distinction is further blurred by the clear multi-ethnic, multi-cultural society in Idumea itself, with seemingly low cultural or ethnical boundaries. This means that the terms "Edomite" or "Idumean" in contrast to individuals with Arabic, Phoenician, Greek or possibly even Judean background is not as sharp as the terminology would suggest. In order to follow the traditional research, this article will first use the termini "Edomite" or "Idumean" as a signal for an "Edomite" background (however defined). This is meant as a counter term to other, clearly identifiable cultural traits, such as Arabic, Phoenician or Yahwistic. In the course of the article, I will problematize and correct the term "Idumean" in its limitation to the "Edomite" (section 6, in this article), then in the external perception all inhabitants of Idumea are considered Idumeans (as is the case for someone from Yehud or Samaria). The Yahwists living in that region are also "Idumeans" – the term says nothing about their religious orientation, only about their geographic or political localization to the Province of Idumea.

1 Religion and Yahwism in Idumea in the Persian Period: An Overview of Onomastic Evidence

The Region and Province of Idumea in the Persian Period

In the Persian and the Hellenistic periods, the territory of Idumea included all the areas of the Beersheba-Arad Valley, the southern Shephelah, and the southernJudean Hills; in other words, territory that had been inhabited mainly by Judeans in the eighth-seventh centuries. The name "Idumea" is first mentioned as a geographical reference in Diodorus' description of the events of the year 312 BCE.[12] The exact course of the northern border of Idumea is still a matter of debate.[13] However, the borders of Yehud seem to have shrunk to a line north of Beth-Zur[14] in the hill country, and Azekah and the Elah Valley in the Shephelah, while most of the Judahite population was concentrated around Jerusalem. A recent article authored by Dafna Langgut and Oded Lipschits[15] puts forth an intriguing thesis for the reasons why the Judean settlement area continually contracted northwards over the centuries. Based on the palynological and sedimentological information, it can be shown that the Southern Levant at the transition of the sixth and fifth centuries BCE – ca. 520 to 450 – experienced an extended period of drought. These dryer climate conditions had serious ramifications in southern Judah, which was hit particularly hard by the drought and was slowly abandoned by the Judeans. It was precisely this retreat by the native population that then allowed other population groups, especially the Edomites, to come and settle into the region.

Moreover, Idumea is part of the double "post-history" of the former kingdom of Edom, which was conquered by the last Babylonian king, Nabonidus, in 552 BCE. In the following period there is evidence for a continued existence of Edomite culture not only in the former core area – the Transjordanian Edomite

12 Diodorus, Siculus. *Bibliotheca Historica*, 19, 94–95, 98. For the Greek text see Siculus. *The Library of History 10*.
13 See, e.g. Levin, "The Genesis of Idumea.", 80–98, esp. 81–86.
14 See for this Josephus, who mentions in several instances that by the second century the region south of Beth-Zur was known as Idumea, and was considered to be separate from Judea, at least until it was taken over by John Hyrcanus I sometime around 107 BCE (Jos., *Antiquities* 13, 256–257; Jos., *Wars* 1.63).
15 Langgut, and Lipschits. "Dry Climate," 151–176.

plateau[16] – but also in Idumea in the Cis-Jordanian area. The name itself, Ἰδουμαία, obviously derived from the kingdom of Edom, in Greek (LXX) "Εδωμ" or Ἰδουμαία. From what we know now, Edomites had begun expanding their mercantile activities and partially migrating into the Judean Negev as early as the eighth century BCE, as confirmed by material evidence found at Lachish,[17] Arad,[18] Beersheba,[19] Maresha,[20] Khirbet el-Kôm/Makkedah,[21] and several other sites in the area.[22] In addition, considering the evidence from the Arabah Valley and the Negev Highlands,[23] it seems likely that areas in southern Judah were already being settled in the 8th century – and probably even earlier. Some of these groups were nomadic, while others were sedentary and engaged in pastoralism, agriculture, and trade with the Edomites.[24]

In the Hellenistic period, this region was called, depending on the source, the *eparchia* (ἐπαρχία), *hyparchia* (ὕπαρχεία) or even "satrapy" (σατραπεία) of Idumea. It is not exactly clear when Idumea as an administrative entity was officially established. The earliest reference to Idumea as an administrative unit can be found in the Zenon Papyri from Cairo, dating to 259 BCE.[25] Here, Zenon mentions the port of Gaza, Marisa and Adoreon in Idumea.[26]

While some therefore argue that a province of Idumea was not established before the early Hellenistic period,[27] there are good arguments for the late Persian period, as might be concluded from the extensive amount of Aramaic official administrative ostraca from the fourth century.[28] According to Diana V. Edelman, the so-called Idumean ostraca (see below) testify to tax collection administered by Persian officials in Makkedah and thus to Idumea as part of the larger Persian financial system.

---

16 On the evidence see now Bienkowski, "Transjordan in the Persian Period." See also the articles gathered in the programmatic volume Hensel, Zvi, and Edelmann, *About Edom and Idumea.*
17 Lemaire, "Un nouveau roi arabe."
18 Naveh, "The Aramaic Ostraca from Tel Arad."
19 Naveh, "The Aramaic Ostraca from Tel Beer-Sheba."
20 See esp. Stern, "The Evolution of an Edomite/Idumean Identity." For the site of Maresha, see Kloner, *Maresha Excavations I* and Stern, *Excavations at Maresha Subterranean Complex 169.*
21 Zadok, "A Prosopography of Samaria and Edom/Idumea," esp. 785–822; Zadok, "On the Documentary Framework"; Stern, "The Population of the Persian-Period Idumea," esp. 212–13.
22 An overview of the surveys in Grabbe, *A History of the Jews and Judaism 1*, 50.
23 For a full review of the available material see Danielson, "Edom in Judah."
24 For an Iron Age I Edomite Kingdom, see Ben-Yosef, "The Architectural Bias."
25 See Bartlett, "Edomites and Idumaeans," esp. 106.
26 See Bartlett, "Edomites and Idumaeans," 106.
27 See, e.g., Levin, "The Genesis of Idumea," 84–86. He already challenged the view that there was a province of Idumea during the Persian Period in a paper published in 2007, see Levin, "The Southern Frontier of Yehud."
28 Edelman, "Economic and Administrative Realia."

It is more than likely that the creation of the province (or sub-satrapy) of Idumea was triggered by the Achaemenid loss of Egypt around 404–400/398 BCE.[29] As a consequence, the southern borders of the Southern Levant became an extremely sensitive frontier of the Persian Empire, all of which paved the way to a higher level of direct imperial involvement in the local administration. One good example is the establishment of the fortified administrative center at Lachish in the area around 400 BCE.[30] More than likely most of the Persian period finds in the various sites of the Negev and the Shephelah, such as Arad, Beer-sheba, Tell el-Far'ah (south), and others, should be dated to the fourth century BCE and show heightened imperial involvement in the area.[31]

Cultural and Ethnic Identities in Idumea: A Complex Phenomenon

One aspect that brings us closer to the topic of our contribution is the question of cultural and ethnic identities in Idumea during the Persian period, which is a highly complex issue in itself.

While the term Ἰδουμαία alone expresses a certain idea of *continuity* with the Edom of old, one of the most urgent and intriguing questions in Idumean research is how this continuity actually transpired in reality; in other words, what cultural, ethnic, and religious traits identifiable in the region point towards a continuity of "Edomite" cultural heritage? Older research typically spoke simply of "Edomites" in the Persian and early Hellenistic periods, which is still widely adapted in modern Hebrew Bible scholarship.[32] However, using the term "Edomite" only blurs the complexity of the various ethnic and cultural identities involved in the region and which will be tangible when we come to the onomastic evidence (see also section 6 below for a detailed discussion on the problematics on identifying ethnical, political or cultural traits). The various findings bring about their own plethora of questions: what of the Idumeans themselves, who lived for over two centuries in what had been southern Judah, without any known political, cultural or religious organization? Did they identify themselves as Idumeans in their own right, or did they instead consider themselves "refu-

29 See Lemaire, *Levantine Epigraphy*, 101.
30 See Fantalkin and Tal, "A Tale of Two Provinces," esp. 177–179.
31 See Fantalkin and Tal, "A Tale of Two Provinces," 177–214.
32 See, among others, the discussion on potential "Edomite" veneration at Hebron, and thus in Idumea of the Persian period, discussed in the context of Gen 17 (P) in De Pury, "Le tombeau des Abrahamides"; also see Schmid, "Judean Identity and Ecumenicity," esp. 26.

gees" from old Edom? Did they think of themselves as "natives"? Can we even think of them in terms of ethnicity? Is there cultural continuity from the Iron-Age Edomites to the people living west of the Arabah in the Persian and Hellenistic periods? What about the Qedarites and other Arab groups who lived in the area, and what about the "Yahwists" in the region?

These questions cannot be fully answered in this article, of course, but they illustrate the problem horizon, and highlight the caution with which one has to approach the onomastic findings in the following. The core problem is that we do not have any testimonies of these "Idumeans," who could give information about their own identity construction and perception. We can only approach this identity, or better, the different identities, in Idumea indirectly via the material findings and namely via onomastics. In the traditional as well as in the current research, however, it can often be observed that linguistic or cultural traits are often raised, which, however, are too hastily explored in the sense of ethnic, cultural, and/or political labels that are possibly also presented mixed with biblical horizons. The following review of the material will give some examples of this.

The Idumean Ostraca: The Unprovenanced Corpus of the 4th Century BCE

In order to understand the complex processes of cultural interaction in Idumea, of which Yahwism was a part, it is essential to study the rich epigraphic evidence of the Persian period. There are nearly 2,100 Ostraca from Idumea that give insight into agriculture, economics, politics, onomastics, and scribal practices from (mainly) the fourth and some from the third-century BCE. Of interest from this corpus are also the land descriptions, which record local landmarks, ownership boundaries, and land registration and thus provide rich complementary material to understanding the region of Idumea. The vast majority of the ostraca are commercial and administrative documents mostly written in Aramaic and mostly, unfortunately, unprovenanced, hence we term in the following the Unprovenanced Corpus. Most stem from the antiquities market, though certain prosopographic connections between individual ostraca and further linguistic and content similarities show that the ostraca originate from the same assemblage as has clearly been shown in several studies by Bezalel Porten and Ada Yardeni. All ostraca are since 2023 accessible through an excellent multivolume critical edition of all the ostraca currently known, edited by Porten and Yardeni ("Textbook of Aramaic Ostraca from Idumea"/TAO 2014; 2016; 2018, 2020; 2023).[33] Many of the

33 *TAO 1–5*.

ostraca are dated according to the Babylonian calendar, typically giving the date, the month and the regnal year of the reigning king, sometimes they are only dated by day. Generally speaking, the dates of the entire corpus range from the 42nd year of Artaxerxes II (362 BCE) until the 5th year of Alexander IV (311 BCE).[34]

The Maresha-Corpus: Suggestions for an Administrative Centre at Maresha in the Late Persian Period

While the "Idumean" corpus is now known to the research community and – mainly due to the excellent critical edition TAO – is now (2023) available in its entirety and thus no longer – as before – to be evaluated only fragmentarily by the research community – the following corpus of inscriptions is, in my estimation, virtually unknown. For the development of Idumea in the late Persian period, however, it is important. For this, however, one must abstain from some of the basic assumptions of previous research ("Hellenistic corpus"), for the case is not as clear-cut as the few small studies occasionally suggest.

While there have been findings of several (but not many) ostraca that are dated to the late Persian period from several smaller sites such as Arad, Beersheba, Tell Jemmeh, Tell el-Far'ah (south), Tell el-Kheleifeh, and the region of Yata, which are believed to belong to the same corpus as the unprovenanced corpus, the excavations at Maresha have yielded more than 1,200 Greek and Semitic (mainly Aramaic) inscriptions (including about 60 inscriptions on jars).[35] However, the publication situation of these ostraca is not very satisfactory and presented only very provisionally. It seems to be the case that about 500 of the ostraca are written in Aramaic with most of the rest in Greek,[36] however, there are contradictory statements about this number in different studies. This is partly due to the fact that the publication of the extensive excavations in Maresha has progressed only very slowly so far. Many of the inscriptions (we do not know precisely how many and from which strata) come from the tell itself, which has not yet been published satisfactorily.

Officially published from the time period in question are until now (September 2023) the following: the first group of ostraca found at Maresha had been published in 2010,[37] including 65 Persian and Hellenistic inscriptions, dated on

34 See Porten and Yardeni. "The Chronology of the Idumean Ostraca."

35 See Eshel, "The Inscriptions in Hebrew, Aramaic, and Phoenician Script" and Eshel, "Iron Age, Phoenician and Aramaic Inscriptions."

36 Eshel, "Hellenism in the Land of Israel," esp. 123.

37 Eshel, "The Inscriptions in Hebrew, Aramaic, and Phoenician Script."

paleographic grounds from the 5th to the 2nd century BCE and written in Aramaic. Additionally, 39 inscriptions have been published in 2014,[38] that have been found in Subterranean Complex 57. 37 of these inscriptions are written in Aramaic and are dated – on paleographic grounds – from the 4th to the 2nd century BCE.[39] Additionally, 360 ostraca are from Subterranean Complex No. 169 (SC 169). According to a preliminary survey, most of these ostraca and inscriptions bear names. Amongst them ca. 127 Aramaic ostraca are known, most of the inscriptions in this group are fragmentary; some of them bear only a few words.[40] The study of this collection was first done by Esther Eshel jointly with Rivka Eltizur-Leiman and it seems to be the case the corpus is now being prepared for publication by Esther Eshel and Michael Langlois. While the specific set of ostraca is paleographically dated to the third or second century BCE.

However, based on further – as yet unpublished – evidence, there seems to be good grounds to question these conclusions. From a discussion with my colleague, Dalit Regev (Israel Antiquities Authorities), it seems quite possible that some (if not the majority) of the inscriptions date from the late Persian period. This is especially the case for the unpublished Aramaic inscriptions found directly at the tell based on their stratigraphic contexts.[41] In addition, the script, writing style and language use of some of the ostraca from Maresha that are generally attributed to the Hellenistic period, has some striking similarities to the Corpus of the unprovenanced ostraca from the 4th century BCE. At least three cases are already known where an ostracon from Maresha (no. 6; no. 12; no. 64) seems to have been written by the same scribe as another Idumean ostracon from the unprovenanced corpus of the 4th century BCE.[42] My suggestion is that at least some of the Aramaic ostraca from Maresha not only stem from the late Persian period but also, that at least some of the unprovenanced ostraca stem originally from Maresha, probably dug up in illegal excavations.

Even more relations between the unprovenanced corpus and the Maresha corpus can be traced in the onomasticon of the "Maresha" Aramaic ostraca. It corresponds in large parts to the findings from the unprovenanced ostraca at Idumea, which clearly date to the late Persian period. For example, the names in the Aramaic corpus from the above-mentioned SC 57 and SC 169 are quite similar

---

38 Eshel, "Iron Age, Phoenician and Aramaic Inscriptions."

39 See e.g., Eshel, "Iron Age, Phoenician and Aramaic Inscriptions," 77.

40 See for a recent treatment of a few of these inscriptions Eshel, Langlois, and Geller, "The Aramaic Divination Texts."

41 While these are not yet published, I was given the opportunity to look into the unpublished materials in 2023.

42 TAO *1*, xvii, xliv, xxxvi.

to those represented in the unprovenanced "Late Persian" corpus, that is usually attributed to Maqqedah. It includes many "Edomite" names, such as *qwsbnh*, *qwsgbr* or *'bdqws*, but also Arabic names such as *whb'l* and *zbd'dh* – as in the Maqqedah-corpus, this makes the vast majority of the names. There are also possible Hebrew names such as Kalkol, Tanḥum and the clearly "Yahwistic" names Azariah and Shemaiah. There is very little evidence (again, as in the unprovenanced corpus) of Babylonian names (only one possible name; "Nabu ben *zbd*"). A study is currently in planning on our part to further advance the question of Persian-period dating of these ostraca. The great advantage of these ostraca, from our point of view, is that they were found in scientifically controlled excavations. We see here a great chance to make further statements about the origin of the remaining Idumea ostraca by paleographic but also content-related comparisons with the unprovenanced text corpus. Last but not least, there is the question of where the administrative center of Idumea may have been in the Persian period. The place name "Maqqedah" – usually spelled *mnqdh*[43] – is recorded more than seventy times in the corpus of the unprovenanced ostraca,[44] which supports the identification of Khirbet el-Kôm – the place believed to be the source of the ostraca – with the biblical city of Maqqedah.[45] The entirely logical conclusion from this finding is that Maqqedah was the administrative center of the province during this period. If, however, it turns out that the Maresha Ostraca are connected with the rest of the corpus (or with parts of it), it cannot be excluded that many of these Ostraca originate from Maresha, which was the administrative and economic center of the province from Hellenistic times onwards. The question, then, is whether Maresha could have had a comparable function already in the late Persian period, which at least cannot be ruled out, and is even quite probable. Mareshah is the only major city in Idumea in

43 The expected spelling *mqdh* appears only rarely in the findings. For a fresh explanation of the surprising addition of the *nun* (traditionally understood as a preservation of the original Hebrew root *nqd* "sheeptender," the assumption then is, that the geminated *qof* in Maqqedah is the consequence of the assimilation of this original nun. The problem however with this explanation: already in older biblical traditions and inscriptions from the First Temple period the proper name in the spelling *mqdh* appears (for the inscriptions see Aḥituv, *Echoes from the Past*, 166–168, 180–181); why should Idumeans have used – centuries later – the assumed original *nun*-form?) see Vainstub, and Fabian, "An Idumean Ostracon From Ḥorvat Naḥal Yatir," 210–211. Clusters of double consonants as *qq* tend to dissimilate, leading to a new consonant being added.
44 See, e.g. Lemaire, *Levantine Epigraphy*, 112–113.
45 This identification was initially proposed by Dorsey ("The Location of Biblical Makkedah") and was then further supported by additional ostraca from the unprovenanced ostraca corpus. On the discussion of the various proposals of Maqqedah see Porten and Yardeni, "Maqqedah and the Storehouse in the Idumean Ostraca."

which extensive modern excavations have uncovered remains that represent a *continuum* from the late Persian period into the early Hellenistic period. If this holds true, then Maresha may as well be the place of the storehouse mentioned in the unprovenanced corpus (*msknt*).[46] While this storehouse is sometimes mentioned together with the placename "Maqqedah," this is not always the case. One may not exclude the possibility for another storehouse in Maresha. The probable function of these storehouse was probably collecting taxes. This would strongly suggest that already in the late Persian period Maresha was the major political and mercantile hub in the region. This is also suggested by the archaeological evidence from the site itself. While the evidence reveals little activity from during the 6th and 5th century BCE, things begin to change by the late Persian period. Aramaic ostraca, aniconic *kernos* lamps and numerous figurines such as horse and rider figurines and pillar figurines, testify to renewed settlement from the Late Persian to the Hellenistic period.[47]

Analysis of the "Yahwistic" Anthroponyms within the Idumean Onomasticon

The names in the ostraca by which the inhabitants of Persian period Idumea called themselves and their children are an important window into their identities. The corpus of the unprovenanced ostraca provides a solid data basis due to the publication quality, on which will be focused in the following.[48] So far about 560 different anthroponyms are recorded in the Idumean corpus. By far the largest groups of anthroponyms can be attributed to either the "Edomite" cultural sphere (for which the theophoric element *qws* is the exclusive indicator – the main Edomite deity) or an Arabic context. Each of these anthroponym-groups make about ca. 33 % of the overall evidence. The next-largest group are the Judean – or, in my terminology (as stated above) "Yahwistic" names (mostly Tetragrammatic). It is important here to be aware that while names with "Yahwistic" and/or Tetragrammatic elements likely (but not necessarily) indicate the presence of individuals of Yahwistic belief, one cannot immediately assume that this also indicates individuals who were formerly Judean that remained in this primarily "ex-Judean"-territory. We simply are not sure how the Idumean people construct-

46 See, e.g., Lemaire, *Levantine Epigraphy*, 204–216; and more generally on the taxation system in Idumea during the Persian period, see Edelman, "Economic and Administrative Realia."
47 See Stern, "The Evolution of an Edomite/Idumean Identity," 99–113 for an overview.
48 See for a recent but still preliminary treatment of the onomastic material from the unprovenanced corpus, Zadok, "Documentary Framework," 178–297.

ed the own self-identification (the Yahwists in this region could potentially understand themselves as Idumeans not as Judeans, simply for the fact that they were living now in the province of Idumea), thus "Yahwists" seems to be more appropriate. The number of clearly identifiable Phoenico or Philistine names lags far behind the Yahwistic ones. They contain popular Egyptian theonyms as theophorous elements. The number of purely Egyptian anthroponyms is very low and that of Greek and Iranian names is negligible.[49]

After this rough assessment of the onomasticon, which is based primarily on certain linguistic markers – Ran Zadok's preliminary study, published in 2021, stands out from the previous ones in methodological quality in this regard, as he steers clear of overly broad speculations about ethnic and political affiliations and tries to work out neat linguistic criteria – the theophoric names are in some ways somewhat more revealing. The fundamental assessment underlying the consideration of the theophoric onomasticon is that the bearers of these names or their eponyms mark persons as members of a particular community of shared *cultic ideologies* or *affiliations*.[50] These names indicate that members of a specific community or group had expressed a feature of their cultural perspectives or a social affiliation through the often highly intentional act of assigning names.[51]

One must be very cautious, however. While the presence of theophoric names within a larger name-corpus is often taken as indicators of one's "cultural," "national" or "ethnic" origins, these concepts too often are inappropriately applied to ancient contexts, as has been convincingly demonstrated by Bruce Routledge.[52] Ancient communities were much less homogenous than is usually assumed. The equation of certain (assumed and clearly distinguishable) identities often risks being too artificial. Especially within the Idumea Corpus it is quite evident that cultural diversity and permeability has to be taken in consideration. For example, not all *qws*-names indicate that its name-bearer is a Qos-worshipper or part of the "Edomite" community. Similarly, theophoric elements do not necessarily indicate that an individual or community worshipped *this deity* solely, as opposed to worshipping this deity as one among many deities. It will be shown in the following section (section 2) that the cases are more complex, especially as within the names theographic elements are mixed with certain linguistic markers usually attributed to other cultural identities (in the case of *qws*-names with Arabic or Aramaic name-elements); and especially from the study of clan-affiliations with

49 For this, see the detailed overview and list of percentages and absolute numbers in Zadok, "Documentary Framework," 193–205.

50 Nyström, "Names and Meaning."

51 Zadok, "Names and Naming."

52 Routledge, "The Antiquity of the Nation."

their remarkable intermixing of various cultural and religious traits, it is immediately visible, that one has to be very careful in his presumption on identities. With these methodological considerations in mind at least a few observations can – with some confidence – be drawn from the pure percentage of distribution of the theophoric elements: the theophoric names from this corpus has 227 names in total.[53] The Edomite deity *Qws* (28,63 % of all theophoric names), *ʾl* (24,66 % of all theophoric names), *Bʿl* (12,77 % of all theophoric names) is followed by the *Yhw*-theophoric element with a percentage of 9,25 % (21 names in total). The other deities are far behind with not even 2 % or less than 1 % of the evidence.

When the theophoric element is in the initial position of the anthroponym, it is always written as *Yhw*, for example *Yhwʿnh*[54] or *Yhwʿqb* (IA 12437 = ISAP 849). In the final position, however, it shows some variation: the most common spelling is *-yh*, as in, for example, *Ḥnnyh*,[55] or *Ṭwbyh*,[56] and its interchanging version *-yw*, as in *Ḥnnyw*[57] or *Ṭbyw*[58] (the name might be homonymous with the *Ṭwbyh).* The form *-yhw* is attested in *ʿbdyhw*[59] and *Yrmyhw.*[60]

If we look at the Maresha-corpus, a comparable situation regarding the percentages of theophoric elements arises. Esti Eshel records twelve *qws*-names, seven *Bʿl*-names, four with *ʾl*, and three with *Yw* or *Yh* in the evidence that she reviewed from the 1989–2000 excavation seasons at Maresha:[61] *Yw'[b]* (or *Yw'[š]*), *ʿbdyw* and *Ṭbyw* and *Šmryh*. The only notable exception in comparison to the corpus of the unprovenanced ostraca is the name *Yw'[b]* (or *Yw'[š]*) with the abbreviated version *yw* in the initial position.

Furthermore, if the suggested reading on the small incense altar from the Persian period is correct, there is the attestation of another Yahwistic name (*mḥlyh*) from a different context (that is, other than from Maresha or Maqqedah). The altar was found in Cave 534 southwest of the city gate.[62]

It is also remarkable that the distribution of anthroponyms is uneven if one looks at the various sites. As Ian Stern had already pointed out in an early publi-

53 I am referring here to the list of theophoric names, arranged by percentage in Zadok, "Documentary Framework," 207–208.

54 *TAO I*, 327.

55 Lemaire, *Nouvelles Inscriptions araméennes d'Idumée II*, 365.

56 Yardeni, *The Jeselsohn Collection*, 681.702–703.

57 Eph'al and Naveh, *Aramaic Ostraca*, 200.

58 Eph'al and Naveh, *Aramaic Ostraca*, 201.

59 *TAO III*, 593.

60 Yardeni, *The Jeselsohn Collection, 683b.*

61 Eshel, "The Inscriptions in Hebrew, Aramaic and Phoenician Script," 35–88.

62 Tufnell, *Lachish III*, 226, no. 534, pls. 49.3 and 68.1. See also below section 4.

cation on "Idumean identity,"[63] in Arad, for example, the percentage of names is 61.22 % Yahwistic (i.e., "Judahites" in Stern's terminology), 14.30 % Idumean (his terminology; he means names with the theophoric element *qws*), and 12.24 % Arabian names. What is remarkable here is the fact, that in Arad most of the "officers" had Yahwistic names, while most of the people to whom the supplies were given had Arabic names. Following these observations, Esti Eshel has speculated that – as she terms the group – "Jews" made up a significant part of the troops in Arad, commanded by the Qedarites in the area.[64] In Beer-sheba, the situation is different: 42.62 % had Arabian names, 24.59 % Idumean, and less than 20 % Yahwistic names.

2 Yahwistic Individuals in Cultural Proximity with Other Groups in Idumea

The following section will look at the larger picture and ask in which cultural context the Yahwistic names appear. As already stated above, we have to be cautious not to risk attributing too artificial identity concepts to these ancient societies. The cultural, social and ideological borders in Idumea are especially blurred, a fact that is easily overlooked when it is suggested that "Edomite," "Arab" and/or "Yahwistic" groups coexisted within Idumea. The reality is much more complex as a variety of cultural backgrounds appear to be mixed within the same name. Most of the theophorous names are a compound of a deity and a verb or noun, especially those with the element *qws* – such as Natanqos ("Qos gave") or Qosrim ("Qos is exalted") have counterparts from the – in my term – "Yahwstic" names that are mainly also attested in the Hebrew Bible, e.g., Natanel ("God gave") or Yehoram ("Yaho is exalted"). Others (but few) display Arabian influence with the theophoric element *qws*, e.g., Qosghayr ("Qos is jealous") or Qosḥair ("Qos is good").[65] Porten/Yardeni also list in their critical edition some 70 predicative elements *that are shared* by the "Yahwistic" and the "Idumean"/"Edomite" theophorous names. Porten/Yardeni here even speak of a – in their terms – "Judeo-Idumean piety."[66] It is not clear, however, what further conclusion they might draw from this finding. They seem to never really follow up to this conclusion.

63 Stern, "The Population of the Persian-Period Idumea," 212–213.
64 Naveh, "The Aramaic Ostraca from Tel Arad," 167.
65 On these see *TAO I*, xx.
66 *TAO I*, xx.

Additionally, in terms of the contexts of these individuals visible in the onomasticon, the clan lists of the (unprovenanced) Idumea Ostraca are very interesting and have been pertinently studied by Bezalel Porten, Ada Yardeni, and André Lemaire,[67] among others. It has been observed that many of the individuals mentioned in the ostraca are defined by their connection to a family, clan, or tribe. Some 230 individuals in the corpus have been identified by filiation to a clan. Porten in particular has undertaken tracing the "dossiers" (his terminology) of several clans over several generations that he constructed through the relationships visible in the various ostraca. These are the clans of Qosḥanan, of Yehokal, of Qoṣi, of Gur, of Ḥori, of Rawi, of Alba'al and of Ba'alrim.[68] These clan-list give an excellent window into the society of Idumea in the fourth century BCE. Remarkable is the level of *cultural fluidity* that is tangible within the generation lists with a substantial amount of flexibility and *intermixing between* the different "ethnic groups." If one, for example, looks at the members of the clan of "Gur," through the generations 31 % had Arabic names, while another 31 % had Edomite/Idumean (that is: names with the theophoric element *qws*) names. Half the members of the Ba'alrim family – the name of the clan leader/founder is of Phoenician origin – had Arabic names, almost 25 % had *qws*-names (and were thus of potential Edomite or Idumean origin), one was Egyptian, and only one was Phoenician.[69]

Remarkable in this context is the clan Yehokal (see Fig. 1 below).[70] Judging from the name, which according to many scholars is a composite name with the theophoric element *yhw*,[71] the progenitor of the family was presumably of a Yahwistic context. Yet, all following generations have, without any exception *non-Yahwistic names*: Qosyinqom, Qoslanṣur, Qosner, Qos'az, Qos'ayr, as well as several Arabic, two Egyptian and one Aramean.[72]

---

67 Porten and Yardeni, "The House of Baalrim"; *TAO 1*: Here are all clan dossiers assembled; see also Stern, "The Population of the Persian-Period," 217–218; Lemaire, *Nouvelles Inscriptions araméennes d'Idumée*, 145; Eph'al and Naveh, *Aramaic Ostraca*, 15.

68 The names are variable in spelling within the ostraca corpus, see Porten and Yardeni, "The House of Baalrim."

69 For both cases see also Stern, "The Population of the Persian-Period," 216–221.

70 All related ostraca can be found in the "Yehokal Dossier" (A5.1–20) in *TAO 1*, 313–362.

71 Lemaire, *Levantine Epigraphy*, 424, holds that the Yahwistic name Yehokal (Yaho is able, has power) is already mentioned in the book of Jeremiah (Jer 37:3; cf 38:1: יְהוּכַל). In the "clan-dossiers", the name Yehokal has five spellings – full: יהוכל that appears most frequently (A5.1–2, 4–8, 10–11, 14–16, 18–20), defective: יהכל (A5.12–13), abbreviated: one יוכל (A5.9), phonetic: יאכל (A5.17), and the unique יואכל (Naveh, "The Aramaic Ostraca from Tel Arad" = ISAP2136). The name appears on four Hebrew seals, bullae, and jar impressions and thrice is affiliated with a Yahwistic theophorous name (cf. also *TAO 1*, 222).

72 *TAO 1*, 222–224.

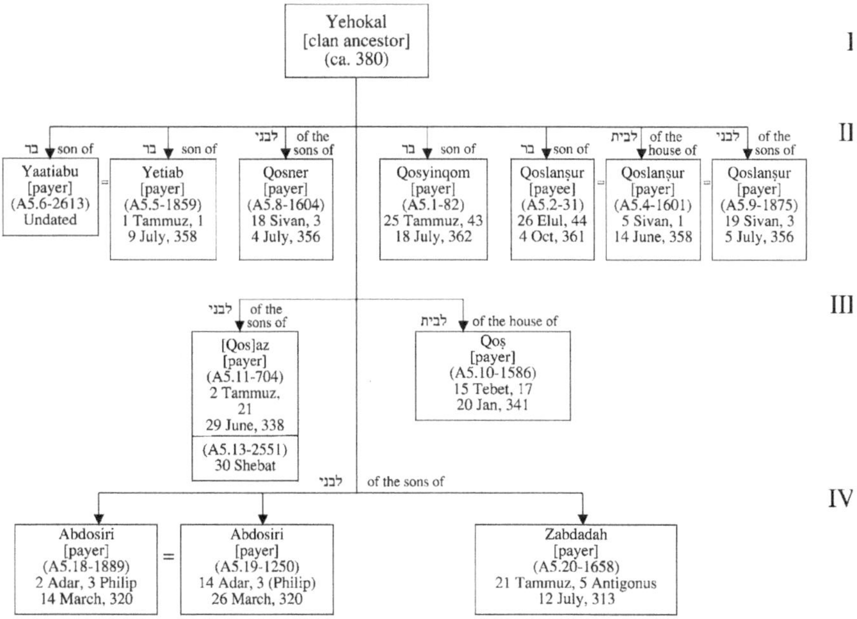

Fig. 1: The Four Generations of the Clan of Yehokal, after Porten and Yardeni, *TAO I*, 223.

One might deduce from this finding that a family of possibly Judean origin found its last representative with Yehokal. The subsequent generations already adapted to the cultural majority. All these clan lists show that cultural borders were rather fluid or low. However, it would be problematic to deduce from this finding that only the generation of the progenitor Yehokal was still Yahwistic, after which one tended towards Qos or another religion – syncretism or acculturation is the term often used for this phenomenon in research.[73] In view of the overall findings in Idumea, however, this term seems to me to be out of place.

Of further interest is the evidence of a *beth yaho*, a temple of Yaho, on one of the Idumean Ostraca (for the detailed discussion of this ostracon see below). If the reading is correct (and the more damaged part in the same line would not

73 See, for instance, Stern, "The Population of the Persian-Period," 216–221. In his words (p. 218): "The onomastic statistics from our database indicate a clear Idumean dominance and it appears reasonable to assume that Ye[ho]kal was a Judahite who was in the process of acculturation into the more dominant Idumean society." Cf. also Porten and Yardeni: "The authors ask whether this is an isolated case of a Jew settled in the midst of pagan Idumeans who gave his children the names of his neighbors or must we understand the Idumean name differently from its Hebrew homonym?" (Porten and Yardeni, "In Preparation of a Corpus of Aramaic Ostraca," 212.

read "the ruins of" the *beth yaho*), this would mean that there was a temple of Yaho in Idumea, possibly situated in Maqqedah or even in Maresha (for this see my arguments below) – this all suggests that at least some Yahwists, potentially ex-Judahites in the area of Idumea remained of Yahwistic belief by the 4th century BCE – thus, even in the 4th century, the Yaho faith had not simply been replaced by a Qos-faith (or the like), and the majority of the inhabitants had become "Edomites" or "Idumeans," so to speak, from "Judahites." One could also put it differently: Yahwism did not share the "streamlined monotheistic, aniconic form" as in Jerusalem (and probably also at Mount Garizim), but was more diverse, with several cultural and religious overlaps with the neighboring cultures and religions in Idumea. Especially since one can never completely exclude the possibility that (such as in the case of Yehokal's clan) qos-containing names of successor generations were used somewhat interchangeably, wherein Yaho, the highest god of the Judeans, was simply translated to the local context wherein the name Qos was more readily understood to be the highest god. Anyway, it remains striking to find so many *qws*-anthroponyms in a Yahwistic clan, even if one is unable to offer a definite solution.

Additionally, there is at least one Judeo-Edomite/Idumean mixed filiation in the evidence of the corpus of unprovenanced ostraca, where Qos and Yaho are also placed in very close proximity: *Qwsytb* son of *Ḥnnyh.*[74]

One may add here also a rather strange name from the biblical corpus: the name Kushaiah (קוּשָׁיָהוּ); according to the biblical tradition he is father of Ethan, a Merarite Levite who accompanies the ark of God on its return to Jerusalem (1 Chr 15:17). Strangely enough, this name may include both, the theophoric element *qws* as well as *yhw*, and the name would better be rendered as "Qosyah": "Qos is YHWH."[75] As is immediately evident, most scholars would reject this understanding on the grounds that Qos is supposedly never spelled with ש but with a ס. Yet, against this speaks the fact that the name *qsmlk* is written in at least one text as *qšmlk* (see Heshbon ostracon A6; late sixth century BCE).[76]

All this evidence together immediately raises the question of the cultural proximity of Qos and Yahweh during the Iron Age. And with good reasons, because after all it is conspicuous that Qos is one of the few non-Israelite deities that is not represented negatively in the biblical traditions. In addition, there are the religious-historical considerations of a common origin of Yahweh and Qos as

74 Lemaire, *Levantine Epigraphy*, 119–120.

75 As Tebes has pointed out, this possibility was raised by Vriezen (original text: "Quš is Jahu"); yet, Vriezen found syncretistic compound names "virtually impossible;" Vriezen, "The Edomitic Deity Qaus," on Kushaiah and the citation from pages 352–353.

76 On the spelling differences see Cross, *Leaves from an Epigrapher's Notebook*, 90–93.

weather deities. As well as the affinity of Yahweh from his origins to Edom (see Kuntillet Ajrud). The mentioning of "YHWH of Teman," as attested in the inscriptions from Kuntillet Ajrud (early eighth century BCE), may point to a close relationship of both deities. However, this depends on whether Teman designates a region or city in Iron Age Edom, as can be argued from the biblical evidence (Jer 49:7, 20; Ezek 25:13; Am 1:11 f.; Obad 8 f.; Hab 3:3). Yet, it has long been presumed that the deity YHWH should be associated with the presence of Shasu nomads in the southern borderlands.[77] Some of the Shasu nomads are also connected in Egyptian texts of the fourteenth/thirteenth centuries BCE with the regions of "Seir" and "Edom." This has, among other reasons, led some scholars to conclude that the Edomites were originally worshippers of YHWH and only "adopted" Qos/Qaus after the establishment of their monarchy.[78] While the cultural interaction between YHWH and Qos/Qaus in the Iron Age is still a matter of heavy debate, I would argue that the Idumean evidence from the Persian and Hellenistic periods shows an interesting fusion of "Edomite" and "Yahwistic" elements.

This also means that the individuals of the clan Yehokal may have understood themselves as Yahwists – despite the Qos-containing names of individuals. Yahwistic identity is not limited to Yahwistic or biblical names as such in this multicultural, ethnically fluid society.

3 The *beth yaho* in Idumea: A Yahwistic Temple in Maqqedah or Marissa – or "in Ruins" since the Late Iron IIC?

In 2002, André Lemaire published an ostracon dating to the fourth century BCE (see Fig. 2 below). The Ostracon, like most of the Idumea Ostraca, unfortunately comes from the antiques market and is therefore unprovenanced. Due to its paleographic references to the rest of the corpus, however, it undoubtedly belongs to the Idumea Ostraca of the 4th century. In 2015, Lemaire presented his most-recent reading of the ostracon,[79] applying several changes in reaction to critical remarks on his readings and reconstructions of the text by Bezalel Porten and Ada Yardeni.[80] The ostracon has now also been included in the final fifth volume

77 See Leuenberger, "YHWH's Provenance from the South," for discussion of the relevant texts.

78 See, e.g., Knauf, "Qôs," esp. 677; see Amzallag, *Esau in Jerusalem*, 39–47.

79 See Lemaire, *Levantine Epigraphy*, 118–119 (with fig. 3.25).

80 See e.g. Porten and Yardeni. "Why the Unprovenienced Idumean Ostraca Should be Published," 87 fig. 8, with page 77; Porten and Yardeni, "The House of Baalrim," 142 fig. 21, with page 112–113; *TAO 1*, liii fig. 40, and page xxi.

of the Textbook of Aramaic Ostraca from Idumea (TAO)-series (under H.1.1).[81] The ostracon reads as follows:

1: תלא[זי] תחת מן בית עזא	1: The hill/ruin that is under the house/temple of 'Uzza
2: וחיבלא זי בית יהו	2: and the rope/portion/ruin of the house/temple of Yaho
3: זבדנבו רפידא זי בטנא	3: ..., the terrace of the terebinth,
4: ברא משכו כפר גלגול	4: ..., the tomb of Gilgul,
5: רקק זי לות כפר	5: the sheet of water *of the monumental tomb*
6: כפר ינקם	6: the tomb of Yinqom.

(Aramaic Ostracon AL 283 = ISAP 1283, 4th century BCE)[82]

Fig. 2: Aramaic Ostracon AL 283 = ISAP 1283, mentioning BYT YHW at the end of line 2; photograph with friendly permission of A. Lemaire from Lemaire, *Levantine Epigraphy*, 118.

81 *TAO V*, 21–22.
82 Text and translation after Lemaire, *Levantine Epigraphy*, 118–119. *Editio princeps*: Lemaire, *Nouvelles Inscriptions araméennes d'Idumée II*, text 283, table XLVIII, 149–156 (= AL 283).

The contents of this ostracon can best be described as a cadastral record where microtoponyms referring to several locales are enumerated. Since the hill (line 1) was located below the two temples mentioned in lines 1 and 2, it is clear that these two were located at a high(er) point of the location. The mention of the temple of the well-known North Arabic goddess al-'Uzza (line 1) accords with the importance of the Arabic "elements" in the other Idumean ostraca.

What is surprising here, however, is the fact that this widespread deity does not appear in the stock of anthroponyms of the Idumean Ostraca. In my opinion, this raises at least two urgent questions:

1. What can actually be learned about the culture, ancestry, religion of the name-bearers or name-givers by the onomastic analysis of the anthroponyms? Without the epigraphic evidence, nothing could have been said about these references in Idumea from the pure onomastic evidence.
2. Is the temple of al-Uzza possibly not connected with the "mainstream" Idumean population (majority Edomite or Arab) at all? It is possibly a sanctuary of other Arabic groups and merchants who trade through the region? A similar phenomenon is known about a recently discovered precinct, which, however, dates to Hellenistic times, but is located not far from Mareshah: Ḥorvat 'Amuda (4 km southeast of Maresha; 3rd/2nd centuries BCE)[83] is interpreted in parts as a sanctuary, but clearly shows cultural influences from (not North, but) South Arabia, more precisely: from Yemen. The classification of this site within the Idumean find is not yet fully clarified, but here, too, the interpretation that it is a sanctuary of merchant travelers is suggested. In the onomastic finding (again) one does not see these references to south Arabia.

Remarkable in this ostracon is the mentioning of a בית יהו in line 2. The reading of this expression is unquestionable. The spelling of the divine name as יהו does not correspond to the expected Judean יהוה, but rather to the form regularly attested in the Elephantine documents (alongside occasional uses of יהה in the ostraca, following the Lozachmeur publications[84]).

The decisive factor is the reading and interpretation of the set of letters immediately before in the same line. The term חיבלא is enigmatic, but it can be interpreted as "length of a rope"/"portion of a field" (Hebrew *ḥbl I, GESENIUS s. v.)* or "ruin" (from the root *ḥbl*$_1$, DNWSI s. v.: "to damage," "to ruin"). The latter interpretation has been favored by Porten/Yardeni in their recent edition of the ostracon.[85] If this would hold true, and a ruined Yahwistic temple is mentioned

83 Haber, Gutfeld, and Betzer. "A Monumental Hellenistic-Period Ritual Compound."
84 Within the Elephantine papyri corpus, יהה is attested only in TAD B2.7:14 (also B3.3:2).
85 *TAO V*, 21–22.

in the document, this immediately raises the question of when the temple was destroyed. One explanation that has been suggested is to connect the temple of Yahu with a pre-exilic temple in the region – Ran Zadok even speculates about a pre-Josian Judean temple.[86] To me this explanation seems not all too convincing. On the one hand it presupposes the immediate historicity of the cult centralization and cult purification under Josiah mentioned only in the Hebrew Bible (2 Kings 23–24) – that this so-called reform is far more complex in historical, religious-historical and literary-historical perspectives has to be considered in a much more differentiated way has already been shown by many studies.[87] On the other hand, why must a ruin of a temple, which is mentioned on an ostracon from the middle of the 4th century B.C., date to the 7th century? A scenario of a damaged temple (e.g., by fire) from the Persian period would also be conceivable.

Interpretating the phrase חיבלא as "portion" (of a land) becomes more plausible if one considers the character of the document as a cadastral and that the בית יהו is mentioned in perfect parallel with the (active temple) בית עזא in line 1.[88] Accordingly, it is an active Yaho-sanctuary in late Persian times in the province of Idumea. This is only surprising if one looks at it with the biblical template of cult centralization (especially Deut 12) in view: historically, however, several Jaho-sanctuaries dating to Persian and also Hellenistic periods outside Judah have been known for quite some time now (one may especially consider the sanctuaries of Mt. Gerizim and at Elephantine[89]).

Furthermore, it is not evident that these sanctuaries were in rivalry with the supposed center of Yahwism in Jerusalem (for the Persian period, this is merely part of the religious reinterpretation of this circumstance in certain scribal circles) – for Garizim[90] as well as for Elephantine,[91] the conflict-free contacts with Jerusalem have been described many times, especially for the Persian period. Accordingly, this can also be assumed for the temple in Idumea as a basic scenario of the religious-historical situation of Yahwism in Idumea.

But where is this sanctuary to be located? Most follow Lemaire's cautious suggestion[92] that it is Maqqedah.[93] However, it has to be said that the interpreta-

---

86 See, most recently, Zadok, "Documentary Framework," 179.

87 Cf. Pietsch, *Die Kultreform Josias*; Uehlinger, "Was There a Cult Reform."

88 See also Lemaire, *Levantine Epigraphy*, 219.

89 For an overview and religious-historical contextualization of the various Yaho-sanctuaries in the post-exilic periods see Hensel, "Cult Centralization."

90 See the comprehensive sketch of the relationship of Juda and Samaria in the Persian period: Hensel, "On the Relationship of Juda and Samaria," 19–42.

91 See Edenburg, "Messaging Brothers in Distant Lands."

92 Lemaire, *Nouvelles Inscriptions araméennes d'Idumée II*, 223; cf. Lemaire, *Levantine Epigraphy*, 118–119.

93 See, e.g., Becking, "Temples across the Border."

tion towards Maqqedah is only based on the fact that the origin of the rest of the Idumea Ostraca are localized in Maqqedah – as already mentioned mainly because of the warehouses mentioned several times in the Ostraca and the locality Ma(n)qqedah. This is of course one possibility. Yet, in the light of my previous considerations on the Aramaic ostraca from Maresha, which possibly stem (this holds true at least for some of the material) from the 4th Century BCE, the temple might more likely be located in Maresha, the – as I interpret it – administrative center of the province of Idumea in the late Persian period (and beyond).

4 Lachish: Indications of Yahwistic Worship in the Persian Period?

Lachish is located on a major road leading from the Coastal Plain to the Hebron hills, bordering the Judean foothills (the Shephelah in the local idiom), some 30 km southeast of Ashkelon. The original British expedition led by Olga Tufnell discovered several areas of Late Persian and early Hellenistic Occupancy of the Tell. A Building Structure in the Residency,[94] was interpreted by the team as a Late Persian/Early Hellenistic temple, which they termed the "Solar Shrine" (see Fig. 3, below). Tufnell dated the establishment of the Lachish temple to the Persian period, while the pottery found inside stemmed from the second half of the second century BCE.[95]

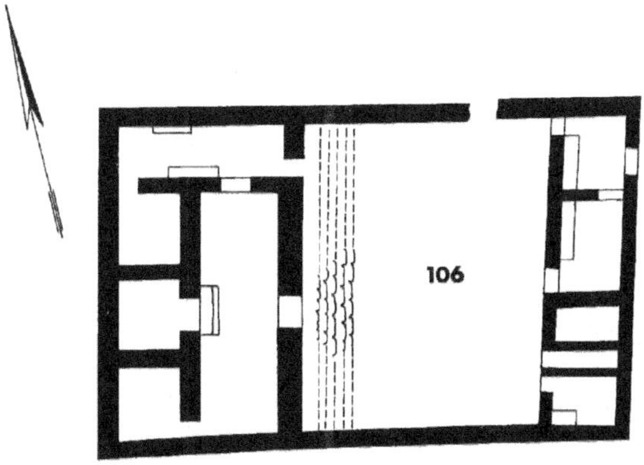

Fig. 3: Lachish, Solar Shrine (building 106), after Aharoni, *Lachish V*, 10 fig. 3.

94 See Tufnell, *Lachish III*, pl. 119.
95 Tufnell, *Lachish III*, 141–145.

When revisiting the site in the year 1966, Yohanan Aharoni related this temple to the Iron Age temple in Arad found during his excavationand related this temple to the Judean Iron Age temple in Arad found during its excavation because of supposed architectural parallels. Unlike Tufnell, however, he dates the temple around 200 BCE and does not see an earlier phase here.[96] Influenced by his findings at Arad, Aharoni attributed the Hellenistic-period cult at Lachish to descendants of the Judeans who remained in the area after its conquest by the Edomites following the fall of the Judean Kingdom in the 6th century BCE, and who continued to practice an existing Yahwistic tradition.[97]

The renewed excavation, led by David Ussishkin, have since shown that the question of Persian and Hellenistic settlement is far more complex – this is primarily due to the evaluation of the Pottery. Yet, Ussishkin also proposed an earlier, Persian-period phase of the Solar Shrine,[98] making it possible to think of a Persian period, Yahwistic Shrine in Lachish.[99] However, the recently published careful reevaluation of the findings processed by Alexander Fantalkin and Oren Tal,[100] this building is the only one with a "secure Hellenistic date."[101] They analyzed and reinterpreted especially the stratigraphy and the pottery in the area, and additionally, none of the finds recovered *in* the Solar Shrine is of Persian date.

However, Fantalkin and Tal have pointed to the fact, that another building in this context (on the map: Grid Squares R/Q/S.15/16: 10–21) (see Fig. 4, below) holds well to an earlier dating, as suggested by Tufnell. Tufnell concluded from the findings in the room that it should be dated to the 4th and 3rd century BCE.[102] Aharoni concluded from this and further findings that this building served as the fourth- to third-century BCE forerunner of the Solar Shrine,[103] which is followed by Fantalkin/Tal.[104]

96 Aharoni, *Investigations at Lachish*, 9.
97 Aharoni, "Trial Excavation," esp. 161–163.
98 Ussishkin, *Biblical Lachish*, 340–342.
99 Ussishkin himself, however, interpreted the shrine in light of his reconstruction of the Solar Shrine as a cultic *Persian* governmental center (Ussishkin, *Biblical Lachish*, 96–97).
100 Fantalkin and Tal, "A Tale of Two Provinces." In more detail on the debate of the dating of the temple see also Tal, *The Archaeology of Hellenistic Palestine*, 68–71.
101 Fantalkin and Tal, "A Tale of Two Provinces," 177–214, citation from page 184.
102 Tufnell, *Lachish III*, 148.
103 Aharoni, *Investigations at Lachish*, 9–11, fig. 3.
104 Fantalkin and Tal, "A Tale of Two Provinces," 184–185.

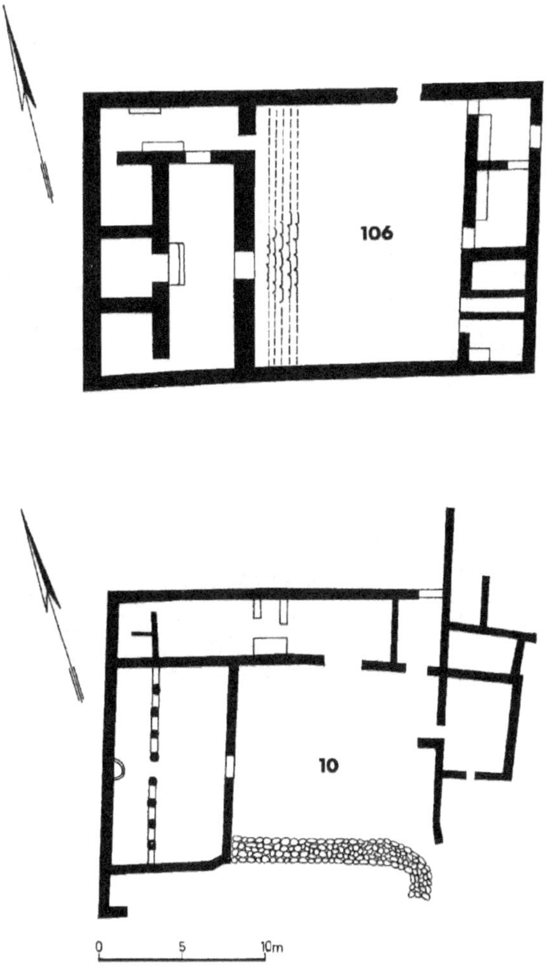

Fig. 4: Lachish, Solar Shrine (top) in context building below in Grid Squares R/Q/S.15/16: 10–21: the Solar shrine forerunner (Aharoni)?; figure from Aharoni, *Lachish V*, 10 fig. 3.

A dedication altar with a possible Yahwistic name incised upon it was found in Cave 534 southwest of the city gate.[105] The suggested reading is *mḥlyh* (see Fig. 5 and Fig. 6, below) – the anthroponym runs from the end of line 2 (*mḥ*) to the beginning of line 3 *(lyh)*.

105 Tufnell, *Lachish III*, 226, no. 534, pls. 49.3, 68.1; and see also 383–384; for its reading, see Dupont-Sommer, "Aramaic Inscription on an Altar"; Aharoni, *Investigations at Lachish*, 5–7, fig. 1, with discussion.

Fig. 5: Lachish; Yahwistic name incised upon dedication altar.

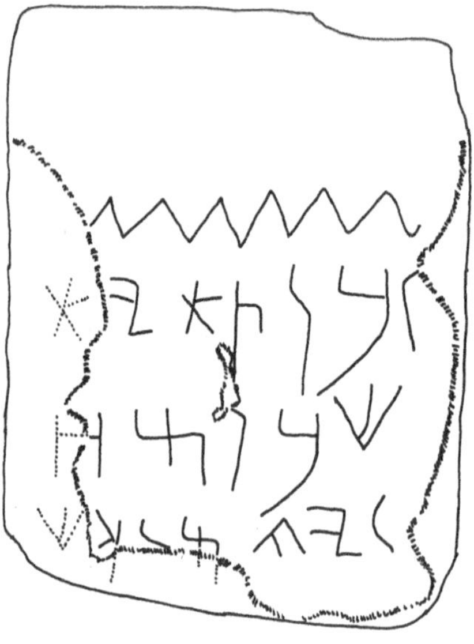

Fig. 6: Drawing of the inscription, figure from Aharoni, *Lachish V*, 6 fig. 1.

The whole inscription reads as follows:

(1) lbnt'y	(1) Incense altar of 'Iyy-
(2) *šbnmḥ*	(2) ōš, son of Maḥa-
(3) *lyhmlk[š]*	(3) lyah from Lachish.

Reproduced here is the balanced reading of Rainer Degen, who has challenged the not unproblematic and since its publication much debated,[106] first reading of Dupont-Sommer (*Lachish III*). The understanding of line 3 is particularly contested: the suggestions range from, amongst others, *lyh mr' [šmy']* "to YH, Lord of the Heaven" (A. Dupont-Sommer) to *lyh mlk[š]* "Maḥliyah from Lachish" (Aharoni and Degen, amongst others) and *ly hmlk* "Maḥlay, the king" (Lemaire[107]). Lemaire's proposal clearly does not see a Yahwistic element here and interprets the *h* as an article for the following substantive with the suggested reading *mlk* ("king"). One argument for Lemaire's reading is certainly that he does not need to add a letter to the end of line 3. In his opinion, no final letter at the end of the line has broken away here. I was not able to check the inscription again in the original, however, it seems to me from the inspection of the photos nevertheless probable that at the breaking line of the inscription (very clearly to see at the final letter at the end of line 2) also in line 3 still another letter must have followed. This would not make it impossible to read "Lachish" and to understand the *h* as part of the proper name previously provided, which would thus clearly be a Yahwistic one.

The altar formed part of an assemblage found in a number of caves southwest of the city gate (506, 515, 522, 534)[108] and was probably cultic in nature. The existence of a Yahwistic name on such an altar at least allows the conclusion that at least from Hellenistic times the installation was used as a place of Yahwistic activity.

Rüdiger Schmitt and others have recently raised the idea that also the Persian-period figurines, that were found outside the borders of Yehud and especially at Lachish[109] could have been used by the Yahwists in or around Lachish.[110] It

106 For the discussion see Degen, "Der Räucheraltar aus Lachisch,“ 40–45.

107 See, most recently, Lemaire, *Levantine Epigraphy*, 100, building on his earlier reading from 1974 in *Revue Biblique* 81.

108 Cf. Tufnell, *Lachish III*, 220–221.224–226.

109 See Tufnell, *Lachish III*, 142–144.

110 See Schmitt, "Continuity and Change," esp. 101. and Negbi, *A Deposit of Terracottas and Statuettes*, 1, n. 5 attributes the Persian figurines and the chalk altars found in the south-west of the site to the Solar Shrine.

has to be said, however, that only one Persian horserider figurine was found actually *in* the Solar Shrine, together with a few other figurines from both earlier and later periods.[111]

5 A Yehud/Yaho-Coin from Idumea? – a Methodological Remark

The finding to be discussed in the following is more of a methodological problem. It illustrates in its curiosity how the research tends to keep the material findings out of an adequate description of the history of religion and culture of early Judaism.

A famous and unique image of a late Persian coin (see Fig. 7 and 8, below) originating from Yehud depicts the governor Bagoas on the obverse,[112] and interestingly shows a deity sitting on a winged wheel on the reverse,[113] which is probably to be identified with YHWH based on its coin legend, traditionally read as יהד.[114] In the meantime Haim Gitler and Oren Tal have proposed the reading יהו, i.e., "Yaho," which is admittedly preferable, because in neo-Paleo-Hebrew writing the consonants ד and ו are very similar, so that the identification is clear. Such an explicit representation of YHWH is absolutely singular and remarkable for the Southern Levantine area, for Yehud (and Judah before) specifically.

However, it is now significant that Gitler/Tal almost reflexively *exclude* the find from the material evidence for *Yehud*, since – in their view – it has no room in the assumed purified and aniconic Yehud cult of the post-exilic period. With reference to other Yaho-sanctuaries in Samaria (Garizim) and Idumea (Maqqedah; see above) they state therefore the following:

> This could suggest that the production of this coin was carried out under Edomite Jews who disregarded the second commandment, or alternatively under Gentiles who consider YHWH as yet another deity of their cultic surface.[115]

---

111 Aharoni, *Investigations at Lachish*, pl. 18.

112 See Barag, "Bagoas and the Coinage of Judea."

113 Hill, *Catalogue of the Coins of Palestine*, XIX 29 and Meshorer and Qedar *Samarian Coinage*, 15.

114 On the possible interpretations of the coin, cf. Niehr, "Götterbilder und Bilderverbot," esp. 243 as well as Blum, "Der 'Schiqquz Schomem'." Also Keel, *Die Geschichte Jerusalems*, interprets the image as a YHWH-image.

115 Gitler and Tal, *The Coinage of Philistia*, 230.

Fig. 7: A famous and unique coin image of a late Persian coin originating from Yehud; photograph with friendly permission of I. de Hulster from his publication de Hulster, *Iconographic Exegesis*, 196).

Fig. 8: Drawing by Izaak de Hulster, Göttingen, for the WiBiLex article "Yahweh" based on the original by Meshorer/Qedar, *Samarian Coinage*, 15.

Already because of the inscription and the context of the find ("Yehud") it is absurd to look for the minting authorities in Idumea. Especially since no minting activities are known for the entire Persian period – this is, among other things, an argument for those researchers who do not want to attribute a provincial status to Idumea for the Persian period.[116]

116 See, e.g., Levin, "The Genesis of Idumea," 85–87.

Of course, the coins do not give any information about a possible group of deviant Yahwists in Idumea. Instead of immediately disqualifying the finding as "deviation," methodological caution must be exercised – as the findings for Idumea show. This coin gives just information about the complexity of the religion-sociological conditions in the Persian province of Yehud and is part of the complex religious-historical developments towards a radically persevered monotheism in later times.

6 Judeans, Judahites, Jews, Hebrews, Samaritans or Yahwists? – Idumean Yahwists or Simply: Idumeans!

The immediate question that arises is, how to term this group of people that is seemingly, within the larger context of the province of Idumea, oriented in cultic affairs to Jaho/YHWH? There is a great deal of disagreement in the research community about how to deal with the "Yahwists" who are believed to be identified via the onomasticon. Important research along this line of the onomastic evidence is connected with the names John R. Bartlett,[117] Bezalel Porten and Ada Yardeni,[118] Ran Zadok,[119] Amos Kloner, Ian Stern,[120] Esti Eshel,[121] Juan M. Tebes,[122] and Yigal Levin.[123] First of all, the linguistic criteria and the terminology of these criteria are very inconsistent and sometimes already very judgmental. Sometimes it creates the impression of an onomastic criteria catalog that can be clearly grasped and clearly delimited. On the other hand, the complexity of the situation, especially in Idumea, is shown by the above explanations. In any case, the following criteria are named. The various studies employ categories of "West Semitic," "Israelite," "Jewish," "Judean," "Judahite" or even "biblical" names – and this is only a selection of the terms used. Because the studies usually do not define

---

117 Bartlett, "Edomites and Idumaeans."
118 See esp. *TAO I*, 1–5.
119 Zadok, "A Prosopography of Samaria and Edom/Idumea," 785–822; Zadok, "Documentary Framework," 178–297.
120 Kloner and Stern, "Idumea in the Late Persian Period"; Stern, "Ethnic Identities."
121 Eshel, "The Inscriptions in Hebrew, Aramaic and Phoenician Script"; and Eshel, "Iron Age, Phoenician and Aramaic Inscriptions."
122 Tebes, "Memories of Humiliation."
123 Levin, "The Genesis of Idumea"; Levin, "The Formation of Idumean Identity"; Levin, "The Southern Frontier of Yehud," 239–252.

what precise linguistic considerations are behind the terminology, they seem to be misleading or at least imprecise. For instance, what would the criterium "Jewish names" as a linguistic category mean in a time period where Judaism is just starting to emerge and the differentiating identity markers (especially the existence of the Torah and its use in everyday life, is not yet a matter of debate).[124] As I have stated on several other occasions now (as have some others before), one should probably not speak about Judaism and Jewish as a religious terminology before the late 2nd/early 1st century, when we have clear indications of Judaism in Antiquity; before is a time of plurality in Yahwism (see my introduction).

The different terminological systems applied by the various studies may have their justification within the interpretative system of each respective researcher; but often solid linguistic criteria are mixed together with assumptions on "ethnic" and "political" identities; in many cases, however, above all the theophoric element is the only unambiguous criterion. From the variety of the criteria and their naming also derives the plurality of the description of this group: the studies speak with reference to the same (depending on their criteria: a roughly similar) group about "Judahites," "Judeans," "Hebrews," "Israelites" or "Jews"[125] – depending on how one correlates the different criteria also the percentage and strength of this group in the onomasticon differs, of course, and ranges from a minimum of 2 % "Yahwists" to 10 % (Ian Stern). Terms like "Judahites" or "Judeans" seem to also always imply their ancestry with the Judean kingdom of old, but which had – nevertheless – long gone (over 200 years) by the time the names are attested. Ran Zadok then discusses and then dismisses the possibility that the group could have been Samaritans – they were Judeans.[126]

With regard to the terminology of the group, I propose to leave these problematic terms, since they are loaded with many presuppositions, and to use instead – at least for the time being – the term "Yahwists." On the basis of the findings, we simply cannot yet make any statement about how exactly these "Yahwists" practiced their Yaho-cult or how they identified themselves. The fact that they still considered themselves Judeans and felt connected to the brothers and

---

124 See for this Adler, *The Origins of Judaism*, esp. 189–221 and Cohen, *The Beginning of Jewishness.*

125 See, for example, Notarius, "The Syntax of the Clan Names," 23: "many Edomite, Arabian, Aramaic, Canaanite (Phoenician) and Jewish names indicate ethnically, linguistically and culturally different groups that were in interaction at that period in the area of Southern Canaan." "Judeans": see e.g., Zadok, "Documentary Framework"; "Jews": Porten and Yardeni, *passim* in most of their works; "Judahite": see, e.g., Stern, "The Evolution of an Edomite/Idumean Identity," 101 and *passim.*

126 Zadok, "Documentary Framework," 234.

sisters in the province of Yehud is a possible, but by no means exclusive, interpretative option.

In addition, there is the following further consideration: That the onomastic evidence has shown how complex the situation in Idumea is, especially in terms of cultural proximity and fluidity. What one can observe, especially in recent publications, is a terminological ambiguity that is, in my opinion, no less simplistic.

Unlike older studies (Bartlett, etc.), one tries – with good reasons – to avoid the category "Edomite" – for the obvious and correct reason that Edom has not existed as a political entity since 552. In its place, in more recent articles, the category of "Idumeans" is used with congruent meaning, especially in the studies of Kloner, Stern and Levin.[127] What is described with this terminological category are ultimately only names with the theophoric element *qws*.

In my opinion, this suggests far too strong a cultural distinction from the other groups – we have already seen how "Edomite"/"Idumean" and "Arabic" cultural traits can intertwine in the names. Above all, however, the category "Idumean" is here also completely inadmissibly restricted to the Qos-Worshippers. At the latest from the Zenon Papyri (3rd century) this province was known as Idumaea; as a geographical term it is already documented in Diodorus (312 BCE). We have already suggested above that there was probably already a Province Idumaea from the late Persian period. This means, nevertheless, that from the outside at least, this region and its inhabitants were known as "Idumeans." This is true for all inhabitants (or – if you subtract the passing traders: at least for most of them) and should not be limited to the Qos-worshippers alone. We simply do not know what the Idumeans – that is, according to my understanding: all the people living in Idumea– thought of themselves. Did they identify themselves as Idumeans in their own right, or did they instead consider themselves "refugees" from old Edom? Did they think of themselves as "natives"? Can we even think of them in terms of ethnicity? Is there cultural continuity from the Iron-Age Edomites to the people living west of the Arabah in the Persian and Hellenistic periods? In order to avoid already introducing too many hypothesis-rich presuppositions with the terminology, I advocate using the term "Idumeans" in a broad sense: the inhabitants of the province. Further linguistic markers, raised via the onomasticon, can then clarify their cultural background on a case-by-case basis – for example, affinity to Qos or affinity to Yaho, etc. Thus, I would plead for calling the Yahwists in the region first of all neutrally as "Idumeans." One must discuss, then, to what extent these (or their subgroups) had family-based ties to Yehud and whether they saw themselves as ex-Judahites. Forthwith, however, I suggest that

127 See their articles quoted in this study.

these Idumeans be referred to as Idumean Yahwists. The geographical and political entity of Idumea is first of all (neutrally speaking) their primary frame of reference. I see the term as analogous to – as I have put it – Judean Yahwism (i.e., that of the province of Yehud) and "Samarian Yahwism" (i.e., that of the Persian province of Samaria).[128] The term "Idumean Yahwism" is clearly to be understood as a provisional term, because at this stage we simply know too little about the social structures and religious structures of the Yahwists in Idumea. The term, however, can claim to look at the group as neutrally as possible from the point of view of religious studies, without immediately bringing in categories such as "deviation" (from an imagined Jerusalem Orthodoxy) or an assumed exiled Judean tradition in Idumea. The Idumean Yahwism is to be studied within the context of the province of Idumea first and added to the panorama of Yahwism in the Persian period in general.

7 The Case of the Edomite-Judean Genealogies in Chronicles and Judean-Edomite Cultic Ties in Genesis 23

The thesis gains further support, I argue, when one turns to the biblical evidence. This can be shown most succinctly in the book of Chronicles, as will be expanded in the following. The origins of the Book of Chronicles can safely be dated with a majority of recent scholars to the 4th or 3rd century BCE[129] – I prefer the later date for reasons that need not to be discussed here.[130]

In its re-telling of the history of Judah, Chronicles sketches an independent conception of what the authors and later redactors envisioned "Israel" to be at the time of writing. This "biblical Israel"[131] of Chronicles is defined – especially

128 See Hensel, *Juda und Samaria.*

129 For a brief discussion of the dating see Nihan, "Cult Centralization and the Torah," esp. 259.

130 The dating, in my view, hinges primarily on the strongly anti-Samaritan perspective of the Chronicles. This perspective develops in the transition from the 4th to the 3rd century B.C., see the following considerations Hensel, "Ezra-Nehemiah and Chronicles" and Hensel, "On the Relationship of Juda and Samaria."

131 For the term see Kratz, "Where to put 'Biblical' Yahwism in Achaemenid Times?" in this volume. In contrast to Kratz, however, it seems appropriate to me to emphasize the plurality of identity constructions that claim to be "biblical Israel." The different concepts are quite different with regard to their factual, literary and theological profiling, thus excluding each other, and in my opinion are historically due to the fact that also historically a certain conception of Yahwistic identities can be found, with which authors, redactors and tradents of the biblical texts deal, see

at the beginning of the Book of Chronicles – primarily through genealogies. These clarify the origin, descent and cultural intertwining of this "Israel" in the context of an imagined mythical pre-past and within the southern Levant and its bordering nations. This definition of the nature of "Israel" may have some historical aspects, but it is above all one thing: the theology or ideology of the contemporary (late Persian, early Hellenistic) authors. Their conception of "Israel" is deduced from the past, grounded there and then given a Jerusalem-centric perspective.

It is not without reason that Chronicles begins with the so-called *Genealogische Vorhalle* (1 Chr 1–9) and defines here quite fundamentally "Israel" via a series of genealogical lists.

In view of Edom and/or Idumea the following is remarkable:

Not surprisingly, the Chronicler's genealogical introduction of the "people of Israel" (1 Chr 2:3–8:40) as such accords more coverage to Judah than to any other tribe in this context (1 Chr 2:3–8:40). The Chronicler clearly emphasizes that although Judah is not the firstborn of Israel, he is still entitled to leadership among his brothers over Reuben (the firstborn of Leah) and Joseph (the firstborn of Rachel). See, for instance, 1 Chr 5:2, the opening part of the genealogy of Ruben: כִּי יְהוּדָה גָּבַר בְּאֶחָיו וּלְנָגִיד מִמֶּנּוּ וְהַבְּכֹרָה לְיוֹסֵף ("though Judah became strong among his brothers and a chief came from him, yet the firstborn-right belonged to Joseph"). The mentioning of the leadership alludes of course to David's kingship, which encompassed all of the Israelite tribes (cf. 1 Sam 13:14; 25:30; Mic 5:1 et al.). This pivotal position of Judah is also the reason why in the presentation of the many groups that comprise – at least in the view of Chronicler – Israel, Judah's offspring is discussed first (1 Chr 2:3–4:23). The genealogy of Judah has received significant scholarly attention, and understandably so. Much of research is thereby focused on textual, source-critical, redactional and literary considerations as there are many problems in the text in its present form, which has been described as difficult, disorderly or incoherent.[132] Above all, however, historical questions of Judah's past are in the foreground for the research and whether the chronicler might not have had earlier "sources" at his disposal. Within the limitations of this article, this research cannot and need not be rehashed here; I leave it at this indication of the problem. However, whatever sources the Chronicler may have used, the crucial question, in my opinion, is what function such a genealogy may have fulfilled in late Persian or early Hellenistic times. Here, the substantial multi-ethnic and multi-cultural character of Judah's genealogy is particularly striking. Not only are there clear connections to other Israelite tribes

on this Hensel, "Who Wrote the Bible," 11–23 and Hensel, "Yahwistic Diversity and the Hebrew Bible," 1–44.

132 For the discussion see, Japhet, *I & II Chronicles*, 73–127.

(Reuben 1 Chr 2:9; 4:1; Manasseh 1 Chr 2:21.22; Simeon 1 Chr 2:43; Benjamin 1 Chr 4:4), but especially striking are the connections to non-Israelites within the genealogy.[133] Here the connection to "Edom" stands out very clearly, especially as – and in contrast to the other non-Israelites – the "Edomites" are *made* Judahite. What do I mean by this? Chronicles presents genealogical lists *linking Judean and Edomite* families or clans through the repetition of eponymous ancestors and descendants from Esau in their literary reception of the Edomite genealogy Genesis 36. It is undoubtedly the case that the Chronicler is very clearly aware of the *text* of Edomite Genealogy in Gen 36 to which he alludes in his version of genealogies. The most striking case of genealogical overlap occurs with regard to Esau's grandson Qenaz (קְנַז), the son of Eliphaz in Genesis 36:11. This name also appears as one of the אַלּוּפֵי בְנֵי־עֵשָׂו in Genesis 36:15 and 42. These "Qenazzites" appear, on the one hand, in the Edomite genealogies in 1 Chr 1:35–54 (קְנַז in vv. 36, 53) – which is of course not surprising –, but, on the other hand, they also appear in the Judahite genealogy in 1 Chr 4:13–15 (בְּנֵי קְנַז). The Qenazzites are here not labeled as "sons of Esau" or "Edomites" or the like, they are simply presented as part of the *Judahite* genealogy, which is opened in 1 Chr 4:1 and stretches till 1 Chr 4:23.

1 Chr 4:1a.13–15:

1 בְּנֵי יְהוּדָה

(…)

13 וּבְנֵי קְנַז עָתְנִיאֵל וּשְׂרָיָה וּבְנֵי עָתְנִיאֵל חֲתַת׃ 14 וּמְעוֹנֹתַי הוֹלִיד אֶת־עָפְרָה וּשְׂרָיָה הוֹלִיד אֶת־יוֹאָב
אֲבִי גֵּיא חֲרָשִׁים כִּי חֲרָשִׁים הָיוּ׃ פ 15 וּבְנֵי כָּלֵב בֶּן־יְפֻנֶּה עִירוּ אֵלָה וָנָעַם וּבְנֵי אֵלָה וּקְנַז׃

1 The sons of Judah….

(…)

13 The sons of Qenaz: Othniel and Seraiah; and the sons of Othniel: Hathath and Meonothai. 14 Meonothai fathered Ophrah; and Seraiah fathered Joab, the father of Ge-harashim, so-called because they were craftsmen. 15 The sons of Caleb the son of Jephunneh: Iru, Elah, and Naam; and the son of Elah: Qenaz.

The Edomites of the literary source Gen 36:11, 15, 42 are by this re-labeled as *Judahites* – rather than that Edomites *became* part of the genealogy. This is, for example, the case in other parts of the Judahite genealogy, where it is clearly said that non-Israelites became part of the Judahite family via intermarriage.

The Edomites of the literary source Gen 36:11, 15, 42 are by this re-labeled as *Judahites* – rather than that Edomites *became* part of the genealogy. This is, for example, the case in other parts of the Judahite genealogy, where it is clearly said that non-Israelites became part of the Judahite family via intermarriage.

133 For these see, instead of many, Knoppers, "Intermarriage, Social Complexity, and Ethnic Diversity," esp., 19–23.

Additionally, there is also a significant overlap between a number of the Jerahmeelite names like Onam (אוֹנָם) and Shammai (שַׁמַּי) (1 Chr 2:28), which are clearly part of the *Judahite* genealogy (1 Chr 2:3–4:23), and the names that appear in the Edomite genealogies in 1 Chronicles 1:35–54 and the Chronicler's *Vorlage*, in Genesis 36, cf. Genesis 36:13/1 Chronicles 1:35 (שַׁמָּה) and Genesis 36:23/1 Chronicles 1:40 (אוֹנָם). As in the case presented before, the literary "template" taken from the Edomite genealogy is presented as an Edomite or more generally speaking: *Foreign* element within the Judahite genealogy (as – again – in other cases of non-Israelites elements in the Judahite tribal system) – they are plainly presented as *Judahites* from the beginning.

1 Chr 2:3a.28:

1 בְּנֵי יְהוּדָה
28 וַיִּהְיוּ בְנֵי־אוֹנָם שַׁמַּי וְיָדָע וּבְנֵי שַׁמַּי נָדָב וַאֲבִישׁוּר

1 The sons of Judah...
(...)
28 The sons of Onam: Shammai and Jada. The sons of Shammai: Nadab and Abishur.

This phenomenon holds true for a variety of other names in the Judahite genealogies: Shobal (שׁוֹבָל), one of the descendants of Hur (1 Chr 2:50, 52) and the immediate son of Judah (1 Chr 4:1), appeared earlier as an Edomite in Genesis 36:20, 23, 29 (= 1 Chr 1:38, 40: שׁוֹבָל). Zerach (זֶרַח), whose name is an outstanding representant of the Edomite genealogy in Genesis 36:13, 17, 33 (cf. its mention within the Edomite genealogy in 1 Chr 1:37, 44), also appears in the list of descendants of Tamar (1 Chr 2:4, 6; cf. Gen 38:30), yet here as a Simeonite (1 Chr 4:24). On a narratological level, Zerah is clearly connected to Esau or Edom, not only on the level of genealogy (Gen 36), but also via allusions, as its name means "sunrise," which alludes to the color of "red" Edom (resp. Esau or Seir). This, via several wordplays, is narratologically connected with Genesis (see esp. Gen 25:30), which plays on the phonetical and written similarity between אָדֹם, "red," and אֱדוֹם. Even in the story of Judah and Tamar, where Zerah is apparently a son of Judah, the story already alludes to the brotherly connection between Esau (Edom) and Judah (Israel) before Gen 25–36. Already the terminology hints or alludes to this connection: The term תּוֹאֲמִם ("twin") occurs only in the Judah–Tamar story Gen 38:27 and in the birth narrative of the famous twins Esau and Jacob (Gen 25:22).

In Gen 38, Perez, Zerah's brother is the firstborn son, while Zerah (alluding to Edom/Esau) is the second born son – here the text emphasizes via genealogical allusion what had been told before: The firstborn Esau/Edom loses his firstborn right in favor of his brother Jacob. I have demonstrated this in more detail in my monograph in the firstborn-blessing (or rather: On the interchange of the natural firstborn with his younger sibling[134]) in the book of Genesis. Remarkably, though, in Chronicles we learn nothing of this "Edomite past" of the *literarische Vorlage* – he is presented as a Judahite.

In my view, while making "Edomites" Judahite within the genealogical (and thus: ideological) thinking of the Chronicler, a certain historical and contemporary (to the Chronicler) situation is reflected. It is the Persian period Idumea where we find this degree of cultural diversity and the very close proximity of "Edomite" and "Judahite" cultural traits, as shown above. As I tried to elaborate in the previous section, the Yahwists in Idumea were part of the Idumean society, while, at the same time, some of them might have or might be remembered as having family ties or ties in the past with Judahite ancestors because of the territory they once lived in. In my understanding this "Edom" that the Chronicler is referring to, when reusing "Edomite" names from the respective genealogy on Gen 36, is not the former Edomite kingdom in Transjordan – he refers to Idumea in the Southern parts of the former Judahite kingdom. This is further supported by the fact, that the Hebrew texts do not terminologically differentiate between Edom (the older kingdom) and Idumea (the later province), all is rendered אֱדוֹם. This also means, not all references to Edom in post-exilic (mostly Persian period) texts are referring to an Iron Age kingdom in Transjordan as traditional and more recent research nearly unanimously tends to assume, they might rather reflect contemporary, that is Persian period, realities in Idumea – I have dealt with this surprisingly influential "blind spot" in research in detail in another article.[135]

Moreover, the Septuagint, which is roughly from the same time period as the Book of Chronicles, provides a possible linguistic differentiation between the two (Εδωμ and Ἰδουμαία). The term Ἰδουμαία for the kingdom of Edom and the Hebrew אֱדוֹם in LXX is especially used in Gen 36:16, thus within the "Edomite" genealogy:

> Gen 36:16 LXX:
> ἡγεμὼν Κορε, ἡγεμὼν Γοθομ, ἡγεμὼν Αμαληκ· οὗτοι ἡγεμόνες Ελιφας ἐν γῇ **Ιδουμαίᾳ**· οὗτοι υἱοὶ Αδας.
>
> Which translates the Hebrew Original:
> אַלּוּף־קֹרַח אַלּוּף גַּעְתָּם אַלּוּף עֲמָלֵק אֵלֶּה אַלּוּפֵי אֱלִיפַז בְּאֶרֶץ **אֱדוֹם** אֵלֶּה בְּנֵי עָדָה

There is no clue why the translator used Ἰδουμαία in this particular instance, while he uses Εδωμ in all other occurrences of the Hebrew אֱדוֹם MT in Gen 36.

---

134 Hensel, *Die Vertauschung des Erstgeburtssegens in der Genesis*, 139, 206–208.
135 See Hensel, "The Complexity of a Site," 13–37, esp. 30–37.

There is no apparent reason why Eliphaz, of all people, the firstborn son of Esau (Gen 36:15), and his descendants (Gen 36:16) should be identified territorially with Idumea, which is not the case with the other Edomite or Seirites in these genealogies. It seems to be the case that the terms Εδωμ and Ἰδουμαία are used synonymously. Further instances for the use of Ἰδουμαία are Josh 15:1; 2 Sam 8:12, 13, 14; 1 Kgs 11:1, 14, 15, 16; 2 Kgs 14:10; 1 Chr 18:11, 12, 17; 25:19. This opens up the possibility that also the Chronicler might have understood or envisioned with "*Edom*" the *Idumean* realities of his time period.

The reason behind making Edomites (Idumeans) Judahite seems to be, that in the Chronicler's conception of "biblical Israel," as he unfolds it first in his *genealogische Vorhalle* and then later narratively, the Idumeans are *integrated* into the main Israelite tribe: Judah. The Idumeans are part of this envisioned "Israel." Consequently, Idumea/Edom can only mean that the chronicler wants to understand the Yahwist individuals in Idumea (probably because there were regional references to Judah earlier) as part of his "Israel."

These observations fit seamlessly with other traditions or redactions, independent of the Book of Chronicles, that can be attributed to the Persian period. I have already suggested elsewhere and elaborated more broadly that both the role of "Edom" as it is further developed in Persian times in the Jacob Cycle (Gen 25–35; in P and Post-P redactional layers),[136] as well as the mention of "Edom" as a brother of Israel (Deut 2; 23, also very likely a Persian text),[137] are part of this literary strategy of integrating Idumeans into the respective image of Israel.

I add here, very briefly, a further case, which I assume is connected with this strategy. Genesis 23 is a text that several recent researchers evaluate as late-P, written in the Persian period. This story narrates the etiology of the grave that Abraham purchased from the Hittites in Hebron and seems to reflect the historical reality of the Persian period in which the southern lands of Judah, including Hebron, were occupied by Edomites.[138] All this is, of course, the territory of Idumea: It is possible that Abraham's cave represents a Yahwistic cultic site in the land of Idumea.[139] The late-P-related revision of Gen 23 possibly makes space for the diversity of the Yahwistic cults (in this case in Idumea) and presents a counter-position to a geographically centralized cult (i.e., only one temple) in Jerusalem.

---

136 See Hensel, "Tightening the Bonds."

137 See Hensel, "Think Positive."

138 Wöhrle, "'Gebt mir einen Grabbesitz bei euch.'."

139 See discussion in, esp. Hensel, "Tightening the Bonds," 397–417; Hensel, "Edom in the Jacob." See also De Pury, "Abraham," esp. 85–86.

Conclusions

To sum up the major observation presented above:

a) It can be concluded that while there is a very strong influence of individuals or groups with an Edomite or Arab affiliation/background, the group of individuals with a Yahwistic background is the next largest group in Idumea.

b) The picture that emerges is that of a mixed population, with Arabs, Edomites, Yahwists and others living side-by-side and probably intermixing as well. It has now become clear, that ethnic boundaries seem to have been very fluid in this region over several centuries; only a minority of persons, for example, maintained their progenitors' ethnic onomastica. The various findings testify more to a mixture of certain cultural and religious traits or a set of cultural options, for example Greek, Phoenician, Edomite, Qedarite or proto-Arabic, Nabatean, Southern Arabian, and Idumean-Yahwistic.

c) As stated before, this Yahwism adds to my general perception of multiple Yahwisms in the Persian period, which are characterized by regional diversification and pluriform sociological and religious forms. To me, the Yahwism of the Persian period is primarily characterized by a set of cultural, social, and religious options that only *realized* their formative power by the 2nd/1st century BCE. Via this long process, early Judaism emerges from this multiplicity. The different groups existed alongside each other in the previous periods, even if they display differences in detail regarding religious practice and the sociology of religion. So, for example, monotheism is a *possible* option during the Persian period (Judah and Samaria) but not an *exclusive* option for faith in the God of Israel, so, e.g., in Elephantine and possibly also in Idumea, where we see a strong cultural and religious affiliation and family ties of (Idumean Yahwists with Qos, the former state deity of Edom).

d) Certain biblical traditions – as was been shown in the case of the Book of Chronicles (which is of Late Persian or Early Hellenistic origin) and in the case of the Post-P text Gen 23 reflect Idumean realities of this time period. They take into account the cultic and cultural fluidity in this period. In the case of the Chronicler, he makes Edomites (= Idumean Yahwist in my understanding) part of his envisioned "biblical Israel."

In any case, the material and possibly biblical evidence of an Idumean Yahwism grants us a unique glimpse into a non-biblical (one might say) Judaism from the Persian period. Yahwism participates in the phenomenon of cultural fluidity in the region and as such is a much larger phenomenon. It can only be hoped that future research and studies of the archaeological material (especially the epigraphic corpus from Maresha) will help clarifying the many still open question.

Bibliography

Adler, Yonatan, *The Origins of Judaism: An Archaeological-Historical Reappraisal*, The Anchor Yale Bible Reference Library. New Haven: Yale University Press, 2022.

Aharoni, Yohanan, *Investigations at Lachish: The Sanctuary and the Residency (Lachish V)*, Tel Aviv University Publications of the Institute of Archaeology 4. Tel Aviv: Gateway Publishers, 1975.

Aharoni, Yohanan, "Trial Excavation at the 'Solar Shrine' at Lachish. Preliminary Report," *IEJ* 18 (1968): 157–169.

Aḥituv, Shmuel, *Echoes from the Past: Hebrew and Cognate Inscriptions from the Biblical Period*, Jerusalem: Carta, 2008.

Amzallag, Nissim, *Esau in Jerusalem: The Rise of a Seirite Religious Elite in Zion at the Persian Period*, CahRB 85. Leuven: Peeters, 2015.

Barag, Dan, "Bagoas and the Coinage of Judea," In *Proceedings of the XIth International Numismatic Congress Hackens*, edited by Tony Hackens, Ghislaine Moucharte, Catherine Courtois, Harry Dewit, and Véronique Van Driessche, 261–265. Louvain la Neuve: Séminaire de Numismatique Marcel Hoc, 1993.

Barnea, Gad, "Yahwistic Identity in the Achaemenid period." *Zeitschrift für die Alttestamentliche Wissenschaft* 136.1 (2024): 1–14.

Bartlett, John R., "Edomites and Idumaeans," *PEQ 131* (1999): 102–114.

Becking, Bob, "Temples across the Border and the Communal Borders within Yahwistic Yehud," *Transeuphratène 35* (2008): 39–54.

Ben-Yosef, Erez, "The Architectural Bias in Current Biblical Archaeology," *VT* 69/3 (2019): 361–387.

Bienkowski, Piotr, "Transjordan in the Persian Period: The Archaeological Evidence and Patterns of Occupation," In *Transjordan and the Southern Levant. New Approaches Regarding the Iron Age and the Persian Period from Hebrew Bible Studies and Archaeology*, edited by Benedikt Hensel in collaboration with Jordan Davis. In press, forthcoming 2024.

Blum, Erhard, "Der 'Schiqquz Schomem' und die Jehud-Drachme. BMC Palestine S. 181, Nr. 29," *BN* 90 (1997): 13–27.

Cohen, Shaye J. D., *The Beginning of Jewishness: Boundaries, Varieties, Uncertainties*, Hellenistic Culture and Society 31. Berkeley: University of California Press, 1999.

Cross, Frank M., *Leaves from an Epigrapher's Notebook: Collected Papers in Hebrew and West Semitic Paleography and Epigraphy*, HSS 51. Winona Lake: Eisenbrauns, 2003.

Danielson, Andrew J., "Edom in Judah: Identity and Social Entanglement in the Late Iron Age Negev," pages 117–150 in *About Edom and Idumea in the Persian Period: Recent Research and Approaches from Archaeology, Hebrew Bible Studies and Ancient Near East Studies*. Worlds of the Ancient Near East and Mediterranean. Edited by Benedikt Hensel, Ehud Ben Zvi, and Diana V. Edelman. Sheffield: Equinox Publishing Limited, 2022.

Degen, Rainer, "Der Räucheraltar aus Lachisch." *Neue Ephemeris für semitische Epigraphik* 1 (1972): 39–48.

De Hulster, Izaak J., *Iconographic Exegesis and Third Isaiah*, FAT II 36. Tübingen: Mohr Siebeck, 2009.

De Pury, Albert, "Abraham: The Priestly Writer's 'Ecumenical' Ancestor," In *Die Patriarchen und die Priesterschrift / Les Patriarches et le document sacerdotal: Gesammelte Studien zu seinem*

70. Geburtstag / Recueil d'articles, à l'occasion de son 70e anniversaire. AThANT 99. Edited by Jean-Daniel Macci, Thomas Römer, and Konrad Schmid, 73–89. Zürich: Theologischer Verlag Zürich, 2010.

De Pury, Albert, "Le tombeau des Abrahamides d'Hébron et sa fonction au début de l'époque perse," *Transeu* 30 (2005): 183–184.

Diodorus, Siculus, *Bibliotheca Historica: Books XVIII–XX*, Edited by Immanuel Bekker, Ludwig Dindorf, Friedrich Vogel, and Kurt Theodor Fischer. Leipzig: aedibus B. G. Teubneri, 1903–1906.

Diodorus, Siculus, *The Library of History: Vol. 10: Books 19.66–20*, Loeb Classical Library 390. Translated by Russel M. Geer. Cambridge: Harvard University Press, 1954.

Dorsey, David, "The Location of Biblical Makkedah," *TA 7* (1980): 185–193.

Dupont-Sommer, André, "Aramaic Inscription on an Altar," In *Lachisch III, The Iron Age*, edited by Olga Tufnell, 358–359. London: Oxford University Press, 1953.

Edelman, Diana V., "Introduction," pages 1–5 in *The Triumph of Elohim: From Jahwisms to Judaism.* CBET 3. Edited by Diana V. Edelman, Kampen: Kok Pharos Publishing, 1995.

Edelman, Diana V., "Economic and Administrative Realia of Rural Idumea at the End of the Persian Period," pages 277–301 in *About Edom and Idumea in the Persian Period: Recent Research and Approaches from Archaeology, Hebrew Bible Studies and Ancient Near East Studies*. Worlds of the Ancient Near East and Mediterranean. Edited by Benedikt Hensel, Ehud Ben Zvi, and Diana V. Edelman. Sheffield: Equinox Publishing Limited, 2022.

Edenburg, Cynthia., "Messaging Brothers in Distant Lands. Biblical Texts in Light of Judean, Samarian and Diaspora Target Audiences," pages 204–223 in *Mass Deportations – To and From the Levant during the Age of Empires in the Ancient Near East*. HeBAi 11. Edited by Ido Koch. Tübingen: Mohr Siebeck, 2022.

Eph'al, Israel, and Naveh, Joseph, *Aramaic Ostraca of the Fourth Century BC from Idumaea*, Jerusalem: Magnes Press, 1996.

Eshel, Esther, "Iron Age, Phoenician and Aramaic Inscriptions," pages 77–94 in *The Excavations of Maresha Subterranean Complex 57: The Heliodorus Cave*, BAR International Series 2652. Edited by Ian Stern. Oxford: Archaeopress, 2014.

Eshel, Esther, "The Inscriptions in Hebrew, Aramaic, and Phoenician Script," pages 35–88 in *Maresha III: Epigraphic Finds from the 1989–2000 Seasons.* IAA Reports 45. Edited by Amos Kloner, Esther Eshel, Hava Korzakova, and Gerald Finkielsztejn. Jerusalem: Israel Antiquities Authority, 2010.

Eshel, Esther, Langlois, Michael, and Geller, Mark, "The Aramaic Divination Texts," pages 302–317 in *About Edom and Idumea in the Persian Period: Recent Research and Approaches from Archaeology, Hebrew Bible Studies and Ancient Near East Studies*. Worlds of the Ancient Near East and Mediterranean. Edited by Benedikt Hensel, Ehud B. Zvi, and Diana V. Edelman. Sheffield: Equinox Publishing Limited, 2022.

Eshel, Hanan, "Hellenism in the Land of Israel from the fifth to the Second Centuries BCE in Light of Semitic Epigraphy," pages 116–24 in *A Time of Change: Judah and Its Neighbors in the Persian and Early Hellenistic Period*. Library of Second Temple Studies 65. Edited by Yigal Levin. London: T & T Clark, 2007.

Fantalkin, Alexander, and Tal, Oren, "A Tale of Two Provinces: Judah and Edom During the Persian Period," pages 177–214 in *About Edom and Idumea in the Persian Period: Recent Research and Approaches from Archaeology, Hebrew Bible Studies and Ancient Near East Studies*. Worlds of the Ancient Near East and Mediterranean. Edited by Benedikt Hensel, Ehud B. Zvi, and Diana V. Edelman. Sheffield: Equinox Publishing Limited, 2022.

Frevel, Christian. "Alte Stücke – Späte Brücke? Zur Rolle des Buches Numeri in der jüngeren Pentateuchdiskussion," pages 255–299 in *Congress Volume München 2013*. VTS 163. Edited by Christl M. Maier. Leiden: Brill, 2014.

Gertz, Jan C., Levinson, Bernard M., Rom-Shiloni, Dalit, and Schmid, Konrad eds. *The Formation of the Pentateuch: Bridging the Academic Cultures of Europe, Israel, and North America*, FAT 111. Tübingen: Mohr Siebeck, 2016.

Gitler, Haim, and Tal, Oren, *The Coinage of Philistia of the Fifth and Fourth Centuries BC. A Study of the Earliest Coins of Palestine*, Collezioni Numismatiche 6. Mailand: Edizioni Ennerre S.r.l., 2006.

Grabbe, Lester L., *A History of the Jews and Judaism in the Second Temple Period: Vol. 1. Yehud: A History of the Persian Province of Judah*, LSTS 47. London: T & T Clark, 2004.

Haber, Michal, Gutfeld, Oren, and Betzer, Pablo, "A Monumental Hellenistic-Period Ritual Compound in Upper Idumea: New Findings from Ḥorbat ʿAmuda," pages 230–249 in *About Edom and Idumea in the Persian Period: Recent Research and Approaches from Archaeology, Hebrew Bible Studies and Ancient Near East Studies*. Worlds of the Ancient Near East and Mediterranean. Edited by Benedikt Hensel, Ehud B. Zvi, and Diana V. Edelman. Sheffield: Equinox Publishing Limited, 2022.

Hensel, Benedikt, "Cult Centralization in the Persian Period: Biblical and Historical Perspectives," *Sem 60* (2018): 221–272.

Hensel, Benedikt, *Die Vertauschung des Erstgeburtssegens in der Genesis. Eine Analyse der narrativ-theologischen Grundstruktur des ersten Buches der Tora*, BZAW 423. Berlin/New York: De Gruyter, 2011.

Hensel, Benedikt, "Edom in the Jacob Cycle (Gen *25–35): New Insights on Its Positive Relations with Israel, the Literary-Historical Development of Its Role, and Its Historical Background(s)," pages 55–134 in *The History of the Jacob Cycle (Genesis 25–35). Recent Research on the Compilation, the Redaction and the Reception of the Biblical Narrative and Its Historical and Cultural Contexts*. ArchB 4. Edited by Benedikt Hensel. Tübingen: Mohr Siebeck, 2021.

Hensel, Benedikt, "Ezra-Nehemiah and Chronicles – New Insights into the Early History of Samari(t)an-Jewish Relation," *Religions* 11(2) (2020): 1–24.

Hensel, Benedikt, *Juda und Samaria: Zum Verhältnis zweier nach-exilischer Jahwismen*, FAT I 110. Tübingen: Mohr Siebeck, 2016.

Hensel, Benedikt, "On the Relationship of Juda and Samaria in Post-Exilic Times: A Farewell to the Conflict Paradigm," *JSOT 44.1* (2019): 19–42.

Hensel, Benedikt, "Tightening the Bonds between Edom and Israel (Gen 33:1–17*): On the Further Development of Edom's Role within the Fortschreibung of the Jacob Cycle in the Exilic and Early Persian Periods," *Vetus Testamentum 71* (2021): 397–417.

Hensel, Benedikt, "The Complexity of a Site: 'Edom' in the Persian Period from the Perspectives of Historical Research, Hebrew Bible Studies, and Ancient Near Eastern Studies," pages 13–37 in *About Edom and Idumea in the Persian Period: Recent Research and Approaches from Archaeology, Hebrew Bible Studies and Ancient Near East Studies*. Worlds of the Ancient Near East and Mediterranean. Edited by Benedikt Hensel, Ehud B. Zvi, and Diana V. Edelman. Sheffield: Equinox Publishing Limited, 2022.

Hensel, Benedikt, "Think Positive! How the Positive Portrayal of Edom in Late Biblical Texts Leads to New Perspectives on Understanding the Literary History of Genesis, Deuteronomy, and Chronicles," pages 338–362 in *About Edom and Idumea in the Persian Period: Recent Research and Approaches from Archaeology, Hebrew Bible Studies and Ancient Near East Studies*. Worlds of the Ancient Near East and Mediterranean. Edited by Benedikt Hensel, Ehud B. Zvi, and Diana V. Edelman. Sheffield: Equinox Publishing Limited, 2022.

Hensel, Benedikt. "Yahwistic Diversity and the Hebrew Bible: State of the Field, Desiderata and Research Perspectives in a Necessary Debate on the Formative Period of Judaism(s)," pages 1–44 in *Yahwistic Diversity and the Hebrew Bible: Tracing Perspectives of Group Identity from*

Judah, Samaria, and the Diaspora in Biblical Traditions. FAT II 120. Edited by Benedikt Hensel, Dany Nocquet, and Bartozs Adamczewski. Tübingen: Mohr Siebeck, 2020.

Hensel, Benedikt, "Who Wrote the Bible? Understanding Redactors and Social Groups behind Biblical Traditions in the Context of Plurality within Emerging Judaism," pages 11–23 in *Social Groups behind Biblical Traditions: Identity Perspectives from Egypt, Transjordan, Mesopotamia, Persia, and Israel in the Second Temple Period.* FAT 167. Edited by Benedikt, Hensel, Dany Nocquet, and Bartosz Adamczewski. Tübingen: Mohr Siebeck, 2023.

Hensel, Benedikt, Adamczewski, Bartosz, and Nocquet, Dany, eds., *Social Groups behind Biblical Traditions: Identity Perspectives from Egypt, Transjordan, Mesopotamia, Persia, and Israel in the Second Temple Period,* FAT 167. Tübingen: Mohr Siebeck, 2023.

Hensel, Benedikt, Ben Zvi, Ehud, and Edelmann, Diana V., eds., *About Edom and Idumea in the Persian Period: Recent Research and Approaches from Archaeology, Hebrew Bible Studies and Ancient Near East Studies,* Worlds of the Ancient Near East and Mediterranean. Sheffield: Equinox Publishing Limited, 2022.

Hill, Georg F., *Catalogue of the Coins of Palestine. A Catalogue of the Greek Coins in the British Museum,* London: British Museum, 1914.

Japhet, Sara, *I & II Chronicles. A Commentary*, OTL. Louisville: John Knox Press, 1993.

Keel, Othmar. *Die Geschichte Jerusalems und die Entstehung des Monotheismus (2 vol.)*, Göttingen: Vandenhoeck & Ruprecht, 2007.

Kloner, Amos. *Maresha Excavations Final Report I: Subterranean Complexes 21, 44, 70*. IAA Reports 17. Jerusalem: Israel Antiquities Authority, 2003.

Kloner, Amos. "The Identity of the Idumeans Based on the Archaeological Evidence from Maresha," pages 563–573 in *Judah and the Judeans in the Achaemenid Period. Negotiating Identity in an International Context,* edited by Oded Lipschits, Gary N. Knoppers, and Rainer Albertz. Winona Lake: Eisenbauns, 2011.

Kloner, Amos, and Ian Stern. "Idumea in the Late Persian Period," pages 139–144 in *Judah and the Judeans in the Fourth Century B.C.E.*, edited by Oded Lipschits, Gary N. Knoppers, and Rainer Albertz. Winona Lake: Eisenbrauns, 2007.

Knauf, Ernst A. "Qôs," pages 674–77 in *Dictionary of Deities and Demons in the Bible,* edited by Karel van der Toorn, Bob Becking, and Pieter van der Horst, 2nd revised ed., Leiden: Brill, 1999.

Knoppers, Gary N., "Intermarriage, Social Complexity, and Ethnic Diversity in the Genealogy of Judah," *JBL* 120 (2001): 15–30.

Kratz, Reinhard G., "The Analysis of the Pentateuch: An Attempt to Overcome Barriers of Thinking," *ZAW* 128 (2016): 529–561.

Kratz, Reinhard G., "Where to put 'Biblical' Yahwism in Achaemenid Times?" (*in this volume*).

Langgut, Dafna, and Lipschits, Oded, "Dry Climate During the Early Persian Period and Its Impact on the Establishment of Idumea," pages 151–176 in *About Edom and Idumea in the Persian Period: Recent Research and Approaches from Archaeology, Hebrew Bible Studies and Ancient Near East Studies*. Worlds of the Ancient Near East and Mediterranean. Edited by Benedikt Hensel, Ehud B. Zvi, and Diana V. Edelman. Sheffield: Equinox Publishing Limited, 2022.

Lemaire, André, "Edom and the Edomites," pages 225–243 in *The Books of Kings; Sources, Composition, Historiography and Reception.* VTSup 129. Edited by André Lemaire, Baruch Halpern, and Matthew J. Adams. Leiden: Brill, 2010.

Lemaire, André, *Levantine Epigraphy and History in the Achaemenid Period (539–332 BCE)*, Oxford: British Academy, 2015.

Lemaire, André, *Nouvelles Inscriptions araméennes d'Idumée du Musée d'Israël*, STrEu 3. Paris: Peeters, 1996.

Lemaire, André, *Nouvelles Inscriptions araméennes d'Idumée, Tome II. Collections Moussaieff, Jeselsohn, Welch et divers*, STrEu 9. Paris: Peeters, 2002.
Lemaire, André, "Un nouveau roi arabe de Qédar dans l'inscription de l'autel à encens de Lakish," *RB* 81 (1974): 63–72.
Leuenberger, Martin, "YHWH's Provenance from the South," pages 157–179 in *The Origins of Yahwism*. Beihefte zur Zeitschrift für die alttestamentliche Wissenschaft 484. Edited by Jürgen van Oorschot, and Markus Witte. Berlin: Walter de Gruyter, 2017.
Levin, Yigal, "The Formation of Idumean Identity," *ARAM* 27 (2015): 187–202.
Levin, Yigal, "The Genesis of Idumea," pages 80–98 in *About Edom and Idumea in the Persian Period: Recent Research and Approaches from Archaeology, Hebrew Bible Studies and Ancient Near East Studies*. Worlds of the Ancient Near East and Mediterranean. Edited by Benedikt Hensel, Ehud B. Zvi, and Diana V. Edelman. Sheffield: Equinox Publishing Limited, 2022.
Levin, Yigal, "The Southern Frontier of Yehud and the Creation of Idumea," pages 239–252 in *A Time of Change: Judah and Its Neighbors in the Persian and Early Hellenistic Periods*, edited by Yigal Levin. London: Bloomsbury, 2007.
Meshorer, Ya'akov, and Qedar, Shraga, *Samarian Coinage*, Publications of the Israel Numismatic Society: Numismatic Studies and Researches 9. Jerusalem: Israel Numismatic Society, 1999.
Naveh, Joseph, "The Aramaic Ostraca from Tel Arad," 153–176 in *Arad Inscriptions*, edited by Zwi Aharoni. Jerusalem: Israel Exploration Society, 1981.
Naveh, Joseph, "The Aramaic Ostraca from Tel Beer-Sheba (Seasons 1971–1976)," *TA* 6 (1979): 182–198.
Negbi, Ora, *A Deposit of Terracottas and Statuettes from Tel Ṣippor ('Atiqot 6)*, Jerusalem: Israel Department of Antiquities, 1966.
Niehr, Herbert, "Götterbilder und Bilderverbot," pages 227–247 in *Der eine Gott und die Götter. Polytheismus und Monotheismus im antiken Israel*. ATANT 82. Edited by Manfred Oeming, and Konrad Schmid. Zürich: Theologischer Verlag Zurich, 2003.
Nihan, Christophe, "Cult Centralization and the Torah Traditions in Chronicles," pages 253–288 in *The Fall of Jerusalem and the Rise of Torah*. FAT I/107. Edited by Peter Dubovsky, Dominik Markl, and Jean-Pierre Sonnet. Tübingen: Mohr Siebeck, 2016.
Notarius, Tania. "The Syntax of the Clan Names in Aramaic Ostraca from Idumea." *Maarav* 22/1–2 (2018): 21–43.
Nyström, Staffan, "Names and Meaning," pages 39–51 in *The Oxford Handbook of Names and Naming*, edited by Carole Hough. Oxford: Oxford University Press, 2016.
Pietsch, Michael, *Die Kultreform Josias. Studien zur Religionsgeschichte Israels in der späten Königszeit*, FAT I/86. Tübingen: Mohr Siebeck, 2013.
Porten, Bezalel, and Yardeni, Ada, "In Preparation of a Corpus of Aramaic Ostraca from the Land of Israel: The House of Yehokal," pages 207–223 in *Shlomo. Studies in Epigraphy, Iconography, History and Archaeology in Honor of Shlomo Moussaieff*, edited by Robert Deutsch. Tel Aviv: Archaeological Center Publication, 2003.
Porten, Bezalel, and Yardeni, Ada, "Maqqedah and the Storehouse in the Idumean Ostraca," pages 125–170 in *A Time of Change: Judah and Its Neighbors in the Persian and Early Hellenistic Periods*, edited by Yigal Levin. London: Bloomsbury, 2007.
Porten, Bezalel, and Yardeni, Ada, "The Chronology of the Idumean Ostraca in the Decade or So after the Death of Alexander the Great and its Relevance for Historical Events," pages 237–249 in *Treasures on Camels' Humps: Historical and Literary Studies from the Ancient Near East Presented to Israel Eph'al*, edited by Mordechai Cogan, and Dan'el Kahn. Jerusalem: Hebrew University Magnes Press, 2008.

Porten, Bezalel, and Yardeni, Ada, eds., *Textbook of Aramaic Ostraca from Idumea (TAO): Vol. 1: Dossiers 1–10: 401 Commodity Chits*. Winona Lake: Eisenbrauns, 2014.

Porten, Bezalel, and Yardeni, Ada, eds. *Textbook of Aramaic Ostraca from Idumea (TAO): Vol. 2: Dossiers 11–50: 263 Commodity Chits.* Winona Lake: Eisenbrauns, 2016.

Porten, Bezalel, and Yardeni, Ada, eds. *Textbook of Aramaic Ostraca from Idumea (TAO): Vol. 3.* Winona Lake: Eisenbrauns, 2018.

Porten, Bezalel, and Yardeni, Ada, eds. *Textbook of Aramaic Ostraca from Idumea (TAO): Vol. 4.* Winona Lake: Eisenbrauns, 2020.

Porten, Bezalel, and Yardeni, Ada, eds. *Textbook of Aramaic Ostraca from Idumea (TAO): Vol. 5.* Winona Lake: Eisenbrauns, 2023.

Porten, Bezalel, and Yardeni, Ada, "The House of Baalrim in the Idumean Ostraca," pages 99–147 in *New Seals and Inscriptions, Hebrew, Idumean, and Cuneiform*. HBM 8. Edited by Meir Lubetski. Sheffield: Sheffield Phoenix Press, 2007.

Porten, Bezalel, and Yardeni, Ada, "Why the Unprovenienced Idumean Ostraca Should be Published," pages 73–98 in *New Seals and Inscriptions, Hebrew, Idumean, and Cuneiform*. HBM 8. Edited by Meir Lubetsk. Sheffield: Sheffield Phoenix Press, 2007.

Römer, Thomas, "Zwischen Urkunden, Fragmenten und Ergänzungen. Zum Stand der Pentateuchforschung," *ZAW* 125 (2013): 2–24.

Routledge, Bruce, "The Antiquity of the Nation? Critical Reflections from the Ancient Near East," *Nations Nationalism* 9 (2003): 213–233.

Schmid, Konrad, "Judean Identity and Ecumenicity: The Political Theology of the Priestly Document," pages 3–26 in *Judah and the Judeans in the Achaemenid Period: Negotiating Identity in an International Context,* edited by Oded Lipschits, Gary N. Knoppers, and Manfred Oeming. Winona Lake: Eisenbrauns, 2011.

Schmid, Konrad, "Textual, Historical, Sociological, and Ideological Cornerstones of the Formation of the Pentateuch," pages 29–51 in *The Social Groups behind the Pentateuch.* AIL 44. Edited by Jaeyoung Jeon. Atlanta: The Society of Biblical Literature, 2021.

Schmid, Konrad, and Schröter, Jens, *The Making of the Bible. From the First Fragments to Sacred Scripture*, Cambridge: Harvard University Press, 2021.

Schmitt, Rüdiger, "Continuity and Change in Post-Exilic Votive Practices," pages 95–109 in *A "Religious Revolution" in Yehûd? The Material Culture of the Persian Period as a Test Case.* OBO 267. Edited by Christian Frevel, Katharina Pyschny, and Izak Cornelius. Göttingen: Academic Press Fribourg, 2014.

Schöpf, Friederike, *Purity without Borders? Purity Concerns in the Early Jewish Diaspora during the Second Temple Period Regarding the Case of Tall Zira'a, Northern Jordan*. Unpublished PhD-thesis: Frankfurt am Main, 2022.

Stern, Ian, "Ethnic Identities and Circumcised Phalli at Hellenistic Maresha," *Strata* 30 (2012): 57–87.

Stern, Ian, *Excavations at Maresha Subterranean Complex 169. Final Report*, Jerusalem: Nelson Glueck School of Biblical Archaeology, 2019.

Stern, Ian, "The Evolution of an Edomite/Idumean Identity. Hellenistic Maresha as a Case Study," pages 99–113 in *About Edom and Idumea in the Persian Period: Recent Research and Approaches from Archaeology, Hebrew Bible Studies and Ancient Near East Studies*. Worlds of the Ancient Near East and Mediterranean. Edited by Benedikt Hensel, Ehud B. Zvi, and Diana V. Edelman. Sheffield: Equinox Publishing Limited, 2022.

Stern, Ian, "The Population of the Persian-Period Idumea According to the Ostraca: A Study of Ethnic Boundaries and Ethnogenesis," pages 205–238 in *A Time of Change: Judah and its Neighbors in the Persian and Early Hellenistic Period*. LSTS 65. Edited by Yigal Levin. London: T & T Clark International, 2007.

Tal, Oren, *The Archaeology of Hellenistic Palestine: Between Tradition and Renewal,* Jerusalem: The Bialik Institute, 2006.

Tebes, Juan M., "Memories of Humiliation, Cultures of Resentment towards Edom and the Formation of Ancient Jewish National Identity." *Nations and Nationalism* 25/1 (2019): 124–145.

Tufnell, Olga, *Lachish III: The Iron Age.* London: Oxford University Press, 1953.

Uehlinger, Christopher, "Was There a Cult Reform under King Josiah? The Case for a Well-Grounded Minimum," pages 297–316 in *Good Kings and Bad Kings: The Kingdom of Judah in the Seventh Century.* ESHM 5. Edited by Lester L. Grabbe. London: T & T Clark International, 2007.

Ussishkin, David. *Biblical Lachish: A Tale of Construction, Destruction, Excavation and Restoration,* Jerusalem: Israel Exploration Society, 2013.

Vainstub, Daniel, and Fabian, Peter, "An Idumean Ostracon From Ḥorvat Naḥal Yatir." *IEJ* 65 (2015): 205–213.

Vriezen, Theodorus C., "The Edomitic Deity Qaus," *OTS* 14 (1965): 330–353.

Wöhrle, Jakob, "'Gebt mir einen Grabbesitz bei euch.' Zur Entstehung und Intention der Erzählung von Abrahams Grabkauf in Genesis 23," pages 63–76 in *Eigensinn und Entstehung der Hebräischen Bibel. Erhard Blum zum siebzigsten Geburtstag*. FAT 136. Edited by Joachim J. Krause et al., Tübingen: Mohr Siebeck, 2020.

Yardeni, Ada, *The Jeselsohn Collection of the Aramaic Ostraca from Idumea*, The Jeselsohn collection. Archaeology – writing. Jerusalem: Yad Ben-Zvi Press, 2016.

Zadok, Ran, "A Prosopography of Samaria and Edom/Idumea," *UF* 30 (1998): 781–828.

Zadok, Ran, "Names and Naming," In *OEANE. Vol. 4*, edited by Eric Meyers, 91–96. Oxford: Oxford University Press, 1997.

Zadok, Ran, "On the Documentary Framework, Terminology, and Onomasticon of the Ostraca from Idumea," pages 178–297 in *New Perspectives on Aramaic Epigraphy in Mesopotamia, Qumran, Egypt and Idumea: Proceedings of the Joint RIAB Minerva Center and the Jeselsohn Epigraphic Center of Jewish History Conference. Research on Israel and Aram in Biblical Times II.* ORA 40. Edited by Aren M. Maeir, Angelika Berlejung, Esther Eshel, and Takayoshi M. Oshima. Tübingen: Mohr Siebeck, 2021.

Tawny L. Holm

Samarians in the Egyptian Diaspora

1 Introduction

A nostalgic passage in Aramaic Papyrus Amherst 63[1] views Samarians and Judeans as siblings who arrive in a new land together (xvii 1–6). In this poem, a troop of Samarians comes before an unnamed king, who addresses a young man in the troop: “Where are y<ou> from,[2] young man; from where are the [peo]ple of your speech?” The man responds in lines 3–4,

> I come from [J]udah,
> my brother has been brought from Samaria,
> and now, a man is bringing up my sister from Jerusalem.

This idealized poetic description suggests different groups or even stages of arrival. The Judean/Yehudite spokesperson arrives with the Samarian troop, and he gives information about both a Samarian “brother” who was brought from Samaria (either referring to a previous emigration or the troop of which the speaker himself is a part), and a “sister” who is separately being brought from Jerusalem. The new land is likely to be Egypt, since this papyrus written in Aramaic, but using Demotic script, is from that land, and rulers of Egypt famously employed foreign troops stationed in various garrisons, especially during the Persian period.[3] Jewish/Judean units were based in places like Elephantine and Memphis, and evidence suggests that Elephantine’s well-known *yĕhûday*[4] community – part of the larger Aramean community at Aswan, both on Elephantine and at nearby Syene – included Samarians or had a Samarian religious element.[5] The island of

1 It was an honor for me to participate in this conference in the memory of Prof. Shaul Shaked, and I am very grateful to Dr. Gad Barnea for inviting me to do so. The importance and impressive scope of Prof. Shaked’s contributions to Aramaic, Iranian, and Jewish Studies would be impossible to overstate. His scholarship can only inspire humbleness, and it is in that spirit that I offer here an approach to the Samarian element in that most challenging of texts, Papyrus Amherst 63.
2 Or translate, “From ⌜where⌝, O young man.” See below, where this passage is discussed in detail.
3 Contra van der Toorn, *Papyrus Amherst 63*, 6–13, who suggests Palmyra. See below.
4 For a very recent discussion on Yahwistic identity in the Achaemenid period, see Barnea, “Yahwistic Identity.”
5 For example, van der Toorn, *Becoming Diaspora Jews*; Barnea, *Khnum is Against Us*, 102 ff.; Holm, “Wandering Arameans.”

Tawny L. Holm, Pennsylvania State University, USA

https://doi.org/10.1515/9783111018638-005

Elephantine itself was home to a temple of Yahō that seems to have had legitimation from both Judah and Samaria, whose officials approved its rebuilding and the renewal of its cult after its destruction in 410 BCE (*TAD* A4.9).

While Samarians and Samaria, alongside Judah and Jerusalem, are only explicitly mentioned on the papyrus in the short poem in xvii 1–6, this composition and others on Papyrus Amherst 63 may hold evidence for the history and culture of the ancient Samarians in the Western Diaspora. Alongside the Samarian-Judean arrival poem, the papyrus' anthology preserves "northern" psalms exalting Yahō (Yahweh) amongst other deities,[6] including the Syrian gods Baʕal/Hadad and Bethel, and describes deportations of unnamed groups and destructions of unnamed cities, which may or may not be connected to the need for Samarians and Judeans to seek refuge elsewhere. In what follows, I intend to elucidate what seems to be evidence in the papyrus for Yahwists in Egypt, especially Samarians, as well as the view of Samaria and the Levant from the papyrus' Aramaic-speaking community in Egypt.[7]

2 Papyrus Amherst 63: A New Year's Celebration Anthology

Papyrus Amherst 63 is a multi-composition text of twenty-three columns on a papyrus about 30 centimeters high and about 3.5 meters in length, written on both recto and verso. Cols. i–xvii consist of poems of various sorts, while cols. xviii–xxiii comprise a long narrative about the seventh century BCE rivalry between the Assyrian royal brothers, Assurbanipal and Shamash-shum-ukin, and the revolt of the latter against the former centered in Babylon.[8] The papyrus is mostly housed in the Morgan Library in New York, but portions of cols. iv–v and xxiii are at the University of Michigan, and are there labeled as Papyrus Amherst

6 But see discussion in Ingo Kottsieper's contribution "From יהה צבאת to יהו מרא שמיא" in this volume, p. 245, note 5.

7 This study relies on my own direct reading of the text, with Demotic transliteration, Aramaic normalization, and translation of the papyrus, found in my book, Holm, *Aramaic Literary Texts*. I am also working on a scientific edition, solicited by De Gruyter.

8 The narrative has been titled both "A Tale of Two Brothers" (Steiner and Nims, "Ashurbanipal and Shamash-shum-ukin") and "The Revolt of Babylon" (Vleeming and Wesselius. *Studies in Papyrus Amherst 63*, 35–38). The latter is preferable to the former, since the former ignores the main character, the two brothers' sister Saritrah, modeled on the historical Šērūʔa-ēṭirat (Holm, "Royal Women Sages").

43b.[9] The text is famously written in the Aramaic language but using Demotic Egyptian script, a unique or nearly unique case of this situation.[10] The papyrus is from Egypt, but otherwise unprovenanced, since it was acquired by Lord Amherst of Hackney via the antiquities market in the 1890s. A case has been made for an Elephantine or Upper Egyptian origin,[11] but this remains impossible to determine with any certainty.[12] The date of the papyrus is probably fourth century or perhaps early third century BCE, with a terminus *ante quem* set at about 250 BCE because the Demotic {r} sign is used to represent both Aramaic /l/ or /r/.[13] The first complete editions of the papyrus are those by Richard Steiner and Charles Nims,[14] and Karel van der Toorn,[15] with a new edition by Holm in press.[16] The Aramaic dialect or dialects represented seem to be of a western sort, based on a variety of features.[17]

While the anthology seems to represent a multi-ethnic or multi-religious community, the "liturgical portions" of the anthology (cols. i–xvii) appear to focus on the New Year, as Richard Steiner first suggested in 1991. The term *rš šnn*, "beginning of years" or "beginning of our year"[18] appears in the context of the fruit

9 I thank both the Morgan Library and the Papyrology Collection at the University of Michigan for allowing me to visit as well as providing me with photos. I am also grateful to the University of Chicago for the earliest photos of the papyrus taken by Spiegelberg in the 1890s.

10 For a possible other example of this within an otherwise Demotic spell (from Wadi Hammamat), see Steiner, "The Scorpion Spell."

11 Tawny Holm, "Nanay and Her Lover," 3.

12 It is also true that the only Egyptian place name on the papyrus is *yb*(3), "Elephantine," although this name is used in the Demotic only to provide the consonants {y} and {b} for the rendering of an Aramaic verb, *ybny*, "will build" (xiv 4–5; see Holm, "Nanay and Her Lover," 3 and Holm, "Sacrifice and Feasting," 142.

13 Vleeming and Wesselius, "An Aramaic Hymn," 501 and Vleeming and Wesselius, *Studies in Papyrus Amherst 63* 1, 7–8, dated the papyrus to the fourth century BCE generally (cf. Zauzich, *Hieroglyphen mit Geheimnis*, 15 and Vittmann, "Arameans in Egypt," 262), versus Steiner ("The Aramaic Text in Demotic Script," 310), who suggested the early third century BCE. It is Günter Vittmann (at the "Elephantine in Context" symposium at the Humboldt University of Berlin in May 2018) who noted that the use of Demotic {r} for both Aramaic /r/ and /l/, and the absence of a distinct Demotic {l} on the papyrus ({r} with a line through it), is diagnostic. The latter does not occur until after 250 BCE.

14 Steiner and Nims, *The Aramaic Text in Demotic Script*, online.

15 Van der Toorn, *Papyrus Amherst 63*, in book form.

16 Holm, *Aramaic Literary Texts*.

17 For some initial comments, see Vleeming and Wesselius, "Betel the Saviour," 121 and Vleeming and Wesselius, *Studies in Papyrus Amherst 63* 2, 23, and Steiner, "Papyrus Amherst 63." On the spelling of *pym*, "mouth," as a representation of western /pem/, instead of eastern /pum/, see also Steiner and Nims, "The Aramaic Text in Demotic Script," 10, 66. For a more comprehensive examination of the Aramaic on the papyrus, see Holm, "Western Aramaic Elements."

18 The latter is possible if this is a Hebrew rather than Aramaic phrase.

(i.e., grape) harvest in v 7, and other activities are done annually; e.g., "the harvest of our years" i.e., "our annual harvests," (*ḫml šntyn*) in ix 21 and annual offerings of sheep in "the series/order of your year" (*sdrt-šntk*) in xiii 4.

Moreover, certain events occur in the Egyptian month of Epiph (see ix 13 and possibly xvi 2), roughly the equivalent to the month of Tishrītu/Tishrei, the first month of the Babylonian-Jewish New Year in the Fall. In addition, multiple compositions appear to refer to activities that are connected to ancient Near Eastern New Year's celebrations, such as the Babylonian *Akītu*. The New Year was a time for remembering the past and looking to the future for renewal and rejuvenation, especially of kingship and the land.[19] For instance, the papyrus frequently references an unnamed king who is sponsored by deities: in cols. i–iv, the goddess Nanay nurses a king at her breast and her spouse Nabû presents him for his enthronement; in col. vii a king laments to his god and is assured of his deity's support; in xiv 18, the throne of a king of *Rēšā* ("the Head," the main place name on the papyrus) is guarded by the sentinels of Nanay; and in col. xvi, a young man ascends to his throne under the aegis of the deities Ash(im)-Bethel and Nabû.[20] Moreover, laments for lost lands and cities (e.g., vi 1–11) are countered by the hope for renewal and rebuilding (e.g., xvii 17b–19). A close look at the contents of the liturgical portions (cols. i–xvii) demonstrates many connections to the *Akītu* or other ancient Near Eastern New Year traditions.[21]

Contents

(with New Year elements emphasized)

cols. i–xv	– Enthronement of deities Nanay and Nabû amongst the gods, followed by the enthronement of an unnamed king.
col. v	– Celebration of New Year's fruit from the vineyards for El (broken).
col. vi	– Lament on destruction, deportation (unnamed cities)

19 On the Hellenistic texts concerning the Babylonian *Akītu* festival, see Debourse, "A New Hope" and Debourse, *Of Priests and Kings*, among others. On P. Amherst 63 xvii and the connection of the sacred marriage text to the New Year, see Holm "Nanay and Her Lover."

20 This is not to mention the unnamed king in the Samarian-Judean arrival poem (xvii 1–6), or the king addressed in the prologue to the "Revolt of Babylon" narrative in xviii 1, neither of whom are presumably related to the other unnamed kings. The latter king is, however, either associated with Baʕal of Heaven or the word ("king") is an epithet of that deity (xviii 3).

21 For further details about the contents, see esp. Holm, "In Praise of Gods & Goddesses, 306–309, Holm, "Papyrus Amherst 63 and the Arameans of Egypt, 331–334, Holm, "Sacrifice and Feasting," 137–140 and Holm, *Aramaic Literary Texts*.

col. viii	– Blessings of all the gods and a procession of sacrifices, esp. in sets of "sixty."
col. ix	– Selection of a priestess to offer bulls in *Rēšā* for the deity Bethel in Epiph (= Tishrei), at same time as a bed is brought down.
cols. x–xi	– *Mār* and *Mārā* ("Lord" and "Lady") cycle with refrains (prayers for canals and rain).
col. xii 1–11a	– Lament for unnamed city.
col. xii 11b–xiii	– Yahō Cycle: Three Psalms of Yhw/Adonay, perhaps at Fall New Year's festival
cols. xiv–xv	– Nanay poems and scribal colphon (end of recto: "Amen, amen. May Nabû cause the time of desolation to pass.")
col. xvi	– Poems celebrating a young man's ascension to the throne before Ash(im)-Bethel and Nabû (name of month uncertain, but perhaps Epiph), followed by descriptions of a divine banquet and further poems
col. xvii	– Samarian-Judean arrival poem; "Sacred Marriage" of Nanay and Baʕal-Shamayn; conclusion of liturgical portion: call to rebuild a city and land.
cols. xviii–xxiii	– Short lament for Nineveh (lns. 1–6) followed by the "Revolt of Babylon" narrative, a literary rendering of the seventh century BCE sibling rivalry between the Assyrian kings Assurbanipal (in Nineveh) and Shamash-shum-ukīn (of Babylon), with sister *Šērūʔa-ēṭirat* as royal mediator.[22]

Although the contents of cols. i–xvii, the liturgical portion of the papyrus, are nowhere divided into units of time as in many festival texts, the New Year's elements are obvious, beginning with the enthronement of Nanay and Nabû among the gods, followed by the presentation and enthronement of the king himself after various rituals (include standing at his station and washing his hands) in cols. i–xv. The nursing of the king at the breast of Nanay (i 17; ii 14; iii 3, 14; iv 3), a goddess who was identified with Ishtar in Mesopotamia and Isis in Egypt, surely echoes the divine wetnurse duties performed by both Ishtar and Isis for their royal sons.[23] Col. v's celebration of the New Year is unfortunately

22 See Holm, "Royal Women Sages" and Holm, *Aramaic Literary Texts* for an interpretation of the narrative that differs from Vleeming and Wesselius *Studies in Papyrus Amherst 63* (1985); Steiner and Nims "Ashurbanipal and Shamash-shum-ukin"; and van der Toorn *Papyrus Amherst 63*, 215–239.

23 Holm, "Nanay(a) among the Arameans," 101–103.

quite broken, so many details are lost, but col. vii's negative confession of the king declaring that he has done no evil, followed by a message of divine support for the king's reign, recalls day five of the Hellenistic-era *Akītu* festival.[24] For its part, col. viii's "Blessings of All the Gods" upon an unnamed masculine singular "you" (perhaps the king again) provides a "who's who" list of ancient Near Eastern deities stretching from Mesopotamia to the Levant (lns. 1–7). This column concludes with a procession of sacrifices, some of which are said to be offered in remembrance (*ldkrw*) and to process in sets of "sixty" – likely a symbolic number representing the totality of the Aramean divine realm. This event recalls the Emarite *zukru*-festival ("remembrance"-festival) at the New Year, wherein "seventy" lambs, symbolizing all the Emarite gods and goddesses, are sacrificed. Moreover, the timing of the selection in col. ix of a priestess (*khnh*) to sacrifice bulls for *Rēšā* is in the month of Epiph, a stipulation which assumes an annual event. The Fall New Year seems also to be the setting for the Yahō psalms in cols. xii and xiii – this is particularly clear in psalm 2, which mentions annual offerings of sheep accompanying the drinking of wine and feasting at a new moon festival, presumably at the time of the annual Fall grape harvest.[25] The papyrus' recto ends in cols. xiv–xv with a desire for the rebuilding of Nanay's shrine and broken statue, and its scribal colophon asks Nabû, the Mesopotamian god of scribes, to allow the "time of desolation" to pass.

The verso picks up in col. xvi with another description of an unnamed king's enthronement, possibly in Epiph (cf. cols. iii–xv), sponsored by the deities Ashim-Bethel and Nabû, followed by a banquet. For its part, the sacred marriage text in the concluding liturgical column (col. xvii), describes the union of the goddess Nanay with a western deity, probably Baʕal-Shamayn, but possibly Bethel.[26] Sacred marriage texts in the Ancient Near East inherently invoke the divine sponsorship and renewal of kingship and land, but this same column – and thus the entire liturgy – ends with a few lines asking for the rebuilding of an unnamed fallen city and land (see below). The lament for Nineveh invoking Baʕal-Shamayn and an unnamed king, which begins the narrative in cols. xviii–xxiii, provides a

---

24 However, the king is not ritually humiliated with a slap by a priest here, as in day five of the *Akītu* (see Debourse, "Debita Reverentia," 183–200, among others). On col. vii, see also Vleeming and Wesselius, "Betel the Saviour."

25 Van der Toorn, "Celebrating the New Year With the Israelites," astutely observed that the three Yahō psalms in particular might be connected to a Fall New Year celebration at the time of the wine harvest and found parallels for this in the Ugaritic new wine celebrations.

26 The former interpretation is that of Holm "Nanay and Her Lover," 19 (cf. Steiner and Nims *The Aramaic Text in Demotic Script* (2017), 67), and the latter is van der Toorn's view (*Papyrus Amherst 63*, 210–211).

link between the sacred marriage in col. xvii and the "Revolt of Babylon" narrative, featuring both the city of Nineveh and of Babylon.

The themes of loss and lament combined with renewal and rebuilding throughout the papyrus thus offer a landscape of cultural nostalgia for the community that produced it.[27] But who is celebrating the New Year? The location of the community that preserved the anthology in Egypt, as well as the location and dates for the original composition of individual works on the papyrus are much debated. The main place name, which appears at least thirty times, however, seems to be Aramaic *rēšā*, "the Head," or "the Capital." This name has no fixed Demotic spelling, and uniquely uses a seated-woman determinative (found in Demotic after the word for goddess, *ntr.t*, or noblewoman, *rpy.t*),[28] rather than the hand-to-mouth or foreign-land determinatives used for all other place names on the papyrus. However, it seems to be a physical location with a land (xi 8), cities (i 13; xi 9), a population ("daughters of *Rēšā*" in ix 16), a pair of deities throughout who are often simply called Mār and Mārāh ("Lord" and "Lady"[29] of *Rēšā*); and an unnamed king whose throne is in *Rēšā* (xiv 18). One poem's narrator even recalls his youth in the "land of *Rēšā*" (xi 8–11).

The presumably hendiadic phrase *dargā warēšā* "the high rank and head," or "the supreme head/capital," used twice, also refers to this location. Suggestions for the identification of *Rēšā* include a Levantine high place (a cape or mountain peak/range)[30] or the Iranian land of Rashi/u or Arashu (in the Zagros mountains).[31] Nadav Na'aman's proposal that this is the home of the gods cannot precisely be correct,[32] given the evidence for *Rēšā* as a land, but it is likely that the name *Rēšā* is also a metaphor in some sense. The toponym may well be both a religious site (cf. the interest in other cultic sites in col. viii), as well as a geographic location.[33] One is left wondering if *Rēšā* is a purposely ambiguous term, a

27 Holm, "Papyrus Amherst 63 and the Arameans of Egypt."

28 See Erichsen, *Demotisches Glossar*, 233–234, 244–245. This determinative is never used in Demotic text to mark place names, so its use on P. Amherst 63 to do so is significant.

29 It seems to be the god Bethel who is the "Resident of *Rēšā*" in vi 15. An unnamed deity *Mār*, "Lord," is "god of *Rēšā*" in vii 7, 11, 13; viii 2, 15, 16; ix 20; xi 1, 3, 6; xvi 17; and a/the? goddess is from *Rēšā* in x 1; xiv 2. A "god of *Rēšā*" is also mentioned in ix 3, 16, 18, and the refrains in col. x–xi.

30 Reading "Ladder (*drg*) and Resh" in vii 13 and xvi 17, Vleeming and Wesselius suggest that "Resh" is Raʔs en-Naqoura and "the Ladder" is the famous promontory near it called the "Ladder of Tyre" ("Betel the Saviour," 111, 113 and *Studies in Papyrus Amherst 63* 1, 9), while van der Toorn suggested this is Jebel Ansariya, the Syrian coastal range (*Papyrus Amherst 63*, 13–18).

31 Steiner and Nims, "Ashurbanipal and Shamash-shum-ukin," 107–108.

32 Na'aman, "Papyrus Amherst 63," 250–266.

33 Cf. Hebrew *rʔš*, "head, capital," as a designation of both Damascus, the "capital of Aram," and Samaria, the "capital of Ephraim/Israel" in Isa 7:8.

prospect that may have multiple implications (see below). Moreover, wherever *Rēšā* is to be located, Yahō is associated with it (in Yahō psalm 1) as are the other main deities of the papyrus: Nanay (xiv 2 and xiv 18); Bethel (cols. ix–xi); and Baʕal-Shamayn (xvii 15).

3 Yahwism in Egypt before Papyrus Amherst 63

While the existence of a temple of Yahō and Yahwists at Elephantine was revealed from the Elephantine documents that came to light in the early twentieth century, excavations on the island were slow to disclose the physical remains of a temple. It was only in a 2003 publication that excavator Cornelius von Pilgrim outlined what he discerned to be the contours of the temple of Yahō at Elephantine, utilizing information from the legal texts describing adjacent properties.[34] This temple may well have been as large as the Jerusalem temple,[35] and seems to have had legitimation from both Judean and Samarian officials, as the memorandum authorizing its rebuilding indicates (*TAD* A4.9). After the temple's destruction by Naphaina, commander of the Syenian garrison, along with Egyptian troops in 410 BCE (A4.7:8–9), the Elephantinian leaders wrote to the governors of Judah and Samaria in 407 BCE to ask for permission to rebuild. Documents from Elephantine dated after 404 BCE may indicate the temple was indeed rebuilt by then, even if the remains of this second temple have not been uncovered.[36] Moreover, in the preserved "request" letter, the authors claim that the temple had already been built before Cambyses arrived in Egypt (A4.7:13–14 and A4.8:12–13). The time of the arrival of this community and its sister Aramean community on nearby mainland Syene is much debated, but most scholars do agree that this dates to a time before Persian conquest.[37]

---

34 See von Pilgrim, "Tempel des Jahu"; von Pilgrim, "'Anyway, We Should Really Dig on Elephantine Some Time'"; von Pilgrim, "On the Archaeological Background." See also Tuplin, "The Fall and Rise of the Elephantine Temple."

35 Porten, *Archives from Elephantine*, 110; Barnea, *Khnum is Against Us*, 49–50.

36 Von Pilgrim, "On the Archaeological Background." For example, *TAD* B3.12:18–20 from 402 BCE describes a house with the temple of Yahō on its west, whose sellers are Anani and his wife the lady Tapamet, servitors of "Yahō, the god dwelling in Elephantine the fortress." Moreover, the so-called Collection account with donations of 2 shekels of silver per person to Yahō the god may date to 400 BCE.

37 On the origins of the Elephantine community, see Porten, "Settlement of Jews at Elephantine"; Rohrmoser, *Götter, Tempel und Kult*, 73–81; post-587 BCE: Kahn, "The Date of the Arrival of the Judeans"; 550–540 BCE: Barnea, "The Migration of the Elephantine Yahwists," among others.

The Yahwism at Elephantine is best described as henotheistic. While Yahō is described as "the god who dwells in Elephantine the fortress" (e.g., *TAD* B3.3:2; B3.5:2; B3.10:2; B3.11:2; and B3.12:2), many letters written by authors with Yahwistic names frequently mention other deities, sometimes even greeting their addressees with blessings from "all the gods" (e.g., *TAD* A3.5:1; 3.9:1; A4.7:2; A6.1:1–2). Moreover, a certain Micaiah writes to Giddel: "I bless you by Yahō and Khnum" (*TAD* D7.21:2–3), and the freedwoman of substance, Mibtahiah, takes an oath by the Egyptian goddess Satis (*TAD* B7.4). For his part, Menahem son of Shallum takes an oath "by He[rem] the [god] in/by the place of prostration and by Anat-Yahō" (*TAD* B7.3:3), and Malchiah son of Jashobiah swears by the god Ḥerem-Bethel (*TAD* B7.2). It also seems that the goddess Anat was worshiped at Aswan both as Anat-Bethel and as Anat-Yahō (i.e., Anat in her relationship to both Bethel and Yahō as their consort).[38] Finally, donations to Yahō in the Collection List (*TAD* C3.15) include individual community members' two-shekel contributions for not just Yahō, but two other deities as well, Ashim-Bethel and Anat-Bethel.[39] It is clear that Yahwism at Elephantine included veneration for multiple deities, probably even at Yahō's own temple.[40] Members of the Elephantine military garrison (*ḥylʔ*) designated themselves as both *yĕhûdayyā*, "Jews / Judeans / Yahwists," as well as *ʔaramayyā*, "Arameans," a general term for Syrians; i.e., those who came to Egypt most recently from Syria, even if they originally hailed from elsewhere, such as Mesopotamia. As "Arameans" on the first cataract of the Nile, the *yĕhûdayyā* were thus part of the larger military colony that included the non-Judean Arameans on the nearby mainland at Syene, where there were temples of the deities Nabû, Banit (Nanay), Bethel, and the "Queen of Heaven."

---

38 Note also the mix of theophoric elements in names within families; e.g., a certain Bethelnathan ("Bethel has given") is the son of one Jehonathan ("Yahō has given") in *TAD* B6.4:10.

39 Gad Barnea has suggested that this particular triad is a translation of both an Achaemenid Zoroastrian and an Egyptian divine triad at Elephantine (Ahuramazda-Mithra-Anahita and Khnum-Satis-Anukis); see Barnea, *Khnum is Against Us*, 291–330 and Barnea, "*Interpretatio Ivdaica.*" See Schipper, "Die Judäer/Aramäer von Elephantine" for the view that it is only the reconstructed, second Temple of Yahō (post 407 BCE) that contained this Yahō-triad, oriented toward Egyptian requirements.

40 Interestingly, almost all the same deities that are found in Elephantine and other Aramaic documents in Aramaic script from Egypt appear on P. Amherst 63 too, with only a few exceptions. The deities from Syria-Palestine include: Bethel, Yahō/ū (also designated "Adonay" in cols. xii–xiii), Baʕal or Baʕal of Heaven (Baʕal-Shamayn/Bʕel-Shamayn); Baʕalat; Had/Hadad, El, Pidray, Ashim-Bethel, Ḥerem-Bethel, ʕAnat, Asherah, and perhaps Śahar (the Aramean moon god). For their part, the Mesopotamian deities on the papyrus include: Nanay/Nanā (Nanaya or Nanā in cuneiform texts); her Babylonian spouse Nabû; Marduk, with his epithet Bēl (Akk. "Lord"); Bēltu (Akk. "Lady," the title for a consort of Marduk); Shamash (the sun god); and Sîn (the moon god).

On the other hand, discussion over exactly what it meant to be *yĕhûday* at Elephantine during the Persian period continues.[41] Preserved Elephantine texts nowhere mention the Torah or its major characters – even those such as Joseph or Moses who spent time in Egypt[42] – and very few of the religious practices in the Hebrew Bible find a counterpart at Elephantine.[43] The Sabbath (*šbh*), Passover (*psḥ?*), the *mrzḥ* drinking institution, and possibly the Festival of Unleavened Bread (*TAD* A4.1)[44] or a new moon's day might have been observed,[45] but there is little to indicate that any of these, not even Sabbath and Passover, resembled what is known of their equivalents from the Ḥebrew Bible.[46]

It is also notable that nowhere in the Elephantine documents are "Israel" or "Samaria" mentioned; the Elephantinians call themselves Judeans and not Israelites or Samarians. Yet, this community seems to have felt linked to both Judah and Samaria at the end of the fifth century BCE, as the letter requesting to rebuild the Elephantine temple (*TAD* A4.7 and A4.8) indicates. It is sent to Bagavahya, governor of Judah, but states that the same letter was also sent to Delaiah and Shelemiah sons of Sanballat, governor of Samaria, and an even earlier (unanswered) letter on the same topic had apparently also been sent to Jehohanan the High Priest and Judean nobles in Jerusalem.[47] In the end, it is the leaders of both Judah and Samaria, Bagavahya and Delaiah, who authorize the reconstruction (*TAD* A4.9). The Elephantine Yahwists thus clearly felt a connection to Samaria, and the fact that they venerated Yahō alongside the Syrian deity Bethel, as seems to have been done in Israel (cf. Jer 48:13),[48] and even may have identified the

---

41 See Becking, "Yehudite Identity in Elephantine"; Becking, *Identity in Persian Egypt*, esp. 18–53, and Becking, "The Identity of the People at Elephantine"; van der Toorn, *Becoming Diaspora Jews*, esp. 15–18, 39–41; Barnea "Yahwistic Identity," among many others.

42 See, for example, Grabbe, "Elephantine and the Torah."

43 See, among others, Knauf, "Elephantine und das vor-biblische Judentum"; Grabbe, "Elephantine and the Torah"; Kratz, "Arameans and Judeans," and Adler, *The Origins of Judaism* esp. 202–205. An Elephantine context for the composition or development of the Joseph story is, however, frequently proposed (see, for example, several contributions in Schmid, et al. *The Joseph Story between Egypt and Israel*).

44 For a detailed analysis of *TAD* A4.1 and its significance, see Barnea, "P. Berlin 13464, Yahwism and Achaemenid Zoroastrianism at Elephantine," in this volume.

45 Holm, "Sacrifice and Feasting," 147 ff.

46 See Barnea, "*Interpretatio Ivdaica*," among others.

47 Jerusalem was perhaps only one month away in distance from Elephantine, and thus Elephantine was much closer to Jerusalem than Babylon was (Granerød, *Dimensions of Yahwism*, 6–9).

48 The prophet predicts that Moab will be ashamed of Chemosh, "as the house of Israel was ashamed of Bethel (*mibbêt-ʔel*), their confidence (*mibṭeḥām*)." Other mentions of the deity Bethel in the Bible are debated (Holm, "Wandering Arameans"),

two, may also be an indication of some Samarian elements among the community obscured by the gentilic *yĕhûday*. It is worth noting that P. Amherst 63's Samarian-Judean arrival poem presents a Judean as the spokesman of what is otherwise a "Samarian" troop, a fact that may reflect the sense in Egypt that Judeans may well have been latecomers to the land of refuge, but they led or represented their brothers, the Samarians.

4 Evidence for Yahwists, including Samarians, in Egypt on Papyrus Amherst 63

The evidence for Yahwists, including Samarians, on the papyrus, which seems to date from a few decades to up to a century later than the *floruit* of the Elephantine community, can be gathered from at least a few key passages. These include: the Samarian-Judean arrival poem, wherein Samaria and Samarians are both explicitly mentioned alongside Jerusalem and Yehud/Judah, and the five compositions in which the name Yahō appears, including the three psalms to Yahō/Adonay in cols. xii–xiii, if not other compositions as well. In the Yahō psalms, Yahō may be identified with Bethel,[49] but it is not clear that this is the case for the Bethel psalms found throughout the papyrus. The name "Bethel" appears in vi 22 and viii 13, and this god is probably the main deity in cols. ix–xi (explicitly named in ix 9, 13; x 9). Bethel also appears in Yahō psalm 1 (xii 17) and at the end of the sacred marriage text in xvii 15. Moreover, two members of Bethel's usual entourage are also found on the papyrus: Her(em)-Bethel in xvii 14 and Ash(im)-Bethel in xvi 1, 14, and 15. Given that the Syrian deity Bethel was likely worshiped in Israel/Samaria, the prominence of Bethel on the papyrus, as at Elephantine and Syene, is of note.

4.1 The "Samarian-Judean Arrival" Poem in xvii 1–6

The "Samarian-Judean Arrival" poem appears at the beginning of the last liturgical column and before the sacred marriage text describing the union of the Aramean-Mesopotamian goddess Nanay and a western deity, probably Baʕal-Shamayn.[50] The beginning of the poem is fragmentary, but seems to reference events in Babylon and Nineveh.

49 Holm, "Bethel and Yahō."
50 On the sacred marriage text, see Holm, "Nanay and Her Lover" and Holm, *Aramaic Literary Texts* (with updated reading in the latter).

1) [. . . has (OR: have) c] ⸢ome⸣ unto/upon[51] Ba<by>lon,
your/my . . . in Nine[veh].[52]
[With] my own two eyes a tr ⸢oo⸣ [p] 2) (I) was wa ⸢tch⸣ ing;
people were coming;[53]
a b[a] ⸢n⸣ d of Samar[i]ans sought out my lord [the] king.
3) " ⸢Where⸣ are y<ou> from, young man, (OR: From ⸢where⸣ , O young man,)
from where are the [peo]ple of your speech?"[54]
"I come from [J]udah,
my brother from Samar ⸢ia⸣ 4) has been brou ⸢gh⸣ t,
and now, a man ⸢is br⸣ inging up my sister from Jerusalem."
"Enter, young man – we 5) will host you.
Raise a kab of ⸢wh⸣ eat on your sho ⸢ul⸣ der (OR: in your j ⸢a⸣ r), lad.[55]

---

51 Or "Ba<by>lon has entered." The translation "has gone up" from the root *\ʕly* would be a Hebraism.

52 With the correct placement of a loose fragment by Steiner, it is now clear that both Babylon and Nineveh are mentioned in this prologue (Steiner and Nims, "The Aramaic Text in Demotic Script," 63, contra my early interpretation in Holm "Nanay and Her Lover," 5–7). Steiner's restorations, however, are by no means obvious. He reads the following Aramaic: [*smt*] *ʕl* <*b*>*bl*{*l*} ⸢*s*⸣ [*bl*]*tky bnn*[*ʔw*], and translates: "[You have placed] upon <Ba>bylon your ⸢bu⸣ [rden]s, Nine[veh]." The first visible sign group in ln. 1 seems to be what is read here as **tyw** (Vleeming and Wesselius' **d**$_5$ and Steiner's **ty** with an overline), which may indicate Aramaic *ty*/*w* or *dy*/*w*. van der Toorn reads **[ʔ**$_2$**ʔ]t**$_5$**ʔ** | **ʕl.C** | **brrt** ⸢| **nš**$_2$⸣ **[|] dqy** | **bʔnm**$_3$**ʔ[rt |]** in his transliteration system, and translates, "They [came(?)] toward the evening watch. Broken men during [the mor]ning watch" (*Papyrus Amherst 63*, 203). Among other problems, he does not read the foreign-land determinative that follows **brr**, which indicates this must be a place name. In spite of the odd spelling of the name "Babylon" as **br** ⸢**r**^{f}**•**⸣ , the foreign-land determinative would indicate this is the correct reading. The most common spelling this GN on the papyrus is something like **bʔbr**^{f} (xix 3; cf. viii 4; xiv 19; xix 3, *et passim*); but compare these spellings as well: **brbr**^{f} in xviii 15 and xx 1; **bʔrʔ**^{f} in xix 1; **bnʔbr**^{f} in xix 3; and **br**[**ʔ**^{f}] xxii 12). As for Nineveh, its Demotic spellings are quite varied: **nʔnʔ•ʔw** in xix 2; **nʔʔw**$_2$**ʔ•** in xix 4; **nʔnʔ•ʔw** in xx 3; **nʔnʔ•ʔwʔ•** in xxi 12, etc.

53 Demotic **s[ʔ]** ⸢**k**⸣ **y•** is either to be considered together with the **ty•** that follows it as one word, resulting in Aramaic *skyty*, "I watched" (Peal Perfect 1cs of *sky*, with a –*ty* afformative as in TA), or as a single word *sk*(*h*). It seems preferable to take both **s[ʔ]** ⸢**k**⸣ **y•** and **ty•** as separate words – Aramaic participles *s* ⸢*k*⸣ (*h*) and (*ʔ*)*t*(*h*) – since this would give **nš** (Aramaic *ʔnš* "person, people") its own verb: (*ʔ*)*t*(*h*) *ʔnš*, "People were coming," instead of placing it in construct with the following noun (cf. Steiner and Nims, "The Aramaic Text in Demotic Script").

54 In the first part of this line there is no room or trace for any Demotic **t** in the phrase to indicate Aramaic *ʔt* or *ʔnt* "you," *pace* Steiner's translation in *COS* 1.99: "Who/From where are y ⸢ou⸣ , lad? Who/From where is your . . .?" This may simply be scribal error, and the phrase should be emended to *mn* ⸢*ʔn*⸣ *ʔ*<*t*> *ġlmʔ*, "Where are y<ou> from, young man?" ("The Aramaic Text in Demotic Script," 321).

55 The reading is either Demotic **bʔgʔ** ⸢**t**⸣ **pk•** = Aramaic *bk* ⸢*t*⸣ *pk*, "on your sho ⸢ul⸣ der," or **bʔkʔ** ⸢**t**⸣ **ʔk•** = *bk* ⸢*d*⸣ *k*, "in your ja ⸢r⸣ ."

> We will *fee<d> your people* (OR: Let us *know your people*), every *refugee* (OR: *the entire standard*).[56]
> 6) On your table one will place b⌜o⌝wls,
> and from every fountai⌜n⌝ wine;
> bowls, and from every vessel an excellent portion."

In this origin tradition, Samarians and Judeans arrive as brothers and sisters. Once he learns from the Judean spokesman their identities, the king of the new land welcomes them and promises to provide food and luxuries. While van der Toorn has suggested this place of refuge is Palmyra in the Syrian desert,[57] there is no historical basis for this, and a description of a mixed troop's arrival appearing on a papyrus found in Egypt, a place famous for its ethnically-mixed units at such sites as Elephantine and Syene, would appear to suggest they are arriving in Egypt.[58]

While Elephantine Yahwism seems to have been uninformed by biblical Yahwism/Judaism,[59] this papyrus from Egypt records in this poem some of the same traditions and tropes found in the Bible. First of all, the portrait of Judeans/Jerusalemites and Samarians as siblings is reminiscent of the metaphorical sororal relationship between the two cities, Jerusalem and Samaria – the capitals of, and metonyms for, the twin kingdoms of Judah and Israel in the Hebrew Bible. For example, in Ezekiel 23, the cities of Samaria and Jerusalem are depicted as rebellious and promiscuous sisters under the symbolic names of Oholah (Samaria) and Oholibah (Jerusalem).[60] Another familial metaphor is also found on the papyrus in col. xii's short psalm lamenting a city (before the Yahō psalms). There, someone's father and brothers are described as weak and puny, but the narrator claims they are (or once were) "like a stable of war horses" and "like eagles and <wi>ld asses," before the narrator laments his brother's diminishment and current sad state (he has lost his "portion" and his city is fallen).

56 *nys* may be a nominal form of the root *nws*, "to tremble, move," which in the Haphel form means "to remove," and is common in Official Aramaic; e.g., *KAI* 202 B:20, *KAI* 225:6, *KAI* 226:8, 9 and the Bukân stela 1. The Aphel participle *mns*, "refugee, fugitive," appears in OfA (Hermopolis 2:3 = *TAD* A2.2:3). For the suggestion that this is *nēs*, "standard," (cf. *degel*, "carrying pole," as a metonym for "military unit"), see van der Toorn, *Papyrus Amherst 63*, 203–204.

57 Van der Toorn, *Papyrus Amherst 63*, 203.

58 Holm, "Papyrus Amherst 63 and the Arameans of Egypt," 328–29.

59 E.g., Grabbe, "Elephantine and the Torah." That there is no knowledge of the Torah or biblical characters set in Egypt seems clear. For Elephantine as the background to the Joseph story, however, see several of the contributions in Schmid et al. *The Joseph Story*.

60 The pejorative names have religious and other meanings: *ʔOhŏlāh* means "Her tent," or "She who has a tent" (i.e., owns a cultic shrine of her own) and *ʔOhŏlîbāh* means "My tent is in her" (with reference to Yahweh's Temple in Jerusalem).

Secondly, the view of Egypt as a land of refuge is also a common theme in the Bible, appearing in, for instance, the story of Abraham and Sarah in Egypt in Gen 12; the Joseph narrative in Gen 37–50; Jeroboam's flight to Egypt in 1 Kings 11:40 and 12:2; and Jeremiah and other Judeans' journey to Egypt to escape the Babylonians in Jer 43:5–6. Moreover, the tradition of a foreign king who supplies shelter for Levantines finds a parallel in the Elephantinian documents too.[61] In the letter from 407 BCE requesting the rebuilding of the Yahō temple at Elephantine, the Judean leaders recount that the temple had been built during "the days of the kings of Egypt" (*mlky mṣryn*) and that Cambyses the Persian saw the Yahō temple already standing there when he entered Egypt (*TAD* A4.7:13; cf. A4.8:12). The letter writers thus distinguish between native Egyptian kings, presumably the Twenty-Sixth Dynasty (ca. 685–526 BCE), in which Egypt was ruled from Sais in the Nile delta, and the Persian period, the Twenty-Seventh Dynasty, in which non-Egyptian Persians ruled.

Finally, the (broken) mention of Babylon and Nineveh at the beginning of the poem in xvii 1–7 is intriguing – it seems to offer some prelude to the troop's arrival in the new land, and echoes the biblical preoccupation with the historical invasions of Israel/Samaria by Assyria and Judah by Babylonia. Babylon precedes Nineveh in the broken first lines, however, rather than the reverse. Historically, of course, Nineveh, a capital of the Neo-Assyrians, was destroyed by Babylonia in 612 BCE. In the tradition of the sister kingdoms, it is Israel/Samaria who falls to the Assyrians in 721 BCE, while Judah lives on to be destroyed by the Babylonians in 587 BCE.[62] What is especially resonant in the poem, however, is the leadership of the spokesman from Judah over the Samarian troop, even if priority in the new land might belong to the (elder?) Samarian "brother."

4.2 The deity Yahō

The name of the deity Yahō appears about fifteen or more times on the papyrus, mostly in the three Yahō poems (xii 11b-19; xiii 1–10; xiii 11–17), but also in the divine epithet "Throne-of-Yahō" in viii 7, and perhaps in a shortened form *Yah*(?) in xvi 14. The fixed Demotic spelling behind this name is **ʔḥ̱r**$_{2}$**w**$_{2}$/**w**$_{3}$, a spelling which looks nothing like either the Hebrew Tetragrammaton (*Yhwh*) or the Ara-

61 On the Elephantine tradents of the lost and rebuilt temple, see Granerød, "The Former and the Future Temple."

62 There is a connection here as well to the "Revolt of Babylon" narrative in xviii–xxiii, which begins in the next column. This starts with a lament for Nineveh's downfall, but the story itself describes the destruction of Babylon by Ninevites.

maic forms of the divine name in Egypt, *Yhw* and *Yhh*. On the other hand, in the Yahō psalms it is opposite the very familiar biblical term *ʔdny*, "Adonay," which only appears there and nowhere else on the papyrus.

The most plausible explanation for reading the divine name in question is a combination of the theories of the Demoticist Karl-Theodor Zauzich[63] and the Semiticist Richard Steiner.[64] In 1985, Zauzich read the name as follows: **ʔ**=*y*; **ḥr**$_2$= *h*; **w**$_2$/**w**$_3$= *w*, rendering an Aramaic *yhw*. The biggest (and to my mind, only) problem with this suggestion is in reading the Demotic *aleph* here as an Aramaic /y/, since an initial *aleph* in Demotic would always indicate a vowel and not a consonant.[65] For his part, Richard Steiner reads the entire name differently, but offers a good suggestion for understanding the *aleph*. He reads the name as *ʔ* + the divine name Horus (*ḥr*) + divine determinative,[66] with the Horus sign group as a stand-in for *Yhw* and the initial *aleph* indicating that the name was to be read as the euphemism *ʔadonay*, "the Lord."[67] While Steiner's reading of this Demotic *ḥr* as "Horus," seems incorrect (the sign group is instead to be read as *ḥr*, "upon," which can be read as /h/), his proposal that the euphemistic replacement of *yhw* by *ʔadonay* is signaled by the Demotic *aleph* at the beginning of the word seems highly likely.

The avoidance of the divine name *Yhwh* in the Levant, which may have begun in the Persian period, was especially prevalent in Aramaic by the mid Second Temple period.[68] For instance, the Aramaic inscriptions from Mount Gerizim from 200–168 BCE do not use the Tetragrammaton, but the Hebrew inscriptions from the same location do.[69] Neither the Aramaic of Ezra nor of Daniel uses

---

63 Zauzich, "Der Gott des aramäisch-demotischen Papyrus Amherst 63."

64 Steiner, "Papyrus Amherst 63: A New Source" and Steiner and Nims, "The Aramaic Text in Demotic Script," 42–43.

65 Allen, *Ancient Egyptian Phonology*, 30.

66 Demotic **w**$_3$ and the divine determinative are the same character.

67 Steiner, "Papyrus Amherst 63: A New Source" and Steiner and Nims, "The Aramaic Text in Demotic Script," 42–43. The word in question is not *ḥr*, "Horus" but *ḥr*, "upon," and is simply used here to indicate /h/ (see Erichsen *Demotisches Glossar*, 316). Demotic *ḥr*, "Horus," and Demotic *ḥr*, "upon," are discrete Demotic words, whose distinct spellings are differentiated even on the papyrus.

68 On divine name use and avoidance, especially in Aramaic texts, see Meyer, *Naming God in Early Judaism* (but note that his comments in pages 64–67 on reading the name on P. Amherst 63 are inaccurate). On the evidence for the beginning of divine name avoidance in the Persian period, and the replacement by *ʔlhym* or *ʔl* (Hebrew) or *ʔlhʔ* (Aramaic), see Meyer *Naming God*, 17 ff. and Stegemann, "Religionsgeschichtliche Erwägungen zu den Gottesbezeichnungen."

69 Meyer, *Naming God*, 74. For a discussion of the Mt. Gerizim temple, its context and inscriptions, see Edelman, "Yhwh Shomron and Yhwh Elohim in the Achaemenid Province of Samaria," in this volume.

the sacred name, but Hebrew Daniel 9 uses it several times (and *ʔdny* appears in Dan 1:2). On the other hand, there is no divine name avoidance in fifth-century Egyptian Aramaic documents in Aramaic script, so finding it here in the papyrus is very curious.[70] Whoever wrote the papyrus is certainly concerned with representing this divine name appropriately and inoffensively, in perhaps the earliest example of this tendency in Aramaic tradition.

But who is Yahō in the context of the papyrus? Nowhere is he explicitly identified with Samaria or Judah (no deity is mentioned in the arrival poem in col. xvii), but he is instead directly connected with Mount Zaphon (xii 13–14) and Syria (xiii 12), and indirectly connected with *Rēšā* (xii 13) in the Yahō psalms. Moreover, he is perhaps connected to "the South" in his hypostasis "Throne-of-Yahō" in the "Blessings of the All the Gods" poem in viii 7. In the latter instance, the "Throne-of-Yahō" and the goddess Asherah are asked to bless "from the South (*ngb*)." This hypostasis of Yahō with a female associate or consort is reminiscent of the late ninth- or eight-century inscriptions at Kuntillet ʕAjrud in the northern Sinai, where Yhwh of Teman (the "South") and *ʔšrth* – either Asherata, a form of Asherah, or "his Asherah" – are asked for blessings.[71] Moreover, if Yahō is identified with Bethel in any portion of the papyrus, as has been suggested,[72] he is not explicitly espoused to Anat, Bethel's traditional consort, but is rather linked to Asherah.

The final appearance of the sacred name is possibly in the short form "Yah" in the poem about a victorious warrior deity in xvi 13b–17, where it is parallel to the name Ash(im)-Bethel in lns. 13–14:[73]

The strength of the divine bull (lit. bull of El) is your strength, Yah.[74]

---

70 It is not avoided in the fourth-century Idumean ostraca either (cf. the Idumean "house of Yhw"; Meyer *Naming God*, 67–68).

71 Cf. *ʔšrth* in Khirbet el-Qôm lns. 3 and 5. For the view that the Yhwh of Teman in the Kuntillet ʕAjrud inscriptions was the name of the God of the southern desert whose temple was located at Beersheba, see Na'aman, "In Search of the Temples of YHWH." Na'aman thinks that it is the Beersheba temple that is mentioned here in col. viii (personal communication).

72 van der Toorn, "Celebrating the New Year," and Holm, "Yaḥō and Bethel," 39–41.

73 Holm "Bethel and Yahō," 48–49.

74 The name spelled **ʔḥ̱r** in Demotic at the beginning of l. 14 is reminiscent of both Yahō (spelled **ʔḥ̱r**$_2$**w**$_2$ or **ʔḥ̱r**$_2$**w**$_3$ on the papyrus) and Ḥerem (spelled as **ḥ̱r** in **ḥ̱rb**⌜**y**⌝ **tr**^{d} "Ḥer(em)-Bethel," in xvii 14); however it is probably neither, and may even be a merger of the two names. For the shortened form, see Yah (*Yh*), that is, the shortened form of *Yhw*/*Yhwh* also found in Hebrew (e.g., Ps 68:19, 77:12, etc.), and at least once in Egyptian Aramaic in Aramaic script (*TAD* B3.4:25). The Demotic *aleph* signals the euphemism *ʔadonay*, as it does in the fuller spelling of the divine name on the papyrus. See the above discussion of the use of Demotic *aleph* in this name. The sign that represents Demotic *ẖr* "under" (Erichsen *Demotisches Glossar*: 385; designated in the transliteration system used by me for this papyrus as **ḥ̱r**) is also another form of Demotic **h** (Erichsen *Demotisches Glossar*: 265). Van der Toorn reads the sign **ḥ̱r** as **p**$_2$, but the latter sign is

Ash(im)-Bethel, the strength of divine bulls is your strength.

If this reading is correct, Yah is identified here with Ash(im)-Bethel; that is, Ashim in relation to Bethel or in his Bethel-characteristics. The rest of this poem describes the weapons of the deity – venom "like that of serpents," a "bow in heaven," and a hammer (*pṭyš*), to be raised forcefully against the country of Elam. The military context is quite appropriate to a deity, Ashim-Bethel, whose name literally means "Name-of-Bethel." In several passages in the Hebrew Bible, the Name-of-Yahweh does battle against Israel's enemies (cf. the Name-of-Yahweh in Isa 30:27–33; 1 Sam 17:45; Ps 20:2, 6, 8). In Isa 30:27–33, the Name-of-Yahweh's weapons include fire, storm, and thunder, and in 1 Sam 17:45, the full name for this hypostasis is "the Name of Yahweh of Armies (*ṣĕbāʔôt*)" (cf. [*yh*]*h ṣbʔt* at Elephantine; *CG* 167). The "bow in heaven" and the god's hammer in P. Amherst 63 xvi may well depict the celestial weaponry of Ashim-Bethel, as a storm god (see col. x where Bethel is explicitly portrayed as such). Moreover, just as the "Name" in Isa 30:27–33 is paralleled to Yahweh, one wonders if the author of col. xvi is setting up the same kind of parallel: Yah and his Name ("Ashim-Bethel/ Ashim-Yahō") go into battle against Elam, the enemy of Ashim-Bethel/Ashim-Yahō's people.[75]

The three Yahwistic psalms, to be discussed next, weave both Hebrew and Aramaic traditions together. In each, Yahō is paralleled with both the Hebrew term Adonay and with the Aramaic, Mār, "Lord," thereby embedding the worship of Yahō in the Aramean-Aramaic frame of the rest of the anthology on the papyrus.[76]

4.3 Three Psalms to Yahō amongst Other Deities

The three communal psalms, using the first-person plural "we, us, our" and featuring Yahō/Adonay, appear in cols. xii–xiii (xii 11b–19; xiii 1–10; and xiii 11–17). The first of these (xii 11b–19) is a version of biblical Psalm 20 in Hebrew, and was one of the first portions of the papyrus to be edited.[77] It has continued to receive great attention, and is often designated an "Israelite" psalm, in deference to its northern features, which in reality all three Yahō psalms share. The three Yahō psalms include additional shared features as well.

shaped slightly differently. Steiner reads "Horus" as the euphemism for the Tetragrammaton (Steiner and Nims *Aramaic Text in Demotic Script*, 61; see also above discussion).

75 Holm, "Bethel and Yahō," 49.

76 Holm, "Wandering Arameans," 177.

77 Vleeming and Wesselius, "Aramaic Hymn," and Nims and Steiner, "A Paganized Version of Psalm 20:2–6," followed by others.

4.3.1 Henotheistic Yahwism

The three psalms promote Yahō as the highest deity but are not monotheistic. In Yahō psalm 1, Yahō appears foremost as the focus of the psalm for six lines (11b–17a). Most notably lns. 16b–17a state that, while others may trust in weapons (bow and spear, *qšt* and *ḥnt*), "as for us, *Mār*/Lord is our god!"[78] In the close of the psalm, however, the deities Bethel and Baʕal appear in some relation to Yahō. Yahō and Bethel are paralleled and thus identified with each other as deities who aid and respond to the psalmist,[79] while Baʕal of Heaven (Baʕal Shamayn) is displaced from his traditional Syrian home on Mount Zaphon by Yahō, whom Baʕal is said to "bless."

> O Bow in Hea⌜ven⌝, 13) shine forth;
> send your envoy(s) from the temple (OR: all) of *Rēšā*,
> and from Zaphon 14) may Yahō aid us ...
> 17) ... May Yahō, our Bull, be with us;
> may Bethel ⌜a⌝nswer us 18) ⌜to⌝morrow.
> May Baʕal of Heaven bless Mar/the Lord;
> (and) for your pious ones (be) 19) your blessings.

In the second Yahō psalm, no other deity besides Yahō is named, but the psalmist claims that "we will sacrifice to you among the gods." Moreover, the human banquet which Yahō is invited to join is specifically said to be for Yahō/Adonay (alone) "out of the Mighty Ones of the people" (*mn-ʔdyry ʕm*; xiii 2–3). Since the sacrifices of lambs and sheep are to Yahō "among the gods," then presumably the "Mighty Ones" are those gods. The notion of Yahō as the supreme deity over many others is taken even further in Yahō psalm 3, wherein Yahō's kingship over the entire council of heaven (*dr šmyn*) is lauded, and Baʕal, who is there said to be "from Zaphon" (xiii 15), is asked to bless Yahō.

> 13b) Beneath you, Yahō,
> 14) beneath you, Adonay, is the council of heaven;[80]
> like sand, Yahō, is the council of heaven.
> 15) Proclai⌜m⌝ to us your kingship among harassers (OR: our harassers),
> and make u⌜s⌝ strong again!
> May Baʕal from Zaphon 16) bless Yahō.

---

78 Cf. *yhwh ʔlhynw* in Deut 6:4.

79 van der Toorn, "Celebrating the New Year," and Holm, "Wandering Arameans."

80 Aramaic *dr šmryn*, read as "the generation of Heaven" in Vleeming and Wesselius *Studies in Papyrus Amherst 63* (1985), 73, 76. Van der Toorn notes a comparison with the Ugaritic phrase, *dr dt šmm* in *KTU*[3] 1.10 i 3–5 ("Celebrating the New Year," 644).

4.3.2 Abundant Hebraisms/Canaanitisms and some Ugaritic borrowings

Each of the three Yahō psalms is especially full of Hebraisms or Canaanitisms. In the first place, as already mentioned, all three poems use both the Hebrew epithet *ʔadonay* and Aramaic *mār* for Yahō (both meaning "Lord"). Besides this, one notices these lexemes: *mṣwryn* ("distresses"); *mšʔl*, "request"; *ḥsyd*, "pious one"; *k*[*b*]*s*, sh[ee]p"; *zbḥ*, "to sacrifice"; *ʔdyr*, "mighty one"; *gdl*, "to be big" (Pa. "to make big"); *šḥʔ*, "the downcast"; *m*(*y*), "who?"; and possibly *ʕkb*, "those who follow closely" (cf. BH *ʕqb*, "heel"). Yahō psalm 3 in particular stands out for its Syrian tones, and likely the use of Ugaritic loan expressions, if not also Ugaritic vocabulary. For instance, the emphasis on Yahō's supremacy over the gods is demonstrated in the beginning lines:

> 11) Who among the gods, among humankind, Yahō –
> who among the gods, king (or) commoner,
> 12) who is like you, Yahō, among the gods?

Vleeming and Wesselius noted long ago that ln. 11b's *my bʔlhn bmlk bl mlk*, "who among the gods, king (or) commoner," is a borrowing from Ugaritic;[81] cf. *KTU*[3] 1.4 vii 43: *u mlk u bl mlk*. Moreover, the expression *my bʔlh(y)n*, "who among the gods?" is quite reminiscent of *my bilm*, "who among the gods ...?" in the Ugaritic epic of *Kirta* (*KTU*[3] 1.16 v 10, 14, 20).[82] Finally, the Aramaic phrase, *dr šmyn*, "council of heaven," over which Yahō is superior in lns. 13–14 ("Beneath you, Yahō, beneath you, Adonay, is the council of heaven") can be compared with the Ugaritic phrase, *dr dt šmm* in *KTU*[3] 1.10 i 3–5.[83] Specific Ugaritic lexical borrowings may include *gl*, "cup" (cf. Hebrew *glh*) and Ugr. *ṣʕ*, "bowl," if not others.

A loose parallel to this psalm may be found in biblical Ps 89:6–13, in which Yahweh is compared to the other deities in the divine assembly (Hebrew *bny ʔlym*, vs. 7), and his rule over Sea, Rahab, heaven, the netherworld (*ʔrṣ*), and the world (*tbl*) is proclaimed. Moreover, in Ps 89:13, the "North" (*ṣpwn* = Zaphon) and "South" (*ymyn*) are described as created beings and paired with the sacred mountains, Tabor and Hermon, who are said to praise the name of God. One notes the nexus of Syrian traditions here; in the Ugaritic *Baʕlu Epic*, Baʕal, who has been granted kingship by El, asks Mot, "Will it be a king or a non-king (*u mlk u bl mlk*) who establishes dominion in the earth (netherworld)?" The poets of both Aramaic Yahō psalm 3 on P. Amherst 63 col. xiii and Hebrew Psalm 89 must

---

81 Vleeming and Wesselius *Studies in Papyrus Amherst 63* 1, 72.

82 In Hebrew, note Ex 15:11 (*my-kmkh bʔlm yhwh my kmkh nʔdr bqdš*) and Ps 71:19 (*ʔlhym my kmwk*); cf. Ps 86:8.

83 van der Toorn, "Celebrating the New Year," 644.

be consciously reversing the Canaanite Baʕal tradition: Baʕal from Zaphon blesses Yahō on P. Amherst 63, and Mt. Zaphon praises the God of Israel in Ps 89:13. Yahō (and probably Bethel in Yahō psalm 1) are superior to Baʕal, the Canaanite king of the gods.

4.3.3 Northern Geographic Associations

As just noted, the geographical focus of the Yahō psalms is not explicitly Jerusalem, the heart of biblical Yahwism and site of the most well-known temple of Yahweh. Instead, Yahō's geographical associations in the Yahō psalms are a temple in *Rēšā* from which his "Bow in Heaven" appears (Yahō psalm 1); the famous mountain Zaphon, the Ugaritic home of Baʕal that is equated with Mount Zion in biblical Hebrew psalms (Yahō psalm 1); and possibly Syria, as the place from which Yahō should take vengeance on the enemies of his people (Yahō psalm 3, xiii 3: "from Syria, Adonay take vengeance for those who call upon you").[84] In addition, in contrast to the very similar psalm in Hebrew (Psalm 20), Aramaic Yahō psalm 1 on P. Amherst 63 does not mention Zion (a euphemism for Jerusalem) as the location of Yahō, but *Rēšā* and Zaphon in parallel. For its part, Yahō psalm 2 has no setting and Yahō has no geographical associations *per se*, but the lyre to which Yahō listens is described as "Sidonian" (xiii 9). Thus, if one can identify a geography in the poems, it is "northern."

4.3.4 New Year's Celebration in the Fall

Read singly and together, the three psalms fit the New Year theme of the rest of cols. i–xvii very well.[85] The first seems to be a victory psalm, a version of biblical Hebrew Psalm 20, in which trust in Yahō as God is superior to relying on military weaponry. The second Yahō psalm seems to clearly indicate its Fall New Year setting (cf. the Jewish Rosh Hashanah), at which sacrifices are brought and the old or new wine at the time of the New Moon is imbibed in banquets with the

---

84 Cf. the toponym **š?**$\mathbf{w_2r_2}$**[?]** ⌜•⌝ in the Demotic of viii 2. It seems likely that here Demotic **š?**$\mathbf{r_2}$**w** represents the same name "Syria" (or "Assyria"), although the scribe has transposed **w** and $\mathbf{r_2}$. Steiner and Nims read this as *mn-šwr-*(X *šrw*) (*?*)*t*(*y*)*-ny*, "*Come from Shur*" (Steiner and Nims, "The Aramaic Text in Demotic Script," their italics) and van der Toorn has interpreted this as Siryon ("Celebrating the New Year," 643), or *šrw*, "beginning," from the root **šry* (*Papyrus Amherst 63*, 173).
85 van der Toorn "Celebrating the New Year"; Holm, "Wandering Arameans."

deity. The final Yahō psalm celebrates the kingship of Yahō over all of the other gods, a perfect motif for the New Year, reminding one also of the enthronement of Nanay and Nabû over the gods in P. Amherst 63 i–xv.

In sum, these "northern," henotheistic Psalms exalt Yahō over other deities, especially Baʕal, but at least one of them may identify Yahō with Bethel, the Syrian deity probably also worshiped in Israel. Steiner has noted that 2 Kgs 17:24–41 and Ezra 4:9–10, which describe the Assyrian deportations of southern Mesopotamians to Samaria where they worshiped their own gods alongside Yahō, may well inform part of the background of some of the community behind P. Amherst 63.[86] These displaced Mesopotamians may be part of the Levantine waves of population that came to Egypt.[87]

5 Purposely Ambiguous Laments – for Samaria or Another City or Land?

In the New Year-oriented compositions in cols. i–xvii, several poems do not specifically name the places lamented (not even using the term *Rēšā*, "the Head") and may be purposely ambiguous, allowing the possibility for identifying these with any number of lands or cities, including Samaria. This is the case of the description of a destroyed city in vi 1–11, whose people are variously killed or deported, and the depiction of a city in xii 1–11a, which precedes the three Yahō psalms. The composition in vi 1–11 begins:

> The [ho]rrors, Mār/Lord, [the] ho[rrors] –
> we are terrif[ied of the horrors [that we have s]een!
> They [de]stroyed for you (OR: the land,) all your cities;
> in the country, trembling dwells.

The sorrowful poem continues with a description of the deportation of leaders and families, and the humiliation and killing of other members of society, including bakers, butchers, priests, and musicians. But it nowhere names the land, cities, or the deportees. The same is true in the difficult poem in xii 1–11a, which contains a description and perhaps a lament for a city. The beginning is fragmentary, however, so perhaps the place name that was once there has simply disap-

---

86 Steiner, "The Aramaic Text in Demotic Script," 310. The names of the foreign deities are corrupted in the Masoretic Text, but may include Banit and Ashim (2 Kgs 17:30–31).
87 While Steiner located the Samarian community in Bethel (confusing some of the mentions of Bethel the deity with Bethel the place), this is not an obvious conclusion.

peared. Yet, since this poem immediately precedes the three Yahō/Adonay psalms, one wonders if it is connected to them somehow. Vleeming and Wesselius identified the city of col. xii with Jerusalem,[88] while both Richard Steiner and Karel van der Toorn saw an Israelite location. Steiner, who incorrectly reads "ivory" at the end of this poem, and who thought many of the occurrences of the name "Bethel" on the papyrus were the place instead of the deity, viewed the city as Bethel.[89] For his part, although his reading of the poem closely follows that of Vleeming and Wesselius, Karel van der Toorn believed it to be Samaria.[90] More recently, in a rather speculative piece, Bob Becking has suggested that place is to be identified with the north Syrian city of Carchemish.[91]

Not all of these suggestions are of equal worth, but one wonders if laments for places whose identities are not specified are meant to be "all-purpose" set liturgical pieces to be utilized on multiple occasions, much as in the case of Mesopotamian laments.[92] For instance, the narrator in the sad poem in vi 1–11 does not ask for *Mār*, "Lord," to do anything to save or restore the cities. Mār is simply called upon to notice the disasters that have befallen his land and his people. In this connection, one may return to col. xvii, which begins with the Samarian-Judean arrival poem, followed by the sacred marriage text with the union of Nanay and Baʕal of Heaven (Baʕal Shamayn). While there is no obvious link between the arrival poem and the sacred marriage, the column ends with an entreaty to rebuild an unidentified land:

Demotic[93]	**Aramaic**
bʔnʔn• ʔ$_2$tmmʔ• 18) ʔr•	bn(y)-n(y) ʔdm- 18) r
p$_2$r$_3$ qrt•	pr(q) qr(y)t(ʔ)
ʔ$_2$bʔn ⸢y⸣ • kryt• npʔrn•	ʔbn ⸢y⸣ qryt np(y)ln
⸢b⸣ ny ʕryt• rʔ•ḥm	⸢b⸣ ny ʕlyt-lḥm
bʔnʔn• 19) ʔrk• rbʔ•	bn(y)-n(y) 19) ʔrq rb(h)
ḥʔyr ⸢•⸣ rʔ•m$_2$m ⸢y⸣ skn•	ḥyl lm{m} ⸢y⸣ skn
b ⸢ʔr• ʔ$_2$⸣ tm mk• sp	b ⸢r-ʔ⸣ dm mk sp

88 Vleeming and Wesselius, *Studies in Papyrus Amherst 63* 2, 72–74.
89 Steiner, *The Aramaic Text in Demotic Script*, 317.
90 van der Toorn, *Papyrus Amherst 63*, 161–165.
91 Becking, "An Elegy for a Conquered City."
92 Gabbay, *Pacifying the Hearts of the Gods*, 15–16; Gabbay, "Defeat Literature in the Cult of the Victorious."
93 I have changed my reading since my 2017 publication of col. xvii, and thus I offer both the Demotic transliteration as well as an Aramaic rendering before an English translation.

Translation

Rebuild, make won- 18) drous,[94]
rescue the city;
rebuil⌜d⌝ a city of ruins;
⌜reb⌝uild a supreme (place) of sustenance;
rebuild 19) a great land –
a rampart for the c⌜om⌝moner,[95]
so⌜n⌝ of a lowly ⌜m⌝an.

These words at the end of col. xvii provide a fitting conclusion to the entire Near Year's anthology in cols. i–xvii. However, one cannot miss that the most immediate section with displaced people is at the beginning of the column: the Samarians and Judeans, who have had some experience connected to Babylon and Nineveh. Viewed in light of the Samarian-Judean arrival poem in lines 1–7, the end of this column is a reminder that, even when welcomed to a new land, refugees never cease dreaming of the home they have left.

6 Conclusion: Samarians in the Egyptian Diaspora according to P. Amherst 63

While there is only one section on P. Amherst 63 that mentions Samaria and Samarians explicitly – the Samarian-Judean arrival poem in xvii 1–6, certain psalms elsewhere focus on lauding Yhw(h)/Adonay, the national God of Israel and Judah (e.g., xii 11b–xiii 17 and perhaps col. xvi). These poems, one of which is related to or even a version of Hebrew Psalm 20 (Yahō psalm 1 in xii 11b–19), have northern connections and demonstrate that Yahō may be identified with the Aramean deity Bethel but is otherwise superior to all the gods, including Baʕal, the paramount Syrian deity and the "Canaanite" god par excellence in the Bible. While there is limited-to-no evidence that the Elephantine community of Yahwists, despite their devotion to Yahō and their cultic connections with Judah and Samaria, knew the Torah or any part of what would become the Hebrew Bible, the Aramaic-speaking community behind P. Amherst 63, written in a western Aramaic dialect some decades later, at least knew a version (or the stock lan-

94 This takes *ʔdmr* as the Aphel Imperative of **dmr*. Cf. the Pael or Ithpael form of **dmr* in i 17–18; ii 14–15; iii 14; iv 3.

95 Or read the Aramaic as *ḥy(y){l} lm⌜y⌝skn*, "keep alive the commoner."

guage) of Hebrew Psalm 20's victory psalm. Moreover, the papyrus and the Bible share certain traditions about Israel/Samaria and Judah/Yehud, such as: a sibling relationship; devotion to Yahō (with some association to Asherah), whose name is spelled in Demotic in a manner that suggests it is to be said aloud as the biblical euphemism "Adonay"; and certain points of history, including the seeking of refuge in Egypt and a background of some kind in Babylon and Nineveh (xvii 1–2).

On the other hand, in P. Amherst 63's Samarian-Judean arrival poem in xvii 1–7, Judah assumes authority over both Samaria and Judah through the spokesman who speaks for the entire group of siblings entering the new land, even though the former may have arrived earlier. Much as the Hebrew Bible presents Jerusalem and Judah as the center of the concept "Israel" and the heart of Yahwism,[96] and just as the term *yĕhûday* in the Elephantine documents subsumes the identity of the Elephantine community's Samarian religious or other elements, the papyrus gives priority to Judah over Samaria. In its Yahwistic components, however, the papyrus reflects henotheistic views that diverge from the core Yahwism of Judah's Bible.[97]

Bibliography

Adler, Yonatan, *The Origins of Judaism: an Archaeological-Historical Reappraisal*, Yale University Press, 2022.

Allen, James, *Ancient Egyptian Phonology*. Cambridge: Cambridge University Press, 2020.

Barnea, Gad, *Khnum is Against Us Since Hananiah has been in Egypt: Yahwistic Reform and Identity in the Prism of Elephantine: 419–399 BCE*. Ph.D. dissertation, University of Haifa, 2021.

Barnea, Gad, "*Interpretatio Ivdaica* in the Achaemenid Period," *Journal of Ancient Judaism* 14 (2023): 1–37.

Barnea, Gad, "The Migration of the Elephantine Yahwists under Amasis II," *Journal of Near Eastern Studies* 82.1 (2023): 103–18.

Barnea, Gad, "Yahwistic Identity in the Achaemenid period," *Zeitschrift für die Alttestamentliche Wissenschaft*, 136.1 (2024): 1–14.

Becking, Bob, "Yehudite Identity in Elephantine," pages 403–419 in *Judah and the Judeans in the Achaemenid Period: Negotiating Identity in an International Context*, Oded Lipschits, Gary N. Knoppers, and Manfred Oeming (eds.), Winona Lake, IN: Eisenbrauns, 2011.

96 As Michael Stahl has noted, the Hebrew Bible, written in Judah, defines Yahweh with the epithet "God of Israel" in 160 out of 202 references to that title. See Stahl, "The 'God of Israel' in Judah's Bible," esp. 744, and Stahl, *The "God of Israel" in History and Tradition*, 41–45.

97 As I have noted elsewhere, the difficulty of distinguishing Judeans from Samarians in Egypt in the Persian era may be comparable to the situation in the Hellenistic period (Holm, "Wandering Arameans," 174), wherein inhabitants of towns named "Samaria" call themselves Jews/Judeans (*Ioudaioi*).

Becking, Bob, *Identity in Persian Egypt: The Fate of the Yehudite Community of Elephantine.* University Park, PA: Eisenbrauns, 2020.
Becking, Bob, "An Elegy for a Conquered City. Or: Does Papyrus Amherst 63 xii 1–11 Reflect the Fall of Samaria?" *Die Welt des Orients* 51 (2021): 136–49.
Becking, Bob, "The Identity of the People at Elephantine," pages 1–16 in *Elephantine Revisited: New Insights into the Judean Community and Its Neighbors*, ed. Margaretha Folmer. University Park, PA: Eisenbrauns, 2022.
Debourse, Céline, "Debita Reverentia: Understanding Royal Humiliation in the New Year's Festival Texts," *Kaskal* 16 (2019): 183–200.
Debourse, Céline, "A New Hope: The New Year's Festival Texts as a Cultural Reaction to Defeat," pages 139–164 in *Culture of Defeat: Submission in Written Sources and the Archaeological Record. Proceedings of a Joint Seminar of the Hebrew University of Jerusalem and the University of Vienna, October 2017*, K. Streit and M. Grohmann (eds.), Gorgias Studies in the Ancient Near East 16. Piscataway, NJ: Gorgias, 2020.
Debourse, Céline, *Of Priests and Kings: The Babylonian New Year Festival in the Last Age of Cuneiform Culture.* CHANE 127. Leiden: Brill, 2022.
Erichsen, Wolja, *Demotisches Glossar.* Kopenhagen: Ejnar Munksgaard, 1954.
Gabbay, Uri, *Pacifying the Hearts of the Gods: Sumerian Emesal Prayers of the First Millennium BCE.* Heidelberger Emesal-Studien 1. Wiesbaden: Harrassowitz, 2014.
Gabbay, Uri, "Defeat Literature in the Cult of the Victorious: Ancient Mesopotamian Sumerian City Laments," pages 121–38 in *Culture of Defeat: Submission in Written Sources and the Archaeological Record. Proceedings of a Joint Seminar of the Hebrew University of Jerusalem and the University of Vienna, October 2017*, K. Streit and M. Grohmann (eds.), Gorgias Studies in the Ancient Near East 16. Piscataway, NJ: Gorgias, 2020.
Grabbe, Lester L., "Elephantine and the Torah," pages 125–135 in *In the Shadow of Bezalel: Aramaic, Biblical, and Ancient Near Eastern Studies in Honor of Bezalel Porten*, ed. A. F. Botta. Leiden: Brill, 2013.
Granerød, Gard, "The Former and theFuture Temple of Yhw in Elephantine: A Traditio-Historical Case Study of Ancient Near Eastern Antiquarianism." *Zeitschrift für Alttestamentliche Wissenschaft* 15 (2015): 63–77.
Granerød, Gard, *Dimensions of Yahwism in the Persian Period: Studies in the Religion and Society of the Judaean Community at Elephantine.* BZAW 488. Berlin: de Gruyter, 2016.
Holm, Tawny, "Nanay and Her Lover: An Aramaic Sacred Marriage Text from Egypt." *Journal of Near Eastern Studies* 76 (2017): 1–37.
Holm, Tawny, "Royal Women Sages in Aramaic Literature: The Unnamed Queen in Daniel 5 and Saritrah in the 'Revolt of Babylon,'" pages 151–74 in *From Mari to Jerusalem and Back: Assyriological and Biblical Studies in Honor of Jack Murad Sasson*, A. Azzoni et al. (eds.). University Park: Eisenbrauns, 2020.
Holm, Tawny, "In Praise of Gods & Goddesses in Aramean Egypt: Papyrus Amherst 63," pages 301–24 in *Hymnen und Aretalogien im antiken Mittelmeerraum: Von Inana bis Isis*, L. Bricault and M. A. Stadler (eds.), Philippika 154. Wiesbaden: Harrassowitz, 2021.
Holm, Tawny, "Nanay(a) among the Arameans: New Light from P. Amherst 63," pages 92–116 in *New Perspectives on Aramaic Epigraphy in Mesopotamia, Qumran, Egypt and Idumea: Proceedings of the Joint RIAB Minerva Center and the Jeselsohn Epigraphic Center of Jewish History*, Aren Maeir et al. (eds.), Research on Israel and Aram in Biblical Times 2. ORA 40. Tübingen: Mohr Siebeck, 2021.
Holm, Tawny, "Papyrus Amherst 63 and the Arameans of Egypt: A Landscape of Cultural Nostalgia," pages 323–51 in *Elephantine in Context: Studies on the History, Religion and Literature*

of the Judeans in Persian Period Egypt, Reinhard Kratz and Bernd Schipper (eds.), Forschungen zum Alten Testament 155. Tübingen: Mohr Siebeck, 2022.

Holm, Tawny, "Sacrifice and Feasting in Papyrus Amherst 63," pages 135–68 in *Ceremonies, Feasts and Festivities in Ancient Mesopotamia and the Mediterranean World: Performance and Participation. Proceedings of the 11th Melammu Workshop, Barcelona, 29–31 January 2019*, ed. Rocío Da Riva, et al., Melammu Workshops and Monographs 7. Münster: Zaphon Verlag, 2022.

Holm, Tawny, "Bethel and Yahō: A Tale of Two Gods in Egypt." *Journal of Ancient Near Eastern Religions* 23 (2023): 25–55.

Holm, Tawny, "The Wandering Arameans in Egypt: Papyrus Amherst 63." *Hebrew Bible and Ancient Israel* 12 (2023): 157–79.

Holm, Tawny, *Aramaic Literary Texts*. Writings from the Ancient World. Atlanta: SBL, in press.

Holm, Tawny, "Western Aramaic Elements in Papyrus Amherst 63, the Aramaic Text in Demotic Script," in *Syria, Mesopotamia, and the Comparative Study of Semitic Languages*, ed. Tawny Holm and Juan Pedro Monferrer-Sala. University Park, PA: Eisenbrauns, in press.

Kahn, Dan'el, "The Date of the Arrival of the Judeans at Elephantine and the Foundation of Their Colony." *Journal of Near Eastern Studies* 81 (2022): 139–163.

Knauf, Ernst A., "Elephantine und das vor-biblische Judentum," pages 179–88 in *Religion und Religionskontakte im Zeitalter der Achämeniden*, ed. R. G. Kratz. Veröffentlichung der Wissenschaftlichen Gesellschaft für Theologie 22. Gütersloh: Kaiser, 2002.

Kratz, Reinhard G., "Arameans and Judeans: Ethnography and Identity at Elephantine," pages 56–85 in *Israel in Egypt: The Land of Egypt as Concept and Reality for Jews in Antiquity and the Early Medieval Period*, ed. A. Salveson et al. Leiden: Brill, 2020.

Meyer, Anthony R., *Naming God in Early Judaism: Aramaic, Hebrew, and Greek*. Studies in Cultural Contexts of the Bible 2. Leiden: Brill Schöningh, 2022.

Na'aman, Nadav, "In Search of the Temples of YHWH of Samaria and YHWH of Teman." *Journal of Ancient Near Eastern Religions* 17 (2017): 76–95.

Na'aman, Nadav, "Papyrus Amherst 63: Shifting between the Heavenly and Earthly Spheres." *Tel Aviv* 29 (2002): 250–266.

Nims, Charles, and Steiner, Richard, "A Paganized Version of Psalm 20:2–6 from the Aramaic Text in Demotic Script," *Journal of the American Oriental Society* 103 (1983): 261–74.

Porten, Bezalel, *Archives from Elephantine.* Berkeley: University of California Press, 1968.

Porten, Bezalel, "Settlement of Jews at Elephantine and Arameans at Syene," pages 451–470 in *Judah and the Judeans in the Neo-Babylonian Period*, O. Lipschits and J. Blenkinsopp (eds.) Winona Lake, IN: Eisenbrauns, 2003.

Rohrmoser, Angela, *Götter, Tempel und Kult der Judäo-Aramäer von Elephantine: archäologische und schriftliche Zeugnisse aus dem perserzeitlichen Ägypten*. AOAT 396. Münster: Ugarit-Verlag, 2014.

Schipper, Bernd U., "Die Judäer/Aramäer von Elephantine und ihre Religion," *Zeitschrift für die Alttestamentliche Wissenschaft* 132 (2020): 57–83.

Schmid, Konrad et al., *The Joseph Story between Egypt and Israel*. Archaeology and Bible 5. Tübingen: Mohr Siebeck, 2021.

Stahl, Michael J., "The 'God of Israel' in Judah's Bible: Problems and Prospects." *Journal of Biblical Literature* 139 (2020): 721–745.

Stahl, Michael J., *The "God of Israel" in History and Tradition*. VTSup 187. Leiden: Brill, 2021.

Steiner, Richard, "The Aramaic Text in Demotic Script: The Liturgy of a New Year's Festival Imported from Bethel to Syene by Exiles from Rash," *Journal of the American Oriental Society* 111 (1991): 362–63.

Steiner, Richard, "Papyrus Amherst 63: A New Source for the Language, Literature, Religion, and History of the Aramaeans." pages 199–207 in *Studia Aramaica: New Sources and New Approaches, Papers Delivered at the London Conference of The Institute of Jewish Studies University College London, 26th–28th June 1991*, M. J. Geller et al. (eds.). JSS Sup 4. Oxford: Oxford University Press, 1995.

Steiner, Richard, "The Aramaic Text in Demotic Script," pages 309–27 in *The Context of Scripture*, William Hallo and Lawson Younger (eds.), vol. 1. Leiden: Brill, 1997.

Steiner, Richard, "The Scorpion Spell from Wadi Ḥammamat: Another Aramaic Text in Demotic Script." *Journal of Near Eastern Studies* 60 (2001): 259–68.

Steiner, Richard, and Nims, Charles, "Ashurbanipal and Shamash-shum-ukin: A Tale of Two Brothers from the Aramaic Text in Demotic Script, Part 1." *Revue Biblique* 92 (1985): 60–81.

Steiner, Richard, and Nims, Charles, "The Aramaic Text in Demotic Script: Text, Translation, and Notes," 2017. https://yeshiva.academia.edu/RichardSteiner

van der Toorn, Karel, "Celebrating the New Year With the Israelites: Three Extra-Biblical Psalms from Papyrus Amherst 63." *Journal of Biblical Literature* 136 (2017): 633–49.

van der Toorn, Karel, *Papyrus Amherst 63*. AOAT 448. Münster: Ugarit-Verlag, 2018.

van der Toorn, Karel, *Becoming Diaspora Jews: Behind the Story of Elephantine*. The Anchor Bible Reference Library. New Haven and London: Yale University Press, 2019.

von Pilgrim, Cornelius, "Tempel des Jahu und 'Strasse des Königs': Ein Konflikt in der späten Perserzeit auf Elephantine," pages 303–17 in *Egypt: Temple of the Whole World: Studies in Honour of Jan Assmann = Ägypten: Tempel der gesamten Welt*, ed. S. Meyer. SHR 97. Leiden: Brill, 2003.

von Pilgrim, Cornelius, "'Anyway, We Should Really Dig on Elephantine Some Time': A Short Tour Through the Research History of the Towns along the First Nile Cataract," pages 85–96 in *Zwischen den Welten: Grabfunde von Ägyptens Südgrenze = Between Worlds: Finds from Tombs on Egypt's Southern Border*, L. D. Morenz et al. (eds.). Rahden/Westf.: VML, Marie Leidorf, 2011.

von Pilgrim, Cornelius, "On the Archaeological Background of the Aramaic Papyri from Elephantine in the Light of Recent Fieldwork," pages 1–16 in *Elephantine Revisited: New Insights into the Judean Community and Its Neighbors*, ed. M. Folmer. University Park, PA: Eisenbrauns, 2022.

Stegemann, Hartmut, "Religionsgeschichtliche Erwägungen zu den Gottesbezeichnungen in den Qumrantexten," pages 195–217 in *Qumrân: Sa piete, sa theologie et son milieu*, M. Delcor (ed.). BETL 46. Leuven: Leuven University press, 1978.

Tuplin, Christopher J., "The Fall and Rise of the Elephantine Temple," pages 344–372 in *Aršāma and his World*, Christopher J. Tuplin and John Ma (eds.). Oxford: Oxford University Press, 2020.

Vittmann, Günter, "Arameans in Egypt," pages 229–79 in *Wandering Arameans: Arameans Outside Syria, Textual and Archaeological Perspectives*, A. Berlejung et al. (eds.), LAS 5. Wiesbaden: Harrassowitz.

Vleeming, Sven P. and Wesselius, Jan-Wim, "An Aramaic Hymn from the Fourth Century B.C." *Bibliotheca Orientalis* 39 (1982): 501–509.

Vleeming, Sven P. and Wesselius, Jan-Wim, "Betel the Saviour." *Journal of the Ancient Near Eastern Society "Ex Oriente Lux"* 28 (1983–1984): 110–40.

Vleeming, Sven P. and Wesselius, Jan-Wim, *Studies in Papyrus Amherst 63: Essays on the Aramaic Texts in Aramaic-Demotic Papyrus Amherst 63*. 2 vols. Amsterdam: Juda Palache Instituut, 1985, 1990.

Zauzich, Karl-Theodor, "Der Gott des aramäisch-demotischen Papyrus Amherst 63," *Biblische Notizen* 85 (1985): 89–90.

Zauzich, Karl-Theodor, *Hieroglyphen mit Geheimnis: Neue Erkenntnisse zur Entstehung unseres Alphabets*. Darmstadt: Philipp von Zabern., 2015.

Itamar Kislev

The Cultic Fire in the Priestly Source

In seeking evidence of the manifold ways in which Achaemenid Persia influenced the Hebrew Bible, one avenue of inquiry should relate to whether, and how, the Persian/Zoroastrian fire cult impacted the Bible. This paper identifies six late interpolations that arguably provide evidence of an effort to inject the Zoroastrian/Iranian concept of ever-burning fire into the Israelite priestly cult.

Even a brief consideration demonstrates the central status of fire in the Persian religion and cult. As summed up by Mary Boyce,

> the ancient Iranian cosmogonists regarded fire moreover as the seventh "creation," forming the life-force, as it were, within the other six, and so animating the world. Fire was thus of great theoretical, ethical, ritual, and practical importance in ancient Iranian life and thought. Zoroaster developed this cultural inheritance yet further when he apprehended fire as the creation of Aša Vahišta (= the best truth – IK), and when he saw fire as the instrument of God's judgment at the Last Day.[1]

Zoroastrian praxis venerated fire and "the cult of fire is at the very heart of Zoroastrian devotional life."[2] When making an offering to fire Zoroaster thought of truth and commanded his followers to always pray before some form of fire.[3] The frequent references in the *Avesta* to fire as the "son of Ahura Mazda" further underscore its importance.[4]

Whether fire temples date to the Achaemenid or the later Parthian period is a debated issue;[5] nonetheless, there is evidence for Persian fire altars in the Achaemenid period, such as the registers above two tombs of the Achaemenid kings, Darius I and perhaps Xerxes, in Naqsh-e Rostam.[6] Direct evidence for the ever-burning cult fire of the Zoroastrians is only known from later periods, but a new reading in the *Avesta* by Alberto Cantera shows the antiquity of the concept of eternal fire. He suggests that the eternal fire was kept in the royal Achaemenid

1 Boyce, "Ātaš."
2 Boyce, "Zoroastrian Temple Cult of Fire," 454.
3 Potts, "Fire in Zoroastrianism."
4 See the texts quoted by Cantera, "Fire, the Greatest God," 25, 35, 38–39, 52. On pp. 24–27 he cites some texts in which fire is called "the greatest god."
5 See Boyce, "Zoroastrian Temple Cult of Fire," 454–62.
6 Root, *King and Kingship*, 176–179; von Gall, "Naqš-e Rostam."

Itamar Kislev, University of Haifa, Israel

https://doi.org/10.1515/9783111018638-006

palace and taken from there for an open-air ritual.[7] This evidence makes it germane to seek Persian influence on biblical practice in this respect.

Gad Barnea convincingly argues that a fragmentary papyrus from Elephantine (dated ca. 410 BCE) concerning the destroyed Yhw temple mentions a fire altar. Following a reference to a *minḥa* offering to Yhw, the text uses the unique term אתרודן (A 4.5:17).[8] Barnea plausibly identifies this term with the later technical one for fire altar: *Ātašdān*. The word אתרודן in the Elephantine document includes the Avestan element Atār, fire, which later became Ātaš.[9] Although the document's fragmentary nature hampers our ability to draw definitive conclusions, nonetheless, we can make two observations: first, that the Jews in Elephantine were familiar with the Persian term for fire altar: אתרודן; second, they used it in relation to their Yhw temple.

We cannot determine with certainty what this Persian cultic term stands for in this Elephantine document. It may indeed indicate substantial penetration of the Persian cult into the Yahwistic temple of Elephantine, namely, that the altar in the Yhw temple was a functioning fire altar with all the related Persian customs. It is also possible, however, that the Jews in Elephantine simply adopted a Persian term for their Yahwistic altar, leaving their temple cult uninfluenced by the Persian one. Furthermore, it is even possible that their use of the term אתרודן simply inhered in the fact that the letter was addressed to Persian officials, whereas the Elephantine Jews did not themselves apply it to their temple altar. In any event, as the Jewish community in Elephantine had some, even if limited, acquaintance with the Persian fire cult, this supports a search for signs of awareness of this cult in the Bible.

In actuality, fire already possesses an important place in older Israelite beliefs and religion, as reflected in biblical sources predating the Persian period. Thus, fire is at times an aspect of YHWH's theophanies as, for example, at the burning bush (Exod 3:2) where the messenger of YHWH or YHWH himself (cf. v. 4) appeared in the fire, and at Horeb (Deut 5:4, 19), where YHWH speaks out of the fire. Pillars of cloud and fire accompanied the Israelites during their wandering in the wilderness (Exod 13:21). The connection revealed by these instances between YHWH and fire made the Israelite religion a convenient platform for absorbing aspects of the Persian concept of fire. Scholars have attempted to identify references to the Zoroastrian fire cult in the Bible, especially in Prophets; for

7 Cantera, "Fire, the Greatest God," 19–61.

8 *TAD* A4.5:17.

9 Barnea, "Interpretatio Ivdaica," 363–64; Barnea, "Some Achaemenid Zoroastrian Echoes."

example, Isa 50:11 has been interpreted as manifesting hostility to those who turned to the Zoroastrian fire cult.[10]

In his article about pants in the priestly source, S. David Sperling has shown that the noun מכנסיים "trousers," which appears only five times in the Hebrew Bible (four in the priestly parts of the Pentateuch and once in Ezekiel – Exod 28:42, 39:28; Lev 6:3, 16:4; Ezek 44:18) and only in the context of the priestly vestments, has Persian roots.[11] In concluding, he remarks: "Despite the general consensus to date P and thus the bulk of the Pentateuch in the Achaemenid period, Biblicists have expended relatively little effort in exploring Iranian influences on Torah-literature." He further adds: "it behooves us to call attention to other elements in the P source that invite further study against an Iranian backdrop."[12] He briefly considers three examples in order to illustrate possible Zoroastrian influence on the priestly writings, one of which is the influence of the Zoroastrian fire cult on the perpetual fire commandment in Lev 6.[13] Although correct, his short comment was ignored. Moreover, Sperling neither develops his insight nor analyzes the relevant passage in Lev 6, leaving room for further study of this issue.

One aspect that requires consideration is the question of dating. Notwithstanding the strong scholarly tendency to date the entire body of priestly writings in the Torah as late as the Persian period, this in my opinion is not necessarily the case with respect to all priestly texts and further evidence is required in order to date a priestly element to the Persian era.[14] I therefore confine the discussion to late additions to the priestly source, in an attempt to demonstrate the existence of a thin priestly editorial layer relating to the altar fire that shares conceptual affinity to the Persian fire cult.

---

10 E.g. Kohut, "Antiparsische Aussprüche," 719–20; Winston, "The Iranian Component," 187. Winston thinks that the expression קדחי אש in the verse is a "verbatim translation of πύραιθοι, the designation of the Magi in Strabo … and equivalent to the Avestan *athravan.*" Although the verse may be directed against those who participate in the fire cult, no real scriptural support for that interpretation exists and there are other, more solid, options; see e.g. Blenkinsopp, *Isaiah 40–55*, 319–22.

11 Sperling, "Pants, Persians and the Priestly Source," 373–82.

12 Sperling, "Pants, Persians and the Priestly Source," 382.

13 Sperling, "Pants, Persians and the Priestly Source," 383–84.

14 For a discussion of the dating of the priestly materials in the Pentateuch, see e.g. Carr, "Changes in Pentateuchal Criticism," 455–56.

Perpetual fire

The directive regarding perpetual fire in Lev 6:5–6 is found in a passage that focuses on the burnt offering, as its heading indicates. The passage reads as follows:

> וידבר יהוה אל משה לאמר. צו את אהרן ואת בניו לאמר זאת תורת העלה הוא העלה על מוקדה על המזבח כל הלילה עד הבקר ואש המזבח תוקד בו. ולבש הכהן מדו בד ומכנסי בד ילבש על בשרו והרים את הדשן אשר תאכל האש את העלה על־המזבח ושמו אצל המזבח. ופשט את בגדיו ולבש בגדים אחרים והוציא את הדשן אל מחוץ למחנה אל מקום טהור. והאש על המזבח תוקד בו לא תכבה ובער עליה הכהן עצים בבקר בבקר וערך עליה העלה והקטיר עליה חלבי השלמים. אש תמיד תוקד על המזבח לא תכבה
>
> YHWH spoke to Moses, saying: Command Aaron and his sons thus: This is the instruction of the burnt offering: the burnt offering remains on its hearth upon the altar all night until morning, while the fire on the altar burns (in) it. The priest shall dress in linen raiment, with linen trousers next to his body; and he shall take up the ashes to which the fire has reduced the burnt offering on the altar and place them beside the altar. He shall then take off his vestments and put on other vestments, and carry the ashes outside the camp to a pure place. The fire on the altar shall be kept burning, not to go out: every morning the priest shall feed wood to it, lay out the burnt offering on it, and turn into smoke the fat parts of the offerings of well-being. A perpetual fire shall be kept burning on the altar, not to go out. (Lev 6:1–6)

Although this is its sole occurrence in the priestly writings and in the Hebrew Bible in general, the perpetual fire instruction appears in this pericope only in passing. It is the *olah* 'burnt offering' which is the main topic of the passage. The passage treats the ashes remaining on the altar after the offering has been burnt at night. Whereas the fatty parts from most offerings burn readily, leaving little ash, in the case of an *olah*, where the entire animal is burnt on the altar, there may well be leftovers. The heading – "This is the instruction of the burnt offering" (v. 2) – thus precisely addresses the issue of leftovers, which encompasses mainly what remains from the burnt offering, and their treatment. In preparing the altar for the offerings of the new day, the leftovers must be removed by the priests.[15] But, as part of a sacrificial offering, these leftovers are holy; accordingly, they must be taken to a pure place (v. 4).[16] The reader may wonder what prompted the appending of the perpetual fire instruction to the burnt-offering ritual and why no independent passage was devoted to such a seemingly important topic. No clear answer to these questions emerges from the verses and it appears that two unrelated issues were juxtaposed in one passage.

---

15 Cf. Levine, *Leviticus*, 35; Hartley, *Leviticus*, 94.
16 Cf. Milgrom, *Leviticus 1–16*, 387.

Another consideration should be taken into account here. At the beginning of the sacrificial legislation, in a pericope devoted to the burnt offering, we find a directive to light a fire when sacrificing the offering: ונתנו בני אהרן הכהן אש על המזבח וערכו עצים על האש "The sons of Aaron the priest shall put fire on the altar and lay out wood upon the fire" (Lev 1:7). Presumably, this reflects an underlying assumption that the fire may be extinguished; it is therefore necessary for the priests to relight and stoke the fire when sacrificing a new burnt offering. This contradicts Lev 6:5–6's directive regarding the ever-burning fire on the altar, which obviates any need to relight the fire.[17]

Furthermore, in Lev 6:1–4, according to which in the morning the priest removes the leftovers of the sacrifices burned by the fire at night in order to make room for the new day's sacrifices, there is no indication that the priest leaves something burning on the altar, nor is there a warning not to put the fire out while removing the leftovers.[18] Actually it seems that the original meaning of the instruction in Lev 6:1–4 is a total clearing of the altar. After all, this is the goal of the action; there is no hint that the removal is not complete.

Moreover, the preparatory instructions for the journey in the wilderness mandate that the tabernacle utensils, including the altar, must be covered with cloth (Num 4:13); it is not possible, however, to cover the burning perpetual fire with cloth. This means that, for the author of that instruction the concept of ever-burning fire was outside his frame of reference. But apart from the different viewpoint, this instruction mandates that the altar be prepared for the journey by removing the ashes: ודשנו את המזבח ופרשו עליו בגד ארגמן "They shall remove the ashes from the altar in order to enable spreading a purple cloth over it." The purpose of removing the ashes is to completely extinguish the fire by removing all the leftovers, including the coals and every potential flame, to allow the altar to be covered by a cloth. This treatment of the ashes means a total emptying of the altar, without even specifying that the removal must be complete. This is

17 The rabbis solve the problem through the artificial solution that although fire permanently burns on the altar, there is a need to light additional fire (b. Yoma 21b). The contradiction between Lev 1:7 and 6:5–6 is noted by many scholars such as Baentsch, *Exodus, Leviticus, Numeri*, 312, but cf. Milgrom, who sought to solve the contradiction by rendering the expression ... ונתנו אש as "stoke the fire" (*Leviticus 1–16*, 157).

18 M. Tamid 1:4 reflects another understanding of this instruction, in which the rabbis say that only a small quantity of ashes should be removed every morning. I hope to devote a special study to this shift. Milgrom thinks that vv. 5–6 were written here as a warning not to extinguish the fire while removing the ashes (*Leviticus 1–16*, 387), but if this was the reason, we would expect the warning to come earlier, closer to the reference to the removal of the ashes, namely after v. 3. In addition, the short passage on the ever-burning fire (vv. 5–6) in no way refers to the removal of the leftovers.

probably also the intention of the injunction to remove the leftovers in Lev 6:3, namely total clearance; fire does not continue to burn after that action.[19]

Interestingly, the tension between the concept of perpetual fire and the instruction to cover the altar before a journey was recognized even in ancient times. The Septuagint does not reflect the verb ודשנו (את המזבח), but states καὶ τὸν καλυπτῆρα ἐπιθήσει (ἐπὶ τὸ θυσιαστήριον) "And he shall put the covering on the altar." Similarly, R. Yehuda states that during the journey a large copper vessel called *psykter* (ψυκτήρ) was placed on the perpetual altar fire in order to keep it burning.[20] The effort to harmonize these two instructions, which involves changing the plain meaning of Num 4:13, indicates the conceptual difference between them.

The one-time directive in Lev 6:5–6 is connected neither to the previous verses nor to the main topic of the pericope. The verses not only contradict the instruction to light the altar fire in Lev 1:7,[21] and that in Num 4:13, they probably also reflect a concept that differs from and is opposite to the passage in which they appear. This suggests that the verses that command perpetual fire (Lev 6:5–6) are a late addition to the passage. In their verses, the interpolators twice quoted an expression from v. 2, namely from the original passage: ואש המזבח תוקד בו, twice adding the essential element of the new directive לא תכבה "not to go out." The original meaning of the expression ואש המזבח תוקד בו in v. 2, is, however, that the altar fire will continue to be lit at night, burning the burnt offering. The masculine suffix in the word בו can relate either to the sacrifice,[22] or the hearth

---

19 This is probably also the meaning of the verb לדשנו in Exod 27:3.

20 *Sifra, Ṣav* 2:5. Note that R. Shimon says there that the altar was indeed evacuated before the journey. Based on similar considerations, Victor Avigdor Hurowitz concludes that *tamid* in Lev 6:5–6 "does not mean 'non-stop', but 'over and over' … and refers only to when the tabernacle is standing" ("Review: Ancient Israelite Cult in History," 230). We cannot expect, however, that glossators, such as those who inserted Lev 6:5–6, would take such a "realistic" consideration into account. Moreover, as Levine has correctly noted "the rendering 'perpetual' is appropriate because our verse states explicitly that the fire is not to go out but must burn incessantly" (*Leviticus*, 36).

21 The injunction to put fire on the altar and then to place wood on the fire in Lev 1:7 is well planted in its context. In some verses these activities are assumed, such as the next verse: וערכו בני אהרן הכהנים את הנתחים את־הראש ואת־הפדר על־העצים אשר על־האש אשר על־המזבח "and Aaron's sons, the priests, shall lay out the sections, with the head and the suet, *on the wood that is on the fire upon the altar.*" Note that the final part of the verse is formulated using the same words as Lev 1:7, but in reverse order as required by the context; see similar formulations in Lev 1:12, 17; 3:5. As all these references relate to Lev 1:7, this means that the verse is original in the sacrificial legislation in Lev 1–7.

22 Either to קרבן or עולה, although there is no match in gender; see Baentsch, *Exodus, Leviticus, Numeri*, 333.

(מוקד);[23] it cannot be attributed to the altar, because if it referred to the altar, we would find the preposition על.[24] In any case this is not a command; the verse simply describes the situation of the altar in the morning: the altar fire burned the sacrifice at night and the leftovers need to be removed in the morning. The command begins only in v. 3. Accordingly, the meaning of the verb תוקד in this case is not that the fire continues to burn overnight, but that it continues to burn the sacrifices at night. Only following the interpolation of vv. 5–6, however, does the meaning of that expression become more command-like: "the fire on the altar is *kept going* on it" (NJPS).[25] But this rendering, which already inserts the concept of perpetual fire in v. 2, is incongruous in that context and is accepted only because of its similarity to the expressions inserted in vv. 5 and 6; note the absence of the prohibition לא תכבה in relation to that expression in v. 2.[26]

In v. 5 the interpolators quoted the original phrase almost verbatim, but now the antecedent of the masculine suffix in the word בו is even less clear, because neither the sacrifice nor the מוקד is in sufficient proximity to the word בו. This obscurity strengthens the supposition regarding the secondarity of vv. 5–6 and reveals the artificiality of the interpolators' use of the phrase from v. 2 as a hook for their addition.[27] Following the repetition of the phrase and the essential addition of לא תכבה, some additional instructions appear: "every morning the priest shall feed wood to it, lay out the burnt offering on it, and turn into smoke the fat parts of the offerings of well-being," according to which the fueling of the fire precedes the sacrifices and the fire possesses independent importance. This contrasts with the aforementioned verse: "The sons of Aaron the priest shall put fire on the altar and lay out wood upon the fire" (Lev 1:7), which appears in the basic law of the burnt offering (vv. 1–17) after the preparation of the parts of the sacrifice for burning (vv. 4–6) and creates the impression that the kindling of the fire is not important in and of itself, but is just for purpose of burning the offering.

The second use of the expression ואש המזבח תוקד בו is found in v. 6, where it is a paraphrase: אש תמיד תוקד על המזבח לא תכבה "A perpetual fire shall be kept

---

23 See Milgrom, *Leviticus 1–16*, 384. The word מוקדה earlier in this verse should be read with *mappiq* in the *heh*, namely "its hearth" with the LXX and many researchers; see e.g. Bertholet, *Leviticus*, 19; Kiuchi, *Leviticus*, 120. Accordingly, the word מוקדה is a masculine noun with a suffix.

24 Milgrom notes that Lev. Rab. 7:5 is the first to note this peculiarity (*Leviticus 1–16*, 384).

25 And similarly in other versions.

26 In the main textual witnesses of the LXX the prohibition "not to go out" does appear at the end of the verse; see Wevers, *Leviticus*, 82–83. In line with that, the concept of perpetual fire is already inserted in v. 2, but this version is probably secondary and was influenced by the formulations in vv. 5 and 6; cf. Wevers, *Notes on the Greek Text of Leviticus*, 69.

27 Bertholet explains the repetition of the phrase in v. 5 as a transition from the first priestly activity in the morning to the second (*Leviticus*, 19).

burning on the altar, not to go out." This duplication not only intensifies the concept of perpetual fire, but also creates a structured two-verse unit with a similar opening and closing.[28] In this case, however, the interpolators rephrased the original expression, replacing the ambiguous word בו with the much clearer expression על המזבח "on the altar," now making it clear that the fire burns on the altar. In addition, the interpolators coined the term אש תמיד "a perpetual fire," thereby underscoring their new notion.

Lev 6:5–6 is a small two-verse unit, which was added to the passage about removing sacrificial leftovers from the altar. The reason for its insertion is probably the complete evacuation of the altar as reflected in the original passage (Lev 6:1–4). The interpolators sought to clarify that extinguishing the altar fire is not part of the treatment of the ashes, adding vv. 5–6 and using the phrase ואש המזבח תוקד בו from v. 2.[29]

One consideration for dating the passage is that the original passage is itself not part of the basic layer of the priestly offering law; as many scholars have observed, chapters 6–7 are a supplement to the core of the priestly sacrificial legislation in Lev 1–5.[30] A second is the occurrence of the aforementioned noun מכנסיים in v. 3, which, as Sperling has shown, has Persian roots.[31] This leads to the conclusion that, as an addition to a not early priestly passage, these two verses were probably composed later in the Persian period. The interpolators, who were active in that period, made discernible textual efforts to insert their new idea. Accordingly, we must ask what underlies the invention of perpetual fire? Why did the interpolators change the previous legislative procedure relating to fire in the late Persian period? Does this not make it likely that these verses reflect Persian influence?

Divine fire

This discussion leads to an inquiry about the underlying concept behind the notion of perpetual fire in Leviticus. What is the importance of this fire? What are its origins? The explanation that the fire which is not allowed to die out is that which came forth from YHWH at the end of the inauguration of the tabernacle

28 See Milgrom, *Leviticus 1–16*, 389.

29 Cf. Noth, *Leviticus*, 53–54.

30 E.g. Baentsch, *Exodus, Leviticus, Numeri*, 332; Nihan, *From Priestly Torah to Pentateuch*, 256–69.

31 See above.

(Lev 9:24) appears to be correct;[32] below I provide further backing for this opinion. However, the description of this appearance of the fire on the eighth day of the inauguration has puzzling aspects.

The verses state: ויבא משה ואהרן אל אהל מועד ויצאו ויברכו את העם וירא כבוד יהוה אל כל העם ותצא אש מלפני יהוה ותאכל על המזבח את העלה ואת החלבים וירא כל העם וירנו ויפלו על פניהם "Moses and Aaron then went inside the Tent of Meeting. When they came out, they blessed the people; and the glory of YHWH appeared to all the people. Fire came forth from before YHWH and consumed the burnt offering and the fat parts on the altar. And all the people saw, and shouted, and fell on their faces.". First of all, I note the uncertain nature of the relationship between the appearance of "the glory of YHWH" in v. 23 and the appearance of the fire in v. 24. It is not clear whether the verses describe a single or two theophanies.[33] The question is heightened when one considers the beginning of the chapter, where Moses says: כי היום יהוה נראה אליכם "For today YHWH will appear to you" (v. 4) and ויאמר משה זה הדבר אשר צוה יהוה תעשו וירא אליכם כבוד יהוה "Moses said: This is what YHWH has commanded that you do, that the glory of YHWH may appear to you" (v. 6). Here Moses makes no mention of fire, but only of YHWH's glory, and the Israelites and the readers of the text alike have no other expectations. The appearance of YHWH's glory is the goal, the climax, and the end of the eighth day; nothing additional is necessary.[34]

Moreover, throughout the story the priests make offerings; regarding all it is stated that Aaron "turned [them] into smoke on the altar" ויקטר (vv. 10, 13, 14, 17, 20 and see vv. 15–16). During the previous seven days the sacrifices were also turned into smoke on the altar, but by Moses (Lev 8:16, 20, 21, 28). The reader wonders: if divine fire is essential to the cult, given that it is the only fire used for the cult thereafter, how was it possible to use nondivine fire at the inauguration of the tabernacle? The question is more acute regarding the eighth day: if divine fire was slated to appear shortly, why turn that day's offering into smoke

32 E.g. Calvin (quoted in Wenham, *Leviticus*, 119); Noth, *Leviticus*, 82; Milgrom, *Leviticus 1–16*, 389. For other explanations, see Wenham, *Leviticus*, 119–20; Hartley, *Leviticus*, 96; and cf. *Sifra: Nedaba* 5:10. Gerstenberger, connecting the heading of the Lev 6:1–6 passage: "This is the instruction of the burnt offering" with the daily burnt offering (Num 28:3–8), explains that the daily offering requires a "perpetually burning altar fire" (*Leviticus*, 94).

33 Whereas according to Hartley, for instance, the glory of YHWH is manifested in a cloud, and the fire came from the glory (*Leviticus*, 124), Milgrom thinks that in this case the presence of YHWH reveals itself in the form of fire (*Leviticus 1–16*, 588–90).

34 Some scholars indeed point to the difference between v. 4, which indicates the appearance of YHWH himself, and v. 6, which mentions the appearance of the glory of YHWH; e.g. Noth, *Leviticus*, 77. It seems, however, that Christoph Nihan is correct in rejecting this distinction (*From Priestly Torah to Pentateuch*, 119–20).

before its appearance? Note that the fire does consume the offerings on the altar (v. 24), which were already turned into smoke and even the fatty parts that are readily consumed.[35] All these comments provide a solid basis for suspicion that the appearance of the fire, which is described in 9:24a, is a secondary addition, as some scholars, following Wilhelm M. L. de Wette, correctly observed.[36]

Therefore, the basic stratum of the account of the inauguration of the tabernacle (Lev 8–9) contains no divine fire, and probably assumes use of "human" fire, namely, fire lighted by human beings, whereas a thin redactional layer inserted divine fire into the narrative. The basic stratum is consistent with the primary stratum of the chapters relating to the laws of offerings (Lev 1–7), in which priests light the fire, presumably every morning anew for the first offering and after cleaning the altar by totally removing the previous day's leftovers. In my opinion, the addition of the appearance of the divine fire is an integral aspect of the concept of the ever-burning fire.[37] Based on the postulation that the notion of perpetual fire developed through Persian influence, it may then also be the case that divine cultic fire also has a Persian source.

We know of the beginning of Persian sacred fires only from late texts. Some Pahlavi texts recount that, during creation, Ahura Mazda installed the three sacred fires of the highest grade in their places.[38] Perhaps in this case too, the priestly text can serve as indirect evidence for the antiquity of the view regarding a divine source for sacred fire.

Alien fire

Another text pertinent to this discussion is the story of Nadab and Abihu. Immediately after the termination of the inauguration of the tabernacle at the end of chapter 9, we are informed of the death of Aaron's elder sons, Nadab and Abihu, in the wake of their actions: ויקחו בני אהרן נדב ואביהוא איש מחתתו ויתנו בהן אש וישימו

35 Scholars deal with that problem by stating that the fire quickly consumed the sacrifices that slowly smolder on the altar (e.g. Hartley, *Leviticus*, 124; Milgrom, *Leviticus 1–16*, 590). This is only a partial solution, however.

36 de Wette, *Beiträge zur Einleitung in das alte Testament*, 121–23. For a detailed survey of the bibliography and considerations for the originality of 9:24a, see Nihan, *From Priestly Torah to Pentateuch*, 111–19.

37 Note the similarity between the wording of 9:24aβ ותאכל על המזבח את העלה ואת החלבים "and consumed the burnt offering and the fat parts on the altar" and 6:5b וערך עליה העלה והקטיר עליה חלבי השלמים "lay out the burnt offering on it, and turn into smoke the fat parts of the offerings of well-being," which is more similar to the 11QLev[b] version of 9:24: את העו]לה ואת החלב השלמ[ים.

38 For the text, see Boyce, "The Pious Foundations of the Zoroastrians," 288–89.

עליה קטרת ויקרבו לפני יהוה אש זרה אשר לא צוה אתם "Now Aaron's sons Nadab and Abihu each took his fire pan, put fire in it, and laid incense on it; and they offered before YHWH alien fire, which he had not commanded them" (Lev 10:1). Many explanations have been suggested for the nature of Nadab's and Abihu's transgression, as described in this verse.[39] Prima facie the account is clear, because the verse explicitly states that they brought אש זרה 'alien fire', namely, fire not taken from the divine fire on the altar. Scholars observe, however, that as formulated the verse is difficult. First, the meaning of the second part of the verse is strange, because it states that the fire is the object of the offering, whereas incense should be the object.[40] Second, the location of the phrase "alien fire, which he had not commanded them" is incongruous; it should have come earlier, closer to the reference to fire at the beginning of the verse.[41] Accordingly, it seems reasonable to assume that this phrase is secondary and was added in order to change the nature of their transgression to one that now involves alien fire.

It appears that initially a different transgression was meant, probably approaching too near to YHWH.[42] In the original verse, the meaning of the word ויקרבו was "they approached," וַיִּקְרְבוּ which, following the addition, was changed through a slight difference in vocalization to "they offered" וַיַּקְרִבוּ. It may be true that the short story of Nadab and Abihu represents political interests in the context of the relationships between priestly families.[43] It is interesting to note that, in the non-priestly tradition in Exod 24:9–11, Nadab and Abihu were part of the group that "saw the God of Israel" but remained unharmed. It seems that the

39 For a survey of the ancient Jewish interpretations, see Kirschner, "The Rabbinic and Philonic Exegeses." For partial surveys of the research, see e.g. Greenstein, "Deconstruction and Biblical Narrative," 57–62; Nihan, *From Priestly Torah to Pentateuch*, 578–80. See more recently Feder, "Playing with Fire."

40 This strange concept led some scholars to doubt whether alien fire is the pair's sole transgression; e.g. Noth, *Leviticus*, 85; Gerstenberger, *Leviticus*, 117, and cf. Nihan, *From Priestly Torah to Pentateuch*, 579–80, who thinks that the use of fire not from the altar itself is not the transgression, but that alien fire "results from the addition of incense on the fire burning in Nadab's and Abihu's censers." He suggests that they acted contrary to the rule that the "performance of the incense rite is always a competence reserved to the high priest." His suggestion, however, is not without difficulties. Exod 30:7 instructs that Aaron shall burn the incense, but the subject there is the daily incense burned on the incense altar, not incense censer as in the case of Nadab and Abihu; in contrast Num 17:5 prohibits burning incense by non-Aaronites, but does not restrict performance of this rite to the high priest.

41 Dillmann, *Die Bücher Exodus und Leviticus*, 579.

42 The enigmatic phrase בקרבי אקדש in v. 3 could be related to the original nature of the transgression and rendered: "In those who trespass upon me I will show myself holy"; see Segal, "The Divine Verdict," and cf. Milgrom's reservations (*Leviticus 1–16*, 601).

43 See e.g. Noth, *Leviticus*, 84; Gerstenberger, *Leviticus*, 116–17.

priestly story used, and reworked, this non-priestly tradition or a similar one in order to remove Nadab and Abihu from the priestly genealogy;[44] according to the priestly version their breaking of the divine-human barrier was a transgression and caused their death.

The interpolators, who added the phrase אש זרה אשר לא צוה אתם, made Nadab and Abihu's transgression an exemplar for those who do not use the divine fire for the cult. The addition underscores the very dangerous, potentially deadly, use of alien fire. The expression אש זרה conveys an idea quite opposite to that of אש תמיד (Lev 6:6). This notion supports the assumption that both expressions were coined by the school that amplifies the importance of fire in the Israelite cult.

Making use of the dreadful divine reaction to Nadab and Abihu's deed: ותצא אש מלפני יהוה ותאכל אותם וימתו לפני יהוה "And fire came forth from YHWH and consumed them; thus, they died before YHWH" (Lev 10:2), the interpolators duplicated the initial part of this reaction in the original story, inserting it several verses earlier, at the end of the inauguration of the tabernacle, a sophisticated means of creating divine fire on the altar.[45] At first, in its original appearance, the divine fire was a violent, destructive fire activated only within the tabernacle; it was Nadab and Abihu's encroachment on the fiery deity that caused their death by burning. The new appearance of the divine fire differs totally. It appears on the outer altar and is integrated in the context as a sign of YHWH's satisfaction with the tabernacle and the sacrifices offered at its inauguration.[46]

Attention should also be paid to the other references to the death of Aaron's elder sons, mentioned three more times in the Pentateuch. As I discuss the reference in Lev 16 at greater length in the next section, I briefly discuss the other two, Num 3:4 and 26:61, here: both mention the offering of alien fire. The reference in Num 3:4, which reads as follows: וימת נדב ואביהוא לפני יהוה בהקרבם אש זרה לפני יהוה במדבר סיני "But Nadab and Abihu died before YHWH, when they offered alien fire before YHWH in the wilderness of Sinai," reflects the current form of Lev 10:1. This passage is part of the arrangement of the camp as recounted in Num 1–4. Elsewhere I argued that, in their current form, Num 1–2 represents a second stage from the Persian period,[47] and we can assume that their continuation in

44 See Rendtorff, "Nadab and Abihu," 359–60. Rendtorff notes the connection between the references to Nadab and Abihu in Exod 24 and Lev 10, but in a different fashion.

45 The similarity between these five words in Lev 9:24 and Lev 10:2 led commentators and scholars to various suppositions. Rashbam (ad loc.), for instance, thinks that both accounts describe the same event. The fire, on its way to the outer altar, struck Nadab and Abihu, who were about to burn the incense. Noth claims that this similarity suggests that the short story of Nadab and Abihu is late, in line with his conclusion regarding the secondarity of Lev 9:24a.

46 See Noth, *Leviticus*, 82; Hartley, *Leviticus*, 124.

47 Kislev, "The Numbers of Numbers," 200–202.

chapters 3–4 also dates to that period. Note that, because the passage that refers to the death of Nadab and Abihu is somewhat exceptional, some scholars maintain its lateness as compared to its context.[48]

The second reference resembles the first and it too reflects the current form of Lev 10:1: וימת נדב ואביהוא בהקריבם אש־זרה לפני יהוה "Nadab and Abihu died when they offered alien fire before YHWH" (Num 26:61). Elsewhere I showed that this chapter was composed in the Persian period and noted its great affinity to the composition of Num 1–2.[49] And, in a separate paper I claimed that Num 26:58aβ–61 is a secondary addition.[50] Although it may belong to the composer, it seems more likely that this was not a unified addition and that the reference to the death of Nadab and Abihu is even later. As both references are very late it is therefore not surprising that they reflect the current form of Lev 10:1.

Lev 16

This chapter is devoted to the ritual that enables the high priest to enter the adytum. Because of the danger inherent in this action, the high priest must adhere to a strict protocol: ואל יבא בכל עת אל הקדש ... ולא ימות ... בזאת יבוא אהרן אל הקדש "he is not to come at will into the Shrine ... lest he die ... Thus only shall Aaron enter the Shrine" (vv. 2–3). The opening of the chapter refers to the death of Nadab and Abihu: וידבר יהוה אל משה אחרי מות שני בני אהרן בקרבתם לפני יהוה וימתו "YHWH spoke to Moses after the death of the two sons of Aaron who died when they drew too close to the presence of YHWH." Although this opening may be secondary, as some scholars suggest,[51] uniquely, it reflects the original form of Lev 10:1: the phrase אש זרה is missing and the meaning of קר"ב is undoubtedly "to approach."[52] Moreover, the notion that, in its original form, the transgression of Aaron's elder sons was encroaching on YHWH is in harmony with the topic of

---

48 See Baentsch, *Exodus, Leviticus, Numeri*, 456; Noth, *Numbers*, 31.

49 Kislev, "The Numbers of Numbers," 200–202.

50 Kislev, "The Census of the Israelites," 243–46.

51 See Nihan, *From Priestly Torah to Pentateuch*, 150 and note 203 there for additional bibliography.

52 The ancient versions (the Old Greek, the Aramaic versions, the Vulgate, the Peshitta) to Lev 16:1 reflect the current form of Lev 10:1, including the phrase אש זרה אשר לא צוה אתם. Mark A. Awabdy thinks that 11QpaleoLev[a] may also reflect the longer version ("Did Nadab and Abihu Draw Near," 588–91). Nevertheless, this version is secondary, adapting the current form of Nadab's and Abihu's account to Lev 16:1; see e.g. Anderson, "'Through Those Who Are Near to Me," 11, note 30.

Lev 16, which treats entering the adytum. Accordingly, Lev 16:1 provides supporting evidence that, in Lev 10:1, the phrase אש זרה אשר לא צוה אתם is a secondary addition.[53]

Another segment of Lev 16 that requires examination is vv. 12–13, which treat the ingress of the high priest to the inner sanctum while carrying incense on a fire pan. This pericope explicitly instructs that the high priest take fire from the altar: ולקח מלא המחתה גחלי אש מעל המזבח "and he shall take a panful of glowing coals scooped from the altar." Actually, vv. 12–13 interrupt the sequence between vv. 11 and 14, which deal with the slaughtering of the *ḥattat* offering of a bull and the sprinkling of its blood over the *kaporet,* respectively. This interruption of the sequence leads many scholars to conclude that vv. 12–13 are secondary.[54] In contrast, based on his observation that without these verses Aaron's entry to the adytum is not mentioned, Christoph Nihan concludes that vv. 12–13 are original.[55] Indeed, the entrance to the inner sanctum is mentioned only in vv. 12–13, not, however, with reference to the blood of the bull, but the incense. The missing reference to the bull's blood is more conspicuous in comparison to v. 15's instruction relating to the goat, which explicitly mentions the entry to the adytum: "He shall then slaughter the people's goat of חטאת, bring its blood behind the curtain, and do with its blood as he has done with the blood of the bull: he shall sprinkle it over the כפרת and in front of the כפרת." Accordingly, we can surmise that in the original legislation the missing detail appeared between the slaughtering in v. 11 and the sprinkling of the blood in the inner sanctum in v. 14. Thus, the instruction in vv. 12–13 either suppressed the reference to the entrance or, what seems more likely, used it, and the phrase והביא מבית לפרכת "and bring behind the curtain" in v. 12, which is similar to the wording in the parallel verse (v. 15), may be a vestige of that ingress, whereas the reference to the object that was brought inside, the blood, was removed. In any event, the missing reference to bringing the blood into the adytum and the interruption of the sequence by vv. 12–13 are in my opinion significant considerations that the issue of the incense in vv. 12–13 are a late addition to this passage.

By situating their addition at Aaron's first entry into the inner sanctum, the interpolators bestowed a unique function on the incense. Here the cloud of incense covers the כפרת: וכסה ענן הקטרת את הכפרת "so that the cloud from the incense screens the כפרת" (v. 13) and the warning ולא ימות "lest he die" at the end of the

---

53 In a forthcoming paper I treat the short story of Nadab and Abihu at length and in detail: Kislev, "The Story of Nadab and Abihu – Revisited" (Hebrew).

54 For bibliography, see Nihan, *From Priestly Torah to Pentateuch*, 364, note 416. Martin Noth discusses, and rejects, this possibility (*Leviticus*, 122).

55 Nihan, *From Priestly Torah to Pentateuch*, 364–65.

verse indicates that danger of death accompanies entry to the adytum and that the screening off of the כפרת eliminates this danger. There are clear affinities between vv. 12–13 and v. 2, which states: ואל־יבא בכל עת אל הקדש ... ולא ימות כי בענן אראה על הכפרת "he is not to come at will into the Shrine ... lest he die; for I appear in the cloud over the כפרת"; the phrases ענן, כפרת, and ולא ימות are shared by both passages.[56] We can then extrapolate that, according to v. 13, the cloud of incense prevents the priest from looking at YHWH who appears on the כפרת. The incense indeed serves an apotropaic function in Num 17:6–15; here, however, the function is not apotropaic, but a unique one – creation of a physical screen that blocks the field of view.[57]

It should be noted that v. 2 does not assert that there is a need to avoid seeing YHWH. Rather, the verse states that because of the divine presence in the adytum a ceremony is required to enable Aaron to enter it safely. It is not the sight of the divine that is dangerous, but the divine presence itself. The interpolators of vv. 12–13, however, interpret v. 2 differently, granting the phrase כי בענן אראה על הכפרת "for I appear in the cloud over the כפרת" a new meaning: "only by means of the cloud (of the incense) I shall appear over the כפרת."[58] In reading the clause כי בענן אראה על הכפרת, the interpolators perhaps recalled the account in Ezek 8:11 and the phrase ועתר ענן הקטרת עלה "and a thick cloud of incense smoke ascended," and added vv. 12–13, which reinterpret v. 2, creating a unique function for the incense – producing a smoke screen. This change provides further evidence for the secondarity of vv. 12–13.

What motivated this interpolation? It appears that the interpolators sought both to insert the issue of incense into the ceremony and to grant it centrality, as the first entry to the adytum involves the incense offering. It seems likely that the interpolators also sought to blur the impression gained from v. 2 that it is possible to see God and live. In any event, the instruction to take the fire from the altar, which is consistent with the notion of ever-burning fire, appears in that addition to Lev 16. Perhaps the reference to the story of Nadab and Abihu in v. 1 triggered sensitivity to that issue, prompting a need to clarify that the fire comes from the altar.

---

56 Nihan, *From Priestly Torah to Pentateuch*, 365. I reject his conclusion that "most likely the two passages stem from the same hand" as I immediately explain.

57 So already Rashbam in his comment to v. 2; see also Nihan, who thinks that the incense here also has another function (*From Priestly Torah to Pentateuch*, 377). Many scholars, however, define the function of the incense here as apotropaic and some connect it to the function of the incense in the plague story in Num 17:6–15; see, e.g., Nielsen, *Incense in Ancient Israel*, 73; Levine, *Leviticus*, 104; see also Rendtorff, "Nadab and Abihu," 361, who indicates that the incense functions differently in both texts, but emphasizes the similarity between them.

58 See Milgrom, *Leviticus 1–16*, 1014–15.

Num 16–17

Offering incense on fire pans appears twice in the book of Numbers, in the story of Korah in Num 16,[59] and in the story of the plague that appears as its continuation in Num 17:6–15. In the first, offering incense is mentioned in the context of the contest between Aaron and the 250 chieftains, but the source of the fire is not explicitly identified (vv. 7, 18), creating the impression that this is immaterial. In the second story, however, Moses specifically commands Aaron to take fire from the altar for the incense: ויאמר משה אל אהרן קח את המחתה ותן עליה אש מעל המזבח ושים קטרת "Then Moses said to Aaron, Take the fire pan, and put on it fire from the altar, and add incense."[60]

As it emerges from the story, the death by divine fire of the 250 chieftains who offered incense on firepans is not their use of fire from a source other than the altar but rather inheres in the divine choice of Aaron over the chieftains. Furthermore, it is unlikely that Moses would knowingly entrap the chieftains by not ordering them to take fire from the altar. David Frankel is certainly correct in noting that "the original priestly story in Num. 16 was simply unaware of the cultic taboo of the 'strange fire.'"[61] In line with the previous conclusion that the phrase אש זרה אשר לא צוה אתם is a gloss in Lev 10, this means that this part of Num 16 was unaware of that interpolated phrase.

In Num 17:11, however, in order to terminate the plague, Moses commands Aaron to take fire from the altar and burn incense. The words מעל המזבח "from the altar" in v. 11 are not reflected in the Peshitta and it is tempting to surmise that they are secondary, inserted in accordance with the notion of perpetual

59 The composite nature of Num 16 is evident, but the exact process of formation is disputed; for a brief survey of the history of the research, see Nihan, *From Priestly Torah to Pentateuch*, 581–82.

60 Num 17:6–15 seems to be a continuation of Korah's story in Num 16, as many scholars think; see e.g. Holzinger, *Numeri*, 66–67; Gray, *Numbers*, 191–92; Jeon, *From the Reed Sea to Kadesh*, 272–73. This appears unlikely because the short story of the cessation of the plague differs from the basic priestly story in chapter 16. For instance, in Num 16 incense is offered in the tabernacle and the phrase לפני יהוה appears in that account (vv. 7, 16–17), whereas in the plague story the incense functions outside the tabernacle. Moreover, according to the Korah's story, Moses and Aaron fell on their faces in response to the divine announcement of the approaching plague (16:21), appealed to God, and prevented the plague (16:22), whereas in the latter, after a very similar announcement and falling on their faces (17:10), there is no appeal and no attempt to prevent the plague, which surprisingly breaks out. Therefore, it seems that composers linked two separate stories in which incense on a fire pan and Aaron the priest play an important role. Through the addition of some introductory verses (17:6–10), they create the impression of continuity between the stories; see Frankel, *The Murmuring Stories*, 238–41.

61 Frankel, *The Murmuring Stories*, 254.

fire.[62] It seems reasonable to assume that the glossators did not want to add these words to chapter 16 in relation to the burning of incense by the chieftains, namely, they did not want to suggest that unauthorized persons took fire from the altar for burning the incense, but with regard to Aaron the priest in 17:11 they sought to demonstrate the correct use of incense.

In order to reinforce this conjecture, another element must be discussed. With regard to Num 17:2, there is a difference between the LXX and the MT. The MT states ואת האש זרה הלאה "and scatter the coals abroad." The Septuagint renders καὶ τὸ πῦρ τὸ **ἀλλότριον** τοῦτο σπεῖρον ἐκεῖ, which reflects the Hebrew ואת האש **הזרה** זרה הלאה "and scatter the *alien* coals abroad." Some scholars assume that the LXX version is interpretative, in line with the case of Nadab and Abihu in Lev 10:1.[63] They fail to explain, however, what motivates the desire to make the stories similar. Moreover, the similarity between the two adjacent words הזרה זרה in the reconstructed *Vorlage* suggests that the word הזרה was omitted due to haplography.[64] But the main question is: why mention scattering the coals, if not for the purpose of inserting the issue of alien fire? We can conclude, therefore, that in this case the LXX reflects the original formulation. This then raises the question of the cultic offence of the 250 chieftains according to the passage in Num 17:1–5: the use of alien fire as v. 2 suggests, or that they were themselves unauthorized persons as v. 5 indicates? Because the issue of unauthorized persons offering incense is not only part of the passage's intent, but also of the entire priestly story in Num 16, it seems that the clause mentioning alien fire in v. 2 is secondary.[65]

The conclusion that the clause about the alien fire in Num 17:2 is secondary lends slight support to the previous conjecture that the words מעל המזבח in 17:11 are secondary too. In the current form of the passage, the issue of alien fire versus fire from the altar appears in chapter 17. The accusation that the chieftains transgressed by offering alien fire in v. 2 is connected to the injunction to Aaron by Moses to take fire from the altar in v. 11. Both assumed additions were inserted in order to promote the notion of cultic fire.

---

62 Frankel connects another element to the issue under discussion, suggesting that the complaint of the people against Moses and Aaron אתם המתם את־עם יהוה "You two have brought death upon YHWH's people" (17:6) is based on the interpretation that Moses cunningly led the rebels to their deaths by having them transgress the fire taboo (*The Murmuring Stories*, 254–55). There is no clue that this sophisticated meaning indeed stands behind the complaint, and it seems preferable to accept the solid interpretation as suggested by most scholars that the complaint focuses on the incense ordeal suggested by Moses; e.g. Rashbam; Nahmanides; Gray, *Numbers*, 212; Milgrom, *Numbers*, 140.

63 See Milgrom, *Numbers*, 139; Wevers, *Notes on the Greek Text*, 277.

64 Frankel, *The Murmuring Stories*, 254n 87.

65 Frankel too thinks that this clause is secondary, basing himself on other considerations (*The Murmuring Stories*, 237–38n 56).

Concluding Remarks

This study noted six interpolations of differing levels of certainty. The first is the instruction to maintain a perpetual fire on the altar, which was joined secondarily to the directive regarding treatment of the leftovers from the burnt offering (Lev 6:5–6). The second is the description of the fire that came from YHWH and burnt the offerings on the altar at the end of the inauguration of the tabernacle (Lev 9:24a). This addition, which transforms the altar's fire into divine fire, constitutes the rationale for maintaining an ever-burning fire. The third addition is the clause אש זרה אשר לא צוה אתם "alien fire, which he had not commanded them,", which was inserted into the account of the transgression of Aaron's elder sons in Lev 10:1. According to this gloss, Nadab and Abihu died because they used alien fire, not divine fire from the altar. This apparently constitutes a warning against independent lighting of cultic fire. Two other references to Nadab's and Abihu's deaths were formulated in line with this addition (Num 3:4; 26:61). The fourth interpolation appears in Lev 16, in which there is an injunction to Aaron to take the fire from the altar for the incense offering (v. 12–13). The fifth and sixth are found in Num 17 following the burning of the 250 chieftains. The first inserts an accusation of offering alien fire into the passage about the chieftains' fire pans (v. 2); the second inserts the words מעל המזבח in the command to Aaron regarding the fire to be used to burn the incense (v. 11). This thin hexafold layer, derived from textual analysis, that accentuates the ever-burning cultic fire and was introduced in the Persian period raises the question of what motivated its insertion into the Pentateuch in that period. It seems reasonable to suggest that it represents an effort to insert the Zoroastrian concept of divine cultic ever-burning fire into the Israelite priestly cult. This probably took place very late in the Persian period, as some of these insertions were interpolated into passages themselves dating to the Persian period; this is consistent with the assumed dating of the development of the Achaemenid fire temples.

This by no means represents a dramatic change to the priestly Israelite cult, and the altar did not become an אתרודן, namely, a real fire-altar. For example, Zoroastrian priests offer only the suet of the sacrifices on the fire altar, and not their flesh, because flesh defiles fire.[66] In the Israelite priestly cult, however, the burnt offering had a central role in the sacrificial array. The main change is that fire itself became an independent cultic object; as we have seen, this receives only limited expression in the Torah. In the later Second Temple period, however, this increasingly came to fore. Here I only briefly mention for instance the term

66 Boyce and Kotwal, "Ātaš-zōhr."

קרבן העצים "the wood offering," that appears twice in the book of Nehemiah (10:35; 13:31), and which I plan to treat in the future.

Bibliography

Anderson, Gary A., "'Through Those Who Are Near to Me, I Will Show Myself Holy': Nadab and Abihu and Apophatic Theology," *CBQ* 77 (2015): 1–19.

Awabdy, Mark A., "Did Nadab and Abihu Draw Near before Yhwh? The Old Greek among the Witnesses of Leviticus 16:1," *CBQ* 79 (2017): 580–92.

Baentsch, Bruno, *Exodus, Leviticus, Numeri*, HKAT 1/2 (Göttingen: Vandenhoeck & Ruprecht, 1903).

Barnea, Gad, "Interpretatio Ivdaica in the Achaemenid Period," *Journal of Ancient Judaism* 14 (2023): 355–91.

Barnea, Gad, "Some Achaemenid Zoroastrian Echoes in Early Yahwistic Sources," *Iran* (forthcoming).

Bertholet, Alfred, *Leviticus*, KHC 3 (Tübingen: Mohr Siebeck, 1901).

Blenkinsopp, Joseph, *Isaiah 40–55* (AB 19; New York: Doubleday, 2002).

Boyce, Mary, "Ātaš," *Encyclopædia Iranica*, https://www.iranicaonline.org/articles/atas-fire.

Boyce, Mary, "On the Zoroastrian Temple Cult of Fire," *JAOS* 95 (1975): 454–65.

Boyce, Mary, "The Pious Foundations of the Zoroastrians," *BSOAS* 31 (1968): 270–89.

Boyce, Mary and Kotwal, Firoze M. "Ātaš-zōhr," *Encyclopædia Iranica* https://www.iranicaonline.org/articles/atas-zohr-or-atas-zor-persian-zor-e-atas-a-middle-persian-term-for-the-zoroastrian-ritual-offering-to-fire-of-fat.

Cantera, Alberto, "Fire, the Greatest God (*ātarš … mazišta yazata*): The Cult of the 'Eternal' Fire in the Rituals in Avestan," *Indo-Iranian Journal* 62 (2019): 19–61.

Carr, David M., "Changes in Pentateuchal Criticism," pages 433–66 in *The Twentieth Century: From Modernism to Post-Modernism*, vol. 3/2 of *Hebrew Bible/Old Testament: The History of Its Interpretation*, ed. M. Sæbø (Göttingen: Vandenhoeck & Ruprecht, 2015).

Dillmann, August, *Die Bücher Exodus und Leviticus* (Leipzig: F. Hirzel, 1897).

Elliger, Karl, *Leviticus*, HAT (Tubingen: Mohr Siebeck, 1966).

Feder, Yitzhaq, "Playing with Fire: Indeterminacy and Danger in the Nadab and Abihu Episode," pages 451–69 in *Ve-'Ed Ya'aleh (Gen 2:6): Essays in Biblical and Ancient Near Eastern Studies Presented to Edward L. Greenstein* ed. Peter Machinist et al. (Atlanta, GA: SBL Press, 2021).

Frankel, David, *The Murmuring Stories of the Priestly School*, VTSup 89 (Leiden: Brill, 2002).

Gall, Hubertus von, "Naqš-e Rostam," *Encyclopædia Iranica* https://www.iranicaonline.org/articles/naqs-e-rostam#prettyPhoto.

Gerstenberger, Erhard S., *Leviticus*, OTL (Louisville, KY: Westminster John Knox, 1996).

Gray, George B., *Numbers*, ICC (Edinburgh: T & T Clark, 1903).

Greenstein, Edward, "Deconstruction and Biblical Narrative," *Prooftexts* 9 (1989): 43–71.

Hartley, John E., *Leviticus*, WBC (Dallas, TX: Word Books, 1992).

Holzinger, Heinrich, *Numeri*, KHC; (Leipzig: Mohr Siebeck, 1903).

Hurowitz, Victor Avigdor, "Review: Ancient Israelite Cult in History, Tradition, and Interpretation," *AJS Review* 19 (1994): 213–36.

Jeon, Jaeyoung, *From the Reed Sea to Kadesh: A Redactional and Socio-Historical Study of the Pentateuchal Wilderness Narrative*, FAT 159 (Tübingen: Mohr Siebeck, 2022).

Kirschner, Robert, "The Rabbinic and Philonic Exegeses of the Nadab and Abihu Incident (Lev 10:1–6)," *JQR* 73 (1983): 375–93.

Kislev, Itamar, "The Census of the Israelites on the Plains of Moab (Numbers 26): Sources and Redaction," *VT* 63 (2013): 236–60.
Kislev, Itamar, "The Numbers of Numbers: The Census Accounts in the Book of Numbers," *ZAW* 128 (2016): 189–204.
Kislev, Itamar, "The Story of Nadab and Abihu – Revisited" (forthcoming, Hebrew).
Kiuchi, Nobuyoshi, *Leviticus*, ApOTC 3 (Nottingham: Apollos, 2007).
Kohut, Alexander, "Antiparsische Aussprüche im Deuterojesajas," *ZDMG* 30 (1876): 709–22.
Levine, Baruch A. *The JPS Torah Commentary: Leviticus* (Philadelphia: Jewish Publication Society, 1989).
Milgrom, Jacob, *Leviticus 1–16*, AB 3A (New York: Doubleday, 1998).
Milgrom, Jacob, *The JPS Torah Commentary: Numbers* (Philadelphia: Jewish Publication Society, 1990).
Nielsen, Kjeld, *Incense in Ancient Israel*, VTSup 38 (Leiden: Brill, 1986).
Nihan, Christophe, *From Priestly Torah to Pentateuch: A Study in the Composition of the Book of Leviticus*, FAT 2/25 (Tübingen: Mohr Siebeck, 2007).
Noth, Martin, *Leviticus*, trans. J. E. Anderson, OTL (London: SCM, 1965).
Noth, Martin, *Numbers: A Commentary*, trans. James D. Martin, OTL (Philadelphia: Westminster, 1968).
Potts, Daniel "Fire in Zoroastrianism," in *The Oxford Dictionary of Late Antiquity*, ed. Oliver Nicholson (Oxford: Oxford University Press, 2018) https://www.oxfordreference.com/view/10.1093/acref/9780198662778.001.0001/acref-9780198662778-e-5615?rskey=I6gG9n&result=1939.
Rendtorff, Rolf, "Nadab and Abihu," in *Reading from Right to Left: Essays on the Hebrew Bible in Honour of David J. A. Clines*, ed. Hugh G. M. Williamson and J. Cheryl Exum, JSOTSup 373 (London: Sheffield Academic Press, 2003), 359–63.
Root, Margaret C., *The King and Kingship in Achaemenid Art: Essays on the Creation of an Iconography of Empire*, Acta Iranica 19 (Brill: Leiden, 1979).
Segal, Peretz, "The Divine Verdict of Leviticus X 3," *VT* 39 (1989): 91–95.
Sperling, S. David, "Pants, Persians and the Priestly Source," in *Ki Baruch Hu*: *Ancient Near Eastern, Biblical and Judaic Studies in Honor of Baruch A. Levine*, ed. R. Chazan et al. (Winona Lake, IN: Eisenbrauns, 1999), 373–85.
Wenham, Gordon J., *Leviticus* (NICOT; Grand Rapids, MI: Eerdmans, 1979).
Wette, Wilhelm M. L. de, *Beiträge zur Einleitung in das alte Testament, Band II* (Halle: Schimmelpfennig, 1807).
Wevers, John W., *Leviticus*, Septuaginta 2, 2 (Göttingen: Vandenhoeck & Ruprecht, 1986).
Wevers, John W., *Notes on the Greek Text of Leviticus*, SCS 44 (Atlanta, GA: Scholars Press, 1997).
Wevers, John W., *Notes on the Greek Text of Numbers*, SCS 46 (Atlanta, GA: Scholars Press, 1998).
Winston, David, "The Iranian Component in the Bible, Apocrypha, and Qumran: A Review of the Evidence," *History of Religions* 5 (1966): 183–216.

Ingo Kottsieper

From יהה צבאת to יהו מרא שמיא: Aspects of religious development on Elephantine

The extant documents written in the Achaemenid Jaho community on Elephantine date roughly from the beginning of the fifth century BC down to the beginning of the fourth and thus cover a period of about hundred years. Nevertheless, in the vast literature on this community the diachronic aspect of a religious development on Elephantine plays a minor role.[1] Some religious changes are obvious in the context of the appearance of Hananja and the ensuing conflict over the Jaho-temple and the sacrificial cult permitted in it, but they are mainly discussed as induced by external influence.[2] Thus, the struggle for permission to rebuild the temple after its destruction led to the cultic decision to renounce bloody sacrifices. But the extant sources make it clear that this decision had been a concession to outsiders who took offense at these sacrifices or were against the Jaho-temple because for other reasons. Whether these outsiders had been religious leaders from Judea, the Egyptian priests of Chnum or the Persians is a matter of debate.[3]

The fact that diachronic considerations have played such a minor role in Elephantine scholarship is certainly due to the fact that no religious or cultic texts have survived and thus the religious life of the Jaho community can only be inferred by indirect data.[4] However, a diachronic evaluation of these data reveals the presence of religious development within the Jaho community.

1 In this paper, I restrict myself for the sake of space mainly to hint to the most recent literature which discusses the older contributions.

2 A rare exception is Rohrmoser's surprising statement in the summary of her book that the priesthood of Elephantine may owe itself to a development within the Jaho community, cf. Rohrmoser, *Götter, Tempel und Kult*, 375. Unfortunately, as far as I can see, this hypothesis is not further substantiated in the book.

3 Cf., e.g., Kottsieper, "Die Religionspolitik der Achämeniden"; Rohrmoser, *Götter, Tempel und Kult*, 56–60, 198–218, 238–90, 334–359; Becking, *Identity in Persian Egypt*, 128–46; Schipper, Die Judäer/Aramäer von Elephantine, 65–82; Becking, "That Evil Act," 194–201, and the literature cited in those contributions.

4 Pap. Amherst 63 does not come into consideration here, although it is quite possible – but not certain – that it was written in the Aswan area (Holm, "Nanay and Her Lover," 3; Holm, "Sacrifice

Note: I would like to thank Dr. Bronson Brown-deVost for reading the manuscript and improving my English.

Ingo Kottsieper, Hanover, Germany

https://doi.org/10.1515/9783111018638-007

Before turning to the texts, however, I would like to deal with the question of when at the latest a Jaho-community on Elephantine had been established.

The terminus *ante quem* is of course provided by the erection of the Jaho-temple. It is common knowledge that the Jaho-community itself claimed in 407 BC as an argument for the rebuilding of their temple that had already existed before the conquest of Egypt by Cambyses, i.e., before 526 BC.[5] While one may question the extent to which the destruction of the Egyptian temples was carried out by Cambyses, there can be no serious doubt that the reference to a Jaho-temple

---

and Feasting," 142). Since the papyrus was written at the earliest in the late 4th century BC after the end of the Achaemenid rule, it remains completely unclear in which relation the Jaho community of Elephantine of the 5th century stands to the syncretistic community which express their traditions in this papyrus (cf., e.g., Kottsieper, "Anmerkungen zu Pap. Amherst 63: Teil II–V," 398–9). The fact that the Elephantine texts do not show such syncretism and that apparently the worshippers of the different gods which appear in the papyrus even in direct juxtaposition (cf. esp. VIII 1–7), still went their separate ways in the 5th century, means either that the group of the papyrus is not identical with these earlier groups or that it owes its existence to a later combination of different religious traditions after the end of the Achaemenid rule. However, the latter is rather unlikely, since the papyrus itself does not contain any Egyptian influence and all its traditions refer to the time before the arrival of its group(s) in Egypt. Corresponding to this is the fact that the interpretation of the god's name *ʾ-ḥr* as Jaho as proposed by Zauzich ("Der Gott des aramäisch-demotischen Papyrus," 89–90) is very questionable for philological reasons. Contrary to Holm's claims ("Nanay and Her Lover," 3; Holm, "Wandering Arameans," 165; cf. also "Sacrifice and Feasting," 141), Zauzich has *not* demonstrated the possibility of interpreting the demotic aleph at the beginning of the word as a spelling for *consonantal* [y]. Zauzich's argument only proves that demotic *Aleph* (ꜣ) could be used as a spelling for a *vowel* in places where the *yod* of the Phoenician-Aramaic alphabet was used as *mater lectionis* also for a *vowel* (cf. Kottsieper, "El – ferner oder naher Gott," 51–2) – a finding that surprises no Demotist or Semitist – and that Demotic *ỉ* (the single read leaf) could also be exchanged by the *Aleph*. However, this is something categorically different from the assumed rendering of a *consonantal* [y] with *Aleph* which is – as one would indeed expect – consistently written with Demotic *y* (cf. already Vleeming and Wesselius, *Studies in Papyrus Amherst 63* (1985), 40–1). By the way, also the information given by Holm, "Wandering Arameans," 165, that the reading Jaho would be "accepted by most scholars but not Steiner" is misleading. It ignores the philological objections raised by me (cf. Kottsieper, "Anmerkungen zu Pap. Amherst 63: I: 12,11–19," , 224–5; Kottsieper, "El – ferner oder naher Gott," 51–2), as well as the verdict of demotists like Quack (cf. "The Interaction of Egyptian and Aramaic," 390); cf. also Salo, *Die judäische Königsideologie*, 63–65. Thus, the *reading* Jaho is obviously not intended by the writer who uses *ʾ-ḥr* for the god's name. This of course does not exclude that this god was meant though with a different name or designation (thus. e.g. Steiner and Nims, *The Aramaic Text in Demotic Script*, 42–3). But even if this were the case, the difference with the Jaho community, who *called* their God simply Jaho, cannot be overlooked.

5 Cf. TAD A4.7:13–4; 8:12–3; also in A4.6:17, a letter from about 410 BC, probably the time "before Cambyses" is referred to. For the date of Cambyses' conquest of Egypt cf. now Quack, "Zum Datum der persischen Eroberung."

existing before Cambyses is historically accurate.[6] Several reasons argue for this assessment:

1) If the temple had been built under the rule of the Achaemenids, then it would have been authorized by the Achaemenids and its destruction would have been an act against an authorized temple and thus against the Achaemenid government itself. Would there be a better argument to make before the Achaemenids authorities to demand the authorization for rebuilding the temple if you could adduce this fact? That the Jaho community did not adduce this striking argument can only be explained that it would have been a lie.[7]

2) Even if the community would have had reasons unknown to us to date their temple in the pre-Achaemenid time, despite it having been built only after Cambyses, such an assertion probably would be really dangerous. Given the archival management of the Achaemenid bureaucracy, it would have been quite optimistic to hope that the Achaemenid administration would forget that the temple had in fact been built under its rule. Thus, the Jaho community could easily have been debunked as liars to the administration which would have thwarted their cause.

3) The fact that the Achaemenid governors Bagohi and Delaiah themselves use the argument that the temple had been built before Cambyses in their advice to the Egyptian Achaemenid administration (TAD A4.9:4–5), clearly shows that the administration had no reason not to doubt this.

That a temple or sanctuary of Jaho existed on Elephantine already in Saitic times can be made probable on the basis of archaeological evidence. As the recent

6 The part of the argument brought up by the Jaho community that Cambyses destroyed the Egyptian temples might be exaggerated, though there are hints that in the context of the conquest of Egypt by Cambyses temples were also damaged (Sternberg-el Hotabi, "Die persische Herrschaft in Ägypten," 114). But it is important to distinguish between the two different parts of the argument of the Jaho community (cf. Granerød, *Dimensions of Yahwism*, 217). That the temple was found by Cambyses as already built is different information than that it was the only one which was not destroyed. Thus, the possibility that the last information was not correct or at least exaggerated cannot be used to cast doubt on the first one as is done e.g. by Becking, *Identity in Persian Egypt*, 141–2; cf. Becking, "The Identity of the People," 108, where he comments on the statement that Cambyses found the Jaho-temple already built: "this claim might be classified as an example of a 'claimed tradition'".

7 This also refutes Briant's argument (cf. "Curieuse affaire," 123–4) that the fact that Vidranga went along with the Chnum priests' request to proceed against the Jaho-temple shows that the Judeans' argument was not valid and that Vidranga knew this. If he did know, however, it must be assumed that it was generally known in the administration too or had come up at the latest during the trial of Vidranga (TAD A4.7:15–17; A4.8:14–16). But this would have exposed the "swindle" of the Judeans. If, however, the permission to build was nevertheless granted, it may be assumed that the statement of the Judeans was essentially correct.

findings and their interpretation suggest, a massive wall was built at latest during the reign of Amasis as a boundary to the northwest of the Chnum sanctuary.[8] Von Pilgrim considers that "the advent of larger contingents of soldiers and mercenaries in the town created the impetus to wall in the temple precincts" (Background, 13) but this seems to be unlikely. Given the fact that the so-called Aramaic quarter which was constructed after 526 BC in the adjacent north-eastern area of this wall to provide houses for the mercenaries of the Achaemenid period, one wonders which "larger contingents of soldiers and mercenaries" von Pilgrim thinks of which would arrived in the Saite period. As is well known, there had been mercenaries on Elephantine before[9] and obviously during this time there was no need to build a barrier between them and the sanctuary of Chnum. But given the fact that the temple of Jaho which was "built in the traditional Egyptian way with sun-dried mud-bricks" (Background, 11) is found exactly on the opposite site of this wall and thus this wall separates the Jaho sanctuary from the sanctuary of Chnum, it seems to be the easiest assumption that this wall was erected as a reaction to or in the context of the establishment of the Jaho-temple. There is a difference between strangers living in the neighborhood of your sanctuary and strangers building their own cult building next to it.

The construction of the Jaho-temple also led to the relocation of the old central main street. Obviously, the temple was built in the former area of the old main road that cut the island since ancient times. Based on the archaeological and epigraphic evidence, it can be assumed that this ancient road was routed around the north-eastern and north-western side of the temple as the "street" (ארח) or "Souq of the king" (שוק מלכא).[10] Initially, von Pilgrim,[11] taking up a suggestion by Briant,[12] saw this as the reason for the action by the Chnum priests against the Jaho-temple, which was then broken up and rebuilt in a reduced size, so that the old street layout between the temple and the enclosing wall of the Chnum temple was now restored.

However, on the basis of further findings and their reassessment, von Pilgrim now concludes that the Jaho-temple and the boundary wall of the Chnum sanctuary were designed from the beginning in such a way that the main street, which would have been used partly also as "Way of the God Chnum" (תמי/א זי חנום אלהא, TAD B3,4:8; B3.5:10) for processions, passed between the two. Nevertheless, he still maintains that the later action against the temple of Jaho, which probably did not lead to the destruction of the buildings but only to some damages, had a

8 Cf. von Pilgrim, "On the Archaeological Background," 13.
9 See, e.g., the Stele of Ns-Ḥr treated below.
10 Cf. von Pilgrim, "Tempel des Jahu," 315.
11 Cf. von Pilgrim, "Elephantine," 262–4; von Pilgrim, "Tempel des Jahu," 315–7.
12 See Briant, "Curieuse affair," 123–8; but cf. above, note 8.

juridical background. Thus, he speculates that the Judeans would have illegally extended the temple afterwards into the area of the street.

With this change of von Pilgrim's argument there is no longer need to assume that the Jaho-temple had been built only in the 5th century B.C. Nevertheless, considerable doubts also about this interpretation arise. The main observations that justify these doubts are:

1) The extension of the temple area into this street cannot be proved archaeologically and therefore remains completely speculative.

2) If one follows the scale of the map provided by von Pilgrim,[13] this obviously important processional road would have been only about 2–3 m wide, which does not exactly speak for the importance of the road, especially since the road leading around on the other side of the temple was at least three times as wide.

3) While a boundary wall can be proved for the northeastern and northwestern side of the temple, such a wall – according to von Pilgrim – would be missing between the temple area and the processional way running southeast of it. Would the Jaho community have designed their sanctuary as open to a processional route of Chnum? This may be considered extremely unlikely.

4) If one follows von Pilgrim, then the "way of the god Chnum" would have led directly without demarcation past the Jaho sanctuary, but would have been deliberately demarcated from its own sanctuary with a strong wall, which would have been built as a demarcation to the foreign mercenaries. Why then was the wall not placed immediately northwest of the processional way as a demarcation from the Jaho sanctuary?

5) If for whatever reasons the Chnum community wanted to separate the Chnum sanctuary even from their own "way of the god Chnum", which, as said, would be a strange assumption, then why did they not just build the Jaho-temple somewhat further to the northwest, particularly since the houses belonging to the later Persian time had not yet been built. Does this mean that the temple already existed and it was in fact the boundary wall to the Chnum sanctuary which finally made the processional way so narrow?

All these observations speak for the assumption that in the area between the Jaho-temple and the boundary wall of the sanctuary of Chnum no "way of the god Chnum" was existent. This accords with the fact that no positive archaeological evidence for the existence of such a way in this area for the late Saite and Persian period can be adduced.[14] Nor is it contradicted by the fact that this way

13 Cf. von Pilgrim, "On the Archaeological Background," 3.

14 Thus, von Pilgrim can offer just two weak, indirect hints for the existence of this way also at this time: it had been there in former times ("On the Archaeological Background," 3–4) and a comparable way on the southeastern side of the demarcation wall would be archaeological excluded ("On the Archaeological Background," 13).

was mentioned in the papyri as an orientation mark for the localization of a (single!) building-complex and thus could also be localized from it.[15] Thus, it is mentioned only in the context of the house complex of Anani located northeast of the temple of Jaho (TAD B3.4:8; B3.5:10), being located beyond the "Way of the King," which thus ran between these two localities. However, there is no evidence that the "Way of the God Chnum" ran further southwest between the Jaho-temple and the Chnum sanctuary.

On the other hand, as recently suggested by Quack,[16] the "Way of the God Chnum" could be the one that led into the Chnum sanctuary through a gate at its northwest corner. This gate was probably opposite the northeast corner of the property Anani acquired, so the description that the "Way of the God Chnum" lay "below", i.e. southeast, and the "Souq of the King" was in between, may well refer to this way.[17] The expression could also well refer to a wider area or forecourt of the path that then led through the gate into the Chnum sanctuary. The assumption that the processional way had been diverted through the Chnum sanctuary or past it through the old city area at the latest when the Jaho-temple had been built directly next to the Chnum sanctuary and had been separated from it by the massive wall, is obvious, even if at the present time it can only be speculated where exactly it ran.[18]

Thus, the simplest solution is that the Jaho-temple had been built directly next to the Chnum sanctuary and the main public road was led around it on the other side while the procession way was led through or along the Chnum sanctuary.

Be that as it may, this finding suggests that the Jaho-temple existed no later than the time of Amasis.[19] At the same time it results that the damages of the

---

15 Cf. von Pilgrim, "On the Archaeological Background," 12.

16 Cf. Quack, "Stadt des Chnum."

17 Probably later, this way was prolonged to the northwest leading to a small shrine and this extension was called by the Egyptians simply "Way of the God" (תמואנתי; TAD B3.10:9). That this designation is just a different name for the "Way of the God Chnum", as, e.g., assumed by von Pilgrim, "On the Archaeological Background," 12, is not convincing. It is mentioned for a way in the same area but not at exactly the same place.

18 Cf., however, the considerations about such a processional way branching off from the main road at von Pilgrim, "On the Archaeological Background," 14.

19 Cf. also Barnea, "The Migration of the Elephantine Yahwists," 103–18, who argues for the assumption, that the Judeans migrated from Syene to Elephantine during the time of Amasis but only "after their temple had been built and functioned there for some time" (116); but his assumption that they were settled on the island as "a replacement contingent" after a revolt during the time of Apries (110) is based on a questionable interpretation of the stele of Ns-Ḥr, cf. the discussion of this stele below; for an overview of the different views of the time of arrival cf. also Kahn, "The Date of the Arrival," 139–164.

Jaho-temple, which even led to the cessation of the sacrificial cult in 410 B.C., cannot be interpreted as a consequence of an unlawful extension of the temple area to the Egyptian procession road, since obviously the procession road had not run between the Jaho-temple and the Chnum sanctuary for more than 100 years.

It should be noted only in passing that such a structural encroachment would not have justified the damage to the temple itself, even according to Egyptian law, as e.g. the Codex Hermopolis West attests.[20] The code does regulate quite clearly that in the case of such structural encroachment, the guilty party is obliged to undo it, though he himself may recover the material he used for the unlawful construction (VI 3–10), but VIII 1–2 also suggests that even in the case of a structural encroachment on a public road, only the extension is the object of the lawsuit, but not the original construction (cf. Rohrmoser, Götter, 257–8). Thus, one would have to assume that the entire construction of the temple was not lawful even at the time of the Saites. However, this would ultimately lead to the completely improbable assumption that the Egyptians would have tolerated this blatant breach of law and encroachment on public space by a not insignificant construction, which would have even affected an important road, not only during construction but for over a century. Moreover, instead of opposing its construction, they would have preferred to distance themselves from it through their own construction activity, i.e. the construction of the boundary wall of the Chnum sanctuary. Therefore, this interpretation, which would hardly be probable already with the assumption that the temple would have been built only in Persian time, as considered by Briant,[21] is to be rejected as absurd in view of the result that the Jaho-temple dates at the latest from the Saite period.

This leads to the question, why the Egyptians should have allowed or tolerated at all the erection of such a foreign sanctuary in close proximity to the Chnum sanctuary, which moreover massively affected the traditional topology of the island. Even if a sure answer is ultimately not possible due to the meager sources, the well-known stele of Ns-Ḥr (Hussein, 2016) from the time of Apries, the predecessor of Amasis, could offer a solution.

The inscription on the back of this stele reports in lines 6–7 about conflicts with the mercenaries stationed on Elephantine and in Syene, which also included people from the Levant. These had evidently rebelled – whatever that meant in detail – and threatened to defect to the Nubians. Ns-Ḥr, who was in charge of Upper Egypt at that time, emphasizes that he was able to prevent this change of sides, which would have been fatal for the protection of the southern border. In

20 And as was adduced by Briant, "Curieuse affaire," 126–7, still followed, e.g., by von Pilgrim, "On the Archaeological Background," 14–5.

21 Cf. Briant, "Curieuse affair."

doing so, he left further action to the pharaoh, whose reaction, however, has not been preserved. Since only two or three hieroglyphs are missing here at the beginning of line 7, the formulation: "What was done by his majesty was their ..." leaves many possibilities open. But one will agree with the conclusion of the latest editor of the inscription, Hussein Bassir, that "Neshor was able to reach a reasonable solution *accepted by all parties* at Elephantine, and stop the revolt of Apries' foreign mercenaries."[22]

This event teaches that the mercenaries in southern Egypt were a power factor, and the Egyptians did well to secure their loyalty. A revolt or withdrawal of the mercenaries to the south would have severely compromised Egypt's security, and Ns-Ḥr's actions indicate that they were well aware of the need to resolve conflicts with the mercenaries *diplomatically.* Thus, the assumption that one could not expect the Egyptians to allow the Judeans mercenaries to build their own temple after the revolt and thus the temple should have been built before the revolt, is based on the further assumption that the Egyptians must have made no decisions in favor for the mercenaries.[23] But if Ns-Ḥr managed to get the mercenaries to end their revolt and return to loyalty with the pharaoh, it is likely that he was able to offer them something in return. It is tempting to assume that the right to build their own sanctuary at such a prominent place as the side of the central sanctuary of Chnum could have been part of the concessions made by Ns-Ḥr to regain the loyalty of the mercenaries and to convince them not to change sides. Or, at least, it could have taught the Egyptians that they had to improve their attempts to integrate mercenaries into the local society and thus made them open to the desires of Judean mercenaries, who might have arrived later, to establish a sanctuary not just somewhere out of the way, but in a prominent place. That the Chnum priests would not be amused about such a diplomatic decision is understandable and could explain why, in turn, they built a massive wall to demarcate their sanctuary from the newly build Jaho-temple.

Thus, it seems quite plausible that the Jaho-temple on Elephantine would have been built under Apries or Amasis – whether by Judeans already serving as mercenaries under Apries or by those arriving on the island later. It cannot be decided whether the massive dividing wall to the Chnum sanctuary was built together with the Jaho-temple or only later. In the first case the construction of the Jaho-temple would have to be dated into the time of Amasis and possibly attributed to new Judean mercenary groups, in the second case it would have to

22 Bassir, "Neshor at Elephantine," 89; italics by me.
23 Thus Barnea, "The Migration of the Elephantine Yahwists," 108, following Anneler, *Zur Geschichte der Juden*, 105.

be considered whether the then later built wall did not replace an original wall of which, following von Pilgrim (Background, 13) nothing would have survived.

Be that as it may, also the early Aramaic documents found at Elephantine indicate a pre-Persian origin for the Jaho community, with the later documents bearing witness to a gradual "modernization" or assimilation of the community to the new Persian supremacy.

This is particularly clear in the designations of the deity itself. Though from the perspective of Imperial Aramaic grammar the name should be written as יהו with ו at the end, it never appears with this writing on the ostraca which can be dated to the first quarter of the fifth century BC. Instead, we find about sixteen instances written as יהה.[24] Since those ostraca contain messages between members of the local community, one may safely assume that the habit to write Jaho as יהה was common in the Jaho community of Elephantine at the beginning of the fifth century BC.[25]

Apparently, this custom was maintained within this community until the middle of the fifth century. Thus, the spelling יהה is found twice more in documents written by Natan bar Ananiah in 449 and 446 BC (TAD B3.3:2; B2.7:14). But all later documents afterwards use the spelling יהו corresponding to the common Aramaic orthography. It is of particular importance that also the son and – as evidenced by his handwriting – also student of Natan bar Ananiah, Mauziah bar Natan, now – in contrast to his father and teacher Natan – uses the spelling יהו (TAD B2.10:6 [416 BC]; B3.5:2 [434 BC], 10; B7.1:4 [413 BC]). This suggests that at some point around 440 BC[26] the "official" Imperial Aramaic orthography יהו for the traditional spelling יהה had also been adopted by scribes within the Jaho community.

That this change from יהה to יהו is an alignment with the generally used orthography within the Jaho community is also supported by the observation that the scribes who did not belong to the Jaho community always wrote the name of God יהו. Thus, the oldest datable instance of the writing יהו can be found in the papyrus B2.2:4, 6, 11, which was written 464 BC in Syene by the scribe איתו בר אבא for the Khwarezmian Dargamana. Obviously, the scribe bears an Aramaic[27] or

---

24 See CG 30 r. 5'; 40, v. 3; 41 v. 5; 56 r. 7; 70 (= D7.21) r. 3; 152 (= D7.16) r. 3; 167 r. 1; 174 r. 2; 185 r. 6; 186 (= D7.35) r. 1; 236 v. 4; J8 r. 6, 9; X8 v. 4; 14 r. 1; D7.18 r. 3; in CG 14 v. 1 and 103 v. 2 the last sign(s) are not preserved.

25 For an additional perspective on the divine element in Yahwistic theophoric names, see Porten, "*Yahu* and Its Cognates in Personal Names: The Problem of Yama," in this volume.

26 TAD B2.7, written 446 BC, is the last text in which יהה is found; the first instance for יהו written by a scribe from the Jaho community appears in 437 BC in a document written by Haggai bar Shemaiah (B3.4:3, 10).

27 See, e.g., Grelot, *Documents araméens d'Egypte*, 462, 475; Porten, "The Aramaic Texts," 158.

possible an Egyptian[28] name, but not a "Judean" one. But also the instance in B3.2:2, written in 451 BC, is found in a document written by a scribe with the Akkadian name בוני בר מנכי,[29] who obviously was not a member of the Jaho community.

But also in TAD A3.3:1, a letter sent probably by a Judean stationed in Memphis Jaho is spelled יהו. Though, therefore, the sender probably belonged to the Jaho community in Memphis, we do not know from which community the scribe of the letter came. If he should have been a Judean of Memphis as well, this would be a proof that in the Jaho community of the residence city Memphis the official orthography was already adopted before 450 BC.[30] But he could be a professional scribe from any other group just writing the letter according to the dictation of the sender and of course using the common orthography.[31]

Thus, a clear picture emerges: though one would expect Jaho written as יהו in Imperial Aramaic texts and though this is accordingly found throughout the fifth century BC in texts not written by scribes from the Elephantine Jaho community, this orthography was taken over by those scribes only after 440 BC. Before, they adhered to the traditional writing יהה which reflects the Israelite/Judean orthography until the sixth century BC.[32] This is also corroborated by the only other instance of writing -[ō] with ה, which is found in פרעה "Pharaoh" in A1.1:1, 3, 6, a letter written by the king of Ekron, Adon to the Pharao at the end of the seventh century. It does not only provide an additional proof for writing -[ō] in the Southern Levant with ה, but also a nice example that in writing foreign terms one easily could stick to a traditional orthography. But the fact that the scribes of the Yaho community on Elephantine kept this traditional writing for such a long time in accordance with their own normal writing system, even though in their environment the same name was already written differently, can be taken as a

---

28 For איתו one could compare Egyptian names like *ỉtw* (Ranke, *Die ägyptischen Personennamen I*, 50, nos. 7–8); for אבא cf. e.g. *ꜣbꜣ* (Ranke, *Die ägyptischen Personennamen I*, 1, no. 21; Lüddeckens, *Demotisches Namenbuch*, 8).

29 For מנכי see, e.g., Grelot, *Documents araméens d'Egypte*, 478; Porten, "The Aramaic Texts," 206. The name בוני is found in Persian time as a name of a Levite (Neh 11,15), but the text seems to be corrupt (cf. Gesenius, *Hebräisches und Aramäisches Handwörterbuch*, 132, s. v. בּוּנִּי). Given the clear Akkadian background of the father's name, one best connects בוני with the Akkadian name *būnî* testified by Neo-Assyrian sources, cf. Radner, *The Prosopography of the Neo-Assyrian Empire* 1, II: B-G, 352.

30 According to Porten, "The Calendar of Aramaic Texts," 17, the letter should even be dated before 473 BC.

31 The only remaining text which might date from before 450 BC and in which the writing יהו is found would be the fragment TAD D4.9 lacking any information at which place and by which scribe it had been written.

32 See, e.g., Zevit, *Matres Lectionis*, 24 and 31.

deliberate act of preserving their own religious tradition and identity, which they must have brought with them at the latest in the sixth century BC.[33]

That the Jaho community continued to adhere to older Hebrew traditions into the fifth century is also evident from a look at the designation of Jaho as יהה צבאת (CG 167 r. 1; J8 r. 9). Since צבאת is derived from the root *ḌB'*,[34] which is supposed to appear as קבא or עבא in Imperial Aramaic, but in no case as צבא, the epithet צבאת is a clear Hebraism. Given the fact, that in Hebrew the plural morpheme -[ōt] was not yet written with ו in the seventh or sixth century BC,[35] the defective writing could have been taken over from ancient Hebrew sources, just as the ה in יהה, and thus there would be no need to assume a partial Aramaization of Hebrew -[ōt] to Aramaic -[āt].[36]

צבאת is encountered only in ostraca from the first quarter of the century (CG 167 r. 1; J8 r. 9). Since only a few texts have survived for the second quarter, which moreover show no comparable epithets we cannot exclude that the term could have been used also after 475 BC.

However, this changes at the latest in the last quarter of the fifth century where new designations of Jaho appear in the text but not צבאת.

---

33 That Jaho as an element of personal names could be written on Elephantine at any time with יהו does not contradict this. One must distinguish between the explicit naming of a god as a deity in its own right and the use of its name as part of a personal name. Furthermore, since personal names serve to identify individuals, it also made sense to write the names in an orthography that would allow any reader to also correctly identify the name. Nevertheless, names with יהה are still common in the documents written before 475 (cf. יההאור TAD B5.1:2, cf. D3.7:2; יההרם B4.2:13; עבדיהה C3.4:6; against יהורם CG X17 v. 1 and יהוטל CG 42 v. 8; 115 v.7; 163 r. 3). Only after 475 BCE the writing יהו became mandatory in personal names. Since the writing יהה does not appear in Israelite/Judean inscriptions which normally use the longer version [yahwē] (beside some possible instances of the short form [yah]; see Renz, *Handbuch der althebräischen Epigraphik* II/1., 89–90), this seems to be a spelling of the colloquial from [yahō] used in informal texts. Less likely, though not impossible, would be the assumption that the Jaho community chose this spelling ad hoc using the traditional Hebrew orthography when they established their Jaho cult on Elephantine to mark their god as their own and foreign to the gods of their environment. This would have been a very strong act of creating an identity as a religious group. In any case, the writing יהו is clearly a later adaption to the Imperial Aramaic orthography and thus cannot be used as an argument for an original Samarian/Israelite background of the Jaho community as proposed by Barnea, "The Migration of the Elephantine Yahwists," 112.

34 Cf. *ḌB'* and its derivatives in Old South Arabic and in some dialects of the North Arabian Peninsula; for this, see the information on the root *ḍb'* and its derivatives given in the Sabaean Online Dictionary http://sabaweb.uni-jena.de/SabaWeb.

35 Cf. Renz, *Handbuch der althebräischen Epigraphik* II/2, 41–2.

36 This does not exclude the possibility, that Aramaic speaking readers would have read the word with -[āt] – it is the (dis-)advantage of a non-vocalized writing system that a reader can adopt the written texts to his own pronunciation and interpretation.

Thus, in some texts אלה שמיא "the God of heaven" appears as a designation of Jaho, which, with one exception (TAD A4.7:28 ‖ 8:26–7), replaces rather than supplements the name of God (A3.6:1; 4.3:3, 5; 4.7:2 ‖ 8:2; 4.9:3–4). The designation is found especially in the prescript of letters in the context of blessings for the addressee:

a) In the formula שלם ... אלה שמיא ישאל בכל עדן "may the God of Heaven seek after the welfare of <the addressee> all them times": A3.6.1, A4.3:2, A4.7:1-f ‖ A4.8:1–2.1[37]

b) Additionally A4.3:2–3 לרחמין הוו קדם אלה שמיא "may they (the addresses) be in favor before the God of Heaven".

It is striking that in letters from the Jaho community from the second half of the fifth century, the שלם-formula is also used with other names of gods such as אלהיא כלא "all the gods" (A3. 7:1) or simply אלהיא "the gods" (A4.4:1), but never with Jaho. This is encountered only once in the first quarter of the fifth century on an ostracon, though it remains unclear whether יהה [אלהא or יהה [צבאת is mentioned there.[38] Be that as it may, evidently at the end of the fifth century, for whatever reasons, it was preferred to avoid explicitly naming Jaho in such letter-introduction formulas and to replace it with other names of God, although it is clear that אלה שמיא refers to Jaho.

That אלה שמיא was perceived as a special designation within the Jaho community is shown by the remaining evidence from letters attributable to members of this community. For example, in the aforementioned letter TAD A4.3, Mauziah reports to the leaders of the Jaho community that אלה שמיא helped the Egyptians Ṣeḥa and Ḥor in their advocacy of Mauziah before Vidranga. The use of this phrase both in the prescript and in reference to two people not belonging to the Jaho community is all the more striking, as Mauziah does use the Jaho name in reference to the representatives of the Jaho community, whom he refers to as כהניא זי יהו אלהא "priests of the god Jaho."

The impression that אלה שמיא was perceived by the Jaho community as a designation of Jaho, which can have the connotation of relationship to the outside world, is confirmed by the letter to Bagohi A4.7 ‖ A4.8. In this letter, too, אלה שמיא occurs not only in the aforementioned prescript as the god who is to take care of the addressee's salvation, but once again at the end, where the senders assure Bagohi that his appearance צדקה יהוה לך קדם יהו אלה שמיא "will be a merit for you before Jaho, the God of Heaven" (l. 27–8 ‖ 26–7). Although Jaho is mentioned here

37 Cf. Schwiderski, *Handbuch*, 115–8.

38 D7.35:1–2 שלמך יהה | [... ישא]ל בכל עדן. Since the right margin of the ostracon is completely lost, the reading צבאת suggested by Dupont-Sommer, "Un ostracon araméen inédit," 404–5) remains uncertain, though quite possible.

also by name, he appears explicitly as "God of Heaven" in his attitude against Bagohi, who does not belong to the Jaho community. In contrast, wherever in the very same letter the Jaho community of Elephantine comes into focus, Jaho is never referred to as "God of Heaven," but simply as יהו אלהא "the God Jaho" used in the designation of the temple or the altar (A4. 7:6, 26; A4.8:7, 24, 25). And in the central statement about the fasting and prayers of the Jaho community itself they refer to their god as יהו מרא שמיא "Jaho, Lord of Heaven" (A4.7:15).

The background for this particular use of אלה שמיא can be seen in the fact that this designation was apparently established within the Achaemenid administration as a designation of Jahwe/Jaho. Otherwise it cannot be understood that the governors Bagohi and Delaiah in their memorandum to Aršames, in which they advise him to approve the restoration of the temple and to allow vegetal sacrifices again, refer to the temple simply as בית מדבחא זי אלה שמיא "altar house of the God of Heaven" and do not use the name Jaho (A4. 9:3). Particularly in the context of Elephantine, this designation must not only have been familiar within the administration, but also have had positive connotations, so that the senders considered it helpful to designate the temple accordingly.

How foreign this had remained to the Jaho community on Elephantine itself is shown by the fact that in their own letter, in which they offer a bribe to Aršames, they call the temple, as was usual with them elsewhere, the אגורא זי יהו אלהא "temple of the god Jaho" (A4.10:8).

That אלה שמיא is an Aramaic name for Yahweh that arose during the Achaemenid period can be demonstrated as probable by other observations. It is found primarily in biblical Aramaic texts, where it appears eleven times always in place of the name of Yahweh and never as an extension (Dan 2:18, 19, 37, 44; Ezra 5:11, 12; 6, 9, 10; 7, 12, 21, 23bis). Only rarely, and then only in recognized late sections, does its Hebrew translation אלהי השמים also appear in Hebrew texts of the Bible, though it is mostly used as an apposition to the name of God (Gen 24:3, 7; Jonah 1:9; Ezra 1:2; Neh 1:5; 2 Chron 36:23) and only in Nehemiah as a stand-alone name of God (Neh 1:4; 2:4, 20). More significantly, this designation disappears in the post-biblical literature. Thus, it is absent from Qumran and is mentioned in the rabbinic texts only in connection with its biblical evidence.[39] Only in the Palestinian Targum tradition does it occur more frequently as a rendering of שדי (אל).[40]

---

39 The expression is also found only rarely in the Piyyutim. Since it is well known that the Paytanim used the Hebrew Bible *ad libitum* as a source for their phraseology, however, this cannot serve as evidence that the expression was in common use in post-biblical Judaism.

40 Tg^{Neoph} Gen 28:3; 35:11; 43:13; 48:3; 49:25; Ex 6:3; Tg^{Frg} Gen 49:25; Ex 6:3; Palestinian Targums from the Genizah (cf. Klein, *Genizah Manuscripts*) Ms. C to Gen 35:11 and Ms. D to Gen 48:3; Ex 6:3. Cf. otherwise the Targums to Ps 136:26 for אל and without a direct reference word only Tg^{Jon} to Lev 24:10 and the Targums to Songs 7:13; Qoh 10:10.

From this finding it can be clearly seen that the designation “God of Heaven” was evidently used as a primarily Aramaic designation for Yahweh in the Achaemenid period, but it remained largely foreign to the Jewish tradition and, with only few exceptions, was not further received. The most likely interpretation of this fact is that this designation was coined by circles who, in their dealings with the Achaemenid suzerainty, on the one hand wanted to lend greater weight to the significance of the cult of Yahweh as a cult of the “God of Heaven,” and on the other hand, by replacing the exclusive name Yahweh with the more inclusive designation “God of Heaven,” also wanted to open this cult to the outside world.[41] This would explain why within most of Yahweh/Jaho communities this designation was received only sporadically and – as the evidence from Elephantine shows – more with regard to the outside world.

In any case, a clear distinction must be made between the “external” God designation אלה שמיא “God of Heaven” and the “internal” epithet מרא שמיא “Lord of Heaven” used side by side in A4.7 ‖ A4.8. In contrast to external orientation of אלה השמיא, Jaho appears as מרא שמיא precisely in the context of the existential need of the Jaho community itself. One should note, that the former יהה צבאת, by which Jaho is referred to as the “Lord of the (heavenly) hosts”, corresponds very well to his designation as “Lord of Heaven”. Thus, it is quite possible to see in מרא שמיא the Aramaic replacement for the older Hebrew צבאת, which had apparently become obsolete – especially since the direct translation as יהו חיליא in the Elephantine context would certainly have been misleading in the sense of “Jaho of the armies (of Elephantine)”.[42]

Be that as it may, these observations suggests that the designation אלה שמין had not been part of the ancient tradition of the Elephantine Jaho community. On the contrary, it is probably an adoption of a terminology that emerged only during the Achaemenid period outside Elephantine with the aim of better integrating the cult of Yahweh into the context of Persian suzerainty.[43]

---

41 This would be supported by the use of אלה שמיא by Bagohi and Deliah towards Aršames.

42 On the other hand, the connection of אלה שמין, to which מרא שמין would then be only a variant, with the well-known בעל שמים/ן, which Meyer (*Der Papyrusfund von Elephantine*, 67) drew and which was then asserted in particular by Kraeling (*The Brooklyn Museum Aramaic Papyri*, 84), Niehr (e.g., *Baʿalšamem*, 191–5), and his student Angela Rohrmoser, *Götter, Tempel und Kult*, 120–1, cannot be assumed. It overlooks the different contexts and thus connotations of the two terms and cannot explain why they appear so late in the texts. And one should take the following critical remark of Bolin, “The Temple of יהו at Elephantine,” 136, seriously: “While the term’s origins may lie in Bronze Age Syria-Palestine, its meaning for a Jewish community in their correspondence with the Persian adminstration a millenium later is another issue.” For further interpretations of אלה שמיא and מרא שמיא cf. Becking, *Identity in Persian Egypt*, 36–8.

43 This has already been considered by Rohrmoser, *Götter, Tempel und Kult*, 121–2, who, however, overlooks the difference between מרא שמיא and אלה שמיא (cf. the previous note).

This draws attention to another terminological innovation that can be observed for the same period and is closely connected with the intervention of the Achaemenid administration in respect to the calendar of the Jaho cult on Elephantine. However one may interpret the so-called Passover letter A4.1 from the year 419 in detail, it is clear that the sender Hananiah communicates decisions of the Persian central administration, which had been sent first to the satrap Aršames, to the Jaho community of Elephantine. In this connection, Hananiah also gives instructions for the date and some rules of a festival in Nisan, whereby it is disputed whether it concerns the Massot or Passover festival.[44] In doing so, Hananiah explicitly addresses this letter referring to cultic measures to the חילא יהודיא "the Judean 'troop'" (l. 1, 10), which is also the first evidence of this expression.

That this designation obviously refers to the Jaho community on Elephantine is also made clear by its second record. Thus, the famous list of contributions for the temple of Jaho is introduced with the words: "This is (a list of) the names of the חילא יהודיא who gave silver to the god Jaho". In fact, this list is a collective manuscript, in which individual lists of people from different groups were compiled. Thus, it begins with a small group of three people (l. 2–5) and ends with a large group of 91 people (l. 32–122). Both groups are not further specified. This is also true for two lists of seven and three more people respectively on the verso, which are added at the end (l. 129–38). Lines 6–31, however, provide two lists of individuals assigned to the military units of a century led by commanders bearing Babylonian names.[45] Since only 13 respectively 11 persons bearing Judean names are mentioned for each of these two centuries, it can be assumed that not all members of the mentioned centuries of Siniddin and Nabuakab belonged to the חילא יהודיא, but only those who counted themselves to the cult community of Jaho. חילא יהודיא is therefore also in this text related to this cult community, to which members of different military units could belong.

Another observation supports the assumption that the term חילא יהודיא means the Jaho community, although it formally corresponds to the term חילא סונכניא "the Syenian troop." Thus, Haggai bar Shemaiah, who is known from several

---

44 On this letter, see van der Toorn, *Becoming Diaspora Jews*, 120–4; Becking, *Identity in Persian Egypt*, 24–8; Schipper, "Die Judäer/Aramäer von Elephantine," 67–71. The following argumentation takes up a thesis of Kottsieper, "Die Religionspolitik der Achämeniden," 150–8, which has been adopted *inter alia* by van der Toorn, "Ethnicity at Elephantine," 156 and van der Toorn, *Becoming Diaspora Jews*, 120–4, and adds additional observations to it. For a different – in my opinion less convincing – reading and interpretation see Barnea. "P. Berlin 13464, Yahwism and Achaemenid Zoroastrianism at Elephantine," in this volume.

45 See the closing l. 19 מאת שנדן "the century of Siniddin" and the opening line of the next section, l. 20 מאת נבועקב "the cenutry of Nabuakab".

documents from the Jaho community on Elephantine as a witness and scribe (B2.7:19; 3.4:23; 3.8:43; 3.10:22; 3.11:17; 3.12:32),[46] is nevertheless attributed to the חילא סונכניא in the ration list C3.14:3 from the year 400.[47] If one does not want to speculate that this was a different person or that he had left the Jaho community at the end of his career, this is probably another proof, that one person could be member of a certain Achaemenid troop unit and the חילא יהודיא at the same time. This suggests that חילא יהודיא is not simply a troop designation, but refers to the members of the Achaemenid garrison who were also members of the Jaho community.[48]

That יהודי has acquired a religious connotation even outside the designation חילא יהודהיא can be shown by further observations regarding the use of יהודי in other contexts.[49] Thus, in legal documents, the term יהודי זי בבירת יב "a Judean who is in the fortress of Jeb" or יהודי זי יב (בירתא) "a Judean of (the fortress) Jeb" is frequently found, but only until September 420 BC.[50] From October 420 on, bearers of Judean names on Elephantine are referred to by scribes belonging to the Jaho community as ארמי זי יב בירתא "an Aramean of the fortress Jeb" in such legal texts whenever Jeb is mentioned.[51]

Particularly telling in this regard is the latest instance of the use of יהודי in the first phrase. Thus, in B5.5:1–2 (September 420), Miptahiah is probably first referred to as a "Judean who is in the fortress of Yeb," as it had been common in the documents written earlier. But obviously the scribe got unsure whether this would be still the right designation and thus he added the notion לדגלה ארמ[יה] „according to her detachment an Aramean". Thus we can observe that with the year 420 the term יהודי lost its meaning as a simple ethnic designation and became a term connoting membership in the Jaho community on Elephantine.

That this was not a development in the scribal habit of different scribes is evidenced by the observation that two different scribes follow this evolution and

---

46 Based on the handwriting, TAD B4.6 may also be attributed to him. The documents date from the period 446–400 BCE.

47 Cf. TAD C3.14:3. The fact that Haggai does not appear in the levy list for the temple of Jaho is not a counterargument, since the list is not completely preserved.

48 Cf. van der Toorn, "Ethnicity at Elephantine," 154–155.

49 For the older discussion of this subject, cf. now Barnea, *Yahwistic Identity*, who reaches a similar conclusion; I would like to thank the author for drawing my attention to this essay prior to its publication after I had completed my manuscript.

50 Cf. TAD B2.2:3 (464); B2.4:2 (460); B3.1:3 (456); B3.6:2 (427); B2.9:2 (August 420); B5.5:1–2 (September 420).

51 Cf. TAD B3.8:2 (October 420; B2.10:2 (216); B3.12:2–3 (403); B4.6:2 (400); cf. also B7.2:2–3 (401) ארמי מהחסן בי ב[ירתא. This is also the case in D2.12:4 (403). The reading יׄ[הו]דׄיׄ proposed in by Porten and Yardeni, Textbook of Aramaic Documents 4, 71, would clearly be too long for the gap. In contrast, אׄ[ר]מׄיׄ fits the preserved letters at the beginning and end and would fill the gap perfectly.

changed their habit accordingly. Thus, Mauziah bar Natan still uses the old formula in September 420 (B2.9), only to be the first to use the new formulation in October 420 (B3.8), which is then also found in the document B2.10 written by him in 416. And Haggai bar Shemaiah offers the old designation with יהודי in 427 (B3.6), only to use the new version with ארמי in later documents written by him in 402 (B3.12) and 400 (B4.6).

A last observation adds a small detail from the perspective of a non-Judean scribe outside of Elephantine. Thus, the Elephantine Anani bar Haggai is called – as expected – an "Aramean who is in the fortress of Jeb, belonging to the degel of Nabukudurri" in a document written by Haggai bar Shemaya on Elephantine in 402 (B3.12:2–4). But the very same person is called in the very same year by the non-Judean scribe Shaweram bar Eshemram in Syene simply יהודי לדגל נובכדרי "a Judean belonging to the detachment of Nabukudduri," while his counterpart is referred to as ארמי זי סון לדגלא זך "an Aramean *of Syene*, belonging to the same detachment" (B3.13:2). Though we do not know how Shaweram exactly understood the term יהודי it is clear that for him this term needs no further localization – in contrast to ארמי which is still just an ethnic term needing the additional information where the person dwells. Obviously, for such a non-Judean scribe from Syene of the year 402 a יהודי is in any case one who lives on Elephantine – a fact which earlier was not obvious for scribes from Syene. Thus, e.g., in B2.2:3 (464) and B2.4:1–2 (460) זי (בבירת) יב is still used in apposition to יהודי.

It results from this that the term יהודי got a new meaning around 420 BC, which obviously connects it closely with the Yaho cult on Elephantine. Consequently, for people outside Elephantine, a יהודי is naturally to be looked for on Elephantine, so that the place specification can be omitted here. For the scribes on Elephantine, however, the term יהודי is manifestly no longer a simple ethnic indication, but defines him as a member of the חילא יהודיא as a recognized cultic community in the realm of the Persian military in southern Egypt. Accordingly, when referring to membership in a particular Persian command unit, the term is avoided and replaced by ארמי. If, however, one means decidedly the members of the Yaho cult community, then, like in the letter to Bagohi, B4.7 and 8, they are now referred to simply as יהודיא.[52]

52 Of course, the different uses of יהודי and ארמי even with the same persons had puzzled scholars for long time and different explanation had been offered, cf. e.g. Becking, *Identity in Persian Egypt*, 18–20; id., Identity of the People, and the literature mentioned there. But the earlier attempts suffer from the lack of a thorough categorization of the instances according to time *and* the different scribes and their background at the time they wrote a certain document. Thus, it had not been taken into account that even one and the same scribe may change his habit for diachronic reasons. For an exception compare van der Toorn, "Ethnicity at Elephantine," and

The fact that this shift in meaning coincides with
- the establishment of the name of the Jaho community as חילא יהודיא,
- the appearance of Hananiah, who wrote the famous so-called Passover letter to the חילא יהודיא in 419 but was probably in contact with it earlier,
- and the adoption of the term אלה שמיא "god of heaven"

is certainly no coincidence. Rather, it may be assumed that around 420 the status of the Jaho community had fundamentally changed to the point that it had now evidently acquired a recognized position as a cult community in the context of the Achaemenid ruling structure. This is shown not only by the term חילא יהודיא with its military component חיל, but also by the observation that with אלה שמיא the Yaho community had taken over a designation of Jaho that was actually foreign to it and that also arose at the same time in Judah.

The well-known statement of Mauziah that the Chnum priests were opposed to the Judeans since the appearance of Hananiah (A4.3:7) confirms, on the one hand, that this change of status was carried out by the official Hananiah at Elephantine, and on the other hand, that it was not insignificant. However, it is a well-known, though unpleasant, phenomenon that indigenous religious groups are allergic to the social advancement of immigrant groups and their religious communities. Von Pilgrims' attempt to place the ultimate responsibility for the Chum priests' action against the Jaho-temple on the Jaho community to the effect that it was the result of a building code violation has proven untenable both archaeologically and in terms of legal history.[53] Thus, the devastation of the temple may have been a consequence of the agitation of the Chnum priests against the Jaho community, whose change of the social status the Chnum priests did not want to accept.

To sum up: the consolidation of the Jaho community with a temple on Elephantine must be dated to the time of Amasis at the latest, but may well have even older antecedents. The spelling יהה and the use of the Hebrew word צבאת show that this community conservatively adhered to its traditions brought from Judah and/or Israel into the Persian period.

However, the later adoption of the Aramaic orthography יהו for the name of Jaho as well as the disappearance of the designation צבאת, which probably was replaced by מרא השמיא, which become visible at the latest around 450 BC, show that the younger generations modernized their tradition step by step.

---

van der Toorn, *Becoming Diaspora Jews*, 116–143, who, nevertheless, underestimates the diachronic aspect of the use of the single terms.

53 See above.

A decisive break in the history of the Yaho community on Elephantine was apparently their establishment as the חילא יהודיא around 420, possibly initiated by the Achaemenid side itself, or at least actively supported, which brought this community not only a new terminology but also garnered the hatred of the Chnum priests. It also caused a shift in meaning of יהודיא which turned from being used as a simple ethnic term to designate now the members of the Jaho community.

Bibliography

Anneler, Hedwig, Zur Geschichte der Juden von Elephantine. Bern: Akademische Buchhandlung Max Dechsel, 1912.

Barnea, Gad, The Migration of the Elephantine Yahwists under Amasis II, Journal of Near Eastern Studies 82 (2023), 103–118.

Barnea, Gad, P. Berlin 13464, Yahwism and Achaemenid Zoroastrianism at Elephantine, in this volume.

Barnea, Gad, Yahwistic Identity in the Achaemenid period, Zeitschrift für die Alttestamentliche Wissenschaft 136.1 (2024): 1–14.

Bassir, Hussein, Neshor at Elephantine in Late Saite Egypt, Journal of Egyptian History 9 (2016), 66–95.

Becking, Bob, 2020. *Identity in Persian Egypt. The Fate of the Yehudite Community of Elephantine*, University Park, Pennsylvania: Eisenbrauns 2020.

Becking, Bob, "'That Evil Act': A Thick Description of the Crisis around the Demolition of the Temple of Yahô in Elephantine," pages 183–207 in: R. G. Kratz / B. U. Schipper (eds.), Elephantine in Context: Studies on the History, Religion and Literature of the Judeans in Persian Period Egypt (Forschungen zum Alten Testament 155), Mohr Siebeck: Tübingen 2022.

Becking, Bob, "The Identity of the People at Elephantine," pages 106–123 in: M. Folmer (ed.), Elephantine Revisited: New Insights into the Judean Community and Its Neighbors, University Park, Pennsylvania: Eisenbrauns 2022.

Bolin, Thomas M., "The Temple of יהו at Elephantine and Persian Religious Policy," pages 127–42 in: D. V. Edelman (ed.), *The Triumph of Elohim: From Yahwisms to Judaisms*, Grand Rapids: William B. Eerdmans 1996.

Briant, Pierre, "Une curieuse affaire à Éléphantine en 410 av.n.e.: Widranga, le sanctuaire de Khnum et le temple de Yahweh," pages 115–131 in: B. Menu, Égypte pharaonique: pouvoir, société (Méditerranées 6/7), Paris: Harmattan 1996.

Dupont-Sommer, André, „Un ostracon araméen inédit d'Éléphantine," Rivista degli studi orientali 32 (1957), 403–9.

Gesenius, Wilhelm, *Hebräisches und Aramäisches Handwörterbuch über das Alte Testament*, 18. Auflage bearbeitet und herausgegeben von Herbert Donner, Heidelberg: Springer 2013.

Granerød, Gard, *Dimensions of Yahwism in the Persian Period: Studies in the Religion and Society of the Judaean Community at Elephantine* (Beihefte zur Zeitschrift für die alttestamentliche Wissenschaft 488), Berlin: de Gruyter 2016.

Grelot, Pierre, *Documents araméens d'Egypte* (Littératures anciennes du Proche-Orient 5), Paris: Les Éditions du CERF 1972.

Holm, Tawny L., "Nanay and Her Lover: An Aramaic Sacred Marriage Text from Egypt," Journal of Near Eastern Studies 76 (2017): 1–37.

Holm, Tawny L., "Sacrifice and Feasting in Papyrus Amherst 63," pages 135–169 in: R. Da Riva, A. Arroyo and C. Debourse (eds.), Ceremonies, Feasts and Festivities in Ancient Mesopotamia and the Mediterranean World: Performance and Participation: Proceedings of the 11th Melammu Workshop, Barcelona, 29–31 January 2020 (Melammu Workshops and Monographs 7), Münster: Zaphon 2022.

Holm, Tawny L., "The Wandering Arameans in Egypt: Papyrus Amherst 63," Hebrew Bible and Ancient Israel 12 (2023): 157–179.

Kahn, Dan'el, "The Date of the Arrival of the Judeans at Elephantine and the Foundation of Their Colony," Journal on Near Eastern Studies 81 (2022): 139–164.

Klein, Michael L., *Genizah Manuscripts of Palestinian Targum to the Pentateuch* I, Cincinnati: Hebrew Union College Press 1986.

Kottsieper, Ingo, "Anmerkungen zu Pap. Amherst 63: I: 12,11–19 – Eine aramäische Version von Ps 20," *Zeitschrift für die alttestamentliche Wissenschaft* 100 (1988), 217–244.

Kottsieper, Ingo, "Anmerkungen zu Pap. Amherst 63: Teil II-V," *Ugarit-Forschungen* 29 (1997): 385–434.

Kottsieper, Ingo, "El – ferner oder naher Gott? Zur Bedeutung einer semitischen Gottheit in verschiedenen sozialen Kontexten im 1. Jtsd.v.Chr," pages 25–74 in: R. Albertz / S. Otto (eds.), *Religion und Gesellschaft: Studien zu ihrer Wechselwirkung in den Kulturen des Antiken Vorderen Orients* (Veröffentlichung des Arbeitskreises zur Erforschung der Religions- und Kulturgeschichte des Antiken Vorderen Orients [AZERKAVO] 1 = Alter Orient und Altes Testament 248), Münster: Ugarit-Verlag 1997.

Kottsieper, Ingo, "Die Religionspolitik der Achämeniden und die Juden von Elephantine," pages 150–178 in: R. G. Kratz (ed.), *Religion und Religionskontakte im Zeitalter der Achämeniden* (Veröffentlichungen der Wissenschaftlichen Gesellschaft für Theologie 22), Gütersloh: Chr. Kaiser/Gütersloher Verlag 2002.

Kraeling, Emil G., *The Brooklyn Museum Aramaic Papyri: New Documents of the Fifth Century B.C. from the Jewish Colony at Elephantine*, New Haven: Yale University Press 1953.

Lüddeckens, Erich, *Demotisches Namenbuch*: Band 1,1, Wiesbaden: Reichert 1986.

Meyer, Eduard, *Der Papyrusfund von Elephantine: Dokumente einer jüdischen Gemeinde aus der Perserzeit und das älteste erhaltene Buch der Weltliteratur*, Leipzig: J. C. Hinrich 1912.

Niehr, Herbert, *Baʿalšamem: Studien zu Herkunft, Geschichte und Rezeptionsgeschichte eines phönizischen Gottes* (Studia phoenicia 17), Leuven, Paris, and Dudley: Peeters and Department oosterse studies 2003.

Porten, Bezalel. "*Yahu* and Its Cognates in Personal Names: The Problem of Yama." Pages 373–378 in Yahwism under the Achaemenid Empire, Prof. Shaul Shaked in memoriam. Gad Barnea and Reinhard Kratz, eds. (BZAW; Berlin: de Gruyter, forthcoming 2024).

Porten, Bezalel, "The Aramaic Texts," pages 74–264 in: B. Porten (ed.), *The Elephantine papyri in English: Three millennia of cross-cultuiral continuity and change* (Documenta et monumenta Oriens antiqui: Studies in Near Eastern Archaeology and Civilisation 22), Leiden: Brill 1996.

Porten, Bezalel, "The Calendar of Aramaic Texts from Achaemenid and Ptolemaic Egypt," pages 13–32 in: Sh. Shaked and A. Netzer (eds.), *Irano-Judaica II: Studies relating to Jewish contacts with Persian Culture throughout the ages*, Jerusalem: Ben Zvi 1990.

Porten, Bezalel and Yardeni, Ada, *Textbook of Aramaic Documents from Ancient Egypt 4: Ostraca & assorted inscriptions*, Jerusalem 1999.

Quack, Joachim F., „Zum Datum der persischen Eroberung Ägyptens unter Kambyses," *Journal of Egyptian History* 4 (2011): 228–246.

Quack, Joachim F., “The Interaction of Egyptian and Aramaic Literature,” pages 375–411 in: O. Lipschits, G. N. Knopper and M. Oeming, *Judah and the Judeans in the Achaemenid Period: Negotiating Identity in an International Context*, Winona Lake: Eisenbrauns 2011.

Quack, Joachim F., “Stadt des Chnum oder Weg des Chnum? Zu einem Problem der historischen Topographie Elephantines,” in: V. Lepper (ed.), *Essays on Elephantine*, Leiden and Boston: Brill (forthcoming).

Radner, Karen, *The Prosopography of the Neo-Assyrian Empire*: Volume 1, Part II: B–G, edited by Karen Radner, Helsinki: The Neo-Assyrian Text Corpus Project 1999.

Ranke, Hermann, *Die ägyptischen Personennamen I: Verzeichnis der Namen*. Glückstadt: J. J. Augustin 1935.

Renz, Johannes, *Handbuch der althebräischen Epigraphik*: Band II/1. Darmstadt: Wissenschaftliche Buchgesellschaft 1995.

Renz, Johannes, *Handbuch der althebräischen Epigraphik*: Band II/2. Darmstadt: Wissenschaftliche Buchgesellschaft 2003.

Rohrmoser, Angela, *Götter, Tempel und Kult der Judäo-Aramäer von Elephantine: Archäologische und schriftliche Zeugnisse aus dem perserzeitlichen Ägypten* (Alter Orient und Altes Testament 396), Münster: Ugarit-Verlag 2014.

Salo, Reettakaisa Sofia, *Die judäische Königsideologie im Kontext der Nachbarkulturen: Untersuchungen zu den Königspsalmen 2, 18, 20, 21, 45 und 72* (Orientalische Religionen in der Antike: Ägypten, Israel, Alter Orient 25), Tübingen: Mohr Siebeck 2017.

Schipper, Bernd U., 2020, “Die Judäer/Aramäer von Elephantine und ihre Religion,” *Zeitschrift für die Alttestamentliche Wissenschaft* 132 (2020) 57–83.

Schwiderski, Dirk, *Handbuch des nordwestsemitischen Briefformulars. Ein Beitrag zur Echtheitsfrage der aramäischen Briefe des Esrabuches* (Beihefte zur Zeitschrift für die alttestamentliche Wissenschaft 295), Berlin / New York: de Gruyter 2000.

Steiner, Richard C. and Nims Charles F., *The Aramaic Text in Demotic Script: Text, Translation, and Notes*, 2017, https://hdl.handle.net/20.500.12202/51.

Sternberg-el Hotabi, Heike, “Die persische Herrschaft in Ägypten,” pages 111–149 in R. G. Kratz (ed.), Religion und Religionskontakte im Zeitalter der Achämeniden (Veröffentlichungen der Wissenschaftlichen Gesellschaft für Theologie 22), Gütersloh: Chr. Kaiser/Gütersloher Verlag, 2002.

Van der Toorn, Karel, *Becoming Diaspora Jews* (The Anchor Yale Bible Reference Library), New Haven and London: Yale University Press 2019.

Van der Toorn, Karel, “Ethnicity at Elephantine: Jews, Arameans, Caspians,” *Tel Aviv* 43 (2016): 147–164.

von Pilgrim, Cornelius, “Elephantine – (Festungs-)Stadt am Ersten Katarakt,” pages 257–70 in: M. Bietak, E. Czerny and I. Forstner-Müller (eds.), *Cities and Urbanism in Ancient Egypt: Papers from a Workshop in November 2006 at the Austrian Academy of Sciences* (Denkschriften der Gesamtakademie LX), Wien: Österreichische Akademie der Wissenschaften 2010.

von Pilgrim, Cornelius, “On the Archaeological Background of the Aramaic Papyri from Elephantine in the Light of Recent Fieldwork,” pages 1–16 in: M. Folmer (ed.), *Elephantine Revisited: New Insights into the Judean Community and Its Neighbors*, University Park, Pennsylvania: Eisenbrauns 2022.

von Pilgrim, Cornelius, “Tempel des Jahu und ‘Straße des Königs’: Ein Konflikt in der späten Perserzeit auf Elephantine,” pages 303–17 in: S. Meyer (ed.), *Egypt – Temple of the Whole World: Studies in Honour of Jan Assmann* (NumenBook Series 97), Leiden: Brill 2003.

Vleeming, Sven P. and Wesselius, Jan-Wim, *Studies in Papyrus Amherst 63: Essays on the Aramaic Texts in Aramaic-Demotic Papyrus Amherst 63*. 2 vols. Amsterdam: Juda Palache Instituut, 1985, 1990.

Zauzich, Karl-Theodor, "Der Gott des aramäisch-demotischen Papyrus Amherst 63," *Göttinger Miszellen* 85 (1985): 89–90.

Zevit, Ziony, *Matres Lectionis in Ancient Hebrew Epigraphs*, Cambridge, M.A.: American School of Oriental Research 1980.

Reinhard G. Kratz

Where to put "Biblical" Yahwism in Achaemenid Times?

1 The Problem

In this paper I would like to address a fundamental methodological problem of the sources on Judaism in Persian times, which is well known but widely ignored in scholarship. I do not have a solution to the problem, but I would like to strongly advocate that we do not continue to pretend that we have a solution or even that the problem does not exist at all. Instead, we should concede the limits of our knowledge and take them into account in our historical reconstruction. Otherwise, biblical scholarship simply makes a fool of itself in relation to other sciences, especially the historians of antiquity, and turns out to be a purely apologetic enterprise of theologians.

The problem I am talking about concerns the literary sources of the Persian period that have been incorporated into the Hebrew Bible and thus – for purely pragmatic reasons – can be called "biblical" sources. These are primarily the books of Ezra and Nehemiah, the prophets Haggai and Zechariah (1–8), the book of Esther as well as parts of the book of Daniel, which explicitly speak about the Persians. Furthermore, one can also include Chronicles, Second Isaiah (chap. 40–55 or 40–66) and the prophet Malachi, which are usually dated to Persian times. I will refrain here from other parts of the Hebrew Bible that for conceptual and/or linguistic reasons are also dated to late Babylonian, Persian or early Hellenistic times , such as the Priestly Writing in the Pentateuch, late redactions and parts in Torah and Former Prophets, or late poetry in Psalms and Wisdom; however, the following remarks also apply to them.

In scholarship, represented by both special monographs and textbooks, the literary, i.e. biblical sources are normally used on an equal footing with archaeological and epigraphic evidence for the history of the two provinces of Samaria and Yehud, of the Samarian and Judean population both in the land and in the diaspora, and of the religion, i.e. Yahwism in Achaemenid times. It is true that the dating, authenticity and historicity of the biblical sources are disputed in detail. But the overall opinion in scholarship seems to be that these sources are more or less reliable and – in this way or the other – reflect the reality of the Achaemenid period.

Reinhard G. Kratz, University of Göttingen, Germany

https://doi.org/10.1515/9783111018638-008

The problem is that, in fact, we do not know and hardly anyone wonders, what kind of reality do the biblical sources depict? Or in other words: where do the sources come from, who wrote them, from which perspective they were written and thus for whom and of what they are actually representative. It is undisputed that these sources were written by professional scribes and intellectual elites who also could afford the necessary material means for writing such texts. However, who were these scribes and what was the historical context of the intellectual elites responsible for the biblical literature? Do we find them in the Samarian or Judean, Persian-controlled administration, at the temples of Mt Gerizim,[1] Jerusalem, or any other temple, in public or private scribal schools or families? And for whom did they write the biblical literature: for the ruling political class and elites in the provinces of Samaria and Yehud, for the priests or other officials at the temples, for the general population or just for fun for themselves?

In short, I want to raise the question: where do we have to put the literature of the Hebrew Bible and its specific, Torah-centered form of Yahwism in the historical and social context of Judaism in the Achaemenid period? As far as I can see, this question was and still is not raised in scholarship very often yet but earns particular reflection.[2] And this is what I am trying to do here, concentrating on Yahwism in Achaemenid times.

2 Yahwism in the Hebrew Bible

I begin with Yahwism in the Hebrew Bible, more specifically with the writings and texts that speak about the Persian era or are usually dated to Persian times. What characterizes Yahwism in the said writings of (what became) the Hebrew Bible and what is special about it? I cannot discuss everything in detail here, but will simply recall five characteristics that I think are not controversial and are familiar to everyone.

a) The first characteristic to mention here is of course the role of the God YHWH. In the biblical sources speaking about the Persian period he is quite often referred to as the "God of Heaven,"[3] but it is clear and occasionally explicitly stated that this is the "God of Israel" who dwells in Jerusalem.[4] He is considered

1 For a detailed discussion of the Samarian community in the Achaemenid period, see Edelman "Yhwh Shomron and Yhwh Elohim in the Achaemenid Province of Samaria," in this volume.

2 See Kratz, "Zwischen Elephantine und Qumran," 129–146; Kratz, *Historical and Biblical Israel*.

3 2 Chr 36:22/Ezra 1:2; Neh 1:4–5; 2:4, 20; in Aramaic Jer 10:11; Dan 2:18, 28, 37, 44; 5:23; Ezra 5:11; 6:9; 7:12, 21, 23; see also Gen 24:3, 7; Jon 1:9.

4 Ezra 1:3; 6:14, 21–22; 7:6, 11, 15; "God of our fathers" Dan 2:23 (cf. Daniel 1 and 9).

not only the highest, but – so especially in Isa 40–48 – also the only God beside whom there is or should be no other. Other gods are regarded as gods of the nations and defamed as idols and actually non-existent.[5]

b) Secondly, this one and only God YHWH has a particularly close relationship with a certain nation – expressed in the covenant formula "I will be their God, they shall be my people".[6] This nation is called "his people", i.e. the people of this God, and bear the name "Israel" or "Jacob-Israel". Even though the biblical sources on the Persian period speak almost exclusively of Judah and Judeans, both those in the land and those who are said to have been in the Babylonian Gola and to have returned, they too are called "Israel" or "people of Israel". Occasionally this is referred to as the people of the twelve tribes of Jacob-Israel.[7]

c) Thirdly, the God YHWH and "his people", the people of "Israel", are connected by a common history that goes back to the Exodus from Egypt or – as in Nehemiah 9 – to the creation of heaven and earth and the choosing of Abraham. This history is the very specific, constructed sacred history of the Hebrew Bible told in Torah and Former Prophets (Genesis to 2Kings). It is often alluded to or recapitulated in prayers such as Ezra 9, Nehemiah 1 and 9, and Daniel 9.[8]

d) Fourthly, the sacred history that connects the God YHWH and the people of "Israel", is consistently marked by sin and punishment, more specifically the sin of the people against their God and the judgement of God on "his people" Israel. The criterion is the Law of Moses and its commandments, which the God YHWH gave to the people of "Israel" (at Sinai/Horeb) and instructed them to keep. The sin thus consists in the apostasy from the one and only God and the Law of Moses; the judgment consists in the destruction of the temple in Jerusalem and the exile and deportation of the people among the nations.[9] Another peculiarity of the biblical sources is that this fatal history of sin and punishment is said to have been ended by the grace of the God YHWH to "his people" called Israel in the Persian era. With Cyrus and the Persians, according to the sacred history of the biblical sources, the time of salvation begins or is promised: The return of the people from the Babylonian exile, the rebuilding of the temple, the reintroduction and application of the Mosaic Law, the teaching and purification of the people, the rebuilding of the city and wall in Jerusalem and the restoration of

---

5 Ezra 6:21; cf. Ezra 9–10; Nehemiah 1 and 9; Daniel 9.

6 Zech 8:8; cf. Gen 17:7; Exod 6:7.

7 Zech 2:2; 8:7–8, 13; Ezra 2:1–2, 70/Neh 7:6–7, 72; Ezra 4:3; 6:16–17, 21; 7:10; 9:1; Neh 8:1; Dan 1:3; Isa 40:27; 41:8, 14; 42:24; 43:1, 22, 28; 44:1, 5, 21; 45:4; 46:3; 48:1, 12; 49:5.

8 See also Hag 2:5; Ezr 5:11–13.

9 See Hag 2:14, 17; Zech 1:2–6; 7:7–14; Isa 40:2; Ezra 5:12; Nehemiah 1 and 9; the Torah as criterion Ezra 3:2, 4; 6:18; Ezra 7–9 and Nehemiah 9.

the political structures of the province of Yehud, and all this under the care of the Achaemenid kings (Cyrus, Darius, Artaxerxes) appointed by the God YHWH himself.[10]

d) This leads me to the fifth characteristic, namely the relationship of the God YHWH and "his people" to the other nations. The nations outside "Israel" are seen either as the epitome of idolatry or as enemies of "Israel" and instruments of God to punish "his people". The other nations are either to be punished and destroyed or they are to repent and join the people of "Israel" and its God YHWH. An exception, as mentioned, are the Persians and the dynastic line of the Achaemenids, whom the "God of Heaven" (YHWH) himself appointed as successors of the Davidic line for the salvation and protection of "Israel".[11]

These are the five characteristics of Yahwism in the literary sources of the Hebrew Bible that deal with the Persian period and possibly date from it or from somewhat later. However, the characteristics do not occur everywhere in the same way. The great exception is, for example, the book of Esther, in which neither YHWH nor Israel are mentioned and only in a few places do we find an indirect reference to the sacred history of the Hebrew Bible. The situation is similar when we analyse the other sources in terms of their literary history and come across older traditions that have entered into the writings of the Hebrew Bible, such as the basic writing of the Nehemiah memoir[12] or the correspondence to the building of the temple in Ezra 5–6;[13] the oldest stages of the Daniel legends in Dan 2–6 should also be mentioned here.[14] Esther and these older components of the Hebrew Bible open a window to a form of Yahwism that is not (yet) affected by the biblical features and therefore does not exhibit the characteristics of biblical Yahwism. Rather, it is a different form of Yahwism that is also found in the epigraphic sources on Judaism in Achaemenid times.

3 Yahwism in the Epigraphic Sources

In addition to the literary, biblical sources, we are – in contrast to earlier historical phases – quite well informed about the provinces of Samaria and Yehud as

10 Ezra-Nehemiah, see esp. 2 Chr 36:20–23/Ezra 1:1 ff; 6:14; Isa 40–66, esp. 44:28; 45:1; Haggai and Zechariah 1–8; Dan 1:1–2,21; 6:29.

11 Hag 2:6–8; 2:21–23; Zech 1:7–17; 2:1–4, 10–17; 6:1–8; 8:20–23; cf. Isa 40–66 passim; for the exception of the Persians see n. 9.

12 See Kratz, *Composition*, 62–68; Wright, *Rebuilding Identity*.

13 Kratz *Composition*, 52–62.

14 Kratz, *Translatio imperii*.

well as about Yahwists and Judeans in the Babylonian and Egyptian diaspora of the Persian and Hellenistic-Roman periods through a wealth of epigraphic sources: the documents of Elephantine and Al-Yahudu, some small epigraphic evidence (seals, bullae and coins), the Samaria papyri of Wadi Daliyeh, the inscriptions from Mount Gerizim and, last but not least, the Dead Sea Scrolls.[15]

Most of these sources, as far as they originate from the Achaemenid period, are discussed in this volume. Therefore, I do not have to and cannot go into them in detail here, but would only like to examine whether the five characteristics of biblical Yahwism listed above can be found in them.

The answer is a clear "no." Among the wealth of the epigraphic sources, only the Dead Sea Scrolls and some of the inscriptions from Gerizim, both coming from the Hellenistic-Roman period, contain evidence of biblical and parabiblical literature. The sources from the Achaemenid period, i.e. the epigraphic finds in Samaria and Yehud as well as the two archives of Elephantine and Al-Yahudu, on the other hand, do not reveal any knowledge of or references to the literature which eventually became the Hebrew Bible. And so the five characteristics of biblical Yahwism are also unknown to the epigraphic sources from Achaemenid times.

Let me briefly review the five characteristics:

a) The epigraphic sources do indeed also speak of YHWH as the "God of Heaven", who in Ostraca of Elephantine occasionally even bears the title "YHWH Zebaoth" also used in the Hebrew Bible.[16] This God is without doubt the main God of the Judeans on Elephantine (YHW or YHH) and in Al-Yahudu (*yāḫû-* or *-yāma*), as can be seen from the onomasticon and other direct witnesses. But in religious and legal practice he is not the one and only God for the Judeans on Elephantine and in Al-Yahudu, and in no place is he called the "God of Israel".[17]

b) The self-designation of the Yahwists is "Judeans" and – this only at Elephantine – "Arameans".[18] There is no mention of a people called "Israel" or "Jacob-Israel". These are also nowhere referred to as the "people of the God YHWH" which would be in a close covenant relationship with their God.

15 For an overview, see Jacobs and Rollinger (eds.), *Companion* (esp. sections III and IV); Kratz, *Historical and Biblical Israel* (see n. 1 above).

16 "God/Lord of Heaven" TAD A4.7: 2, 15, 27; 4.8: 2, 14, 26–27; "YHH Zebaoth" CG 167 and probably 175 and 186 (= TAD D7.35 conj.); for the latter epithet, see Porten, *Archives*, 106 n. 6; Lemaire, "Everyday Life," here 369. See also Kottsieper, "From יהה צבאת to יהו מרא שמיא: Aspects of religious development on Elephantine," in this volume.

17 On the religion of the Judeans at Elephantine, see Granerød, *Dimensions of Yahwism*; Becking, *Identity in Persian Egypt*, 23–53; for the discussion also Barnea, *Interpretatio Ivdaica*; on Al-Yahudu, see Alstola, *Judeans in Babylonia*.

18 See Kratz, "Arameans and Judeans," 56–85. See also Barnea, "Yahwistic Identity."

c) Nowhere in the relevant epigraphic sources from Achaemenid times does the idea of sin and punishment, an offence against one's own deity and a divine judgement occur; the Torah of Moses is not mentioned, not even in the so-called Passover letter from Elephantine. The destruction of the temple at Elephantine by local Egyptians with the help of a Persian officer is lamented and accompanied by mourning rites and fasting familiar also from the Hebrew Bible.[19] But the event is not interpreted – as we would expect on the basis of our knowledge from the Hebrew Bible – as God's judgement on "his people" or the people of "Israel" for apostasy and transgression of the Torah. Nor does the rebuilding of the Temple and the celebration of the feasts take place with reference to the prescriptions of the Law of Moses as in Ezra-Nehemiah.

d) Nowhere in the epigraphic sources is there any allusion to or recapitulation of the sacred history of the Hebrew Bible. The only historical reminiscence in the Elephantine papyri is the reference to the conquest of Egypt by Cambyses and his handling of the Egyptian sanctuaries as distinct from the Yahu-Temple of the Judeans on Elephantine for apologetic reasons.[20]

e) Finally, nowhere in the epigraphic sources does the biblical view of the other nations as idol worshippers and enemies facing their destruction appear. The Persians are accepted as the ruling political class, the indigenous population in Egypt or Babylonia as the ruling social class, with whom one comes to terms politically, legally and administratively. With other ethnic groups stationed at Elephantine or settled in the area of Al-Yahudu, there are occasional legal disputes or struggles, including the conflict of the destruction of the temple by the neighbouring Chnum priests on Elephantine. But otherwise, the Judeans live peacefully with the other ethnic groups in the diaspora as well as in the country, do business, conclude treaties and fraternize with them. This also includes – in contrast to the ideology of Ezra-Nehemiah – mixed marriages as well as oaths or contracts in the name of gods of other nations and ethnic groups.[21]

After all, we can say: there is no doubt that we are dealing with Yahwists in the epigraphic sources. They are Judeans with a distinct Judean identity, partly also with specifically Judean customs and legal provisions. They apparently worship the god YHWH as their main ethnic deity, though not as the only god, and live and arrange themselves in a multinational and multi-religious environment shaped by the Achaemenid political and administrative class, the indigenous population, and other ethnic groups and their cultures.

---

19 TAD A 4.7: 15–18, 19–21; A4.8: 13–16, 18–20.

20 TAD 4.7:13–14; 4.8: 12–13.

21 On Elephantine, see Becking, *Identity in Persian Egypt*, 54–77 and 78–98; on Al-Yahudu, see Alstola, *Judeans in Babylonia*.

4 Scholarly Narratives and Explanations

The evidence of the sources is actually crystal clear and leaves no room for doubt: quite obviously we are dealing with two fundamentally different forms of Yahwism in the literary, biblical sources on the one hand and the epigraphic sources on the other. While the historical and sociological location of the epigraphic sources is mostly clear from the sources themselves or from the archaeological context in which they were found, the historical and sociological context of the biblical sources is just unknown. How does scholarship deal with this state of affairs?[22]

Well, most scholars follow – some completely, others with some historical-critical reservations – the narrative of the biblical sources and think that the narrative in Ezra-Nehemiah represents the ideology of the Judeans of the time. As far as the evidence of the epigraphic sources is concerned, they either ignore it or declare it to be an exception or some marginal phenomenon which somehow coincides with the narrative of the biblical texts. Characteristic of this position is, for example, the heading in a recent textbook in which the chapter on the Achaemenid period is entitled "History of Israel in the Persian Period".[23] The subject of the account here is the biblical "Israel"; biblical Yahwism then naturally also serves as a yardstick for the history of religion. The fact that neither is documented in any epigraphic source is mentioned in this textbook, but plays no role in the reconstruction of historical events and the religious-historical situation. To be quite honest: even if this is the usual view and represents the firm consensus in scholarship, in my opinion it no longer has anything to do with scientific standards.

The strategy for holding on to the view of the literary, biblical sources essentially consists of levelling the historical and social impact of the evidence of the epigraphic sources. Thus, scholars emphasize the fact that the most important epigraphic sources do not come from the land but from the diaspora, i.e. from peripheral areas (such as Elephantine and Al-Yahudu). Here, it is argued, people either held on to old, outdated ideas or adapted to the foreign environment ("syncretism"). In addition, scholars argue that Yahwism in the epigraphic sources is the popular religion (so-called *Volksreligion*), while the biblical sources are witnesses of the "official religion" or at least of the political and cultural elites, the so-called *literati*, who are considered more representative or more important for the course of religious history. And finally, an argument of genre is also put forward by some scholars: since the documents of Elephantine and Al-Yahudu

22 For the following, see Kratz, "Fossile Überreste," 23–39.
23 Frevel, *Geschichte Israels*, 328.

are mainly of administrative nature, they claim that a comparison with the literary texts of the Hebrew Bible is not possible at all. The fact that there is no reference to the Hebrew Bible in the epigraphic sources is thus justified by the genre and considered as *argumentum e silentio*.

However, none of these arguments stand up to closer scrutiny. As far as the location of the sources is concerned, it is clear from Elephantine that the Judeans in the Egyptian diaspora were in close contact with their own people and the Persian administration in the provinces of Samaria and Yehud. Thus, Elephantine is not a forgotten place on the edge of the world. Moreover, although few epigraphic sources have been found in the Palestine itself, they are certainly speaking and are in accordance with the documents from Elephantine and Al-Yahudu.[24]

The distinction between the religion of the elites and *literati* on the one hand, and that of the general population on the other, does not hold water either. In the documents from Elephantine and Al-Yahudu we find very different groups of the Judean population, some of whom seem to have been very highly placed socially. It is rather unlikely that there were no *literati* among them or among the scribes of the documents. And after all, two literary documents have been found in Elephantine, the Aramaic *Aḥiqar* and the Aramaic version of the Bisutun inscription, which are undoubtedly the work or subject of study of the *literati*.[25]

In addition, the two literary works (*Aḥiqar* and Bisutun inscription) also speak against the argument of genre and the assumption of an *argumentum e silentio*. At least these two writings, as well as the correspondence about the destruction and rebuilding of the temple of Yahu from Elephantine,[26] offer sufficient points of comparison with the literature of the Hebrew Bible.[27] If we take only these few literary witnesses, it is evident that we are dealing here and there with two different expressions of Judaism or Yahwism respectively. The same is also evident from the onomasticon and the administrative sources. As Gard Granerød has shown for Elephantine and Tero Alstola for Al-Yahudu, the outlines of an ethnic identity of the Judean community and the religion of this community can be reconstructed relatively completely from these documents.

---

24 See Kratz, *Historical and Biblical Israel*, 165–187 (German version ^{2}2017, 232–268); Kratz, "Biblical Sources," 133–148.

25 See Kratz, "Ahiqar and Bisitun," 301–322 (repr. in: Folmer [ed.], *Elephantine Revisited*, 67–85).

26 TAD A4.9–9.

27 This is especially true for the correspondence on the rebuilding of the temple in Jeb and in Jerusalem as well as the memoir of Nehemiah and the figures of Ezra and Nehemiah who are colleagues of the ambassador Hananiah mentioned in the papyri of Elephantine. See Kratz, "Second Temple," 247–264 (German version in: Kratz, *Das Judentum*, 60–78); Kratz, "Judean Ambassadors," 421–444 (German version: Allison et al. [eds.], From Daena to Din, 377–398).

There is thus nothing to prevent a comparison of the ethnic identity and specific form of Yahwism in the epigraphic sources with the Judean or "Israelite" identity and Yahwism of the literary, biblical sources. Both forms of ethnic identity and Yahwism move on a comparable level, but are fundamentally different, whereby one form can be clearly classified historically and sociologically, the other hangs – in terms of historical origin and context – somehow in the air.

In the discussion of this paper during the meeting in Haifa in December 2022, the legitimate question arose whether one should not take much more account of the many, even conflicting, voices of the Hebrew Bible itself. These too would document different forms of Judaism ("Judaisms") and Yahwism ("Yahwisms"). Therefore, according to another contribution to the discussion, it seems obvious that Judaism and Yahwism of the epigraphic sources should simply be considered as one form alongside the many voices and forms of Judaism of the Hebrew Bible, and therefore one should rather speak of an equal coexistence of biblical and non-biblical Judaism or Yahwism.[28]

But it is just not that simple. Thus, a categorical difference consists in the fact that the epigraphic sources usually are a direct witness of those who speak or are addressed in them, while the biblical sources neither come from the time nor originate from those or are addressed to those of whom they deal with. That is why it is hardly possible to conclude without further ado on the basis of the different voices and contents of the Hebrew Bible the authors and "social groups behind biblical traditions". This is exactly the problem and not the solution of our problem! If one puts both kinds of epigraphic and literary sources on the same level, two fundamentally different kinds of sources and in this way two different historical levels are mixed.

5 Conclusion

In conclusion, the question remains: What can we do with the findings? What can we say and how should we proceed in the historical reconstruction of Yahwism in Achaemenid times?

As I said at the outset, I have no answer to the question of where the "biblical", Torah-centered Yahwism of the Hebrew Bible should be placed historically or sociologically. But there is no one who knows the answer to this question,

28 This is also the direction taken by the programmatic article by Hensel, "Who wrote the Bible?," 11–23.

and that is why I would like to promote a rethinking and a more consistent methodological approach.

We need to stop pretending that we know the answer and treating the literary, biblical sources as if they were equal to or even superior to the archaeological and epigraphic sources just because they offer more information and, unlike the archaeological and epigraphic sources, provide a nice and seemingly compelling historiographical narrative.

Rather, we should – as is actually customary in historiography and is also practiced for other comparable regions and ethnic groups (such as Arameans, Phoenicians, Moabites, Ammonites, Edomites, etc.) – use the archaeological and epigraphic sources as a starting point for the historical reconstruction of the history of Judaism and Yahwism in Achaemenid times and take the picture that emerges from this as the historical blueprint for everything else.

Only in a second step should the literary, biblical sources then be examined to see if anything fits into the picture gained on the basis of the archaeological and epigraphic evidence. At the same time, the fundamental differences to these sources in regard to the history of the Judeans and Yahwism should be worked out and observed in order not to contaminate the sources with each other in an inadmissible way and to appreciate the literary, biblical sources in their historical distinctiveness.

Where the biblical sources have their historical and sociological place, who is responsible for them and in which circles of the Judean population they circulated, I can, as I said, no more answer than anyone else. What can be said, however, is this, that the specific Yahwism we find in the Hebrew Bible cannot have been very widespread in the land or in the diaspora. Otherwise, some reference to it in the epigraphic sources would be expected, but there is none.

This is not an *argumentum e silentio*, but is confirmed by later archaeological and epigraphic evidence. As recently shown by Yonatan Adler in his study on the "Origins of Judaism",[29] the archaeological evidence for the dissemination and observance of the Torah of Moses does not begin until the 2nd century BCE; the same is the case with the epigraphic sources found at Qumran. This confirms the conclusion that the absence of references to the Yahwism of the Hebrew Bible in the archaeological and epigraphic sources of the Persian and early Hellenistic period is not due to the coincidence of tradition, but to the fact that biblical, Torah-centered Yahwism was not widespread in this period and had little to no historical or sociological impact yet.

Personally, I suspect that the biblical sources come from and were handed down by a (politically and religiously historically) marginalized elite, which only

29 Adler, *The Origins of Judaism*.

gained historical importance and had an influence on the broader population in the Hasmonean period. However, in whatever circles of scribes or *literati* the biblical sources may have originated and transmitted – we just do not know for sure. This means that while these sources must be included as a definite factor in the historical reconstruction of the religious history of Judaism, they should be regarded as a (still unexplained) marginal phenomenon within the history of ancient Judaism, and Yahwism in particular, but the historical reconstruction should not be based on them. We should therefore stop pretending that we know more than can be known. If this is achieved, a great deal would already have been achieved.

Bibliography

Adler, Yonathan, *The Origins of Judaism: An Archaeological-Historical Reappraisal* (The Anchor Yale Bible Reference Library), New Haven: Yale University Press 2022.

Alstola, Tero, *Judeans in Babylonia: A Study of Deportees in the Sixth and Fifth Century BCE* (Culture and History of the Ancient Near East 109), Leiden: Brill 2020.

Barnea, Gad, "*Interpretatio Ivdaica* in the Achaemenid Period," JAJ 14 (2023): 1–37.

Barnea, Gad, "Yahwistic Identity in the Achaemenid period." *Zeitschrift für die Alttestamentliche Wissenschaft* 136.1 (2024): 1–14.

Becking, Bob, *Identity in Persian Egypt: The Fate of the Yehudite Community of Elephantine*, University Park Pennsylvania: Eisenbrauns/The Pennsylvania State University Press 2020.

Edelman, Diana, "Yhwh Shomron and Yhwh Elohim in the Achaemenid Province of Samaria," Pages 35–80 in *Yahwism under the Achaemenid Empire, Prof. Shaul Shaked in memoriam*. Edited by Gad Barnea and Reinhard G. Kratz. *BZAW*. Berlin: de Gruyter, 2024.

Frevel, Christian, *Geschichte Israels* (Kohlhammer Studienbücher Theologie), Stuttgart: Kohlhammer Verlag ^{2}2018.

Granerød, Gard, *Dimensions of Yahwism in the Persian Period: Studies in the Religion and Society of the Judean Community at Elephantine* (BZAW 488), Berlin: De Gruyter 2016.

Hensel, Benedikt, Adamczewski, Bartosz, Nocquet, Dany (eds.), *Social Groups behind Biblical Traditions: Identity Perspectives from Egypt, Transjordan, Mesopotamia, and Israel in the Second Temple Period* (FAT 167), Tübingen: Siebeck Mohr 2023.

Jacobs, Bruno, Rollinger, Robert R. (eds.), *A Companion to the Achaemenid Persian Empire*, 2 vols. John Wiley & Sons inc. 2021

Kratz, Reinhard G, *Translatio imperii: Untersuchungen zu den aramäischen Danielerzählungen und ihrem theologiegeschichtlichen Umfeld* (WMANT 63), Neukirchen Vluyn: Neukirchener Verlag 1991.

Kratz, Reinhard G, *The Composition of the Narrative Books of the Old Testament*, translated by John Bowden, London: T & T Clark International 2005 (German original version *Die Komposition der erzählenden Bücher des Alten Testaments*, Göttingen: Vandenhoeck & Ruprecht 2000).

Kratz, Reinhard G, "The Second Temple of Jeb and Jerusalem," pages 247–264 in: O. Lipschits and M. Oeming (eds.), *Judah and the Judeans in the Persian Period*, Winona Lake: Eisenbrauns 2006, (German version in: R. G. Kratz, *Das Judentum im Zeitalter des Zweiten Tempels: Kleine Schriften I* [FAT 42], Tübingen: Mohr Siebeck ^{2}2013, 60–78)

Kratz, Reinhard G, "Zwischen Elephantine und Qumran: Das Alte Testament im Rahmen des Antiken Judentums," pages 129–146 in A. Lemaire (Hg.), *Supplements to Vetus Testamentum, Congress Volume Ljubljana 2007*, Leiden: Brill 2010.

Kratz, Reinhard G, "Judean Ambassadors and the Making of Jewish Identity: The Case of Hananiah, Ezra, and Nehemiah," pages 421–444 in O. Lipschits et al. (eds.), *Judah and the Judeans in the Achaemenid Period: Negotiating Identity in an International Context*, Winona Lake: Eisenbrauns 2011. (German version in: C. Allison et al. [eds.], *From Daena to Din: Religion, Kultur und Sprache der iranischen Welt* [Festschrift Philip Kreyenboek zum 60. Geburtstag], Wiesbaden: Harrassowitz 2009, 377–398).

Kratz, Reinhard G, *Historical and Biblical Israel: The History, Tradition, and Archives of Israel and Judah*, translated by Paul Michael Kurtz, Oxford: Oxford University Press 2015 (German original version: *Historisches und Biblisches Israel: Drei Überblicke zum Alten Testament*, Tübingen: Mohr Siebeck Verlag, 2013, 2nd. revised and enlarged edn. 2017).

Kratz, Reinhard G, "Arameans and Judeans: Ethnography and Identity at Elephantine," pages 56–85 in A. Salvesen et al. (eds.), *Israel in Egypt: The Land of Egypt as Concept and Reality for Jews in Antiquity and the Early Medieval Period* (Ancient Judaism and Early Christianity 110), Leiden: Brill 2020.

Kratz, Reinhard G, "'Fossile Überreste des unreformierten Judentums in fernem Lande'? Das Judentum in den Archiven von Elephantine und Al-Yaḫudu," ZAW 132 (2020): 23–39.

Kratz, Reinhard G, "Ahiqar and Bisitun: The Literature of the Judeans at Elephantine," pages 301–322 in: R. G. Kratz and B. U. Schipper (eds.), *Elephantine in Context: Studies on the History, Religion and Literature of the Judeans in Persian Period* (FAT 155), Tübingen: Mohr Siebeck 2022, (repr. in: M. Folmer [ed.], *Elephantine Revisited: New Insights in the Judean Community and Its Neighbors*, University Park, Pennsylvania: Eisenbrauns/The Pennsylvania State University Press 2022, 67–85).

Lemaire, André, "Everyday Life according to the Ostraca of Elephantine," pages 365–373 in O. Lipschits et al. (eds.), *Judah and the Judeans in the Achaemenid Period: Negotiating Identity in an International Context*, Winona Lake: Eisenbrauns 2011.

Porten, Bezalel, *Archives from Elephantine*, Berkeley: University of California Press 1968

Wright, Jacob L., *Rebuilding Identity: The Nehemiah Memoir and its Earliest Readers* (BZAW 348), Berlin: De Gruyter 2004.

Oded Lipschits

“Those who live in these ruins in the land of Israel” (Ezekiel 33:24): Some Thoughts on Living in the Shadow of Ruins in Persian-period Judah

This paper aims to add another layer of understanding to the Jerusalemite theology of the Persian period as reflected in the biblical texts. It proposes that the tensions between the poor living conditions, the longing for the glorious past, and the expectations for a divine change in the near future, which are so clear in biblical texts written throughout this period, are also reflected in the archaeology of Jerusalem. This was a reality of daily life in Jerusalem throughout the Persian period, and it probably continued into the early Hellenistic period and until the construction of the Hasmonaean city in the 2nd century BCE.

Unlike in the rural settlements that continued to exist in the vicinity of Jerusalem, the city itself was destroyed by the Babylonians and left in ruins. Not much changed in the Persian period, and from an archaeological perspective, Jerusalem did not really return to being a “city” until the late 2nd century BCE. Until this time, it was no more than a very small, poor, and sparsely populated settlement that existed around the temple – quite similar in many respects to the sparse residential quarter that existed below the temple on Mount Gerizim during the same time span.[1] This situation changed only in the Hasmonaean period (the second half of the 2nd century BCE), when Jerusalem established itself as a major city for the first time since the early 6th century BCE. In this period, Jerusalem was well populated, surrounded by strong fortifications, and had rich material culture.

In the following, I suggest that for “the people of the land” (those who were not deported to Babylon before and after the destruction of Jerusalem), the ruined city symbolized the punishment that came upon the sinful Jerusalemite elite, contrary to the fate of those who remained in Judah in their villages and on their land. For the exiled elite in Babylon and for the very few among them who came

1 See Magen, “The Dating of the First Phase”; Magen, *Mount Gerizim Excavation II*. See also Edelman, “Yhwh Shomron and Yhwh Elohim in the Achaemenid Province of Samaria,” in this volume.

Oded Lipschits, Tel Aviv University, Israel

https://doi.org/10.1515/9783111018638-009

back to Judah during the Persian period, the interpretation of the fate of Jerusalem and the condition of the ruined city were totally different. Priests, Levites, and other temple servants who lived around the temple in this still-ruined city during the Persian and early Hellenistic periods developed, based on these ruins, the image of a glorious Jerusalem of the past. For them, these ruins were proof of the city's grandeur in ancient times and the source of their hope for a glorious future.

As much as it contrasted with the reality of the city in the Persian period, the legendary image of glorious Jerusalem was both the "source of" and the "fuel for" the glorification of Jerusalem, which shaped the image of the city within the memory of the people. In my opinion, the main theological question was to what extent they could and whether they were allowed to actually change the fate of Jerusalem.[2]

The tension between their present situation and the hopes for a change, as well as bitter disappointments for the change that did not come, was not limited to biblical texts but was a daily reality in Jerusalem during the entire Persian and early Hellenistic periods. This was partially an expression of the poverty prevalent in this period, but another part of it was an expression of the intentional reality of living in the shadow of the ruins of the past, an action designed to perpetuate the past.

This reality should be viewed as a Persian-period Jerusalemite "landscape of memory"[3] that served as a physical and active reminder of the glory of the past

2 This question has continued to preoccupy the Jewish world throughout its history even after the destruction of the Second Temple. One of the main discussions of this question is based on the text in the Gemara (*Ketubot* 111a). Rabbi Yossi bar Hanina interprets certain passages of the Song of Songs (2:7; 3:5; 8:4) as suggesting that there are three oaths binding the Jewish people in their relationship with the non-Jewish world. The first is that the Jews should not "go up as a wall," meaning that they should not return to the land of Israel by force, interfering with nature and against the will of the nations of the world, but should wait for God to decide to return Israel to the land.

3 "Landscapes of memory" are a well-known and well-defined phenomenon throughout history and are usually described as a social phenomenon: Practices of memory contextualize certain places as meaningful in relationship to the past. For the definition of this phenomena, see Maus, "Landscapes of Memory." Geographers like Lowenthal ("Past Time, Present Place") and historians such as Schama (*Landscape and Memory*) use the term "landscape" in conjunction with memory to describe geographical imaginations of the pastness of our world. For the much wider definition of this phenomenon in archaeology, where "all landscapes are 'historical', provided that they are now – or were once – altered, inhabited, visited, or interpreted by people ... In fact, it can be argued that very few parts of the world do not fulfil the criterion of being 'historical landscapes'; landscapes in which the past accumulates or is created through human action," see Holtorf and Williams, "Landscapes and Memories." The bibliography on this subject is vast; see, e.g., Van Dyke and Alcock, *Archaeologies of Memory.*"

and was intended to perpetuate this memory against the reality of the present. It may have also been part of the attempt to speed up the long-awaited divine intervention into the present situation. This is a common phenomenon throughout history, and recent decades of archaeological research have dealt with this subject since becoming cognizant of its existence.[4] It seems that the ruins of Jerusalem had a similar status for the inhabitants of Judah as Hazor and Megiddo had for the inhabitants of these Canaanite cities' ruins and Troy for the inhabitants of its ruins, which stood visible for hundreds of years. The place of Jerusalem throughout the Persian and early Hellenistic periods can be compared to the place of Troy throughout the centuries after its destruction, and it seems that Morris's summary for Troy is also applicable to Jerusalem:

> The ruined city functioned as the primary backdrop to events imagined at Troy or rites performed before its walls ... For several centuries, the site was primarily a locus of pilgrimage and homage, a true 'landscape of memory,' prior to the Hellenistic revival of the site as a rebuilt city with a new temple to Athena.[5]

In this paper, after **(a)** a short introduction to problems of the study of the Persian period in Judah and the recent progress in understanding the material culture of the period, I describe **(b)** the origin and history of the rural Persian-period settlement in Judah, demonstrating that it provides evidence for the continued existence of the "people of the land" (עם הארץ) – the people who remained in the tiny, peripheral province of Judah after the destruction of Jerusalem, the deportation of the elite, and end of its urban society. These people are the rural communities who preserved the traditional material culture in Judah from before the Babylonian destruction into the periods following it. These are the countryside settlements that display the continuity of the imperial administration in Judah. They are the portion of the people that, according to their own understanding of history, did not sin and were not punished with destruction and exile. For them, Jerusalem's fate was the ultimate proof of the elite class's sin and the divine punishment they got in return.

---

4 See Zuckerman, "Ruin Cults at Iron I Hazor." Cf. Na'aman, "Memories of Canaan," 140, n. 18. See differently, however, Kleiman, "Living on the Ruins," 27–38. Similar phenomena have also been observed at other sites in the southern Levant. See, e.g., the suggestions regarding the destruction of Stratum VIA at Megiddo (Kleiman, et al., "Cult Activity at Megiddo," 26; Fig. 13; Kleiman and Dunseth, "Area W," 166–179. Cf. also the explanation for the treatment of the inhabitants of the Iron I village at Tel Aphek, who refrained from building over the ruins of the Egyptian estate (Gadot, "Iron Age," 88. For other studies relating to this subject, see, e.g., Prent, "Glories of the Past in the Past," 81–103; Greenberg, "The Afterlife of Tells," 337–343.

5 Morris, "Troy between Bronze and Iron Ages," 65.

(c) The destruction of Jerusalem stands in contrast to the continuity of the rural settlement surrounding the city and to the continuity that is clearly evident in the administration and rural economy. The fate of the city reflects the fate of the local elite that were deported to Babylon. But from an archaeological point of view, Jerusalem evinces no major changes from the time after the 586 BCE destruction through the Babylonian, Persian and early Hellenistic periods. Without the biblical descriptions, we would not know about the existence of the "return to Zion" and the reconstruction of the temple. Against this background and that of the biblical descriptions, the change in Jerusalem must be understood as **(d)** evidence of the "sons of the exile" (בני הגולה), the "holy seed" (זרע הקודש) returning to Jerusalem after receiving approval from Persian authorities to go to Jerusalem and rebuild the temple.[6] These "returnees" were a small, representative group of the elite who were deported to Babylon about two generations earlier, after the Babylonian destruction of Jerusalem. They were probably a very small community, one that had no expression in the material culture, and there is no evidence of demographic change in Judah throughout the Persian period.

This is the basis of my attempt to **(e)** understand the reality revealed through the archaeological excavations in Jerusalem, especially the Persian-period building exposed in the Giv'ati Parking Lot in the City of David. This building was constructed right next to and within the ruins of the Iron Age city, a situation that lasted into the early Hellenistic period. From the biblical descriptions, it appears that **(f)** the "returnees" to Jerusalem had difficulties in rebuilding the temple, which was delayed for an entire generation. The rebuilding of the city was also delayed, and it remained impoverished and empty for several generations. This is evidence not only for the small number of these "returnees" and the tensions with those who remained in the land. It also seems that there were questions and doubts among the small group of returnees: Is it indeed the time to build the temple? The city? Is this even necessary? Should we wait for divine intervention and approval? Based on this, I suggest that a "landscape of memory" existed in this period, and people from the community of "returnees" preferred to live alongside the glory of the past without any real attempt to actually change it, waiting instead for the divine signal and divine change that was to come.

---

6 See also Pearce, "Through a Babylonian looking glass: a perspective on foreign wives," in this volume.

1 Problems with the Study of the History and Archaeology of Persian-period Judah and Recent Developments in Understanding Its Material Culture

From a historical point of view, the 205 years between 539/538 and 333 BCE, the so-called Persian period, constitute a well-defined phase. A clear opening to this period is marked by Cyrus the Great's conquest of Babylon, and a defined end is marked by the fall of the Persian empire into the hands of Alexander the Great's army. However, no clear chronological foothold for any historical or archaeological aspect of the study of Judah in the Persian period has been found in or around the 206-year slot between 539 and 333 BCE. There is also no apparent indication of any variation between this period and the preceding one (the so called "Babylonian period" or "exilic period" of the 6th century BCE) nor with the subsequent period (the early Hellenistic period in the late 4th and 3rd centuries BCE). This is a long period with only minor and gradual changes in the material culture, and there is not even a single clear destruction layer after 586 BCE that can be used as an archaeological and chronological anchor and historical tool for reconstructing actual events described in biblical and extrabiblical texts.

On one side of this period stands the Babylonian destruction of the early 6th century BCE. Even without the biblical description – and only on the basis of the archaeological evidence – archaeological research could easily have reconstructed that the destruction layers, demographic crisis, and changes in many aspects of the material culture were all part of a single crisis at the beginning of the 6th century BCE.[7] This destruction could easily have been connected to the Babylonian empire and compared with parallel processes in neighboring areas such as Ammon and Ashkelon, which show a similar fate.[8] Many fundamental features of the material culture that developed over the hundreds of years preceding the 586 BCE event disappeared, the Judahite urban centers were destroyed, and the settlement pattern changed to a rural one, which stayed typical of Judah until the 2nd century BCE.[9]

There are only minor changes in the material culture at the end of the 6th century BCE, and the beginning of the postexilic period does not exist from the archaeological point of view. No demographic change can be detected, nor can

7 Lipschits, *The Fall and Rise of Jerusalem*, 185–191.
8 Lipschits, "Ammon in Transition"; Fantalkin, "Why Did Nebuchadnezzar."
9 Lipschits, "Shedding New Light." Cf. Faust, *Judah in the Neo-Babylonian Period.*

any changes in settlement patterns, administration, economy, pottery production, or any other aspect of the material culture, probably aside from a marked change in glyptic traditions and the disappearance of icons in seals used for stamping jar handles.[10] There are only small and gradual changes in all aspects of the material culture (from script to pottery) that slowly brought new shapes and characteristics and created the “classic” Persian-period shapes and features that crystallized in and characterized the second half of the 5th and the early 4th centuries BCE. Later, there are further slow and gradual changes that created the so-called “late Persian–early Hellenistic” material culture of the late 4th and early 3rd centuries BCE – again, with no single, clear chronological/historical foothold for the date of the change.[11]

The outcome of this situation is that there are no clear archaeological, chronological or historical anchors between the events of 586 and the second half of the 2nd century BCE – both before and after the 206-year interlude of the Persian period. Furthermore, in contrast to the detailed historical information from before this period (esp. in 1–2 Kings and other biblical sources that shed light on the late First Temple period, as well as Assyrian, Babylonian and other historical sources) and the detailed sources about the Hasmonean period that followed (esp. the book of Maccabees, but also other Jewish Apocryphal texts as well as Hellenistic and Roman writings), the historical sources concerning this 450-year period are few and far between, which also makes it a “dark age” from a historical point of view.[12]

The main difficulty with this period, and the reason for the paucity of historical sources, is that it is indeed an intermediate period in which Judah existed as a small and poor province under the rule of the Babylonian, Persian, Ptolemaic, and Seleucid empires. The starting point of this period – the destruction of Jerusalem in 586 BCE by the Babylonians and the deportation of a large number of the elite – marked not only the change in status of Judah from a semi-independent kingdom to a province; it also led to a sharp decline in all aspects of material culture. All of the Jerusalemite elite were deported to Babylon, including “all the men of valor, seven thousand, and the craftsmen and the smiths, one thousand,

---

10 On the lions that characterize the Judahite stamp impressions of the 6th century BCE, see Ornan and Lipschits, “The Lion Stamp Impressions from Judah.” The use of symbols in the stamp impression system ceased to exist and during all the Persian and early Hellenistic periods the seals in this system contained only script. See Lipschits and Vanderhooft, *Yehud Stamp Impressions*.

11 Lipschits, *Fall and Rise of Jerusalem*, 185–206; Lipschits, “Persian Period Judah.” Cf. Faust, Settlement Dynamics.”

12 Grabbe, “A History of the Jews.”

all strong and fit for war" (2 Kgs 24:16). The situation did not improve in the Persian period, and the poor province with its nominated governors did not acquire the means, ability, or perhaps even permission to undertake building projects in Jerusalem or in any other urban center in the land. The lack of skilled artisans during the Persian period in every field of the economy, administration, and daily life is one of its prominent characteristics. The inferior building techniques, the poor quality of the pottery, and the seals, all of which probably resulted from the lack of raw materials and the need to reuse existing resources such as building stones and metals, or to use inexpensive substitutes, are all expressions of this situation in the Persian-period material culture. It seems to me that this is one further explanation for the lack of architectural and other finds from this period and for the relatively ease in which Persian-period building remains and other finds could have been removed and lost during and after the Hellenistic period. It is worth noting that this characteristically low quality of the material culture continued throughout the 450 years of the Babylonian, Persian and early Hellenistic periods, and a noticeable change occurred only at the beginning of the Hasmonean period, with the renewal of the monarchy in Jerusalem.[13]

Progress in the study and understanding of the material culture – mainly of the 200 years of the Persian period but also of the 50 years of the Babylonian period that preceded it and the 150 years of the early Hellenistic period that followed – came largely on the basis of the excavations at Ramat Raḥel.[14] The excavations there aided in progressing the study of the stamp impressions on the handles and bodies of storage jars,[15] and they contributed to the ability to identify pottery assemblages from these periods and to define their context and development processes.[16]

Most studies on the archaeological material in Second Temple Judah start with the beginning of the Persian period following the obvious periodization. However, despite the hard blow that the Babylonians dealt to the Judahite urban and military centers, it has become clear that all the different aspects of Persian-period material culture were continuations from the late Iron Age through the 6th century BCE, with only marginal changes in material culture during the transition from Babylonian to Persian-Achaemenid rule. Most of the characteristics of Babylonian and early Persian-period material culture (like the script, stamp

---

13 Lipschits, *Fall and Rise of Jerusalem*, 185–206; Lipschits, "Persian Period Judah."

14 Lipschits, Freud, Oeming, and Gadot, *Ramat Raḥel VI.*

15 Lipschits, *Age of Empires.*

16 Lipschits, *Fall and Rise of Jerusalem*, 192–206; Freud, *Judahite Pottery*; Freud, *Pottery of Babylonian-period Jerusalem*, 231–262; Sandhaus (Reem), *The Nexus of Culture.*

impressions, and pottery) can be defined as intermediate Iron Age–Persian-period material.[17]

Furthermore, although most studies on the material culture of the early Second Temple period describe the Persian period as a marked and defined period from an archaeological point of view, there are three distinctive sub-phases within the 200 years of Persian rule in Judah, with a marked continuity and development between them:[18]

a) The early Persian period in the late 6th and early 5th centuries BCE is a transitional period from the Babylonian period, with no marked change in the material culture. Besides the disappearance of the use of icons in stamps used for stamping jar handles, all other aspects of material culture (including pottery and script) look like a clear continuation. For this period, one should also include the early *yhwd* stamp impressions on jar handles.[19]
b) The typical, "classic," and well-known material culture of the Persian period can be dated to the second half of the 5th century BCE and the first half of the 4th century BCE. The main change in the form, style, paleography, and orthography of the *yhwd* stamp system occurred during the late 5th or even early 4th century BCE, probably as a result of tighter Persian control in the administration. As part of this change, some secondary administrative centers took on a much more important role in the system, and the most important Persian-period pottery and other finds were discovered at these sites.[20]
c) The late Persian–early Hellenistic material culture is well dated to the late 4th and early 3rd centuries BCE.[21] The changes in the material culture (especially the script and pottery) were probably slow and gradual, and as can be seen from the *yhwd* stamp impressions, there is a clear continuity in administration and economy from the late Persian to the early Hellenistic period in nearly every aspect.[22] The marked changes in almost every facet of the material culture occurred in the middle of the 2nd century BCE, but examining this change is beyond the scope of this essay.[23]

---

17 Freud, *Judahite Pottery*; Freud, *Pottery of Babylonian-period Jerusalem*.
18 Lipschits, *Fall and Rise of Jerusalem*, 185–206; Lipschits, *Persian Period Judah*.
19 Lipschits and Vanderhooft, *Yehud Stamp Impressions* (2011), 81–252; Freud, *Judahite Pottery*.
20 Lipschits and Vanderhooft, *Yehud Stamp Impressions* (2011), 253–592; Freud, *Judahite Pottery*.
21 Sandhaus and Kreimerman, "Late 4th/3rd Century BCE Transition"; Shatil, *Persian Period and-Early Hellenistic Pottery*.
22 Lipschits and Vanderhooft, "Yehud Stamp Impressions" (2007); Lipschits and Vanderhooft, "Yehud Stamp Impressions," (2011); Shatil, *Persian Period and-Early Hellenistic Pottery*; Shalom, Lipschits, Shatil, and Gadot, "Judah in the Early Hellenistic Period," 63–79.
23 Tal, *The Archaeology of Hellenistic Palestine*; Bocher and Lipschits, *The Corpus of yršlm Stamp Impressions*.

The meager finds from the Persian period at all the main sites is a basic fact that all scholars excavating sites, surveying areas, or studying the history of Judah during this period have had to deal with and explain. It is clear that there was a cessation of urban life during this period and a concentration of the population in rural settlements, and as part of that, it might be that in some former Iron Age settlements, the Persian-period private dwellings were built outside the defined areas of the earlier destroyed towns. Undoubtedly, the Persian-period occupation levels were damaged in some cases by intensive building activities conducted during the Hellenistic-Roman periods.

2 The Origin and History of the Rural Settlement in Persian-period Judah

The rural settlement that existed in Judah in the Persian and early Hellenistic periods and characterized its settlement and economy until the establishment of the Hasmonaean kingdom in the late 2nd century BCE is rooted in its settlement, economy, and administration after it became a vassal Assyrian kingdom and especially in the history of the land after Sennacherib's military campaign (701 BCE) and the loss of the Shephelah. During this period, the rural settlement around Jerusalem and in the region of Benjamin grew and became stronger. It was closely linked to the administrative center that existed during that period of time in Ramat Raḥel and was part of the economy and administration of Judah under the rule of the Assyrian empire.[24] It is also the outcome of the Babylonian conquest of Jerusalem in the early 6th century BCE, the destruction of the other urban and military centers, and the transition of Judah from vassal kingdom to Babylonian province.[25] During this period, the Judahite population that continued to subsist in the northern Judean highlands, as well as in the Benjamin region, was able to preserve its economy, ways of life, administration, and material culture, and it probably also preserved its identity as the "people of land" (עם הארץ) – those who kept their pre-exilic Judean identity.[26]

The area of Benjamin became an important part of the Judahite economy and administration already in the 7th century BCE, probably after the Shephelah

24 Koch, and Lipschits, "The Rosette Stamped Jar Handle"; Lipschits, "The Changing Faces"; Gadot, "In the Valley of the King."

25 Lipschits, "Nebuchadrezzar's Policy"; Lipschits, *The Fall and Rise of Jerusalem*, 68–97.

26 Lipschits, "The Rural Economy of Judah." Cf. also Lipschits, "The Rural Settlement in Judah"; Lipschits, "Shedding New Light."

was cut off from Judah as a result of Sennacherib's campaign. The region was not destroyed during the Babylonian military campaign against Jerusalem in the early 6th century BCE.[27] Likewise, the area to the south of Jerusalem, with Ramat Raḥel at its center, probably had the same fate as the Benjamin region.[28] It seems that the Babylonian period was the historical point in time when the imperial administration separated Jerusalem from the agricultural area that surrounded it and the city became an independent district (the district of Jerusalem). This was probably done in an attempt to isolate the city from its surroundings, leave it in ruins with minimum role and function in the new province, and let the region around it to continue to function as agricultural land. The area to the north of Jerusalem became the district of Mizpah (= Benjamin) with its center in Tel en-Nasbeh,[29] and the area to the south of Jerusalem became the district of Beth-haccerem with its center in Ramat Raḥel.[30]

---

27 Lipschits, "The History of the Benjaminite Region";Lipschits, *The Fall and Rise of Jerusalem*, 237–249; Lipschits, "Benjamin in Retrospective." It may be assumed that even before the fall of Jerusalem, the Babylonians had chosen Mizpah (Tel en-Nasbeh) as the alternative capital of the Babylonian province and had already appointed Gedaliah son of Ahikam as its first governor. See Lipschits, *The Fall and Rise of Jerusalem*, 68–125, 237–249. On Tel en-Nasbeh (Biblical Mizpah), see Zorn, *Tell en-Naṣbeh*. On the history of the site in the 6th century BCE, see Zorn, "Tell en-Nasbeh and the Problem."

28 Lipschits, *The Fall and Rise of Jerusalem*, 250–258. The Rephaim Valley, with its rich alluvial soil and moderately terraced slopes, as well as the Moza Valley along the Naḥal Sorek have historically been the prosperous agricultural districts in the environs of Jerusalem, vital to the economy of the city. There is clear evidence for associating the development of the Rephaim basin and the agricultural area to the south of Jerusalem, especially in the 7th century BCE, with the emergence of Ramat Raḥel as an administrative center in the region under Assyrian rule and with the organization of royal estates in the kingdom of Judah – probably after the period when Judah became an Assyrian vassal kingdom – and even more so after the loss of the Shephelah. The Rephaim basin and the rural settlement around Jerusalem flourished in the 7th century BCE more than in any other period in the history of Judah; see Gadot, "In the Valley of the King," 3–26. This settlement phenomenon fits the centralized processing demonstrated by the concentration of winepresses not associated with village infrastructure, the process of organized decanting and shipping of the wine, and the function of Ramat Raḥel in all periods in question as an administrative center in the region. See Gadot and Lipschits, "Ramat Raḥel and the Emeq Rephaim Sites," 88–96. (Hebrew); Lipschits, Gadot, Arubas, and Oeming, *What Are the Stones Whispering?*. The mounting archaeological data from this area confirms that the Rephaim and Moza Valleys continued to flourish agriculturally during the same periods in which Ramat Raḥel functioned as the main administrative center, i.e., from the very late Iron Age to the Persian and early Hellenistic periods, with no signs of hiatus. See Gadot and Lipschits, "Ramat Raḥel and the Emeq Rephaim Sites," 88–96.

29 On the importance of the change in the status of the Benjamin region during this period, see the detailed discussion in Lipschits, "Benjamin in Retrospective," 161–200.

30 On the importance of this district and its role in the district system of the province of Judah, see Lipschits, "Rural Economy of Judah," 239–240, 244–246.

The administrative situation did not change in the Persian period, and these three districts continued to exist even after the Persians authorized the reconstruction of the temple. Each district continued to function as a separate entity, each with its own specific role: Jerusalem once again became the cultic center of the province, but remained isolated from its close surroundings. Mizpah had become the political center of the province already during the Babylonian period and continued to function as such, while also serving as the center of the Mizpah (= Benjamin) district. Ramat Raḥel remained the main administrative center for the collection of agricultural produce and continued to function as the center of the district that included most of the rural settlement to the west and south of Jerusalem – the district of Beth-haccerem. Each site – Jerusalem, Mizpah and Beth-haccerem (= Ramat Raḥel) had its own specific function and also served as the center of its own district.[31]

Judah continued to exist as a rural society with the same geopolitical structure until the 2nd century BCE. It is not only the role of Ramat Raḥel that points in this direction but also the continuation of the stamped jar administration. The corpus of stamped and incised jar handles found in Judah, especially in and around Ramat Raḥel, is the key to understanding this period. About 3,000 stamped jar handles have been discovered in archaeological excavations and surveys of Judah from the 600 years when the kingdom/province of Judah was under imperial rule.[32] This is precisely the period in which Ramat Raḥel served as the region's administrative and main collection center for agricultural products,[33] primarily wine and oil stored in jars.[34] Ramat Raḥel was the main center of stamped jar handles throughout the Babylonian, Persian, and Hellenistic periods,[35] and all in

31 For more details on the rural settlement during this period, see Lipschits, "Rural Economy of Judah," 237–264.

32 Lipschits, "Age of Empires."

33 For a general summary of Ramat Raḥel during the "Age of Empires," see Lipschits, Gadot, Arubas, and Oeming, *What Are the Stones Whispering?*.

34 No other Judahite site, not even Jerusalem, can challenge Ramat Raḥel's record: Over 300 stamped handles from the late Iron Age were found at the site (see Lipschits, Gadot, Arubas, and Oeming, "Palace and Village," 16–17), including *lmlk* and "private" stamp impressions (late 8th and early 7th centuries BCE; see Lipschits, Sergi, and Koch, "Royal Judahite Jar Handles"), concentric circle incisions (mid-7th century BCE; see Lipschits, Sergi, and Koch, "Judahite Stamped and Incised," 7–8), and rosette stamp impressions (late 7th–early 6th centuries BCE; see Koch and Lipschits, "The Rosette Stamped Jar Handle System," 60–61).

35 About 77 lion stamped handles dating to the 6th century BCE (Ornan, and Lipschits, "The Lion Stamp Impressions," 69–91), more than 300 *yhwd* stamp impressions dating from the late 6th to mid-2nd centuries BCE (see Lipschits and Vanderhooft, "Yehud Stamp Impressions" (2011), 107–110), and 33 *yršlm* stamp impressions dating to the 2nd century BCE (see Bocher and Lipschits, *The Corpus of yršlm Stamp Impressions*, 103–104).

all, the phenomenon of jars with stamped handles being collected and stored at Ramat Raḥel continued over these six centuries in a constant, systematized administrative system continually based on agricultural settlements, royal estates, administrative centers, and the system of districts in Judah.[36]

The origin and history of rural settlement in Persian-period Judah provides evidence of the continued existence of the "people of the land" (עם הארץ) – the people who remained in Judah after the destruction of Jerusalem and the deportation of the elites and urban denizens. They lived mainly in the rural area around Jerusalem, in the districts of the small province of Judah, dwelling at the peripheries of the empires.[37] This is the settlement that expresses the continuity in the material culture and puts the continuity of the imperial administration in Judah on display. This is also the place that preserved the local Judahite identity, alongside memories, traditions, and beliefs.

The deportation from Jerusalem, and probably from other (mainly urban) population centers, brought to an end the rule of the Jerusalemite elite in Judah and created the major separation between those who remained in the land and the exiles in Babylon.[38] Furthermore, even the first Babylonian deportation of about 10,000 people of the kingdom's elite in 597 BCE, but especially the 586 BCE deportation of another group of approximately the same size,[39] left the two communities – the exiles and those who remained in Judah – facing essential questions for the continued existence of each, and all the more so concerning their identities and their relationships to each other.

For the people who remained in the land and became the local rural community already in the exilic period, the fate of Jerusalem was the ultimate proof of the exiled elite's sin and the divine punishment that they received as a result. This argument recalls Jer 2:5 and highlights the source of the Judahite world view,[40] which apparently was expressed in the prophecies of Isaiah (6:11–13). In response to this argument, Ezekiel (11:17–21) promised that those deported from their land would be destined to return to Israel (vv. 17–20); he prophesied a grim future for "those who remained" (v. 21).[41]

---

36 See a detailed summary in Lipschits, "Age of Empires," 143–153.

37 Cf. Smith, *Palestinian Parties and Politics*. But see against it the critique of Grabbe, *A History of the Jews and Judaism*, 257–258.

38 See the wide discussion and the definition of the two different groups in: Rom-Shiloni, *Exclusive Inclusivity*, 1–30, with further literature.

39 On the numbers of the two deportations, see the discussion and summary in Lipschits, *The Fall and Rise of Jerusalem*, 258–271.

40 See the references in Japhet, "People and Land," 123 n. 21; Rom-Shiloni, *God in Times of Destructions*, 279–280.

41 See Albertz, *Israel in Exile*, 363; Rom-Shiloni, *God in Times of Destructions*, 244; Rom-Shiloni, *Exclusive Inclusivity*, 144–156.

"Those who remained" saw themselves as "the people of God." Their presence in the land was the fulfillment of the promise given to Abraham (Ezek 33:24).[42] However, Ezekiel prophesied that they would be utterly destroyed (vv. 25–29).[43] Both of these arguments, as well as the prophet's harsh reply to them, reveal the profound ideological rift between the two segments of the people already during the time between the two exiles (597–586 BCE). In my opinion, the rift stemmed primarily from the blow to the status of the people's leaders who were deported to Babylon and the attempt by "those who remained" to take the place of the deported elite and their property, as expressed, for example, in Gedaliah's call to the local Judahites who were left in the land (Jeremiah 40:10).[44]

3 Jerusalem and the Fate of the Judahite Elite

The destruction of Jerusalem stands in contrast to the rural settlement continuity surrounding the city and the clear continuity evident in the administration and the rural economy. The fate of the city reflects the fate of the local elite who were deported to Babylon, but even in view of the heavy destruction of Jerusalem and the description of the deportations that took place as part of it, the picture of a complete emptying of the city seems problematic.[45] Furthermore, from an

42 On Ezek 33:24 as a citation of the people who remained in the land, see Garffy, *A Prophet Confronts His People*, 122–123; Rom-Shiloni, God in Times of Destructions, 70, n. 51, 244; Rom-Shiloni, *Exclusive Inclusivity*, 144–156.

43 On the connection between these arguments and the prophecies of Second Isaiah and the changes these arguments underwent during the exile, see Japhet, "People and Land"; Rom-Shiloni, *God in Times of Destructions*, 58–62, 70–71.

44 See on this Albertz, *Israel in Exile*, 90–96.

45 There is general agreement that Jerusalem and its immediate environs were destroyed during the Babylonian military campaign against the kingdom of Judah, which took place between 588 and 586 BCE. This was the most severe crisis in the region in the first millennium BCE. The finds from the excavations in Jerusalem show a clear picture of the Babylonian destruction, and evidence of the destruction was revealed in various parts of the city from the end of the First Temple period. These destruction layers were uncovered in excavations conducted by Avigad in the Jewish Quarter, Kenyon in the eastern slope of the City of David, Shiloh in Areas D, E, and G in the City of David, at the citadel, by E. Mazar in some of the buildings in the Ophel, and by Gadot and Shalev in the new excavations at the Giv'ati Parking Lot. For a detailed discussion on the size and status of the city in the Babylonian, Persian, and early Hellenistic periods, see Lipschits, "Judah, Jerusalem and the Temple"; Lipschits, *The Fall and Rise of Jerusalem*, 206–271; Lipschits, "Achaemenid Imperial Policy"; Lipschits and Vanderhooft, "Jerusalem in the Persian and Hellenistic Periods," 106–115 [Hebrew]. For a comprehensive methodological discussion and a detailed archaeological survey concerning Persian-period finds in Jerusalem, see Lipschits, *Persian Period Judah*, 187–212. For modern methods of dating and understating the destruction

archaeological point of view, no change can be recognized in the transition from the 6th to 5th centuries BCE, from the time of the Babylonian exile to the days of the "return to Zion." The "*myth* of the mass return" is clear from an archaeological perspective, and it also seems that careful analysis of the biblical texts can support the conclusion that there is no clear boundary between the Babylonian and Persian periods.[46]

Furthermore, no clear finds have been exposed in the excavations conducted in the city from the nearly 400 years of the Persian and early Hellenistic periods, and until the Hasmonaean establishment of Jerusalem as their capital. Besides some remains of poor buildings constructed in the Persian and early Hellenistic periods among the ruins from the Babylonian destruction, without clearing these ruins (see further below), only potsherds, stamp impressions, and other small finds have been recovered, quite similar to what has been found in Jerusalem from the 6th century BCE – the time of the Babylonian exile.[47] In addition, most of the finds were exposed in later fills and without any clear stratigraphic or architectural context.[48]

Based on archaeological data from the Persian and early Hellenistic periods, it seems that during these four centuries, Jerusalem was no more than a small, unwalled, sparsely populated settlement. There is no way of knowing the extent of settlement on the Temple Mount, but in view of the existing data, the settlement in the City of David throughout this period comprised an area of about 50 dunams. The population of Jerusalem did not include more than 250–300 families, or approximately 1,000–1,250 people.[49] In the light of the archaeological data, this estimate seems maximalist, and based on the same data there are other estimations that set the population in Jerusalem at approximately 1,000 people,[50] and even ultra-minimalistic estimations of about a half this number.[51]

In light of this clear archaeological evidence, we should interpret the "return to Zion" as a slow and gradual process of a very small number of priests, together

---

of Jerusalem, see Vaknin, et al. "Earth's Magnetic Field"; Shalom, et al. "Destruction by Fire"; Shalom, "Babylonian Destruction."

46 See summary in Lipschits, *The Fall and Rise of Jerusalem*, 258–271; Lipschits, "Between Archaeology and Text"; Lipschits, "Jerusalem as a Symbol."

47 See the recent summary in Shalev, Shalom, Bocher, and Gadot, "New Evidence" (with further literature). The main new suggestion of this publication is that the center of Persian and early Hellenistic Jerusalem shifted to the western slope of the City of David ridge.

48 On the very slow and gradual development processes of Jerusalem in the Persian period, see Lipschits and Vanderhooft, "Jerusalem in the Persian and Hellenistic Periods," 106–115.

49 For further details, see Lipschits, "Jerusalem between Two Periods."

50 Geva, "Jerusalem's Population in Antiquity."

51 See Finkelstein, "Jerusalem in the Persian." Cf. the very similar estimation based on the interpretation of the biblical material by Zwickel, "Jerusalem und Samaria."

with other temple servants and members of the exiled elite, who did not leave an imprint on the archaeological data.

4 The "Returnees" in Jerusalem

Against the background of the biblical descriptions, especially in Ezra-Nehemiah, Haggai, and Zechariah, and assuming that they contain some historical reliability, the change in Jerusalem must be understood as evidence of the return of the "sons of the exile" (בני הגולה), the "holy seed" (זרע הקודש), to the city.[52] They were part of the core exilic community that continued to exist in Babylon and received approval from the Persian authorities to send representatives back to Jerusalem with one main goal: to renew the cult in Jerusalem and to rebuild the temple.[53]

As stated, the deportation from Judah was selective and limited in scope. At the center of the exile were the Jerusalem elite, who had led the people in Judah since the beginning of its history. At the same time, most of the population of the kingdom of Judah remained in place – on their land and in their villages around Jerusalem. For the first time, this population had to live without the religious, political, and economic elite who had always dominated it. The tension between the two parts of the people was clear and understandable and included serious disagreements – economic, political, social, and religious.

The days of exile – when the people's elite were cut off from the people in the land – was an exceptional and short period of time, and fifty years after the destruction and the deportation, the representatives of the exilic community in Babylon were authorized to return to Jerusalem and build the temple. As discussed above, during this short period, the ideological and theological gap between the exilic community and the "people who remained" in Judah, as well as the questions of identity of these two groups, had already developed. The approval to the exilic community given by Cyrus, who had just conquered Babylon and

52 On the "holy seed," see Becking, Continuity and Community," 270–272.

53 On the core-periphery relationship between the community in Babylon and its representatives in Jerusalem, see Bedford, "Diaspora." I tend to agree with Bedford that the local leadership was consistently sent from the "home" community in Babylon, and this community initiated and was responsible for everything that was done in Judah. However, I agree with Rom-Shiloni, (*Exclusive Inclusivity*, 34), that these points are also valid for the late 6th and 5th centuries BCE and thus cannot accept Bedford's suggestion that this situation reflects only the 4th century BCE. On this issue, see already Kessler, "The Diaspora in Zechariah," 129–137. Cf. Knoppers, "Ethnicity, Genealogy, Geography, and Change," 168.

inherited its vast empire, allowed them to rebuild the temple and thus restore their status over the "people who remained" in Judah.

This was a new phase in the relationship between the two Judahite communities, and a new phase in the much more direct conflict between them: Who was entitled to participate in the restoration of the temple?[54] The target audience of the Edict of Cyrus was part of the Judean exilic community in Babylon, who were chosen to return to Jerusalem to build the temple.[55] There is no wider authorization here – to go to Judah for any other purpose or to change the legal or demographic situation in Judah. The return was only to Jerusalem and solely for the purpose of building the temple, while all those who remained in Babylon were required to help the project via donations. Even during the detailed execution of the Edict of Cyrus, the emphasis is exactly the same: the returnees were those chosen to build the temple and to return to Jerusalem for this purpose, and the rest of the people who remained in Babylon were to assist via donations. Moreover, the description goes on to include the return of the temple vessels taken by the Babylonians during the destruction. This closes the cycle of destruction and exile, the pause in the temple service. Things finally fell into place – the Second Temple period could begin. The exclusion of those who remained in the land from the new political entity is also mentioned in connection with the reinstitution of the sanctuary (Ezra 3), the reconstruction of the temple (Ezra 4–6), and the reconstruction of the walls of Jerusalem (Neh 2:19–20).[56]

5 The Reality Revealed by the Archaeological Excavations in Jerusalem

Excavations of the Giv'ati parking lot, on the northwestern side of the City of David ridge, have uncovered a rich and monumental house, securely dated to the late Iron Age and with clear and strong indications of the Babylonian destruction

54 Many scholars have assumed that the return of the exilic community was the starting point for the conflict between the two communities. See in this direction, e.g., Smith, *The Religion of the Landless*, 179 and Kessler, "The Diaspora in Zechariah," 119–145. In the opposite direction, some scholars assume that this conflict started much later, during the 5th or even the 4th centuries BCE. See, e.g., Japhet, "People and Land," 42–61; Bedford, *Temple Restoration*, 42–61; Bedford, "Diaspora," 150–151.

55 See: Grabbe, *A History of the Jews*, 271–276.

56 See Rom-Shiloni, *Exclusive Inclusivity*, 33–47. On the place of Neh 2:19–20, see Wright, *Rebuilding Identity*, 112–118.

in 586 BCE.[57] This destroyed monumental building stood for decades, exposed for anyone to see, and was finally resettled during the early Persian period. A small, rectangular chamber was built into the collapse of the late Iron Age building. Throughout this structure's short-lived existence in the Persian period, it remained within the ruins of the ancient Iron Age construction, which had not been cleared away.[58] Moreover, walls, floors and tabun-ovens of two superimposed domestic structures were discovered ca. 30 m south of this building, dating to the same Persian period phase.[59] Persian-period pottery was also found in a large pit dug out slightly to the north, and analysis of this pottery dates it to both early and late Persian period (5th to 4th centuries BCE).[60]

Since Shiloh also observed similar Persian-period reuse of a partly destroyed Iron Age structure in the "Ashlar House" of Area E,[61] it is possible to reconstruct the characteristics of the settlement in Jerusalem during the Persian period as sparse and poor residences built into the ruins of the Iron Age city. Over hundreds of years, from the 5th to 2nd centuries BCE, the inhabitants of Jerusalem continued to live in and around the Iron Age ruins, generally without removing or clearing them out.

This poor architectural reality of life in the shadow of the Iron Age ruins stands in sharp contrast to the nature of the finds in these buildings, which is surprisingly rich. They include a large concentration of fish bones,[62] a rich collection of animal bones indicating accessibility to quality meat supply and premium meat cuts, some of which were redistributed from feasts and sacrifices,[63] and

---

57 On some of the impressive finds in this house, see Avisar, et al. "Jerusalem's Ivories.": 57–74. On the structure itself and the indications of its destruction, see Vaknin et al., "Earth's Magnetic Field"; Shalom et al., "Destruction by Fire"; Shalom, "Babylonian Destruction," 85–107.

58 See Shalev, Shalom, Bocher, and Gadot, "New Evidence," 160–161.

59 The structure was erroneously dated by its excavator to the Iron Age. See Ben-Ami, *Jerusalem*, 16–18. However, a reexamination of the pottery associated with this building proves that it should be dated to the early Persian period, very similar to the adjacent structure in the Giv'ati Parking Lot. See Freud, *Judahite Pottery*, 251–253.

60 See Shalev et al., "New Evidence," 160–161.

61 A large Iron Age structure was uncovered that was destroyed by a fierce fire, probably also as part of the Babylonian destruction of Jerusalem. Shilo noticed that in the Persian period, new floors were laid inside the destroyed building in several places and a small chamber was built in the corner. See De Groot and Bernick-Greenberg, *Excavations at the City of David*, 21–22.

62 See Spiciarich, *Religious and Socioeconomic Diversity*, table 5.30. This is the largest assemblage of fish bones found in Persian-period Jerusalem to-date.

63 Study of the animal remains demonstrates that the populations in Jerusalem continued to have access to livestock and their by-products. Moreover, Jerusalem continued to obtain meat in the same manner as before the destruction and abandonment of the city – although it does not appear that outside producers, as in earlier periods, exclusively supplied them. See Spiciarich, et al. "Continuity and Change."

also a fragment of a Bas vessel (depicting a human face) that also indicates trade and cultural contacts with the Phoenician coast. The relatively rich finds indicate that the settlement of this long, 400-year period was not merely temporary life in ruins but rather a planned reuse of the structure that continued to exist as it was until the end of the Persian period.[64]

It seems that the residents of Jerusalem ascribed great importance to returning and settling in the city in the very places that had been burned and destroyed at the end of its glory days and were still visible until the 2nd century BCE, when these structures were partly reused and rebuilt.[65] The fact that at this stage, some of the Iron Age walls were used while others became a source of building stones, and that the general plan of the new neighborhood established there continued the direction and general orientation from the Iron Age, indicates that the Iron Age remains continued to be seen on the surface and were known throughout the subsequent centuries.

This is an important example of the reality of life of the Persian-period Jerusalem elite, who had trade relations and a material culture that testifies to the status of those who lived in the houses close to the temple, although these houses were built into the ruins of the Iron Age city. We should remember that every time someone opened the door and stepped out from their house, they saw all around them the ruins of Iron Age buildings that had not been cleared away throughout the Persian period. This is the meaning of living in these "ruins in the land of Israel" (Ezek 33:24), inside a "landscape of memory," a daily reminder of the glorious past and a daily reflection of the impoverished present.

6 The Destroyed City as a Symbol

From the biblical descriptions, it appears that the "returnees" had difficulties in building the temple, which was delayed for an entire generation. They had even more difficult problems in building and inhabiting the city, which remained in misery for many generations, and the construction of a wall around Jerusalem was postponed for at least three generations. According to Ezra 1–6 (probably with some support from the prophecies in Haggai and Zechariah and with no support from any other source), the reconstruction of the temple was delayed for at least one generation after the first returnees arrived to Jerusalem with the old temple vessels from Babylon in order to renew the cult in Jerusalem.[66] According

64 See Shalev et al., "New Evidence," 167–168.

65 Shalev et al., "The Givʿati Parking Lot Excavations," 31.

66 See Bedford, *Temple Restoration*, and further below.

to the description in Nehemiah (with neither archaeological nor further textual support), the reconstruction of the city wall was completed only in the time of Nehemiah, in the mid-5th century BCE.[67] The narrative then claims (again without archaeological or further textual support) that it was only at this stage that Jerusalem reached population as high as one tenth of the province's inhabitants.[68]

Together with the wretched and poor material reality in Jerusalem throughout the Persian period as indicated by the archaeological findings, this attests to much more than the small number of these "returnees" and to their tensions with the "remainees" who lived with no temple in Jerusalem for many decades, and who probably understood the destruction of Jerusalem as part of the punishment of the elite, finding it difficult to accept the new return and the reestablishment of the old Jerusalemite elite's rule in Judah. This seems to me to much more broadly display an understanding, and perhaps even an ideological, theological, and moral belief and conception, that one should wait for the divine decision regarding the restoration of the ruins and the building of the temple and the city rather than to "force the issue" ("לדחוק את הקץ") and start building without the divine signal to do so. This was part of a desire not to change the existing situation in Jerusalem, to live within a landscape of memory of the city's glorious past, which evidences a tension between the poor reality, the longing for the glorious past, and the expectations for divine intervention in the near future. It might even be part of the attempt to speed up the long-awaited divine signal for coming change.

Based on the great gap between the architectural poverty of the houses built within the ruins of late Iron Age Jerusalem and the findings excavated in these houses – indicating trade relations with the Phoenician coast, rich food served to the small population in the city, and a material culture of higher quality than the houses in which the archaeological evidence was found – it seems that the ruins played a role beyond functionality and everyday comfort. In my opinion, among the people who came from Babylon and among the people who remained in Judah, two different perceptions prevailed regarding the question of rebuilding temple and city: should they wait for the divine signal, God's confirmation of the forgiveness of the people and their sins that led to the destruction, or should they start building without a sign from God, perhaps even as a step to earn God's approval and hasten the forgiveness of the sins? How was one to determine that

67 See Lipschits, "Nehemiah 3."
68 See Lipschits, "Literary and Ideological."

now was the time to rebuild the temple?[69] It is also possible that the two views did not fall neatly along the division between the "Golah community" who had returned to Jerusalem and those who had not been deported but remained living in Judah, and both groups had to deal with differing opinions on the matter.

The existence of both perspectives is most clearly expressed in the prophecy of Haggai, who encourages the people to build the temple in response to the explanation given for the delay in construction: "This people says: 'It is not yet time to rebuild the temple of Yahweh'" (Hag 1:2) (הָעָם הַזֶּה אָמְרוּ לֹא עֶת־בֹּא עֶת־ בֵּית יְהוָה לְהִבָּנוֹת).[70] Zechariah 1:12–17 can also be interpreted in this direction, and Ezekiel, for example (36:10, 33–38), speaks of the ruins in the land as evidence of God's existence and power and of the restoration of the ruins as related to the purification of sins, God's forgiveness, and the rebuilding of the land that will come only at the appointed time.

This is the basis of my attempt to understand the reality revealed in the archaeological excavations in Jerusalem. Furthermore, in my opinion, the small number of priests, Levites, and other temple servants who lived in this small "temple-village" below the Temple Mount during the Persian and early Hellenistic periods developed the image of the past glorious Jerusalem based on these ruins. For them, the ruins were a testament to the city's greatness in ancient times and the source of their hope for the glorious future. The legendary image of a glorious Jerusalem, as much as it contrasted with the actual reality of the Persian-period city, was both the "source of" and the "fuel for," so to speak, the glorification of Jerusalem, which shaped the image of the city within the memory of the people. The question was how much they were able, or if they were allowed at all, to change the fate of Jerusalem. The tension between the present situation and the hope for change, as well as the bitter disappointments for the change that did not come, exists not only in biblical texts but was a daily reality in Jerusalem throughout the Persian and early Hellenistic periods. This was a "landscape of memory" when people preferred to live alongside the glory of the past without any real attempt to actually change it, waiting instead for the divine signal and divine change that was to come.

---

69 As expressed very clearly in the discussion by Bedford, *Temple Restoration*, 85–181 (with further literature). Cf. also Bedford, *Temple Restoration*, 270: "the initial ideological problem to be addressed by Judeans who sought to rebuild the Jerusalem temple was determining that the deity did indeed wish to have his shrine rebuilt; that it was indeed 'time' to rebuild the temple."

70 On the MT text of this version, see Rudolph, *Haggai – Sacharja*, 29, n. 2 b; Wolff, *Haggai*, 14, n. 2 a-a.

Bibliography

Albertz, Rainer, *Israel in Exile: The History and Literature of the Sixth Century B.C.E.* Atlanta: SBL, 2003.

Avisar, Reli, Shalev, Yiftah, Shochat, Harel, Gadot, Yuval and Koch, Ido, Jerusalem's Ivories: A Collection of Decorated Ivory Panels from Building 100, Giv'ati Parking Lot Excavations and their Cultural Setting. *'Atiqot* 106 (2022): 57–74. http://www.atiqot.org.il/.

Becking, Bob, "Continuity and Community: The Belief System of the Book of Ezra," pages 256–275 in B. Becking and M. C. A. Korpel (eds.). *The Crisis of Israelite Religion: Transformation of Religious Tradition in Exilic and Post-Exilic Times* (OTS 42). Leiden: Brill, 1999.

Bedford, Peter R., *Temple Restoration in Early Achaemenid Judah* (JSJSup 65), Leiden: Brill, 2001.

Bedford, Peter R., "Diaspora: Homeland Relations in Ezra–Nehemiah," *Vetus Testamentum* 52 (2002): 147–166.

Ben-Ami, Doron, *Jerusalem: Excavations in the Tyropoeon Valley (Giv'ati Parking Lot)* (IAA Reports 52) Jerusalem: The Israel Exploration Society, 2013.

Bocher, Efrat and Lipschits, Oded, "The Corpus of yršlm Stamp Impressions – The Final Link," *Tel Aviv* 40 (2013): 99–116.

De Groot, Alon and Bernick-Greenberg, Hannah, *Excavations at the City of David 1978–1985 Directed by Yigal Shiloh, Vol. VIIA: Area E: Stratigraphy and Architecture* (Qedem 53). Jerusalem, 2012.

Edelman, Diana, "Yhwh Shomron and Yhwh Elohim in the Achaemenid Province of Samaria." Pages 35–80 in Yahwism under the Achaemenid Empire, Prof. Shaul Shaked in memoriam. Gad Barnea and Reinhard Kratz (eds.), (BZAW; Berlin: de Gruyter, forthcoming 2024).

Fantalkin, Alexander, "Why Did Nebuchadnezzar II Destroy Ashkelon in Kislev 604 B.C.E.?," pages 87–112 in I. Finkelstein, and N. Na'aman (eds.), *The Fire Signals of Lachish: Studies in the Archaeology and History of Israel in the Late Bronze Age, Iron Age, and Persian Period in Honor of David Ussishkin.* Winona Lake: Eisenbrauns, 2011.

Faust, Avraham, "Settlement Dynamics and Demographic Fluctuations in Judah from the Late Iron Age to the Hellenistic Period and the Archaeology of Persian-Period Yehud," pages 23–51 in Y. Levin ed., *A Time of Change: Judah and Its Neighbors in the Persian and Early Hellenistic Periods.* London: Bloomsbury, 2007.

Faust, Avraham, *Judah in the Neo-Babylonian Period: The Archaeology of Desolation* (Society of Biblical Literature Press 18). Atlanta: SBL, 2012.

Finkelstein, Israel, "Jerusalem in the Persian (and Early Hellenistic) Period and the Wall of Nehemiah," *JSOT* 32 (2008): 501–520.

Freud, Liora, *Judahite Pottery in the Transitional Phase between the Iron Age and the Persian Period: Jerusalem and Its Environs* (Ph.D. dissertation, Tel Aviv University), 2018 (Hebrew with English abstract).

Freud, Liora, "The Pottery of Babylonian-period Jerusalem: Stratum 9/10 at the Summit of the Southeastern Hill," *Tel Aviv* 50 (2023): 231–262.

Gadot, Yuval, "Iron Age (Strata X11- X6)," pages 88–109 in Y. Gadot, E. and Yadin (eds.), *Aphek-Antipatris II: The Remains on the Acropolis: The Moshe Kochavi and Pirhiya Beck Excavations.* (Monograph Series of the Sonia and Marco Nadler Institute of Archaeology, 41). Tel Aviv: Kedem, 2009.

Gadot, Yuval, "In the Valley of the King: Jerusalem's Rural Hinterland in the 8th–4th Centuries BCE," *Tel Aviv* 42 (2015): 3–26.

Gadot, Yuval and Lipschits, Oded, "Ramat Raḥel and the Emeq Rephaim Sites: Links and Interpretations," pages 88–96 in D. Amit and G. D. Stiebel (eds.), *New Studies in the Archaeology of Jerusalem and its Region (Collected Papers)*, Vol. 2. Jerusalem:IAA, 2008. (Hebrew).

Garffy, Adrian, *A Prophet Confronts His People* (Analecta Biblica 104). Rome: Biblical Institute Press, 1984.

Geva, Hillel, "Jerusalem's Population in Antiquity. A Minimalist View," *Tel Aviv* 41 (2014): 131–160.

Grabbe, Lester L. *A History of the Jews and Judaism in the Second Temple Period, Volume I: Yehud: A History of the Persian Province of Judah*. London and New York: Bloomsbury, 2004.

Greenberg, Raphael, "The Afterlife of Tells," pages 337–343 in I. Thuesen (ed.), *Proceedings of the 2nd International Congress on the Archaeology of the Ancient Near East* (22–26 May 2000, Copenhagen, Vol. 1). Bologna: Department of History and Cultures, University of Bologna and Eisenbrauns, 2016.

Holtorf Cornelius and Williams, Howard, "Landscapes and memories," pages 235–254 in D. Hicks and M. C. Beaudry (eds.), *The Cambridge Companion to Historical Archaeology*. Cambridge: Cambridge University Press: 2006.

Japhet, Sara, "People and Land in the Restoration Period," pages 103–125 in G. Strecker (ed.), *Das Land Israel in biblischer Zeit*. Göttingen: Vandenhoeck & Ruprecht, 1983.

Kessler, John, "The Diaspora in Zechariah 1–8 and Ezra–Nehemiah: The Role of History, Social Location, and Tradition in the Formulation of Identity," pages 119–145 in G. N. Knoppers and K. A. Ristau (eds.), *Community Identity in Judean Historiography: Biblical and Comparative Perspectives*. Winona Lake: Eisenbrauns, 2009.

Kleiman, Assaf, "Living on the Ruins. The Case of Stratum XII/XI at Hazor," pages 27–38 in A. Berlejung, A. M. Maeir, T. M. and Oshima (eds.), *Writing and Re-Writing History by Destruction* (Proceedings of the Annual Minerva Center RIAB Conference, Leipzig, 2018, Research on Israel and Aram in Biblical Times III). Tübingen: Mohr Siebek 2022.

Kleiman, Assaf, Cohen, Margaret E., Hall, Erin, Homsher, Robert S. and Finkelstein, Israel, "Cult activity at Megiddo in the Iron Age: new evidence and a long-term perspective," *Zeitschrift des Deutschen Palästina-Vereins* 133 (2017): 24–52.

Kleiman, Assaf and Dunseth, Zachary C., "Area W: Sounding in the Northeastern Sector of the Mound," pages 166–179 in I. Finkelstein and M. A. S. Martin (eds.), *Megiddo VI: The 2010–2014 Seasons*, Volume I (Monograph Series of the Sonia and Marco Nadler Institute of Archaeology, 41). Winona Lake: Eisenbrauns, 2023.

Knoppers, Gary N., "Ethnicity, Genealogy, Geography, and Change: The Judean Communities of Babylon and Jerusalem in the Story of Ezra," pages 147–171 in G. N. Knoppers and K. A. Ristau (eds.), *Community Identity in Judean Historiography: Biblical and Comparative Perspectives*. Winona Lake: Eisenbrauns, 2009.

Koch, Ido and Lipschits, Oded, "The Rosette Stamped Jar Handle System and the Kingdom of Judah at the End of the First Temple Period," *ZDPV* 129 (2013): 55–78.

Lipschits, Oded, "Nebuchadrezzar's Policy in 'hattu-Land' and the Fate of the Kingdom of Judah," *Ugarit-Forschungen* 30 (1999): 467–487.

Lipschits, Oded, "The History of the Benjaminite Region under Babylonian Rule," *TA* 26 (1999): 155–190.

Lipschits, Oded, "Judah, Jerusalem and the Temple (586–539 BCE)," *Transeuphraténe* 22 (2001): 129–142.

Lipschits, Oded, "Literary and Ideological Aspects of Nehemiah 11," *JBL* 121 (2002): 423–440.

Lipschits, Oded, "Ammon in Transition from Vassal kingdom to Babylonian Province," *BASOR* 335 (2004): 37–52.

Lipschits, Oded, "The Rural Settlement in Judah in the Sixth Century B.C.E.: A Rejoinder," *PEQ* 136/2 (2004): 99–107

Lipschits, Oded, *The Fall and Rise of Jerusalem: The History of Judah under Babylonian Rule*. Winona Lake: Eisenbrauns, 2005.

Lipschits, Oded, "Achaemenid Imperial Policy, Settlement Processes in Palestine, and the Status of Jerusalem in the Middle of the Fifth Century BCE," pages 19–52 in O. Lipschits and M. Oeming (eds.), *Judah and the Judeans in the Persian (Achaemenid) Period* (Proceedings of the Conference held in Heidelberg University, July 2003). Winona Lake: Eisenbrauns, 2006.

Lipschits, Oded, "Persian Period Judah: A New Perspective," pages 187–212 in L. Jonker (ed.), *Texts, Contexts and Readings in Postexilic Literature: Explorations into Historiography and Identity Negotiation in Hebrew Bible and Related Texts* (FAT 2/53). Tübingen: Mohr Siebeck, 2011.

Lipschits, Oded, "Shedding New Light on the Dark Years of the 'Exilic Period': New Studies, Further Elucidation, and Some Questions Regarding the Archaeology of Judah as an 'Empty Land,'" pages 57–90 in B. Kelle, F. R. Ames, and J. L. Wright (eds.), *Interpreting Exile: Interdisciplinary Studies of Displacement and Deportation in Biblical and Modern Contexts* (SBL's Ancient Israel and Its Literature series). Atlanta: SBL, 2011.

Lipschits, Oded, "Jerusalem between Two Periods of Greatness: The Size and Status of Jerusalem in the Babylonian, Persian and Early Hellenistic Periods," pages 163–175 in: O. Lipschits and L. L. Grabbe (eds.), *Judah between East and West: The Transition from Persian to Greek Rule (ca. 400–200 BCE)*. London: Bloomsbury, 2011.

Lipschits, Oded, "Between Archaeology and Text: A Reevaluation of the Development Process of Jerusalem in the Persian Period," pages 145–165 in M. Nissinen (ed.), *Congress Volume, Helsinki 2010* (VT.S 148). Leiden: Brill, 2012.

Lipschits, Oded, "Nehemiah 3: Sources, Composition and Purpose," pages 73–99 in I. Kalimi ed., *A New Perspective on Ezra-Nehemiah Story and History, Literature and Interpretation*. Winona Lake: Eisenbrauns, 2012.

Lipschits, Oded, "The Rural Economy of Judah during the Persian Period and the Settlement History of the District System," pages 237–264 in M. L. Miller, E. Ben Zvi, and G. N. Knoppers (eds.), *The Economy of Ancient Judah in Its Historical Context.* Winona Lake: Eisenbrauns, 2015.

Lipschits, Oded, "The Changing Faces of Kingship in Judah under Assyrian Rule," pages 116–138 in: A. Gianto and P. Dubovský, *Changing Faces of Kingship in Syria-Palestine 1500–500 BCE* (AOAT 459). Münster: Ugarit-Verlag, 2018.

Lipschits, Oded, "Benjamin in Retrospective: Stages in the Creation of the Territory of the Benjamin Tribe (7th–5th Centuries BCE)," pages 161–200 in: J. Krause, O. Sergi, and K. Weingart (eds.), *Saul, Benjamin and the Emergence of Monarchy in Israel: Biblical and Archaeological Perspectives* (Ancient Israel and its Literature, 40). Atlanta: SBL, 2020.

Lipschits, Oded, *Age of Empires: The History and Administration of Judah in the 8th–2nd Centuries BCE in Light of the Storage-Jar Stamp Impressions* (Mosaics: Studies on Ancient Israel 2). Tel Aviv and University Park, PA: Eisenbrauns, 2021.

Lipschits, Oded, "Jerusalem as a Symbol and in Reality," *HeBAI* 12 (2023): 69–84.

Lipschits, Oded, Gadot, Yuval, Arubas, Benjamin and Oeming, Manfred, "Palace and Village, Paradise and Oblivion: Unraveling the Riddles of Ramat Raḥel," *NEA* 74 (2011): 2–49.

Lipschits, Oded, Gadot, Yuval, Arubas, Benjamin and Oeming, Manfred, *What Are the Stones Whispering? 3000 Years of Forgotten History at Ramat Raḥel.* Winona Lake: Eisenbrauns, 2017.

Lipschits, Oded, Sergi, Omer, and Koch, Ido, "Royal Judahite Jar Handles: Reconsidering the Chronology of the *lmlk* Stamp Impressions," *TA* 37 (2010): 3–32.

Lipschits, Oded, Sergi, Omer, and Koch, Ido, "Judahite Stamped and Incised Jar Handles: A Tool for the Study of the History of Late Monarchic Judah," *TA* 38 (2011): 5–41.

Lipschits, Oded and Vanderhooft, David S., "Jerusalem in the Persian and Hellenistic Periods in Light of the Yehud Stamp Impressions," *EI* 28 (Tedi Kolek's volume), 2007: 106–115. (Hebrew).

Lipschits, Oded and Vanderhooft, David S., *Yehud Stamp Impressions: A Corpus of Inscribed Stamp Impressions from the Persian and Hellenistic Periods in Judah.* Winona Lake: Eisenbrauns, 2011.

Lowenthal, David, "Past Time, Present Place: Landscape and Memory," *Geogr. Rev.*, 65.1 (1975): 1–36.

Magen, Yitzhak, "The Dating of the First Phase of the Samaritan Temple on Mount Gerizim in Light of the Archaeological Evidence," pages 157–212 in O. Lipschits, G. N. Knoppers, and R. Albertz (eds.), *Judah and the Judeans in the Fourth Century BCE*. Winona-Lake: Eisenbrauns, 2007.

Magen, Yitzhak, *Mount Gerizim Excavation II: A Temple City* (Judea and Samaritan Publications 8). Jerusalem: Israel Antiquities Authority, 2008.

Maus, Gunnar, "Landscapes of memory: a practice theory approach to geographies of memory," *Geogr. Helv.* 70 (2015): 215–223.

Morris, Sarah P., "Troy between Bronze and Iron Ages: Myth, Cult and Memory in a Sacred Landscape," pages 59–68 in S. P. Morris and R. Lafineur (eds.), *Epos: Reconsidering Greek Epic and Aegean Bronze Age Archaeology* (Aegaeum 28). Liège: Université de Liège, 2007.

Na'aman, Nadav, "Memories of Canaan in the Old Testament," *Ugarit Forschungen* 47 (2016): 129–146.

Ornan, Tallay and Lipschits, Oded, "The Lion Stamp Impressions from Judah: Typology, Distribution, Iconography, and Historical Implications. A Preliminary Report," *Semitica* 62 (2020): 69–91.

Pearce, Laurie, "Through a Babylonian looking glass: a perspective on foreign wives," pages 351–372 in Yahwism under the Achaemenid Empire, Prof. Shaul Shaked in memoriam. Gad Barnea and Reinhard Kratz (eds.), (BZAW; Berlin: de Gruyter, forthcoming 2024).

Prent, Mieke, "Glories of the Past in the Past: Ritual Activities at Palatial Ruins in Early Iron Age Crete," pages 81–103 in R. M. Van Dyke and S. E. Alcock (eds.), *Archaeologies of Memory*. Malden: Blackwell, 2003.

Rom-Shiloni, Dalit. *God in Times of Destructions and Exile: Tanakh (Hebrew Bible) Theology*. Jerusalem: Magnes Press, 2009.

Rom-Shiloni, Dalit, *Exclusive Inclusivity: Identity Conflicts Between the Exiles and the People who Remained* (6th–5th Centuries BCE), New York and London: Bloomsbury, 2013.

Rudolph, W., *Haggai – Sacharja 1–8 – Sachaja 9–14 – Maleachi* (KAT 13/4). Gütersloh: Mohn, 1976.

Sandhaus (Reem), Débora, *The Nexus of Cultures: The Central Shephelah during the Persian and Hellenistic Periods* (Ph.D. Dissertation, Tel Aviv University), 2022.

Sandhaus, Débora and Kreimerman, Igor, "The Late 4th/3rd Century BCE Transition in the Judean Hinterland in Light of the Pottery of Khirbet Qeiyafa," *Tel Aviv* 42 (2015): 251–271.

Schama, Simon, *Landscape and memory*. London: Harper Perennial, 1995.

Shalev, Yiftah, Shalom, Nitsan, Bocher, Efrat, and Gadot, Yuval. "New Evidence on the Location and Nature of Iron Age, Persian and Early Hellenistic Period Jerusalem," *Tel Aviv* 47.2 (2020): 149–172.

Shalev, Yiftah, Gadot, Yuval, Bocher, Efrat, Bejerano, Oscar, Gellman, David, Sindel, Marion, Har-Tuv, Riki Z., Machline, Helene, Roth, Helen, and Shalom, Nitsan. "The Giv'ati Parking Lot Excavations: Four Years of Renewed Excavations,"*Qadmoniot: A Journal for the Antiquities of Eretz-Israel and Bible Lands* (2022): 24–35.

Shalom, Nitsan, "The Babylonian Destruction of Jerusalem as a Symbol? New Archaeological Evidence of the Babylonian Conquest," *HeBAI* 12 (2023): 85–107.

Shalom, Nitsan, Lipschits, Oded, Shatil, Noa, and Gadot, Yuval, "Judah in the Early Hellenistic Period: An Archaeological Perspective," pages 63–79 in S. Honigman, C. Nihan, and O. Lipschits (eds.), *Times of Transition: Judea in the Early Hellenistic Period*. Tel Aviv and University Park, PA: Eisenbrauns, 2021.

Shalom, Nitsan, Vaknin, Yoav, Shaar, Ron, Ben-Yosef, Erez, Lipschits, Oded, Shalev, Yiftah, Gadot, Yuval, and Boaretto, Elisabetta, "Destruction by fire: Reconstructing the evidence of the

586 BCE Babylonian destruction in a monumental building in Jerusalem," *Journal of Archaeological Science* 157 (2023) :105823. https://doi.org/10.1016/j.jas.2023.105823

Shatil, Noa, *Persian Period and-Early Hellenistic Pottery from Tell Azekah: Typology, Chronology and Identity* (MA Thesis, Tel Aviv University), 2016.

Smith, Morton, *Palestinian Parties and Politics that Shaped the Old Testament* (Lectures on the History of Religions 9). New York: Columbia University Press, 1971.

Smith, Daniel L., *The Religion of the Landless. The Social Context of the Babylonian Exile.* Bloomington: Meyer-Stone, 1989.

Spiciarich, Abra, *Religious and Socioeconomic Diversity of Ancient Jerusalem and its Hinterland during the 8th–2nd centuries BCE: A View from the Faunal Remains* (Ph.D. Dissertation, Tel Aviv University), 2020.

Spiciarich, Abra, Gadot, Yuval, Shalev, Yiftah, Har-Even, Binyamin, Lipschits, Oded and Sapir-Hen, Lidar, "Continuity and Change: Animal Economies of Jerusalem and its Hinterland during the Persian and Hellenistic Periods," *ZDPV* 139 (2023): 193–217.

Tal, Oren, *The Archaeology of Hellenistic Palestine. Between Tradition and Renewal.* Jerusalem: The Bialik Institute, 2007.

Vaknin Yoav, Shaar Ron, Gadot Yuval, Shalev Yiftah, Lipschits Oded, Ben-Yosef Erez, "The Earth's magnetic field in Jerusalem during the Babylonian destruction: A unique reference for field behavior and an anchor for archaeomagnetic dating," *PLoS ONE* 15.8 (2020): e0237029. https://doi.org/10.1371/journal.pone.0237029.

Van Dyke, Ruth M. and Alcock, Susan E., *Archaeologies of Memory.* Oxford: Blackwell, 2003.

Wolff, Hans W., *Haggai: A Commentary.* Minneapolis: Augsburg, 1988.

Wright, Jacob L. *Rebuilding Identity: The Nehemiah Memoir and Its Earliest Readers* (BZAW 348), Berlin: De Gruyter, 2004.

Zorn, Jeffrey R., *Tell en-Naṣbeh: A Re-evaluation of the Architecture and Stratigraphy of the Early Bronze Age, Iron Age and Latter Periods.* (Ph.D. dissertation, University of California, Berkeley), 1993.

Zorn, Jeffrey R., "Tell en-Naṣbeh and the Problem of the Material Culture of the Sixth Century," pages 413–447 in O. Lipschits and J. Blenkinsopp (eds.), *Judah and the Judeans in the Neo-Babylonian Period.* Winona Lake: Eisenbrauns, 2003.

Zuckerman, Sharon, "Ruin Cults at Iron I Hazor," pages 387–394 in I. Finkelstein and N. Naʾaman (eds.), *The Fire Signals of Lachish: Studies in the Archaeology and History of Israel in the Late Bronze Age, Iron Age, and Persian Period in Honor of David Ussishkin.* Winona Lake: Eisenbrauns, 2011.

Zwickel, Wolfgang, „Jerusalem und Samaria zur Zeit Nehemias. Ein Vergleich," *BZ* 52.2 (2008): 201–222.

James D. Moore

Administering Cult at Elephantine

Shaul Shaked's work models the very best of the historical investigation of religion. With expertise and integrity he demonstrated how to use textual evidence to reconstruct history and religious phenomena, and I am honored to contribute this paper to a collection dedicated to the memory of his scholarship.

Introduction

This contribution aims to provide a different perspective on references to notions of cult in the Aramaic documents from Persian period Elephantine by viewing them through the lens of the scribal cultural perspective of the administrators who wrote the documents. This perspective holds the following presuppositions: (1) the writers of the Elephantine Aramaic documents were foremost administrators rather than authors of literary compositions, such as biblical writers who encoded religious ideology into narrative. (2) The Yahô temple at Elephantine was a community and economic center. (3) In this sense, the temple's personnel reciprocally built and maintained cultural cohesion among the Judean community (i.e., "troop," Aram. ḤYL). (4) This culture was not a systemized religion but rather involved cultic activity designed to maintain order within the community's economy and to promote self-governance within the scope of imperial allowances. (5) The temple of Yahô was a center for the diffusion of Persian imperial culture in southern Egypt, and therefore, its economic and cultic agendas ensured that the Judean community was in right standing with the Persian administration in Egypt and by extension within the empire more broadly.

These presuppositions are an outgrowth of a forthcoming history of Elephantine within its imperial and administrative context.[1] That work argues that the Judeans at Elephantine and Syene were not mercenaries, but rather an imperial colony of Persian loyalists. This is based on the fact that no surviving document

1 This contribution is an outgrowth of the forthcoming study. Both are funded in part by the Deutsche Forschungsgemeinschaft grant "Judeans/Arameans at Elephantine: Their Social and Economic Status in Light of New Persian Period Texts from Egypt and Babylonia" (Project Number 432563380; active 2019–2024), hosted at the Humboldt Universität zu Berlin, Theological Faculty, under the Lehrstuhl of Bernd U. Schipper.

James D. Moore, Ohio State University, USA

https://doi.org/10.1515/9783111018638-010

from the site describes (or alludes to) Judeans as a community involved in military action nor as controllers for imperial taxation of imports or exports at Elephantine or Syene. As of now (after six decades of excavations), no archaeological evidence of Persian period military weaponry survives from the site of Elephantine, and women were active in taxation, property ownership, and business, as full members of the various social "ranks" (DGL-unit and century-unit) of state dependency within the community (ḤYL). Terms referring to ranks of state dependency and communities have long been mistakenly thought to be military terminology.

Furthermore, recent advances in ancient Near Eastern studies have shown that temples in the Persian period were foremost economic centers overseen by Persians or Persian loyalists. If religious textual production occurred it was a marginal enterprise, likely driven by historically contextual circumstances. This knowledge is heuristically important for understanding the Yahô temple's administration at Elephantine. The data from the Ebabbar temple at Sippar is an example of a Persian period major temple archive in a provincial district that was overseen by the regional (and subsequently imperial) administration.[2] Excavated there were two cuneiform archives which were operational until the beginning of the reign of Xerxes.[3] The major archive (Sippar 1; room 55) contained at least 60,000–70,000 tablets, all pertaining to the economic activities of the temple, its lands, labor, and royal interactions. Across the temple's complex was found a much smaller archive (Sippar 2; room 351) described as a "temple library," which comprised approximately 800 tablets of mostly literary content. From the available published data, the religious literary texts are part of the Mesopotamian canon known from earlier Standard Babylonian texts in addition to (traditional) royal inscriptions. Of the known genres, the only literary advances may be in the

2 The *qīpu* served as the senior royal representative in the major Babylonian temples in the Neo-Babylonian period. This role worked closely with the *šatammu*, the priestly temple administrator, who operated an independent administration. This Neo-Babylonian system was taken over and expanded by the Persians, at least at the Ezida temple in Borsippa, where the Persians began to claim eminent domain of temple lands. The *qīpu*'s role was expanded to control and directly oversee the organization of state labor of dependents within the temple economy/administration (Kleber, "Taxation and Fiscal Administration," 70–71). This destroyed the notion of autonomy previously held by the Neo-Babylonian temple administrators. Similar situations are found at Elephantine in the reign of Darius according to the so-called Pharendates correspondences, which demonstrate provincial approval was needed for the election of the *lesonis*-priest of the temple of Khnum (Pap. Ber. P. 13540). Such activity appears to have also been in place at the temple of Amun in Karnak (Pap. Louvre E 7128).

3 For possible reasons as to why the archive ends at this point see MacGinnis, "The Use of Writing Boards."

genre of "pseudo-biographical works."[4] From the current state of the archive, it seems that priests of the Ebabbar temple at Sippar were not engaged in the formation of organized religion, but rather in the practice of understanding the traditional religious culture of Babylonia and its interaction with royal propaganda in order to maintain the temple's economic interests. The archives of Sippar (and other major temple sites in the Persian provinces of Mesopotamia and Egypt) are heuristically valuable for framing how cult was administered at Elephantine given the surviving Aramaic evidence from the Persian period.

It must further be remembered that all but two Aramaic textual objects from Elephantine are documentary textual sources. The two literary texts (the Story of Ahiqar and the Darius Inscription) are not of Judean origin and do not speak directly to practices of the Judean cult nor a notion of Judean religion. Scholarship has focused disproportionately on these sources. Therefore, it will be shown in this study that when the references to the Judean cult that do survive are interpreted from the perspective of administrative scribal culture and with a sensitivity to the documents' various administrative genres, new historical interpretations are fleshed out. Although references to cult are few, this study does not aim to be comprehensive. Instead, it will focus on a collection of texts dating to the fifth year of Darius II (419 BCE), discuss facets of the temple's services offered to its own community and the state administration, and end with a discussion of cultic days and festivals.

As a caveat, for this study I will forego an in-depth discussion of the copies of Yedanyah's letter to Bagavahya the Governor of Judah (Pap. Ber. P. 13495 = TAD A4.7 ‖ Pap. Cairo EM JdE 43465 = TAD A4.8), which are generally the central texts studied for information about the religion and cult of Elephantine. The letter's charged emotive language is designed to elicit political sway from Bagavahya to effect change in the Egyptian province that would result in the Persian provincial administration of Egypt approving, financing, and rebuilding the Yahô temple at Elephantine. The letter provides (1) important architectural information in its report of the damage made to the temple and the cultic accoutrement therein; (2) references to mourning attire, mourning rites, and the act of fasting, (3) and shows that meal-offerings (Aram. MNḤH), burnt animal offerings (Aram. ʿLWH), and sacrifices (Aram. DBḤ) were, at least, occasionally performed in the temple. Other than this, it is a political and cultural letter, that was written out of political necessity because the responsible Persian administrators had gone rouge by favoring the native Egyptian population over the Judean Persian loyalists in a dispute between their cultural centers at Elephantine.

4 Pedersén, *Archives and Libraries*, 194–197.

Documents from the Fifth Year of Darius II (419 BCE)

The so-called Passover Letter has been at the center of the discussion of Judean festivals since its publication because it deals with instructions from someone named Ḥananyah to the priest Yedanyah at Elephantine regarding activity within a particular week of the month of Nisan. In recent years some, particularly Reinhard Kratz and Bernd Schipper, have focused on the role of Ḥananyah, the letter's sender, in the Judean community often equating him to an instigator of cultural conflict found in another letter (TADAE A4.3).[5] When we view the letter of Ḥananyah through the lens of the imperial administration, different concerns come into view. These issues are important to work out for understanding the history of the community, however, the question remains: what is the *purpose* of the letter?[6]

A conservative translation of the fragmentary text is:

The Letter of Ḥananyah, Pap. Ber. P. 13464 = TAD A4.1

r 1. [To my brothers Ye]⸢danya⸣h and his ⸢collea⸣gues, [the] Judean comm[unity,] your brother Ḥanan[y]ah. May God/the gods [seek after] the welfare of my brothers

r 2. [at all times.] And now, this year, year 5 of Darius the King, (word) has been sent from the king to ʾArša[ma ...]

r 3. [... ...] ∘ Yʾ. Now, you (m.p.), thus, appoint/count ʾ{D|R}{B|D|R}[... ...]

r 4. [... ...]{D|R}W. And from day 15 until day 21 of[Nisan ...]

r 5. [... ...] they were/be (m.p.) pure/clean. And beware! Labor ʾ[... ...]

r 6. [... ...]you (m.p.) must ⸢no⸣t drink(,) and anything that is leavened/fermented ʾ⸢S⸣[... ...]

v 1. [... from day 15 (...), at]sunset until day 21 of Nisa[n ...]

v 2. [... b]ring into your (m.p.) chambers and seal (them) during ⸢t⸣[hese] days.

v 3. [... ...]Yʾ

v 4. [To] my brothers Yedanyah and his colleagues, the Judean community, your brother Ḥananyah ⸢s⸣[on of PN].

After the opening salutation, the letter's initial instruction begins after the topical marker "now" (Aram. KʿT). The clause indiactes that in Darius's fifth year instruction was sent from the imperial bureau to the provincial bureau of ʾAršama,

5 Schipper, "The Judeans/Arameans of Elephantine," esp. 216–223 and Kratz, "Judean Ambassadors."

6 For a detailed analysis of this letter, see Barnea, "P. Berlin 13464, Yahwism and Achaemenid Zoroastrianism at Elephantine" in this volume.

whose official title known from other documents was "the prince."[7] The details of that content are either lost in the lacuna of Ḥananyah's letter or perhaps more likely already known by Yedanyah at Elephantine. It should be remembered that a remarkable feature of the Aramaic imperial administration was its hierarchical structure that allowed provincial decisions to be made within the province with minimal imperial interference.[8] In fact, Ḥananyah's statement is the only surviving evidence that the imperial administration could affect Elephantine.

The rarity of imperial involvement means that most certainly the content of Darius's message to ʾAršama had nothing to do with Judean festivals or the Judean temple. The dissemination of the imperial instruction would have been sent to ʾAršama's bureau, which in turn would have made all districts aware of the message. Ḥananyah's letter is not meant to make Yedanyah aware of the imperial instruction, but to advise Yedanyah and the Judean community in light of the imperial instruction. This can be said to be the letter's ultimate purpose.

But what is the empire concerned with in the month of Nisan that would ultimately affect the Judean community? Idan Dershowitz believes it refers to a correction of the calendar due to an intercalated Adar in Darius's fifth year and restores the text as such.[9] His view can be rejected since it does not account for known administrative procedure[10] or known features of Persian period scribal training,[11] nor does it appear to be chronologically

7 ʾAršama is never identified as a "satrap" in the surviving Aramaic sources. See discussion in Moore, "Who Gave You a Decree," esp. 74–76.

8 Moore, "Persian Administrative Process," esp. 51 n. 10 and Moore, "Who Gave You a Decree," 75.

9 Dershowitz, "The Elephantine Passover Papyrus."

10 See note 8 above.

11 The Babylonian calendar was standardized before Persian imperial ambitions. The standardized calendar with its eight or nineteen year cycle was adopted by the reign of Darius II, and the king's authority is lacking on early Persian period texts referring to intercalated months; see Steele, "Making Sense of Time," 475–477. The minor discrepancies in Elephantine documents observed by Stern, "The Babylonian Calendar at Elephantine," esp. table 1 (pp. 162–163) and table 2 (p. 165) are in all but one instance, a discrepancy of a one or two days with the exception being four days. These can be explained as errors owed to miscalculating when synchronizing with the Egyptian calendar. As for TAD B2.3, B2.4, and B3.9, Stern concludes that the contracts are off by one month due to not intercalating a second Adar. Of the two similar texts drafted on the same day TAD B2.3 and B2.4, Stern overlooks that the former exhibits a scribal correction on the date in which a numeral "20" was added between the numeral and the Egyptian month; "day 21 of Kislev, that is, day 1 of Mesore" was corrected to "day 21 of Kislev, that is, day 21 of Mesore," eliminating the word-break. The second manuscript's line containing the date is broken, but even still TAD postulates a correction to the lost text based on spacing and remnants of

viable.[12] Instead, one may reasonably assume that during Nisan, the first month of the year, the empire's concern focused on taxation and/or audits of the inventories of storehouse goods. This is further supported by the letter's content which refers to storing and sealing items (v 2).[13] This type of imperial concern was cause for Ḥananyah to provide advice to Yedanyah regarding matters of the Yahô temple, since it was the primary storehouse and likely taxation center for the Judean and affiliated communities in Syene/Elephantine. Evidence for this comes from the administrative documents written in the same year, only months later, which demonstrate that the Yahô temple collected taxes from the Judean community; that a major Syenean ration distribution occurred in the same year and was accompanied by storehouse audits throughout Upper Egypt; and that likely a census and taxation of taxable Egyptian families occurred at the same time.

The Yahô Temple's Collection List (TAD C3.15), is by far, the most cited administrative papyrus from Elephantine. It is worth noting that of the list's 128 names only 8 possible correspondences can be found when compared to the other documents. It represents a large group of Judeans whom we know nothing about and a population that is likely too large to be living solely on the island. It is, I believe, an example of a community collection in anticipation of the royal tax (likely a *mandattu*-tax, Aram. MNDH) owed on the community lands.

The temple functions as an intermediary between the state and the Judean and affiliated communities of colonists. The Yahô Temple's Collection List states only that the money was collected on "the 3rd of Phamenoth, year 5" (r 1) without an eponym. Arthur Cowley[14] and others dated the list to 419 BCE during the reign

---

stokes. Porten, "Calendar of Aramaic Texts," esp. 24, rightly observed that 21 days into Marcheshvan, the writer was thinking of Kislev and wrote that instead. In further support of Porten's argument, I would add that the notary was likely referencing a formulaic manual while at the same time reading TAD B2.2 (cited in B2.3:23–27), which was written in the Babylonian month of Kislev – the same month erroneously appearing in B2.3 and B2.4. The notary wrote Kislev in B2.3 then it was copied into B2.4. The notary's error in TAD B3.9 is not as apparent. But if I am understanding the data correctly, Darius II's eighth regnal year (c. 416 BCE) would have included a second Adar, but the misdated document B3.9 comes 5 months earlier than the first Adar of that year. Porten, "Calendar of Aramaic Texts," 23 opted to see the monthly error owed to a miscalculation of the Egyptian month, and this seems to be the obvious answer.

12 The letter appears to have been written in the first two weeks of Darius II's fifth year, before the 15th of Nisan, which is the start of the range of time cited in the letter. The 15th of Nisan has no pragmatic bearing on intercalation, which would still be over twelve months away.

13 The word for "chamber" (Aram. TWN) refers to an enclosed room without windows; see CAL "twn."

14 Cowley, *Aramaic Papyri*, 65.

of Darius II and rightly suggested a connection with Ḥananyah's letter.[15] Porten argued on paleographic and onomastic grounds that the fifth year of Amytraeus in 400 BCE is meant and that the collection may have been in preparation of the Feast of Weeks.[16] He also postulates that the lack of the king's name may be "further confirmation of the unofficial character of the document."[17] Others have discussed at length the end of the account which provides a statement regarding the deities Yahô, Anatbethel, and Eshembethel.[18] While the collection of the gods were part of the same administrative activity, it does not necessarily mean that these deities occupied the same temple. Only Yahô and Anatyahô (TAD B7.3:3) are referred to as Northwest Semitic deities at Elephantine. Moreover, Bethel and the Queen of Heaven, presumably Bethel's consort Anatbethel,[19] were worshiped in a temple at Syene according to a Hermopolis letter (TAD A2.1). Recognizing this, Karel van der Toorn writes of the gods in the Yahô Temple's Collection List, "One would have expected to find Anat-Bethel and Eshem-Bethel on the[other] side of the river."[20] There is no administrative reason to assume that they were not. The deity Eshem remains somewhat elusive as is clear in Bob Becking's recent review of the evidence.[21] Others have noted that Eshem-type names can be found in the corpus, but as far as I can tell they have overlooked the fact that Eshem-type names (in addition to Bethel-type and Ḥerem-type names) appear as witnesses on a contract that was written by a scribe who identified the region as Syene, not Elephantine (TAD B3.9). There is no reason to assume from an administrative perspective that the collection events recorded in the document occurred at Elephantine rather than among Judean lands off the island, where affiliated Persian approved communities also resided.

As I have argued elsewhere, using paleography to date fifth century Aramaic sources is dubious.[22] Furthermore, I, unlike Porten, believe that the Collection

15 Grelot, *Documents araméens d'Égypte*, 366 rejected Porten's dating for similar reasons: "Dans les deux cas, la date est donc proche de la fête des Semaines. On peut donc déjà supposer que la proximité de la Pentecôte a fourni l'occasion de cette quête pour le 'denier du culte.' Mais plusieurs raisons plaident en faveur de l'année 419, si l'on veut expliquer cette attestation claire d'un Judaïsme non réformé. Le 'Papyrus pascal,' antérieur à la Pâque de 418 (n° 96), constitue un indice de réforme qui rend peu probable la persistance d'un tel état de choses dans les dernières années du siècle."

16 Porten, *Archives from Elephantine*, 160–164.

17 Porten, *Archives from Elephantine*, 164.

18 For a recent discussion see Barnea, "Interpretatio Ivdaica."

19 See van der Toorn, *Becoming Diaspora Jews*, 33 and references therein.

20 Toorn, *Becoming Diaspora Jews*, 34.

21 Becking, *Identity in Persian Egypt*, 47–48.

22 *NAP*, pp. 219–221.

List is an official account. The data show that state accountants did not need to use royal eponyms in dates on taxation documents or storehouse audits, as indicated by the Syene Ration List's summary of storehouse goods as well as administrative documents from Saqqara.[23]

The Syene Ration List (*NAP* no. 2.2.3 and TAD C3.14) is an excellent example of an official account which refers to state activity at Syene in a document found at Elephantine. It includes summaries of total storehouse expenditures from the month of Mehir in year four through Mehir year five from the districts of Thebes to Syene. Preceding these audits of the storehouse expenditures is a list of ration distributions to fifty-four persons, who are called members of the Syenean Troop (Aram. ḤYL' SWNKNY', r iv 1). Both the reference to district storehouses and to Syeneans are a sign that the document refers to those performing their service obligation in the active labor team or military units of the Syenean district. The document represents an annual accounting or audit of the storehouses in Darius's fifth year and, therefore, may be seen as a (by)product of the imperial order sent to Aršama's bureau, which was referred to at the beginning of Ḥananyah's letter.

Similar to the Yahô Temple's Collection List is a fragmentary account that recent research in the form of new readings and newly published fragments has shown to be a tax collection on the taxable Egyptian population at Elephantine (*NAP* no. 2.2.1).[24] It is enticing to see the document connected to the wave of taxation and storehouse auditing that the Judeans and the Syenean troop experienced in Darius's fifth year. Like the Syene Ration List, there is no indication that the Judean community participated in writing the document. In this case the document is solely concerned with Egyptian family units and may be the prerogative of the Khnum temple's administration and the Persian authorities who oversaw it. Thus, the administrative backdrop of the taxation and auditing event in Darius's fifth year can be used to better understand the Yahô Temple's Collection List. The collection need not have occurred at Elephantine but may be part of the temple's role in collecting community taxes in the farmlands off the island. The temple likely sent representatives to collect community taxes among its farmland inhabitants, which explains why so few of the names are known in the other documentation.[25]

Now having broadened the historical picture of the administrative context of Darius's fifth year, Ḥananyah's letter is understood in a new light. His instructions

23 Here I also include the accounts on the palimpsest of the Ahiqar Manuscript (TAD C1.1 and C3.7), which refer to only years ten and eleven, without an eponym.

24 Formerly TAD C3.9.

25 This model of tax collection appears on a solely civil-level among the Persian period Judean community at al-Yahudu under the auspice of the Judean *dēkû*. See Wunsch, *Judaeans by the Waters of Babylon*, 55–56 and Zadok, "Yamu-Iziri the Summoner of Yahūdu."

to Yedanyah at Elephantine seem less likely to refer to a matter of timing regarding festivals in the week of Nisan, as most have previously argued, but rather to the temple's ability to finance and provide the resources for such festivals in view of the year's upcoming taxation and auditing. On this point, it should be remembered that the impetus for seasonal festivals was the careful administration of food and storage. The letter's prohibition on drinking and possible reference to leavened or fermented goods could refer to a conservation of resources (r 6).[26] This is further supported by the statement regarding the sealing and storage of goods (v 2). The letter may simply be a warning (r 5) to not over indulge in the upcoming festival and to (surreptitiously ?) store away resources in view of the coming tax and audit.[27] Religious or cultic festival activity was often merely the cultural and administrative expression of taxation.

Only after establishing the purpose of the letter in view of the historically accurate administrative practices, can one speculate about the festival to which Ḥananyah refers. It is possible that the festival was not mentioned in the letter. While Passover was practiced at Elephantine (see below), there is no evidence it is connected with a temple service. So while the dates mentioned align with the biblical Feast of Weeks, it is not clear that that festival was celebrated among Judeans at Elephantine. It should be remembered that a variety of festivals may have been held in the first month of the year, including Iranian festivals.[28] Perhaps it is historically irresponsible to even speculate what festival may have been referred to here, but if I were to hazard a guess, I would tentatively suggest the letter refers to the wide-spread Near Eastern/Mediterranean festival held in the month of Nisan associated with taxation, the Marzeaḥ (see below) because it is the only festival mentioned (so far) in the Aramaic sources from Elephantine that is associated with temple activities. Nonetheless, the point to be made is that the Letter of Ḥananyah demonstrates an intimate relationship between the priestly functions of the temple of Yahô and the Persian taxation and rationing scheme. The documents indicate that cultic activity exists within the limitations of civil allowances for the Judean community of state dependents.

---

26 The end of line r 6 may be restored as an imperative, "anything that is leavened pa⌈ck⌉[age up!] (Aram. ʾ⌈S⌉[RW])."

27 As for the fragmentary statement regarding purity (Aram. DKYN), note that in the ostraca terms that are typically associated with numinous (im)purity by biblical scholars are used pragmatically to refer to an item's quality (e.g., CG nos. 97; 125; 137). See discussion in Lemaire, "Judean Identity in Elephantine," 371 and Lemaire, "The Ostraca of Elephantine," 48.

28 Barnea, "P. Berlin 13464," in this volume.

Some Historical Remarks on the Temple's Services

As the evidence from Darius II's fifth year demonstrates, the Yahô temple was two-facing. On the one hand, it was the community and economic center of the Judean and affiliated communities at Elephantine and Syene. On the other hand, it was a provincial and imperial vehicle for extracting taxes from those communities. In this section I will discuss one of the resources that the temple offered which extended into the civil judiciary followed by observations about sacrifices and offerings.

Oath Statements

The civil administration recognized the role of the temples, which extended into the domain of civil law by providing a venue in which state recognized oath statements could be made in lieu of evidential documentation. The papyri contracts are the most often studied legal documents[29] from Elephantine. Contracts are highly formulaic and deal with civil matters of the state, not matters of religion or cult. That said, in legal disputes the state could request that an oath be made in lieu of documentary evidence. Oaths or references to oaths made before Yahô (TAD B2.2; B2.3; B7.1), Anatyahô (B7.3), and Sati (B2.8) can be found in the sources. Beyond these explicit references one finds an allusion to the oath making practice in one of the fragmentary ostraca missives. CG no. 265 refers to some sort of reed construction (Aram. ḤṢṢ, line cc 1) and an associated box. The text clearly states that "the documents are not in my box" (cc 4). After a statement concerning one named Malkyah and a karš (presumably of silver), the text insists, "And if Maʿûzyah did not swear [...] for/to Tat'ay, he must swear it [...] Malkyah send/sent" (cv 4–6).[30] It is probable that here we have a discussion of missing documentary evidence for which an oath statement must be made to quell a

29 In Mesopotamia, the Persians elevated registries and other administrative texts to the level of "legal" documentation, so much so that these administrative sources were consulted in court cases and trumped contractual evidence; see Stolper, *Entrepreneurs and Empire*, 29–31. This is also true of the Aramaic sources from Egypt, but unfortunately, most of the higher-level administrative documents that may be deemed "legal" survive only from Saqqara.

30 Additionally, in DAIK/SI O 5018, Fund-Nr. 45200 (unpub.), swearing may be meant in the context of silver; see discussion in Moore, "Aramaic Ostraca."

dispute. Beyond this missive and the references to oaths in contracts, two examples of actual oath statements survive.

The first TAD B7.3 is a nearly complete Aramaic oath statement that was claimed to have been made in a chapel (Aram. MSGDʾ) and before Anatyahô; this is presumably a designated area in the Yahô temple's complex. The writer of the document is not stated. It is possible that the notary of the court followed the oath-maker into the sacred complex to write the document, but as evidence from the next document will show, it is more likely that a priest or temple oblate recorded the legal condition that the oath-maker was compelled to swear.[31] This is a very important social-historical observation because it demonstrates a relationship between the administrative scribal training of the advanced notary, who could write contracts and trail records for the state, and the training of at least one administrative personnel in the temple complex.

The second source, TAD B7.4, is a small fragment which contains an Aramaic docket indicating it is an oath statement. The recto however, is written in Demotic and preserves the end of the oath's first eight lines. Until recently, this text has evaded translation, even though the photograph was published in Sachau's 1911 volume for which Wilhelm Spiegelberg gave comments without translation. Jan Moje claims to have read a few words in the document, including the eponym Artaxerxes in the first line.[32] The next five lines are too difficult to decipher, but Moje restores lines 6–8 with a stock legal phrase. The last lacuna ends in a male's name, according to Moje, then he sees the female's name Meritptah.[33] If the reading is correct, it is enticing to see this as the oath statement of Mib/pṭaḥyah,[34] which she made in the Sati temple to dispel the suit which the Egyptian Pîaʾ son of Paḥî brought against her in TAD B2.8. Regardless, it is certain from this Demotic/Aramaic oath statement that an Egyptian temple administrator, perhaps Ḥmny ∘ ... who is indicated on the Aramaic docket, recorded the oath in a temple, and by comparison we can assume the same was true of the Aramaic oath (B7.3).

31 I do not rule out the possibility that this notary was a priest serving his *ilku*/HLK-service obligation and, therefore, was the same person as the administrative priest. The point is that the state judicial and cultic administrative roles were distinct though in theory they could be held for a time by the same person (see below).

32 Moje, "References to Persians and Judeans."

33 The name itself is highly unusual and may be foreign.

34 If Mibṭaḥyah's name was Egyptian-ized, this may explain why some writers spell the name with /p/ rather than /b/. Furthermore, in TAD B2.3:36 on the address of one of her contracts, she is called Mibṭaḥ, which is phonetically close to Meritptaḥ, for which the -rit- may not have been pronounced. This Egyptian-ization added to her social advantage as a businesswoman on the island.

From these two documents we glimpse an important yet not often seen function of the temple complexes on the island: they supplemented the needs of the state's legal system in civil cases, and were, therefore, a recognized extension of the state judiciary. The temples' albeit minor role in the civil judiciary point to their more active role in arbitrating conflict within their own communities. To their own patrons temples offered additional services to rectify community specific disputes. The clearest example comes in the form of pardoning community members by means of sacrifices or fees paid in place of a sacrifice.

Sacrifices and Offerings

The state's recognition of the temple's judicial role can be seen to originate in the services and resources that temples offered patrons and their respective communities. This is especially true regarding the service that allows community members to give sacrifices and offerings to rectify an offense made or incurred within the community – an offense that does not directly affect the state's interest in property or the legal (and taxable) status of humans.

A Community Offense and Expiation in HL no. J8 with a Comment on CG no. X8

The ostracon CG no. 175 + 185 which Hélène Lozachmeur joined and published as no. J8 has recently drawn attention due to its use of the Aramaic root KPR, which refers to the act of expiating or pardoning within a temple setting. Guilia Grassi has argued that the ostracon's content infers a purification ritual within a medical context.[35] This is based on her reading of words, which I do not believe agree with the surviving letters and strokes. I argue here, instead, that in the context of Elephantine, this ostracon refers to a social offense that was understood as a sin against the temple or the deity and more pragmatically the community. As such, reparation was to be paid to the temple for its service in pardoning (Aram. √KPR) the offenders. The fragmentary text reads:

---

35 Lemaire, "The Ostraca of Elephantine," 48–49 makes note of the content but concludes that "[a]ll these words are suggestive, but their fragmentary context means that their interpretation can only be conjectural."

CG no. 175 + 185 = HL no. J8[36]

cc 1. [...] ∘
cc 2. [...] I stayed the night
cc 3. [... t]od⸢a⸣y
cc 4. [... so]n of Yedanyah
cc 5. [...]’ 10 (...)
cc 6. [... daugh]ter of Saraka
cc 7. [...]⸢by the li⸣fe of Yahô
cc 8. [...]{N|K} on top of
cc 9. [...](the) [d]⸢a⸣y which I shall die,
cc 10. may Yahô of Hosts carry you (f.s.)
cc 11. Setaryah is pardoned
cc 12. Each woman is pardoned.
cc 13. –
cv 1. That/who(m) ⸢{’|Y}N⸣[...]
cv 2. you (f.s.) ma[d]e[...]
cv 3. to your (f.s.) heart TM[...]
cv 4. [st]omach pain[...]
cv 5. and I said to you[...]
cv 6. Now, if B[...]
cv 7. Now, until he comes to you (f.s), Yahô
cv 8. do not approach!

I tentatively hold that the text refers to Judean women who may have been charged with illicit sexual activity. They were granted the cultic pardon of expiation – probably by paying for it – but are warned to refrain from cultic interaction if either a child was conceived as a result the offense (cv 4) or if the event happens again (cv 7–8). While I am filling many gaps to draw this conclusion, the fact that two women are pardoned within a cultic context is clear. What is also clear from historical evidence is that the pardon would have been costly.

In no ancient Near Eastern Semitic context did priests regularly offer a temple’s service free of charge. Perhaps the most relevant historical evidence for understanding this pardon at Elephantine comes from the Carthaginian Marseille Tariff Text (KAI 69) because it comes from a nearly contemporary Semitic and Mediterranean temple context.[37] It describes the taxes owed to a Phoenician/Punic temple of Baalṣapon and the distribution of those taxes in the event of sin as well as how one can bring either an animal for sacrifice or make a monetary payment equivalent to the price of the animal.[38]

---

36 I have collated and translated all ostraca in this contribution.

37 I date the inscription to the 4th century BCE.

38 I do not take the biblical reference to the Hebrew root KPR to be reliable historical information in this regard, even though nearly all occurrences appear in the so-called priestly source, which scholars generally date to the Persian period. That said, HL no. J8 and the Carthaginian

At Elephantine, in addition to HL no. J8 we find CG no. X8 which appears to be a reference to another sin against the community. In this case perhaps slander or libel between two members of the community is in view. This community matter brings cultic guilt, which needs to be adjudicated and expiation performed for the guilty party/parties. The text reads:

CG no. X8

cc 1. [...] ∘ [...]
cc 2. [∘ (∘)] ∘ [∘] son of Tmyl'. Now,
cc 3. [...]⸢H⸣R'. Indeed, to Yislaḥ
cc 4. [...] ∘ T a word which you/I/she spoke
cc 5. [...] ∘ M and it was not. Moreover,
cc 6. that (word ?) (f.s.) shall be so.
cv 1. ⸢And they shall say,⸣ it/she (f.s.) pardoned us / expiation is ours ([...]).
cv 2. Indeed, I am he, a si⸢nn⸣er
cv 3. who be⸢lo⸣ngs to them. (4) No (3) man
cv 4. shall sin against Yahô
cv 5. We have feared him. Now,
cv 6. [∘ ∘] ∘ them, but not Y[∘ (∘) ∘]
cv 7. [...]my ⸢b⸣oat [∘ ∘ ∘]

These two Elephantine ostraca indicate that the temple served a judicial function within the Judean community whereby it dealt with community and cultural offenses that were outside the domain of the state. By comparison with known Semitic and Mediterranean practices it can be determined that the offenses cost the offenders a monetary price to regain right stand within the community. It should further be noted that HL no. J8 and probably the content of CG no. X8 refer to issues that would not have been tried in the Persian imperial judicial system because they dealt with internal cultural maters rather than matters of imperial property, the property of imperial personnel, or the legal (and taxable) status of humans. In both cases, these texts survive likely because the administrators are concerned with tracking the money paid for the expiation rite or tracking the resolution of the conflict. Whether these are temple records or descriptive receipts issued to the offenders who paid for pardoning is unknown.

TAD A4.9 and A4.10

Given the importance of sacrifice within the Judean community, this study's administrative perspective contributes to arguments regarding the history of the

Marseille Tariff Text (KAI 69), could be used to understand how in Leviticus 5, an offender could pay in monetary terms for their offense. For further discussion of the Mediterranean and tariff context of Leviticus see Darshan, "The Casuistic Law."

right to make animal sacrifices in the Judean temple. For several reasons beyond restoring offenders to the community, Semitic temples provided their patrons services in the form of sacrificing and offering. As could be the case in the Letter of Ḥananyah, temples were responsible for providing a venue for festivals, which included sacrifices and/or offerings. Taxation collected by the temple, even if it was funneled to the state, was a form of offering. As is clear from a reference in Yedanyah's Letter to Bagavahya (TAD A4.7 ‖ A4.8), the temple also extends the service of offerings and sacrifices "in the name of" someone in order to advance their fortunes psychologically and socially (A4.7:25–26).

A couple of documents, which Porten edited as "letters" and included in the so-called Jedaniah Archive (which is better understood as the Yedanyah Dossier) have been interpreted to be acknowledgments by either the Judeans or the Persians that if the Yahô temple, which was damaged by a coalition of Egyptian priests and rouge Persian officials, were to be rebuilt, then blood sacrifices would no longer be practiced therein. One of the two texts often cited as evidence that the rebuilt temple of Yahô would abstain from blood sacrifice is TAD A4.9. The document is a memorandum-entry (or better two memorandum-entries in one) – not a letter, and the conclusions scholars have drawn from the document are the result of a fundamental misunderstanding of the administrative genre of memorandum-entries.

The memorandum-entry (Aram. DKRN or ZKRN) is an emic administrative genre that was taught across the empire to Aramaic administrators and used throughout the duration of the fifth and fourth centuries BCE. In a forthcoming study on all known attestations of the term,[39] I show that memorandum-entries are précis of official legal documents, from decrees to tax ledgers. All attestations can be linked to storehouse management, often in the domains of storage, tax collection, or the issuing of food rations. While each précis may include a few phrases copied from the actual document, the language of memorandum-entries remains terse, often in note form. This is perhaps because Persians elevated the function of "official" state documentation (see note 29), and therefore, it was likely inappropriate, if not legally dangerous, to possess exact or near exact copies of official legal documents. The memorandum-entry served as an *aide-mémoire* for the administrator who wrote it. It was evidence that a legal document that affected his domain of work existed or said document permitted or required his institution to engage in the stipulations noted in the memorandum-entry.

The memorandum referring to the Yahô temple's offerings has been mined for its content, but its administrative function as a memorandum-entry has been

39 Moore, "The Legality of Persian."

wholly overlooked. Scholars are correct to assume that TAD A4.9 demonstrates that the temple renovation was approved by the authorities, but the document itself is not "official" nor is it an indication that the approved project was ever undertaken. This is due in part to the fact that the damage caused by the Egyptian priests was repairable and did not disturb the building's foundations.[40] In this vein, the cessation of offerings and animal sacrifices is likely owed to damaged altars (see note 51). Furthermore, the papyrus lacks reference to blood sacrifices, but this cannot be construed as meaning the Persians prohibited the renovated temple from performing sacrifices. The document reads:

Pap. Ber. P. 13497 = TAD A4.9[41]

Memorandum of Bagavahya and Delayah. They said
to me: Memorandum. Quote: "It shall be to you in Egypt to say
before ʾAršama: 'Concerning the altar-house of the God of
the Heavens which (was) built in Fort Elephantine–
it was previously before Kanbûzî (i.e. Cambyses)
(and it) which that wicked Vîdranga demolished.'
(Dated) on the 14th (year) of Daryûhûš (i.e. Darius II), the king.
(It shall be to you in Egypt) to (re)build it in its place, as it was formerly.
And the grain-offerings and incense-offerings they may present on
that altar, just as formerly
had been done."

When understood in view of the established administrative genre of memorandum-entries, and considered for its terse administrative language, the most obvious interpretation is that the document was a note made by a storehouse administrator, who was responsible for distributing grain and dried goods to the temple personnel for the grain-offerings. There is ample evidence both archaeological (here I refer to house *k* of the Rubensohn and Zucker excavations[42]) and documentary (e.g., TAD A4.5) that the administration surrounding the temple of Yahô included large grain stocks, which were managed by personnel who were not priests, such as ʾAḥuṭab the dry-goods storage manager referred to often in the ostraca missives. Therefore, the administrator who wrote this memorandum sim-

40 According to von Pilgrim, there is currently no archaeological evidence of temple renovation at his proposed site for the Yahô Temple ("On the Archaeological Background," 11). The formatting here is intentional. The third line has a correction in the margin, and the second line is an interlinear insertion.

41 The transliteration is certain and agrees with TAD. The translation is my own. TAD indicates the composition's erasures on lines 2–3, which I have left out for clarity. For two different proposals of the administrator's compositional acts see Moore, "'Who Gave You a Decree,'" 81–86, esp. 84 and Porten, "Aramaic Papyri and Parchments," esp. 98–101.

42 Honroth, Rubensohn, and Zucker, "Bericht über die Ausgrabungen," esp. 23–24, Taf. III.

ply summarized the parts of the official petition and decree that granted approval for the temple to continue grain offerings after its repair. Animal sacrifice was not a function of this administrator's domain and thus not mentioned in the document.

In a similar vein, it is important to study A4.10, which is a roster of backers, who support the rebuilding of the Yahô temple. It is formatted as a report, not a letter, and uses the terse administrative language of a memorandum-entry, though the administrative title DKRN is not mentioned. From an administrative point of view, the text may be understood as a petition, but if so, this is not an official petition, of which one survives from Elephantine,[43] but rather a draft in note form. The reconstruction of the papyrus by Sachau has essentially never been challenged,[44] and the document has been taken to mean that if the temple is rebuilt, the Judeans agree to omit burnt offerings from the temple's services.[45] As can be seen from the photograph, the document is difficult to read due to lacuna that affect the relevant lines (see Fig. 1).

TAD translates the relevant lines as:

> [We 5 persons] say thus: If our lord [...] and our temple of YHW the God be rebuilt in Elephantine the fortress as it was former[ly bu]ilt – and sheep, ox, and goat are [n]ot made there as burnt-offering but [they offer there] (only) incense (and) meal-offering – and should our lord mak[e] a statement [about this, then] we shall give to the house of our lord si[lver ... and] a thousa[nd] ardabs of barley.

Grelot similarly renders:

> [Nous 5 hommes] parlent ainsi : Si notre Seigneur le veut, le sanctuaire de Yahô notre Dieu sera construit à Éléphantine-la-forteresse comme il était construit auparavant, et il n'y sera pas fait d'holocauste de béliers, bœufs (et) boucs, mais on offrira l'encensement (et) l'oblation. Et que notre Seigneur fasse une enquête là-dessus; Quant à nous nous donnerons à la maison de notre Seigneur une somme de ... ainsi que de l'orge : mille ardabes.[46]

---

43 Moore, "Persian Administrative Process."

44 Sachau, *Aramäische Papyrus*, 31–33.

45 Porten, *Archives from Elephantine*, 291–292. Grelot, *Documents araméens d'Égypte*, 417 believes that the order to rebuild the temple had been issued, and this document is a receipt of the order. It seems unlikely that receipt of decrees were part of the imperial administration.

46 Grelot, *Documents araméens d'Égypte*, 417–418 (no. 104).

Fig. 1: Photograph of Pap. Cairo EM JdE 43467 = TAD A4.10.[47]

47 Photograph from Sachau, *Aramäische Papyrus und Ostraka*, Taf. 4. The publication, and photograph is in the public domain. Ruler added for scale by J. D. Moore.

The document records a proposal by Yedanyah and his colleagues that the five listed men would be willing to offer ʾAršama's bureau 1,000 ardabs of grain, if their temple be rebuilt. It should be made clear that they are not requesting permission to rebuild their temple using their own labor or financing, but rather that the state should rebuild the temple, and in return the community through these five men will pay a surcharge, a one-time tax to support the state's investment in the temple's repair.[48] The tax is enormous and can be estimated between 25,000–55,000 liters of barley, depending on how one calculates the size of an ardab.[49]

The reconstruction of the effaced text on lines 8–9 in TAD rightly matches the surviving strokes. The question then becomes how does one interpret lines 10–11? Clearly line 10 uses a conjunctive-*waw* indicating that it begins an independent clause. It may be the apodosis of the condition of petition beginning with "if" (Aram. HN) in line 7. In such a case, the *waw* can be translated as "then," but it must be coordinated with LHN at the beginning of line 11, which is likely the preposition meaning "except for, but." In addition to these matters, one must consider the restoration of the short word ending in *alef* in the middle of line 10. Sachau restored [L]ʾ "not," and to my knowledge, no one has proposed an alternative. In fact, one may read here [L]ʾ but also [KL]ʾ or [H]ʾ. The latter two options render the opposite meaning than what is traditionally thought.

Additionally, the Aramaic noun MQLW poses a problem because it is so far only attested here. The word is a loan from Akkadian *maqlû*,[50] where it refers most often to a ritual series by that name, but its etymological meaning is simply "burning" (CAD M1, 251–252 meaning 2).

Lastly, the clause's verb is singular. This means that the list of animals should be construed distributively or as a list of options translated with "or," rather than as a compound series translated with "and." In this sense, *maqlû* may be an appositive noun. Interestingly, Akkadian lexical texts indicate that *maqlû* may be construed as a place for burning, such as an "oven" or "grate" (CAD M1 251–252 "*maqlû*" and "*maqlûtu*"). Given the context of TAD A4.10, a specialized "place of burning" also produces a compelling reading. In addition to those traditional translations with the restored [L]ʾ "not", the following alternatives should be seriously considered:

---

48 This may be (akin to) the *iškaru-* or *urašu-*labor tax; see Kleber, "Taxation and Fiscal Administration in Babylonia," 74–75 and Schütze, "The Aramaic Texts," 418–419.
49 See recently Bivar, "Weights and Measures I."
50 Kaufman, *Akkadian Influences on Aramaic*, 70.

Alternative renderings of lines 10–11:

Alt. a. Then sheep, ox, (or) goat [in]deed (h') shall be made there (as) *maqlû* (a burning-ceremony), but incense, grain-offering, [...]

Alt. b. Then sheep, ox, (or) goat – [each/all] (KL') shall be made there (as) *maqlû* (a burning-ceremony), but incense, grain-offering, [...]

Alt. c. Then sheep, ox, (or) goat – the burning of the [whole] (KL') shall be made, but incense, grain-offering, [...]

Alt. d. Whether sheep, ox, (or) goat – (a place for) burning [in]deed (H') shall be made, but incense, grain-offering, [...]

The final clause "but incense, grain-offering, [...]" is probably a reference to a different location in which incense and grain-offering are performed. One is tempted to restore, "but incense (or) grain-offering [shall be made in the altar house.]" It must be remembered that Semitic-Mediterranean temples often contained a four-horned altar, or a variation thereof, where incense and small grain-offerings were made, but animal sacrifice and large-scale immolation occurred on a larger altar, which unlike the four-horned altars was always located outside of the temple's building (Aram. BYT) though still within the temple complex (Aram. 'GWR'). Keeping this in mind, it is compelling to see TAD A4.9 as a reference to the repair of the "altar house" (Aram. BYT MDBḤ'),[51] while A4.10 focuses on the exterior altar complex.

The point to made is that like A4.9, when the roster of A4.10 is understood within its administrative context it cannot be construed as clear evidence of a prohibition on animal sacrifice. While all have followed Sachau's restoration and interpreted A4.10 as such, other restorations are possible which produce the opposite meaning. Because animal sacrifice was an integral part of the services the temple offers its community, it seems unlikely that it would (agree to) forego this practice. Besides, the revived practice of animal sacrifices was seen as a selling point for Persian interests in Yedanyah's proposal to Bagavahya the Governor of Judah (TAD A4.7:25–26).

CG no. 103 Votive Offerings and the Accounting of Sacrifices with a Comment on CG no. 17

A final text regarding sacrifice and offerings should be mentioned because it may demonstrate an administrative feature of votive promises made by a suppliant.

51 In the Persian report of the events (TAD A4.5), the Iranian loanword 'TRWDN may be used to describe what in Aramaic is the MDBḤ' "altar." However, see Barnea, "P. Berlin 13464," in this volume, note 33.

The relevant text is CG no. 103, which is difficult to read. Unlike other ostraca, CG no. 103 contains a bore hole, and evidence of wear from hanging on a string is found in the bore hole as though it were worn as a triangular shaped amulet. Furthermore, a text was written on the concave side of the ostracon then erased and a different text was written with a different pen on the convex side of the sherd. It is rare for Aramaic texts to have been written this way at Elephantine/ Syene. The notes of Cowley and André Dupont-Sommer show that both struggled to read the ostracon; Lozachmeur provided a more judicial reading and translation. After collating the document in person and from high-definition infrared photographs, I argue for the following translation:

CG no. 103
cv 1. This clay(-receipt) (f.) is | of ⸢the grai⸣n offe⸢rings⸣
cv 2. which he shall offer to Yah⸢ô⸣
cv 3. one is ʾAbah's
cv 4. Just as are his offerings to be burned/Just as are Yaqaryah's.
cv 5. ⸢Now, 2, are⸣ his ⸢mo⸣ther⸢'s⸣.

The ostracon appears to be a type of promissory note written in the form of a temporary amulet, reminding an offerer ʾAbah to fulfill his family's promised offering. Temporary amulets, by definition, are not likely to survive in the archaeological record, but some are known from Mesopotamia and written in contemporary Babylonian.[52] Promised offerings are generally understood as votive vows which are made then paid at a later date, normally after the deity has fulfilled his/her end of the vowed request.[53] This ostracon is our only glimpse into how the offering and perhaps sacrificial system at Elephantine worked. (As a reminder, the statements found in the Yedanyah Dossier refer to the system as a concept but do not describe it.)

I should mention that reference to sacrifice is also found in one of the administrative missives. CG no. 17 was sent to one named Natan, who appears to be directed to go to one named ʾÛryah. There is something written about a garment, and there is found the statement "[...] the sacrifice and you/she shall bring in" (CG no. 17 cv 4). The study mentioned in this article's introduction, which is in progress, argues that Natan was a courier who administers the transport of goods to and from the island, and ʾÛryah appears to be an administrator on the island

52 Finkel, "Amulets against Fever."
53 No historically reliable source discusses the practice of making vows and issuing temporary amulets, however, biblical narratives such as Hannah's vow during her family's yearly trip to Shiloh (1 Sam 1) come to mind.

responsible for living animals, specifically sheep, wool, and garments. The text reads:

CG no. 17

cc 1.	[(Greetings,) Na]⸢t⸣an. Now, I/you/she sent (word)[...]
cc 2.	[...] and I/you/she sent (word) ⸢to⸣
cc 3.	[...]go (m.s.) to ʾÛrya⸢h⸣[...]
cc 4.	[...] ∘ (∘) ∘ [...]
cv 1.	[...]the garment
cv 2.	[...]I shall make it
cv 3.	[...] ∘ was with me
cv 4.	[...] the sacrifice and you/she shall bring in
cv 5.	[...] to Paḥî
cv 6.	[...] ∘ ∘ [...]
cc pal. 1.	[...] this. And not [...]

I would suggest that an administrative priest, like ʾÛryah may have issued temporary amulets in the form of promissory notes to suppliants who journeyed across the river to the Yahô temple to perform a vow. As with legal promissory notes known from Mesopotamia, when the promissory vow was paid and the amulet delivered to the temple, the note was erased, to be reused or destroyed. CG no. 103 and indirectly supported by CG no. 17 provides enticing evidence of the temple economy engaging in votive offering practices and how the temple administered those vows. Vows in antiquity could have been made for several reasons, but a known time at which vows were made was during festivals, to which this study now turns.

Cultic Festivals

The distribution of commodities appears to have occurred within the scope of the needs of the community. The ostraca indicate that items could be requested within a day's notice and sometimes on the same day, and the courier system maintained an efficient mode of transport that ferried items across the river. Beyond the references to "yesterday," "today," "evening," "tomorrow," "another day, "1 day," "3 days," "that day," and "quickly" are a few references to specific calendrical moments or events.[54] As is typical of previous Elephantine research, scholars have looked at these references to the calendar through a solely religious lens. Unfortunately, the contexts of these events yield hardly any useful religious

54 Lemaire, *Levantine Epigraphy*, 50–51.

or cultic information. Nearly all of the references appear in the ostraca missives, which is a large collection of administrative documents. Reference to calendrical moments are foremost about administrative time or the technicalities of the administration surrounding these calendrical moments.[55]

Shabbat

The ostraca's references to Shabbat have been discussed at length by scholars.[56] I wish only to emphasize here that it seems to be a reference to a single day; its spelling with a final *heh* rather than *tav* remains a curiosity; and only two clear readings can be securely interpreted as the calendrical Shabbat (CG no. 152 and CG no. 186). Of these references it is well noted that CG no. 152 demands the addressee to meet the boat on Shabbat, so much has been said about the biblical prohibition against work on Shabbat and this reference, which clearly encourages work.[57] Nonetheless, it should be noted that this is one of only two clearly defined "days" in the corpus (see note 55). Whether it was a weekly moment in time as in later Hebrew or a bi-monthly occurrence as in Akkadian,[58] it served as an indication to the community as a marker of time. In my view it functioned as a way of demarcating the otherwise monotonous days for administrators and laborers who did not meticulously maintain the calendar. Other than the fact that the temple, as the administrative center of the community, maintained the calendar, it remains unclear if Shabbat served any religious, cultic, or festive purpose.

---

55 Due to the fragmentary state of the texts, I have excluded for the sake of space references to fasting, something called "the day of wind/spirit," and a Ḥanukhah-dedication. For fasting, see Lemaire, "Ostraca of Elephantine," 48. Additionally the verb "to fast" may be found on CG no. 154 cv 2 which reads either [...] ∘ ṢYM or [...] ∘ ŠYM. Lozachmeur struggled to read the line. For the "day of wind/spirit" see CG no. 12 cc 4, but compare the Ahiqar Manuscript (TAD C1.1) pl. K r i 10. For what may be a reference to a Ḥanukhah-dedication, see CG no. 50 cc 4.

56 Recently see Lemaire, "Ostraca of Elephantine," 47; Becking, *Identity in Persian Egypt*, 28–31.

57 Note Lemaire's reservation about interpreting the relevant verb as "to meet" ("Ostraca of Elephantine," 47).

58 Compare the view of Lemaire, "Ostraca of Elephantine," 47 that the biblical references referred to a full moon feast.

Passover

Passover is only found in the ostraca on two fragmentary ostraca missives, TAD D7.24 and CG no. 155, as well as on a third fully preserved ostracon missive, TAD D7.6.[59] The latter of these reads:

Oxford Bodl. Aram. Inscr. 7 (TAD D7.6)
cc 1. To Hôšeʿyah.
cc 2. Your greetings. Now, look
cc 3. over the children until
cc 4. ʾAḥuṭab (3) can come. (4) Do not entrust(?)
cc 5. them to another.
cv 1. If their bread is ground,
cv 2. knead bread, 1 qab, until
cv 3. their mother will come. Send (word)
cv 4. to me when you will make the Passover.
cv 5. Continue sending greetings(-notes) of
cv 6. the children.

As in this case, many of the ostraca focus on the ordering or shipment of food rations. Here again, the sender is concerned with timing: when the Passover will be made. This suggests that an administrative concern is in view. The Elephantine Passover is traditionally understood – from the biblical point of view – as a sacrifice prescribed on the 14th of Nisan (at least in Leviticus) followed the next day by the Feast of Weeks. But in this ostracon, the Passover does not appear as a defined point in time. It's timing is selfreferential. While it seems possible the temple would have made the Judeans aware of when the Passover occurred, it is unclear if the festival was rigidly tied to the calendar and if it took place in the temple, in the Judean households, or both. A further difficulty with this ostracon is identifying Hôšeʿyah. He clearly runs in the orbit of ʾAḥuṭab, who is the primary storehouse manager of dry-goods on the island. And ʾAḥuṭab runs in the orbit of ʾÛryah, who appears to be the manager of animals and animal products. So could it be that the sender is simply responsible for transporting the Passover animal(s) to or from the temple to the community homes? One can envision the Passover animal sent to the temple, slaughtered there, then returned across the river for consumption in the home. While this is conjecture, it is clear from other sources (e.g., TAD D7.8) that herdsmen residing off the island communicated with management (such as ʾÛryah) on the island about animals and shipments of meat.

---

59 For the possibility of the appearance of the term on CG no. 62 see Lemaire, "Ostraca of Elephantine," 47–48.

Whether the Passover resembles the biblical Passover, cannot be known. What is known is that those at Elephantine celebrated ritual feasts that are not prescribed in the biblical text, such as the Marzeaḥ. Rather than imposing the biblical descriptions on the large gaps in our knowledge of Judean religious life at Elephantine,[60] scholars should rather contextualize the documents using reliable historical and cultural information, leaving questions open for future research.

Marzeaḥ

Lastly, and perhaps most importantly of the cultic festivals, is the Marzeaḥ.[61] Its appearance on an ostracon ascribed (and I think correctly)[62] to Elephantine further demonstrates the pan-Mediterranean and Northwest Semitic nature of the Judean community at Elephantine. Furthermore, given that fasting (see note 55) is an impromptu cultic activity, Shabbat could be a calendrical marker more than an event, and Passover may be a household event rather than a temple festival, the Marzeaḥ stands out as the only community festival in the Elephantine documentation associated with the Yahô temple.

Most scholarship has discussed the Marzaeḥ from the point of view of the late second millennium BCE Ugaritic evidence, in which it is depicted as a cultic association of professional (I would say administrative) businessmen within a temple context who engage in a festive drinking ceremony.[63] This general description for the event is not contradicted by the Persian period evidence, and therefore, Marzeaḥ may safely be assumed to be a festival for temple associates and businessmen conducted at or under the auspices of the temple. Whether it extended to the public remains unclear. In 2018 Maria Giulia Amadasi Guzzo and José Zamora collected the three previously known Phoenician/Punic references

60 Previous scholars working on the ostraca have concluded that "there is no meaningful indication in the Elephantine ostraca of real religious syncretism among the Judeans at Elephantine (Lemaire, "Ostraca of Elephantine," 49–50). Similarly, Lozachmeur, *La collection Clermont-Ganneau*, 533. I hold that the Marzeaḥ should not be seen as syncretism, but as a native practice of this Judean community.

61 Becking has studied the Elephantine Marzeaḥ the most. For a synthesis of his views and a bibliography on the topic see *Identity in Persian Egypt*, 33–35, 152–153.

62 Sayce, "An Aramaic Ostracon," 154–155, claims to have found the ostracon in the Cairo Museum but that it was from Elephantine.

63 See most recently, Mandell, "When Form is Function." Note that she rightly argues that the Marzaeḥ was not a funerary festival (55). Its continued association with the temple in Phoenician/Punic times supports this. The temple was not a location where rites for the dead were practiced, but rather the administrative center for the living.

to the Marzeaḥ, (Carthage [KAI 69], Cyprus or Lebanon [Avigad and Greenfield], and Sidon [KAI 60]) and studied them in conjunction with a new ostracon or vessel label referring to a food-offering to Ashtart and Melqart found at excavations of the acropolis of Idalion in Cyprus (IDA 974 [2001]). That same year Hans-Peter Mathys and Rolf A. Stucky published a few inscriptions from the excavations of the Eshmun sanctuary at Sidon (Bostan esh-Sheikh), one of which was a marble votive inscription referring to "reserving" the Marzeaḥ and includes references to Ashtart and perhaps Shamash. All these sources date to or around the same time as the Persian period Judean settlement at Elephantine. The Phoenician evidence is becoming clearer that the Marzeaḥ was a pan-Mediterranean and native Northwest Semitic festival, often associated with Ashtart/Astarte and other major deities. The festival focused on feasting in the context of a temple economy and on taxation for which votive payments could be made.

The sole reference to the Marzeaḥ at Elephantine nicely fits this general temple economic context. The ostracon reads:

Ost. Cairo EM JdE 35468 a = TAD D7.29

cc 1. To Ḥaggay. I spoke
cc 2. to ʾAšyan about the silver of
cc 3. the Marzeaḥ. Thus he said
cc 4. to me: there is none.
cc 5. Now, I shall give it
cc 6. to Ḥaggay or
cc 7. Yigdol. Send (a person)
cc 8. to him,
cc 9. and he shall give it
cc 10. to you (m.p.).[64]

Whether the Marzeaḥ refers to a ceremony at the Yahô temple or at a Northwest Semitic temple at Syene is unclear, but the reference to Yigdal, who can be identified as a messenger to the Yahô temple's Judean administrators, is a good sign that this is in reference to a Marzaeḥ practiced among the Judeans. The lines of interest read, "I spoke to ʾAšyan about the silver of the Marzeaḥ. Thus he said to me: There is none" (cc 1–4). Some have interpreted this as a silver payment, in which case the notion would align with the option in the Carthaginian Marseille Tariff Text (KAI 69) for a person to compensate the temple in virtual currency. That said, here silver is not accompanied by a measurement, which is common

64 It is unclear if ʾAšyan's statement is simply "there is none" (cc 4) or if it comprises the rest of the ostracon (cc 4–10). Since Ḥaggay, the addressee, is mentioned in the third person, I suspect lines 4–10 are ʾAšyan's instruction.

in the sources when it refers to payment. So we could read the reference to silver as a reference to silver-ware. Such an interpretation would align with the drinking and feasting activities for which the Marzeaḥ is known. But this interpretation further calls to mind the votive silver feasting vessels known from Egypt,[65] which were offered in a temple context, but some of which eventually may have been taxed by the Persians and sent to Persepolis.[66] This is especially compelling if we understand ʾAšyan as an Iranian name and, therefore, as an imperial representative, perhaps an accountant. The point to be made in this short study is that the Marzeaḥ was a native pan-Northwest Semitic (including Judean) festival celebrated across the Mediterranean. It nicely fits the Persian program of ritualized feasting and taxation, and it stands out among the references at Elephantine as perhaps the only ceremony practiced at the Yahô temple according to the surviving sources. It was depicted as the party of the year, so to speak, in which wealthy businessmen came together to feast and drink. The temple may have used this festival as a strategy to incentivize the wealthy to come pay their taxes, which they might be more likely to do while inebriated at a party where they can engage in drunken contests of devotion.

What Historical Conclusions Can Be Drawn from the Data?

Gap-filling is needed to reconstruct any history, particularly one with only partially surviving documentation. My approach here has been to understand and interpret the Elephantine documents within their administrative contexts, and to avoid gap-filling with biblical data. From the surviving evidence, the temple of Yahô appears to have been a type of civil center, akin to those known in other ancient Near Eastern contexts, that served as the Judean community's access portal to the Persian administration. It was foremost an economic institution

---

65 Brooklyn nos. 54.50.32; 54.50.33; 54.50.34; 54.50.35; 54.50.36; 54.50.37; 54.50.38; 54.50.39; 54.50.40; 54.50.43a-c; 54.50.44a–b; 55.183; 57.121; 54.50.41 (handle); 54.50.42 (handle). The bronze vessels from the Achaemenid period, which are similar in typology, may have served the same function (e.g., Brooklyn 76.108 [Egyptian acquisition] or Muscarella, *Bronze and Iron*, 218–219 [Iranian acquisition; but see notes therein to similar excavated objects]).

66 See Moore, "The Legality of Persian," particularly the discussion of text no. 3 (= TAD C3.13). In note 68 I write: "None have yet claimed, to my memory, a tax function for the silver bowls from Egypt. But Henkelman, "Imperial Signature," esp. 97–109 (and notes) discusses how precious vessels are part of the taxation system in the eastern provinces, and I thank him for suggesting to me that the Egyptian silver bowels may serve this purpose."

designed to ensure the stability of the Judean community of colonists, who lived mostly off the island on presumably state owned/allotted land.

Additionally, the temple also served the moral needs of the community by being a place in which vows could be made, but this cultural function was by no means its primary function.

This paper has further argued that the temple also served as a culturally specific judicial center for the Judean community, and likely also for other Persian colonists (much like the Khnum temple served for the Egyptian population). It adjudicated community disputes that were not elevated to the Persian authorities. The Persian authorities were concerned with very few types of disputes, mostly issues regarding state owned property or the legal (taxable) status of humans, particularly if the status of a human changed through emancipation or marriage. Only in the event of missing evidentiary documentation was the temple evoked to oversee oaths made by legal parties in the state judiciary.

Where the administrative training of the Yahô temple's personnel occurred is yet to be determined, but I agree with André Lemaire, who sees scribal education at Elephantine located within small home-school or small state institutional settings and not in the temple proper.[67] It is entirely possible that priests or temple oblates conducted scribal education in their own homes. Certainly priests or oblates would have learned skills – on the job training – but their basic education seems to have occurred formally under the auspice of a private apprenticeship or public institution that was not the temple.

To summarize, while it is incredibly difficult to find evidence of religion or religious systems in ancient Near Eastern documentation pertaining to temples and their administrative practices, there is enough evidence at Elephantine to tease out vignettes of cultic activity. These vignettes are possible when interpreted in the social and historical context of the temple economy, and they lead to different perspectives on the history of Judeans at Elephantine and Syene than those which have been constructed through the lens of the biblical texts.

Bibliography

Barnea, Gad, "P. Berlin 13464, Yahwism and Achaemenid Zoroastrianism at Elephantine." In *Yahwism under the Achaemenid Empire, Prof. Shaul Shaked* in memoriam. Edited by Gad Barnea and Reinhard G. Kratz. *BZAW*. Berlin: de Gruyter, 2024.

Barnea, Gad, "Interpretatio Ivdaica in the Achaemenid Period." *Journal of Ancient Judaism* 14.3 (2023): 1–37.

67 Lemaire, "Aramaic Literacy and School in Elephantine."

Becking, Bob, *Identity in Persian Egypt: The Fate of the Yehudite Community of Elephantine*. University Park: Eisenbrauns, 2020.

Bivar, Adrian D.H., "Weights and Measures I. Pre-Islamic Period." In *Encyclopaedia Iranica Online Edition*. New York: Encyclopaedia Iranica Foundation, Inc., 2000. https://www.iranicaonline.org/articles/weights-measures-i#prettyPhoto.

Cowley, Arthur E., *Aramaic Papyri of the Fifth Century B.C.* Oxford: Clarendon Press, 1923.

Darshan, Guy, "The Casuistic Law in Leviticus, the New Marmarini Inscription, and the Eloulaia and Nisanaia Festivals." *Zeitschrift für die alttestamentliche Wissenschaft* 134 (2022): 483–99. https://doi.org/10.1515/zaw-2022-4003.

Dershowitz, Idan, "The Elephantine Passover Papyrus: Darius II Delays the Festival of Matzot." TheTorah.com." https://thetorah.com/article/darius-ii-delays-the-festival-of-matzot-in-418-bce. (Accessed August 31, 2022).

Finkel, Irving L., "Amulets against Fever," pages 232–271 in *Mesopotamian Medicine and Magic: Studies in Honor of Markham J. Geller*, edited by Strahil V. Panayotov and Luděk Vacín, Ancient Magic and Divination 14. Leiden: Brill, 2018.

Grelot, Pierre, *Documents araméens d'Égypte*. Littératures Anciennes du Proche-Orient 5. Paris: Éditions du Cerf, 1972.

Henkelman, Wouter F. M., "Imperial Signature and Imperial Paradigm: Achaemenid Administrative Structure and System across and beyond the Iranian Plateau," page 45–256 *in Die Verwaltung im Achämenidenreich: imperiale Muster und Strukturen = Administration in the Achaemenid Empire: Tracing the Imperial Signature: Akten des 6. internationalen Kolloquiums zum Thema "Vorderasien im Spannungsfeld klassischer und altorientalischer Überlieferungen" aus Anlass der 80-Jahr-Feier der Entdeckung des Festungsarchivs von Persepolis, Landgut Castelen bei Basel, 14.–17. Mai 2013*, edited by Bruno Jacobs, Wouter Henkelman, and Matthew W. Stolper. Classica et Orientalia 17. Wiesbaden: Harrassowitz, 2017.

Honroth, Wilhelm, Rubensohn, Otto and Zucker, Friedrich, "Bericht über die Ausgrabungen auf Elephantine in den Jahren 1906–1908." *Zeitschrift für Ägyptische Sprache* 45 (1910): 14–61.

Kaufman, Stephen A., *Akkadian Influences on Aramaic*. Assyriological Studies 19. Chicago: Oriental Institute of the University of Chicago, 1974.

Kleber, Kristin, "Taxation and Fiscal Administration in Babylonia," pages 13–153 in *Taxation in the Achaemenid Empire*, ed. Kristin Kleber. Classica et Orientalia 26. Wiesbaden: Harrassowitz, 2021.

Kratz, Reinhard G., "Judean Ambassadors and the Making of Jewish Identity: The Case of Hananiah, Ezra, and Nehemiah," pages 421–44 in *Judah and the Judeans in the Achaemenid Period: Negotiating Identity in an International Context*, edited by Oded Lipschits, Gary N. Knoppers, and Manfred Oeming. Winona Lake: Eisenbrauns, 2011.

Lemaire, André, "The Ostraca of Elephantine: A Further Light on the Judeans in Elephantine," pages 45–54 in *Elephantine Revisited: New Insights into the Judean Community and Its Neighbors*, edited by Margaretha L. Folmer. University Park: Eisenbrauns, 2022.

Lemaire, André, "Aramaic Literacy and School in Elephantine," *Maarav* 21 (2017): 295–307.

Lemaire, André, *Levantine Epigraphy and History in the Achaemenid Period (539–332 BCE). Schweich Lectures on Biblical Archaeology 2013*. Oxford: Oxford University Press, 2015.

Lemaire, André, "Judean Identity in Elephantine: Everyday Life According to the Ostraca," pages 265–373 in *Judah and the Judeans in the Achaemenid Period: Negotiating Identity in an International Context*, edited by Oded Lipschits, Gary N. Knoppers, and Manfred Oeming. Winona Lake: Eisenbrauns, 2011.

Lozachmeur, Hélène, *La collection Clermont-Ganneau: Ostraca, épigraphes sur jarre, étiquettes de bois*. 2 vols. MPAIBL N.S. 35. Paris: Boccard, 2006.

MacGinnis, John, "The Use of Writing Boards in the Neo-Babylonian Temple Administration at Sippar." *Iraq* 64 (2002): 217. https://doi.org/10.2307/4200524.

Mandell, Alice, "When Form Is Function: A Reassessment of the *Marziḥu* Contract (*KTU* 3.9) as a Scribal Exercise." *Maarav* 23 (2019): 39–67. https://doi.org/10.1086/MAR201923104.

Moje, Jan, "References to Persians and Judeans/Arameans in the Demotic Sources from Elephantine," in *Advances in Elephantine and Persian Period Research*, edited by James D. Moore and Petra Schmidtkunz. Studies on Elephantine. Leiden: Brill, Forthcoming.

Moore, James D., "Who Gave You a Decree? Anonymity as a Narrative Technique in Ezra 5:3, 9 in Light of Persian Period Decrees and Administrative Sources." *Journal of Biblical Literature* 140 (2021): 69–89.

Moore, James D., "The Persian Administrative Process in View of an Elephantine ʾAršāma Decree (TAD A6.2)." *Semitica et Classica* 13 (2020): 49–62. https://doi.org/10.1484/J.SEC.5.119664.

Moore, James D., "Aramaic Ostraca from the Deutsche Archäologische Institut, Kairo's Excavations of Elephantine." *Mitteilungen des deutschen archäologischen Instituts Abteilung Kairo*. (Tentative Title, Contracted, forthcoming).

Moore, James D., "The Legality of Persian Period Memoranda." In *The Dynamics of Early Judaean Law: Studies in the Diversity of Ancient Social and Communal Legislation*, edited by Sandra Jacobs. BZAW 504. Boston: De Gruyter, forthcoming.

Muscarella, Oscar W., *Bronze and Iron: Ancient Near Eastern Artifacts in the Metropolitan Museum of Art.* New York: Metropolitan Museum of Art, 1988.

Pedersén, Olof, *Archives and Libraries in the Ancient Near East, 1500–300 B.C.* Bethesda, MD: CDL Press, 1998.

Pilgrim, Cornelius von, "On the Archaeological Background of the Aramaic Papyri from Elephantine in the Light of Recent Fieldwork," pages 1–16 in *Elephantine Revisited: New Insights into the Judean Community and Its Neighbors*, edited by Margaretha L. Folmer. University Park, Pennsylvania: Eisenbrauns, 2022.

Porten, Bezalel, "The Calendar of Aramaic Texts from Achaemenid and Ptolemaic Egypt," pages 13–32 in *Irano-Judaica II: Studies Relating to Jewish Contacts with Persian Culture throughout the Ages*, edited by Shaul Shaked and Amnon Netzer. Jerusalem, Ben-Zvi Institute, 1990.

Porten, Bezalel, "Aramaic Papyri and Parchments: A New Look." *The Biblical Archaeologist* 42.2 (1979): 74–104. https://doi.org/10.2307/3209370.

Porten, Bezalel, *Archives from Elephantine: The Life of an Ancient Jewish Military Colony.* Berkeley: University of California Press, 1968.

Sachau, Eduard, *Aramäische Papyrus und Ostraka aus einer jüdischen Militär-Kolonie zu Elephantine.* 2 vols. Leipzig: Hinrichs, 1911.

Sayce, Archibald H., "An Aramaic Ostracon from Elephantine." *Proceedings of the Society of Biblical Archaeology* 31 (1909): 154–55.

Schipper, Bernd U., "The Judeans/Arameans of Elephantine and Their Religion – An Egyptological Perspective," pages 209–336 in *Elephantine in Context*, edited by Reinhard G. Kratz and Bernd U. Schipper. Forschungen zum Alten Testament 155. Mohr Siebeck, 2022.

Schütze, Alexander, "The Aramaic Texts from Arachosia Reconsidered," pages 405–424 in *Taxation in the Achaemenid Empire*, edited by Kristin Kleber. Classica et Orientalia 26 (Wiesbaden: Harrassowitz, 2021).

Steele, John M. "Making Sense of Time: Observational and Theoretical Calendars," pages 470–485 in *The Oxford Handbook of Cuneiform Culture*, edited by Karen Radner and Eleanor Robson. Oxford Handbooks. Oxford: Oxford University Press, 2011.

Stern, Sacha, "The Babylonian Calendar at Elephantine." *Zeitschrift für Papyrologie und Epigraphik* 130 (2000): 159–71.

Stolper, Matthew W., *Entrepreneurs and Empire: The Murašû Archive, the Murašû Firm, and Persian Rule in Babylonia.* Uitgaven van Het Nederlands Historisch-Archaeologisch Instituut Te Istanbul = Publications de l'Institut Historique et Archéologique Néerlandais de Stamboul 54. Istanbul: Nederlands Historisch-Archaeologisch Instituut te Istanbul, 1985.

Toorn, Karel van der, *Becoming Diaspora Jews: Behind the Story of Elephantine*. Anchor Yale Bible Reference Library. New Haven: Yale University Press, 2019.

Wunsch, Cornelia, *Judaeans by the Waters of Babylon: New Historical Evidence in Cuneiform Sources from Rural Babylonia Primarily from the Schøyen Collection*. Babylonische Archive 6. Dresden: ISLET, 2022.

Zadok, Ran, "Yamu-Iziri the Summoner of Yahūdu and Aramaic Linguistic Interference." N.A.B.U. 2015/3: 142–144, 2015.

Antonio Panaino

Cyrus as Mašiaḥ or Χριστός, and the Implications of this Title on the Theology of Power in Late Antiquity

One of the most interesting aspects of the cultural interconnections between Israel and Persia can be found in the story of the Jewish liberation from the Babylonian captivity under the kingdom of Cyrus the Great. His triumph over the Babylonian king Nebuchadnezzar, and the progressive creation of a universal empire changed ancient geopolitics and created a new perception of the political space, in which the limits of the world were perceived as having been expanded beyond the traditional, ethnoreligious and ethnocultural borders. Thus, despite the fact that we cannot uncritically repeat the *ritornello* of the "Achaemenid tolerance", whose reasons and meanings must on the contrary be framed within the prudent definition of intelligent and prudent Persian politics of governance and alliance with other ethno-political subjects, without evoking abstract and unhistorical forms of generosity *a priori*, the strategy chosen by the Persian king with his open support for the reconstruction of the Temple of Jerusalem opened the way to a solid and durable cooperation with the Jewish community. The Persian behavior was taken as different and favorable, and in any case it was worthy of deep consideration and appreciation.

It is within this historical context that we must frame the famous sentence through which Deutero-Isa 45,1, presents the Persian king as "the Anointed" of the Lord:

> יְהוָה לִמְשִׁיחוֹ לְכוֹרֶשׁ אֲשֶׁר־הֶחֱזַקְתִּי בִימִינוֹ לְרַד־לְפָנָיו גּוֹיִם וּמָתְנֵי מְלָכִים אֲפַתֵּחַ לִפְתֹּחַ לְפָנָיו דְּלָתַיִם וּשְׁעָרִים לֹא יִסָּגֵרוּ׃
> כֹּה־אָמַר
>
> Thus, YHWH says to my anointed Cyrus, whose right hand I have held to subdue nations before him; and I will let loose the loins of kings [...].
>
> *haec dicit Dominus Christo meo Cyro cuius adprehendi dexteram ut subiciam ante faciem eius gentes et dorsa regum vertam* [...] *(Vulgata)*.

Despite the various and controversial approaches to this passage, it is evident that at a certain point, even if this was not the true intention of the original redactor (a conclusion which I do not accept, but that some scholars advanced and that we must take into consideration), literally and simply, Cyrus was consi-

Antonio Panaino, University of Bologna, Italy

https://doi.org/10.1515/9783111018638-011

dered a "Messiah" (*mašiaḥ*).[1] This interpretation, probably valid already for the times of the Achaemenian Empire, assumed and then continued to exercise its influence in later times, and it is so that it was received in the Hellenistic and Late Antiquity periods, underpinning new speculations particularly within the Christian environment.

The Greek version of *Deutero-Isaiah* 45,1, as attested in the *Septuaginta*, reads as follows:

> Οὕτος λέγει κύριος ὁ θεὸς τῷ χριστῷ μου Κύρῳ οὗ ἐκράτησα τῆς δεξιᾶς ἐπακοῦσαι ἔμπροσθεν αὐτοῦ ἔθνη καὶ ἰσχὺν βασιλέων διαρρήξω (...)
>
> Thus says the Lord God to my anointed Cyrus, whose right hand I have held, that nations might be obedient before him; and I will break through the strength of kings]),[2]

This sharply confirms that the qualifying title of *Mašiaḥ* was understood as Χριστός.[3] For this reason, we cannot doubt that this text promoted a special image of the Old Persian kingship in the tradition of Late Antiquity, and that this title created a model for the "best" royal person. Certainly, the way in which Cyrus is presented by *Isaiah* 2 attributes a very positive list of qualities to the Persian king, which Lisbeth Fried has summarized well:[4] not only "anointed", but "shepherd", and beloved, so fully legitimized in his royal commitments. The present passage emphasizes the special role of this king with respect to the other ones, and explicitly exalts his role as king of kings, of a superior royal authority under the legitimation of the divine oil that anointed him. In this respect, the messianic function can be equally considered as political, and its model inspired further unpredictable developments. Although this is a delicate matter, we can assume that the general atmosphere of this text implies that "the god of Cyrus" was a universal god, and that the Iranian Ahura Mazdā might, at least for a while, be even perceived as a foreign equivalent of the Hebrew supreme god, or, in a reversed formulation, that behind him the universal creative force of YHWH could be imagined as well.

In a series of previous studies, I have emphasized some very peculiar outcomes stemming from this occurrence, which created a direct trajectory linking

---

1 On this complex matter, see the detailed discussion offered by Fried, "Cyrus the Messiah?."

2 Rahlfs, *Septuaginta*, vol. II, 627.

3 About the title of *mašiaḥ* and its implications, see again Fried, "Cyrus the Messiah?," 373–393; Paul, "Deutero-Isaiah and Cuneiform"; Filippone, "Ciro il Grande tra storia e mito," 178–189. See also Basello, "Il Cilindro di Ciro (ME 90920)," (https://www.academia.edu/944786/_DRAFT_Il_cilindro_di_Ciro_ME_90920_tradotto_dal_testo_babilonese, here quoted with the authorization of the author), note 16, with reference to the comments offered by Elliger, *Deuterojesaja*. 1, 482 and 485–486. Cf. Briant, *Histoire*, 56–58.

4 See again Fried, "Cyrus the Messiah?" *passim*.

the role of the Persian King, Cyrus the Great, to that of Jesus Christ. In this proposal, the witness of a legendary cycle concerning Cyrus and the journey of the Magi to Bethlehem is very fitting, even though its existence is not well known. Actually, this narration underpins the idea that the prophecy of the appearance of a star pointing to the birth of a new supreme king and savior was previously given to another earlier king, worthy of this privilege. The privilege of this dignity was attributed to the only king to have been appointed within the Biblical tradition with the superb title of *Mašiaḥ* and Χριστός, i.e., Cyrus the Great. In this way, we can observe a special application of the doctrine of the *Translatio imperii*, in which the supreme power is transferred from the highest emperor of the ancient world, the founder of the Persian Empire, as the leading manifestation of human and historical authority, to Jesus Christ, taken as the highest incarnation of the divine and eternal power on the earth.[5]

Greek Byzantine and Arabic sources actually knew the present legendary story concerning the appearance of the star to Cyrus, who was asked to order his own priests, i.e., the Magi, to start their journey to Bethlehem and then find the new king of the world. Byzantine manuscripts eventually still preserve a beautiful series of illustrations which visually narrate this extraordinary legend.

A Greek text preserving this tradition is known as Ἐξήγησις τῶν πραχθέντων ἐν Περσίδι, while in Latin it is referred to as *Disputatio de Christo in Persia*, as *De Gestis in Perside* or even as *Narratio de rebus Persicis*. In the present contribution I cannot focus on the philological tradition concerning the present text, whose origin can be framed in the 6th or 7th century and to which many other studies have been dedicated. Here, we can give the essential references to the classical German edition of Bratke,[6] and to the more recent French one by Bringel.[7] While in Bratke's edition the name of Cyrus is quoted just once, although the king, whom we can easily associate with him, would be called just in a single and doubtful situation as Μιθροβάδης,[8] the new critical edition of the text, according to the new edition by Bringel,[9] presents the name of Cyrus at least twice, in both the short and long redactions of this work.

---

5 See Aus, "The Magi," 95–111; Melasecchi, "Il Messia regale," 63–105, esp. 69–90; Panaino, *I Magi evangelici*, 17–18; Panaino, *I Magi e la loro stella*.

6 Bratke, *Das sogenannte Religionsgespräch*; cf. Wirth, *Aus orientalischen Chroniken*, 143–210. See Heyden, *Die "Erzählung des Aphroditian"*. Very useful is the English translation by Eastbourne, *Religious Discussion*. Translated according to the respective editions of Bratkes and Bringel. Cf. also Usener, *Religionsgeschichtliche Untersuchungen*. 1.

7 Bringel, *Une polémique religieuse*, 264–265, 276–277, 330–331, 372–373.

8 See below.

9 Bringel, *Une polémique religieuse*, 264–265, 276–277, 330–331, 372–373.

The text in any case narrates that, one night, a Persian high priest invited Cyrus to come immediately to a pagan temple, where the statues of the gods had begun to dance out of enthusiasm.[10] The main goddess there worshipped is presented with the name of Pegé (Πηγή) "source",[11] a designation which must be explained as a metaphoric reference to the identity of Mary (Μυρία), the mother of Christ. Furthermore, the text states that she would have married a "carpenter", so confirming her identity. Being a "source", as the text affirms, she guarantees a perennial flow of the Spirit, through which only one fish, i.e., Jesus,[12] can proceed. Then, a shining star descends from heaven, stopping on the pillar of the statue of the "Source" revealing to the Persian king the future virginal birth of a child, presented as "the Beginning of Salvation and the End of Destruction". This child would be the son of the great Sun (Ἥλιος), that is presented as the son of a divinity with three names (τριώνυμος). In this case too, it is clear the Trinitarian reference. At that point, all the statues, except the one atop which the star had stopped, collapsed upon the ground. The star stands out not only for its splendor, but for the diadem (διάδημα βασιλικὸς),[13] another evidence recalling the different motifs of the Iranian royalty, if we consider that the diadem was one of the most recognizable regalia of a Persian king in late antiquity. A celestial voice from the star then orders the Persian king to send his Magi to Jerusalem. Finally, the god Dionysus makes his appearance, and manifests himself by predicting that the child would have chased away all the false gods and declaring that "Pegé" would no longer be a human figure, but a superhuman one, for having conceived a being generated from divine Fortune.

Obviously, the image of "Fortuna" (Τύχη),[14] in her turn, recalls again a series of Iranian themes typical of the sphere of royalty and religious sacredness, well known in a late antique context. We are here referring to the well-known concept of *xwarrah* in Middle Persian (but also *farn, farr*; cf. Av. *x*^{v}*arənah-*, and O.P. *farnah-*), the "royal fortune", or *fortuna regia*, which distinguished the superior dimension of divinities, heroes, kings, and saints. This mixture of Iranian and Christian elements confirms the late antique dimension of this source and shows how an ancient tradition, such as the one of Deutero-Isa, was re-adapted to a new

10 About the animation of the statues, a custom attested in Syria and Egypt, cf. Bringel, *Une polémique religieuse*, 46.

11 See Kaufmann, "La Pegè du temple"; cf. Bringel, *Une polémique religieuse*, 264–267, 332–333, *passim*.

12 About the image of the fish in this text, see Heyden, *Die "Erzählung des Aphroditian"*, 243–245 and *passim*. Cf. Dölger, ΙΧΘΥΣ. Cf. Bringel, *Une polémique religieuse*, 266–267, 335–336.

13 Bratke, *Das sogenannte*, 13, 21, 14, 15; Bringel, *Une polémique religieuse*, 268–269, 340–343.

14 Bratke, *Das sogenannte*, 14, 18; 21, 21; 202, 203; Bringel, *Une polémique religieuse*, 268–269, 244–245.

environment. In fact, we cannot forget that the starting point in these conceptions of the Messiah was the idea of power, the royal and divine investiture, which qualified the different authority of the king above the rest of the existing crowns of the world.

I must specify that the narrative context in which the story of Cyrus, the temple and the Magi sent to Bethlehem, is framed within a larger literary work, which presents a theological dispute among Pagans, Christians and Jews, probably placed at the Sasanian court of king Cosroes, presumably the 1st (although that of Cosroes the 2nd is not impossible as well), in which a pagan philosopher, reasonably Mazdean, Aphroditianos, plays the role of an apparently neutral referee, despite the fact that he shows himself to be, at least *in pectore*, a good Christian. Given these general premises, we can come back to the story contained in the *Disputatio*.

King Cyrus ordered the Magi[15] to go to Bethlehem following the star to adore Jesus and Mary, whom they eventually would find, according to the most consolidated tradition of the Christian Nativity, only after having met Herod and his elders. As a variant of the traditional narration, well preserved in the Apocryphal or deuterocanonical tradition, however, it should be noted that Herod's fellows tried to corrupt the Magi, offering them superb gifts[16] in exchange for their silence about the birth of the Savior and the immediate return to their homeland. The Magi responded by reminding them of their captivity in Babylon as a punishment for their wickedness.[17] Thus, this source evokes and contains many other themes and intriguing references, which I cannot deal with on this occasion, but strictly regarding our main subject under discussion we simply can observe that here the link between Cyrus and Jesus is strikingly evident and clear.

We must in particular remark that all the objections raised against these connections in the name of a patent chronological implausibility of the synchronism (Cyrus belongs to the 6th century BCE, while the birth of Jesus should be placed between the year 7 and the year 4 of the same era) between Cyrus and Jesus are completely misleading and ineffective. These arguments completely miss the true point. In light of the evocation of the present messianic connection or trajectory, we are evidently not dealing with a true history or a direct historical link between the two kings in crude empirical terms, but with an ideological and symbolical association, which plays with the fact that the unction of the king, his

15 Bringel, *Une polémique religieuse*, 47–48.

16 Cf. Bringel, *Une polémique religieuse*, 270–273, 352–357. About the gifts of the Magi, and the different versions attested in the mss tradition, see again Bringel, *Une polémique religieuse*, 50–52, 272–273, 364–365.

17 Bringel, *Une polémique religieuse*, 54–61, 361–362.

being anointed by God himself, and thus his transformation into a special person, created a different and special link. Both Cyrus and Jesus were treated as a *persona sacra*, who embodies a number of symbolic and spiritual powers and functions. Cyrus becomes the prototype of the royal identity, as a new David, who, as the best among his contemporary kings above whom he has been placed, sends his own priests, the Magi (who presumably had previously anointed him in God's name as a supreme terrestrial king) to anoint Jesus as the supreme king of the world, as a superhuman hero, the central protagonist of human history. Then, the unction of the king becomes a sacred mark and a legitimization, a charisma, whose distinctive force is additionally emphasized in the Biblical passage from the idea that Cyrus was also God's "shepherd" in I. 44,28 (*ro'ī*).

If these ideological elements did not particularly change or impress the self-representation of the Persian royal power and identity within the Achaemenian cultural milieu, this tradition exercised an enormous influence on the Christian traditions, thanks to the preservation of the Jewish biblical corpus and its commentaries. The material, which favored the inclusion of the Persian (or Parthian) Magi among the protagonists of the Jesus Nativity already within the theatrical composition of the *Infancy Gospel*, certainly was inspired by the role attributed to Cyrus in the *Bible*, and his specific Messianic commitment. The mutual recognition between them is considered, obviously *post eventum*, as a fact developed within the Christian propaganda, and the elaboration of the story of Cyrus' vision fully enters into this tradition, in which it developed the idea that the Iranian Magi would have been the true guardians of a secret originally revealed by Seth and handed down through a book kept in great secrecy amongst them. In few words, they would have preserved the promise of Jesus' birth from immemorial time.

According to the *Armenian Gospel of Childhood* 11,10–11,[18] the Magi, when they came to visit Herod, would have declared, that their travel to Israel would have been due to a divine order, which they kept as a written source, transmitted directly by the Lord to Adam, exactly at the time of the birth of his son Seth. Other sources attributed Seth, in particular, with the redaction of a *Book of Revelation*.[19] He would have delivered the letter sealed by the finger of God to his

18 See now Terian, *The Armenian Gospel*. Peeters, *Évangiles Apocryphes*, 137–139. Cf. Craveri, *I Vangeli apocrifi*, 168–169; de Villard, *Le Leggende Orientali*, 76.

19 The tradition about the direct transmission of a secret message to Seth by Adam is found in the apocryphal text named *Descent into Hell*, chap. 3, and its known also in the *Opus Imperfectum in Matthaeum*, hom. 2,2 (see Migne, *Patrologiae* LVI, cols 637–638). Cf. in particular Messina, *I Magi a Betlemme*, 65–66. This text is known also from the Gnostic Coptic Library of Nag Hammadi. See Craveri, *I Vangeli apocrifi*, 168–169, n. 2; 353. Cf. Moraldi, *Tutti gli Apocrifi*, 692.

descendants, who passed it on to Noah and, through him, from Shem to Abraham and Melchizedek. Finally, it was Melchizedek, at the time of Cyrus, king of Persia, that the divine letter would finally be entrusted to the Magi. Furthermore, we must recall that, according to the *Book of the Cave of Treasures*,[20] Adam would have hidden the three gifts of the Magi in a cave so that this secret, at a certain point, would be transmitted specifically to Seth in order to be finally transmitted to the Magi.[21] Other sources, such as the *Opus Imperfectum in Matthaeum*,[22] also insist on the fact that twelve Magi would have observed the sky every night on a peak named *Mons Victorialis*, until the star announcing the expected event would be finally shown to them and then, they would have undertaken the long-awaited journey to Bethlehem. Some other traditions (from the *Book of the Cave of Treasures* to the *Chronicle of Zuqnin*, etc.)[23] refer to a prediction, made by Zoroaster himself, about the birth of Jesus. This motif presents the synthesis of two traditions in which the role of the messianic figure of Cyrus and the knowledge of the Zoroastrian doctrine concerning the miraculous birth of the three posthumous sons of the Iranian prophet, the last of whom, i.e., the *Saošiiaṇt-* (in Pahlavi *Sōšyans*),[24] merge together and are finally mixed. We must actually emphasize the role of the Mazdean *Saošiiaṇt-* and his two brothers in the final process of resurrecting all the dead. Obviously, as we have seen, from time to time, in this complex cycle, Cyrus the Great also appears, given his importance in the history of Israel.

It is important to recall that this tradition occurs also in an important Arabic source, the *Golden Meadows* by Mas'ūdī,[25] (a work of the 9th century), in which the story narrated in the *Disputatio* is shortly mentioned. This narration insists on the idea that the star can reveal only a "true" king, fully worthy of divine recognition and appointed to as the only person in a condition to transfer it to the Magi. In few words: from an extraordinary (earthly) king to a (superhuman) king. But the memory was not limited to these facts. We must actually observe that a prestigious subtler reference to the anointment of Cyrus becomes the ex-

---

20 See chap. V; cf. Ri, *La Caverne des trésors*, 17–18; Ri, *Commentaire de la Caverne*, 191–197.

21 Bezold, *Die Schatzhöle*, 7–9. Moraldi, *Tutti gli Apocrifi*, 318 in the note. See also Moraldi (ed. and tr.), *Vangelo arabo apocrifo*, 64–66; de Villard, *Le Leggende Orientali, passim*.

22 See de Villard, *Le Leggende Orientali, passim*.

23 See de Villard, *Le Leggende Orientali*, 20–68; cf. also Landau, *The Sages*.

24 Messina, *I Magi a Betlemme*, 84–85, *passim*. Cf. also Panaino, "Jesus' trimorphisms," 167–209; Panaino, "The Esoteric Legacy," 368 – 382.

25 See chapter 68 of the *Golden Meadows*, according to the edition by Barbier de Meynard and Pavet de Courteille, *Maçoudi. Les prairies d'or* 4, 79–80; this chapter has been re-edited with the number 1405 in the revised edition by Pellat, *Les prairies d'or*, 542; cf. van Tongerloo, "*Ecce Magi*," 57–74, in particular 73.

plicit mark of exemplary legitimate kingship. This character was clearly evoked during the Nestorian Synod of the year 544,[26] when the *katholikós* Mār Ābā invoked God's blessing upon the *šāhān šāh* Xusraw Anōširwān, who was present at the event, formally chairing the synodal assembly. On the occasion of the opening session of this religious event, Mār Ābā wished his king as a sort of "new Cyrus", with a clear evocation of the most fitting passage in *Deutero-Isaiah* 45,1:[27]

> By the grace of God, creator, lord and governor of all things, and by the care of the new Cyrus, who is superior to all kings, the gentle and merciful Kosrau, King of kings, to whom, because of his good will, Christ the redeemer of all creatures has suggested to constantly pour out all the goods on his holy Church.

A simple intertextual comparison would confirm that the present reference to Cyrus, who trumps all kings, clearly evokes the submission of the other earthly royal powers (*məlāḵîm*/βασιλέων/*regum*) just mentioned at the beginning of the Biblical chapter pointing to Cyrus as the Messiah. Thus, we can again observe that the evocation of Cyrus was still working in the most appropriate context of the Christian Church of the East with direct pertinence to the Sasanian king, whose profile was equated with the one of his "spiritual" Old Persian ancestors. Mār Ābā did not dare to explicitly call his king Xusraw as "Χριστός", but he was trending very close to this result, because the image of a new Cyrus, winning over all the other contemporary kings, functions as a mirror of the elder one. We should also consider that Xusraw and Mār Ābā were personally in good terms, and that Xusraw saved the Christian Patriarch from the death penalty, which a Zoroastrian tribunal had inflicted against him.[28] Although the Persian king was moved by political reasons, and not just by personal sentiments of human sympathy or friendships,[29] nobody could deny that the Katholikos, who was a Zoroastrian converted to Christianity, was highly considered by Xusraw, and that Xusraw himself considered a good cooperation with the Christian authorities as a necessary instrument underpinning his secular power despite any confessional bias. What we cannot affirm, however, is whether Xusraw had, in his turn, any specific knowledge and conscience of the very singular wish directed toward his own person by Mār Ābā during the opening session of the synodal meeting, or whether

---

26 Chabot, *Synodicon orientale*, 320.

27 Chabot, *Synodicon orientale*, 320: « Par la grâce de Dieu, créateur, seigneur et gouverneur de toutes choses, et par les soins du nouveau Cyrus, qui l'emporte sur tous les rois, le doux et miséricordieux Kosrau, Roi des rois, auquel, à cause de sa bonne volonté, le Christ rédempteur de toutes les créatures a suggéré de répandre constamment tous les biens sur sa sainte Église ».

28 Panaino, "La Chiesa di Persia," 765–863. Cf. Peeters, "Observations," V, 69–112.

29 Panaino, "La Chiesa di Persia," 817–820.

he had a certain knowledge of the Achaemenian fasts. Although the discussion on these matters is still difficult and obviously open, in my opinion, the close relations between the highest members of the intellectual élites of the Christian Church and the contemporary *šāhān šāh*, with whom they interacted, created a cultural space in which the Christians had the chance to use all the opportunities in order to emphasize the good relations between the Iranian royalty and the Jewish-Christian background, of course presented in a way more favorable to the Christian (and not Jewish) interpretations. In this respect, the formula adopted by Mār Ābā during this synodal meeting cannot be considered just as a sort of *captatio benevolentiae*, but it continues a long-aged tradition in which the commitment of the king of Persia assumed a special value in the history of human salvation according to a Christian perspective. This opportunity, of course, was not lost or forgotten by the Christian communities, especially by those who were trying to convert Iranian peoples. In particular, we must think about the Christian strategy toward the conquest of the religious power, which probably tried to imitate what already had happened in Armenia. A religious triumph might have been attained only through the direct conversion of members of the royal family and, finally, of the king himself. It is for this reason that the center of the Christian Church was erected in proximity to the royal palace of Ctesiphon, so that the search for a direct political and spiritual dialogue was openly pursued. At the same time, the Mazdean Church, well conscious of the risks, reacted with the most brutal violence, in particular when Zoroastrian aristocrats or members of the highest priestly family were baptized.[30] Strange episodes such as the ones concerning the personal story of one of the most interesting philosophical and intellectual authorities of the age of Xusraw 1st, the translator and fine commentator of Aristotle and Plato, i.e. Paul the Persian,[31] originally Zoroastrian, then converted to Christianity, elected to the highest ranks of the Church, and again probably re-converted to Zoroastrianism, shows the complexity of these intercultural exchanges taking place within Persian society of late antiquity. It is difficult to imagine that Paul and his king, for whom this peculiar scholar translated and interpreted many Greek philosophical sources, had not spoken of Cyrus and his role as Messiah as well as of other Persian details in the Jewish and Christian literatures.

On the other hand, one cannot forget that the Iranian lands were places in which the intellectual role played by the Jewish schools of commentators and

30 Panaino, "La Chiesa di Persia," 820–834.
31 See Panaino, ABĒBĪM, 59–61. Gutas, "Paul the Persian," 231–240; Teixidor, *Aristote en syriaque*; Bruns, "Paul der Perser," 28–53; King, "The Study of Logic."

interpreters who created the Babylonian *Talmud* had a special influence,[32] and that the interference between Mazdean and Jewish traditions was not at all rare or impossible.[33] We should even reflect on the cultural impact of the Jewish historical literature on the Persian intellectual world, and assume as a working hypothesis that Jewish authorities were active,[34] sometimes in plausibly prudent, but not hostile, relations with the royal power. The Jewish authorities might have even created summaries and *excerpta* of their literary and historical pieces of information about the Achaemenians and their power to give a substantial witness to the good relations already existing between the Iranian world and the Hebrew culture and its people. Concerning Widengren's overly optimistic evaluation of the later Jewish sources,[35] for instance concerning Yezdegird I and the exilarch, Neusner[36] expressed some prudent *caveats*, but, although these assumptions were ungrounded or excessive, we at least must observe that in the Rabbinical literature the memory of Isaiah and the Persians of past times were still usable within the Sasanian context, despite its limited value. Actually, we must also take into consideration that some *Ravas* of the 4th century commented on Isa 45:1, stating that Cyrus was not really referred to as the Messiah, and even assumed that all the Persians would be destined to Gehenna.[37] I wonder if these arguments actually circulated as a common opinion or if they were limited to the scope of a few religious authorities, because the impact of these invectives would have been certainly negative from the Persian side. Some Talmudic and Midrashic sources deal with the embarrassing definition of Cyrus as a "Messiah" to justify or even to deny it. We know, for instance that, in the *Megillah* 12a, it is assumed that Cyrus was obviously *not* the Messiah, while the *Roš Hašanah* 3b at least stated that it was *kāšēr* under the influence of a pseudo-etymological speculation about his name, *Kōreš* in Hebrew, interpreted as an anagram of *kāšēr*.[38] Another solution was that of accepting the messianic definition, but at the price of denying his full Iranian origin, so introducing the assumption that he would have been the son of Esther and Ahasuerus. This story was later developed in the Judaeo-Persian literary tradition by Šāhīn, in the *'Ezrā-nāma*,[39] a poem written in the

32 Secunda, *The Iranian Talmud*. Cf. Neusner, "How Much Iranian," 184–190.

33 See Neusner, *History of the Jews* 4 & 5.

34 For instance, we cannot forget the role of the Exilarches already since Parthian times, and their influence also during the Sasanian era, as well shown by Herman, *Prince*.

35 Widengren, "The Status of the Jews," 117–162, in particular 140.

36 Neusner, *History of the Jews*, 5, 12–13.

37 Neusner, *History of the Jews*, 4, 375–383.

38 Netzer, "Some Notes," 35–52, in particular 42.

39 Bacher, "Le livre d'Ezra," 249–280; Bacher, *Zwei jüdisch-persische*, 66–71. Netzer, "Some Notes," 35–52; Netzer, *'Ezrā-nāma*, 131, accessible online on the website https://www.iranicaonline.org/articles/ezra-nama.

year 1372. The reception of this tradition can be found even in Islamic sources, such as Ṭabarī.

Thus, we apparently face a problem: it seems that the Christians have played with the Biblical tradition about the Messiah and royal power, using a deliberate revival of the image of the sacred royalty from a Christian point of view, with the patent scope of sympathizing with the dominating Iranian element, and within the perspective of a conversion of the king. It is reasonable to wonder whether the Jews, in their turn, had used their literary background and their secular presence in the Iranian and Babylonian lands to improve all the potentially positive resonances with the leading powers, or if their approach had been more skeptical, as some Rabbinical sources invite us to presume, in particular when we observe that the apparent universalism of Isaiah was implicitly denied recurring to the explanation that Cyrus was nothing but a hidden Jew, son of Esther, or that his genealogy could justify the role given to him by god.[40] Other reasons against the image of Cyrus, belonging both to the Palestinian and the Babylonian Rabbinical traditions, have been previously collected by Louis Ginzburg,[41] Ephraim E. Urbach,[42] and later with new arguments by Jason Sion Moktarian.[43] From these studies it is now more clear that a number of striking evidences shows the presence of strong criticisms against the image of Cyrus within the exegetic tradition of the Babylonian *Talmud*, so that we must at least infer a remarkable difference between Jews and Christians in the strategies concerning the interpretation of Cyrus's role. While the latter tried to be inclusive, the other part marked the ethno-cultural borders in a radical way. In this respect, the political dimension of the Messiah remained a crucial problem, and its treatment a sensible matter, especially within the Iranian milieu, despite the fact that we still need further investigations.

Bibliography

Aus, Roger D., "The Magi at the Birth of Cyrus, and the Magi at Jesus' Birth in Matt. 2:1–12," pages 95–111 in *Barabbas and Esther and Other Studies in the Judaic Illumination of Earliest Christianity*. Edited by Roger David Aus. Atlanta: Scholars Press, 1987.

Barbier de Meynard, Charles and Pavet de Courteille, Abel, *Maçoudi. Les prairies d'or*, Tome 4: Texte et traduction par Charles Barbier de Meynard. Paris: Société Asiatique, 1865.

40 Netzer, "Some Notes," 42–43. Despite the Jewish mother, even the *'Ezrā-nāma* calls Cyrus "pagan", as noted by Netzer.

41 See Ginzburg, *The Legends of the Jews*, 433, n. 7.

42 Urbach, "Koresh"; reprinted in *The World of the Sages*, 407–410.

43 Mokhtarian, "Rabbinic Depictions," 114–141.

Bacher, Wilhelm, "Le livre d'Ezra de Schahin Schirazi," *Revue des études juives* 55 (1908): 249–280.
Bacher, Wilhelm, *Zwei jüdisch-persische Dichter Schahin und Imrani*. 31. Jahresbericht der Landes-Rabbinerschule in Budapest für das Schuljahr 1907–1908, Zweite Hälfte. Budapest: Adolf Alkalay & Sohn, 1908.
Basello, Gian P., "Il Cilindro di Ciro (ME 90920)," (http://unior.academia.edu/GianPietroBasello/Papers/982178/_DRAFT_Il_cilindro_di_Ciro_ME_90920_tradotto_dal_testo_babilonese
Bezold, Carl, *Die Schatzhöle aus dem syrischen Text dreier unedirten Handschriften in's Deutsche übersetzt und mit Anmerkungen versehen*. Erster Abteilung. Leipzig: Hinrichs, 1883.
Bratke, Eduard, *Das sogenannte Religionsgespräch am Hof der Sasaniden*. Texte und Untersuchungen zur Geschichte der altchristlichen Literatur, 18. Bd., Heft 3. Leipzig: Hinrichs, 1899.
Briant, Pierre, *Histoire de l'Empire Perse de Cyrus à Alexandre*. Paris : Fayard, 1996.
Bringel, Pauline, *Une polémique religieuse à la cour perse : le* De gestis in Perside. *Histoire du texte, Edition critique et traduction*. Paris, Thèse présentée par Pauline Bringel, sous la direction de Jean Gascou. Sorbonne, 2007.
Bruns, Peter, "Paul der Perser. Christ und Philosoph im spätantiken Sasanidenreich," *Römische Quartalschrift für christliche Altertumskunde und Kirchengeschichte* 104 (2009): 28–53.
Chabot, Jean-Baptiste, *Synodicon orientale ou recueil de synodes nestoriens*. Paris, Imprimerie Nationale.
Ginzburg, Louis, *The Legends of the Jews*. Vol. 6: *From Moses to Esther.* Philadelphia: The Jewish Publication Society of America, 1928.
Herman, Geoffrey, *A Prince without a Kingdom. The Exilarch in the Sasanian Era*. Texts and Studies in Ancient Judaism 150. Tübingen: Mohr Siebeck.
Landau, Brent C. *The Sages and the Star-Child: An Introduction to the Revelation of the Magi, An Ancient Christian Apocryphon*. A dissertation presented by Brent Christian Landau to The Faculty of Harvard Divinity School in partial fulfillment of the requirements for the degree of Doctor of Theology in the Subject of New Testament and Early Christianity. Harvard University, Cambridge, Massachusetts, 2008.
Elliger, Karl, *Deuterojesaja*. 1. Teilband. *Jesaja 40,1–45,7.* Biblischer Kommentar Altes Testament, 11/1. Neukirchen-Vluyn: Neukirchener Verlag, 1978.
Filippone, Ela, "Ciro il Grande tra storia e mito: Il sovrano ideale e l'iscrizione che non c'è," pages 178–189 in *Hinc illae lacrimae Studi in memoria di Carmen Maria Radulet*. Edited by Gaetano Platania, Cristina Rosa, and Mariagrazia Russo. Vol. 1. Viterbo: Sette Città, 2010.
Fried, Lisbeth S., "Cyrus the Messiah? The Historical Background to Isaiah 45:1," *The Harvard Theological Review* 95/4 (2002): 373–393.
Gutas, Dimitri, "Paul the Persian on the Classification of the Parts of Aristotle's Philosophy: A Milestone Between Alexandria and Baghdad," *Der Islam* 60/2 (1983): 231–240.
Heyden, Katharina, *Die "Erzählung des Aphroditian": Thema und Variationen einer Legende im Spannungsfeld von Christentum und Heidentum*. Studien zur Antike und Christentum 53. Tübingen: Mohr Siebeck, 2009.
Kaufmann, Carl M., "La Pegè du temple de Hierapolis. Contribution à la symbolique du christianisme primitive." *RHR* 2 (1901) : 529–548.
King, David, "The Study of Logic in Syriac Culture," pages 163–208 in *La philosophie en syriaque*. Édité par Henri Hugonnard-Roche et Emiliano Fiori. *Études syriaques* (2019) 16. Paris: Geuthner.
Melasecchi, Beniamino, "Il Messia regale di Matteo: ascendenze zoroastriane, 1," pages 63–105 in *Il Salvatore del mondo. Prospettive di salvezza nell'Oriente antico*. A cura di Beniamino Melasecchi. Roma: IsIAO, 2003.
Messina, Giuseppe, *I Magi a Betlemme e una predicazione di Zoroastro*. Sacra Scriptura Antiquitatibus Orientalibus illustrata, 3. Romae: apud Pontificium Institutum Biblicum, Scuola Tipografica Pio X, 1933.

Migne, Jacques P., *Patrologiae Cursus Completus Series Graeca*, Tomus LVI, Lutetiae Parisorum: J. P. Migne Editor, 1862.
Monneret de Villard, Ugo, *Le Leggende Orientali sui Magi Evangelici*. Studi e Testi 163. Città del Vaticano: Biblioteca Apostolica Vaticana, 1952.
Mokhtarian, Jason S., "Rabbinic Depictions of the Achaemenid King Cyrus the Great: The *Babylonian Esther Midrash* (bMeg. 10b–17a) in Its Iranian Context," pages 114–141 in *The Talmud in Tts Iranian Context*. Edited by Carol Bakhos and M. Rahim Shayegan. Texts and Studies in Ancient Judaism / Texte und Studien zum Antiken Judentum 135. Tübingen: Mohr Siebeck, 2010.
Moraldi, Luigi, *Vangelo arabo apocrifo dell'apostolo Giovanni da un manoscritto della Biblioteca Ambrosiana*. Milano: Jaca Book, 1991.
Moraldi, Luigi, *Tutti gli Apocrifi del Nuovo Testamento*. Casale Monferrato: Piemme, 2007.
Netzer, Ammon, "Some Notes on the Characterization of Cyrus the Great in Jewish and Judeo-Persian Writings," pages 35–52 in *Commemoration Cyrus*. *Acta Iranica* 2, Téhéran – Liège: Peeters, 1974.
Netzer, Ammon, *ʿEzrā-nāma*, in *Encyclopeœdia Iranica*, vol. IX, ed. by Ehasan Yarshater. New York: Routledge & Kegan Paul, 1999, 131; accessible also online on the website https://www.iranicaonline.org/articles/ezra-nama
Neusner, Jacob, "How Much Iranian in Jewish Babylonia," *Journal of the American Oriental Society* 95 (1975): 184–190.
Neusner, Jacob, *The History of the Jews in Babylonia*. Part 4: *The Age of Shapur II*. Eugene, Oregon: Wipp & Stock, 1999.
Neusner, Jacob, *The History of the Jews in Babylonia*. Part 5: *Later Sasanian Times*. Eugene, Oregon: Wipp & Stock, 1999.
Panaino, Antonio, *I Magi evangelici. Storia e simbologia tra Oriente e Occidente*. Ravenna: Longo, 2004.
Panaino, Antonio, "La Chiesa di Persia e l'Impero Sasanide: Conflitto e integrazione," pages 765–863 in *Cristianità d'Occidente e Cristianità d'Oriente (secoli VI–XI). LI Settimana di Studio della Fondazione CISAM, Spoleto, 24–30 aprile 2003*. Spoleto: CISAM, 2004.
Panaino, Antonio. *I Magi e la loro stella. Storia, scienza e teologia di un racconto evangelico*. Parola di Dio, II serie, 67. Cinisello Balsamo: San Paolo, 2012.
Panaino, Antonio. *"Jesus' trimorphisms and tetramorphisms in the meeting with the Magi,"* pages 167–209 in *From Aṣl to Zā'id: Essays in Honour of Éva M. Jeremiás*. Edited by Iván Szántó. Acta et Studia XIII. Piliscsaba, The Avicenna Institute of Middle Eastern Studies, 2015.
Panaino, Antonio, "The Esoteric Legacy of the Magi of Bethlehem in the Framework of the Iranian Speculations about Jesus, Zoroaster and His Three Posthumous Sons," pages 368–382 in *Apocryphal and Esoteric Sources in the Development of Christianity and Judaism: The Eastern Mediterranean, the Near East and Beyond*. Edited by Igor Dorfmann-Lazarev. Brill: Leiden, 2021.
Panaino, Antonio, ABĒBĪM. *"Fearless". Who Was Afraid of the End of the Millennium? New Approaches to the Interpretation of the Traditional Date of Zoroaster.* With contributions by Domenico Agostini, Jeffrey Kotyk, Paolo Ognibene and Alessia Zubani. Milan: Mimesis, 2022.
Paul, Shalom M., "Deutero-Isaiah and Cuneiform Royal Inscriptions," *Journal of the American Oriental Society* 88/1 (1968): 180–186.
Peeters, Paul, *Évangiles Apocryphes*, II, *L'Évangile de l'enfance*. Rédaction syriaque, arabe et arméniennes traduites et annotées. Paris: A. Picard Éditeur, 1914.
Peeters, Paul, "Observations sur la Vie syriaque de Mar Aba, Catholicos de l'église perse (540–552)," pages 69–112 in *Miscellanea Giovanni Mercati pubblicata sotto gli auspici di Sua Santità Pio 12. in occasione dell'ottantesimo natalizio dell'e.mo Cardinale bibliotecario e archivista di Santa Romana Chiesa*, vol. V. Città del Vaticano: Biblioteca Apostolica Vaticana, 1946.

Pellat, Charles, Mas'ūdī, *Les prairies d'or*, Traduction française de Barbier de Meynard et Abel Pavet de Courteille, revue et corrigée par Charles Pellat. Tome II. Paris: Société Asiatique, Collection d'ouvrages orientaux, 1964.
Rahlfs, Alfred, *Septuaginta, Id est Vetus Testamentum graece iuxta LXX interpretes*, Duo volumina in uno. Stuttgart: Deutsche Bibelgesellschaft, 1979.
Ri, Su-Min, *La Caverne des trésors : les deux recensions syriaques*, éditées [et traduites], 2 vols, CSCO 581, Subsidia 103. Lovanii: Peeters, 1987.
Secunda, Shai, *The Iranian Talmud. Reading the Bavli in Its Sasanian Context.* Divinations: Rereading in Late Ancient Religion, Philadelphia: University of Pennsylvania Press, 2013.
Teixidor, Javier, *Aristote en syriaque. Paul le Perse, logicien du VIe siècle*. Paris: CNRS éditions, 2003.
Terian, Abraham, *The Armenian Gospel of the Infancy with three early versions of the Protevangelium of James*. Oxford: Oxford University Press, 2008.
Urbach, Ephraim E., "Koresh vehakhrazato be'einei hazal." *Molad* 157 (1961) 368–374.
Urbach, Ephraim E., *The World of the Sages Collected Studies*. Jerusalem: The Magnes Press, 1988.
van Tongerloo, Alois, "*Ecce Magi ab Oriente venerunt*," *Acta Orientalia Belgica* 7 (1992): 57–74.
Widengren, Geo, "The Status of the Jews in the Sassanian Empire," *Iranica Antiqua* 1 (1961): 117–162.

Laurie E. Pearce

Through a Babylonian looking glass: a perspective on foreign wives

As Ezra and his company of travelers camped outside of Jerusalem and prepared offerings prior to their entry into the city, he received from his officers this message concerning the Israelites' behavior:

> They have taken their daughters as wives for themselves and for their sons; so that the holy seed has become intermingled with the peoples of the land; and it is the officers and prefects who have taken the lead in this trespass. When I heard this, I rent my garment and robe, I tore hair out of my head and beard, and I sat down desolate. Around me gathered all who were concerned over the words of the God of Israel because of the returning exiles' trespass, while I sat desolate until the evening offering. (Ezra 9:1–4)[1]

The news of intermarriage between the people of Israel, including priests and Levites, and peoples of foreign lands, may have rendered Ezra disconsolate, but it can hardly have surprised him.[2]

Ezra resided in Babylonia, a generation after revolts against Xerxes accelerated a shifting economic landscape and transformed the power and standing of the urban prebendary elite.

His immediate elders belonged to the generation of the "end of archives," in which elite northern Babylonians were removed from power derived from connections to the temples they served. Social change in Babylonia in the generation immediately preceding Ezra's time is also reflected in marriage records. The once-strong divide that precluded intermarriage between the urban elite and non-elite families gave way to a more homogeneous set of social and economic norms. Indeed, the language that recorded intermarriage between non-elite Babylonians and non-Babylonians preceding the "end of archives" was widely adopted in marriage documents in the period following it. Intermarriages of Ezra's predecessors into the Babylonian host community would have conformed to the norms defining non-elite Babylonian marriages; they would have likewise been aware of the social barriers that precluded their marriage into families of the elite. The offspring of this generation would have learned, at their parents' knees and by

---

1 Translation of the Jewish Publication Society (JPS) 1985.

2 Ezra 9:1 records that the Israelites mingled with and adopted practices of Canaanites, Hittites, Perizzites, Jebusites, Ammonites, Moabites, Egyptians, and Amorites.

Laurie E. Pearce, University of California, Berkeley, USA

https://doi.org/10.1515/9783111018638-012

their own observation, of the social barriers that defined the life of Babylonians and of foreigners resident in Babylonia. But by the time Ezra assumed his leadership position, both the Judean community and its Babylonian host were transformed with respect to personal (e.g., marriage), as well as public (e.g., cultic) practices. The similarities in these transformations suggest that a broader understanding of the Babylonian background should shed light on motivations for Ezra's ban on foreign marriages. This paper begins with a description of transformations in Babylonian society in the fifth century BCE, focusing on marriage practices and the realignment of the professional cult families. Against this background, it then turns to identify the main reasons Bible scholars label as the motivation for Ezra's foreign marriage ban. Finally, it considers Ezra's marriage ban as part of a broader pattern of social change and restoration of cultural norms following a series of political disruptions.

Transformation in Babylonian Society

A widely accepted date of 458 BCE for Ezra's mission situates the foreign marriage ban one generation after revolts against Xerxes which resulted in the "end of archives," a marked break in the production of cuneiform documentation of the activities of the prebendary urban elite.[3] In 484 BCE, Xerxes' second year, production of records associated with the homogeneous social sector of the temples of Sippar, Borsippa, Babylon, Dilbat, and Kish ceased. This resulted when Xerxes suppressed revolts led by Šamaš-erība and Bēl-šimânni,[4] and removed from power the prebendary elite who had lent support to the insurrections. Records of their activities, which constituted the vast temple and private archives of the long sixth century, ended with the termination of their association with the northern temple cults. The disruption is further reflected in transformations of other social and economic institutions, notably marriage practices, and, to a degree, the early stages of the re-establishment of a venerable cult. It is in this period of complex realignment of social structures that Ezra's marriage ban emerges.

---

3 For the date of Ezra's mission, see, e.g., Demsky, "Who Came First?" and Williamson, *Ezra and Nehemiah*. For more recent sources, see Carr, "Criteria and Periodization," 12, Lemaire, *Levantine Epigraphy*, 87.

4 Waerzeggers, "The Babylonian Revolts," 159–60.

Changes in Babylonian Marriage Practices

Marriage constraints were not unique to the Judean community. Although Babylonian texts contain no explicit ban similar to the Deuteronomic injunction,[5] recent studies of surviving cuneiform marriage documents identify the existence of parameters and guidelines for marriage and intermarriage in Babylonia.[6] In *Babylonian Marriage Agreements* (BMA), Martha Roth outlined the structure and terminology of the genre, and focused her discussion on legal and economic implications of the material goods – dowry and marriage gifts – associated with marriage.[7] Her discussion of intermarriage was limited to noting the different linguistically-defined ethnic backgrounds of contracting parties.[8] As new publications expanded the corpus of marriage texts, recent investigations employing social science tools and approaches have produced more nuanced understandings of the practices and social location of intermarriage, including between Babylonians and Judeans.[9]

Two recent studies have transformed our understanding of marriage practices in the long sixth century and beyond. Their important points are summarized here to provide Babylonian context for the treatment of marriages of foreign

5 Deut 7: 1–4; cf. Exod 34: 11–16.

6 In the Babylonian context, intermarriage is defined as marriage between a Babylonian and a non-native Babylonian; in the Assyriological literature, it is increasingly termed an "ethnically mixed marriage." The labels "ethnically mixed marriage" and "intermarriage" suggest a distinction without a difference. The two terms have established a foothold in their respective scholarly communities and serve as discourse markers in each: Assyriology and biblical scholarship, respectively (Waerzeggers, "Changing Marriage Practices," 101–9). In cuneiform sources, the determination of an individual's background relies on two points: (1) members of the urban elite are identified by the presence of a family name in the third position of their name formulae (Personal Name son of Father's Name descendant of Family Name). The families so identified enjoyed the prestige associated with prebendary, priestly offices in the cults of the major cities., and (2) the linguistic background of a person's name. Although names of non-Babylonian origin can be relatively easy to identify in the onomasticon, the difficulties of relying on onomastics to determine an individual's geographic or ethnic origin are well-known.

7 Roth, *Babylonian Marriage Agreements*, 8–10. She delved into details of specific social and legal components of marriage in the following studies: "Age at Marriage"; "She Will Die"; "Contested Status"; "Women in Transition"; "Material Composition"; "Dowries of the Women"; "Neo-Babylonian Widow."

8 Roth, *Babylonian Marriage Agreements*, 24–25, and in the commentary to individual texts where foreign (i.e., non-Babylonian) names appear.

9 Neo-Babylonian and Achaemenid marriage agreement texts identified and studied subsequent to Roth's study include: Wunsch, *Urkunden zum Ehe*, texts 1–7; Jursa, "Babylonian Economy"; Abraham, "West Semitic and Judean Brides"; Bloch, "Judeans in Sippar and Susa"; Waerzeggers, "Locating Contact."

wives.[10] In his 2019 study, *The Social World of the Babylonian Priest*, Bastian Still analyzed the world of the Babylonian elite of Borsippa, as reflected across four relationship rubrics: landholding, lending of silver, friendships, and marriage.[11] Relevant here is his analysis of eighty-one marriages that occurred over a 140-year period. He concluded that marriages in the priestly class adhered to a strict hypergamous system, dependent on the social rank of the priestly families. Daughters of prebendary-holding priestly families married into families of higher rank than of their families of origin, eventually depleting the ranks of daughters eligible for marriage to sons of the lowest priestly families. The solution was to accept women of non-priestly background as brides for the sons of the lowest ranking elite families. The women who were married into this system were wealthy and urban, their economic standing augmenting their social capital.[12] Such movement across levels of social standing helped perpetuate the urban elite's social and economic privileges and was:

> closely monitored and continuously re-negotiated through such hypergamous marriage bonds. *The pervasive necessity to preserve ritual fitness ("purity") and to affirm and defend status determined all social choices made by the priestly clans, as well as their economic outlook* (emphasis added).[13]

Although the circle of priestly families was defined by religiously determined stability and immutability, the marriage documents themselves do not address cultic purity, although it was a requisite for admission to the priestly, prebendary ranks.[14] However, prosperity could also grant social mobility and entrée into the priestly sphere, as evidenced by those few occasions in which "entrepreneurial non-priests managed to marry into established priestly houses – invariably because of the latter's financial difficulties."[15] In pre-484 BCE Babylonian marriage

10 Still, *Social World*; Waerzeggers, "Changing Marriage Practices."

11 Still, *Social World*, 5.

12 Still emphasized that there isn't sufficient evidence to demonstrate widespread implementation of this hypergamous system outside of the Borsippa archives. Although the Sippar marriage agreement of the Judean bride, Kaššaya, to Gūzānu of the Miller family, does not represent a true instance of such hypergamy, it suggests that the system operated, at varying degrees of strictness, in multiple urban settings.

13 Jursa, "Neo-Babylonian Empire," 154–55.

14 Caroline Waerzeggers briefly describes the purity requirements to which members of the (Neo-)Babylonian priesthood were subject (*The Ezida Temple*, 51–54). In addition to meeting standards of physical and moral cleanliness, candidates for the Neo-Babylonian priesthood were also required to register with the king, who retained the right to deny individuals access to the cult. The potential negative consequences of the close connection between crown and palace are apparent in the fate of the priestly class following the revolts against Xerxes.

15 Jursa, "The Neo-Babylonian Empire," 155.

documents, the limited degree of such movement is observed in and across four categories of marriage:[16]

1. Elite endogamous marriages joined individuals from elite families of the same social hierarchy.[17] Inclusion of family names in their name formulae served to mark individuals' membership in this group connected to priestly offices of the temples.[18]

2. Non-elite endogamous marriages united members of the upper class to other members of the upper-class,[19] primarily wealthy merchants or members of the court, whose professions granted them social and financial standing.

3. Exogamous marriages occurred between elite and non-elite individuals, the former identified by presence of a family name, the latter, lacking the same. Most instances of this common form of mixed marriage occurred between Babylonians.[20]

4. Ethnically mixed marriages united members of non-elite status and persons of non-Babylonian background. Waerzeggers notes that the difficulty of assigning such marriages a place in the overall system of marriages is impacted by the limitations of onomastic evidence, the openness of Babylonia to newcomers, and the widely differing status of individuals with non-Babylonian names.[21]

The clear social boundaries are evident in the language and structure of specific components of marriage contracts. Those of the elite focus on dowry, whereas less than twenty percent of non-elite marriage documents do so.[22] Language in the marriage documents of the non-elite controlled the marriage partners' sexual behavior through institution of various punishments. The divorce clause imposed a fine in silver on husbands who were unfaithful or otherwise wrongly dismissed a wife. Unfaithful wives were condemned to death by the iron

16 Following Waerzeggers, "Changing Marriage Practices," 101–31.

17 For a description of the hierarchy among priests (and by extension, priestly families), see the discussion in Waerzeggers, *The Ezida Temple,* 42–51.

18 Still, *Social World,* 30. These marriages belong to Group B in Waerzeggers, "Changing Marriage Practices," 124–26.

19 Group A in Waerzeggers, "Changing Marriage Practices," 121–23.

20 Group C in Waerzeggers, "Changing Marriage Practices," 127–28.

21 Waerzeggers, "Changing Marriage Practices," 108.

22 Information about the composition and disposal of dowries is also found in: (1) dowry receipts, legal texts recording the bride's family transfer of the dowry to the groom's family (Wunsch, *Urkunden zum Ehe,* 2), and (2) dowry lists. The hundreds of preserved dowry receipts outnumber the marriage contracts themselves and are the primary source for the study of the composition of the dowry (Roth, "Material Composition"). A fourth category of text is the dowry promise, a record of the intention of the bride's family to transfer the dowry at the time of marriage (Waerzeggers, "Changing Marriage Practices," 104).

dagger.[23] This harsh threat, of which there is no record of having been effected, appeared exclusively in marriage documents of brides lacking a traditional family name, regardless of the groom's standing, social connections, professional or administrative titles or material wealth. The iron dagger clause marked and reinforced such brides' outsider status vis-à-vis the elite status of the groom's family. Such signals of social location were of particular importance to the urban elite, for whom preservation of the purity of family lines was intrinsically tied to their prebendary temple service.

Even prior to the "end of archives," the language of marriage documents evidenced change, reflecting incipient shifts in the fabric of Babylonian society. BMA 25, written at the end of Darius I's reign (year 35, 486 BCE), records the marriage of a woman without a family name. Among the innovations from previous contractual patterns was the fact that she negotiated the terms for herself, contributed dowry to the marriage and avoided inclusion of the iron dagger clause, which had previously appeared in all marriage documents of non-elite women. This is a pivotal document, as subsequent marriage documents all omit penalty clauses, rendering non-elite marriages in the same terms as those of the elite. These changes signal "a departure from the communal values that had underpinned lower class marriage at least since the second half of the seventh century BCE."[24]

The Judean Marriages

As the interest here is in ways that marriage practices in Babylonia might inform understanding the circumstances that prompted Ezra's marriage ban, evidence of ethnically-mixed marriages involving Judeans and Babylonians should be considered. The cuneiform marriage documents of Judeans in Babylonia all pre-date 484 BCE and adhere to the patterns attested in the contemporaneous sources. Limitations of the data as a means of assessing the impact of Babylonian social conditions on Judean marriages include: (1) The gender balance in marriages of Judean brides to Babylonian grooms does not parallel that attested in the Ezra narrative, concerned with the marriage of Judean men to *foreign wives*. Thus, a direct correspondence of social praxis, e.g., hypergamy, that functions in gender-specific ways may not be evident.; (2) The small size of the Judean marriage text corpus provides a limited perspective on the scope of social and economic condi-

23 Roth, "She Will Die," 186–206.

24 Waerzeggers, "Changing Marriage Practices," 118.

tions associated with Judean marriages in Babylonia.[25] Surely, more than two marriages took place in the Judean community, even taking into consideration the *communis opinio* that a verbal agreement sufficed to effect a contract for marriages which included no special circumstances;[26] (3) As the entire marriage corpus spans nearly 150 years, each document provides a snapshot of the details of a specific marriage at a singular point in time. It is to the two prominent cases that this study now turns, the marriages of the Judean brides, Nanaya-kanāt and Kaššaya to their respective grooms.

Nanaya-kanāt's Marriage Contract

Nanaya-kanāt's marriage document was written in the fifth year of Cyrus (533 BCE) in Yahudu, a Babylonian mirror town in which many Judean deportees were settled. Indirect onomastic evidence identifies Nanaya-kanāt as Judean, even though her mother's West Semitic name, Dibbi, is of uncertain etymology and her maternal grandfather bore the Akkadian name Dannâ. The large number of

---

25 The two most frequently discussed Judean marriage texts are those of Nanaya-kanāt and of Kaššaya. Together they constitute but 4 % of the total number of texts (50) on which Waerzeggers based her 2020 study of the evolution of Babylonian marriage practices. A third text, BMA 17 (YOS 6 188), belongs to this category but is much less informative than the Nanaya-kanāt and Kaššaya contracts. BMA 17, written in ālu-ša-Lanē (27.ix.14 Nabonidus = 542 BCE) should be considered another instance of a ethnically-mixed marriage, notably of a Judean groom to a Babylonian bride (see also Alstola, *Judeans in Babylonia*, 132 and Lemos, *Marriage* Gifts, 237). The groom bears the good Babylonian name Nabû-aḫ-uṣur, but is identified as Judean by his Yahwistic patronymic, Hatāma (*ᵐha-ta-a-ma*) (Zadok, *The Jews in Babylonia*, 39.) The patronymic of the final witness, [...] son of Amma (*ᵐam-ma-a*), is West Semitic (Zadok, "Representation of Foreigners," 498; Zadok. "New Documents," 495.

As witnesses are drawn from the social circles of the contracting parties, this supports locating the groom's family among individuals of foreign origin in southern Babylonia. Zadok located the town ālu-ša-Lanē in the vicinity of Uruk but noted that the final element of the toponym may be emended to -Banē [RG 8 p. 13], a town located on the Middle Euphrates RG 8: 424 (Appendix), at a remove from the Babylonian heartland, perhaps reducing the impact of Babylonian practice on this specific marriage.

26 This is deduced from the text of Neo-Babylonian law §9A, which reads: "A man who makes an oral promise of the dowry for his daughter, or writes it on a tablet for her, and whose estate later decreases – he shall give to his daughter a dowry in accordance with the remaining assets of his estate; the father-in-law (i.e., the bride's father) and the groom will not by mutual agreement alter the commitments." (*amēlu ša nudunnû ana mārtišu iqbûma lu ṭuppi išṭurušu u arki nikkassīšu imṭû akî nikkassīšu ša rēḫi nudunnû ana mārtišu inandin eme u ḫatanu aḫāmeš ul innû*) (Roth, *Law Collections*, 146–47: iii 23–31.

witnesses bearing Yahwistic names locates the marriage in the Judean community, as witnesses were typically drawn from the circle of a principal's associates, friends, or colleagues.[27] Thus it is reasonable to suggest that Nanaya-kanāt's father, absent from this document and presumed deceased, was himself of Judean descent. Taking 572 BCE, the date of the earliest known Yahudu text, as a reference point, and approximating the length of a generation at 25 years, her marriage occurred as early as the second generation of Yahudu's existence as a deportee settlement. Her family would have lived in Mesopotamia for a long enough period to have observed marriage practices among their Babylonian neighbors, and perhaps, to have incorporated those practices into its own family customs.[28] The lack of clan affiliation in the groom's name and absence of the bride's dowry establish Nanaya-kanāt's marriage as one of Waerzegger's "non-elite marriages."[29]

---

27 Von Dassow, "Introducing the Witnesses," 15. The request by a groom (or a member of his family), for the purposes of marriage, of the hand of a sister from a brother or mother, is an indication that the bride's father has died or is otherwise no longer in the picture (see Roth, "Age at Marriage," 724). Further support for the connections between Nanaya-kanāt's family and the broader Judean community is evident from the fact that two of the witnesses to her marriage contract, Šilim-Yāma son of Nadab-Yāma and Ṣidqī-Yāma son of Natīn, may be attested in two other Yahudu documents: CUSAS 28 10 and BaAr 6 3. Alstola (*Judeans in Babylonia*, 130 f.) discusses Nanaya-kanāt's marriage text. He cautions against concluding, on the sole basis of the witnesses' names, that the bride's family was of Judean origin and warns that the Babylonian names of the groom and his father may conceal their own foreign origins. Nonetheless, Alstola considers this a Judean marriage.

28 However, Nanaya-kanāt's marriage document may reflect a more complex process of cultural borrowings and integration. Abraham ("Negotiating Marriage," 36 f.) suggests unusual expressions in the contract resemble phrases in Elephantine marriage documents, and thus reflect influence from the foreign participants' origins. Abraham believes that the parties could choose to add phrases and to emend standard Babylonian marriage document terminology to suit their cultural paradigms, even though they were marrying in Babylonia and adhering primarily to a Babylonian model.

29 Abraham notes that poor brides typically did not receive dowries ("West Semitic and Judean Brides," 202). Wunsch discusses the link between socio-economic status and the iron dagger clause (*Urkunden zum Ehe*, 6 f.). Waerzeggers explains that this identification is predicated on the assumption that the groom and his family were in fact of Babylonian origin, and that their Babylonian names didn't conceal foreign (potentially even Judean) origins ("Changing Marriage Practices," 121). Another non-elite marriage that should be mentioned in this connection is BMA 11, originally published as tablet 23 in Dhorme, "Les Tablettes babyloniennes." BMA 11 was written during the reign of Nabonidus (555–539 BCE) in a town called Neirab, like Yahudu, a mirror town named for the hometown of a majority of its residents. It remains the only town for which cuneiform texts confirm a return of descendants of deportees to their homeland. The Neirab marriage text, which demonstrates that intermarriage between deportees and (presumably) native Babylonians was practiced beyond the Judean community and that such marriages were

The Marriage of Kaššaya

Two texts reference the marriage of Kaššaya, daughter of Amuše and Guddad-dītu.[30] Although her brothers bore Babylonian names, and she shared a good Babylonian name with one of Nebuchadnezzar's daughters,[31] the family's Judean background is confirmed by the Yahwistic name of her uncle, Aḫī-Yāma. He and his brother were *tamkar šarri*, royal merchants, and thus they and the family were considered to be upper class.[32] Kaššaya's marriage contract resembles that of Nanaya-kanāt in its standard components but differs significantly in its inclusion of a dowry presentation,[33] indicative of her family's standing.

At first glance, the marriage of Kaššaya to Gūzānu, son of Kiribati of the Miller clan, might appear to have been a rare example of an individual of non-elite origin marrying into the elite circle of temple priests and prebend holders, of the type of hypergamy Still identified occurring at the bottom level of the Sippar priesthood. However, this was unlikely, as "Miller" was not an elite family name tied to prebendary temple service in the Neo-Babylonian period.[34] Thus Kaššaya's marriage differs technically from marriages in which attested family names refer to professionals at different levels of the temple priestly culture and prebendary environment. However, in Kaššaya's marriage contract, the groom's

---

contracted contemporaneously with the Judean exilic period. Although the Neirab marriage took place in Babylonia, it is unlikely that the bridal couple returned to its ancestral homeland. The chronological distribution of the tablets carried back to the Aleppo region point to a return date in the reign of Darius. For the most recent discussion of the Neirab texts, see Tolini, "Le Rôle de la famille," and Gauthier Tolini, "From Syria to Babylon."

30 BM 65149, and its near duplicate, BM 68921, have been treated in the following: BMA 26; Abraham, "West Semitic and Judean Brides," 198–219; Bloch, "Judeans in Sippar and Susa," 119–72; Jursa,"Eine Familie von Königskaufleuten."

31 Joannès, "Kaššaia, fille de Nabuchodonosor II"; Beaulieu, "Ba'u-Asītu and Kaššaya."

32 Aḫī-Yāma and Basia, uncles of Kaššaya, are identified as *tamkar šarri* in her marriage contract. Her father, Amušê, whose name appears only as a patronym in the marriage document, was likely also a royal merchant, based on the payment of 5½ minas of silver he received for its equivalent of gold. These commodities, and especially in these quantities, reflect access to the largesse of the temple or palace coffers. See Wunsch, *Judaeans by the Waters*, 57 n. 104.

33 It consisted of 1/3 shekel of jewelry, one pair of gold earrings worth one shekel, one Akkadian bed, five chairs, one table, a goblet and a platter made of bronze.

34 Wunsch, *Judaeans by the Waters*, 57. The only attestation of a miller's prebend appears in the Hellenistic period text OECT 9 62, which combines responsibility for prebends of a baker and a miller for a period of ten years (van Driel, *Elusive Silver*, 120 n. 131). In the Borsippa documentation, millers are associated with bakers and brewers, but their work, subordinate to and supportive of the prebendaries' offices, does not carry prebendary compensation or status (Waerzeggers, *The Ezida Temple*, 39 n. 206).

use of a family name identifying one of the groups of subordinate, non-prebendary laborers in the lowest circles of temple workers, suggests his family's aspiration to greater social standing; marriage into a family with an elite name may have been additional enticement for the Ariḫ family to conclude Kaššaya's marriage with Gūzānu. However, the social connection that resulted from this marriage was ultimately (and indirectly) to a family involved with a non-priestly family in a prominent Babylonian social circle, namely the Babylon-based entrepreneurial Egibi.[35]

Recent analysis of the onomastic and prosopographic evidence for the Miller family name connects the family to the circle of Egibi activities, and establishes a Judean connection, through marriage, to the entrepreneurial firm. In the marriage document, the family name "miller" is written logographically: ^{lu_2}ÀR.ÀR.[36] In a half-dozen Egibi texts, the family name of a certain Marduk son of Gūzānu is written pseudo-logographically as ^{lu_2}*kàṣ-ṣì-dak-ku*/*ka*. The genealogical information preserved in the marriage contract made it possible for the two orthographies to be identified as referring to the same family group, and to establish Kaššaya's groom as Marduk's father.[37] This information provides the indirect link necessary to connect the Judeans to the circle of the Egibi.

In a handful of texts dated to 497–496 BCE, Marduk son of Gūzānu appears as a witness together with a Tattannu son of Nabû-kāṣir of the Dābibi family, who regularly appears in Egibi texts concerned with payments for services owed the state and for bulk commodity shipments.[38] In at least one case, he co-occurs in a text with a scribe from the Dēkû family, whose activities connect the Egibi firm to the *bīt mār šarri*, the "house of the crown prince," that is, to the royal household, which supported endeavors of the Egibi as well as those of royal merchants. Marduk son of Gūzānu and Tattannu son of Nabû-kāṣir of the family of Dābibi share a closer connection to each other than to other witnesses in the texts, few of whom reoccur in this small corpus. Their positions near or at the top of witness lists also suggests a close connection to the principals and officials ordering the

35 For general overviews of the Egibi family and its entrepreneurial activities, see Wunsch, "The Egibi Family," and Wunsch, "The Egibi Family's Real Estate."

36 The logographic writing is typically ^{lu_2}GAZ.ZÍD.DA. Additional examples of the orthography ^{lu_2}ÀR.ÀR are attested in VAS 3 53:13; Nbn 600:4; RA 19 85:14 (cited in CAD A/2 233). In the Borsippa texts, the verb *ṭênu*, rather than *arāru*, is used to refer to milling activity; the miller was *ṭē'inu* (Waerzeggers, *The Ezida Temple*, 213). This distinction in terminology corroborates Wunsch's assertion that the family name Ararru was a late invention (*Judaeans by the Waters*, 56), and perhaps suggests that millers, who were subordinate to and provided labor necessary for the prebendary bakers' work, found a means to express desired social standing.

37 For this identification, see Wunsch, *Judaeans by the Waters*, 55–7.

38 Abraham, *Business and Politics*, texts 22, 38, 43, 50, 54, 59, and 61.

transactions.[39] These connections illustrate a network of relationships between individuals associated with financial firms and the royal court. Thus, the offspring of Kaššaya's marriage to Gūzānu extend the activity of the Ariḫ family from the days of the Neo-Babylonian kings down to the reign of Darius. The link between Marduk son of Gūzānu and Tattannu son of Nabû-kāṣir of the Dābibi family connects a Judean family of royal merchants to the Egibi family in the decade or so preceding the revolts in Xerxes' reign. Although the Judean family of royal merchants never achieved the wealth of the Egibi family, the sources demonstrate a potential path by which the control of Judean assets, in the form of dowry, could be reassigned outside the family, at least until the dissolution of a marriage. This pattern could have represented a threat to the financial stability of the Judean family and community. The question that remains to be asked is whether any of these features related to marriage and intermarriage in Babylonia offer parallels to the reasons adduced for Ezra's marriage ban.

What Prompted Ezra's Marriage Ban?

Ezra declaims the foreign marriages as he is poised to enter Jerusalem to fulfill the mission initiated by Artaxerxes' letter:

> Artaxerxes, king of kings, to Ezra the priest, scholar of the law of the God of heaven, and so forth. And now, I hereby issue an order that anyone in my kingdom who is of the people of Israel and its priests and Levites who feels impelled to go to Jerusalem may go with you. For you are commissioned by the king and his seven advisers to regulate Judah and Jerusalem according to the law of your God, which is in your care, and to bring the freewill offering of silver and gold, which the king and his advisers made to the God of Israel, whose dwelling is in Jerusalem, and whatever silver and gold that you find throughout the province of Babylon, together with the free will offerings that the people and the priests will give for the House of their God, which is in Jerusalem. (Ezra 7: 12–17)

Ezra's experience in Babylonia as a scribe and community leader led Hugh Williamson to label Ezra uniquely qualified "to reconcile the sometimes conflicting demands of 'the law of your God and the law of the king'."[40] But Ezra was not the only individual who had to confront tensions between the realms of sacred and secular law. In Babylonia, one generation before Ezra's mission, disruptive political events and shifts in economic practices in early Achaemenid Babylonia

39 A royal courtier orders the transaction recorded in Abraham, *Business and Politics*, no. 38; the governor of Babylon does the same in texts 54 and 59.
40 Williamson, *Ezra and Nehemiah*, 74–5.

triggered change in several Babylonian institutions, including marriage and manifestations of individuals' and families' identification with offices of the traditional temple cults.

Scholars have identified five major areas of concern that could have contributed to Ezra's extreme call for the expulsion of wives and children some Judean men had married. None, however, provides sufficient justification for the action. In this paper, the five areas are summarized and serve as a jumping off point for consideration of similar rationales in the social and economic environment of the Neo-Babylonian and Achaemenid periods. The following sketch of the shape and transformations of social processes in Babylonia across the long sixth century to the period following the revolts in Xerxes second regnal year (484 BCE),[41] which corresponds to the period of Judean history from the first deportations under Nebuchadnezzar and the destruction of the Jerusalem temple through the time of Ezra's mission. It will not resolve all the questions pertaining to the motivation and justification of Ezra's actions, but it will locate the Judean community and its own responses to challenges to its composition and identity within the broader context, making more evident that "restructuring Jewish life in the aftermath of military, economic and religious devastation" occurred in a "pivotal era" not only for the Judeans, but for Babylonian society more broadly.[42]

Scholars have identified these themes as primary concerns driving the foreign marriage crisis: apostasy; inheritance and land tenure; status, class, and money; purity; identity and ethnicity.[43] The threat posed by each is summarized to facilitate identification of comparable evidence and social situations in Babylonia, and therefore elucidate the context in which Ezra's intermarriages may be viewed.

1. Apostasy. Some scholars suggest a primary motivation for Ezra's foreign marriage ban was the concern that foreign brides would lead the Judeans toward idolatry, especially as children adopted their mothers' religious beliefs.[44] According to Katherine Southwood, the scholarly argument that apostasy was a significant reason for the ban's implementation is tied to matters of Israelite (i.e., national), rather than religious, identity. She further suggests that an example of religious conversion appears in Ezra 6:21, but the text preserves no other indica-

---

41 For a definition of the long sixth century, see Jursa and Baker, *Approaching the Babylonian Economy*, v.

42 Eskenazi, "Out from the Shadows," 25.

43 The rubrics presented here follow the terminology in Tiemeyer, *Ezra-Nehemiah*, 86–94. Although other scholars apply different labels to these topics, there is consensus on the areas of concern.

44 Fensham, *The Books of Ezra and Nehemiah*, 124.

tion that the foreign wives were offered an option that would have addressed issues of continuity of religious identity and distinctiveness.[45] Indeed, apostasy is not explicitly identified as problematic in Ezra 9–10, despite the text's allusion to the foreign marriage prohibition in Deuteronomy 7.[46] In the Babylonian record, concerns over apostasy, renunciation of a religious philosophy or practice, are not evident. While biblical scholars frame the loss of distinctive Judean/Israelite identity as a major consequence of association with foreign populations, Babylonian society was historically and notably receptive to foreigners, regardless of the newcomer's religious affiliation or preference, as is evident in marriages between Babylonians and non-Babylonians, where social standing is a defining principle.

2. Inheritance and Land Tenure. The notion that social, economic, and legal issues associated with the potential loss of inheritance served as the motivation for the foreign wives ban reflects a scholar's belief that forced divorces "sought to make sure that the land of Yehud would not leave Jewish ownership. If women could inherit property, then foreign wives-turned-widows who, in turn, remarried men from their community of birth would endanger the rights of the Jewish community to their ancestral land."[47] This perceived threat to the land holdings of the Jewish community could have become a reality if legal conventions allowed wives to inherit real property in the case of divorce or death. Such was the practice at Elephantine,[48] where women could inherit real and movable property

---

45 In support of a reference to conversion in Ezra, Southwood (*Ethnicity and the Mixed Marriage*, 78) notes John Kessler's exegesis of Ezra 6:21, discussing inclusivist tendencies, among them broadening eligibility to participate in the Passover "to all who purify themselves from the uncleanness of the surrounding nations." ("Persia's Loyal Yahwists," 109).

46 Deut 7:1–4: "When your God יהוה brings you to the land that you are about to enter and possess, and [God] dislodges many nations before you – the Hittites, Girgashites, Amorites, Canaanites, Perizzites, Hivites, and Jebusites, seven nations much larger than you – your God יהוה delivers them to you and you defeat them, you must doom them to destruction: grant them no terms and give them no quarter. You shall not intermarry with them: do not give your daughters to their sons or take their daughters for your sons. For they will turn your children away from Me to worship other gods, and יהוה's anger will blaze forth against you, promptly wiping you out." (JPS translation 1985).

47 Tiemeyer, *Ezra-Nehemiah*, 87. Harold C. Washington expresses the problem thus: "Exogamous marriages could result in alien claims to land belonging to the Judean collective." ("The Strange Women," 235).

48 The date of the marriage contract written in Yahudu is damaged. The regnal year is preserved (5), but the name of the king is not. Either proposed reconstruction (Cyrus [Bloch, "Judeans in Sippar and Susa," 152; Jursa, "Kollationen," 99] or Darius I [Wunsch "Judaeans by the Waters," 59] positions the marriage in the post-return period. It is thus contemporaneous to the Elephantine material.

and initiate divorce.[49] Proponents of this perspective argue that, for the Golah community, marriage to women of non-Israelite background opened the possibility, upon the grooms' demise, of eventual loss of Judean control of the land.[50]

Indeed, most scholars do not contend that the rights of women at Elephantine to inherit and divorce were a major motivation to Ezra's marriage ban. First, the number of instances in which an inheritance issue appears in connection with the Judean women at Elephantine is small. And, second, Kathleen Abraham understands the occurrence of Aramaic marriage practice in a Yahudu document of a Judean woman's marriage as important enough to characterize it as "non-Babylonian in an Akkadian garb."[51]

The Yahudu text demonstrates the marriage of Judean women to foreign men, setting up a gender balance opposite that encountered in Ezra's marriage ban. But the text does not mention land, either as a dowry component or as a portion of inheritance, which therefore cannot be included as an explanation of any aspect of the marriage ban. In short, claims that concerns over inheritance could justify Ezra's call for divorce in a significant portion of the Golah community run counter to the situation in Babylonia, his home and familiar territory.

There, strict patriarchal rules of inheritance meant that women rarely, if at all, acquired property or the ability to dispose of it. Social convention constrained women from full participation in those activities, even though they had, in principle, the legal capacity to acquire and dispose of property, manage businesses, and enter legal obligations. Normally, neither daughters nor wives had the right to inheritance, but could receive a share of the paternal estate in the form of a dowry or marital gift.[52] When land is listed in the dowry component of Babylonian marriage documents of the urban elite, it is "precisely because its value made the drafting of a written record advisable."[53] Notably, and not surprisingly, land

---

49 For general sketches of Elephantine documentation of women's rights to inherit property in their own names, as well of circumstances in which they could do so, see Eskenazi, "Out from the Shadows," 25–43; Azzoni, "Women and Property."

50 Washington, "The Strange Women," 236: "In the post-exilic setting, if families outside the recognized paternal estates became related to community members through marriage, there could be no assurance that such laws would preserve the economic base of the Judeaean collective."

51 Abraham, "West Semitic and Judean Brides," 198–219; Abraham, "Negotiating Marriage," 33–57.

52 Wunsch, "Women's Property"; Oelsner, Wells, and Wunsch "Neo-Babylonian Period," 941–43 describe a limited number of scenarios in which women were heirs to real estate holdings of their father. Notably, the fathers headed wealthy families and the marriages of their daughters were arranged to further the social standing of the family.

53 Westbrook, *Property and the Family*, 143 n. 2. Parcels of land are included in five of the twenty Babylonian marriage documents between members of the urban elite, all of which occurred

is not mentioned in any of the non-elite marriages in the Neo-Babylonian corpus,[54] the category to which the marriages of the Judean brides belonged.

Regarding the degree to which inheritance was an important factor in the pronouncement of the foreign marriage ban, the cuneiform marriage documents referencing Judean brides are not informative. Neither the document written at Yahudu nor the one written in Sippar references land in connection with the transaction, consistent with the non-elite status of the families involved.

3. Status, class and money. Some argue that those who returned to Yehud belonged to the elite, and because they "traced their lineage back to the pre-exilic men of power [they] also hold key leadership positions in post-exilic Yehud."[55] Daniel L. Smith-Christopher argues the opposite, namely that the dissolution of mixed marriages in Ezra is not compatible with the view that returning exiles belonged to the privileged elite.[56] He suggests that hypergamy defined status-minded exilic men's marriages to women from Yehud, as they "attempt to 'marry up' and thus to climb the social ladder."[57] While Smith-Christopher's invocation of hypergamy as an explanation of the foreign marriage problem has been deemed circular,[58] recent studies of the role of hypergamy in the social and cultic organization of long sixth century Babylonian society provide greater context and clarification of its potential impact on marriage, and may offer insights into Ezra's rejection of such marriages.

4. Purity as a justification for the foreign marriage ban is a broad category with wide-ranging discussion. It is considered in the scholarly literature in terms of concerns over cultic and moral purity, as hallmarks and assurances of Israel's distinctiveness, its holy status, and ethnic sanctity. Impurity labels used in Ezra-Nehemiah to mark persons as unwelcome in the community bind the issue of purity to ethnic standing.[59] Southwood notes that the various explanations "fail to go beyond describing the significance of purity itself within the text, and the mechanics of how it operates."[60] As the concern here is to consider issues associated with the marriage ban and their possible Babylonian contexts, it should be noted that in the Babylonian cult, purity is also a prerequisite to serve in the

before the end of the archives in 484 BCE: BMA 9, (Borsippa, 6 Nbn); BMA 15 (Babylon, 12 Nbn); BMA 18 (Babylon, 16 Nbn); BMA 21 (Borsippa, Camb. [year broken]); BMA 22 (Borsippa, 1 Darius).

54 Details of these marriages are presented in tabular form in Waerzeggers, "Changing Marriage Practices," 121–23.

55 Tiemeyer, "Hope and Disappointment," 68–9.

56 Smith-Christopher, "The Mixed Marriage," 256.

57 Tiemeyer, *Ezra-Nehemiah*, 88.

58 Southwood, *Ethnicity and the Mixed Marriage*, 89.

59 Southwood, *Ethnicity and the Mixed Marriage*, 90–3.

60 Southwood, *Ethnicity and the Mixed Marriage*, 97.

temple and its associated prebendary offices.[61] But Babylonian sources provide few explicit statements of what constitutes purity, and make no claim for purity's value as an identity marker.

5. Identity and Ethnicity. For Ezra, mixed marriages and return migration endangered Israel's identity, for they defied boundaries of who was understood to be "in" and "out" of the people. Identity and ethnicity are considered in connection with family and kinship, issues intimately tied to marriage. For Babylonia, identity and ethnicity do not seem to have been problematized, as reflected in the rare inclusion of a marker of a person's or group's place of origin. Indeed, Babylonia had a long-standing tradition of integrating individuals and groups of people into the mainstream of society. In the first millennium BCE, even prior to Nebuchadnezzar's deportations, large numbers of non-Babylonian populations, particularly West Semites, entered the Mesopotamian heartland, impacted the demographic landscape, and found integration into most strata of society, save the urban elite.[62] This is reflected in marriages, where economic standing, rather than geographic or ethnic background was a defining factor.

Situating Ezra's Problem with the Foreign Wives

None of the above topics alone offers sufficient motivation for Ezra's foreign marriage ban. They reflect the complex intertwining of legal, economic, and religious factors, which permeated the social fabric of the diverse, multicultural environment of Babylonia in which Ezra resided, as well as of the Judean experience. For some Judeans who returned to the land, behavior that ran counter to biblical law (i.e., marrying foreign wives) may have been influenced through exposure to Babylonian practices. However, to attribute the foreign marriages simply to acculturation would not provide justification for Ezra's ban. Rather, consideration of marriage patterns in Babylonia before and after 484 BCE in connection with the purpose of Ezra's mission provides broader context for Ezra's response.

In this connection, it is worth revisiting a century-old commentary on the books of Ezra and Nehemiah that offers a suggestion that can be reconsidered with the help of recent knowledge of Babylonian marriage practices. In 1913, with respect to the charge that the Judeans had taken foreign wives, Loring Batten

61 See the discussion in Waerzeggers, *The Ezida Temple*, passim.

62 For discussion of the arrival and treatment of foreign groups into the Babylonian heartland during the first millennium, and especially the Neo-Babylonian and Achaemenid periods, see Zilberg. "At the Gate of All Nations," II, 21–220.

commented: "There is no hint that Jewish women had married foreign men. The condition is attributable to the scarcity of women in the new community."[63] The Judean-Babylonian marriage texts demonstrate that Judean (Jewish) women indeed did marry foreigners in Babylonia. As the two Judean cuneiform marriage texts date to the period preceding and immediately after Cyrus' decree of return, they suggest that at the time of the first wave of Judeans returning from the exile, the Judean population of the land could have experienced a gender imbalance. Once married, women were tied to their grooms' households; Judean brides, now rooted in Babylonia, were unlikely to have returned to Judah. Judean men in Babylonia could have married local women, as BMA 27 demonstrates. Such marriages may be assumed to have taken place, based on the parallel situation evident in the marriage document in which a Neirabean man resident in Babylonia married a non-elite Babylonian woman.

Participants in non-elite marriages between Judean men and non-Judean women might have returned to Judah, as the men aimed to reclaim their heritage, and possibly, their real property. In the period before 484 BCE, marriages in Babylonia that united two individuals of non-elite standing would have posed no threats to the financial or social standing of individual Judeans or to their community. However, by 458 BCE, Ezra's return to Jerusalem "to teach laws and rules to Israel,"[64] coincided with accelerating social changes in Babylonia. With the elimination of the social restrictions of hypergamy that applied to marriages for members of the Babylonian priesthood, the language of elite and non-elite contracts resembled each other. Members of the Judean elite who accompanied Ezra back to Judah lived in a cultural environment in which the standing of people traditionally tasked with temple service were removed from their positions of power. Memory of limitations on marriages may have circulated among members of the Babylonian priesthood, whose families had been adversely affected by the social shifts, and in the network of Judeans who had contact with the court. Ezra's work associated with Temple restoration, however, required adherence to traditional social and cultic norms, including preservation of priestly lines. And in this task, there is evidence for cultic continuity and restoration in traditional Babylonian cults in the late Achaemenid and early Hellenistic periods.

Some Babylonian families which had not supported the revolts against Xerxes relocated to the south where the priesthood remained intact and prebendary personnel continued to staff temples. In Uruk, these families initiated restoration of the venerable Anu cult, which, by the period of Neo-Babylonian and early

---

63 Batten, *A Critical and Exegetical Commentary*, 331.

64 Ezra 7:10 (JPS 1985 translation).

Achaemenid rule, had been supplanted by that of the goddess Ištar.[65] Reasons for this must remain speculative, but Beaulieu suggests local interest and pride in the Anu cult as an identity marker.[66] He argues that under the reign of Nebuchadnezzar II, Uruk "had been forced to acknowledge the theological dominance of Babylon" with introduction to the Eanna temple of a form of Ištar-of-Babylon worship, as a form of religious centralization. This may have instigated a migration of prebendaries from Babylon and other northern cities to Uruk, where their participation in the Eanna priesthood continued until the reign of Xerxes. Following the revolts at the beginning of Xerxes' reign, even the members of families from Babylon who were now resident in Uruk found their influence constrained. The conditions were right for a return to the former dominance of the local gods, under the titular Anu.[67]

Conclusion

The reasons Ezra promoted his ban on marriages to foreign wives are many and complex in their interconnections. They hint at the economic conditions associated with marriage, divorce, and inheritance. In Babylonia, marriage was likewise subject to social norms. Prior to 484 BCE, marriages among the elite at Borsippa (and likely elsewhere) enforced the pattern of hypergamy, designed to protect the hierarchy of the prebendary priesthood, entrance into which was predicated not only on class standing, but on fitness (purity) to serve the cult. Ezra's marriage ban is issued one generation after the revolts against Xerxes, when, in northern Babylonia, impacts of the demotion of the prebendary elite is reflected in the leveling of the language associated with marriage documents of elite, upper class, and non-elite persons. In this same era, some prebendary families relocated to Uruk, which was not impacted by the "end of archives." There, they implemented changes that led to the restoration of the venerable Anu cult, which had been replaced early in the Neo-Babylonian era by that of Ištar. Ezra's marriage ban restores members of Judahite society to social patterns that adhered to biblical law and which assured the cultic fitness of those who would serve in the restored Temple. These similar sets of cultural changes that appear over the course of the long sixth century into period of the end of archives suggest that Ezra's marriage ban, with its specifically Judean or Jewish concerns, may be understood as one

65 Beaulieu, "Uruk Before and After Xerxes"; Hackl, "The Esangila Temple," 185.
66 Beaulieu, "Uruk Before and After Xerxes," 203.
67 Beaulieu, "Uruk Before and After Xerxes," 204.

of many instances of change and reaction to the political and economic events of the early fifth century BCE.

Bibliography

Abraham, Kathleen, *Business and Politics Under the Persian Empire: The Financial Dealings of Marduk-nāṣir-apli of the House of Egibi (521–487 B.C.E.)*. Bethesda: CDL Press, 2004.

Abraham, Kathleen, "West Semitic and Judean Brides in Cuneiform Sources from the Sixth Century BCE. New Evidence from a Marriage Contract from Āl-Yahudu." *Archiv für Orientforschung* 51 (2005–2006): 198–219.

Abraham, Kathleen, "Negotiating Marriage in Multicultural Babylonia: An Example from the Judean Community in Āl-Yāhūdu," pages 33–57 in *Exile and Return. The Babylonian Context*. BZAW 478. edited by Jonathan Stökl and Caroline Waerzeggers. Berlin: De Gruyter, 2015.

Alstola, Tero, *Judeans in Babylonia: A Study of Deportees in the Sixth and Fifth Centuries BCE*. CHANE 109. Leiden: Brill, 2020.

Azzoni, Annalisa, "Women and Property in Persian Egypt and Mesopotamia," in *Women and Property in Ancient Near Eastern and Mediterranean Societies*, edited by Deborah Lyons and Raymond Westbrook (Center for Hellenic Studies, 2003), available online at: https://classics-at.chs.harvard.edu/wp-content/uploads/2021/05/ca1.2-azzoni.pdf, accessed 12/1/2023.

Batten, Loring W., *A Critical and Exegetical Commentary on the Books of Ezra and Nehemiah*. New York: Scribner, 1913.

Beaulieu, Paul-Alain, "Ba'u-Asītu and Kaššaya, Daughters of Nebuchadnezzar II," *Orientalia NS* 64 (1998): 173–201.

Beaulieu, Paul-Alain, "Uruk Before and After Xerxes: The Onomastic and Institutional Rise of the God Anu," pages 189–206 in *Xerxes and Babylonia. The Cuneiform Evidence*. OLA 277. edited by Caroline Waerzeggers and Maarja Seire. Leuven: Peeters, 2018.

Bloch, Yigal, "Judeans in Sippar and Susa during the First Century of the Babylonian Exile: Assimilation and Perseverance under Neo-Babylonian and Achaemenid Rule," *Journal of Ancient Near Eastern History* 1 (2014): 119–72.

Carr, David McLain, "Criteria and Periodization in Dating Biblical Texts to Parts of the Persian Period," pages 11–18 in *On Dating Biblical Texts to the Persian Period*, edited by Richard J. Bautch and Mark Lackowski. Tübingen: Mohr Siebeck, 2019.

Dassow, Eva von. "Introducing the Witnesses in Neo-Babylonian Documents," pages 3–22 in *Ki Baruch Hu: Ancient Near Eastern, Biblical, and Judaic Studies in Honor of Baruch A. Levine*, edited by Robert Chazan, William W. Hallo, and Lawrence H. Schiffman. Winona Lake: Eisenbrauns, 1999.

Demsky, Aaron, "Who Came First, Ezra or Nehemiah? The Synchronistic Approach," *Hebrew Union College Annual* 65 (1994): 1–19.

Dhorme, E., "Les Tablettes babyloniennes de Neirab," *Revue d'Assyriologie et d'archéologie Orientale* 25 (1928): 53–82.

Fensham, F. Charles, *The Books of Ezra and Nehemiah*. Grand Rapids: Eerdmans, 1983.

Hackl, Johannes, "The Esangila Temple during the Late Achaemenid Period and the Impact of Xerxes' Reprisals on the Northern Babylonian Temple Households," pages 165–188 in *Xerxes and Babylonia. The Cuneiform Evidence*. OLA 277. edited by Caroline Waerzeggers and Maarje Seire. Leuven: Peeters, 2018.

Joannès, Francis, "Kaššaia, fille de Nabuchodonosor II," *Revue d'Assyriologie et d'archéologie orientale* 74 (1980): 183–184.

Jursa, Michael, "Kollationen," *NABU* 2001–102.

Jursa, Michael, "The Babylonian Economy in the First Millennium BC," pages 220–31 in *The Babylonians: An Introduction*, edited by Gwendolyn Leick. London: Routledge, 2003.

Jursa, Michael, and Heather Baker, eds. *Approaching the Babylonian Economy: Proceedings of the START Project Symposium Held in Vienna, 1–3 July 2004*. AOAT 330. Münster: Ugarit-Verlag, 2005.

Jursa, Michael, "Eine Familie von Königskaufleuten judäischer Herkunft," *NABU* 2007–22.

Jursa, Michael, "The Neo-Babylonian Empire," pages 91–173 in *The Oxford History of the Ancient Near East, Volume V: The Age of Persia*, edited by Karen Radner, Nadine Moeller, and D. T. Potts. Oxford: Oxford University Press, 2023.

Kessler, John, "Persia's Loyal Yahwists: Power Identity and Ethnicity in Achaemenid Yehud," pages 91–121 in *Judah and the Judeans in the Persian Period*, edited by Oded Lipschits and Manfred Oeming. Winona Lake: Eisenbrauns, 2006

Lemaire, André, *Levantine Epigraphy and History in the Achaemenid Period*. Oxford: Oxford University Press, 2015.

Lemos, T. M., *Marriage Gifts and Social Change in Ancient Palestine, 1200 BCE to 200 CE*. Cambridge: University Press, 2010.

Oelsner, Joachim, Bruce Wells, and Cornelia Wunsch, "Neo-Babylonian Period," pages 911–74 in *A History of Ancient Near Eastern Law*. HdO 72. edited by Raymond Westbrook and Gary M. Beckman. Boston: Brill, 2003.

Roth, Martha T., "Age at Marriage and the Household: A Study of Neo-Babylonian and Neo-Assyrian Forms." *Comparative Studies in Society and History* 29 (1987): 715–47.

Roth, Martha T., "'She Will Die by the Iron Dagger': Adultery and Neo-Babylonian Marriage." *Journal of the Economic and Social History of the Orient* 31 (1988): 186–206.

Roth, Martha T., "A Case of Contested Status," pages 481–89 in *dumu-e2-dub-ba-a: Studies in Honor of Åke W. Sjöberg*, edited by Hermann Behrens, Darlene Loding, and Martha T. Roth. Philadelphia: Samuel Noah Kramer Fund University Museum, 1989.

Roth, Martha T., *Babylonian Marriage Agreements: 7th–3rd Centuries B.C.* AOAT 222. Neukirchen: Neukirchener Verlag, 1989.

Roth, Martha T., "Women in Transition and the *bīt mār banî*." *Revue d'Assyriologie et d'archéologie orientale* 82 (1989): 131–38.

Roth, Martha T., "The Material Composition of the Neo-Babylonian Dowry." *Archiv für Orientforschung* 36–37 (1989–1990): 1–55.

Roth, Martha T., "The Dowries of the Women of the Itti-Marduk-Balāṭu Family." *Journal of the American Oriental Society* 111 (1991): 19–37.

Roth, Martha T., "The Neo-Babylonian Widow." *Journal of Cuneiform Studies* 43/45 (1991–1993): 1–26.

Roth, Martha T., *Law Collections from Mesopotamia and Asia Minor.* WAW 6. Atlanta: Scholars Press, 1997.

Smith-Christopher, Daniel L., "The Mixed Marriage Crisis in Ezra 9–10 and Nehemiah 13: A Study of the Sociology of the Post-Exilic Judean Community," pages 243–65 in *Second Temple Studies 2: Temple Community in the Persian Period*, edited by Tamara C. Eskenazi and Kent H. Richards. Sheffield: JSOT Press, 1994.

Southwood, Katherine E., *Ethnicity and the Mixed Marriage Crisis in Ezra 9–10: An Anthropological Approach*. Oxford: Oxford University Press, 2012.

Still, Bastian, *The Social World of the Babylonian Priest*. CHANE 103. Leiden: Brill, 2019.

Tiemeyer, Lena-Sofia, "Hope and Disappointment: The Judahite Critique of the Exilic Leadership in Isaiah 56–66," pages 57–73 in *New Perspectives on Old Testament Prophecy and History: Essays in Honour of Hans M. Barstad*, edited by Rannfrid I. Thelle, Terje Stordalen, and Mervyn E. J. Richardson. Leiden: Brill, 2015.

Tiemeyer, Lena-Sofia, *Ezra-Nehemiah: An Introduction and Study Guide: Israel's Quest for Identity.* London: Bloomsbury, 2017.

Tolini, Gauthier, "Le rôle de la famille de Nusku-Gabbe au sein de la communauté de Neirab*," pages 591–98 in *La famille dans le proche-orient ancient: réalités, symbolismes et images. Proceedings of the 55th Rencontre Assyriologique Internationale, Paris, July 6–9, 2009*, edited by Lionel Marti. Winona Lake: Eisenbrauns, 2014.

Tolini, Gauthier, "From Syria to Babylon and Back: The Neirab Archive," pages 58–93 in *Exile and Return. The Babylonian Context*. BZAW 478. edited by Jonathan Stökl and Caroline Waerzeggers. Berlin: De Gruyter, 2015.

van Driel, Govert, *Elusive Silver: In Search of a Role for a Market in an Agrarian Environment Aspects of Mesopotamia's Society*. Leiden: Nederlands Instituut voor het Nabije Oosten, 2002.

Waerzeggers Caroline, "Changing Marriage Practices in Babylonia from the Late Assyrian to the Persian Period." *Journal of Ancient Near Eastern History* 7 (2020): 101–31.

Waerzeggers, Caroline, "The Babylonian Revolts against Xerxes and the 'End of Archives.'" *Archiv für Orientforschung* 50 (2003–2004): 150–73.

Waerzeggers, Caroline, *The Ezida Temple of Borsippa: Priesthood, Cult, Archives*. Achaemenid History 15. Leiden: Nederlands Instituut voor het Nabije Oosten, 2010.

Waerzeggers, Caroline, "Locating Contact in the Babylonian Exile: Some Reflections on Tracing Judean-Babylonian Encounters in Cuneiform Texts," pages 131–46 in *Encounters by the Rivers of Babylon: Scholarly Conversations Between Jews, Iranians, and Babylonians in Antiquity.* Texte und Studien zum antiken Judentum 160. edited by Uri Gabbay and Shai Secunda. Tübingen: Mohr Siebeck, 2014.

Washington, Harold C., "The Strange Women of Proverbs 1–9 and Post-Exilic Society," pages 217–42 in *Second Temple Studies 2: Temple Community in the Persian Period*, edited by Tamara C. Eskenazi and Kent H. Richards. Sheffield: JSOT Press, 1994.

Westbrook, Raymond, *Property and the Family in Biblical Law.* Sheffield: JSOT Press, 1991.

Williamson, Hugh G. M., *Ezra and Nehemiah.* Sheffield: Society for Old Testament Study, 1987.

Wunsch, Cornelia, "The Egibi Family's Real Estate in Babylon (6th Century BC)," pages 391–419 in *Urbanization and Land Ownership in the Ancient Near East: A Colloquium Held at New York* University, November 1996, and the Oriental Institute, St. Petersburg, Russia, May 1997, edited by Michael Hudson and Baruch A. Levine. Cambridge: Harvard University, 1999.

Wunsch, Cornelia, *Urkunden zum Ehe-, Vermögens- und Erbrecht zum verschiedenen neubabylonischen Archiven*. Babylonische Archive 2. Dresden: ISLET-Verlag, 2003.

Wunsch, Cornelia, "The Egibi Family," pages 236–247 in *The Babylonian World*, edited by Gwendolyn Leick. New York: Routledge, 2007.

Wunsch, Cornelia, "Women's Property and the Law of Inheritance in the Neo-Babylonian Period," in *Women and Property in Ancient Near Eastern and Mediterranean Societies*, edited by Deborah Lyons and Raymond Westbrook (Center for Hellenic Studies, 2003), available online at: https://classics-at.chs.harvard.edu/wp-content/uploads/2021/05/ca1.2-wunsc/2023h.pdf, accessed 12/1/2023.

Wunsch, Cornelia, *Judaeans by the Waters of Babylon New Historical Evidence in Cuneiform Sources From Rural Babylonia Primarily from the Schøyen Collection*. Babylonische Archive 6. Dresden: ISLET-Verlag, 2022.

Zadok, Ran, *The Jews in Babylonia during the Chaldean and Achaemenian Periods According to the Babylonian Sources*. Haifa: University of Haifa, 1979.

Zadok, Ran, “The Representation of Foreigners in Neo- and Late- Babylonian Documents (Eighth through Second Centuries B.C.E.),” pages 471–589 in *Judah and the Judeans in the Neo-Babylonian Period*, edited by Oded Lipschits and J. Blenkinsopp. Winona Lake: Eisenbrauns, 2003.

Zadok, Ran, “New Documents about Uruk, and Its Countryside,” pages 491–534 in *Des Polythéismes aux monothéismes. Mélanges d'Assyriologie offerts à Marcel Sigrist.* Études bibliques NS 82. edited by Uri Gabbay and Jean Jacques Pérennès. Leuven: Peeters, 2020.

Zilberg, Peter, “At the Gate of All Nations. A Study of Displaced and Migrant Minority Groups in the Center of the Persian Empire.” Hebrew University, 2019.

Bezalel Porten

Yahu and Its Cognates in Personal Names: The Problem of Yama

Before diving into the topic of this article, I would like to pay my respects to Shaul Shaked with a memory and an homage.

Shaul Shaked in Memoriam

Making my way from the elevator to my office at The Hebrew University of Jerusalem, I would always pass the office of Shaul Shaked. Even though he had long since retired, he invariably had a trio of students whom he was teaching, clearly drawn to his expertise and charisma. I can remember the candor of the conversations I would overhear, the debates and the lessons – clear evidence that his legacy lives on in the students he inspired.

Names and Ethnicity

Among his many publications and projects, he and Amnon Netzer published a well-known periodic anthology called *Irano-Judaica*. We are much indebted to the rigor of these anthologies, and I was lucky enough to publish articles in the two of the editions – in 1990 and 2003. My latter article was part of a series that I researched on names in the Aramaic Elephantine documents, having taken a keen interest in onomastics of the era and what these naming traditions reveal about the communities that they built. I had already worked in consultation with Günter Vittmann the year before (2002) to publish an article on Egyptian names, so I contacted Shaul Shaked afterwards to seek a similar collaboration on Iranian names. Shaked obliged, and I published my 2003 article in consultation with him. Imagine my surprise when I learned that Shaked was also collaborating with an Aramaic scholar whom I had met on a visit to London, Siam Bhayro, who consulted with Shaked in his research on Aramaic bowl spells – and had even stayed with him in his house in Jerusalem!

Note: With the assistance of Matt Kletzing.

Bezalel Porten, The Hebrew University of Jerusalem, Israel

https://doi.org/10.1515/9783111018638-013

Onomastics has always struggled with the degree to which personal names reflect ethnicity in different times and places. The post-modern parent, detached from their ethnic origins, may pick up a "baby names" book and flick through it until they find one with a pleasing sound, without attaching any meaning to it. Yet, in most times and places, naming traditions have a depth and breadth that reveal meaningful ethnic and cultural – and sometimes even political – data.

There is a parcel of family letters discovered at Hermopolis (*Hermopolis papyri* or TAD A2.1–70) that provides good evidence for the assumption that personal names testify to ethnicity. Not one of the names in these papyri is compounded with the element *YH(W)*, which is a theophoric element regularly featured in the many names of the Elephantine papyri. Indeed, as the greetings to Bethel, Banit, Nabu and the Queen of Heaven at the beginning of these letters show, they were sent to Syene by non-Jews. As indicated by one of the Elephantine letters, addressed to Bagavayah, the deity of the Elephantine Judeans was *YHW*, and to this god they had a temple on the island (TAD A4.7–8).

Even in very conservative or closed ethnic communities, naming conventions change through time. While names might come and go, and even theophoric elements within them might be altered, this sort of evolution is not strange in and of itself. What is intriguing, however, is that certain naming conventions within diaspora Judean communities changed *concomitantly* despite long distances between separate communities. And yet, in other communities, very distinct elements emerged that are hard to explain.

YHW and Its Cognates

This paper deals with one theophoric element in particular – *YHW* – and three specific questions:

1) Why was the theophoric ending in pre-exilic personal names always written *YHW* while in exilic names it was abbreviated to *YH*?
2) How did this development happen both at Elephantine and in the names in the books of Ezra and Nehemiah at the same time?
3) How does this usage comport with the use of *YĀMA* in clearly Judean names on some of the clay tablets found in Babylonia?

Let's start by looking at the early history of this onomastic tradition.

According to the Biblical text, the name *YHW(H)* was first revealed to Moses at the burning bush (Ex. 3:15), whereas to the Patriarchs he was known as El Shaddai (Ex. 6:3). There are no Yahwistic names for a very long time. None of the twelve spies who appear in Numbers 13:4–15, for example, bore names with the element *YHW*. In fact, the first person to bear a Yahwistic name in the literature was Joshua, and that was only *after* his name was changed by Moses from הושע to יהושע. This is a creative renaming: the former was a hypocoristicon of the verbal sentence name הושעיה, whereas the new name became a nominal sentence name unrelated to the original. There is only one exception in this period, the puzzling name of the wife of Moses' father Amram – יוכבד (Num. 26:59). In this name יו is clearly an abbreviation of יהוה. What are we to make of this?

Much later, however, Yahwistic names appear to have become popular. In Jeremiah 36–38, we have an interesting list of persons who accompanied the reading of the scroll in the royal chambers, and many of them bore Yahwistic names – דליהו בן שמעיהו, מיכיהו בן גמריהו, יאשיהו, ירמיהו, צדקיהו, יהוכל, צפניהו, and גדליהו. This attests to the fact that during the pre-exilic period, the dominant form of the Yahwistic element in a personal name was *YHW*. (Of particular note is יהוכל: we will come back to this.) This convention is confirmed by a sample of seals and bullae.[1]

1. Seal from Arad: לברכיהו בן {– – –י}הו בן שלמיהו
2. Bulla from Jerusalem: יהוכל בן שלמיהו בן שבי
3. Bulla from Lachish: לירמיהו בן צפניהו בן נבי
4. Seal from Jerusalem: למתניהו בנהו{ } נ{ }
5. Bulla from Jerusalem: לשמעיהו {ב} (?) {ן} (?) מחסיהו

As an initial element, *YHW* was popular in pre-exilic female names, too, which we can see from a collection list at Elephantine, with no less than eight such names (TAD C3.15:86–110):

1. Line 87: יהושמע ברת נתן
2. Line 90: יהושמע ברת משלם
3. Line 95: יהוחן ברת יגדל
4. Line 101: יהושמע ברת הושע
5. Line 102: יהושמע ברת חגי
6. Line 104: יהוחן ברת גדליה
7. Line 106: יהוטל ברת יסלח
8. Line 108: יהועלי ברת עמניה

From this common background, we see various localized traditions develop, even in pre-exilic times. In Samaria, for example, the *he* of the theophoric proponent was assimilated to the following *waw*, creating a new diphthong *aw* (YW) that did not reduce to *ō*. We have two names like this in six different ostraca:

1. Ostraca 13, 14, 21: שמריו
2. Ostraca 16A, 17A, 18A: גדיו

---

1 Taken from Demsky, "Three-Tier Names," 213.

In post-exilic communities, one might imagine that even more localized variants would proliferate, as diaspora communities spread and became disconnected from each other. However, we find precisely the opposite phenomenon occurring: a distinct convention arose *simultaneously* in two separate fifth century communities, as attested in fifth century names at Elephantine and in the names in the books of Ezra and Nehemiah. In both of these sources, the divine elementיהו (YHW) was abbreviated in personal names to יה (YH).

Looking first at Ezra and Nehemiah, we find dozens of such names (Ezra 2, 8:1–12, 10:10 ff, and Nehemiah 3). Here is a sample of ten of them:

1. עזריה בן מעשיה בן ענניה
2. נחמיה בן חכליה
3. ישעיה בן עתליה
4. שמעיה בן שכניה
5. חנניה בן שלמיה
6. מתניה
7. זכריה
8. עזריה
9. בניה
10. רפיה

Turning to material from Elephantine, the witnesses in a contract bear names with the theophorous element abbreviated to *YH*, as well (TAD B2:4–16–21):

1. פלליה
2. זכריה
3. גמריה בר מחסיה
4. זכריה בר משלם
5. מעזיה בר מלכיה
6. שמעיה בר ידניה
7. ידניה בר מחסיה
8. ענניה
9. צפניה
10. דעויה/רעויה
11. מחסה בר ישמעיה

In 4th century BCE Idumea, however, we have a very problematic name – יהוכל – the very same name which appeared in the pre-exilic text of Jeremiah, cited above. "Yehokal" was the name of one of the five main clans that appear in unprovenanced ostraca, which I published together with Dr. Ada Yardeni in a five volume series called *Textbook of Aramaic Ostraca* (TAO).[2] Although the smallest

2 See discussion in Hensel, "Reconsidering Yahwism in Persian Period Idumea in Light of the Current Material Findings," in this volume.

clan, some of the names within it also show Yahwistic elements, which feature is distinct from the other clans that appear in these ostraca, who take theophoric elements from many other ethnic origins. Interestingly, moreover, "the name Yehokal has five spellings: a full one, יהוכל, that appears most frequently (TAO A5.1–2, 4–8, 10–11, 14–16, 18–20), a defective spelling יהכל (A5.12–13), an abbreviated one יוכל (A5.9), a phonetic variant יאכל (A5.17), and the unique יואכל (Naveh 1981 [Arad No. 36 {sic!} = ISAP2136])."[3] So the most frequent spelling appears to carry on the pre-exilic tradition of using YHW, although the defective spelling could be confused for the post-exilic tradition of using just YH, while the abbreviated spelling looks most like the Samarian tradition of using just YW. What was happening in Idumea?

Let's move across ancient Babylonia, where an altogether different evolution occurred. A number of clearly Judean names found on clay tables in Babylonia attest to the use of *YĀMA* as the theophoric element. No less than 46 Biblical equivalents are found with the use of this element, not to mention another 20 without Biblical equivalents![4] To illustrate, here is a selection of 10 of these, five with Biblical equivalents and five without:

1. Azar-Yama – equivalent to עזריה
2. Dala-Yama – equivalent to דליה
3. Matan-Yama – equivalent to מתניה
4. Rapa-Yama – equivalent to רפיה
5. Yarim-Yama – equivalent to ירמיהו
6. Dagal-Yama – no equivalent
7. Manuni-Yama – no equivalent
8. Pigla-Yama – no equivalent
9. Uhli-Yama – no equivalent
10. Lihim-Yama – no equivalent

It is by no means straight-forward to explain this localized variant. However, "On the face of it, Ia-(a-)ma renders /Yaw/, but since /h/ is often rendered as <0> in NB/LB, Ia-(a-)ma can render /Yahw/ as well. The sequence <a-ma> stands for /a(h)w/ as originally intervocalic (i.e. VmV) = /w/. ... So far there are no ascertained cuneiform renderings of YH."[5] In other words, in Babylonia, the Judean diaspora community's naming tradition more closely resembles either the localized variant in Samaria (YW) or the pre-exilic onomastic tradition (YWH), meaning that it differs noticeably from the localized tradition in post-exilic Elephantine (YW) and

3 TAO VOL.1, page 222.

4 Pearce and Wunsch, *Documents of Judean exiles*, 308–311.

5 Communication from Ran Zadok on June 6, 2023.

Ezra-Nehemiah (YW). Is it incidental that the two communities associated most with centralized Temple worship developed similar, abbreviated naming conventions, whereas other diaspora communities held on to more ancient forms?

Conclusions and Questions

In tracing the evolution of Yawhistic names in different communities, it is not always straightforward to explain why certain variants arose when they did, and even less straightforward to explain why at least one variant arose simultaneously in two different places. Why was YHW abbreviated in the first place in theophoric names? What does it mean that the scribes at Elephantine followed the same tradition as the scribes in the Bible? How does the ending *Yama* comport with the spelling at Elephantine and in the Bible?

While we might only be able to begin to guess at the answers to these questions, what Yahwistic onomastic tradition hints at is the clear identity-marker that Judean communities felt compelled to maintain from generation to generation. As the diaspora grew and expanded, *Yahu* names and its cognates became both a marker of distinction from the surrounding ethnic milieu, as well as a point of connection between different diaspora communities who drew on a common Yahwistic ancestry, tradition, and religious practice.

Bibliography

Demsky, Aaron, "Three-Tier Names: An Onomastic Formula from Jewish Antiquity," pages 207–226 in *Ve-'Ed Ya'aleh (Gen 2:6): Volume 1: Essays in Biblical and Ancient Near Eastern Studies Presented to Edward L. Greenstein*. Edited by Peter Machinist et al. WAWS; Atlanta: Society of Biblical Literature, 2021.

Pearce, Laurie E. and Wunsch, Cornelia, *Documents of Judean exiles and West Semites in Babylonia in the collection of David Sofer*, Cornell University studies in Assyriology and Sumerology (CUSAS) volume 28. Bethesda, Maryland: CDL Press, 2014.

Benedikt Hensel, "Reconsidering Yahwism in Persian Period Idumea in Light of the Current Material Findings," pages 151–196 in *Yahwism under the Achaemenid Empire, Prof. Shaul Shaked in memoriam*. Edited by Gad Barnea and Reinhard G. Kratz. *BZAW*. Berlin: de Gruyter, 2024.

Michael Shenkar

The 'Eternal Fire', Achaemenid Zoroastrianism and the Origin of the Fire Temples

Zoroastrianism has long been associated with the worship of fire since ancient times. Historical evidence unequivocally links this reverence for fire to the era of Indo-European unity. This devotion is notably evident in the Roman worship of Vesta, whose sacred flame symbolized a similar reverence. The prominence of ritualistic fire within Indo-Iranian religious practices and ceremonial customs is unmistakable, particularly reflected in the profound emphasis on fire within the Vedic cult.[1]

In today's Zoroastrianism, two key aspects stand out: the focus on the eternal fire, tended by priests within special rooms, and the fact that this fire is kept in closed buildings known as *Ātaškada*, *Dar-e Mehr*, or *Agyari*. Yet, determining the historical context and emergence of these practices has posed a significant challenge in the study of Zoroastrianism.[2] This article aims to reassess this subject, drawing insights from recent excavations in Afghanistan and Uzbekistan, particularly focusing on the Achaemenid period.

The era of the Achaemenid dynasty likely played a pivotal role in shaping Zoroastrianism. Scholars have rightly emphasized the significance of this period, delving deeply into exhaustive yet often repetitive debates on the religion of the Achaemenid kings. These discussions primarily focused on how the evidence we possess about their religious practices aligns or differs from the tenets of Zoroastrianism as known from texts codified as late as the Abbasid period.[3] However, there has been little clarity on what exactly "Zoroastrianism" meant in the second half of the first millennium BCE. I believe it is crucial to define this term before engaging in discussions about pre-Sasanian Iranian religious material. Analyzing and comparing the relevant material should follow this initial definition.

1 Jamison and Brereton, *The Rigveda*, 25–30.

2 Boyce, "On the Zoroastrian Temple Cult of Fire," 1975; Boucharlat, "Fire Altars and Fire Temples." For the discussion of the Iranian religious architecture, see also Canepa, "Transformation," and most recently Martinez-Sève, "The Sanctuary of the *Temple*."

3 See a recently published collection of articles dedicated entirely to the Achaemenid religion (Henkelman and Redard, *Persian Religion*), and also the entries on religions and cults in (Jacobs and Rollinger, *Companion*).

Michael Shenkar, The Hebrew University of Jerusalem, Israel

https://doi.org/10.1515/9783111018638-014

Scholars increasingly consider the presence of the liturgy in the Avestan anguage as a defining trait of Zoroastrianism.[4] In my view, the second critical criterion is the status of Ahura Mazdā, the distinctively Zoroastrian deity, as the supreme god and creator. While Ahura Mazdā's presence in this role in the Achaemenid royal inscriptions is undeniable, it is important to note that initially, Ahura Mazdā was the patron god of the Achaemenid dynasty, less popular than some other local deities even in Pars itself.[5] It is likely that the worship of Ahura Mazdā was introduced from the eastern regions only by Darius I or shortly before his ascent.

Pinpointing the first condition proves notably challenging due to the well-known fact that the Avestan language and the Zoroastrian liturgy were written down centuries after the Achaemenid era. Efforts were made to link certain formulations in the Achaemenid royal inscriptions and names within the Achaemenid family to potential Avestan quotations, suggesting the presence of the Avestan liturgy in the Achaemenid court.[6] However, as highlighted by Alberto Cantera, most of these Achaemenid 'Avestan' names align with formulations found in the Rig-Veda.[7] Rather than specifically stemming from Avestan compositions, these may reflect a shared Indo-Iranian heritage. Yet, there is a tangible piece of evidence that points to the existence of the Avestan liturgy in connection with the Achaemenid royal dynasty. This evidence lies within a Zoroastrian calendar, recorded for the first time in Aramaic documents from the archive of the Achaemenid satrap of Bactria, published by Shaul Shaked and Joseph Naveh.[8] Introduced by the Achaemenids after the conquest of Egypt, this calendar, distinct from the Old Persian or Babylonian calendars, was specifically tailored for ritual purposes, unequivocally indicating the existence of Avestan rituals within the Achaemenid court.[9]

In summary, I believe the Achaemenids practiced Zoroastrianism, albeit not necessarily in accordance with the doctrines that emerged during the Sasanian and Early Muslim periods. Similar to how early Christians differed in their religious practices from their medieval European descendants. It is essential to exercise caution, refraining from projecting all the concepts outlined in much later

4 Cantera, "La liturgie longue," 24.

5 Henkelman, "Practice of Worship."

6 Skjærvø, "Avestan Quotations."

7 Cantera, "La liturgie longue," 30–33.

8 Naveh and Shaked, *Aramaic Documents*; Shaked, "Zoroastrian Calendar." See, however, Henkelman, "God is in the Detail," n. 100.

9 Cantera, "La liturgie longue," 53–61. Based on his analysis of the Avestan liturgy, Cantera believes that these rituals took their shape in the Achaemenid period and were spread by the imperial administration, see Cantera, "On the Edge," 217.

Zoroastrian texts onto the Achaemenid period or imposing them upon the non-religious nature of Achaemenid inscriptions.

Considering these observations, let us return to the fire cult. Often, structures in the Iranian context displaying evidence of non-functional use of fire are hastily labelled as "fire temples".[10] However, similar to "Zoroastrianism", it is essential to establish a common understanding of this term. In my view, a "fire temple" is a closed building dedicated exclusively to housing and perpetuating a sacred, continuously burning fire. This fire serves as the focal point for rituals held within this building. A key archaeological criterion for identifying such a structure is the presence of meticulously preserved layers of pure ashes.[11] Notably, the reverence for ashes and their careful preservation, is observed already in the BMAC/Bronze Age Oxus Civilization of Central Asia, which was not Indo-Iranian.[12] Therefore, the occurrence of this custom alone at Central Asian Bronze and Iron Age sites may not necessarily signify a Zoroastrian cult.

The Indo-Iranians in general, and the people who composed the Old Avestan texts toward the end of the second or the beginning of the first millennium BCE, did not use specific closed structures for worship. Instead, they worshipped their deities while focusing on a sacred fire under the open sky. For a considerable period, the earliest known closed temple associated with the Iranians, specifically with the Medes, was Tepe Nush-i Jan.[13] Dating back to around 700 BCE and located in western Iran, this temple had a cross-shaped layout characterized by near-perfect axial symmetry. Within the main room, a mud-brick altar was constructed in the western section, partitioned by a low wall. Standing at 85 cm tall, the altar has a square top measuring 1.41 m. Notably, atop the altar there was a small depression, 23 cm in diameter and 7.5 cm deep, bearing traces of intense burning. It seems clear that this altar was not intended to sustain a continuously burning fire, and no layers of pure ashes were discovered within the temple. Nevertheless, it seems that fire veneration played an important role in the cult conducted at Tepe Nush-i Jan.

Recent excavations at the site of Haji Khan, situated in the core of historical Media, have revealed remnants of another temple, strikingly similar in layout to that of Tepe Nush-i Jan.[14] Within this temple, a remarkably akin three-stepped

---

10 See also the remark by Frantz Grenet ("Mary Boyce's Legacy," 29), who warns against a hasty approach of many archaeologists "who were prone all too often to label any heap of ashes found in any context a 'fire altar'".

11 As noted by Boucharlat, "Fire Altars and Fire Temples," 10.

12 Lyonnet and Dubova, "Questioning the Oxus Civilization," 26.

13 Stronach and Roaf, *Nush-i Jan I.*

14 Hamati Azandaryani et al. "Haji Khan."

mud-brick altar (measuring 60 cm in height and 100 × 100 cm at the top) was unearthed in the northeastern section. Similar to Tepe Nush-i Jan, there is no evidencc suggesting a perpetually burning fire at Haji Khan. However, this discovery prompts interesting questions regarding the consistency of the Median religious practices. Of relevance to our discussion is the confirmation that the fire-related rituals held a significant place within Median cult. Notably, the design of Median altars persisted into the Achaemenid period.

The reliefs adorning the Achaemenid tombs at Naqsh-e Rostam, coupled with accounts from Classical authors, firmly attest to the fire worship practiced by Persian kings. Additionally, depictions from the Persepolis archive portraying the reverence of fire on an altar,[15] provide compelling evidence that starting from the reign of Darius I, not only the royal family but also the Persian elites engaged in fire worship. The pertinent questions that arise are: where did these rituals take place? And, if they involved an "eternal fire," where was it perpetually kindled (or rather, smouldered)?[16]

Answering the first question seems relatively straightforward. Similar to their Indo-Iranian ancestors, the Achaemenids likely conducted their fire rituals under the open sky – upon elevated locations or on constructed podiums like those found at Pasargadae. Achaemenid monumental imagery portrays solely the king engaging with the fire altar and the floating representation of Ahura Mazdā. However, in practice, it is probable that the principal rites around the fire were overseen by priests. It is more difficult to determine whether the fire depicted in the reliefs of the royal tombs or the sealings from Persepolis represents an "eternal fire," as known from the later Zoroastrian practice. Common sense suggests that a perpetually burning fire would require shelter from the elements, being housed within a dedicated structure – a practice observed from the Sasanian era to the present day. Hence, if the Achaemenids possessed an eternal fire, it should have been housed within a building. However, such structures have not been identified in the Achaemenid centres in western Iran.[17] Evidently, the Achaemenids did not seem to follow the tradition of closed temples observed at sites like Tepe Nush-i Jan and Haji Khan.

---

15 Garrison, *Ritual Landscape.*

16 For a consideration of a possible reception of the concept of the "eternal fire" in the Hebrew Bible, see Kislev, "The Cultic Fire in the Priestly Source," in this volume.

17 The famous Achaemenid towers of Ka'ba-ye Zardosht at Naqš-e Rostam and Zendān-e Soleymān at Pasargadae were probably ritual structures, perhaps indeed belonging to the type of "tower temples" as recently argued by Martinez-Sève, "The Sanctuary of the *Temple,*" 242–243. However, they were certainly not intended to house a constantly sustained fire. On the existence in the vicinity of Persepolis of sanctuaries called *ziyan* in Elamite, see Henkelman, "Practice of Worship," 1247–1249.

Valuable insights into this question are offered by a recent reconstruction of Avestan fire rituals by Götz König and Alberto Cantera.[18] Their interpretation suggests that the fire was kept in the "houses of men" (*nmāna-maṣ̌iiānąm*), maintained continuously burning and receiving offerings twice a day. During public sacrifices, it was brought to a designated open-air ritual area and returned to the same "houses of men" upon ritual completion. Some rituals were even conducted within these houses. It means that perpetually burning fire existed already within the Avestan community. These "houses of men" might have belonged to priests, yet it is more plausible that they refer to the dwelling of a *daŋ́hupati* – "lord of the country". Essentially, this ritual fire could have been the same domestic hearth of a ruler. The Achaemenid royal cult likely followed a similar practice. The fire was probably housed within a structure or chamber, conceivably linked to the royal household. It would be taken outdoors for ritual ceremonies and then returned. While such structures or chambers await archaeological identification, they may be represented by the so-called "tower-like structures" depicted on the Persepolis sealings and coins from the Hellenistic period issued by the local rulers of Pars.[19]

Fortunately, a written source sheds light on the practice of maintaining a burning fire for an extended duration. It is found in the account by Diodorus Siculus (17.114.4) narrating details of the funeral of Hephaistion, Alexander the Great's closest companion:

> As part of the preparations for the funeral, the king [Alexander] ordered the cities of the region to contribute to its splendour in accordance with their ability, and he proclaimed to all the peoples of Asia that they should sedulously quench what the Persians call the sacred fire, until such time as the funeral should be ended. This was the custom of the Persians when their kings died, and people thought that the order was an ill omen, and that heaven was foretelling the king's own death. There were also at this time other strange signs pointing to the same event, as we shall relate shortly, after we have finished the account of the funeral.[20]

Another historian of Alexander's life, Curtius Rufus, explicitly refers to the fire accompanying the Persian king during a campaign as "eternal" (*aeternum*) (3.3.9; 4.13.12; 4.14.24). Crucially for our discussion, both Diodorus and Curtius Rufus emphasize that this fire is a royal fire, linked to kingship. Isidore of Charax (11) reinforces this association during the Parthian period, noting the perpetual fire

---

18 König, "Zur Frage 'ewiger' feuer"; Cantera "Fire, the Greatest God."

19 Garrison, *Ritual Landscape.*

20 The translations from the Greek and Roman authors are given according to the editions of the Loeb Classical Library unless stated otherwise.

of Arsak, the founder of the Arsacid dynasty, kept burning in the city of Asaac. As late as the Sasanian period, the inscription on the reverse of coins minted by the first Sasanian king identifies the flame atop the throne-altar as the "fire of Ardashir" (*ādur-ī ardašīr*) – the regnal fire emblematic of the individual Sasanian ruler.

The earliest detailed description of closed temples housing perpetually burning sacred fires is found in Strabo's *Geographica*, completed at the beginning of the first century CE. Strabo notably mentions numerous fire temples (πυραιθεῖα) of the Magi located in Cappadocia (15.314–15).

> But in Cappadocia – for there the tribe of the Magi is large; they are also called fire-kindlers; and there are many sanctuaries of the Persian gods – they do not even sacrifice with a knife, but they beat (the animal to death) with a piece of wood as with a cudgel. And there are fire-sanctuaries, noteworthy enclosures; in the midst of these is an altar, on which there is a large quantity of ashes, and (where) the Magi keep the fire ever burning. And every day, they enter and sing invocations for approximately an hour, holding the bundle of wands before the fire, wearing felt tiaras which fall down on both sides over the cheeks to cover the lips. The same customs are observed in the sanctuaries of Anaïtis and Omanos; these also have enclosures, and the image of Omanos is carried around in a procession. These things we have seen ourselves, but the other things and those which follow are recorded in the histories.[21]

Regrettably, the question that may be crucial for the genesis of fire temples remains unanswered: are the sanctuaries described by Strabo a relic of Achaemenid rule in Asia Minor, or rather a subsequent local evolution influenced by Greek religious practices?

Archaeological evidence from Central Asia is especially important for understanding the origins of fire temples, given that the people behind the Avestan texts were inhabitants of this region. Archaeological findings from Sogdiana and Bactria during the first millennium BCE indicate that rites were conducted outdoors on mudbrick terraces, such as those discovered at sites of Pachmak-Tepe, Pshak-Tepe, and Kok-Tepe in modern Uzbekistan.[22] This ritual practice persisted into the Hellenistic period in Central Asia, as revealed by the discovery of a cultic platform atop the acropolis of Ai Khanoum.[23]

In recent years, however, several important discoveries were made in Afghanistan and Uzbekistan that according to some scholars represent the first examples of fire temples.[24] The earliest is the Topaz Gala site in southern Turk-

21 De Jong, *Traditions of the Magi*, 121–157.

22 Rapin, "Sanctuaires sogdiens," 419–426; Lhuillier 2019, 261.

23 Boyce and Grenet, *History of Zoroastrianism*, 181–183.

24 Grenet, "Mary Boyce's Legacy," 30–31; Xin, "Sacred Landscape," 18. For a critical review of this material, see Canepa, "The Transformation of Sacred Space," 329–333.

menistan, excavated by Polish archaeologists and dated to around 930–745 BCE (Fig. 1).[25] This site comprises four rooms, one notably larger and almost square (measuring 13 × 13.9 m). Supporting the roof are three columns arranged in a line. Within the main room's western section stands a round clay podium, approximately 104 cm in diameter. Archaeologists interpret this as a fire altar due to traces of intense burning. Enclosed within a low, square structure, the podium appears aligned with a likely entrance in the western wall, allowing a direct view.[26] Notably, a storage jar unearthed in the main room's southwestern corner contained ashes, suggesting their symbolic significance akin to the importance of ashes in Zoroastrian fire temples. However, excavators also found evidence indicating the cooling of hot ashes with water,[27] – a practice incompatible with the Zoroastrian tradition.

Another site is Sangirtepa situated in the Kashkadarya region of modern Uzbekistan.[28] According to the excavators, the closed temple existed here before the arrival of the Achaemenids (Fig. 2). It was located outside the fortified area of the city and its dimensions were 34 × 40 m. The structure comprised two wings flanking a central room. Initially, the excavators presumed the existence of four central pillars, yet further analysis of the data unveiled this to be incorrect.[29] Interestingly, the hearth, interpreted as a fire altar by researchers,[30] was not situated in the middle of the central room, but was deliberately moved west and aligned on the axis with the southern entrance. Moreover, also the walls of the eastern passage were not straight, apparently on purpose, allowing a direct view of the hearth. This deviates from the Zoroastrian practice of concealing the fire from outsiders' view.

The purported fire altar was nothing more than a conical earth mound built upon a foundation of pebbles. If this hearth was indeed the focal point of the building's cultic activities, it raises a question about its simplicity, considering the substantial investment of effort and resources into the structure. The suggestion of the cultic function of the building also stems from evidence of a foundation ritual and an atypical burial associated with the site. However, it is plausible that the foundation ritual might simply denote this building as a public structure, not

25 Wagner, "Fire Temple at Topaz Gala depe."

26 This is suggested by an analysis of a room with a very similar layout at Tillya Tepe in Afghanistan. See Sarianidi *Khram i nekropol*, 6–22.

27 Wagner, "Fire Temple at Topaz Gala depe," 337.

28 Rapin and Khasanov, "Sakral'naya arkhitektura," 50–51; Rapin, "Sanctuaires sogdiens;" Martinez-Sève, "The Sanctuary of the *Temple*," 235.

29 Unpublished information from Claude Rapin cited in Martinez-Sève, "The Sanctuary of the *Temple*," 235.

30 Rapin, "Sanctuaires sogdiens," 441.

necessarily a dedicated sanctuary. Nonetheless, from the perspective of Zoroastrian doctrine, the connection between the burial and the sacred area would be considered inappropriate.

During the Achaemenian era, this structure was replaced by a platform, accompanied by hearths and fragments of two human skulls. Eventually, by the third century BCE, this platform fell into disuse. Considering its location beyond the settlement walls, the foundation rituals, and the subsequent installation of a cultic platform, it is probable that the building at Sangirtepa was a sanctuary. While fire probably had a role in the rituals, it was not a fire temple, and any correlation with subsequent Zoroastrian fire temples remains ambiguous.

One of the most interesting structures proposed to be an "early fire temple" is Kindyktepa, in the Surkhandarya valley in southern Uzbekistan.[31] Dating back to the fourth century BCE, this site's primary chamber is rectangular, with four columns placed asymmetrically (Fig. 3). The clay installations identified as fire altars, have significantly deteriorated, with reconstructions primarily relying on traces of intense burning. These reconstructed altars were approximately 1.6 × 1.6 meters, standing at least 20 cm from the floor.[32] Although layers of ashes were discovered on the room's surface, their thickness – only 10 cm – raises doubts regarding their origin from a continuously burning fire. The ceramic assemblage from Kindyktepa is rather ordinary, lacking distinctively cultic vessels or items associated with offerings. Yet, Kindyktepa's architectural layout may suggest a ritual function by restricting access to the main hall and intentionally limiting the visibility of the fire.[33]

Another potential sanctuary dating back to the fifth century BCE, recently uncovered in the Surkhandarya region of Uzbekistan, is Kyzyltepa.[34] This building was constructed atop the citadel's highest point within a sizable city. Despite similar size, its layout was different from that of Kindyktepa, – a central chamber encircled by a corridor (Fig. 4). During excavations, two mud-brick installations were identified as fire altars. These installations had small depressions on their

31 Mokroborodov, "Kindyktepa"; Martinez-Sève, "The Sanctuary of the *Temple*," 234–236.

32 Victor Mokroborodov, email from 12.12.22.

33 Viktor Mokroborodov suggested that the room to the north of the central chamber served as the site for the Zoroastrian purification ritual, *barašnom* (Mokroborodov, "Novye arkheologicheskie"). Frantz Grenet, in a lecture he gave at the Collège de France on March 16, 2023, examined in detail the problems associated with this interpretation. https://www.college-de-france.fr/fr/agenda/cours/argenterie-de-prestige-en-asie-centrale-suite-homere-alexandre-les-temples-non-bouddhiques-en/argenterie-de-prestige-en-asie-centrale-suite-homere-alexandre-les-temples-non-bouddhiques-en-5

34 Sverchkov and Xin, "Khram ognya"; Xin "KYZYLTEPA"; Xin, "Sacred Landscape," 20–23; Martinez-Sève, "The Sanctuary of the *Temple*," 234–236.

tops, filled with ashes. Additionally, layers of ashes were discovered in the central chamber, but they were only 1 cm thick. Notably, small depressions containing pure ashes were also found in the room.[35]

Finally, at Cheshme-Shafa, located south of Baktra in northern Afghanistan, the French archaeological mission uncovered a monumental stepped stone altar, standing at 2.10 meters high and measuring 2.70 × 1.55 meters across its top (Fig. 6).[36] However, due to incomplete excavations, its precise context – whether within an enclosed structure or an open courtyard – remains unclear. Given its elevated location, the altar appears to have stood in an open space. The altar's shape, material, and monumental dimensions suggest a connection with the royal Achaemenid cult rather than local traditions, distinguishing it from the above-mentioned finds in Uzbekistan. Despite the altar's grandeur, the small round depression on its surface seems inadequate for maintaining a continuously burning fire. It is possible that fire was brought to the site, potentially in a metal vessel, and installed for public worship on the altar.

How do these discoveries contribute to our understanding of the genesis of the Zoroastrian fire temples? There can be little doubt that fire, and perhaps also certain cultic activities associated with it, played an important role in the function of these structures. The evidence for the constantly sustained fire and for the rituals that took place there is, however, limited. We should remember that such practices were not unique to Zoroastrianism, but were probably common to all Indo-Iranians, some Indo-European and even non-Indo-European people.

Nevertheless, these sanctuaries, if indeed they represent such, did not influence the Achaemenid cult and were not adopted by the Achaemenids.[37] The layout of Kindyktepa structure might relate to the tetrastyle Bactrian temples from the Hellenistic and the Kushan periods, like Takht-i Sangin and Surkh Kotal. However, whether this suggests solely architectural or perhaps also cultic continuity remains unclear. It is worth noting that both Indo-Iranians and Indo-Europeans attributed particular ritual significance to the fireplaces within important public buildings and the residences of rulers and leaders. In the Greek context, for instance, the fireplace held a political centrality within the community, assuming the role of what initially was the hearth of the king.[38] Additionally, the tetrastyle central hall alone does not necessarily imply a ritual function of the building.

---

35 Sverchkov and Xin, "Khram ognya," 102–103, 108.

36 Besenval and Marquis, "travaux," 997–998. For most recent discussion, see Xin, "Sacred Landscape," 23–25.

37 Martinez-Sève, "The Sanctuary of the *Temple*" 240–241, thinks that Kindyktepa and Kyzyltepa belong to the type of "tower-temples", which was introduced to Central Asia by Achaemenids.

38 Kajava, "Hestia Hearth," 2.

For instance, the arrangement of the Mycenaean megarons, featuring a hearth positioned amid four columns, resembles the layout observed at Kindiktepa.

I believe that some of these buildings from pre-Achaemenid and Achaemenid Central Asia might have functioned as communal or political centres.[39] In some cases, perhaps, the fire burned continuously within them. Other communities had different traditions, which were shared by various Indo-Iranian and potentially non-Indo-Iranian groups in the second and first millennia BCE. As the Iranians migrated to the Iranian plateau, they brought various forms of fire worship with them. The earliest evidence for this can be traced back to the Medes. From the time of Darius I, some Persians also worshipped fire. This royal fire burned continually during a king's reign, probably within an unknown structure or room connected to palace complexes. The Achaemenids actively supported Avestan liturgy and fire worship, effectively promoting Zoroastrianism not just among Persians, but among all Iranians. It seems that the tradition of closed temples in the Iranian world developed after the Macedonian conquest.[40] At present, we lack archaeological evidence for pre-Sasanian fire temples, – closed structures housing the eternal fire and serving as primary sites for rituals instead of moving the fire outdoors. However, textual sources indicate that they already existed in the Parthian period. The earliest mention of fire temples dedicated to a specific deity is found in Cappadocia. This development might be linked to life in the Asia Minor diaspora when the eternal fires lost support from local non-Iranian kings. However, in Iran during the Parthian period, the connection between the sacred fire and kingship was maintained. Later, under the Sasanians, numerous fire temples were established in Iran, dedicated to individual gods and members of the royal family. While the importance of fire temples diminished significantly for the Zoroastrian community in Iran during the twentieth century, in India, they remain central institutions of the Parsee cult, where priests still continue to maintain the eternal flame of their religion, as their ancestors did for centuries.

39 While the lack of residential areas and the placement of Kindyktepa and Sangirtepa outside the settlement walls suggest they might not have served as private residences where a ruler lived.

40 Shenkar, "Temple Architecture."

Bibliography

Besenval, Roland, and Marquis, Philippe, "Les travaux de la délégation archéologique française en Afghanistan (DAFA): résultats des campagnes de l'automne 2007-printemps 2008 en Bactriane et à Kaboul," *Comptes rendus des séances de l'Académie des Inscriptions et Belles-Lettres* 152, no. 3 (2008): 973–995.

Boucharlat, Rémy, "Fire Altars and Fire Temples in the First Millennia BC/AD in the Iranian World: Some Remarks," pages 7–25 in *Proceedings of the 8th International Congress on the Archaeology of the Ancient Near East, 30 April – 4 May 2012*, University of Warsaw. Volume 1. Wiesbaden, 2014.

Boyce, Mary, "On the Zoroastrian Temple Cult of Fire." *Journal of the American Oriental Society* 95 (1975): 454–465.

Boyce, Mary, and Grenet, Frantz, *A History of Zoroastrianism. Vol. 3: Zoroastrianism under Macedonian and Roman Rule*. Leiden: Brill, 1991.

Canepa, Matthew P., "The Transformation of Sacred Space, Topography, and Royal Ritual in Persia and the Ancient Iranian World," pages 319–372 in *Heaven On Earth: Temples, Ritual, and Cosmic Symbolism in the Ancient World*, edited by Deena Ragavan. Chicago, 2013.

Cantera, Alberto, "La liturgie longue en langue avestique dans l'Iran occidental," pages 21–68 in *Persian Religion in the Achaemenid Period / La religion perse à l'époque achéménide*, edited by Henkelman Wouter F. M. and Redard, Céline. Wiesbaden, 2017.

Cantera, Alberto, "Fire, the Greatest God (*ātarš ... mazišta yazata*): The Cult of the 'Eternal' Fire in the Rituals in Avestan." *Indo-Iranian Journal* 62, no. 1 (2019): 19–61.

Cantera, Alberto, "On the Edge between Literacy and Orality: Manuscripts and Performance of the Zoroastrian Long Liturgy," *Oral Tradition* 35, no. 2 (2022): 211–250.

De Jong, Albert, *Traditions of the Magi: Zoroastrianism in Greek and Latin Literature*. Leiden: Brill, 1997.

Garrison, Mark B., *The Ritual Landscape at Persepolis: Glyptic Imagery From the Persepolis Fortification and Treasury Archives*. Chicago, 2017.

Grenet, Frantz, "Mary Boyce's Legacy for the Archaeologists." *Bulletin of the Asia Institute* 22 (2008): 29–46.

Hamati Azandaryani et al., "Haji Khan: A Median Temple in Hamadan province, Iran," Iranica Antiqua, 57 (2022): 43–89

Henkelman, Wouter F. M., "Practice of Worship in the Achaemenid Heartland." In *A Companion to the Achaemenid Persian Empire*, edited by Jacobs, Bruno and Rollinger, Robert, 1221–1243. 2 vols. Hoboken, NJ, 2021.

Henkelman, Wouter F. M., "God is in the Detail: The Divine Determinative and the Expression of Animacy in Elamite with an Appendix on the Achaemenid Calendar," pages 405–477 in *Transfer, Adaption und Neukonfiguration von Schrift- und Sprachwissen im Alten Orient*, edited by Cancik-Kirschbaum, Eva and Schrakamp, Ingo. Wiesbaden, 2022.

Henkelman, Wouter F. M., and Redard, Céline (eds.), *Persian Religion in the Achaemenid Period / La religion perse à l'époque achéménide*. Wiesbaden, 2017.

Jacobs, Bruno, and Rollinger, Robert (eds.), *A Companion to the Achaemenid Persian Empire*. Hoboken, NJ. 2 vols, 2021.

Jamison, Stephanie W., and Brereton, Joel P., *The Rigveda: The Earliest Religious Poetry of India*. Vol. 1. New York: Oxford University Press, 2014.

Kajava, Mika, "Hestia Hearth, Goddess, and Cult," *Harvard Studies in Classical Philology* 102 (2004): 1–20.

König, Götz, "Zur Frage 'ewiger' feuer im Avesta und in der zorastrischen Tradition." *Iran and the Caucasus* 19 (2015): 201–260.

Lhuillier, Johanna, "Central Asia during the Achaemenid Period in Archaeological Perspective," pages 257–273 in *L'orient est son jardin, Hommage à Rémy Boucharlat*, edited by Gondet, Stéphane and Haerinck, Ernie. Leuven, 2019.

Litvinskij, Boris A., *Khram Oksa v Baktrii (Juzhnyj Tadzhikistan). Vol 3. Iskusstvo, khudozhestvennoe remeslo, muzykal'nye instrumenty*. Moscow: Nauka, 2010.

Lyonnet, Bertille, and Dubova, Nadezhda, "Questioning the Oxus Civilization or Bactria-Margiana Archaeological Culture (BMAC): An Overview," pages 7–66 in *The World of the Oxus Civilization*, edited by Lyonnet, Bertille and Dubova, Nadezhda. New York, 2021.

Martinez-Sève, Laurianne, "The Sanctuary of the *Temple à redans* in Ai Khanum (Hellenistic Bactria): Cults and Ritual Practices," *Studia Hercynia* 27/1 (2023): 98–123.

Mokroborodov, Viktor, "Novye arkheologicheskie svidetel'stva ob odnom iz zoroastrijskikh obryadov," pages 13–22 in *Trudy Gosudarstvennogo Ermitazha LXXV. Bukharskij oasis i ego sosedi v drevnosti i srednevekov'e*. Saint-Petersburg, 2015.

Mokroborodov, Viktor, "Kindyktepa: a Temple of the Mid-First Millennium BC in Southern Uzbekistan," pages 343–351 in *A Millennium of History. The Iron Age in southern Central Asia (2nd and 1st Millennia BC)*, edited by Lhuillier, Johanna and Boroffka, Nikolaus: Berlin, 2018.

Naveh, Joseph, and Shaked, Shaul, *Aramaic Documents from Ancient Bactria (Fourth Century BCE) from the Khalili Collection*. London, 2012.

Rapin, Claude, "Sanctuaires sogdiens et cultes avestiques de l'époque de Gava à l'époque hellénistique," pages 417–461 in *Persian Religion in the Achaemenid Period / La religion perse à l'époque achéménide*, edited by Henkelman Wouter F.M. and Redard, Céline. Wiesbaden: Harrassowitz Verlag, 2017.

Rapin, Klod and Khasanov, Mutalib, "Sakral'naya arkhitektura Tsentral'noj Azii s akhemenidskogo perioda po ellinisticheskuju epokhu: mezhdu lokal'nymi traditsiyami i kul'turnym transferom," pages 42–58 in *Kul'turnyj transfer na perekrestkah Tsentral'noj Azii: do, vo vremya i posle Velikogo shelkovogo puti*. Paris-Samarkand, 2013.

Sarianidi, Viktor I., *Khram i nekropol' Tillyatepe*. Moscow, 1989.

Shaked, Shaul, "The Zoroastrian Calendar in Another Document from Ancient Bactria", pages 249–252 in Tokhtasev, S. and Lurje, P. (eds.), *Commentationes Iranicae*. Vladimiro f. Aaron Livschits nonagenario donum natalicum, Petropoli: ædibus Nestor-Historia, 2013.

Shenkar, Michael, "Temple Architecture in the Iranian World in the Hellenistic Period." In *From Pella to Gandhara. Hybridisation and Identity in the Art and Architecture of the Hellenistic East*, edited by Kouremenos, Anna, Chandrasekaran, Sujatha and Rossi, Roberto, 117–139. Oxford, 2011.

Skjærvø, Prods O., "Avestan Quotations in Old Persian?" pages 1–64 in *Irano-Judaica* IV, edited by Shaked, Shaul and Netzer, Amnon. Jerusalem, 1999.

Stronach, David, and Roaf, Michael, *Nush-i Jan I. The Major Buildings of the Median Settlement*. Leuven, 2007.

Sverchkov, Leonid and Xin Wu, "Khram ognya V-IV vv. do n.e. Kizyltepa". *Scripta Antiqua* 8 (2019): 97–128.

Wagner, Marcin, "The Fire Temple at Topaz Gala depe in Southern Turkmenistan," pages 333–351 in *A Millennium of History. The Iron Age in southern Central Asia (2nd and 1st Millennia BC)*, edited by Lhuillier, Johanna and Boroffka, Nikolaus. Berlin: Dietrich Reimer Verlag, 2018.

Wu, Xin, "KYZYLTEPA." In *Encyclopaedia Iranica Online*, © Trustees of Columbia University in the City of New York, 2021. Consulted online on 23 July 2023 http://dx.doi.org/10.1163/2330-4804_EIRO_COM_362540.

Wu, Xin, "The Sacred Landscape of Central Asia in the Achaemenid Period." *Studia Hercynia* 27/1 (2023): 13–53.

Konrad Schmid

The End of History and the Ends of History: Assessing the Political-Theological Status of the Achaemenid Empire in Persian Period Judaism

1 Persian Period Judaism in Biblical Scholarship: Some Spotlights

The topic "Yahwism under the Achaemenid Rule"[1] was extremely hotly debated at the end of the 19th century between the Hebrew Bible scholar Julius Wellhausen and the ancient historian Eduard Meyer, who in the view of some was one of last universal scholars in the humanities.

Initially, the quarrel between them was about the authenticity of the Aramaic documents in Ezra 4–7, but in the end, it was rather about what role Persian rule played in the development of what both Meyer and Wellhausen called "Judaism." Meyer stated that the genesis of Judaism can only be understood as a product of the Persian empire, whereas Wellhausen found this statement opaque, and he was not willing to accept too much Persian influence in the formation of post-exilic Judaism. According to Wellhausen, everything we need to know about this process we know from the Bible, and this suffices for reconstructing the Persian influence on Judaism. Reinhard Kratz has aptly described this controversy in which Meyer felt deeply insulted by Wellhausen.[2] In the end, the argument between the two was unfruitful. Their positions might even have been closer one to another than the heated and hateful debate would suggest. One shortcoming that both Meyer and Wellhausen suffered from, however, was their lack of sociological differentiation. Although not much older than Emile Durkheim and Max Weber, they did not yet embark on the project of sociological differentiation. Of course, Meyer and Wellhausen were aware of groups in late Second Temple Juda-

1 See the contributions in Edelman et al. eds., *Religion in the Achaemenid Persian Empire*. For an overview of the biblical literature of the period see Schmid, *Literaturgeschichte des Alten Testaments*, 183–231; see also Kratz, "Biblical Sources," 133–148; for (Deutero-)Isaiah see Kratz, "Isaiah and the Persians," 155–168. Silverman, *Persepolis and Jerusalem*, offers a broad assessment of possible influences between Achaemenid Persia and Judah.

2 Kratz, "Die Entstehung des Judentums."

Konrad Schmid, University of Zurich, Switzerland

https://doi.org/10.1515/9783111018638-015

ism like the Pharisees, the Sadducees, the Essenes, and the Zealots, because the sources identify these groups directly, but in the preceding period there are no clear sociological distinctions discernible in their writing. Their account of history is mainly politically determined by national and international actors, but less so sociologically by groups and societal interactions.

Meyer's hypothesis ("Judaism is a product of the Persian empire")[3] was deemed by Wellhausen to be a pointless statement that does not help us any further in understanding Second Temple Judaism. Meyer was not as wrong as Wellhausen thought. Nevertheless, Wellhausen's influence and exceptional standing in biblical scholarship let his own position prevail for quite some decades.

This contribution aims at leaving behind the Meyer-Wellhausen paradigm that tried to assess the influence of the Persian empire on the formation of "Judaism." Rather, I will ask, in an era after Durkheim and Weber, about the interactions *within* Second Temple Judaism, and I will have to limit myself here to positions that found entry into the Hebrew Bible.

One of the pioneers in that regard was Otto Plöger, a professor of Hebrew Bible at the University of Bonn. In 1959 he published a monograph entitled *Theocracy and Eschatology* (German original: *Theokratie und Eschatologie*)[4] that by now is no longer very well known.

Nevertheless, in the first decade after its publication, the book – or rather, the *booklet*, it is only 142 pages long – was quite successful. It saw three editions in German (1959, 1962 and 1968) and was even translated into English (1968).

In his book, Plöger reconstructs a basic bifurcation in the political and theological thinking of Persian period Judaism. Jewish literature of that era, according to him, covers a spectrum between "theocratic" positions that approve of the Achaemenid empire and interpret it as a legitimate expression of God's rule and as something like the "end of history" (represented in texts like P and Chronicles), and "eschatological" positions that instead argue for the contrary – that history has not yet come to an end, and rather Israel has to strive for national sovereignty, a Davidic kingdom, and the return of the diaspora (represented in various Deuteronomistic and prophetic texts from the Second Temple period).

Of course, Plöger's terminology of "theocratic" and "eschatological" is unfortunate, because it is far too general and has very strong doctrinal overtones, as even he himself admits in the very first sentence of this book. Why he still kept it will remain his own secret.[5]

---

3 Meyer, *Julius Wellhausen*, 25.

4 Plöger, *Theokratie und Eschatologie*.

5 There are other points of possible criticism: Firstly, the title is quite misleading. Plöger himself has to justify it in the very first sentence of his book where he explains that his book is not a doctrinal treatise, but that he is proposing a historical hypothesis. Unfortunately, Plöger never

Plöger's main distinction was taken up by Odil Hannes Steck in his inaugural lecture at the University of Heidelberg from 1968.[6] He directly referenced Plöger,[7] but he also highlighted the need to differentiate further the two main strands that Plöger had identified as "theocratic" and "eschatological." Steck and Plöger used different texts to discuss what they called "theocracy" and "eschatology." For the former, Plöger used mainly P, and Steck mainly Chronicles; for the latter, Plöger used mainly Isa 24–27, Zech 12–14 and Joel, while Steck used late Deuteronomistic texts like Neh 9 that he had identified in his dissertation.

A similar distinction along the line of Plöger was introduced into the discussion in 1973 by Paul Hanson's *Dawn of Apocalyptic*.[8]

He differentiates between the two camps of hierocratic priests on the one hand and visionary prophets on the other hand in the Second Temple period. Paul Hanson draws particularly on Karl Mannheim's basic distinction between "ideologians" and "utopians" in order to describe these two groups (it is not difficult to imagine who is who). Hanson also quotes Plöger's book, but only in passing.[9]

This will suffice to explain Plöger's distinction, its genesis, and its early reception in the work of Steck and Hanson. But now the question arises: How accurate is it?

---

added a subtitle to his book which could have been more than helpful. Secondly, its five chapters are relatively unintegrated; some of them are more general in nature, while others are analyses of specific text units like Isaiah 24–27, Zech 12–14 or Joel. The review by Hartman "Theocracy and Eschatology," states: "P.'s detailed analysis of these writings [i.e. Isaiah-Apocalypse, Trito-Zechariah, Joel] is difficult to follow; he seems to get lost in the woods of minute "units" and hardly shows how these writings are the missing links between the older eschatology of the pre-exilic prophets and the fully developed apocalyptic eschatology of Daniel" (634). This is not an unfair evaluation. Thirdly, there is a significant mismatch between the opening question of the book that is asking about the identity of the Ἀσιδαῖοι *Hasidaioi* (in Hebrew: the חֲסִידִים *ḥăsîdîm*) and the basic distinction between "theocracy" and "eschatology" which Plöger proposes in his last chapter that the book became known for. The *Hasidim* are mentioned three times in the first and second book of Maccabees, and Plöger suspects them to be behind the current shape of the book of Daniel and thus wants to shed light on their intellectual and social prehistory. The last sentence of Hartman's review reads as follows: "In all fairness to the author, however, it must be said that he presents his work merely as a possible hypothesis, and as such it is not without real value" (634).

6 Steck, "Das Problem."

7 Steck, "Das Problem," 456.

8 Hanson, *The Dawn of Apocalyptic*. For a broader treatment of "eschatological" positions, one should also add Talmon, "Eschatology and History."

9 Plöger himself uses very little theoretical underpinning. It seems that he was more indebted to his own earlier work that he published in two journal articles: "Priester und Prophet," (a short version of his habilitation), and "Prophetisches Erbe."

As usual, the scholarly balanced answer to this question is: It depends. It depends on how distinct one perceives the two camps to be, and how much fluidity within them and intersection between them one allows. In my view, Plöger's basic proposal – as simple as it is, at least in its basic outline – is plausible. It unlocks the intellectual background of many Persian period texts in the Hebrew Bible, and it is also able to explain certain later redactional historical developments of these texts.[10]

If we, despite all criticism, accept Plöger's basic distinction *in terms of a spectrum*, it is helpful to ask how we can update, refine, and modify his approach in order to take advantage of the progress Hebrew Bible studies have made in the past few decades.

In order to do so, this article will discuss two positions in the Pentateuch that probably belong to the Persian period, the first one is P – in Plöger's terms a "theocratic" text –, the second is Deuteronomy 30 – an "eschatological" text. Due to the Mosaic fiction of the Pentateuch, the Achaemenid empire is, of course, not explicitly mentioned, but it is present overall as the historical background of the authors of P and Deuteronomy 30. For both texts I will ask how they interact with other positions on Plöger's spectrum. Finally, the integration of P and D in the Pentateuch shall be discussed and its significance for the "theocratic" or "eschatological" quality of the Pentateuch. To be sure, the composition of the Pentateuch is a redactional process that also still seems to belong, at least in its basic contours and decisions, to the Persian period.

2 P's vision of the end of history

One of the most prominent theocratic voices of early Persian period Judaism in the Hebrew Bible is the so-called Priestly Document in the Pentateuch, in short P.[11]

---

10 As is well known, the biblical book of Daniel, for example, includes legends and visions. The legends are theocratic, while the visions are eschatological (see e.g. Kratz, "The Visions of Daniel," 91–113; Kratz, *Translatio imperii*. Using Plöger's approach, it becomes possible to understand the legends and the visions in their historical context, but it becomes also possible to understand the *dynamics* of the redactional development from the theocratic legends to the eschatological visions.

11 See the standard text assignments by Elliger, "Sinn und Ursprung"; repr. in *Kleine Schriften zum Alten Testament*; Lohfink, "Die Priesterschrift"; repr. in *Studien zum Pentateuch*; Otto, "Forschungen zur Priesterschrift." For a position against P as a source in Exodus see Berner, *Die Exoduserzählung* (see, however, my review in *ZAW* 123 (2010): 292–294); Albertz, *Exodus 1–18*, 10–26. Wöhrle, *Fremdlinge im eigenen Land*, holds a similar position regarding Gen 12–50. The debate concerning the literary end of P (if seen as a formerly independent literary source text)

Some scholars date it to the pre-exilic period,[12] but the resonances with Persian imperial ideology and its dependency on prophetic books like Ezekiel are so strong, that a date in the late 6th century BCE seems to be preferable, at the beginning of the Achaemenid period.[13] It is probably fair to say that this is the majority position among Hebrew Bible scholars.

P is not interested in national or international politics, as long as the cult in Jerusalem is unaffected. The Achaemenid empire does not negatively interfere with it, so foreign rule is acceptable for P. It basically limits itself to describing how Israel's cultic institutions emerged from its foundation history, and its entire narrative thread is located in the mythical past. As Norbert Lohfink once put it aptly: P, as an overall document, does not describe history, but *primeval* history.[14] P's narrative establishes a perfect cult and describes Israel as centered around that cult, but P does not speak of a monarchy, nor of a state. It only once talks about kings, in Gen 17:6, where God promises to Abraham:

והפרתי אתך במאד מאד ונתתיך לגוים ומלכים ממך יצאו׃

> And I will make you exceedingly fruitful; and I will make you into nations, and kings shall come from you.

This statement is difficult to interpret within the ideological context of P. It might be an explanation why the political system of the ancient world was organized in monarchies. It might even pertain to the Davidic dynasty which for P is already in the past, while for Israel's present, no king is needed, just the temple, the sacrificial cult, its personnel, and the chosen people. Of course, the institution of a Persian great king is a given for the time when P was written, but for P's

arose especially in the wake of Perlitt, "Priesterschrift im Deuteronomium?" Proposals include seeing the literary end at either Exod 29 (Otto, "Forschungen zur Priesterschrift"), Exod 40 (Pola, *Die ursprüngliche Priesterschrift*; Kratz, *Die Komposition der erzählenden Bücher*, 102–117; Bauks, "La signification de l'espace"), Lev 9 (Zenger, "Priesterschrift,": 435–46; Zenger, *Einleitung in das Alte Testament*, 156–75), Lev 16 (Köckert, *Leben in Gottes Gegenwart*, 105; Nihan, *From Priestly Torah*, 20–68) or Num 27 (Ska, "Le récit sacerdotal," 631–653). A staggering of endings within the Priestly document between Exod 40 and Lev 26 is suggested in Gertz (ed.) *Grundinformation Altes Testament*, 236; Frevel, *Mit Blick auf das Land*, supports the traditional conclusion in Deut 34 (cf. Schmidt, *Studien zur Priesterschrift*, 271; Weimar, *Studien zur Priesterschrift*, 17; Blenkinsopp, "The Structure"; Lohfink, "Die Priesterschrift"; Guillaume, *Land and Calendar*; see also the conclusion of P^g in Joshua.

12 Milgrom, "The Antiquity"; Hurvitz, "Once Again."

13 See in more detail: Schmid, "Taming Egypt," 13–29; see also Hartenstein and Schmid (eds.) *Farewell to the Priestly Writing?*. For a discussion of the linguistic shape of P in that regard see Blenkinsopp, "An Assessment"; Levine, *Numbers 1–20*.

14 See Lohfink, "Die Priesterschrift," 183–225 = Lohfink, *Studien zum Pentateuch*, 213–253.

theocratic vision, a foreign political leading structure is not a problem as long as the functioning of the temple cult is guaranteed – particularly, if that guarantee comes from that foreign king.

One exception (at least within P's narrative scenery) is the case of Egypt: Egypt is not part of P's peaceful commonwealth of nations, which might hint towards a date for P before 526 BCE,[15] when Cambyses conquered Egypt. Prior to this, Egypt was not part of the Persian empire, and that could also explain why in P it is particularly Egypt's *army*, but not its population, that is eventually destroyed, in the crossing of the sea (Exodus 14).

Finally, the overall political-theological structure of the world according to P seems to mirror a basic Persian imperial concept. P differentiates between the "world circle" (Genesis 1–9), the "Abrahamic circle" (Genesis 11–Exodus 1) in Genesis and the "Israel circle" (Exodus 1–40) in Exodus. It represents a concentric theological organization of the world in which the creator God is *Elohim* for the world (Gen 9:1), *El Shadday* for the Abrahamic people (Gen 17:1), and YHWH for Israel (Exod 6:2).[16] This conception is quite close to the Persians' own view of center and periphery within their empire, as described by Herodotus in his histories (I, 134):

> τιμῶσι δὲ ἐκ πάντων τοὺς ἄγχιστα ἑωυτῶν οἰκέοντας μετά γε ἑωυτούς, δευτέρα δὲ τοὺς δευτέρους: μετὰ δὲ κατὰ λόγον προβαίνοντες τιμῶσι: ἥκιστα δὲ τοὺς ἑωυτῶν ἑκαστάτω οἰκημένους ἐν τιμῇ ἄγονται, νομίζοντες ἑωυτοὺς εἶναι ἀνθρώπων μακρῷ τὰ πάντα ἀρίστους, τοὺς δὲ ἄλλους κατὰ λόγον τῆς ἀρετῆς ἀντέχεσθαι, τοὺς δὲ ἑκαστάτω οἰκέοντας ἀπὸ ἑωυτῶν κακίστους εἶναι.
>
> They honor most of all those who live nearest them, next those who are next nearest, and so going ever onwards they assign honor by this rule: those who dwell farthest off they hold least honorable of all; for they think that they are themselves in all regards by far the best of all men, that the rest have only a proportionate claim to merit, until those who live farthest away have least merit of all.[17]

One can even – not necessarily as a direct influence, but as a parallel phenomenon – adduce P's programmatic and specific use of *'elohim* without an article in the sense of a proper noun in order to speak of the one and only "God" that mirrors the absolute use of *basileus* in Herodotus' *Histories*, also without an article, in order to designate the one and only Persian great king.[18]

---

15 On 526 instead of 525 BCE see Quack, "Zum Datum."

16 See on this in further detail Schmid, "Judean Identity and Ecumenicity."

17 *Herodotus, with an English translation;* see also Briant, *From Cyrus to Alexander,* 181.

18 See Schmid, "The Quest for 'God'." For a reading of P's calendric system from a Persian period background see Guillaume, "Non-violent Re-readings," 57–71.

P is thus theocratic in nature. But does P show any kind of interaction with diverging positions, and particularly with proponents of the "eschatological" strand in contemporary Persian period Judaism? Yes indeed, in my view, the most prominent elements in this regard can be found in the Priestly Flood account in Genesis 6–9.

ויאמר אלהים לנח קץ כל־בשׂר בא לפני כי־מלאה הארץ חמס מפניהם והנני משחיתם את־הארץ׃

> And God said to Noah, The end (*qṣ*) of all flesh has come before me; for the earth is full of iniquity from them. So then I will destroy them from the earth. (Gen 6:13)

This harsh statement of the "end" that "has come" is not a formulation invented by P, but it is a quote from the book of Amos, from a prophecy of judgment, as had been noted early on by Rudolf Smend.[19]

ויאמר מה־אתה ראה עמוס ואמר כלוב קיץ
ויאמר יהוה אלי בא הקץ אל־עמי ישׂראל
לא־אוסיף עוד עבור לו׃

> Am 8:2: And he said, What do you see, Amos? I answered, A basket of fruit (*qyṣ*). Then Yhwh said to me, the end (*qṣ*) has come for my people Israel; I will no longer forgive them.

ואתה בן־אדם כה־אמר אדני יהוה לאדמת ישׂראל
קץ בא הקץ על־ארבעת כנפות הארץ׃
עתה הקץ עליך ושׁלחתי אפי בך
ושׁפטתיך כדרכיך ונתתי עליך את כל־תועבתיך׃

> You, son of man, say, Thus says the Lord Yhwh to the land of Israel, An end (*qṣ*) is coming! An end (*qṣ*) is coming upon the four fringes of the land! Now the end (*qṣ*) is coming upon you: I will let loose my wrath against you and judge you according to your ways and lay upon you [the punishment for] all your abominations. (Ezek 7:2–3)

Manifestly, P thus takes up the message of earlier prophecies of doom but refracts it prehistorically: There has been a divine decree about the "end," but it is in the past, not in the future. P thus relegates God's comprehensive will of judgment back to the mythic past.[20]

For the present and future, the promises of Gen 9 are the binding expression of God's eternal will: He guarantees the world eternal continuance and the sparing of catastrophes such as the flood, which took place once and for all in the past. In Gen 9, God places the relaxed war bow in the clouds and guarantees the

---

19 See Smend, "'Das Ende ist gekommen'," 67–74 = Smend (ed.), *Die Mitte des Alten Testaments*, 238–243. See also Pola, "Back to the Future"; Gertz, "Noah und die Propheten."
20 See Pola, "Back to the Future."

creation permanent existence. Thus, God renounces here all violence, after he exercised prehistorically, in the previously narrated Flood, once for all violence against כל־בשׂר, "all flesh":[21]

והקמתי את־בריתי אתכם ולא־יכרת כל־בשׂר עוד ממי המבול
ולא־יהיה עוד מבול לשׁחת הארץ׃

> And I establish my covenant with you, that never again shall all flesh be cut off by the waters of a flood, and never again shall there be a flood to destroy the earth. (Gen 9:11)

Both P's theocratic stance and its criticism of the prophetic tradition can be discerned in this relocation of the cosmic catastrophe from the end to the very beginning of world history. But what was P's legitimation to do that?

P is making this argument based on – in ancient terms – *scientific grounds*: The primeval flood is something which could be reliably found in the scholarly Mesopotamian traditions about the past, most prominently in the interlinked flood traditions in Atrahasis and in Gilgamesh.[22] Why should God plan a second cosmic catastrophe after he dealt with the first one in a way that excluded such a possibility in a very decisive way.

A pro-Persian and strictly theocratic text like P was thus not simply stating its position, but it was also interacting with conflicting traditions, for example the earlier prophecy of doom found in Amos and Ezekiel.

Another piece of literature that is clearly theocratic in its outlook is the book of Chronicles. Wilhelm Rudolph in his 1955 commentary on Chronicles put it this way:[23] The Chronicler's work "wants to describe the realization of theocracy on Israel's soil".[24] We are not completely sure whether Chronicles belongs the Persian or rather the early Hellenistic period, but given its theocratic profile, it is probably at least historically rooted in the Persian period.

In 1 Chronicles 16:8–36, King David has the Asafites perform a psalm for the first time. Its text is a compilation of Ps 105:1–15; 96; 106:1,4,7–8, but it also includes new elements, particularly at its end in V. 35:

ואמרו הושׁיענו אלהי ישׁענו וקבצנו והצילנו מן־הגוים להדות לשׁם קדשׁך להשׁתבח בתהלתך׃

> And say: Save us, O God of our salvation, and gather and rescue us from the nations, that we may give thanks to the name of your holiness, and give glory in your praise. (1Chr 16:35)

21 Zenger, *Gottes Bogen in den Wolken*; Janowski, "Schöpfung, Flut und Noahbund"; Schmid, "Das kosmische Weltgericht," 409–434.

22 See Wasserman, *The Flood*.

23 Rudolph, *Chronikbücher*, III.

24 "[Das] chronistische[...] Werk ... will *die Verwirklichung der Theokratie auf dem Boden Israels* schildern."

Within a nearly completely theocratic theology, we can thus find in Chronicles also a very modest element that seems to identify the existence of a diaspora as a problem that is in need of being attended to by God himself.[25]

Another such passage can be found in 2Chr 30:6–9, a text claiming that repentance by those who are in the land will lead to the return of the exiles in Mesopotamia.[26]

What does the other side of the spectrum between “theocracy” and “eschatology” look like? Within the Pentateuch, it is predominantly the later expansions of the D-strand that should be mentioned here. The literary kernel of Deuteronomy probably belongs to the late Neo-Assyrian period or, as some prefer, to the early Babylonian period. For our purposes, this dating is, however, irrelevant. I will focus on the post-deuteronomistic and post-Priestly framework of Deuteronomy, in Deut 4 and Deut 30, that on the one hand clearly belongs to the Persian period and on the other hand exhibits, in Plöger’s terms, an “eschatological” stance.[27]

3 Deuteronomy 30 and the ends of history

Why is Deut 30 a Persian period text? First of all, Deut 30 is one of the very few textual windows in the Pentateuch that provide a look far away from Deuteronomy’s imagined scenery in the Moabite desert immediately before Israel’s conquest of the land into the future of the author’s present. Deut 30 states that all the blessings and the curses will happen to Israel, and that they will be exiled among the nations.

> והיה כי־יבאו עליך כל־הדברים האלה הברכה והקללה אשר נתתי לפניך והשבת אל־לבבך בכל־הגוים אשר הדיחך יהוה אלהיך שמה׃
>
> And when all these things have happened to you, the blessings and the curses that I have set before you, if you bring them back to your heart among all the nations where YHWH your God has scattered you. (Deut 30:1)

But Deut 30 does not only envision the exile, it also speaks of the return from exile and restoration:

25 Mathys, *Dichter und Beter*, 201–217; Klein, *1 Chronicles*, 48.
26 See Hilpert, *Die Komposition der Chronikbücher*, 212–213.
27 For a long term interpretation of “Deuteronomism” see Schmid, “The Deuteronomistic Image,” 369–388.

והביאך יהוה אלהיך אל־הארץ אשר־ירשו אבתיך וירשתה והיטבך והרבך מאבתיך׃

And YHWH your God will bring you into the land that your ancestors possessed, and you will possess it; he will make you morc prosperous and numerous than your ancestors. (Deut 30:5)

This outlook toward the restoration period makes it very likely that Deut 30 was actually written in that very time – it belongs to the Achaemenid period.[28] This can be further corroborated by the very close links of Deut 30 to Deut 4. The post-Priestly origin of Deut 4 is quite well established since Michael Fishbane, in my view correctly, interpreted that text as an innerbiblical exegesis of Gen 1 and other texts.[29] Deut 30 clearly presupposes and even quotes Deut 4; therefore, its dating into the Persian period can be quite safely assumed. A quite clear case is provided by the link from Deut 30:3 back to Deut 4:32:

ושב יהוה אלהיך את־שבותך ורחמך ושב וקבצך מכל־העמים אשר הפיצך יהוה אלהיך שמה׃

And YHWH your God will take back your exile and he will have compassion on you, and he will be gathering you again from all the peoples among whom YHWH your God has scattered you. (Deut 30:3)

This presupposes and takes up the according announcement from Deut 4:27 (also formulated with הפיץ):

והפיץ יהוה אתכם בעמים ונשארתם מתי מספר בגוים אשר ינהג יהוה אתכם שמה׃

And YHWH will scatter you among the peoples; only a few of you will be left among the nations where YHWH will lead you. (Deut. 4:27)

Another motif binding Deut 4 and Deut 30 together can be found in the expression "end of the heavens":[30]

אם־יהיה נדחך בקצה השמים משם יקבצך יהוה אלהיך ומשם יקחך׃

If you are scattered to the end of the heavens, from there YHWH your God will gather you, and from there he will take you [back]. (Deut 30:4)

---

28 Cf. Schmid, "How to Identify," 101–118.

29 Fishbane, *Biblical Interpretation*. See also Otto, *Deuteronomium 1,1–4,43*, 508–592. For the reception of P see specifically 534–535; for the relationship between Deut 4:26 and 4:27–28 see 571.

30 See Otto, *Deuteronomium 1,1–4,43*, 581; see further on this topic Schmid, "Himmelsgott, Weltgott und Schöpfer"; Koch, *Gottes himmlische Wohnstatt*.

כי שאל־נא לימים ראשנים אשר־היו לפניך למן־היום אשר ברא אלהים אדם על־הארץ ולמקצה השמים ועד־קצה השמים הנהיה כדבר הגדול הזה או הנשמע כמהו:

For ask about former days, [long] before your own, ever since the day that God created human beings on the earth; [ask] from one end of heaven to the other: has anything so great as this ever happened or has ever been heard of anything alike? (Deut. 4:32)

In addition, this motif is attested outside the Pentateuch only in Neh 1:9, which also hints towards a setting in the Persian period:

ושבתם אלי ושמרתם מצותי ועשיתם אתם אם־יהיה נדחכם בקצה השמים משם אקבצם והביאותים אל־המקום אשר בחרתי לשכן את־שמי שם:

And if you return to me and keep my commandments and do them, if you are scattered at the end of the heavens, from there I will gather them and bring them to the place at which I have chosen to establish my name. (Neh 1:9)

The pre-Hellenistic origin of Deut 30 on the other hand can be safeguarded by its inclusion into the Pentateuch, which is basically a pre-Hellenistic text.[31]

After having situated Deut 30 in the Persian period, a closer look at its content is in order. Interestingly, Israel's restoration is impossible without a fundamental anthropological transformation of the returnees:

ומל יהוה אלהיך את־לבבך ואת־לבב זרעך לאהבה את־יהוה אלהיך בכל־לבבך ובכל־נפשך למען חייך:

And YHWH your God will circumcise your heart and the heart of your descendants, so that you might love YHWH your God with all your heart and with all your soul, and for your life. (Deut 30:6)

Keeping God's commandments is thus only possible for a renewed Israel with a circumcised heart, a motif that is taken up from prophecy (see e.g. Jer 4:4; Ezek 44:7, besides the prophecies about a "heart of flesh" instead of a "heart of stone" or a "new heart" in Jer 32 and Ezek 36). The writers of this passage in the Persian period were apparently of the opinion that Israel's current condition was deficient and needed to be changed by divine intervention. How important this aspect is can be further deduced from the overall concentric structure of Deut 30:1–10: The circumcision of the heart is at the very heart of that composition.[32] But also the international situation, at least regarding Babylon, is evaluated negatively by Deut 30:

31 See Schmid, "Textual, Historical, Sociological," 29–51.

32 Otto, *Deuteronomium 23,16–34,12*, 2040.

ונתן יהוה אלהיך את כל־האלות האלה על־איביך ועל־שׂנאיך אשר רדפוך:

> And YHWH your God will put all these curses on your enemies and on your haters who pursued you. (Deut. 30:7)

Israel's "heart" (that is, in modern terms: its "mind") must be changed and its enemies must be punished. Of course, one might think first of the Babylonians as these enemies, but probably all empires ruling over Israel and Judah are in view here, including the Persians, the empire active at the time when Deut 30 was written. *And only after that* will God provide all his blessing upon Israel:

והותירך יהוה אלהיך בכל מעשׂה ידך בפרי בטנך ובפרי בהמתך ובפרי אדמתך לטובה

> And YHWH your God will make you abundantly prosperous in all the deed of your hands, in the fruit of your body, in the fruit of your livestock, and in the fruit of your soil for good. (Deut 30:9a)

It is noteworthy how apolitical this outlook is; it is concentrated on the elementary aspects of rural life, but it does not touch upon further social or political aspects of the restoration. It is interesting that Deut 30 in a certain sense is also a "theocratic" text, but it postpones the "theocracy" from the present to the future: There will be no special need for a Davidic king; there may be one, as the king's law in Deut 17 has it, but he is of minor importance and he has to stick to the law.

The overall "eschatological" quality of this perspective of Deut 30 is finally highlighted by the final statement that links protology and eschatology together:

כי ישׁוב יהוה לשׂושׂ עליך לטוב כאשׁר־שׂשׂ על־אבתיך:

> For YHWH will again take delight in you for good, just as he delighted in your ancestors. (Deut 30:9b)

The goal of God's history with his people at its end is identical to its origins.

If we look back on Deut 30 and compare this text with P, then it is fairly obvious that these texts represent two very different intellectual attitudes towards the Achaemenid empire.

If Deut 30 is a text from the Persian period, then it evaluates its own present negatively overall: Israel anthropologically lacks the capacity to follow the law, obeying the laws is the prerequisite to attaining the divine blessing over everyday life, the Babylonian empire is to be cursed, the Persian empire could be as well if it acts in a hostile way towards Israel, and only in a divinely organized new future will good life be possible and guaranteed. The present is deficient; only the future will be bright and positive.

It is probably not too far-fetched to assume that Deut 30, at least in certain parts, is polemicizing against P. Why? Firstly, Human beings, according to P, are created perfectly in the image of God. According to Deut 30, this is not true; humans still must await their divine re-creation in order to comply with God's will. Secondly, P holds a very peaceful worldview, while Deut 30 claims that all the enemies of Israel will be punished by God. Thirdly, P is a diaspora-friendly text. Nothing indicates that living abroad would not be a possible solution for P. Even the sanctuary, the tent of meeting was founded abroad in the sand of the desert of Sinai. Conversely, Deuteronomy 30 only sees a possible and prosperous future for Israel in the land of its ancestors. And to get back to its land, God himself will become active again. The Achaemenid period, according to Deut 30, does not signify the end of history – this would be P's position – but it is a time of decisive divine creational activity.

4 Theocracy and Eschatology in the Final Formation of the Pentateuch

P and D no longer exist as independent texts. They are integrated into the Pentateuch.

The *terminus ante quem* for the formation of the Pentateuch, at least regarding its main components to which both P and D belong, is – according to me and to many others – still within the Achaemenid period, just before the time of Alexander the Great. The following three arguments point towards such an assumption: First, there is the translation into Greek which can be dated to the mid-third century BCE.[33] Although there are some differences between the Hebrew and the Greek text, especially in the second tabernacle account of Exodus 35–40,[34] the textual evidence of the Old Greek basically points to a completed Pentateuch. Second, the books of Chronicles, which probably date to the 4th century or early 3rd century BCE, refer to a textual body called either the Torah of YHWH or the Torah of Moses. It is not fully clear whether these terms denote an already completed Pentateuch, but they at least point in this direction.[35] Third,

33 See, e.g., Siegert, *Zwischen Hebräischer*, 42–43; Görg, "Die Septuaginta im Kontext," 115–130; Kreuzer, "Entstehung und Entwicklung"; Krauter, "Die Pentateuch-Septuaginta," 26–46; Albrecht, "Die alexandrinische Bibelübersetzung." The oldest manuscript of the Greek Pentateuch is Papyrus Rylands 458, dating to the mid 2nd century BCE, cf. Wevers, "The Earliest Witness," 240–244; de Troyer, "When Did the Pentateuch," 277; Dorival, "Les origins de la Septante."

34 Cf., e.g., Wevers, "Building."

35 Cf. García López, "תורה," especially 627–630; Steins, "Torabindung und Kanonabschluss"; Maskow, *Tora in der Chronik*.

the Pentateuch does not seem to presuppose the fall of the Persian empire in the wake of Alexander the Great's conquests.[36] Especially in Prophetic literature, this event was interpreted as a cosmic judgment. But in the Pentateuch, the cosmos – particularly heaven and earth – is supposed to exist forever. The Pentateuch does not exhibit clear influences and reactions to the fall of the Achaemenid empire following the conquest of Alexander. There might be a few exceptions, for instance Num 24:14–24, which mentions the victory of the ships of the כתים,[37] other Hellenistic elements might be found in the specific numbers in the genealogies of Genesis 5 and 11 or in some of the alterations in Exod 35–40.[38] But these exceptions are minor. The bulk of the Pentateuch seems to be pre-Hellenistic.

This is at least what biblical scholars mostly assume. Israel Finkelstein has argued against the assumption that the bulk of the Pentateuch stems from the Persian period.[39] For him, it is unconceivable that in the very modest circumstances of Jerusalem in the Persian period, many and extensive texts might have been written. According to him, there was simply no sufficient infrastructure for a temple administration to handle, develop, and transmit complex textual bodies like the Pentateuch. Finkelstein therefore wants to believe that the 7th and the 3rd and the 2nd century BCE were more important for the composition of the Pentateuch.[40] However, the archaeological evidence for Persian period Jerusalem is admittedly scarce and the relative dating of texts in the Pentateuch hints at the pre-Hellenistic origin of the Pentateuch and the Persian period origin of large text blocks like Leviticus and Numbers.[41]

If the formation of the Pentateuch was, at least in its basic features, a process that took place in the Achaemenid period, how is it to be interpreted regarding its integration of P and D and their respective positions in the "theocracy" – "eschatology" spectrum?

The answer to this question is a specimen of the ideological compromise which characterizes the final Pentateuch. The sheer co-presence of P- and D-elements in the Pentateuch attests to the will of its composers to integrate diverging traditions. Erhard Blum (orally) once used the metaphor of "fire" and "ice"

---

36 See Steck, *Bereitete Heimkehr*, 52–54; Beuken, *Jesaja 28–39*, 300–327; Schmid, "Das kosmische Weltgericht," 409–434.

37 Cf. Rouillard, *La péricope de Balaam*, 467; Crüsemann, *Die Tora*, 403, Schmitt, "Der heidnische Mantiker," 185.

38 Cf. Hughes, *Secrets of the Times*; see the reservations of Hendel, "A Hasmonean Edition," against a dating of the numbers in MT in the 2nd century BCE.

39 See Finkelstein, *Essays in Biblical Historiography*, 5–23, 567–570.

40 See Finkelstein, "Jerusalem and Judah 600–200 BCE"; Finkelstein, *Essays in Biblical Historiography*, 567–572.

41 See n. 27.

for P and D in the Pentateuch. In a conceptual perspective, they do not fit together at all. Nevertheless, at some point during the Achaemenid period, they have been woven together in what eventually became the Pentateuch.

But what can we say about the ideological shape of the Pentateuch in the late Achaemenid period? Briefly, three aspects shall be mentioned: First of all, as all documentarians ever since Wellhausen and even before him (e.g. Nöldeke)[42] have maintained, P is the "Grundschrift" of the Pentateuch: It is the most prominent voice in the Pentateuch, simply because P's narrative thread served as the basic layer into which the older and younger traditions had been inserted. Therefore, the Pentateuch has a basic "theocratic" imprint. Secondly, however, there is one motif that binds all the books of the Pentateuch together, which David Clines called the "Theme of the Pentateuch."[43] What he means by this is the promise of the land to Abraham, Isaac, and Jacob as an oath. This motif appears in comparably few places, only to Gen 50:24; Exod 32:13; 33:1; Num 32:11; Deut 34:4. If one includes Lev 26:42, which is related in terms of its content, then this theological declaration is the only one that carries through all five books of the Pentateuch. Conversely, it never again appears in the rest of the narrative books of the Enneateuch, from Joshua–2 Kings – which is especially conspicuous in this context. And thirdly, in the very final passages of the Pentateuch, in Deut 34:10–12, Moses is presented as the prophet *par excellence*. One could be under the impression that this is also a hint towards a more prophetic or eschatological imprint of the Pentateuch, but I am not so sure about this. Given the prominence of P in the Pentateuch, and given the statement in Deut 34 that Moses is above all other prophets, one could also interpret this interpretation of "Moses" as *the* "prophet" as a theocratic critique of the prophetic tradition within the Nevi'im.

Finally: Was there an external trigger that motivated the combination of D and P? Why would anyone strive to combine what actually does not seem to go together?

The answer offered in a theory developed by Erhard Blum[44] and Peter Frei[45] in the 80s of the last century is: This has to do with the Persian imperial authorization of local regulations, and the Torah might have been the result of such an imperial authorization of local laws. Second Temple Judaism was forced to

---

42 See Nöldeke, "Die s.g. Grundschrift des Pentateuchs."

43 Clines, *The Theme of the Pentateuch.*

44 Blum, *Studien zur Komposition des Pentateuch*, 345 n. 42; Blum, "Esra, die Mosetora," 250 n. 80.

45 Frei, "Zentralgewalt und Lokalautonomie"; Frei, "Zentralgewalt und Lokalautonomie im achämenidischen Kleinasien"; Frei, "Die persische Reichsautorisation" (See also the English translation: "Persian Imperial Authorization").

present a set of laws that represented all its ideological and theological strands, and the result of this enterprise was a Pentateuch comprising both D and P, and also other elements that actually do not really belong together.

Of course, this theory is highly contested,[46] but it has also often been misrepresented. Some critics, for instance, believed that Frei had claimed that the local regulations that were sanctioned by the imperial center had to be collected and to be listed in a central Persian archive. But Frei never claimed that. He rather conceptualized this process of Persian imperial authorization as an ideological means to convey imperial authority to local regulations, but not to establish a real, existing, comprehensive Persian imperial law that included all its local parts. The Persian empire had no central law, rather the imperial law only existed in local law collections that at their specific place were elevated to the status of imperial law.

Another problem is, of course, that among the attested procedures of Persian imperial authorization of local laws there are no such large legal entities like the Pentateuch. But this might have to do with the fact that larger textual bodies were written on parchment or papyrus and not on stone and therefore did not survive. Be this as it may: whoever contests the theory of the Persian imperial authorization of the Torah as an explanation for its diversity would need to come up with a better theory as to why the Pentateuch looks the way it does – combining "fire" and "ice". The Pentateuch implicitly propagates the Achaemenid period as the "end of history," while at the same time it also is shaped in a way that contests this assumption. Foreign rule is difficult to accept. In the eyes of some, however, it nevertheless entailed significant benefits for Judah. The Pentateuch witnesses to both positions: the Persian period is *the* end of history, but at the same time, history may have other ends.

Bibliography

Albertz, Rainer, *Exodus 1–18*. ZBK 2.1. Zürich: TVZ, 2012.

Albrecht, Felix, "Die alexandrinische Bibelübersetzung: Einsichten zur Entstehungs-, Überlieferungs- und Wirkungsgeschichte der Septuaginta," pages 209–243 in Alexandria, edited by T. Georges et al., COMES 1. Tübingen: Mohr Siebeck, 2013.

Bauks, Michaela, "La signification de l'espace et du temps dans l''historiographie sacerdotale'," pages 29–45 in The Future of the Deuteronomistic History, edited by Thomas Römer, BETL 147. Leuven: Peeters, 2000.

Berner, Christoph, *Die Exoduserzählung*, FAT 73. Tübingen: Mohr Siebeck, 2010.

46 See the discussion in: Watts, (ed.) *Persia and Torah*. See also Schmid, "Der Abschluss der Tora," 159–184; Römer, "Der Pentateuch."

Beuken, Willem A. M., *Jesaja 28–39*. HThKAT. Freiburg: Herder, 2010.
Blenkinsopp, Joseph, "An Assessment of the Alleged Pre-Exilic Date of the Priestly Material in the Pentateuch." *ZAW* 108 (1996): 495–518.
Blenkinsopp, Joseph, "The Structure of P." *CBQ* 38 (1976): 275–292.
Blum, Erhard, "Esra, die Mosetora und die persische Politik," pages 231–255 in *Religion und Religionskontakte im Zeitalter der Achämeniden*, edited by Reinhard G. Kratz, Veröffentlichungen der Wissenschaftlichen Gesellschaft für Theologie 22. Gütersloh: Gütersloher Verlagshaus, 2001.
Blum, Erhard, Studien zur Komposition des Pentateuch. BZAW 189. Berlin and New York: de Gruyter, 1990.
Briant, Pierre, *From Cyrus to Alexander: A History of the Persian Empire*. Winona Lake: Eisenbrauns, 2002.
Clines, David J. A., *The Theme of the Pentateuch*. JSOT.S 10. Sheffield: Sheffield Academic Press. 2nd edition, 1997.
Crüsemann, Frank, *Die Tora*. Munich: Kaiser, 1992.
Dorival, Gilles, "Les origins de la Septante: la traduction en grec des cinq livres de la Torah," pages 39–82 in La Bible grecque de Septante, edited by Marguerite Harl et al., Paris: Cerf, 1988.
Edelman, Diana V. et al., (eds.) *Religion in the Achaemenid Persian Empire: Emerging Judaisms and Trends*. ORA 17. Tübingen: Mohr Siebeck, 2016.
Elliger, Karl, "Sinn und Ursprung der priesterlichen Geschichtserzählung," *ZTK* 49 (1952): 121–143. Reprinted in *Kleine Schriften zum Alten Testament*, edited by H. Gese and O. Kaiser, 174–198. TB 32. Munich: Kaiser, 1966.
Finkelstein, Israel, "Jerusalem and Judah 600–200 BCE: Implications for Understanding Pentateuchal Texts," pages 3–18 in: *The Fall of Jerusalem and the Rise of the Torah*, eds., Peter Dubovský, Dominik Markl, and Jean-Pierre Sonnet, FAT 107. Tübingen: Mohr Siebeck, 2016.
Finkelstein, Israel, *Essays in Biblical Historiography: From Jeroboam II to John Hyrcanus I*. FAT 148. Tübingen: Mohr Siebeck, 2022.
Fishbane, Michael, *Biblical Interpretation in Ancient Israel*. Oxford: Clarendon, 1985.
Frei, Peter, "Die persische Reichsautorisation: Ein Überblick." *ZABR* 1 (1995): 1–35. Reprinted in English: "Persian Imperial Authorization: A Summary," pages 5–40 in *Persia and Torah: The Theory of Imperial Authorization of the Pentateuch*, edited by James W. Watts, SBLSymS 17. Atlanta: Scholars Press, 2001.
Frei, Peter, "Zentralgewalt und Lokalautonomie im Achämenidenreich," pages 5–131 in *Reichsidee und Reichsorganisation im Perserreich*, edited by Peter Frei and Klaus Koch. OBO 55. Fribourg: Universitätsverlag. 2nd edition, Göttingen: Vandenhoeck & Ruprecht, 1996.
Frei, Peter, "Zentralgewalt und Lokalautonomie im achämenidischen Kleinasien." *Transeu* 3 (1990): 157–171.
Frevel, Christian, *Mit Blick auf das Land die Schöpfung erinnern*. HBS 23. Freiburg: Herder, 2000.
Gertz, Jan C. (ed.), *Grundinformation Altes Testament*. 2nd edition. UTB 2745. Göttingen: Vandenhoeck & Ruprecht, 2007.
Gertz, Jan C. "Noah und die Propheten: Rezeption und Reformulierung eines altorientalischen Mythos." *Deutsche Vierteljahrsschrift für Literaturwissenschaft und Geistesgeschichte* 81 (2007): 503–522.
Görg, Manfred, "Die Septuaginta im Kontext spätägyptischer Kultur: Beispiele lokaler Inspiration bei der Übersetzungsarbeit am Pentateuch," pages 115–130 in *Im Brennpunkt: Die Septuaginta: Studien zur Entstehung und Bedeutung der Griechischen Bibel*, edited by Heinz-Josef Fabry and U. Offerhaus. BWANT 153. Stuttgart: Kohlhammer, 2001.

Guillaume, Philippe, *Land and Calendar: The Priestly Document from Genesis 1 to Joshua 18*. LHBOTS 391. London: T & T Clark, 2009.

Guillaume, Philippe, "Non-violent Re-readings of Israel's Foundational Traditions in the Persian Period (the Calendar System in P)," pages 57–71 in *Religion in the Achaemenid Persian Empire: Emerging Judaisms and Trends*, edited by Diana V. Edelman et al., ORA 17. Tübingen: Mohr Siebeck, 2016.

Hanson, Paul, *The Dawn of Apocalyptic: The Historical and Sociological Roots of Jewish Apocalyptic Eschatology*. Minneapolis: Fortress, 1973.

Hartenstein, Friedhelm, and Schmid, Konrad, *Farewell to the Priestly Writing? The Current State of the Debate*. SBL.AIL 38. Atlanta: SBL Press, 2022.

Hartman, Louis F., "Theocracy and Eschatology by Otto Plöger, S. Rudman," *CBQ* 30.4 (1968): 633–634.

Hendel, Ron, "A Hasmonean Edition of MT Genesis? The Implications of the Editions of the Chronology in Genesis 5." *HeBAI* 1 (2012): 448–464.

Herodotus, *Herodotus, with an English translation* by A. D. Godley. Vol. 1. LCL. Cambridge: Harvard University Press, 1920.

Hilpert, Andreas, *Die Komposition der Chronikbücher: Redaktionsgeschichtliche Studien zu 2Chr 10–36*. BZAW 526. Berlin: de Gruyter, 2021.

Hughes, Jeffrey, *Secrets of the Times: Myth and History in Biblical Chronology*. JSOTSup 66. Sheffield: Sheffield Academic Press, 1990.

Hurvitz, Avi, "Once Again: The Linguistic Profile of the Priestly Material in the Pentateuch and its Historical Age: A Response to J. Blenkinsopp." *ZAW* 112 (2000): 180–191.

Janowski, Bernd, "Schöpfung, Flut und Noahbund. Zur Theologie der priesterlichen Urgeschichte." *HeBAI* 4 (2012): 502–521.

Klein, Ralph, *1 Chronicles*. Hermeneia. Minneapolis: Fortress, 2006.

Koch, Christoph, *Gottes himmlische Wohnstatt: Transformationen im Verhältnis von Gott und Himmel in tempeltheologischen Entwürfen des Alten Testaments in der Exilszeit*. FAT 119. Tübingen: Mohr Siebeck, 2018.

Köckert, Matthias, *Leben in Gottes Gegenwart: Studien zum Verständnis des Gesetzes im Alten Testament*. FAT 43. Tübingen: Mohr Siebeck, 2004.

Krauter, Stefan, "Die Pentateuch-Septuaginta als Übersetzung in der Literaturgeschichte der Antike," pages 26–46 in *Die Septuaginta und das frühe Christentum / The Septuagint and Christian Origins*, edited by T. S. Caulley and Hermann Lichtenberger. WUNT 277. Tübingen: Mohr Siebeck, 2011.

Kratz, Reinhard G., "Biblical Sources," pages 133–148 in *A Companion to the Achaemenid Persian Empire*, edited by Bruno Jacobs and Rober Rollinger. Blackwell Companions to the Ancient World, Vol. 2. New York: John Wiley & Sons, Inc, 2021.

Kratz, Reinhard G., "Die Entstehung des Judentums. Zur Kontroverse zwischen E. Meyer und J. Wellhausen." *ZTK* 95 (1998): 167–184.

Kratz, Reinhard G., "Isaiah and the Persians," pages 155–168 in *Imperial Visions: The Prophet and the Book of Isaiah in an Age of Empires*, edited by Reinhard G. Kratz and Joachim Schaper. FRLANT 277. Göttingen: Vandenhoeck & Ruprecht, 2020.

Kratz, Reinhard. G., *Die Komposition der erzählenden Bücher des Alten Testaments*. UTB 2157. Göttingen: Vandenhoeck & Ruprecht, 2000.

Kratz, Reinhard G., *Translatio imperii: Untersuchungen zu den aramäischen Danielerzählungen und ihrem theologiegeschichtlichen Umfeld*. WMANT 63. Neukirchen-Vluyn: Neukirchener, 1991.

Kratz, Reinhard G., "The Visions of Daniel," pages 91–113 in The Book of Daniel: Composition and Reception, edited by John J. Collins and Peter Flint. VT.S 83/1. Leiden: Brill, 2001.

Kreuzer, Siegried, "Entstehung und Entwicklung der Septuaginta im Kontext alexandrinischer und frühjüdischer Kultur und Bildung," pages 3–39 in Septuaginta Deutsch: Erläuterungen und Kommentare zum griechischen Alten Testament, edited by Martin Karrer and Wolfgang Kraus. Stuttgart: Deutsche Bibelgesellschaft, 2011.

Levine, Baruch A., *Numbers 1–20*. AB 4A. New York: Doubleday, 1993.

Lohfink, Norbert, "Die Priesterschrift und die Geschichte," pages 183–225 in *Congress Volume Göttingen 1977*, edited by J. A. Emerton. VTSup 29. Leiden: Brill, 1978. Reprinted in pages 213–253 in *Studien zum Pentateuch*. SBAB 4. Stuttgart: Katholisches Bibelwerk, 1988.

López, Federico G., "תורה," pages 597–637 in *ThWAT*, vol. 8, edited by G. J. Botterweck, H Ringgren, and Heinz-Josef Fabry. Stuttgart: Kohlhammer, 1995.

Maskow, Lars, *Tora in der Chronik: Studien zur Rezeption des Pentateuchs in den Chronikbüchern*. FRLANT 274. Göttingen: Vandenhoeck & Ruprecht, 2019.

Mathys, Hans-Peter, *Dichter und Beter: Theologen aus spätalttestamentlicher Zeit*. OBO 132. (Fribourg: Academic Press/Göttingen: Vandenhoeck & Ruprecht, 1994.

Meyer, Eduard, *Julius Wellhausen und meine Schrift Die Entstehung des Judentums: Eine Erwiderung*. Halle: Max Niemeyer, 1897.

Milgrom, Jacob, "The Antiquity of the Priestly Source: A Reply to Joseph Blenkinsopp," *ZAW* 111: 10–22, 1999.

Nihan, Christophe, *From Priestly Torah to Pentateuch: A Study in the Composition of the Book of Leviticus*. FAT II/25. Tübingen: Mohr Siebeck, 2006.

Nöldeke, Theodor, "Die s.g. Grundschrift des Pentateuchs," in *Untersuchungen zur Kritik des Alten Testaments von Theodor Nöldeke*. Kiel: Schwers, 1869.

Otto, Eckart, *Deuteronomium 1,1–4,43*. HThK.AT. Freiburg i. Br.: Herder, 2012.

Otto, Eckart, *Deuteronomium 23,16–34,12*. HThK. Freiburg i. Br.: Herder, 2017.

Otto, Eckart, "Forschungen zur Priesterschrift." *TR* 62 (1997): 1–50.

Perlitt, Lothar, "Priesterschrift im Deuteronomium?" *ZAW* 100 (1988): 65–88. Reprinted: in pages 123–143 in *Deuteronomium-Studien*. FAT 8. Tübingen: Mohr Siebeck, 1994.

Plöger, Otto, "Priester und Prophet." *ZAW* 63 (1951): 157–192.

Plöger, Otto, "Prophetisches Erbe in den Sekten des frühen Judentums." *TLZ* 79 (1954): 291–296.

Plöger, Otto, *Theokratie und Eschatologie*. WMANT 2. Neukirchen-Vluyn: Neukirchener, 1959.

Pola, Thomas, "Back to the Future. The Twofold Priestly Concept of History," pages 39–65 in: *Torah and the Book of Numbers*, edited by Christian Frevel et al., FAT II/62. Tübingen: Mohr Siebeck, 2013.

Pola, Thomas, *Die ursprüngliche Priesterschrift: Beobachtungen zur Literarkritik und Traditionsgeschichte von Pg*. WMANT 70. Neukirchen-Vluyn: Nekirchner Verlag, 1995.

Quack, Joachim F., "Zum Datum der persischen Eroberung Ägyptens unter Kambyses." Journal of Egyptian History 4 (2011): 228–46.

Römer, Thomas, "Der Pentateuch," pages 53–110 in Die Entstehung des Alten Testaments, edited by W. Dietrich et al., ThW 1,1. Stuttgart: Kohlhammer, 2014.

Rouillard, Hedwige, *La péricope de Balaam (Nombres 22–24)*. EtB N.S. 4. Paris: Gabalda, 1985.

Rudolph, Wilhelm, *Chronikbücher*. HAT I/21. Tübingen: Mohr Siebeck, 1955.

Schmid, Konrad, "Der Abschluss der Tora als exegetisches und historisches Problem," in *Schriftgelehrte Traditionsliteratur: Fallstudien zur innerbiblischen Schriftauslegung im Alten Testament*. FAT 77. Tübingen: Mohr Siebeck, 2011.

Schmid, Konrad, "Christoph Berner, Die Exoduserzählung." *ZAW* 123 (2010): 292–294.

Schmid, Konrad, "The Deuteronomistic Image of History as Interpretive Device in the Second Temple Period: Towards a Long-Term Interpretation of 'Deuteronomism'," pages 369–388 in Congress Volume Helsinki 2010, edited by Martti Nissinen,. VTSup 148. Leiden: Brill, 2012.

Schmid, Konrad, "Himmelsgott, Weltgott und Schöpfer. 'Gott' und der 'Himmel' in der Literatur der Zeit des Zweiten Tempels," pages 111–148 in Der Himmel, edited by Dorothea Sattler and Samuel Vollenweider. JBTh 20. Neukirchen-Vluyn: Neukirchener, 2006.

Schmid, Konrad, "How to Identify a Persian Period Text in the Pentateuch," pages 101–118 in *On Dating Biblical Texts to the Persian Period*, edited by Richard J. Bautch and Mark Lackowski. FAT II/101. Tübingen: Mohr Siebeck, 2019.

Schmid, Konrad, "Judean Identity and Ecumenicity: The Political Theology of the Priestly Document," pages 3–26 in *Judah and Judeans in the Achaemenid Period: Negotiating Identity in an International Context*, edited by Oded Lipschits, Gary N. Knoppers, and Manfred Oeming. Winona Lake: Eisenbrauns, 2011.

Schmid, Konrad, "Das kosmische Weltgericht in den Prophetenbüchern und seine historischen Kontexte," pages 409–434 in *Nächstenliebe und Gottesfurcht: Beiträge aus alttestamentlicher, semitistischer und altorientalischer Wissenschaft für Hans-Peter Mathys zum 65. Geburtstag*, edited by Hanna Jenni et al., AOAT 439. Münster: Ugarit, 2016.

Schmid, Konrad, *Literaturgeschichte des Alten Testaments: Eine Einführung*. 3rd ed. Darmstadt: Wissenschaftliche Buchgesellschaft, 2021.

Schmid, Konrad, "The Quest for 'God': Monotheistic Arguments in the Priestly Texts of the Hebrew Bible," pages 271–289 in Reconsidering the Concept of Revolutionary Monotheism, edited by Beate Pongratz-Leisten. Winona Lake: Eisenbrauns, 2011.

Schmid, Konrad, "Taming Egypt: The Impact of Persian Imperial Ideology and Politics on the Biblical Exodus Account," pages 13–29 in Jewish Cultural Encounters in the Ancient Mediterranean and Near Eastern World, edited by Mladen Popović et al., JSJ.S 178. Leiden: Brill, 2017.

Schmid, Konrad, "Textual, Historical, Sociological, and Ideological Cornerstones of the Formation of the Pentateuch," pages 29–51 in The Social Groups Behind the Pentateuch, edited by Jaeyoung Jeon. SBL.AIL 44. Atlanta: SBL, 2022.

Schmidt, Ludwig, *Studien zur Priesterschrift*, BZAW 214. Berlin: de Gruyter, 1993.

Schmitt, Hans-Christoph, "Der heidnische Mantiker als eschatologischer Jahweprophet: Zum Verständnis Bileams in der Endgestalt von Num 22–24," pages 180–198 in "'Wer ist wie du, Herr, unter den Göttern?": Studien zur Theologie und Religionsgeschichte Israels: Festschrift Otto Kaiser, edited by I. Kottsieper et al., Göttingen: Vandenhoeck & Ruprecht, 1994.

Siegert, Folkert, *Zwischen Hebräischer Bibel und Altem Testament: Eine Einführung in die Septuaginta*. Münster: Lit, 2001.

Silverman, Jason M., *Persepolis and Jerusalem: Iranian Influence on the Apocalpytic Hermeneutic*. LHB/OTS 558. London: T & T Clark, 2012.

Ska, Jean-Louis, "Le récit sacerdotal: Une 'histoire sans fin'?," pages 631–653 in *The Books of Leviticus and Numbers*, edited by Thomas Römer,. BETL 215. Leuven: Peeters, 2008.

Smend, Rudolf, "'Das Ende ist gekommen:' Ein Amoswort in der Priesterschrift," pages 67–74 in *Die Botschaft und die Boten. FS für Hans Walter Wolff zum 70. Geburtstag*, edited by Jörg Jeremias and Lothar Perlitt. Neukirchen-Vluyn; Neukirchener, 1981. Reprinted in pages 238–243 in *Die Mitte des Alten Testaments: Exegetische Aufsätze*, edited by Rudolf Smend. Tübingen: Mohr Siebeck, 2002.

Steck, Odil Hannes, *Bereitete Heimkehr: Jesaja 35 als redaktionelle Brücke zwischen dem Ersten und dem Zweiten Jesaja*. SBS 121. Stuttgart: Katholisches Bibelwerk, 1985.

Steck, Odil Hannes, "Das Problem theologischer Strömungen in nachexilischer Zeit." *EvT* 28.9 (1968): 445–458.

Steins, Georg, "Torabindung und Kanonabschluss: Zur Entstehung und kanonischen Funktion der Chronikbücher," pages 213–256 in Die Tora als Kanon für Juden und Christen, edited by Erich Zenger. HBS 10. Freiburg: Herder, 1996.

Talmon, Shemaryahu, *Literary Studies in the Hebrew Bible: Form and Content*. Leiden: Brill, 1993.

De Troyer, Kristin, "When Did the Pentateuch Come into Existence? An Uncomfortable Perspective," pages 269–286 in *Die Septuaginta: Texte, Kontexte, Lebenswelten, Internationale Fachtagung veranstaltet von Septuaginta Deutsch (LXX.D), Wuppertal 20.–23. Juli 2006*, edited by Martin Karrer and Wolfgang Kraus. WUNT I/219. Tübingen: Mohr Siebeck, 2008.

Wasserman, Nathan, *The Flood: The Akkadian Sources. A New Edition, Commentary, and a Literary Discussion*. OBO 290. Leuven: Peeters, 2020.

Watts, James W. (ed.), *Persia and Torah: The Theory of Imperial Authorization of the Pentateuch*. SBLSymS 17. Atlanta: Scholars Press, 2001.

Weimar, Peter, *Studien zur Priesterschrift*. FAT 56. Tübingen: Mohr Siebeck, 2008.

Wevers, John W., "The Building of the Tabernacle." *JNWSL* 19 (1993): 123–131.

Wevers, John W., "The Earliest Witness to the LXX Deuteronomy," *CBQ* 39 (1977): 240–244.

Wöhrle, Jakob, *Fremdlinge im eigenen Land: Zur Entstehung und Intention der priesterlichen Passagen der Vätergeschichte*. FRLANT 246. Göttingen: Vandenhoeck & Ruprecht, 2012.

Zenger, Erich, *Einleitung in das Alte Testament*. 5th edition. Studienbücher Theologie 1,1. Stuttgart: Kohlhammer, 2004.

Zenger, Erich, Gottes Bogen in den Wolken. Untersuchungen zu Komposition und Theologie der priesterschriftlichen Urgeschichte. SBS 112. Stuttgart: Katholisches Bibelwerk, 1987.

Zenger, Erich, "Priesterschrift," pages 435–446 in Theologische Realenzyklopädie, Vol. 27, edited by G. Krause and G. Müller. Berlin: Walter de Gruyter, 1997.

Stefan Schorch

The Torah as a Closed Cluster Text: Conceptualizing the Transmission of the Pentateuch in the Persian Period

Introduction

It is currently agreed by many scholars of the Hebrew Bible that the text of the Pentateuch was completed in the Persian period, more or less in the version known to us today, in terms of content, literary arrangement and even, although to a somewhat diminished degree, in terms of the textual surface.[1] While this conclusion was originally drawn mainly with reference to literary and religious history, it received further support from the data emerging from the text-historical analysis of the Dead Sea Scrolls. Nevertheless, and most obviously, material evidence for the state of the biblical texts during the Persian period is extremely scarce, and our knowledge in this regard stems almost completely from retrojection and reconstruction.

Throughout the history of research, the Masoretic text (MT) has played a major role in this regard, and has often been prioritized. Again, with the ongoing research in the biblical scrolls from Qumran, this situation has started to change, both with respect to the evaluation of non-MT witnesses preserved in Hebrew, especially Qumran fragments and the Samaritan Pentateuch (SP), and with respect to the ancient translations, specifically the Greek, but also the Latin, the Syriac and others. Nevertheless, in spite of all these efforts, an undeniable dominance of the MT in the multifarious efforts to reconstruct and access the Pentateuch texts from the Persian period is generally still well discernible.

From the perspective of textual history, this dominance is only partly justified. To start with, the oldest extant material textual witness in Hebrew, as is well known, are fragments from Qumran, dating to the mid 3rd century BCE.[2] The oldest textual witness that can be expected to cover the whole Pentateuch is

1 See Zenger et al., eds., *Einleitung in das Alte Testament 3*, 79–84; Römer, Macchi, and Nihan *Introduction*, 104–111. See also the discussion in Schmid, "The End of History and the Ends of History: Assessing the Political-Theological Status of the Achaemenid Empire in Persian Period Judaism," in this volume.
2 See Tov, *Textual Criticism*, 110.

Stefan Schorch, University of Halle-Wittenberg, Germany

https://doi.org/10.1515/9783111018638-016

therefore the original Septuagint (G), also named Old Greek translation, dating to the 3rd century BCE., even though G is not preserved as an independent textual witness, but only in the context of the later Septuagint tradition, on the basis of which it has to be reconstructed.[3] Moreover, it should be remembered that it is ultimately not the Greek translation itself that is of interest here, but its Hebrew *Vorlage*, which is also to be accessed only through reconstruction.

Since the original translation of G emerged at the beginning of the Hellenistic period in the Eastern Mediterranean and Egypt, it provides textual evidence from a point in history that is not too distant from the Persian period. The original Septuagint is thus not only in itself a critically important source of information regarding the text of the Pentateuch in the Persian period, but it is also an essential means of evaluation for the contribution of the preserved Hebrew witnesses, above all MT and SP, towards the reconstruction of the text of the Pentateuch during the late Persian period.

I The Septuagint and the text-historical context of the Samaritan Pentateuch

Remarkably, the *Vorlage* of the original Septuagint, as far as we are able to reconstruct it on the basis of the (also) reconstructed Greek text, is not particularly close to the MT, but rather to the contrary: The Hebrew Vorlage of G seems to have deviated to a considerable degree from proto-MT, as we know it especially from the Qumran manuscripts[4] and from the medieval MT, and among all the Hebrew textual traditions of the Pentateuch that can be accessed and evaluated at least partially,[5] the MT is one of its more distant reflections in comparison to the textual tradition represented by the original Septuagint.

The relationship between the *Vorlage* of G and the SP, on the other hand, is much closer, as was demonstrated in great detail and based on a vast amount of data by Emanuel Tov,[6] who came even to the conclusion that the evidence points

3 See Tov, *Textual Criticism*, 215–219.

4 A definition of the term "proto-MT", referring to the late antique textual tradition that became the basis for the medieval MT, and an analysis of the available evidence in this regard is provided in Tov, "'Proto-Masoretic'," 195–213.

5 For a comprehensive overview, see Tov, *Textual Criticism*, 35–203.

6 See Tov, "The Shared Tradition," 357–372; Tov, "From popular Jewish LXX-SP," 19–40.

to a common ancestor for these two textual traditions.[7] This can be substantiated also with respect to the most characteristic features of SP:[8]

First, both the original Septuagint and the Samaritan Pentateuch contain a prominent layer of so-called "harmonizing" elements,[9] representing an editorial attitude that aims at closing apparent narrative gaps, and at adding supposedly lacking complementary elements within narratives or within the general framework of literary structures that build upon repetition. Although the application of these editorial techniques is not entirely identical in the Hebrew *Vorlage* of G and SP, its presence in both of them is quite discernible, which attests to the literary proximity between these two textual traditions of the Pentateuch. At the same time, it sets these two apart from the Masoretic text. Well known examples of similar tendencies in the Greek and the Samaritan text in this regard include the following:[10]

Gen 1:14

MT	SP	G
וַיֹּאמֶר אֱלֹהִים	ויאמר אלהים	καὶ εἶπεν ὁ θεός
יְהִי מְאֹרֹת	יהי מאורות	γενηθήτωσαν φωστῆρες
בִּרְקִיעַ הַשָּׁמַיִם	ברקיע השמים	ἐν τῷ στερεώματι τοῦ οὐρανοῦ
	להאיר על הארץ	εἰς φαῦσιν τῆς γῆς
לְהַבְדִּיל בֵּין הַיּוֹם	ולהבדיל בין היום	τοῦ διαχωρίζειν ἀνὰ μέσον τῆς ἡμέρας
וּבֵין הַלָּיְלָה	ובין הלילה	καὶ ἀνὰ μέσον τῆς νυκτὸς

And God said, Let there be lights in the dome of the sky < ***to give light upon the earth***, > to separate the day from the night; ... (and let them be for signs and for seasons and for days and years, ...

7 Tov, "The Development of the Text," 245–248 and 256.

8 For a categorization of the latter see Schorch, "Die prä-samaritanischen Fortschreibungen."

9 Following Tov, the category "Harmonization" is used here only for small-scale editorial changes of the text that aim at greater coherence, see Schorch, "Die prä-samaritanischen Fortschreibungen," 113–114. The general designation of SP as a "harmonizing" text, as proposed by Eshel and Eshel, "Dating the Samaritan Pentateuch's Compilation," 217–218, has been demonstrated as misleading by Segal, "The Text of the Hebrew Bible," 12–16.

10 The biblical text is quoted from the following sources: MT – *Biblia Hebraica Stuttgartensia*; G – *Septuagint: Vetus Testamentum Graecum, auctoritate Societatis Scientiarum Gottingensis* (Göttingen: Vandenhoeck & Ruprecht, 1931–); SP – Stefan Schorch, ed., *The Samaritan Pentateuch: A critical editio maior* (Berlin and Boston: de Gruyter, 2018–). English translations of the Hebrew Bible are generally presented according to the *New Revised Standard Version* (1989), and English translations of the Septuagint according to Albert Pietersma and Benjamin G. Wright, eds., *A New English Translation of the Septuagint and the Other Greek Translations Traditionally Included Under that Title* (New York: Oxford University Press, 2nd ed., 2009), both with occasional adaptions.

In this verse, both SP and the Hebrew *Vorlage* of G added the phrase להאיר על הארץ, harmonizing the wording in verse 14 with the continuation in verse 15:

– וְהָיוּ לִמְאוֹרֹת בִּרְקִיעַ הַשָּׁמַיִם לְהָאִיר עַל־הָאָרֶץ וַיְהִי־כֵן׃

... and let them be lights in the dome of the sky to give light upon the earth. And it was so.

In the preceding example, "harmonization" refers to the literary structure. The following verse became "harmonized" in accordance with the expectations of contemporary readers:

Gen 4:8

MT	SP	G
וַיֹּאמֶר קַיִן אֶל־הֶבֶל אָחִיו	ויאמר קין אל הבל אחיו	καὶ εἶπεν Καιν πρὸς Αβελ τὸν ἀδελφὸν αὐτοῦ
	נלכה השדה	διέλθωμεν εἰς τὸ πεδίον
וַיְהִי בִּהְיוֹתָם בַּשָּׂדֶה	ויהי בהיותם בשדה	καὶ ἐγένετο ἐν τῷ εἶναι αὐτοὺς ἐν τῷ πεδίῳ

Cain said to his brother Abel, < ***Let us go out to the field,*** > and when they were in the field ... (Cain rose up against his brother Abel, and killed him.)

According to the first sentence of Gen 4:8, Cain spoke to his brother Abel, and the introductory ויאמר seems to indicate that the communication itself follows. However, MT does not present it, but instead a new scene follows immediately. In SP and G, on the other hand, Cain's words are indeed presented at the expected place. From a text-historical perspective, it seems rather unlikely that an entire sentence disappeared from the text in the course of its transmission, all the more so one that makes perfect sense and may even have been seen as required in the context. Therefore, inasmuch a satisfactory explanation can be provided for the *lectio difficilior* found in the MT, the latter should be regarded as preserving an older stage. The problem revolves primarily around the use of אמר *qal*. Although in most cases this verb is followed by direct speech or at least by an indication of the latter's content, alternatives are indeed found in the corpus of Biblical Hebrew.

First of all, a 3rd masculine pronominal object is not always indicated, and this general rule[11] was applicable also to אמר *qal*.[12] Thus, the sentence ויאמר קין אל הבל אחיו may be understood as "Cain said <it> to his brother Abel," referring to the preceding verse. Unfortunately, this latter verse poses great difficulties for comprehension too, and since this appears to have been the case already in an-

11 Gesenius and Kautzsch, *Hebräische Grammatik, 28*, 380 § 117, f.

12 Cf. Exod 19:25 וַיֵּרֶד מֹשֶׁה אֶל־הָעָם וַיֹּאמֶר אֲלֵהֶם׃ – "So Moses went down to the people and told <it> them."

tiquity, this might be one of the reasons that favored the insertion of the passage containing Cain's speech.

A second possibility to make sense of the words in MT is that אמר *qal* could be used here as an absolute, without an object, i.e., "Cain spoke to his brother Abel." While this usage of אמר *qal* would be rare, it is indeed clearly attested in at least one instance, namely in 2 Chr 32:24,[13] and it is therefore obviously legitimate.

In light of these considerations, either on the basis of the first or the second usage, MT is much more likely to have preserved the older version of Gen 4:8, but it also obvious that the text posed difficulties to its readers. The addition of Cain's speech in SP and the Hebrew *Vorlage* of G is thus probably a way to address these difficulties by creating a smooth transition between what must have appeared as an introduction of Cain's speech and the new scene of the narrative. It therefore harmonizes the older text in accordance with the expectations of a readership that was familiar with the common contemporary standard of Hebrew language and Hebrew prose.

While in these two instances the wording of SP and of the Hebrew *Vorlage* of G were shaped under the impact of the same editorial harmonization, there are also many cases where either SP or G contain harmonizing additions that are absent from the other version, as the following two examples demonstrate:

Gen 1:6

MT	**SP**	**G**
וַיֹּ֣אמֶר אֱלֹהִ֔ים	ויאמר אלהים	Καὶ εἶπεν ὁ θεός
יְהִ֥י רָקִ֖יעַ בְּת֣וֹךְ הַמָּ֑יִם	יהי רקיע בתוך המים	Γενηθήτω στερέωμα ἐν μέσῳ τοῦ ὕδατος
וִיהִ֣י מַבְדִּ֔יל	ויהי מבדיל	καὶ ἔστω διαχωρίζον
בֵּ֥ין מַ֖יִם לָמָֽיִם׃	בין מים למים:	ἀνὰ μέσον ὕδατος καὶ ὕδατος.
		καὶ ἐγένετο οὕτως.

And God said, Let there be a dome in the midst of the waters, and let it separate the waters from the waters. < ***And it was so.*** >

G is based here on a Hebrew *Vorlage* in which the statement ויהי כן* followed immediately after God's words, confirming their fulfillment. According to M and SP, on the other hand, the statement is found only in the next verse, where it concludes the account of the deed itself. While the latter arrangement of the text deviates from the general literary structure of the first creation account (cf. 1:9.11.15.24.30), the Hebrew Vorlage of G harmonized the use of ויהי כן* in verse 6 in line with the other occurrences of the phrase. While therefore in this instance

13 See Dillmann, *Die Genesis*, 6, 95.

G displays a greater inclination towards harmonization than SP, the opposite is the case in the plague account in the book of Exodus, where MT and G generally retained the unharmonized text, while SP presents a harmonized version, inasmuch as Yhwh's command to Moses is always followed by an explicit report that the command was fulfilled, e.g. Exod 9:1–5.[14]

Second, apart from this inclination towards harmonization, which is generally shared by G and SP, even though their respective textual traditions materialized it to a somewhat different extent, several of the so-called "sectarian elements" of SP, i.e. textual variants that became the scriptural basis for ideological claims of the Samaritans,[15] appear also in G. This observation seems to prove that these variants too were part of the shared textual basis of G and SP, and they therefore predate the emergence of the Samaritans as an independent group vis-a-vis Judaism in the late 2nd century BCE. This includes even the most prominent of these variants, namely:

- The reading המקום אשר בחר יהוה – "the place that Yhwh has chosen," in the centralization formula in Deuteronomy (Deut 12:5.11.14.18.21.26 etc.), with the verbal form in the past tense instead of the future יבחר "he will chose" (MT), implying that the election of the place of Israel's sanctuary already had happened, and
- The reading הרגריזים in Deut 27:4, stating that the altar to be erected after Israel's entrance into the land of Canaan shall be built on "Mount Gerizim" and not on "Mount Ebal," as MT has it.

In both cases, the original G parallels SP, against MT, as demonstrated by Adrian Schenker and others.[16]

It has been noted by Emanuel Tov that the original G served as Greek translation of the Pentateuch amongst both Jews and Samaritans.[17] This conclusion is based on the fact that the Old Greek translation originated within the joint Israelite Hebrew literary culture, which preceded the split between the two communities, as pointed out by Jan Joosten.[18] In other words, the Old Greek translation of the Pentateuch was jointly used by followers of both the sanctuary at Mount Gerizim, i.e. Israelite proto-Samaritans, and followers of the temple in Jerusalem, i.e. Israelite proto-Jews, in contradiction to what the Aristeas legend aims to infer,

14 Tov, "The Shared Tradition," 371.

15 Tov, *Textual Criticism*, 190–193.

16 See Schenker, "Le Seigneur choisira-t-il," and Schenker, "Textgeschichtliches zum Samaritanischen Pentateuch."

17 Tov, "Pap. Giessen 13, 19, 22, 26," 473–474.

18 Joosten, "Septuagint and Samareitikon," 14–15.

and what was traditionally claimed also in scholarship, namely that the original Septuagint was a distinctively "Jewish" translation.[19] Thus, both the textual tradition called with a later Greek term "*Samareitikon*" as well as the tradition generally known as "Septuagint" ultimately go back to this so-called Old Greek translation.

Due to these connections between the Old Greek translation and the Samaritan Pentateuch, in terms of textual history, it seems justifiable, besides analyzing the Samaritan Pentateuch in light of data gained from our analysis of the Old Greek translation, to proceed also in the opposite direction, i.e. to analyze the Old Greek translation in the light of insights gained from the later transmission of the Samaritan Pentateuch, aiming to identify possible forerunners of phenomena detected in the Samaritan Pentateuch within the Old Greek translation. While this is a task yet to be realized in full, I will come back to some aspects of it in chapter III.

II The Pentateuch – an open or a closed text?

Besides the Old Greek translation, a second central means of evaluating the contribution of the Masoretic text and the Samaritan Pentateuch towards the reconstruction of the text of the Pentateuch during the late Persian period is provided by the Qumran scrolls. With relation to the Samaritan Pentateuch, especially the so-called pre-Samaritan texts are of immediate importance. Since large-scale editorial additions found in the Samaritan Pentateuch also appear in these pre-Samaritan texts, we should conclude that these textual additions pre-date the emergence of the Samaritans, i.e. the *terminus ad quem* of the insertion of these additions can be pinpointed to the second half of the 2nd century BCE. This regards especially the following two large-scale editorial additions:

- The "Gerizim commandment," a compilation of eight verses from the Book of Deuteronomy (Deut 11:29 – 27:2–7 – 11:30) entered in SP after Exod 20:17 // Deut 5:21,[20] and
- The compilation "The prophet Moses," consisting of nine verses from Deuteronomy (Deut 5:28–29 – 18:18–22 – 5:30–31), entered in SP after Exod 20:21.[21]

The origin of the Moses-compilation in a pre-Samaritan stratum of the textual history of the Pentateuch is confirmed beyond any doubt by the observation that

19 Cf. Tov, *The Text-Critical Use of the Septuagint*, 201–206.
20 Schorch, "The So-called Gerizim Commandment," 79–81.
21 Schorch, "The So-called Gerizim Commandment," 88–90.

it is contained in the text of 4QRP[a] (4Q158) and 4QTest (4Q175). As regards the Gerizim-compilation, the situation appears to be similar: Two recent studies of the preserved fragments of 4QpaleoExod[m] (4Q22) have demonstrated that the Gerizim-compilation was probably included in the text of this pre-Samaritan scroll,[22] leading also in this case to the conclusion that the insertion of the compilation pre-dates SP. On the other hand, we have no evidence that either of these two compilations was present in the Hebrew *Vorlage* of the original Septuagint, even though, due to the scarceness of conclusive data, this possibility cannot ruled out completely.

Nevertheless, the available evidence points to the conclusion that the Samaritan Pentateuch contains two different layers of editorial changes that pre-date its emergence and are not found in MT – the older one paralleled by the Old Greek translation, and the younger one paralleled by the pre-Samaritan texts from Qumran. While the *terminus ad quem* for the former is the mid 3rd century BCE,[23] the *terminus ad quem* for the latter is about one hundred years later, in the mid 2nd century BCE.

Obviously, the two editorial layers result from the application of different literary techniques vis-a-vis the text of the Pentateuch. However, both of these literary layers were produced under the influence of the same conceptualization of the Pentateuch, namely that it is a ***closed text***, and not an *open text*.[24]

While an open text is conceived as aiming for continuation and expansion beyond its actual narrative framework, therefore allowing for the addition of new sections, chapters, or even whole new books, a closed text aims at achieving, preserving, and enforcing the linguistic and literary coherence *within* the boundaries of the present text. And while the emergence and growth of the literary collection beyond the Pentateuch that became associated with the Masoretic Text followed the concept that the Pentateuch was an open text, the emergence and monopolization of the Samaritan Pentateuch was the result of conceiving the Pentateuch as a closed text.

The point of departure for the manifestation of the Pentateuch as a closed or an open text is the Book of Deuteronomy, as is clearly demonstrated by the fact that the textual manifestations of both conceptualizations are based on that book: On the one hand, the major editorial additions found in the pre-Samaritan scrolls

---

22 See Schorch, "The So-called Gerizim Commandment," 91–93, and Dayfani, "4QpaleoExod[m]."

23 See Tov, *Textual Criticism*, 218–219.

24 The terminology "closed text" versus "open text" proposed in the present article has a significantly different meaning than the terminological distinction between "open book" and "closed book" applied by Ron Hendel, who refers, following earlier scholarship on textual history, to textual fluidity versus textual stability, see Hendel, "Original and Archetype."

and in SP, aiming for greater coherence within the given textual boundaries of the Pentateuch and expressing the understanding that the textual horizons of the Pentateuch were closed and could not be further expanded, were obviously carried out with reference to the text of Deuteronomy. These editorial changes may therefore be called "retrospective" in the sense that they aim at editing the text of the preceding books under the direct impact of Deuteronomy. On the other hand, the addition of paratexts to the Pentateuch beyond the latter's textual and material boundaries, proceeding from the notion that the Pentateuch narrative continues beyond the end of the Deuteronomy, happened also under the direct influence of a specific understanding of Deuteronomy, specifically in the framework of the so-called Deuteronomistic History. In this case, we may thus speak of a "prospective" literary activity.

Most notably, the "external" paratexts of the so-called Deuteronomistic history do not seem to have been subdued to the same means of literary editing like the "internal" editorial layers. Instead, they obviously applied different scribal techniques. This observation suggests that the two textual manifestations of the Pentateuch, as an open vis-a-vis a closed text, were realized in the context of different scribal circles.

The centralization formula is a prominent example for the impact of Deuteronomy upon the literary manifestation of the Deuteronomistic History, and for the latter as a paratext materializing the literary potential of texts found in Deuteronomy outside the book itself: The centralization formula stipulates, in the wording of MT Deut 12:5

– אֶל־הַמָּקוֹם אֲשֶׁר־יִבְחַר יְהוָה אֱלֹהֵיכֶם מִכָּל־שִׁבְטֵיכֶם לָשׂוּם אֶת־שְׁמוֹ שָׁם לְשִׁכְנוֹ תִדְרְשׁוּ וּבָאתָ שָׁמָּה׃

> you shall seek the place that the Lord your God will choose out of all your tribes as his habitation to put his name there. You shall go there.

Within the Deuteronomistic History, this lead is taken up in MT 1 Kgs 8:16, after the erection of the temple in Jerusalem, in Solomon's citation of what God allegedly told his father David is the meaning of this sanctuary:

מִן־הַיּוֹם אֲשֶׁר הוֹצֵאתִי אֶת־עַמִּי אֶת־יִשְׂרָאֵל מִמִּצְרַיִם לֹא־בָחַרְתִּי בְעִיר מִכֹּל שִׁבְטֵי יִשְׂרָאֵל לִבְנוֹת בַּיִת לִהְיוֹת שְׁמִי שָׁם
וָאֶבְחַר בְּדָוִד לִהְיוֹת עַל־עַמִּי יִשְׂרָאֵל׃

> Since the day that I brought my people Israel out of Egypt, I have not chosen a city from any of the tribes of Israel in which to build a house, that my name might be there; but I chose David to be over my people Israel.

Clearly, as indicated by the parallel use of the same expressions and concepts, the latter verse refers to the centralization formula in Deuteronomy. At the same time, 1 Kings obviously modifies the object of God's choice, thus entering an interpretation of the centralization formula, insofar the "place" is identified here as a "city," within the city a "house" is supposed to accommodate God's name, and the election of the place is paralleled with David's election as king of Israel.[25]

In spite of the close correspondence created between the centralization formula in Deuteronomy and the fulfilment of its historical promise in 1 Kings, the text of 1 Kgs 8:16 did not aim at full congruence from the outset, it was also not harmonized with Deuteronomy in the course of its textual history, and neither was, of course, Deuteronomy with 1 Kings. Instead, 1 Kgs 8:16 is conceived as a paratextual interpretation of the centralization formula, which:

- Links Deuteronomy with traditions otherwise absent in that book, namely that God chose the city of Jerusalem as his sanctuary, and that the election of Jerusalem goes along with the election of the Davidic dynasty for kingship in Jerusalem,
- Applies a literary technique that is neither identical nor congruent with the editorial layers found in the pre-Samaritan and Samaritan texts: While the latter aim at retrospective harmonization of the earlier parts of the narrative with the subsequent ones, the technique applied in the Deuteronomic History aims at the prospective interpretation of the former through the later, and
- Displays a hermeneutical approach towards the Pentateuch that aims at understanding its text in light of traditions from outside the Pentateuch. This approach is dramatically different from the one displayed by the pre-Samaritan and Samaritan texts, where the horizons of understanding are strictly confined by the limits of the text of the Pentateuch itself.

In the tradition of the Masoretic text, the aim of 1 Kings 8:16 and its textual setting, namely to focus the Deuteronomic centralization formula at the city of

25 The logical structure of 1 Kgs 8:16 is based on a double schema of "prophecy and fulfillment," i.e., $A^{Proph.}B^{Proph.}$ // $A^{Fulf.}B^{Fulf.}$. In MT, however, only $A^{Proph.}$ // $B^{Fulf.}$ is expressed verbatim, as part of a rhetorical figure that requires completion by the attentive reader. In MT 2 Chr 6:5–6, the same logical structure is verbalized in full detail: "[$A^{Proph.}$:] Since the day that I brought my people out of the land of Egypt, I have not chosen a city from any of the tribes of Israel in which to build a house, so that my name might be there, [$B^{Proph.}$:] and I chose no one as ruler over my people Israel; [$A^{Fulf.}$:] but I have chosen Jerusalem in order that my name may be there, [$B^{Fulf.}$:] and I have chosen David to be over my people Israel." Japhet, *I & II Chronicles*, 588–589, and other scholars have suggested that the text in 2 Chronicles in fact preserves the oldest form of this statement, but this seems unlikely in light of the observation that the text in MT Kings posits the use of a rhetorical figure and thus presents the more difficult version than MT Chronicles, which in fact contains the most simple text, while at the same time the meaning of the two versions is identical.

Jerusalem, is accompanied by a polemical attitude against the religious tradition of the North, as e.g. expressed in 2 Kings 17.[26]

On the other hand, however, the paratextual expansion of the Pentateuch as preserved in the context of the so-called Deuteronomistic history contains of course also a considerable amount of texts and traditions that seem to shed a rather favorable light on the claims of religious traditions connected with the north of Israel, both large scale, as for instance the Shechem tradition implied in Josh 24, and in small details, as for instance with regard to the motive of a mountain in the immediate vicinity of Shechem which figures under the designation "navel of the land" (טבור הארץ) in Judg 9:37 – probably an allusion to Mount Gerizim. Thus, while undeniably preserving prominent claims in favor of the primacy of Jerusalem, the so-called Deuteronomistic history cannot generally be conceived as an account serving the ideological interests of the sanctuary in Jerusalem. Rather, the so-called Deuteronomistic history, as an external paratext to the Pentateuch, seems to have originated within the same literary culture as the editorial layers found in the pre-Samaritan and Samaritan texts of the Pentateuch, namely the shared literary culture of Israel and Judah, which preceded the break between Samaritan and Jews. Without being entirely coherent, it accommodated both contexts, in spite of profound differences with respect to religious centers, hermeneutical attitudes towards the Torah, literary techniques applied in order to express these attitudes, and the role of external traditions, outside the textual perimeters of the Torah. Thus, in the same way the pre-Samaritan texts were not confined to the north, the paratextual perspective of the Deuteronomistic history was not confined to the south.

There is little doubt that the so-called Deuteronomistic history and thus the conceptualization of the Pentateuch as an open text pre-dates the Hellenistic period and goes back to the Persian period. Moreover, the conceptualization of the Pentateuch as a closed text is most likely to predate the alternative conceptualization as an open text, since the claim of a complete removal of the Deuteronomistic history's post-Pentateuchal narrative from the Pentateuch itself, after the former had become established in the literary culture, seems difficult to entertain in light of the profound literary and textual links between the two. Thus, it is much more probable that it is the focus upon the Pentateuch alone, the conceptualization of the Pentateuch as a closed text, that pre-dates the conceptualization of the Pentateuch as an open text, and we shall therefore conclude that the conceptualization of the Pentateuch as a closed text was already prevalent in the Persian period too. And obviously, although this latter attitude seems to have favored northern

---

26 For a recent in-depth analysis of the anti-northern, and anti-Samaritan attitudes expressed in the different historical layers of this text, see Kartveit, "Anti-Samaritan Polemics."

views and especially claims for the primacy of Mount Gerizim, it was not confined to the north, and not restricted to the circles of followers of Mount Gerizim either.

III The Pentateuch – a unified text or a cluster text?

It is often surmised, explicitly or implicitly, that the transmission of the Pentateuch proceeded from a unified *Urtext*, i.e. a model text displaying the final stage of literary development, which became the point of departure for textual transmission. Most obviously, the great stability of the proto-Masoretic and Masoretic tradition was favorable for the adoption of this theory.[27] Most notably, as demonstrated by Emanuel Tov, already the proto-Masoretic tradition was characterized by a clear tendency towards a unified text, which became even more apparent in the scrolls with Biblical texts that were found at the Judean Desert sites outside Qumran.[28]

On the other hand, however, the Qumran scrolls and fragments demonstrate that in antiquity several textual traditions existed side-by-side, each of them characterized by distinctive textual features, including deviations from the other traditions. Although the prominence of the Masoretic model of transmission might lead us to think that also all the deviating non-MT textual traditions represent unified stabile texts of the Pentateuch, this assumption cannot be taken and the available evidence should be analyzed for alternative paradigms of textual transmission. Again, it is specifically the Samaritan Pentateuch, which seems to provide the basis for the reconstruction of an alternative model.

The surviving manuscripts of the Samaritan Pentateuch display a broad array of internal variation. Not even places that are considered central characteristics of SP are exempted from this diversity, as illustrated by the name הר גריזים, which is mostly spelled as one word, but also appears in several manuscripts with a word separator between הר and גריזים, i.e., in two words.[29] The frequency of these

27 It should be pointed out that the *Urtext*-model was first introduced in the field of "Classical" Latin and Germanic philology, by the German philologist of the age of Romanticism Karl Lachmann (1793–1851), see Timpanaro, *The Genesis of Lachmann's Method*, 120. Its introduction into biblical studies, which happened considerably later, was mainly due to Paul de Lagarde (1827–1891), see Tov, *Textual Criticism*, 342.

28 See Tov, *Textual Criticism*, 74–80.

29 The attestations of הר גריזים, in two words, from the Hebrew manuscripts included in Schorch, *The Samaritan Pentateuch editio maior*, are as follows: Exod 20:17c – G^6M^2; Deut 5:21d – L^2P^2; Deut 11:29 – G^6M^2; Deut 27:4 – C^1.

variants may be demonstrated on the basis of a random verse. Thus, e.g., for three out of thirteen words contained in SP Gen 31:27, i.e., almost one quarter, variants are attested in the manuscripts dating from the 12th to the 14th century, namely: נחבת versus נהבת, בשרים versus ובשרים, and ובכנר versus ובכנור. While these variants affect mainly spelling, etymology, lexical inventory, and syntax, a large portion of further variants from other verses also concerns morphology.[30] The average percentage of variants seems to be somewhat lower than in Gen 31:27, but it is still substantial: Within the Samaritan text of Leviticus, out of the total of 12.012 words, a variant is attested for 1447 words, i.e. in ca. 12 %.[31]

While the preserved manuscripts of SP therefore exhibit the considerable textual variety that characterized the transmission of SP from the 12th century CE onward, the evidence emerging from the Samaritan translations into Arabic and Aramaic demonstrates that this phenomenon is not an innovation, but rather a continuation of the textual transmission of SP in Late Antiquity. This conclusion relies upon the reconstruction of the Hebrew *Vorlagen* of the different Samaritan translations, which can be achieved thanks to the extremely literal translation technique generally applied in the course of their production, as well as upon the fact that neither in the case of the Samaritan Arabic translation nor in the case of the Samaritan Targum an authoritative version emerged, but instead SP was translated repeatedly, and at different points of time. Thanks to that situation, no less than five Samaritan Arabic translations allow for the reconstruction of the transmission of SP in the period between the 11th and the 13th century, and at least seven different translations of SP into Aramaic recorded the transmission of SP in the time span from the 1st to the 11th century CE.[32]

Most of the variants attested by the Samaritan translations are also known from the Hebrew manuscripts. E.g., the variant בשרים versus ובשרים from Gen 31:27 quoted above, involving the absence or presence of conjunctive -ו "and," is mirrored both in the Targumim and the different Samaritan Arabic transla-

30 August Gall, in his 1914–1918 edition of SP aimed to reduce this textual variance through reconstructing an alleged "Urtext" of SP, following the model of MT, see *Der hebräische Pentateuch*. Neither this procedure itself nor the underlying assumption of one unified text correspond to the data available, see Schorch, "A Critical editio maior," 107–108. The new *editio maior* of SP, edited by myself in cooperation with several colleagues, seeks to reflect this evidence and to provide access to the full range of textual variance within the Samaritan tradition, presenting a diplomatic text of SP together with several apparatuses, see Schorch, *The Samaritan Pentateuch editio maior*. The first apparatus, called "var. mss," lists the variants in the transmission of SP in the Hebrew manuscripts dating from the 12th to the 14th century. The data presented above for Gen 31:27 are taken from this apparatus.

31 Numbers are provided according to Schorch, *The Samaritan Pentateuch editio maior*.

32 See Schorch, "The Value of the Samaritan Versions."

tions. However, in a substantial number of cases one or several of the different translations preserve variants that are unknown in the available Hebrew manuscripts, probably because they disappeared from the Hebrew transmission before the medieval period. A prominent and important example for this is found in Gen 2:2. All the extant Hebrew manuscripts of SP read here ויכל אלהים ביום הששי מלאכתו אשר עשה – "and on the sixth day God finished the work that he had done." This reading is confirmed word by word by almost all manuscripts of the Samaritan translations of SP, both Aramaic and Arabic. One manuscript of the Samaritan Targum, however, reads ביומה [שב]יעאה – "on the seventh day", instead "sixth,"[33] which points to a corresponding Hebrew *Vorlage* and shows that the Late Antique Hebrew transmission of SP contained both variants.[34]

We can thus conclude, on the basis of the analysis of these data, that the Samaritan transmission of the Pentateuch was characterized by a considerable internal textual diversity at least since the 1st century CE, but most probably from the outset, i.e. starting with the adoption of one out of several textual traditions of the Pentateuch by the Samaritans in the late 2nd century BCE. In other words: The Samaritan Pentateuch is not to be regarded as one unified text, but rather as a ***textual cluster***, comprising many variants, while at the same time still being conceived as one textual tradition.

The question of whether or not the alternative paradigm of the Pentateuch as a textual cluster, as attested for SP, vis-a-vis the paradigm of a unified text, as attested in the case of proto-MT, reflects a concept of the textual transmission of the Pentateuch that predates the emergence of the Samaritans in the late 2nd century BCE, can be elucidated by the third of the three Samaritan translation traditions of the Pentateuch, namely the Samaritan Greek translation. Although the so-called *Samareitikon* is generally understood as one single and unified Greek translation (or revision), there is in fact ample evidence that the Samaritan Greek tradition of the Pentateuch too is to be conceived as a textual cluster rather than one unified text, as the following observations demonstrate:

First of all, the only source that seems to speak explicitly about the so-called *Samareitikon*, found in the treatise *De mensuris et ponderibus*, which was composed by Epiphanius of Salamis in 392 CE, clearly speaks about several and apparently different Samaritan Greek translations. Describing the Hexapla, Epiphanius writes about Symmachos, the author of one of the recensions of the Septuagint, as follows:[35]

---

33 Tal, "Divergent Traditions," 311.

34 Schorch, "The Value of the Samaritan Versions," 75–76.

35 Epiphanius, *De mensuris et ponderibus*, 16, quoted from the edition of Moutsoulas: Μουτσουλα, "Το «Περι μετρων και σταθμων», 177. The English translation follows Alison Salvesen, with slight adaptions ("Symmachus in the Pentateuch," 284).

> Ἐν τοῖς τοῦ Σευήρου χρόνοις Σύμμαχός τις Σαμαρείτης τῶν παρ᾽ αὐτοῖς σοφῶν μὴ τιμηθεὶς ὑπὸ τοῦ οἰκείου ἔθνους, νοσήσας φιλαρχίαν καὶ ἀγανακτήσας κατὰ τῆς ἰδίας φυλῆς, προσέρχεται Ἰουδαίοις, καὶ προσηλυτεύει, καὶ περιτέμνεται δευτέραν περιτομήν. [...] Οὗτος τοίνυν ὁ Σύμμαχος πρὸς διαστροφὴν τῶν παρὰ Σαμαρείταις ἑρμηνειῶν ἑρμηνεύσας τὴν τρίτην ἐξέδωκεν ἑρμηνείαν.
>
> In the time of Severus lived Symmachus, a Samaritan and one of their sages. Since he received no honor from his own race, being crazed with ambition and indignant with his own people, he went over to the Jews, converted, and was circumcised a second time. [...] So this Symmachus produced the third version, in order to refute the versions held by the Samaritans.

Epiphanius' words are in fact the earliest extant reference for the so-called *Samareitikon*. The source itself, however, might be even older, probably dating to the first half of the 4th century CE, since Epiphanius seems to have relied on Origen, who in turn refers to Symmachos who lived in the 2nd century CE. In any case, using the plural αἱ παρὰ Σαμαρείταις ἑρμηνεῖαι – "the (Greek) versions held by the Samaritans," Epiphanius certainly refers explicitly to more than one Samaritan translation.

Second, the preserved readings from the so-called *Samareitikon*, quoted in the margins of Septuagint manuscripts together with the explicit attribution that they are stemming from a Samaritan source, display a remarkable incoherence with regard to both their translation technique and their reconstructed Hebrew *Vorlagen*.[36]

Thus, both Epiphanius' reference, as an external source, and the analysis of the surviving readings of the so-called *Samareitikon* itself point towards the conclusion that the Samaritan Greek translation did not consist of one unified text, but was in fact a textual cluster of several translations. Admittedly, especially due to the imponderability in dating the origin of the transmitted *Samareitikon* readings, the evidence at hand provides no conclusive answer to the question whether or not this cluster of different parallel Greek translations predates the emergence of the Samaritans as an independent group in the late 2nd century BCE. However, since the so-called Old Greek translation, which became the source for both the Samaritan and the Jewish reception of the Greek Pentateuch, originated in the 3rd century BCE, this does not seem unlikely. In any case, the sources of the so-called *Samareitikon* provide further confirmation that the textual transmission of the Pentateuch amongst the Samaritans followed the concept of a cluster text from the outset, and since according to all available sources the Samaritan transmission of the Pentateuch built upon existing older traditions rather

36 For a detailed analysis of the evidence to which this conclusion refers, see my forthcoming article (in Hebrew) "מקראות הרבה ותרגום אחד?" ,שורש.

than on innovations, it seems likely that the historical origins of the cluster paradigm are considerably older than that date. Moreover, the available sources for the transmission of SP do not seem to display any tendencies towards the reduction of the cluster's textual variety in course of time.

Therefore, the Samaritan Pentateuch represents an alternative paradigm of how the text of the Torah was conceived – not one unified and fixed text, as was apparently the case in relation to the medieval Masoretic text and its late antique forerunners, but a textual cluster with internal variance. While the coherence of the cluster relies upon the presence of the same literary structure and identical editorial techniques in all textual witnesses that belong to the cluster, they display considerable textual variety within these confinements, especially on the level of single words, single morphemes, and spelling. Moreover, the textual variety within the textual cluster is able to accommodate a considerable range of different views on central terms and concepts, in spite of the confinements of the text due to the general literary coherence of the textual cluster. The importance of this conceptual variance can again be illustrated by examples from the Samaritan transmission of the Pentateuch:

– In Exod 15:18, the Samaritan Pentateuch contains two parallel readings, namely יהוה ימלך לעלם ועד – "The Lord will reign for ever and ever," and לעלם ועוד – "... forever and beyond." While these variants might seem minor from a textual point of view, they imply two different concepts of history and eschatology: According to the first, God's rulership is to be conceived as one continuous and eternal period of time, while the second clearly discerns between two subsequent periods – i.e. God's rule in the present aeon, and in the thereafter. Both variants are not only found in SP, but are also well attested as part of the transmission of the Pentateuch in the late Second Temple period[37] – obviously in the context of the transmission of the Pentateuch as a textual cluster with internal variance.
– As demonstrated above, the Samaritan transmission of Gen 2:2 originally contained two parallel variants, namely besides ויכל אלהים ביום הששי מלאכתו אשר עשה – "and on the sixth day God finished the work that he had done," also ביום השביעי* – "on the seventh day." The latter version seems to express that the Shabbat is not only implicitly present in the literary structure of the first creation account, but that it is actually the ultimate and most important achievement of creation. In opposition to this, the first variant – God having completed his creation at the sixth day – points to the view that mankind is the ultimate achievement of creation. Again, both variants were part of the

37 Schorch, "In aeternum et ultra," 378–381.

transmission of the Pentateuch in the Late Second Temple period, which demonstrates that it accommodated quite different basic concepts of anthropology, calendar, and time, within the one and the same textual cluster.

From a historical perspective, the widespread and well established general textual divergency of the Pentateuch within the Qumran scrolls, as well as the discernible, although much more small-scale, specific textual divergency within the so-called "proto-MT"-group of manuscripts from Qumran, suggest that the cluster paradigm was not an innovation of that period, but must have originated before the Hellenistic period. Presumably, it was this paradigm that characterized and governed the textual transmission of the Pentateuch in the Late Persian period.

The emergence of the unified paradigm, on the other hand, most probably post-dates the cluster paradigm. Its adoption is likely to have been occurred in the context of the so-called "reading revolution" of the 2nd–1st centuries BCE, following a suggestion by Adiel Schremer:[38]

> The appeal to the written text of the Torah as an authoritative source for halakhic matters, and as a means by which one is able to discuss halakhic questions, was a revolutionary innovation of first century BCE Judaism, and it was actually unknown prior to that era.

Most probably, it was the impact of this new attitude towards textual authority, aiming to base arguments on the surface structure of a given text, and not on a general idea of the text's content and meaning, which motivated the emergence of the unified paradigm of textual transmission, which relies both on the reduction of textual and of conceptual variety. The unambiguous selection of one out of several variants which became the fundament of the proto-Masoretic/Masoretic-tradition, favoring עד and השביעי while dismissing עוד and הששי, is an expression of this tendency.

Conclusion

Although the transmission of the Samaritan Pentateuch, like that of the Masoretic text, can be traced back materially only down to the 2nd century BCE, it is of high importance for the reconstruction of the transmission of the Pentateuch in the Persian period.

First of all, the Samaritan Pentateuch, *vis-a-vis* the Masoretic text, seems to bear clear witness that the Pentateuch in the Persian period was conceptualized

38 Schremer, "'[T]he[y] did not read in the sealed book'," 123.

in a twofold manner, namely as a closed text, limiting the textual horizons to the Pentateuch alone, and as an open text, expanded by and potentially accessed through added paratexts, as for instance and most prominently in the framework of the so-called Deuteronomistic history. In the latter case, these paratexts became an important means for explicitly connecting the text of the Pentateuch with external traditions and at the same time subduing it to different and explicitly extrinsic hermeneutical perspectives. The concept of the Pentateuch as a closed text, on the other hand, lived on in the pre-Samaritan and Samaritan tradition. It implies strict intrinsic hermeneutic principles, i.e., the Pentateuch is to be read and understood on the sole basis of its own text.

Second, the transmission of the Pentateuch in the Persian period should be understood as a cluster text rather than a unified text. The conceptualization of textual transmission in accordance with the cluster paradigm rather than the paradigm of a unified text can be studied on the basis of the textual evidence preserved through the Samaritan Pentateuch, which seems to have preserved this older paradigm of textual transmission and continuously followed it.

Bibliography

Dayfani, Hila, "4QpaleoExod^{m} and the Gerizim Composition." *Journal of Biblical Literature* 141 (2022): 673–698.

Dillmann, August, *Die Genesis, 6. Auflage*. Kurzgefaßtes exegetisches Handbuch zum Alten Testament. Leipzig: S. Hirzel, 1892.

Eshel, Esther, and Eshel, Hanan, "Dating the Samaritan Pentateuch's Compilation in Light of the Qumran Biblical Scrolls," pages 215–240 in *Emanuel: Studies in Hebrew Bible, Septuagint and Dead Sea scrolls in Honor of Emanuel Tov*, edited by Shalom Paul et al. Supplements to Vetus Testamentum 94, 1. Leiden and Boston: Brill, 2003.

Gall, August, *Der hebräische Pentateuch der Samaritaner.* Giessen: Töpelmann: 1914–1918.

Gesenius, Wilhelm, and Kautzsch, Emil, *Hebräische Grammatik, 28. vielfach verbesserte und vermehrte Auflage.* Leipzig: F. C. W. Vogel, 1909.

Hendel, Ron, "Original and Archetype in Open and Closed Books," in *Urtext – Fluidity – Textual Convergence? The Quest for the texts of the Hebrew Bible*, edited by Frédérique Rey and Stefan Schorch. Contributions to Biblical Exegesis and Theology. Louvain: Peeters, forthcoming.

Japhet, Sarah, *I & II Chronicles: A Commentary.* Old Testament Library. Louisville, Ky.: Westminster/ John Knox Press, 1993.

Joosten, Jan, "Septuagint and Samareitikon," pages 1–15 in *From Author to Copyist: Essays on the Composition, Redaction, and Transmission of the Hebrew Bible in Honor of Zipi Talshir*, edited by Cana Werman. Winona Lake, Indiana: Eisenbrauns, 2015.

Kartveit, Magnar, "Anti-Samaritan Polemics in the Hebrew Bible? The Case of 2 Kings 17:24–41," pages 3–18 in *The Samaritans in historical, cultural, and linguistic perspectives*, edited by Jan Dušek. Studia Samaritana 11. Berlin and Boston: de Gruyter, 2018.

(Moutsoulas, Elias D.:) Μουτσουλα, Ηλια Δ. "Το «Περι μετρων και σταθμων» εργον Επιφανιου του Σαλαμινος." *Θεολογια* 44 (1973): 157–198.

Römer, Thomas, Macchi, Jean-Daniel and Nihan, Christophe (eds.) *Introduction à l'Ancien Testament.* La Monde des la Bible 49. Genève: Labor et Fides, 2004.

Salvesen, Alison, "Symmachus in the Pentateuch," *Journal of Semitic Studies Monograph* 15. Manchester: University of Manchester, 1991.

Schenker, Adrian, "Le Seigneur choisira-t-il le lieu de son nom ou l'a-t-il choisi?: l'apport de la Bible grecque ancienne à l'histoire du texte samaritain et massorétique," pages 339–351 in *Scripture in Transition: Essays on Septuagint, Hebrew Bible, and Dead Sea Scrolls in Honour of Raija Sollamo*, edited by Anssi Voitila. Supplements to the Journal for the Study of Judaism 126. Leiden and Boston: Brill, 2008.

Schenker, Adrian, "Textgeschichtliches zum Samaritanischen Pentateuch und Samareitikon," pages 105–121 in *Samaritans Past and Present: Current Studies*, edited by Menahem Mor and Friedrich Reiterer. Studia Samaritana 5. Berlin and New York: de Gruyter, 2010.

Schorch, Stefan, "A Critical editio maior of the Samaritan Pentateuch: State of Research, Principles, and Problems," *Hebrew Bible and Ancient Israel* 2 (2013): 100–120.

Schorch, Stefan, "Die prä-samaritanischen Fortschreibungen," pages 113–132 in *Schriftgelehrte Fortschreibungs- und Auslegungsprozesse: Textarbeit im Pentateuch, in Qumran, Ägypten und Mesopotamien*, edited by Walter Bührer. Forschungen zum Alten Testament, 2. Reihe, 108. Tübingen: Mohr Siebeck, 2019.

Schorch, Stefan, "In aeternum et ultra: Die Vorstellung eines Zeitenendes nach Gen 8,22 und Ex 15,18," pages 371–383 in *Nichts Neues unter der Sonne? Zeitvorstellungen im Alten Testament: Festschrift für Ernst-Joachim Waschke zum 65. Geburtstag*, edited by Jens Kotjatko-Reeb, Stefan Schorch, Johannes Thon, and Benjamin Ziemer. Beihefte zur Zeitschrift für die alttestamentliche Wissenschaft 450. Berlin and Boston: de Gruyter, 2014.

Schorch, Stefan, (ed.) *The Samaritan Pentateuch: A critical editio maior.* Berlin and Boston: de Gruyter, 2018–.

Schorch, Stefan, "The So-called Gerizim Commandment in the Samaritan Pentateuch," pages 77–97 in *The Samaritan Pentateuch and the Dead Sea Scrolls*, edited by Michael Langlois. Contributions to Biblical Exegesis & Theology 94. Leuven: Peeters, 2019.

Schorch, Stefan, "The Value of the Samaritan Versions for the Textual History of the Samaritan Pentateuch." *Textus* 30 (2021): 64–85.

(Schorch, Stefan:) 2024. שטפן שורש. "מקראות הרבה ותרגום אחד? מסירת התורה השומרונית ושאלת הסמריטיקון." בתוך: כרך לכבוד עמנואל טוב, עורך משה בר-אשר. ירושלים: האקדמיה הלאומית הישראלית למדעים,

Schremer, Adiel, "'[T]he[y] did not read in the sealed book': Qumran Halakhic Revolution and the Emergence of Torah Study in Second Temple Judaism," pages 105–126 in *Historical Perspectives: From the Hasmoneans to Bar Kokhba in Light of the Dead Sea Scrolls. Proceedings of the Fourth International Symposium of the Orion Center for the Study of the Dead Sea Scrolls and Associated Literature, 27–31 January, 1999*, edited by David Goodblatt, Avital Pinnick, and Daniel R. Schwartz. Studies on the Texts of the Desert of Judah 37. Leiden, Boston and Köln: Brill, 2001.

Segal, Michael, "The Text of the Hebrew Bible in Light of the Dead Sea Scrolls." *Materia giudaica* 12 (2007): 5–20.

Tal, Abraham, "Divergent Traditions of the Samaritan Pentateuch as Reflected by its Aramaic Targum," *Journal for the Aramaic Bible* 1 (2003), 297–314.

Timpanaro, Sebastiano, *The Genesis of Lachmann's Method.* Chicago: University of Chicago Press, 2005.

Tov, Emanuel, "From Popular Jewish LXX-SP Texts to Separate Sectarian Texts: Insights from the Dead Sea Scrolls," pages 19–40 in *The Samaritan Pentateuch and the Dead Sea Scrolls*, edited by Michael Langlois. Contributions to Biblical Exegesis & Theology 94. Leuven: Peeters, 2019.

Tov, Emanuel, "Pap. Giessen 13, 19, 22, 26: A Revision of the Septuagint?," pages 459–475 in *The Greek and Hebrew Bible. Collected Essays on the Septuagint*. Supplements to Vetus Testamentum 72. Leiden, Boston and Köln: Brill, 1999.

Tov, Emanuel, "'Proto-Masoretic', 'Pre-Masoretic', 'Semi-Masoretic', and 'Masoretic': A Study in Terminology and Textual Theory," pages 195–213 in *Textual Developments: Collected Essays, Volume 4*. Supplements to Vetus Testamentum 181. Leiden: Brill, 2019.

Tov, Emanuel, *Textual Criticism of the Hebrew Bible, Revised and Expanded Fourth Edition*. Minneapolis: Fortress Press, 2022.

Tov, Emanuel, "The Development of the Text of the Torah in Two Major Text Blocks," pages 237–256 in *Textual Developments: Collected Essays, Volume 4*. Supplements to Vetus Testamentum 181. Leiden: Brill, 2019.

Tov, Emanuel, *The Text-Critical Use of the Septuagint in Biblical Research, Third Edition, Completely Revised and Expanded*. Winona Lake, Indiana: Eisenbrauns, 2015.

Tov, Emanuel, "The Shared Tradition of the Septuagint and the Samaritan Pentateuch," pages 357–372 in *Textual Developments: Collected Essays, Volume 4*. Supplements to Vetus Testamentum 181. Leiden: Brill, 2019.

Zenger, Erich, et al., eds., *Einleitung in das Alte Testament, 3. Auflage*. Stuttgart: Kohlhammer, 1998.

Jason M. Silverman

Yahwism in the Achaemenid Imperial Religious Field: Using Bourdieu as a theorist of religious change in the Persian Empire

Introduction: How to understand Religion in the ANE

It was a very great honor to be at a symposium in the memory of the late Shaul Shaked, a man who pioneered the study of "Irano-Judaica," and a man whose assessments of "Iranian influence" are still some of the most lucid on offer. I only had the privilege of meeting him a handful of times at ASPS meetings, where he was gracious and supportive. I hope he would have found the following ideas of interest.

Everyone in this audience is well aware of the difficulties inherent in attempting to understand or define "religion." These problems are compounded when we try to understand how different or similar ancient religion was from that in our contemporary society; they get even more obstruse when one tries to understand how it fit into the wider social structure (not to mention understanding said wider social structure!). Should religion be treated as an independent phenomenon of human society, subsumed under the wider culture, or dismissed as merely the verbal superstructure of the political economy? Some of these difficulties of course derive from the limited extant evidentiary bases. Some, however, come from the tools with which we think about these things. Perhaps our tools have been too blunt or too influenced by the 19th and 20th centuries to be able to reveal more than they obscure.

Note: This paper was written in the context of the Academy of Finland Centre of Excellence in Ancient Near Eastern Empires, PI Saana Svärd. This essay grows out of ANEE Team 2's work on using Bourdieu for the social history of the ANE, and it expands on ideas sketched for a contribution to Rose and de Jong (eds.) *the Zoroastrian World*. I am grateful to Shai Gordon, Ryan Thomas, and Joanna Töyräänvuori for reading an earlier draft of this essay.

Jason M. Silverman, University of Helsinki, Finland

https://doi.org/10.1515/9783111018638-017

I do not have the space to rehearse the history of these debates in the field.[1] Rather, I will briefly describe some tools of Pierre Bourdieu's Field Theory that I think have the potential of placing old debates in a new, perhaps more productive light. Bourdieu's own foray into Ancient Near Eastern religion was very much dependent on Weber's earlier work, and thus has little to commend it.[2] Nonetheless, his theoretical concepts and orientation remain highly flexible and insightful, inviting a new, more relational assessment of religion in the Persian Empire (and the wider ANE).

Bourdieusian Field Theory

Bourdieu is widely utilized in sociology, anthropology, and more recent history, though he has received rather little engagement from Near Eastern historians. Those who have appealed to him have most often appealed to his most famous concept of *habitus*.[3] The wider breadth and analytical capability of his theory, however, retains much unexplored potential.[4] I find one of the most compelling aspects of his thought to be the effort to resist reductionism while retaining a relatively parsimonious toolkit. For Bourdieu, human society cannot be reduced to a mere epiphenomenon of economics. Neither is it simply a figment of the human imagination, with no reality outside human perception. Humans are neither entirely free to do as they will, nor predetermined to do anything. Despite the fact that many of his own analyses are clearly indebted to the specific historical experience of France, Bourdieu himself was quite insistent that every historical case had to be re-analyzed anew, without assuming similarities to other times and locations.[5]

The concept for which his thought is often named, the *field*, Bourdieu has described as:

---

1 For a variety of overviews on various aspects, cf. Sharpe *Comparative Religion*, Adams, "Ancient Mesopotamian Urbanism," Garcia-Ventura and Verderame *Perspectives*; for a more popular reception cf. McGeough *The Ancient Near East*. The forthcoming *Routledge Handbook of the Ancient Near East and the Social Sciences* will have an entire section devoted to such overviews.

2 Bourdieu, "Genesis and Structure."

3 Cf. the overview given in Silverman et al, "Preface."

4 See the forthcoming Team 2 project arguing this case as well as the relevant chapters in the forthcoming handbook.

5 Bourdieu and Wacquant. *Invitation*, 109–110: "I believe indeed that there are no transhistoric laws of the relations between fields, that we must investigate each historical case separately. [...] Rather, its [his theory of field] major virtue, at least in my eyes, is that it promotes a mode of construction that has to be rethought anew every time."

> a network, or a configuration, of objective relations between positions [that] impose upon their occupants, agents or institutions, by their present and potential situation in the structure of the distribution of capital ... access to the specific profits that are at stake in the field ...[6]

For Bourdieu, a field comprises individuals and institutions with varying degrees of actual and potential access to relevant *capital* – we will return to capital below – and it is the relations between these occupants that define the structure of the field. These relations have both an objective reality (some positions have more capital than others) as well as a subjective reality (the perception of each person of the field and of their own position within it). The interactions between these entities are determined by a shared investment in the field (what Bourdieu calls *illusio* and its resultant *doxa*),[7] a shared understanding of the "rules of the game,"[8] and an organizing *capital* specific to that field.

Each individual and institution in the field will, according to their *habitus*, attempt to increase, maintain, or even decrease their position in the field based on their subjective understanding of their position in said field.[9] Thus, the topography of any given field is constantly changing, as the result of these interactions (Bourdieu prefers to call them struggles). Moreover, the very boundaries of a given field are part of the competition that takes place within a field: contesting who and what are part of a field are a constituent element of a field.[10] Nonetheless, no matter how fierce the competition between players, they share an unspoken, unconscious commitment to the values at stake in the given field (*illusio*) and take the structure of the field for granted (*doxa*).[11]

The field is a segment of society that is "autonomous." What Bourdieu means by this is,

> As I use the term, a field is a separate social universe having its own laws of functioning independent of those of politics and the economy.[12]

By positing a field, therefore, one wishes to describe a segment of society in which the pursuit of specific capitals produces relations of positions independent of those in other fields, and with an internal logic ("rules of the game") that

6 Bourdieu and Wacquant, *Invitation*, 97.

7 E.g., Bourdieu, *Logic*, 82; Bourdieu, *Outline*, 164, 168.

8 Bourdieu, *Logic*, 148, 299 n. 14.

9 Bourdieu, *Field of Cultural Production*, 65, 72.

10 Bourdieu and Wacquant, *Invitation*, 100; Gorski, "Bourdieusian Theory," 331–2.

11 Bourdieu explicitly distinguishes *doxa* from *orthodoxy* and *heterodoxy*, in that the latter two are self-aware of alternate possibilities (e.g., Bourdieu, *Outline*, 164).

12 Bourdieu, *Field of Cultural Production*, 162.

cannot be reduced to those structuring other parts of society. Older studies spoke of four "canonical" Bourdieusian fields (economic, cultural, social, and political), though the existence of any "autonomous" field is an empirical question for any given historical moment.

A key element in analyzing a field is determining the capital(s) at stake. Although borrowed from (Marxist) economics, within Field Theory the point of capitals is to avoid a reduction to *economic* capital. As Bourdieu defines it,

> a species of capital is what is efficacious in a given field, both as a weapon and as a stake of struggle, that which allows its possessors to wield a power, an influence, and thus to exist, in the field under consideration.[13]

This capital may or may not be useful in other fields, but it provides the main structuring principle for its given field. The concepts of political capital[14] and social capital[15] have been widely used in academia, even outside a Bourdieusian context, implying at least their heuristic utility. A key aspect for field theory in this is that the capital provides both a shared orientation for those in the field, as well as providing the basis of power for those in higher positions in the field. Further, capitals can be "exchanged" or "converted" into other types of capital according to the logic of the society.[16] This is also one mechanism for thinking about the relationships between fields in a given society.

In their experience of and attempts to increase their position and access to capital in a given field, individuals and groups develop a *habitus*. In Bourdieu's admittedly abstruse formulation, habitus are,

> systems of durable, transposable dispositions, structured structures predisposed to function as structuring structures, that is, as principles of the generation and structuring of practices and representations which can be objectively 'regulated' and 'regular' without in any way being the product of obedience to rules, objectively adapted to their goals without presupposing a conscious aiming at ends or an express mastery of the operations necessary to attain them and, being all this, collectively orchestrated without being the product of the orchestrating action of a conductor.[17]

In more prosaic language, *habitus* describes the ways of life and expectations for it that are unconsciously internalized by an individual or a group in relation to a particular field. This includes the person's subjective perception of their posi-

13 Bourdieu and Wacquant, *Invitation*, 98.
14 Casey, "Defining Political Capital."
15 Smith, "We All Bantu."
16 Bourdieu, *Logic*, 118–119, 300 n. 6.
17 Bourdieu *Outline*, 72.

tion in the field, and their ability to impact their position. Importantly such perceptions (Bourdieu likes the term *dispositions*) contain what agents consider *desirable* (compare Bourdieu's analysis of taste as part of the practices of distinction inherent in upper class *habitus*).[18] Habitus further comprises what Bourdieu called *hexis*,[19] the way in which one embodies one's *habitus* (clothing, posture, gestures, etc). Recently, Hadas has pointed to the examples of musical and sports training for the ways specific fields can inculcate correct *hexis*.[20] In the latter, Hadas points to the possibility for individuals to have multiple *habitus* related to the various fields which they inhabit. Atkinson has called any individual's combination of *habitus* their "social surface".[21] It is worth noting that one can speak of the *habitus* of a group or class as well as of an individual.

There are many more elements to field theory, but this brief overview of the three central concepts should suffice for setting the stage for this paper's proposal: to see the analytical purchase of thinking about a religious field in the Persian Empire.

Religion as an autonomous field

As noted above, adequately conceptualizing ancient religion is not straightforward. This paper is a thought experiment to see what might be gained from thinking about religion in the Persian Empire as an autonomous field in a Bourdieusian sense.[22] I want to emphasize that autonomous does not mean with no relations or interactions with other fields, but that it operates with its own structuring capital and rules for the game with a logic outside mere politics or economics. A key element to note in this regard is that the Persian king (like the Neo-Babylonian kings before him) was not a priest. Indeed, Darius's depiction of Gaumata as a *maguš*[23] (DBa I 36 ff) implies a societal differentiation between kingship and priesthood, and thus, arguably, between political and religious fields.[24] It is the goal of

18 Bourdieu, *Distinction*.
19 Bourdieu, *Outline*, 93; Bourdieu, *The Bachelors' Ball*, 84.
20 Hadas, Miklós. *Outlines of a Theory*.
21 Atkinson, *Beyond Bourdieu*, 26.
22 First briefly proposed in Silverman forthcoming. The context there, however, was to answer the question of what the HB can tell one about Persian religion. Here the interest is much broader and more theoretical.
23 He is called a *maguš* nine times in the text.
24 As does the myth of Yima, as I have pointed out elsewhere (Silverman, "From Remembering to Expecting," 430–1; Silverman, "Was There an Achaemenid," 175, 188).

this paper, therefore, to attempt to sketch what such a hypothesis would mean for understanding the period. A subsequent task, then, is to think about how such a field would have interacted with the political and economic fields.

I think we are safe in calling the existence of the divine world and the divine origin of society *doxa* in the Persian Empire (as in the ANE generally). It was also a matter of some import to determine divine approval for all kinds of decisions (via divination),[25] and in certain contexts which divine entity was responsible (e.g., 'medical' diagnoses[26] just as the Avestan texts insist on naming the deity being addressed[27]). It was incumbent on a ruler to ensure they were *perceived* as maintaining the divinely ordained order – even while there clearly was never any singularly agreed description what precisely that order ought to be. While the logic of a religious field would operate apart from politics, its structures are likely to be homologous to those of the political field.[28] Therefore, a key element in sketching the structure of the religious field at any given moment in time would be the Great King's own religious practice. We will return to analyzing the relevance of the king in the religious field below.

Other key elements to religion throughout the ANE are of course the various types of priesthoods and sacred sites, most prominently temples. The kinds of priests and their remits are crucial to assessing the types of positions available within the field. This requires assessing not only the relative hierarchies of specific types of priests, but determining the interactions between priesthoods and between cults. Temple institutions are vital actors here as well, with the relative prestige and power of temples no doubt strong elements in the relations between their priesthoods and potentially even the laity. Further, one must not forget the hazier aspects of everyday religion, which were also a major part of the field. Anyone who revered the gods was part of the religious field, even if the lowest levels are likely often to fall outside the extant evidence. Since Culturally Posited Supernatural Entities (CPSEs)[29] were believed to exist, they also ought to be reck-

25 E.g., Koch, *Mesopotamian Divination Texts.*

26 Heeßel, "Diagnosis, Divination and Disease," 99.

27 E.g., the Avestan phrase "aoxtō.nāmana yasna," "ritual in which its name is invoked," cf. Mithra's complaint in his Yašt for not being worshipped by his name (Yašt 10.54–5 [Gershevitch, *The Avestan Hymn to Mithra,* 101]). Cf. Panaino, "Philologica Avestica IV," 172–3.

28 Bourdieu and Wacquant, *Invitation,* 106; Bourdieu, *Field of Cultural Production,* 84, 87–97.

29 This terminology derives from the Cognitive Science of Religion. Spiro ("Religion," 96) defined religion as comprising interaction with 'culturally posited superhuman beings' and CSR scholars write of Culturally Posited Supernatural Agents. The concept is useful for retaining a phenomenological approach to ancient belief systems without imposing modern conceptual categories like "deity" or "ghost" that can be obfuscating. I include gods, demons, ancestors, heroes, *mischwesen,* etc, in this terminology. See, e.g., McCauley and Lawson, *Bringing Ritual to Mind.* By using the term here I do not necessarily imply anything else from CSR.

oned as comprising the topography of the field. Their relative prestige and purported competencies would have had major ramifications for actors' perceptions of positions in the field – and the trajectories they might take to improve their own positions in the field.

A wide swathe of practices of course belongs to the field: these include not just the sacrificial cults, but other rituals, divination, calendars, festivals, funerary and mortuary traditions, etc. That not all practices held sway in all parts of the ANE is entirely in keeping with a Bourdieusian approach, whereby *habitus* is shaped by one's relative position in the field ("social space").

Capital and the structure of the religious field: Religious capital and Supernatural social capital

A field is structured around the distribution of a distinctive capital, so treating religion as a field at a given place and point in time requires one to identify what that distinctly religious capital would comprise. As a note, it is worth remembering in this regard that multiple capitals may be of value in a particular field, but theoretically one ought to provide the dominant structuring principle, though the interactions between several could also be considered. It is also to be expected that the structure and structuring principle of any given field will differ according to time and space.

In his own treatment of the religious field, Bourdieu merely called religious capital the "accumulated symbolic capital" of the priesthood,[30] which is rather vague. Among other issues (such as his dependence on Marx and Weber's depictions of the ANE[31]), his specific analysis resonates more with the development of the Catholic Church in France than religions elsewhere.[32] Bourdieu also underestimates the role of non-priests in the religious field.[33] One is therefore justified in seeking better ways to understand what religious capital might comprise, at least outside France.[34] Nonetheless, his idea of "religious capital" has frequently

30 Bourdieu, "Genesis and Structure," 9.

31 E.g., in terms of urbanism as well as the role of the charismatic prophet vis-à-vis the bureaucratic priest; cf. Rey, "Pierre Bourdieu," 304.

32 Verter, "Spiritual Capital," 151.

33 E.g., Urban, "Sacred Capital," 364.

34 Verter "Spiritual Capital," 150, also thinks Bourdieu is most useful for religion when not utilizing Bourdieu's work on religion; he also notes the role of the image of the Catholic church (151). But Bourdieu often uses ideas or terminology from the Catholic church for the "secular" world, e.g., in Bourdieu, "What Makes a Social Class?," 14–15. For the influence of religious

been received as the form of cultural capital specific to a particular cult,[35] and thus not restricted to the religious field, and this will prove useful below.

In passing we can note the definition of religious capital by Iannaccone,[36] despite the fact his study was based in economic rational choice theory rather than Bourdieu. He considered it to comprise "familiarity with a religion's doctrines, rituals, traditions, and members."[37] This was slightly revised in a more sociological manner by Stark and Finke, who defined religious capital as "the degree of mastery of and attachment to a particular religious culture."[38] They find this comprises both culture and emotions, and posit that people try to preserve their religious capital.[39] Other scholars have occasionally mooted other ideas for capitals belonging to various religious fields, though I find none of them to be useful for the ANE. Urban[40] uses "sacred capital" but never defines it.[41] Baker[42] has offered definitions of "religious capital" and "spiritual capital" that, due to his psychological framework, appears unhelpfully to blend capitals with *habitus*. In the context of the modern USA, Verter argues for defining "spiritual capital" as a sub-species of cultural capital, taking embodied (knowledge, competence), objectified (objects and ideologies), and institutionalized (churches) forms.[43] The individualistic marketplace of religious ideas Verter analyzes, however, is a very different religious world from the ANE. In the specific context of the Anglican Communion, McKinnon et al. see episcopal authority as the key form of religious capital, along with a newly created claim of "orthodoxy."[44]

In a forthcoming article Silverman, Töyräänvuori, and Wasmuth offer two ideas for understanding religious capital in Achaemenid Egypt: one as *numen* and one as supernatural social capital. It is the second one I wish to pick up and elaborate here as useful for analyzing the Persian Empire with a religious field. By supernatural social capital, I mean a similar concept to social capital, but one

---

concepts on Bourdieu's thought, cf. Rey, "Pierre Bourdieu," 302. Rey goes so far as to claim Bourdieu is less useful for less centralized religions ("Pierre Bourdieu," 309).

35 E.g., Baker, "Social, Religious and Spiritual Capitals," 173.

36 Iannaccone, "Religious Practice."

37 Iannaccone, "Religious Practice," 299.

38 Stark and Finke, *Acts of Faith*, 108.

39 Stark and Finke, *Acts of Faith*, 109.

40 Urban, "Sacred Capital."

41 It is perhaps worth noting that Urban critiques Bourdieu's treatment of the religious field for ignoring the strategies of the dominated, though Urban's own model is quite in line with bow Bourdieu describes such strategies in other contexts (particularly in *Homo Academicus*).

42 Baker, "Social, Religious and Spiritual Capitals."

43 Verter, "Spiritual Capital," 159–160.

44 McKinnon, Trzebiatowska, and Brittain, "Bourdieu, Capital, and Conflict."

that includes all purported relationships to Culturally Posited Supernatural Entities (CPSEs) – deities, demons, the dead, etc. This distinguishes the religious field from the cultural field by including all CPSEs within it. This means that CPSEs are real insofar as they comprise part of actors' perceptions and dispositions towards the religious field.[45] Supernatural social capital comprises the relationships individuals are purported to hold with CPSEs as well as their relative prestige. This means the relative popularity and purported competences of CPSEs have a structuring role for the field: those deemed more powerful will attract more interest in relationships (e.g., worship, sacrifice) than others. It also means those with recognized relationships to them will also increase in prestige (such as those associated with institutionalized relationships). This is a positive feedback loop, much like how Gudme[46] has analyzed the function of votive inscriptions. Bourdieu's concept of religious capital, as the religious field's version of cultural capital – i.e., education in appropriate rituals, lifeways, etc – would be one of the prerequisites for humans to gain supernatural social capital. The exact "exchange rates" between the two would of course vary by cult and location. A benefit to this analysis is that it includes official and unofficial forms of religious roles and their attendant activity: centralized cultic priests, popular magicians, exorcists, and family mourners all participated in networks of relations with various CPSEs in various capacities. One can equally analyze royally sponsored sacrifices, the spread of apotropaic amulets, or ancestor veneration within this frame. "Illicit" activities such as witchcraft are analyzable as either heterodox corners of the religious field, or as cultivating different sets of religious capital.

I think this provides a useful way to deal with the undeniable fact that there were copious different deities, demons, and ancestors in the ANE, many of which required very specific cultic traditions. Participation in any given particular cult required a certain amount of religious capital, which could be translated into supernatural social capital in proportion to any particular cult's rules. So, while the "big brother" of the Esagila had the most supernatural social capital with Marduk, he probably had little to none with Anu.[47] The king could maintain or gain some with either or both with gifts to their priests and temples. Further,

45 Since actors' strategies depend on their perceptions both of other positions in the field and the interactions of others with those positions. It also means that the demarcation between such entities is immaterial for a sociological analysis. This is in line with a phenomenological approach to religion, in which we neither have to believe nor disbelieve in the existence of any such CPSE to take the religion's own perspectives seriously.

46 Gudme, "Out of Sight, Out of Mind?"; Gudme, *Before the God.*

47 Although there was a shrine to Anu within the Esagil of Marduk in Babylon (é.giš.ḫur.an.ki.a, Tintir II 18'; see George, *Babylonian Topographical Texts*, 52–3; George, *House Most High*, 95).

since it is clear that ideas of exclusive worship are anachronistic for the Persian Empire, this invites analysis not only of the relative positions of various deities and their cultic sites, but the religious investments needed to gain social capital with any given deity or indeed ancestor.[48] It also invites a dynamic analysis of the religious field, when one recognizes a field as a competition between positions, and structured by the changing positions of actors, human and supernatural. Incidentally, one could therefore read Second Isaiah's program (e.g., use of creation theology, ridicule of Marduk cult, praise of Cyrus, etc)[49] as one to increase the supernatural social capital of YHWH in order to encourage both relations with YHWH and the requisite investment in religious capital to acquire supernatural social capital with him.

The Great King and the Religious Field in the Empire

Even if, as I would argue, the Persian Great King was not a priest, he was part of the religious field as a person claiming relationships with various CPSEs: not just Ahuramazda or other major formerly imperial deities,[50] but also with *farnah*, and likely with royal *fravašis* and/or royal ancestors, to name a few. He also had structural effects on the shape of the field through several different avenues: 1) through patronage of cults and priests (and their vetting); 2) through royal discourse on the divine and worldviews; and 3) through his own religious practices.

A traditional role of kings in numerous times and places in the ANE was the patronage of and indeed building of temples, as well as of various kinds of religious functionaries (priests, diviners, prophets, etc.).[51] As with all patron relations, both the king and the client received benefits from these relationships. Royally patronized deities often became more widely recognized and worshipped, even being moved to the tops of pantheons. Temples received social capital as well as economic capital from these relationships, as did religious functionaries. I have argued elsewhere[52] that the Great King insisted on vetting candidates for the

48 It is worth noting in this respect Sonia's argument that one could "co-opt" the ancestors of others to gain social capital (Sonia, *Caring for the Dead*; one could also analyze it in terms of increasing supernatural social capital.

49 Following my analysis in Silverman, *Persian Royal–Judaean Elite*.

50 For Marduk, see the Cyrus Cylinder, for Ra see Darius's canal inscriptions, for Humban, see the attested sacrifices in the Persepolis tablets.

51 For the Neo-Babylonian Empire, cf. Waerzeggers, "The Pious King."

52 Silverman, "Vetting the Priest in Zech 3"; cf. Silverman, *Persian Royal–Judaean Elite*.

priesthood along social criteria, meaning he and his satraps had a strong influence on the social capital needed for attaining priestly positions and thus their supernatural social capital. This is important for coloring debates over the impact of the king on the cults, as it is not their *religious* capital – i.e. their specific religious knowledge and competence – but their *social* capital that appears to have been a royal criterion in these matters, outside Iran, at least. This nonetheless determined some of the specific rules needed to reach higher positions in the field, thus shaping the effective strategies therein. In other words, to be able to convert one's religious capital into supernatural capital most effectively, one needed social capital within the imperial administration.

While one may be justified in seeing the primary intention of royal propaganda to be to shape the political field, there are at least two mechanisms one could imagine for its effect on the religious field. The first is the fact that dominant positions in the field are able to define what counts as capital and what counts as legitimate categories of evaluation and worth (what Bourdieu calls symbolic capital). The king, holding a relatively high position in the field, would thus have much power within the field (meaning ability to gain and wield religious capital, shape the rules of the game, etc). Further, the principle of homology between the political field and other fields would suggest that similar rules and legitimation principles as in the former would shape the latter. Thus, as I have argued elsewhere, the royal inscriptions manage to redefine the value of deities based on their creative powers and on their benevolence.[53] This is because the king derives his legitimacy from the beneficial and creative powers of Ahuramazda (and which shape the Great King's view of his domain), which, in a homologous turn in the religious field would increase the symbolic value of creation and benevolence within the scope of divine positionality.

Finally, the Great King had effect through his own religious *habitus*. The CPSEs he chose to honor and worship, the rituals he sponsored and attended, the festivals and calendars he participated in, would have increased in status. This is beyond the effects of any royal decrees on any such matters. Those wishing to maintain a high position in the religious field – especially outside the priesthoods – and those wishing to increase theirs would have had every incentive to adjust their own practices accordingly. Topics I can imagine worth analyzing in these terms include

53 Silverman, "Achaemenid Creation"; cf. Silverman, *Persian Royal–Judaean Elite*. In the context of this paper, it is worth noting that Nehemiah stresses the benevolence of YHWH in ch 2 (vv. 8, 18 [2x]).

the worship of Mithra or Anāhitā,[54] ancestor cults,[55] and festivals.[56] One might also wonder about the implications for more restricted priestly practices; those priests whose positions were on an upward trajectory could both impose their understanding of proper priestly *habitus* on other priests, as well as have it copied by the same. I have in mind here questions such as ritual purity and lay roles in relation to cults, not to mention acceptable forms of divination, etc.

Other structural issues in the Religious Field of the Persian Empire

For the sake of time I will only briefly suggest further ways one might investigate the larger structure of the religious field in the empire and some of the ways it was likely changing. The first is the issue of dispersion through the empire. In a previous essay I noted that Judaeans and Iranians shared an experience of dispersal around the empire, though for different reasons.[57] The Judaeans lived around the empire as the result of waves of deportations and, presumably, other forms of migration. Iranian colonists were also settled around the empire, as military colonists, administrators, and satrapal elites. This means that these two groups at least potentially shared the experiences associated with *hysteresis*, or of (religious) *habitus* designed for one context and placed in another, incongruous context. It also means various cults were likely spread among groups of very different composition and with different positions in the religious field (not to mention the political field). One might think of garrisons versus satrapal courts, for example, proximity to temples or shrines, or the likely very different *habitus* of admin-

54 Often debated in terms of the sudden appearance of both deities in the inscriptions of Artaxerxes II (A^{2}Ha, b; A^{2}Sa, d) as well as the claim in Berossus (680 F11) that the same king instituted temples to Anāhitā. For Mithra there is also the perennial question of whether Mihragan dates as far back as the first Persian Empire. Boyce had famously adventurous interpretations of both (eg Boyce, *History of Zoroastrianism*). For various aspects see Boyce, "On Mithra, Lord of Fire"; Boyce, *History of Zoroastrianism II*; Jong, *Traditions of the Magi*, 273–276, 371–377; Bahadori, "Persepolitan Ceremonies." Recently Henkelman has suggested there was a temple to Anāhitā in Fars (Henkelman, "Humban & Auramazdā," 289 n. 70).

55 E.g., Porter, "The Dynamics of Death"; Henkelman, "An Elamite Memorial"; Sonia, *Caring for the Dead*.

56 For Palestine, the origins of Pesach, Shavuot, Sukkot, Rosh HaShanah and Yom Kippur have long been debated. For Babylon and Assyria the most discussed is the Akitu. For Iran the festivals of Nowruz, Tirigan, and Mihragan have long been debated. One might also consider whatever lay behind Purim.

57 Silverman, "Persian Religion in the Hebrew Bible."

istrative scribes (a position likely shared by some Judeans and some Iranians) and that of members of the imperial elite.

Case Study: Nehemiah 8 as Practices of Feasting within the Religious Field

In his study of food in the Hebrew Bible, MacDonald has already pointed to the relevance of Persian feasting practices,[58] which he sees as a good example of conspicuous consumption.[59] However, MacDonald focuses mostly on the post-Persian, Hellenistic use of the Persians as a foil for the Hellenistic ideal of moderation. It also would be remiss of me not to note that Laird has already wielded Bourdieu in her book on Ezra-Nehemiah, though she does not posit a religious field.[60] As will be visible below, her analysis of Ezra 3/Neh 8[61] therefore differs from mine.

Feasting has long attracted social scientific attention as a mechanism that constructs and maintains patterns of relationships.[62] MacDonald has highlighted it as a potential mechanism for the development of what, in Bourdieusian terms, would be the political field.[63] Following several anthropologists on feasting, MacDonald argues that feasting is a major way of converting economic capital into political capital,[64] pointing in particular to the narratives associating Solomon's court with feasts.[65] I would here like to analyze some hints in Nehemiah 8 as potential mechanism for change in the religious field in Yehud, as a subfield of the Imperial religious field and in relationship with the broader political field. I will first draw on Henkelman's work on royally sponsored feasts, and then turn to Nehemiah 8.

Henkelman has argued that attestations of *šip*-feasts in the Persepolis Fortification Tablets and in the Elamite version of XPh represent royally sponsored

---

58 MacDonald, *Not Bread Alone*, esp. ch. 7.

59 Ala Veblen, *Conspicuous Consumption*; MacDonald, *Not Bread Alone*, 203–211.

60 Laird, *Negotiating Power.*

61 Laird, *Negotiating Power*, 123–133.

62 O'Connor, *The Never-Ending Feast*, esp. ch 3; MacDonald, *Not Bread Alone*; Altmann, *Festive Meals*, §2.2 emphasizes the psychological element more; cf. Da Riva, Arroyo, and Debourse, *Ceremonies, Feasts and Festivities*.

63 MacDonald, *Not Bread Alone*.

64 MacDonald, *Not Bread Alone*, esp. 144–5.

65 Joanna Töyräänvuori suggested another side of the equation as one of fasting converting religious capital into social or supernatural social capital (personal communication). This could provide an interesting analysis in light of the developing tradition of penitential prayers and the fact that Zoroastrianism is not congenial to ascetic traditions such as fasting (cf. Boyce, *History of Zoroastrianism* I, 121; Choksy, "Fasting in Persia I").

events for imperial work forces.[66] He sees this as an instance of the royal ideology of gift-giving, but one with religious and sacrificial meanings (so far only the gods Zizkurra [NN 0654] and Auramazdā [XPh_c] are mentioned by name).[67] Large amounts of food were consumed, including duck, which Henkelman sees as a specifically royal prerogative,[68] and these events are attested involving large groups of laborers, up to 520 individuals.[69] They appear to occur in November/December, and Henkelman adduces culling of herds as the practical reason and the king's presence in Fars as the ideological reason.[70] It was held in *paradises* and possibly at the sacred precinct in Pasargadae.[71] Persian feasting also notoriously involved wine (as well as being one option for liquid rations, the other being beer).[72] Henkelman published one text documenting wine distributed at a *šip*-feast (NN 2402).[73]

The political symbolic function of such feasts is fairly transparent, as Henkelman has argued: the king directly or through his agents performs the role of most generous gift-giver, and in line with rules of hospitality demonstrates his superior social status.[74] But the religious elements to this feast – however elusive in details – also have implications for a religious field. Religious elements include any divine dedications or sacrifices made during the feast (so far only two known by name in Fars, one of Elamite origin and one of Indo-Iranian),[75] the location of the feasting in a sacredly tinged environ like a *paradise* or the sacred precinct, any other CPSE patrons named, food taboos created or ignored, or the creation of sacred festivals. Although one might imagine such feasts, if held regularly,

---

66 Henkelman, "Parnakka's Feast"; cf. Henkelman, "Practice of Worship," 1260–2. For higher-level dining practices of the kings, queens, and satraps, see e.g., Henkelman, "Consumed."
67 Henkelman, "Parnakka's Feast," 99, 102–103, 115, 119.
68 Henkelman, "Parnakka's Feast," 104–5.
69 Henkelman, "Parnakka's Feast," 119.
70 Henkelman, "Parnakka's Feast," 119.
71 Henkelman, "Parnakka's Feast," 132.
72 Colburn, *Archaeology of Empire*, ch. 5; Balatti, "Wine Consumption." There may have even been a Persian god of wine, Minam (See Henkelman, "Practice," 1234 [NN 2259]; cf. Silverman, forthcoming on this and Isaiah). At the level of the royal tables this is attested in staggering amounts: Henkelman identifies over 37k quarts of wine at the King's table, and a tenth of that at one queen's table (Henkelman, "Consumed," 681, 695).
73 Henkelman, "Parnakka's Feast," 99. The issue of the distribution of imperial dining ware and its local terracotta imitations would be relevant here, though it goes beyond the present scope. Relevant, perhaps, for below is of course the tradition in Nehemiah of said governor having been a cup-bearer to the king. Cf. Briant, *From Cyrus to Alexander*, 263; Balatti "Wine Consumption," 178.
74 Briant, *From Cyrus to Alexander*, 314; Colburn, *Archaeology*; Gudme, "Guests."
75 Henkelman, "Parnakka's Feast," 103.

might popularize a particular holiday or even a particular deity, it is worth considering more subtle but more important ramifications. In line with the principle of homology, the practice normalizes the patronage of the Persian king or his agents over religiously-tinged public festivals outside of temple complexes. It simultaneously reinforces the position of the king in the field while maintaining a distinction between his position and priestly positions. As we know the satraps mirrored the king, and governors likely mirrored the satraps,[76] this means there is likely to be a ripple effect in the religious *habitus* in the empire. In other words, a strategy for imperial officials of various levels to increase their religious capital would be to sponsor such large feasts for workers. This should not be taken to imply a uniform, "trickle down" of cults from the crown downward; rather, a strategy available to imperial agents to improve their positions would have been choosing appropriate local festivities to sponsor in a conspicuous manner. Further, given the large-scale use of various forms of labor in the empire,[77] this means one might expect being a guest at such events to become incorporated into the *habitus* of the lower layers of society.[78] This involved an implicit recognition of the patron's, and ultimately the king's, position in the religious field.

Then there are the practical considerations of which gods are chosen to be honored, which priests chosen for the respective rites, which sacrifices are offered, which location they are held in, and the status distinctions which are marked among guests, etc. Depending on the historical moment such choices have the potential to reinforce existing positions and rules of the game or to alter them – Bourdieu is as much a theorist of change as of stasis. Further, the precise "table manners" or etiquette of feasting are also implicated. This is most immediately illustratable through the spread of the Achaemenid style bowls and rhyta, which represent manners of eating and drinking that were marked as imperial.[79] As the Persian style of feasting and drinking included reclining on couches with servants holding rhyta and drinkers holding bowls, this is a distinctive *hexis* (embodied *habitus*) with clear imperial connotations. If one believes Nehemiah's attribution as a royal cupbearer (Neh 1:11–2:1), then he would have been intimately familiar with this dining style. One might justifiably relate such matters of *hexis* to the raising of hands in Neh 8:6, which is reminiscent of the royal posture in front of the winged disk.[80]

76 Briant, *From Cyrus to Alexander*, 314–5; Henkelman, "Consumed"; Miller, "Luxury Toreutic."
77 Dandamaev, "Forced Labour"; Aperghis, "War Captives."; Hyland, "Persia's Lycian Work Force."
78 On the neglected aspects of guest etiquette in hospitality and feasting, see Gudme, "Guests."
79 Dusinberre, "Satrapal Sardis"; Dusinberre, *Empire, Authority, and Autonomy*; Katchadourian, *Imperial Matter*, ch 5. MacDonald, *Not Bread Alone*, 196, speaks of table manners as part of the "grammar of identity."
80 Fried, *Nehemiah*, 207, calls this a "common posture of prayer," but does not note the similarity to the royal Persian posture (eg, at DB and DN).

The *šip*-feasts for workers noted above were of course not the only or necessarily most prominent feasting practice of the king and imperial elites (Neh 5:17–18).[81] Nonetheless, they might provide a new angle for considering the material presently in Nehemiah 8. I do not wish to delve into the question of the origin and/or redactions of this chapter, nor do I wish to go into the origins of Sukkot.[82] Recently, Fried has argued this chapter originally concerned a celebration marking the completion of the Jerusalem wall.[83] Whether this is the case or not, the chapter has the governor and his elites give orders for one or two different communal feasts. There is a feast on the first day of the month (v. 10, 12),[84] and then a festival of Sukkot, which one presumes also would have involved food, though this is not specified directly (of course in later tradition, it was/is common to eat in the sukkot). While here v. 12 might indicate it is not a centrally organized distributional feast like the *šip*,[85] both are still centrally mandated. The feasts are meant to be fancy as well, with choice food and wine (v. 10), albeit without much specificity. They are to be minimally distributed at least (to those unprepared, v. 10). Though people are to build sukkot on their own rooves, there are also others in public spaces, suggesting a wider variety of groups envisioned (not just the traditional concern with "pilgrims"). One could also point to the more explicitly rarified gubernatorial table in Neh 5:17–18 for more explicitly distributional dynamics.[86] Edelman has suggested that pilgrimage feasts such as Pesach (and later Sukkot) were designed by the priesthood to develop communal memories that bound land and diaspora.[87] Even if one were inclined to see this as the case, such a development would have occurred within a wider social structure with rules of the game beyond the specific concerns of Judean priests. In this context it looks very much like the governor (in the narrative, Nehemiah) is echoing the

---

81 Cf. Altmann, *Economics*, 270–287; Fried, "150 Men at Nehemiah's Table." Altmann (*Economics*, 244) does not even include our passage in his list of economically relevant passages in Nehemiah.
82 E.g., Batten, *A Critical and Exegetical Commentary*, 109, thought the festival was a Canaanite harvest festival; Rubenstein, *The History of Sukkot*, ch 1, offers an overview of theories of its origins. I agree with Rubinstein (29) in seeing the most probable origin being a rural harvest festival. A handy overview of the textual versions of Sukkot can be found in Fried, "Sukkot." For discussion of literary developments outside present interest, see, eg, Weyde, *The Appointed Festivals of YHWH*; Weyde, "And They Found It."
83 Fried, "Sukkot"; Fried, *Nehemiah*, 193–198, 203.
84 Most commentators appear to ignore this first feast, as they are keen to discuss either the Torah reading or Sukkot (and its relation to Torah).
85 Fried (*Nehemiah*, 211) thinks they remained in Jerusalem, at lodgings there.
86 It may be worth pointing out the specifics of who prepares the food in Neh 8 is passed over in silence. The previous assembly had included women and children. For Neh 5 Altmann avers Nehemiah is depicted reflecting royal feasting glory (*Economics*, 287).
87 Edelman, "Exodus and Pesah/Massot."

feasting practices of the Great King for non-elites, and using it to increase his own supernatural social capital by linking it to religious tradition. The selection of religious functionaries involved (Levites and Ezra as priest and scribe) may have found this a useful moment for ritual innovation as well.[88]

I think the image sketched above of local elites emulating higher imperial elites in patronizing local practices provides an interesting angle to this passage. If we accept that Yehud and Samerina probably had had agricultural festivals marking the harvest and/or threshing of the harvest, we can argue the work forces at the disposal of the higher-level elites in the two provinces were probably well acquainted with these practices. There is no reason to assume that such regular agricultural practices would have been disrupted by the deportations of elites and/or urbanites by the Babylonians. If one accepts Rubenstein's argument that the building of temporary shelters for the purposes of such harvesting was the practical origin of temporary structures later called *sukkot*,[89] it would therefore follow that such agricultural workers would have been used to such practices – and have continued them through the Babylonian and Persian Empires – but that urbanites such as those in Nehemiah 8 would not have been. Through his authority as governor, Nehemiah is able to draw on the administrative resources of the temple establishment – the literate priests and scribes, here depicted as Ezra and the Levites – to increase his supernatural social capital. He does this by having the urbanites adopt as a sacred practice what had been merely a practical practice, thereby imbuing it as part of the cult and demonstrating his fealty to the local deity. In other words, what had been an incidental aspect of tradition only relevant to a portion of the community was taken up and transformed into a religious obligation for all. This is likely to be an effective way to coopt workers into the new "symbolic capital" by requiring minimal change to their *habitus*. As I have argued elsewhere,[90] the issue of written *torah* here is a red herring – what is really at stake is who the legitimate authorities for religious practice are. In this passage it is those who control the ability to read and write, and thus in reality the administration of the province. It is perhaps worth noting that this is an effect on the religious field outside the temple proper (unlike Ezra 3)[91]: it

88 There has been much debate over whether and how the instructions in Neh 8 for the sukkot are related to those in Leviticus or not (eg Weyde 2007), but since the phenomenon of written texts providing social warrants is later, this debate obscures discussion of the social processes involved.

89 Rubenstein, *History*, 17; Fried, *Nehemiah*, 221.

90 Silverman, "Concepts."

91 Laird (*Negotiating Power*, 126) sees a difference in impact between the decentralized and centralized versions in Neh 8 and Ezra 3; I think relating both to different spaces in the same religious field provides a better analysis of the effects. I suspect most major ANE festivals had

concerns the practice of the general "laity." It also has a twofold effect on the rules of the game in the field. First, it implicitly adds a criterion of literacy to the religious capital needed to gain priestly supernatural capital. This presumably would favor those priests who worked in the imperial administration, seeing as those are the most likely to have had the need to learn literacy. Indeed, Ezra is depicted exactly as a dual priest and imperial agent in his book. In this it is immaterial whether or not the practice decreed by the authorities was in fact written in a scroll or not. What matters is the ability to access the scroll and explain it to others. Strictly speaking, literacy had not been necessary for the religious capital to become a cultic priest. Now, however, it increased a priest's religious capital and thus potential for conversion of it into supernatural social capital (thus, contra the analysis of Laird[92] who sees rival authorities in Ezra 3 and Neh 8). Second, it makes what one might have called a cultural practice into an explicitly religious practice.[93] The building of booths becomes part of *torah*, the way things are done, and thus part of general religious capital available to all participants in the field. Of course, as capital available to all it had little value for social distinction (though it would have had value for group-belonging). It would, however, have been the occasion for the development of new patterns for the display of distinction (either in terms of types of wood used for the sukkot, their size, number of guests invited, etc). In this, the priests would have had the incentive to emphasize the temple-centric aspects of the holiday, as a way to heighten the position of the temple within the religious field.[94]

This analysis connects the religious field with both the economic field (through agricultural practices and the utilization of labor forces) and with the political field (through the agency of the governor and the administrators), but the strategies for advancement in the field are autonomous from both. It also highlights how *habitus* and positionality can effect religious change. The administrative *habitus* acquired by the governor and by his administrators shapes their expectations for warrants within the religious field, while the different positions of urbanites from rural workers changes the meaning of a similar practice.

---

temple-centric and more public aspects, making the centralized/decentralized scholarly trope merely an artifact of overly prioritizing the text.

92 Laird, *Negotiating Power*, 131.

93 This is not to say there had not been fertility – and thus religious – elements to the festivities beforehand.

94 Laird (*Negotiating Power*, 123) sees a strong contrast between the home-centric and temple-centric versions of the festival, but relates this to differences in *habitus* due to exilic and local backgrounds (124).

I must contrast my analysis above with that relatively recently offered by Whitters.[95] Whitters argues that Nehemiah 8 represents, in my terms, a deliberate, conscious influence ("borrowing") from Achaemenid imperial ritual to Yehud. While I agree that Iranian influence is an important issue for Persian Period religion, and even that Bourdieu offers useful tools for exploring it,[96] this is not how I have analyzed the passage above. The first problem I have is I disagree with his analysis of the relief program at Persepolis as depicting a "liturgy" in any meaningful sense of the word, so I do not think there is actually something there to compare to Nehemiah. Second, his analysis depends on Neh 8 depicting a specific historical event, which is also problematic. Rather than seeing Nehemiah 8 as an example of pro-Persian elites deliberately inscribing the empire into their ritual practice, my analysis above accepts such an imperial background in the form of elite habitus formation but not in the construction of the feasts *per se* (whichever ones one thinks they are). At the end of his article Whitters helpfully points to a number of issues (what one might call symbolic capital)[97] certainly useful to think about, but my explicit use of Bourdieu highlights how the choice of local practices could still serve the interests of local elites as well as be part of a wider imperial religious game. One need not posit a specific ritual at Persepolis or for any Yehudian elite to have ever visited Persepolis for the structural effects of Achaemenid feasting practices to be relevant. Indeed, I would argue that in this case the structural changes are significant without any similarity in contents. If Neh 8 really does reflect the genesis of new feasting practices for the population, this creates not just new practices (such as the particular feasts in the seventh month or the building of sukkot for religious purposes), it creates new expectations (towards hosting and being hosted, construction and collection), and relationships (between and among families, new possibilities for patronage, the governor and the populace).

Of course, this analysis cannot prove anything about Nehemiah 8's historic dating or origins. If Fried's new theory on the dating of the chapter is correct, then one would have to seriously consider the relation with Ptolemaic Bacchic festivals, as she does.[98] Yet the viability of the toolkit arguably remains, as the religious field within the Ptolemaic Empire was different and would need to be

95 Whitters, "Persianized Liturgy." A similar sort of critique of Fleishman, "The Rebuilding of the Wall of Jerusalem," could also be offered, but is avoided here for constraints of space. However, cf. the discussion of Foroutan, "References to Zoroastrian Beliefs."

96 Silverman, "Cultural and Religious Influence."

97 Whitters, "Persianized Liturgy," 82–4. My take on his topics: Bureaucracy, minimal coercion, hierarchy, multiculturalism, sacred language, book as a replacement for kingship.

98 Fried, *Nehemiah*, 236–9.

analyzed on its own terms. Given a relevance for the Persian Empire, however, this enables a way to think about the potential social dynamics around religious change in Yehud that are not tied merely to redaction and exegesis, but to dynamic competition between positions in a religious field and the relations between this field and the political field.

Afterthoughts

Positing a religious field within the Achaemenid Empire forces one to ask many difficult questions. How did new practices, positions, and capitals change strategies for players in the field? How did Yehud relate to this larger game in Abar-Nahara and the empire at large? Direct influence of specific forms of symbolic or cultural capital are always a possible part of the evolution of the field. Nonetheless, practices that appear either entirely unrelated or only superficially analogous can sometimes be argued to share structural homologues, inviting a broader sociological analysis of what rules were at play in the field to create such similar conditions. I think the concepts of religious capital and supernatural social capital provide a more nuanced way to ask what is at stake in something as seemingly simple as the introduction of a feast or even just the institutionalization of a pre-existing practice with a new interpretation. Though analyses of the political and economic fields are still useful – no field ever operates in isolation – a religious field provides a heuristic for interrogating the relations between the local governors, administrators, and cultic officials beyond the tired old debates around the so-called priestly usurpation of 'Davidic' prerogatives.

One might be automatically inclined to relate the supernatural social capital at stake in our case study to YHWH, as biblical scholars are wont to do. Surely since Sukkot is a practice in the Pentateuch, the only relevant CPSE would be him? However, I think a distinction between religious capital and supernatural social capital is useful here, for taking into consideration the wider imperial religious context. Since we have hints in Third Isaiah (Isa 57: 5–10; 65: 3–5, 11)[99] of alternate practices, concrete proof of multiple deities in Elephantine, and a spread in popularity of apotropaic deities such as Bes, it is worth noting that supernatural social capital – like regular social capital – would not be exclusive. Its effectiveness would be just as situational as the former, based on prestige and "networks". Part of religious capital in the empire would be knowing the CPSEs most relevant in a given situation as well as which practices are appropriate for them.

99 Cf. Edelman, "Possible Rituals."

Just as one needs to know which person to approach to gain entrance to the royal court, one would need to know which CPSE would provide the most supernatural benefits. The fertility and labor aspects I hinted at above lurking behind the agricultural festival could suggest a wider array of relevant cultic practices and CPSEs around Sukkot or whatever other festivals are in Neh 8. Similarly, the chains of political patronage also suggest chains of divine patronage or identification as potential dynamics in the field. This again invites a wider consideration of what Bourdieu would call symbolic capital, or the principles of legitimacy and warrants in the field, requiring a zooming back out from just Yehud proper. Scholars often like to argue that something like monolatry provided power or solidarity for priests and/or scribes, but exact mechanisms for how this would achieve such results remain under-developed. Relations between CPSEs, and with their human counterparts, provide a social structure through which one could analyze any such changes in the rules of the religious game in Yehud. While religious specialists are to be expected to promote the prestige of the deities to which they are devoted, this does not imply a move towards a reduction in pantheon size (consider the rise of Anu in Uruk as a similar phenomenon).[100] A social space would be required in which agents could convert supernatural social capital to political capital and use it to eliminate rivals; this does not appear to be the case in the Persian Levant.

Field Theory is complicated and requires much thought to utilize properly. There are many more aspects to Bourdieu's thought and those who have utilized it than just the basic triad of field, habitus, and capital used here. Further, as a historical "empirical" question (as Bourdieu would phrase it), I remain ambivalent on the existence of an autonomous religious field in the Persian Empire. Nevertheless, asking questions such as "was there a religious field" forces one to ask a series of relational questions: between individuals, social positions, political positions, and social practices. Even though we lack the richness of the anthropological studies upon which Bourdieu cut his teeth, the thought process remains a valuable exercise. If for nothing else, the challenge of matching the necessary relational questions with the limited extant data gives rise to new questions otherwise not necessarily asked in the heavy debates over religion in the Achaemenid Empire.[101]

---

100 Krul, *Revival of the Anu Cult.*

101 This has of course been a very contentious field of debate, for Achaemenid religion itself (eg, recently Henkelman, Redard, *Persian Religion*; Jong, "Religion," 2:1199–1209), relations with local cults (eg. Achenbach, *Persische Reichspolitik*), and for Judaean religions (eg Edelman, Fitzpatrick-McKinley, and Guillaume, *Religion in the Achaemenid Persian Empire*).

Bibliography

Adams, Robert McC., "Ancient Mesopotamian Urbanism and Blurred Disciplinary Boundaries." *Annual Review of Anthropology* 41 (2012): 1–20.

Achenbach, Reinhard, (ed.), *Persische Reichspolitik und lokale Heiligtümer.* Beihefte zur Zeitschrift für altorientalische und biblische Rechtsgeschichte 25. Wiesbaden: Harrassowitz, 2019.

Altmann, Peter, *Festive Meals in Ancient Israel: Deuteronomy's Identity Politics in Their Ancient Near Eastern Context*. BZAW 424. Berlin: De Gruyter, 2011.

Altmann, Peter, *Economics in Persian-Period Biblical Texts: Their Interactions with Economic Developments in the Persian Period and Earlier Biblical Traditions*. FAT 109. Tübingen: Mohr Siebeck, 2016.

Aperghis, Gerassimos G., "War Captives and Economic Exploitation: Evidence Form the Persepolis Fortification Tablets," pages 127–44 in *Économie Antique: La Guerre Dans Les Économies Antiques*, edited by Jean Andreau, Pierre Briant, and Raymond Descat. Entretiens d'archéologie et d'histoire Saint-Bertrand-de-Comminges 5. Saint-Bertrand-de-Comminges: Musée archéologique départemental de Saint-Bertrand-de-Comminges, 2000.

Atkinson, Will, *Beyond Bourdieu: From Genetic Structuralism to Relational Phenomenology.* Cambridge: Polity, 2016.

Bahadori, Ali, "Persepolitan Ceremonies: The Case of Mehrgān." *Ancient West & East* 14 (2015): 51–71. https://doi.org/10.2143/AWE.14. 0. 3108188.

Baker, Chris, "Social, Religious and Spiritual Capitals: A Psychological Perspective," pages 169–87 in *International Handbook of Education for Spirituality, Care and Wellbeing*, edited by M. de Souza, L. J. Francis, J. O'Higgins-Norman, and D. Scott. International Handbooks of Religion and Education 3. Dordrecht: Springer, 2009. https://doi.org/10.1007/978-1-4020-9018-9_10.

Balatti, Silvia, "Wine Consumption in the Achaemenid Empire: Evidence Form the Heartland," pages 169–200 in *Paleopersepolis: Environment, Landscape and Society in Ancient Fars*, edited by Silvia Balatti, Hilmar Klinkott, and Josef Wiesehöfer. Oriens et Occidens 33. Stuttgart: Franz Steiner, 2021.

Batten, Loring, *A Critical and Exegetical Commentary on the Books of Ezra and Nehemiah*. International Critical Commentaries. Edinburgh: T & T Clark, 1913.

Bourdieu, Pierre, and Wacquant, Loïc, *An Invitation to Reflexive Sociology*. Chicago: University of Chicago Press, 1992.

Bourdieu, Pierre, "What Makes a Social Class? On the Theoretical and Practical Existence of Groups." Translated by Loïc Wacquant and David Young. *Berkeley Journal of Sociology* 32 (1987): 1–18.

Bourdieu, Pierre, *The Logic of Practice*. Translated by Richard Nice. Stanford, CA: Stanford University Press, 1990.

Bourdieu, Pierre, "Genesis and Structure of the Religious Field," *Comparative Social Research* 13 (1991): 1–44.

Bourdieu, Pierre, *The Field of Cultural Production: Essays on Art and Literature*. Edited by Randal Johnson. European Perspectives. New York: Columbia University Press, 1993.

Bourdieu, Pierre, *Outline of a Theory of Practice*. Translated by Richard Nice. 19th English printing (orig 1972). Cambridge Studies in Social and Cultural Anthropology 16. Cambridge: Cambridge University Press, 2005.

Bourdieu, Pierre, *The Bachelors' Ball*. Translated by Richard Nice. Cambridge: Polity, 2008.

Bourdieu, Pierre, *Distinction: A Social Critique of the Judgement of Taste*. Translated by Richard Nice. London: Routledge, 2010.

Briant, Pierre, *From Cyrus to Alexander: A History of the Persian Empire*. Translated by Peter T. Daniels. Winona Lake, IN: Eisenbrauns, 2002.

Boyce, Mary, "On Mithra, Lord of Fire." In *Monumentum H. S. Nyberg I*, edited by J. Duchesne-Guillemin, 69–76. Acta Iranica 4. Leiden: Brill, 1975.

Boyce, Mary, *A History of Zoroastrianism: The Early Period*. Vol. I. Handbuch der Orientalistik VIII.1.2.2A.1. Leiden: E. J. Brill, 1975.

Boyce, Mary, *A History of Zoroastrianism: Under the Achaemenians*. Vol. II. Handbuch der Orientalistik VIII.1.2.2A.2. Leiden: E. J. Brill, 1982.

Casey, Kimberly L., "Defining Political Capital: A Reconsideration of Bourdieu's Interconvertibility Theory." *Critique: A Worldwide Student Journal of Politics* Spring 2008: 1–24.

Choksy, Jamsheed K., "Fasting in Persia i. Among Zoroastrians, Manicheans, and Bahais." *Encyclopaedia Iranica* 9.4 (1999 [2012]): 394–96. https://www.iranicaonline.org/articles/fasting.

Colburn, Henry P., *Archaeology of Empire in Achaemenid Egypt*. Edinburgh Studies in Ancient Persia. Edinburgh: Edinburgh University Press, 2020.

Da Riva, Rocio, Arroyo, Ana and Debourse, Céline (eds.) *Ceremonies, Feasts and Festivities in Ancient Mesopotamia and the Mediterranean World: Performance and Participation*. Melammu Workshops and Monographs 7. Münster: Zaphon, 2022.

Dandamaev, Muhammad A., "Forced Labour in the Palace Economy of Achaemenid Iran." *Alt-Orientalische Forschungen* 2 (1975): 71–78.

Dusinberre, Elspeth R. M., "Satrapal Sardis: Achaemenid Bowls in an Achaemenid Capital." *American Journal of Archaeology* 103 (1999): 73–102.

Dusinberre, Elspeth R. M., *Empire, Authority, and Autonomy in Achaemenid Anatolia*. Cambridge: Cambridge University Press, 2013.

Edelman, Diana V., "Exodus and Pesah/Massot as Evolving Social Memory," pages 161–93 in *Remembering (and Forgetting) in Judah's Early Second Temple Period*, edited by Christoph Levin and Ehud Ben Zvi. FAT 85. Tübingen: Mohr Siebeck, 2012.

Edelman, Diana V., "Possible Rituals Involving the Dead Reflected in Isaiah 65:3–5, 66:3, 17," in *Approaching the Dead: Studies on Mortuary Rituals in the Ancient World*, edited by Anne Katrine de Hemmer Gudme and Kirsi Valkama. Helsinki: Finnish Exegetical Society, 2020.

Edelman, Diana V., Fitzpatrick-McKinley, Anne and Guillaume, Philippe (eds.), *Religion in the Achaemenid Persian Empire: Emerging Judaisms and Other Trends*. ORA 17. Tübingen: Mohr Siebeck, 2016.

Fleishman, Joseph, "The Rebuilding of the Wall of Jerusalem: Neh 2:1–9 and the Use of Zoroastrian Principles," *Journal of Northwest Semitic Languages* 34.2 (2008): 59–82.

Foroutan, Kiyan, "References to Zoroastrian Beliefs and Principles or an Image of the Achaemenid Court in Nehemiah 2:1–10?," pages 403–18 in *Political Memory in and After the Persian Empire*, edited by Jason M. Silverman and Caroline Waerzeggers. ANEM 13. Atlanta. GA: SBL, 2015.

Fried, Lisbeth S., "150 Men at Nehemiah's Table? The Role of the Governor's Meals in the Achaemenid Provincial Economy." *Journal of Biblical Literature* 137.4 (2018): 821–31. https://doi.org/10.15699/jbl.1374.2018.200652.

Fried, Lisbeth S., "Sukkot as Resistence in the Days of Nehemiah," pages 191–202 in *Samuel, Kings, Chronicles, Ezra-Nehemiah*, edited by Athalya Brenner and Gale A. Yee, 2. Texts@contexts. London: T & T Clark, 2021.

Fried, Lisbeth S., *Nehemiah: Commentary*. Sheffield: Sheffield Phoenix, 2022.

Garcia-Ventura, Agnès, and Verderame, Lorenzo (eds.), *Perspectives on the History of Ancient Near Eastern Studies*. University Park, PA: Penn State Press, 2020.

George, Andrew R., *Babylonian Topographical Texts*. Orientalia Lovaniensia Analecta 40. Leuven: Peeters, 1992.

George, Andrew R., *House Most High: The Temples of Ancient Mesopotamia*. Mesopotamian Civilizations 5. Winona Lake, IN: Eisenbrauns, 1993.

Gershevitch, Ilya, *The Avestan Hymn to Mithra: Introduction, Translation, and Commentary*. Oriental Publications 4. Cambridge: Cambridge University Press, 1959.

Gorski, Philip S., "Bourdieusian Theory and Historical Analysis: Maps, Mechanisms, and Methods," pages 327–66 in *Bourdieu and Historical Analysis*, edited by Philip S. Gorski. Durham, NC: Duke University Press, 2013.

Gudme, Anne Katrine de Hemmer, "Out of Sight, Out of Mind? Dedicatory Inscriptions as Communication with the Divine," pages 1–15 in *Mediating between Heaven and Earth: Communication with the Divine in the Ancient Near East*, edited by C. L. Crouch, Jonathan Stökl, and Anna Elise Zernecke. LHBOTS 566. London: T & T Clark, 2012.

Gudme, Anne Katrine de Hemmer, *Before the God in This Place for Good Remembrance: A Comparative Analysis of the Aramaic Votive Inscriptions from Mount Gerizim*. BZAW 441. Berlin: De Gruyter, 2013.

Gudme, Anne Katrine de Hemmer, "Guests, Like Fish, Begin to Smell after Three Days: How to Be a 'Good Guest' in the Hebrew Bible." SBL Annual Meeting, Denver, 2022.

Hadas, Miklós, *Outlines of a Theory of Plural Habitus: Bourdieu Revisited*. Routledge Studies in Social and Political Thought 11. London: Routledge, 2022.

Heeßel, Nils P., "Diagnosis, Divination and Disease: Towards an Understanding of the Rationale behind the Babylonian Diagnostic Handbook," pages 97–116 in *Magic and Rationality in Ancient Near Eastern and Graeco-Roman Medicine*. Edited by H. J. F. Hortstmanshoff and Marten Stol. Studies in Ancient Medicine 27. Leiden: Brill, 2004.

Henkelman, Wouter F. M., "An Elamite Memorial: The Šumar of Cambyses and Hystaspes," pages 101–72 in *A Persian Perspective: Essays in Memory of Heleen Sancisi-Weerdenburg*, edited by Wouter Henkelman and Amélie Kuhrt. Achaemenid History XIII. Leiden: Nederlands Institute voor het Nabije Oosten, 2003.

Henkelman, Wouter F. M., "'Consumed before the King': The Table of Darius, That of Irdabama and Irtaštuna, and That of His Satrap, Karkiš," pages 667–776 in *Der Achämenidenhof/The Achaemenid Court*, edited by Bruno Jacobs and Robert Rollinger. Classica et Orientalia 2. Wiesbaden: Harrassowitz, 2010.

Henkelman, Wouter F. M., "Parnakka's Feast: *Šip* in Pārsa and Elam," pages 89–166 in *Elam and Persia*, edited by Javier Álvarez-Mon and Mark B. Garrison. Winona Lake, IN: Eisenbrauns, 2011.

Henkelman, Wouter F. M., "Humban & Auramazdā: Royal Gods in a Persian Landscape," pages 273–346 in *Persian Religion in the Achaemenid Period*, edited by Wouter F. M. Henkelman and Céline Redard. CLeO 16. Wiesbaden: Harrassowitz, 2017.

Henkelman, Wouter F. M., "Practice of Worship in the Achaemenid Heartland," pages 1243–70 in *Companion to the Achaemenid Persian Empire*, edited by Bruno Jacobs and Robert Rollinger. Blackwell Companions to the Ancient World. Hoboken, NJ: John Wiley & Sons, 2021.

Henkelman, Wouter, and Redard, Celine (eds.), *Persian Religion in the Achaemenid Period*. CLeO 16. Wiesbaden: Harrassowitz, 2017.

Hyland, John O., "Persia's Lycian Work Force and the Satrap of Sardis." *ARTA* 2022.002 (2022): 1–20.

Iannaccone, Laurence R., "Religious Practice: A Human Capital Approach," *Journal for the Scientific Study of Religion* 29.3 (1990): 297–314.

Jong, Albert de, *Traditions of the Magi: Zoroastrianism in Greek and Latin Literature*. Religions in the Greco-Roman World 133. Leiden: Brill, 1997.

Jong, Albert de., "The Religion of the Achaemenid Rulers," pages 1199–1209 in *A Companion to the Achaemenid Persian Empire*, edited by Bruno Jacobs and Robert Rollinger, 2. Blackwell Companions to the Ancient World. Hoboken, NJ: John Wiley & Sons, 2021.

Katchadourian, Lori, *Imperial Matter: Ancient Persia and the Archaeology of Empires*. Oakland, CA: University of California Press, 2016. https://doi.org/10.1525/luminos.13.

Koch, Ulla S., *Mesopotamian Divination Texts: Conversing with the Gods: Sources from the First Millennium BCE*. Guides to the Mesopotamian Textual Record 7. Münster: Ugarit-Verlag, 2015.

Krul, Julia, *The Revival of the Anu Cult and the Nocturnal Fire Ceremony at Late Babylonian Uruk*. CHANE 95. Leiden: Brill, 2018.

Laird, Donna, *Negotiating Power in Ezra-Nehemiah*. Ancient Israel and Its Literature 26. Atlanta. GA: SBL, 2016.

MacDonald, Nathan, *Not Bread Alone: The Uses of Food in the Old Testament*. Oxford: Oxford University Press, 2008.

McCauley, Robert N., and Lawson, E. Thomas, *Bringing Ritual to Mind: Psychological Foundations of Cultural Forms*. Cambridge: Cambridge University Press, 2002.

McGeough, Kevin M., *The Ancient Near East in the Nineteenth Century*. 3 vols. Hebrew Bible Monographs 67–69. Sheffield: Sheffield Phoenix, 2015.

McKinnon, Andrew, Trzebiatowska, Marta, and Brittain, Christopher, "Bourdieu, Capital, and Conflict in a Religious Field: The Case of the 'Homosexuality' Conflict in the Anglican Communion." *Journal of Contemporary Religion* 26.3 (2011): 355–70. https://doi-org/10.1080/13537903.2011.616033.

Miller, Margaret C., "Luxury Toreutic in the Western Satrapies: Court-Inspired Gift-Exchange Diffusion," pages 853–97 in *Der Achämenidenhof/The Achaemenid Court*, edited by Bruno Jacobs and Robert Rollinger. Wiesbaden: Harrassowitz, 2010.

O'Connor, Kaori, *The Never-Ending Feast: The Anthropology and Archaeology of Feasting*. London: Bloomsbury Academic, 2015.

Panaino, Antonio, "Philologica Avestica IV. Av. Yaštay-/Yešti-; Yašta-; Phl. Yašt," *Studia Iranica* 23 .2 (1994): 163–85. https://doi.org/10.2143/si.23. 2. 2014302.

Porter, Anne, "The Dynamics of Death: Ancestors, Pastoralism, and the Origins of a Third-Millennium City in Syria." *Bulletin of the American Schools of Oriental Research* 325 (2002): 1–36.

Pyssiäinen, Ilkka, *Supernatural Agents: Why We Believe in Souls, Gods, and Buddhas*. Oxford: Oxford University Press, 2009.

Rey, Terry, "Pierre Bourdieu and the Study of Religion: Recent Developments, Directions, and Departures," pages 299–326 in *The Oxford Handbook of Pierre Bourdieu*, edited by Thomas Medvetz and Jeffrey J. Sallaz. Oxford: Oxford University Press, 2018.

Rubenstein, Jeffrey L., *The History of Sukkot in the Second Temple and Rabbinic Periods*. Open Access edition [2020]. Brown Judaic Studies 302. Atlanta, GA: Scholars Press, 1995.

Sharpe, Eric J., *Comparative Religion: A History*. 2nd ed. London: Duckworth, 2003.

Silverman, Jason M. "Achaemenid Creation and Second Isaiah." *Journal of Persianate Studies* 10.1 (2017): 26–48.

Silverman, Jason M. "Vetting the Priest in Zech 3: The Satan between Divine and Achaemenid Administrations," *Journal of Hebrew Scriptures* 14 (2014): 1–27, <http://www.jhsonline.org/Articles/article_200.pdf>.

Silverman, Jason M., "From Remembering to Expecting the 'Messiah': Achaemenid Kingship as (Re)Formulating Apocalyptic Expectations of David," pages 419–46 in *Political Memory in and after the Persian Empire*, edited by Jason M. Silverman and Caroline Waerzeggers. ANEM 13. Atlanta. GA: SBL, 2015.

Silverman, Jason M., "Was There an Achaemenid 'Theology' of Kingship?," pages 160–85 in *Religion in the Persian Period: Emerging Trends Judaisms and Other Trends*, edited by Diana V. Edelman, Anne Fitzpatrick-McKinley, and Philippe Guillaume. OLA. Tübingen: Mohr Siebeck, 2016.

Silverman, Jason M., “Are the Concepts of ‘Torah’ and ‘the Prophets’ Texts or Something Else? Educational, Media, and Elite Contexts from the Persian Empire Onwards,” pages 3–32 in *Scriptures in the Making: Texts and Their Transmission in Late Second Temple Judaism*, edited by Raimo Hakola, Jesse Orpana, and Paavo Huotari. Leuven: Peeters, 2022.

Silverman, Jason M., “Persian Religion in the Hebrew Bible,” in *The Zoroastrian World*, edited by Jenny Rose, Albert de Jong, and Sarah Stewart. London: Routledge, forthcoming.

Silverman, Jason M., “Cultural and Religious Influence in the Ancient Near East: Re-Conceptualization and New Methodologies,” in *Bloomsbury Handbook on Ancient Near Eastern Religions*, edited by Shana Zaia, Gina Konstantopoulos, and Helen Dixon. London: Bloomsbury Academic, forthcoming.

Silverman, Jason M. *Persian Royal–Judaean Elite Engagements in the Early Teispid and Achaemenid Empire: The King’s Acolytes*. LHBOTS 690. London: T & T Clark, 2019.

Silverman, Jason M., Alex Aissaoui, Rotem Avneri Meir, Jutta Jokiranta, Nina Nikki, Adrianne Spunaugle, Joanna Töyräänvuori, Caroline Wallis, and Melanie Wasmuth. “Social Biography from the Ancient World: Studying ’Ahatabu, Jonathan, and Babatha through Bourdieu,” forthcoming.

Silverman, Jason M., Joanna Töyräänvuori, and Melanie Wasmuth, “’Ahatabu and Her Stela (ÄM 7707): Mortuary Habitus in Achaemenid Egypt,” forthcoming.

Smith, Yda J., “We All Bantu – We Have Each Other: Preservation of Social Capital Strengths during Forced Migration.” *Journal of Occupational Science* 20 (2013): 173–84.

Sonia, Kerry M., *Caring for the Dead in Ancient Israel*. Atlanta, GA: SBL, 2020.

Spiro, Melford E., “Religion: Problems of Definition and Explanation,” pages 85–126 in *Anthropological Approaches to the Study of Religion*, edited by Michael Banton. London: Routledge, 2004 [1966].

Stark, Rodney and Finke, Roger, *Acts of Faith: Explaining the Human Side of Religion*. Berkeley, CA: University of California Press, 2000.

Urban, Hugh B., “Sacred Capital: Pierre Bourdieu and the Study of Religion.” *Method and Theory in the Study of Religion* 15.4 (2003): 354–89.

Veblen, Thorstein, *Conspicuous Consumption*. Penguin Classics. London: Penguin, 1899, 2005.

Verter, Bradford, “Spiritual Capital: Theorizing Religion with Bourdieu against Bourdieu.” *Sociological Theory* 21.2 (2003): 150–74. https://doi.org/10.1111/1467-9558.00182.

Waerzeggers, Caroline, “The Pious King: Royal Patronage of Temples in the Neo-Babylonian Period,” pages 725–51 in *Oxford Handbook of Cuneiform Cultures*, edited by Karen Radner and Elenor Robson. Oxford: Oxford University Press, 2011.

Weyde, Karl W., *The Appointed Festivals of YHWH: The Festival Calendar in Leviticus 23 and the Sukkot Festival in Other Biblical Texts*. FAT 2.4. Tübingen: Mohr Siebeck, 2004.

Weyde, Karl W., “And They Found It Written in the Law: Exegetical Procedures Reflected in Nehemiah 8:13–18.” In *Shai Le-Sara Japhet: Studies in the Bible, Its Exegesis and Its Language*, edited by Moshe Bar-Asher, 143*-164*. Jerusalem: Bialik Institute, 2007.

Whitters, Mark, “The Persianized Liturgy of Nehemiah 8:1–8.” *Journal of Biblical Literature* 136.1 (2017): 63–84.

Karel van der Toorn

Persian Imperialism and the Religious Imagination

This book on Yahwism under the Achaemenid Empire is part of a trend. An increasing number of contemporary scholars look at the Persian period as the time when the Hebrew Bible and early Judaism were beginning to take shape. It was a formative era. Perhaps future generations of scholars will look back to us and say we overrated its significance. How about crucial developments in the monarchic era; the revolutionary experience of the diaspora; and the cultural impact of Hellenism? Trends follow fashion. But also if one takes into account the contributions of earlier and later periods, there is no denying the fact that exposure to Persian imperialism left profound traces in the religious practices and concepts of Judeans in Judah and the diaspora. This contribution focuses on the impact of Persian imperialism rather than Persian religion. Though entangled, the two are to be distinguished. I shall look at several elements in the collective religious imagination that can be traced back to the historical experience of Persian imperialism. The two areas where Persian influence is most tangible are (1) the conceptions of God and the heavenly court; and (2) the transformation of torah into *dāt*, "law." Because in both areas Judean religion responded to the impact of Persia, the Achaemenid Empire left an imprint that still resonates today.

God and the Heavenly Court

For "the sons of the Golah" – the self-designation of the Judean returnees – the migration from Babylon to Jerusalem took place in the wake of the transition from Babylonian to Persian supremacy. The change of rule threw a large shadow. Like many peoples in the ancient world, the Judeans were in awe of the Persians – the efficiency of their military machine, their smooth communications network, the rumored fast of their palaces, and the secrets of their sumptuous court life. It did not mean they hastened to adopt Persian culture. Though some aspects of Israelite religion in its later stages seem to echo certain Zoroastrian notions, the Persian influence was in general more subtle – though not, for that

Karel van der Toorn, University of Amsterdam, The Netherlands

https://doi.org/10.1515/9783111018638-018

reason, any less pervasive.[1] The presence of Persian loanwords, in Hebrew and Aramaic, bears witness to the impact of the new masters. Some of those terms – like *rāz*, "secret," *pardēs*, "park, paradise," *dāt*, "law" – would play a considerable role in later Jewish writings.[2] Under the Persians, the world had entered a new era.

The Judean experience of the Persian hegemony left a mark on the collective religious imagination too. It was to be expected. People have always borrowed their religious metaphors from the world they are familiar with, looking to asymmetric and hierarchical relationships as models of their position vis-à-vis the gods. That is why, in the time of the monarchy, the Israelites thought of God as their king, and themselves as his subjects. During the Persian era, God came to be modelled after the Persian emperor, and the heavenly court came to resemble a Persian palace. One unmistakable indication of the Persian influence upon the new religious speculations is the notion of the seven "angels of the presence." Though found foremost in texts from the Hellenistic period, the Persian background of the idea is not in doubt. The topic merits a demonstration since it throws an intriguing light on some of the major transformations of the way in which the Israelites – Judeans *and* Samarians – thought about God and the world of the gods. So let us take a closer look at the emergence of these seven angels.

In most English Bibles, the book of Tobit has a place in the section of the Apocrypha. Written around 250 BCE, the book tells the story of Tobias son of Tobit, and his journey from Nineveh to Ecbatana, where he ends up marrying his cousin Sarah. Tobias has a traveling companion who eventually reveals his true identity. "I am Raphael, one of the seven angels who stand ready and enter before the glory of the Lord" (Tob 12:15). The theme of the seven angels who have privileged access to God originated in the Persian era. An early occurrence is in the Book of Heavenly Luminaries (1 En. 72–82), also known as the Enochic Astronomical Book. Most scholars hold that this section is the oldest stratum of the Enoch literature and stems from the Persian period.[3] After his tour of heaven, Enoch returns to earth. "Then the seven holy ones brought me and placed me on the ground in front of the gate of my house ..." (1 En. 81:5). These seven "holy

---

1 For the influence of Persian religion on Israelite religion in the Persian and Hellenistic periods, see Boyce, "Persian Religion"; Shaked, "Iranian Influence." Many instances of claimed influence (dualism, predestination, final judgment, etc.) are only compelling in part, some similarities being too general. One indubitable instance of religious borrowing is the demon Asmodeus in the book of Tobit, whose name is only plausibly explained through reference to Aešma-daeva, "wrath demon," see Shaked, "Iranian Influence," 318.

2 On Persian loanwords in Hebrew, see Wilson-Wright, "From Persepolis to Jerusalem."

3 Nickelsburg, "Enoch," 2.508–516, esp. 509, with reference to Black, *Books of Enoch*, 387.

ones" are the seven angels.[4] They are still there in the book of Revelation. "When the Lamb opened the seventh seal, there was silence in heaven for about half an hour. And I saw the seven angels who stand before God, and seven trumpets were given to them" (Rev 8:1–2).

Both the figure of the seven archangels (1 En. 20, in the Greek text from Akhmim; 1 En. 90:21; T. Levi 8:2) and their designation as "angels of the presence" (Jub. 1:27, 29; 2:1, 18; 15:27) go back to the organization of the Persian court. All major political decisions were taken by the king in consultation with his inner circle, consisting of "seven counselors" or "officials." An early reference to this political body occurs in the Artaxerxes edict concerning the mission of Ezra. "You are commissioned by the king and his seven counselors" (*šibᶜat yāᶜăṭōhî*, Ezra 7:14). The book of Esther mentions these men by name and explains that they were "the seven officials (**śarîm*) of Persia and Media, who had access to the king (*rōᵓê pĕnê hammelek*), and sat first in the kingdom" (Esth 1:14, NRSV). Xenophon refers to these men as "seven of the noblest Persians" (*Anab.* 1.6.4), and Herodotus offers an historical explanation why they had free and unannounced access to the king (*Hist.* 3.84, 118). Though the historical relationship between the Persian king and his counselors will have varied over time – the number seven may have included the king himself, and their specific office is uncertain – it is clear that in the popular perception, as reflected in the writings of Greek and Judean authors, the Persian monarch had seven advisors with privileged access.[5]

It is hardly surprising to find that Judean intellectuals came to imagine the heavenly court on the model of the Persian court – as they understood it. When Yehud was under Persian rule, no one wielded more political power than the Persian emperor. He was "the king of kings," as the phrase of the period had it.[6] Little wonder that Judeans began to think of their god in similar terms. Since the introduction of the monarchy in Israel and Judah, YHWH had been given the title King – king of the gods and king of Israel. From the Persian era onward, however, YHWH became the king of kings. He was the cosmic Emperor. Next to him all other gods lost their glory. Though the Elephantine Papyri show that Jewish communities long continued to venerate divine companions of Yaho, the Persian period also witnessed the gradual demotion of other gods to the rank of angels. Up to a point it was a matter of semantics. The Sons of El who once constituted the council of the gods became the council of the holy ones – the latter now a term

---

4 The term also occurs in Job 5:1, "To which of the holy ones will you turn?," here too in reference to mediating angels.

5 For a discussion of the college of seven counselors, see Briant, *From Cyrus to Alexander*, 128–130.

6 See Williamson, *Ezra-Nehemiah*, 100.

for angels.[7] But in the mind of the worshippers, the difference between gods and angels was real. There was only one true God. It made the Judeans monotheists, also in the eyes of their contemporaries.[8] Angels were not gods but beings of a lower rank and a different nature. From colleagues and peers, the other gods turned into God's servants. They ran his errands and did his every bidding. Though every class of angels had its own role to perform, all of them were links in the chain that ultimately connected the individual to God.

One of the consequences of the mediated access to God was a new conception of the communication with the deity. The older notion according to which one could say a prayer on the assumption that one's voice would come to God – the view that informs many of the individual prayers in the book of Psalms – gave way to a different metaphor. The new metaphor was based on the analogy with the Persian postal system, with letter bearers and couriers, much admired by the Greek authors.[9] The book of Tobit offers an illustration. Prior to the journey of Tobias, both Tobit and Sarah, separately but at the same time, the one in Nineveh and the other in Ecbatana, say a prayer. "At that very moment, the prayers of both of them were heard in the glorious presence of God" (Tob 3:17, NRSV). This looks like the old conception. But another passage in the same book shows otherwise. "So now when you (i.e., Tobit) and Sarah prayed, it was I (i.e., the angel Raphael) who brought and read the record of your prayer before the glory of the Lord [...]." (Tob 12:12). The speed of transmission remains miraculous, but the mechanics are new. Angels make a record of the spoken prayer and transmit the message to the inner circle of God, where it is read aloud in his glorious presence. This is how petitions supposedly reached the Persian emperor.

Ideally, communication is a two-way street. In the new conception, God's messages to humankind were mediated by angels too. So too for the Torah – or the Law, as many people came to see it. Whereas the older stories had God give or dictate the commandments to Moses, the new conception holds that the Law was brought down from heaven by angels. Josephus compares these angels to heralds. "[T]he Greeks have declared heralds (*kērux*) to be sacred (*hieros*) and inviolable (*asylos*), and we have learned the noblest of our doctrines and the holiest of our laws through angels (*angeloi*) from God" (Josephus, *Ant.* 15.136; cf. Acts 7:53; Gal 3:19; Heb 2:2). It was like an edict by the Persian emperor, communicated to the most distant corners of the realm by messengers. In the religious

7 See Mullen, *The Assembly of the Gods*, 113–280; Parker, "Saints"; Collins, "Saints of the Most High," 720–722.

8 Hecaraeus of Abdera, writing around 300 BCE, praises the Jews for the sacrifices they are willing to make to hold on to the monotheism of their Law, see Josephus, *C. Ap.* 1.190–193.

9 See Briant, *From Cyrus to Alexander*, 369–371.

imagination, the horizontal separation between the emperor and his subjects was reconfigured along a vertical axis. In both cases, the distance could only be bridged through mediation – "passed on by angels, to the hand of a mediator" (*diatageis di' angelōn en cheiri mesitou*), as the apostle Paul says (Gal 3:19).

From Hebrew *tôrâ* to Persian *dāt*

Ezra was "an expert scribe in the *tôrâ* of Moses," as the Hebrew text puts it (Ezra 7:6). In the Artaxerxes edict, on the other hand, Ezra is qualified as "a scribe of the *dāt* of the God of heaven" (*sāpar dātāʾ dî ʾĕlāh šĕmayyāʾ*, 7:12, 21). On the face of it, *dāt* is simply the Aramaic translation of Hebrew *tôrâ*. But we know there is no such thing as simple translation. Every translation gives a particular twist to the meaning of the original. There is all the more reason to be alert to a possible shift in meaning because the Aramaic term *dāt* is a direct loan from Old Persian *dāta*. The same loan took place in Neo-Babylonian (*dātu*). Apparently, then, Persian *dāta* had a meaning that differed – perhaps just a matter of nuance – from its equivalents in Aramaic and Akkadian.

The literal meaning of *tôrâ* is "instruction." It occurs both in the singular (so mostly) and in the plural (e.g., "all the instructions" concerning the temple, in Ezek 44:5). Such instructions or teachings came from parents (Prov 31:26), the sage (Prov 13:14), and the priest (Deut 33:10). It was, originally, an oral genre (Prov 28:9). People came to "seek torah from [the] mouth" of the priest (Mal 2:7; see also Mal 2:6; Hag 2:11–13).[10] The earliest reference to *written* torah is in Hosea 8:12, where God is introduced as saying that "even if I wrote more copies of my Torah, they would be considered as though they were from an alien."[11] The passage does not refer to "the book of the Torah," as we know it from Deuteronomy and the Deuteronomistic presentation of Josiah's reform but, as circumstantial evidence suggests, to the temple entry torah.[12] The entry *tôrôt* were a reminder of prohibited behavior that would bar one from participation in the cult. They formed the nucleus of the Ten Commandments. The Book of the Torah was the invention of a later period. What period exactly? Scholars have long thought the "book" of the Torah was a notion from the time of King Josiah, and the *sēper hattôrâ* was actually "a product of his time and probably also of his own chancellery."[13] But was it really? Perhaps the attempt at cult centralization was, and

10 See Liedke and Petersen, "*tôrâ* Weisung," 2.1032–1043, esp. 1033–1034.
11 On the antiquity of the passage, see Wolff, *Dodekapropheton 1*, 186.
12 See van der Toorn, "Before the Decalogue."
13 Quotation from Ahlström, *Royal Administration*, 73.

especially the destruction of the Bethel temple. But the different literary frames of the book of Deuteronomy suggest that the "Torah edition" of the work is exilic at the earliest.[14] That brings us close to the Persian period.

Perhaps we should go one step further and posit that the transformation of Torah into a law code is due to the Persian concept of *dāta*, "law." The discussion about the meaning of *dāta* has very much focused on the Babylonian loan *dātu*, and more especially on the expression *dātu ša šarri*, "royal dāt." It makes sense, because the Babylonian texts from the Achaemenid period allow us to grasp the legal innovations brought about by the regime change. All the relevant texts have been collected and discussed by Kristin Kleber.[15] She shows that it is not correct to say that *dātu ša šarri* is by definition an edict rather than a law, as though it were always an ad hoc legal decision ("Einzelfallgerechtigkeit"). Perhaps the most revealing passage on *dātu ša šarri* occurs in a record of a legal decision by the simmagir-official and his colleagues the judges.[16] The case concerns the illegal appropriation of a slave girl by a man who claims she is his sister. During an interrogation (*maš'altu*) he admits he lied, and he loses the case. Follows the verdict:

> *simmāgir u dayyānū kinātšu dāti iptû'i*
> *ultu dāti* [*erbi*]*ta amēlūtu ina muḫḫi* PN [*par*]⌈*saniššu*⌉
>
> The simmagir and his colleagues the judges opened the dātu.
> On the basis of the dātu they imposed on PN (a penalty of) four slaves.

Fourfold restitution of stolen property occurs more often in Persian law, but that is not the issue. What matters here is the reference to the "opening" of the dātu, and the fact that the penalty is "based on the dātu." As one of the editors of the text comments, "[t]hus we may postulate the existence of a royal 'rule book' for regulating different cases of disputes over the status of slaves."[17] Or, in the words of Kristin Kleber, the *dātu* here refers to a "compendium" that was "consulted" to determine the correct penalty.[18] Other texts are only slightly less explicit. In various disputes about a "deposit" or "deposited goods" (the Babylonian term is *paqdu*) – here a legal fiction that allows a promissory note to serve as payment instead of cash – it is said that the judges settled the matter "according to the

---

14 See van der Toorn, *Scribal Culture*, 155–160.
15 Kleber, "*Dātu ša šarri.*"
16 The text is from the 25th year of Darius I, i.e., 497 BCE. For the first publication see Jursa, Paszkowiak, and Waerzeggers, "Three Court Records," 255–268, esp. 255–259.
17 Jursa, Paszkowiak, and Waerzeggers "Three Court Records," 259 [comment by Michael Jursa].
18 Kleber, "Dātu ša šarri," 53.

dātu of the king, that has been written about deposits" (*libbu dātu ša šarri ša ina muḫḫi paqdu šaṭri*).[19]

The evidence just passed in review shows that the *dātu* (or the *dātu ša šarri*) refers to a written compendium containing royal decisions. Those are, moreover, unalterable.[20] The judges have to open the book and consult it to reach a verdict. This concept of law (*dāt*) differs fundamentally both from Hebrew *tôrâ*, "instruction, teaching," and Akkadian *dīnātu*, "verdicts," the term used in the Laws of Hammurabi.[21] Prior to Ezra there is no instance in the Hebrew Bible where people consult the written Torah to establish the proper measures to be taken. After Ezra, however, the situation changes. People study the words of the written Torah, and apply them to the letter (Ezra 10:3; Neh 8:13–18). It bears stressing that in Mesopotamia, too, the various law collections did not serve as legal codes to be consulted and applied in each and every case.[22] The purpose of the royal law collections – edicts are a different matter – was to demonstrate the wisdom of the king and to hone the skills of judges. They were a reference for scribes and legal scholars, but more as exemplary cases than as prescriptions.[23] They were not law codes in the Roman sense of the term. Nor in the Persian sense of the term, we must now add, for Persian *dāta* – Aramaic *dāt* and Akkadian *dātu* – does refer to a legal code, i.e. a compendium of unalterable written rules judges are to consult and to apply.

In the older literature on biblical law, it is not unusual to read that "law" is a mistranslation of *tôrâ* to be blamed on the latter's equation with Greek *nomos*.[24] This judgment contains two errors. The first is a misrecognition of the fact that the *nomos* of the Septuagint had a precedent in the Persian interpretation of the Torah as *dāt*, as evidenced in Artaxerxes's decree about Ezra's mission. The second one concerns the notion of a "mistranslation." It is true, of course, that Torah originally meant "instruction, teaching," which is something different than law. In the Persian period, however, the Torah did in fact become a kind of law code,

---

19 Stolper, *Late Achaemenid*, 28–33, BM 41454:9–10. The text is dated in 218 BCE. On *paqdu*, see *CAD* 12, 137 s. v. *paqdu* B.

20 On the immutability of the *dāt*, see the biblical reference to "the law (*dāt*) of the Medes and the Persians, which cannot be revoked" (Dan 6:9[8]). On the absolute authority of *dāta*, see also Tuplin, "The Justice of Darius," 73–126, esp. 86.

21 The epilogue of the Laws of Hammurabi refers to the preceding articles as "the equitable decisions (*dīnāt mīšarim*) which Hammurabi, the able king, has established" (LH xlvii 1–5), see Roth, *Law Collections*, 133. See also the subscript in a Standard Babylonian copy of LH, quoted in *CAD* 3, 153 s. v. *dīnu* 2, *dīnāni ša Ḫammurabi*, "verdicts by Hammurabi."

22 For a classic statement of this view, see Kraus, "Ein zentrales Problem."

23 For a discussion of these issues, see Charpin, "Le statut," 93–108.

24 See, e.g., Sandmel, *The Genius of Paul*, 46–47.

and was so understood by the leadership of the province Yehud (and by much of later Jewry). To call that development a misunderstanding is a theological judgment. Looked at it from a – hopefully – less biased perspective we can simply say that the new understanding of Torah – as *dāt* – inaugurated a new phase of Judean religion, and one that would prove to be extraordinarily fruitful.

Bibliography

Ahlström, Gösta W., *Royal Administration and National Religion in Ancient Palestine*, SHANE 1, Leiden: Brill, 1982.

Black, Matthew, *The Books of Enoch or 1 Enoch: A New English Edition with Commentary and Textual Notes* (SVTP 7; Leiden: Brill, 1985).

Boyce, Mary, "Persian Religion in the Achaemenid Age," pages 279–307 in *Cambridge Hististory of Judaism*, 1, W. Davies and L. Finkelstein (eds.), Cambridge: Cambridge University Press, 1984.

Briant, Pierre, *From Cyrus to Alexander: A History of the Persian Empire* (trans. Peter T. Daniels; Winona Lake, IN: Eisenbrauns, 2002).

Charpin, Dominique, "Le statut des 'codes des lois' des souverains babyloniens," *Le législateur et la loi dans l'Antiquité: Hommage à Françoise Ruzé*, edited by P. Sineux; Caen: Presses Universitaires de Caen, 2005, 93–108.

Collins, John J., "Saints of the Most High," pages 720–722 in in *Dictionary of Deities and Demons in the Bible*. Toorn, Karel van der, Becking, Bob, and Horst, Pieter Willem van der (eds.), Leiden: Brill, 1999.

Jursa, Michael, Paszkowiak, Joanna, and Waerzeggers, Caroline, "Three Court Records," *Archiv für Orientforschung* 50 (2003–2004): 255–268.

Kleber, Kristin, "*Dātu ša šarri*: Gesetzgebung in Babylonien unter den Achämeniden," *Zeitschrift für altorientalische und biblische Rechtsgeschichte* 16 (2010): 49–75.

Kraus, Fritz R., "Ein zentrales Problem des altmesopotamischen Rechtes: Was ist der Kodex Hammu-rabi?," *Genava* 8 (1960): 283–296.

Liedke, Gerhard and Petersen C., "*tôrâ* Weisung," *Theologisches Handwörterbuch zum Alten Testamenti*, Ernst Jenni, Claus Westermann (eds.), vol. 2, München: Chr. Kaiser Verlag, 1032–1043.

Mullen, E. Theodore Jr., *The Assembly of the Gods: The Divine Council in Canaanite and Early Hebrew Literature* (HSM 24; Chica, CA: Scholars Press, 1980).

Nickelsburg George W. E., "Enoch, first book of," *ABD* 2.

Parker, Simon B. "Saints," pages 718–720 in *Dictionary of Deities and Demons in the Bible*. Toorn, Karel van der, Becking, Bob, and Horst, Pieter Willem van der (eds.), Leiden: Brill, 1999.

Roth, Martha, *Law Collections from Mesopotamia and Asia Minor*, SBLWAW 6; Atlanta: Scholars Press, 1995.

Sandmel, Samuel, *The Genius of Paul*, New York: Farrar, Strauss, and Cudahy, 1958.

Shaked, Shaul, "Iranian Influence on Judaism: First Century B.C.E. to Second Century C.E.," pages 308–325 in *Cambridge Hististory of Judaism*, 1, W. Davies and L. Finkelstein (eds.), Cambridge: Cambridge University Press, 1984.

Stolper, Matthew W., *Late Achaemenid, Early Macedonian, and Early Seleucid Records of Deposit and Related Texts*, AION 53/4, Supplement 77; Napels: Istituto Universitario Orientale, 1993.

Tuplin, Christoph J., "The Justice of Darius: Reflections on the Achaemenid Empire as a rule-based environment," pages 73–126 in *Assessing Biblical and Classical Sources for the Reconstruction of Persian Influence, History and Culture*, Classica et Orientalia 10; ed. Anne Fitzpatrick-McKinley; Wiesbaden: Harrassowitz, 2015.

Van der Toorn, Karel, "Before the Decalogue: In Search of the Oldest Written Torah," *Catholic biblical quarterly* 85 (2023): 385–401.

Van der Toorn, Karel. *Scribal Culture and the Making of the Hebrew Bible*, Cambridge: Harvard University Press, 2007.

Williamson, H. G. M., *Ezra-Nehemiah* (WBC 16. Grand Rapids, MI: Zondervan, 1985).

Wilson-Wright, Aren, "From Persepolis to Jerusalem: A Reevaluation of Old Persian-Hebrew Contact in the Achaemenid Period," *VT* 65 (2015): 152–167.

Wolff, Hans Walter, *Dodekapropheton 1: Hosea* (BKAT 14/1; 2nd ed.; Neukirchen-Vluyn: Neukirchener Verlag, 1965.

Ran Zadok

Issues Pertaining to the Israelite-Judeans in Pre-Islamic Mesopotamia and the Land of Israel as well as Their Encounters with Iranians

Preamble

The main issue which will be discussed here is the presence of Iranians in the Fertile Crescent and their lengthy encounter with Israelites and Judeans from the Sargonid period in Assyria to as late as the end of the Sasanian period in Babylonia (a period of almost 1400 years). This encounter took place also in Achaemenid Palestine. The Judean-Persian interaction in Achaemenid Babylonia must have had a theological impact on Judaism in this formative and critical age. One has to look for plausible scenarios and loci of Judeo-Iranian encounters. Much later, in Sasanian Babylonia, Jewish practitioner-scribes left a sizable corpus of incantation bowls; many of their clients bore Iranian names, an indication of an intensive interaction between both groups. I hope that this treatise of mine, especially the detailed classification and analysis of the onomasticon of the JBA and to some extent other Aramaic incantation bowls is a worthy tribute to the eminent Iranianist, my teacher Prof. Shaul Shaked. This onomasticon has never been subjected to a systematic study, although many names were individually interpreted.

A The pre-Hellenistic periods

1 The Neo-Assyrian period

The earliest encounter of Israelites with inhabitants of the Iranian Plateau was during their deportation to the “cities of Media”, which are identifed with the Assyrian satrapies of Media, namely Harhar, Kishesi(m) and Parsua. However, concrete information about Israelites in Media is lacking: the attempt of Galil

Note: Symbols: ° follows a letter with an uncertain reading. ↑↓ = see above and below respectively. I should like to thank Professors M. Morgenstern and M. Moriggi for sending me the book of Faraj 2010 which is not available in Israel.

Ran Zadok, Tel Aviv University, Israel

https://doi.org/10.1515/9783111018638-019

(2009) to locate two Israelite exiles in the town of Sagbat (in Kišesim) sometime between 732 and 727 BCE was refuted by me.[1] Moreover, Radner[2] observes that the settlement of the deportees in Media probably did not predate 713 BCE,[3] very probably not before 716 BCE.

Non-Indo-Iranian groups and individuals from the Iranian Plateau, viz. Kassites, Harhareans and Elamites, were deported to Assyria[4] as well as Medes who bore Iranian names. The following 23 individuals who were either explicitly Medes or bore Iranian names lived in Upper Mesopotamia between *c.* 810 and 618 BCE:[5]

1. *Ur-ru-da* (perhaps OIran. **Hu-rauda-* "of beautiful appearance") was a dependent head of a family who was granted to an eunuch by Adad-nerarī III (810–783 BCE).[6]

2. *Ú-ar-gi* (OIran. **Hu-arga-*)[7] was perhaps a military official. He is mentioned in a damaged letter concerning hostilities (probably from the time of Tiglath-pileser III). The arena and his domicile are not specified.[8]

3–4. *Bar-zi-i* (OIran.**Bṛziya-*)[9] refers to witnesses from Calah (738 BCE) and Imgur-Illil (734 BCE). Mādāyu (*Mad*-A+A, gentilic > PN) "Mede" was borne by at least four (maximum six) individuals (provided the reading of the polyvalent sign KUR is in all occurrences *mad*):[10]

5. Witnesses from Calah, 738 BCE (listed together with *Bar-zi-i*);

6. Lent silver and copper (with a field as pledge) and also acted as a witness (his title is not preserved), Calah, 717–710 BCE.

7. Recipient of a royal letter (found in Calah), in the reign of Tiglath-pileser III or Sargon II. He is presumably identical with his namesake who was a royal intimate (ša-qurbūti) and an official recorded in a list of offerings from the same time.

---

1 See Zadok, "Israelites and Judeans," 164.

2 Zadok, "Onomastics as a Historical Source," 106–111.

3 For information about exiles there cf. Zehnder, *Umgang mit Fremden*, 186, 194, 217, 224, 226, 246, 263–264 (Israelites are not mentioned).

4 See Zadok, "Onomastics as a Historical Source," 481–482.

5 I do not include here *Mar-tú-'* (PNA 2: 742b) since, in my opinion, the spelling with - *tú-'* is incompatible with the Iranian etymology **Marta-* suggested by Schmitt (*Iranische Personennamen*, 109:89). It can be read *Mar-lih-'*, in which case it would be an Aramaic name (cf. *Mar-li-hi-ia*/*Ma-ri-li-hi*, PNA 2: 740–741).

6 See PNA 3: 1418a. *Ú-ma-nu*, who is recorded in Gozan in the same reign bore a name which – on the face of it – is explicable in Elamite or Iranian terms (see PNA 3: 1378), but this is uncertain.

7 See Zadok "Review of Hinz 1975," 214b and Schmitt, *Iranische Personennamen*, 163:148.

8 See PNA 3:1354–1355.

9 See Zadok, "Five Iranian Names," 388b and Schmitt, *Iranische Personennamen*, 67:40.

10 See PNA 2: 673–674 (cf. Schmitt, *Iranische Personennamen*, 105–106: 85).

8. *Ku-ta-ki* (OIran.**Kutaka-*),[11] had a house in Assur in 724 BCE.[12]

9. *Pa-ra-'-u* (OIran. **Paruva-*[13]), official from the town of Birtu, 717 BCE.[14] BCE;

10. *A-bé-eš-ta-am-ba* (OIran. **Abi-štamba-*),[15] military official, Dūr-Šarru-kēn, sometime between 714 and 705 BCE;[16]

11. *Mādāyu* (*Mad*-A+A), slave, purchased by the manageress of the royal harem of the central city, Nineveh, reign of Sennacherib.

12. *⌜Si⌝-ti-ir-ka-a-nu/Si-t[i-ir-ka-a-nu]*, Aram. *Š[t]rkn* (OIran. **Čiθrakāna-*),[17] slave purchased by a royal official in Nineveh, 684 BCE;[18]

13. *Par-ta-a-ma* (OIran. **Fratama-*),[19] recipient of quantity of wine, Nineveh, 683 BCE.[20]

14. *Ú-ri-ia-a* (OIran. **Varya-* "the desirable"; alternatively Israelie-Judean) refers to a dependent individual from Dadiualla who was pledged with his family by the governor of Talmusu in 681 BCE.[21]

15. *Ú-na-ma-a* (OIran. **Hu-nāma-* "having a good name, reputation", cf. RAE *Ú-na-ma*)[22] acted as a witness for the Egyptian Tapnahte (Assur, 646* BCE).[23]

16. *Pa-ar-nu-u-a* (OIran. **Farnahvā*, nom. of **Farnah-vant-*),[24] a dependent person from an unknown settlement, time of Assurbanipal.[25]

17. *Sa-am-bu-uk* (OIran. **Sambu-ka-*),[26] a dependent person from an unknown settlement, time of Assurbanipal.[27]

---

11 See Zadok, "Two Old Iranian Anthroponyms," 96, 128 with n. 23 and Schmitt, *Iranische Personennamen*, 105:83.

12 See PNA 2: 644b.

13 See Schmitt, *Iranische Personennamen*, 120:102.

14 PNA 3: 988b.

15 See Zadok, "Kassite and Iranian Names," and Schmitt, *Iranische Personennamen*, 39–40:2.

16 See PNA 1: 14b.

17 See Schmitt, *Iranische Personennamen*, 140–141:124 (cf. Sims-Williams, *Bactrian Personal Names*, 130:437).

18 See PNA 3: 1152b.

19 See Schmitt, *Iranische Personennamen*, 123–124:107 with lit.

20 See PNA 3: 990b.

21 See PNA 3: 1414b.

22 See Gershevitch, "Amber at Persepolis," 242 (followed by Mayrhofer *Onomastica Persepolitana*, 8.1742).

23 See PNA 3: 1386b.

24 See Schmitt, *Iranische Personennamen*, 122–123:106.

25 PNA 3: 989b.

26 See Zadok "Review of Hinz 1975," 215 with n. 7, cf. Schmitt, *Iranische Personennamen*, 132–133:116.

27 See PNA 3: 1082b.

18. *Bar-zi-i* s. of Sili (West Sem.), opponent in a lawsuit, Assur, 633 BCE.[28]

19. *Pa-ra-an-ša-ka* (OIran. **Far(a)n-saka- < *Farnah-saka-*),[29] witness in a lawsuit, Assur, 618* BCE.[30]

20. *Bar-zi-ia-*[*a*] (OIran. **Bṛziya-*),[31] military official from Buramma, undated (Sargonid).[32]

21. An isolated occurrence of an Iranian: *Ba-ga-a-nu*, i.e. an *-āna-*(pro-)patronymic of *Baga-* "god"[33] (cf. *Bgn*, below) from **Pap(a)hu* (*kurPa-pa-ha-*A+A), who acted as the sixteenth witness (out of twenty) together with another individual from the same place bearing the Akkadian-Aramaic name Man-nu-kī-Adad (X) in a deed from VII 644 BCE (eponymy of Nabû-šarra-uṣur) belonging to the documentation group of Harrānāyu. The deed is very probably from Ma'allānāte. First recorded are seven witnesses from there, followed by four witnesses with filiations and one with a title (8th, 9th, 11th, 12th and 10th respectively), one from Gozan (13th), two without filiation and provenience (14th, 15th), the Pap(a)hean pair (16th, 17th), one with filiation (19th) and two without (18th, 20th). All the witnesses whose provenance is indicated are without filiations, since a single identifier was sufficient. Yet it should be pointed out that three of the seven witnesses from Ma'allānāte in the northern Jazira bear titles. They and Bēl-šarra-uṣur (judging from his basilophoric name) belonged to the palatial sector (the 1st and 2nd to the queen and the 3rd to the crown prince). The deed is about a pledge of an agricultural domain of Nūrānu on behalf of Harrānāyu. The domain was situated in Kapar (URU.ŠE)-Kuzbi-šarri. It consisted of a field, a vegetable garden and a structure defined as *bīt-ri/tal-pi-ti*. The domain was adjacent to:

The fields of (a) Qar-ha-a and (b) Kur-ri-il-la-A+A (both messengers of the countryside), (c) a meadow (*se-hi*, cf. MA *sa-hi* and SB *sah-hu* in a NA inscription) of the settlement of Kak-mis/š, (d) a watercourse, (f) the threshing flour of the village (presumably that of Kapar-Kuzbi-šarri), (g) half of an unoccupied structure (*bīt-ri/tal-pi-ti*), (h) half of a cistern of water which is situated behind the *bīt-ri/tal-pi-ti*, (i) half of a cistern of water which is emptied into a wadi, and (j) half of a vegetable garden (^{giš}KIRI$_6$ ša ^{ú}SAR). The segments g-j are halves of the original areas and installations due to the fact that Nūrānu's domain was the outcome of partition of the original estate with his unnamed brothers (perhaps the abutters

28 See PNA 1: 274.

29 See Zadok, "Iranians in Cuneiform," 139 and Schmitt, *Iranische Personennamen*, 119–120:101.

30 See PNA 3: 988b.

31 See Schmitt, *Iranische Personennamen*, 67–68:41 with lit.

32 See PNA 1: 274b.

33 Cf. PNA 1: 250–251, s. v. *Bagānu* ("meaning unknown").

a and b above). **Papahu* is perhaps a settlement near Ma'allānāte.[34] Another possibility, if one relies on the Iranian origin of *Ba-ga-a-nu*'s name, is to consider **Papahu* not as his actual domicile, but his ultimate origin, in which case **Papahu*, which is otherwise not recorded in NA, is a late form of **Paphu*, which is the base of MA (*Māt-)Paphî* (invariably with the Akkadian *nisbe*, aptly lemmatized as **Paphû*). Moreover, the MB form of this originally Hurrian geographical designation is *papahhu* "east", cf. Hittite *Pa-pa-ah-hi, Pa-pa-an-hi*[35] and with the Akkadian nisbe *pa-ba-ah-hu-ú* (gen. *pa-ba-ah-hi-im*).[36] "mountain dweller" in OB Mari. The name goes back to Hurr. *pabanhi* "mountainous, Easterner".[37] In Mari it refers to mountaineers of Ṭūr-ʿAbdīn.[38] The land of *Paphi* is to be sought SW of Lake Van.[39] In this case *Ba-ga-a-nu* might have originated from the Iranians (the NW group, viz. Medes and the ancestors of the Kurds) who migrated to the Armenian Plateau during the 1st half of the 1st millennium BCE and eventually replaced the indigenous Hurrian population. At least three Israelite-Judeans are recorded in the documentation from Ma'allānāte. *Yṭyhw* acted as a witness at Qaštu in 700 BCE (archive of Handî).[40] *A-za-ri-iá-u*[41] and *Barak* (BARAG)*-ia/iá-u*,[42] are recorded in the documentation from Ma'allānāte (in 665 and 644 BCE respectively), but there is no evidence that they interacted with Iranians. The latter is mentioned in the same deed as *Hu-ba-na-nu* who acted as a witness in a deed from X.665 BCE (one of the parties is from Ma'allānāte).[43] There is a slight possibility that *Hu-ba-na-nu*'s name is based on the Elamite theonym *Humban*. However, this was two decades before the hostilities between Assyria and Elam resulted in deportations of Elamites to upper Mesopotamia, which weakens the case for considering him an Elamite.

22. The Iranian *Ma-du-ki/ku* (< OIran. **Madu-ka-*, *ka*-hypocoristicon to *madu-* "honey, sweet drink; wine")[44] is recorded as a sealer of a tablet and as a witness in Dūr-Katlimmu in 667–654 BCE (archive of Šulmu-šarri).[45]

---

34 See Bagg, *Rép. géogr.* 7/2–2: 474, s. v. **Pappaha* (his lemmatization with *-pp-* is not justified) of unknown linguistic affiliation (op. cit.: lxxxxvi).

35 Bagg, *Rép. géogr.* 6: 101, s. v. *Papanhi.*

36 CAD P: 101a, s. v.

37 Cf. Richter, *Bibliographisches Glossar*, 295–297, s. v. *paba.*

38 See Kupper, *Lettres royales*, 156, n. c; cf. Durand, "Review of Arnaud," 186.

39 See Nashef, *Rép. géogr.* 5: 190–191, s. v. Māt-Paphî.

40 See PNA 2: 496b, s. v. Yaṭyahu, cf. Lipiński, *Studies in Aramaic Inscriptions*, 37–39.

41 Homès-Fredericq, Garelli *et al.*, *Maʿallānāte*, 17, 4 (eponymy of Nabû-šarra-uṣur).

42 Homès-Fredericq, Garelli *et al.*, *Maʿallānāte*, 16, 7.

43 Homès-Fredericq, Garelli *et al.*, *Maʿallānāte*, 16a, 9 = 16b, 11 (3rd and 2nd witness respectively).

44 See Zadok, "Two Old Iranian."

45 See PNA 2/2: 674b, where the name is not interpreted.

23. Another witness with an Iranian name occurring in the same archive is *Ku-re-e-nu* (631 BCE)[46] < OIran. *-aina*-hypocoristicon of **Kura-*, to **kura-* "seed, clan" (cf. Parth. *Kwryn*).[47] A generation later, descendents of Israelite-Judean exiles dwelt on the lower Habur, notably in Dūr-Katlimmu, at the end of the 7th century BCE.[48] Iranian and Elamite deportees also dwelt there. The Elamites possessed a field in Magdalu in 603–600 BCE,[49] but so far there is no evidence of any contact between them and the Israelite-Judeans who are recorded in the same archive.

2 Babylonia: The Neo-Babylonian and Achaemenid periods

Shortly later, King Jehoiachin, his entourage and other prominent Judean exiles are recorded together with other rulers and prominent figures from the conquered Levant in the royal archive from the Southern Fortress of Babylon during the 1st quarter of the 6th century BCE. Medes, Persians and Elamites sojourned in Babylon at that time according to the same archive,[50] but there is no evidence that the Levantine exiles interacted with Irano-Elamites.

Iranian names among Judeans in Achaemenid Babylonia are rare. Only two individuals from Nippur and its region bore Iranian given names. Their paternal names are Semitic (one is Yahwistic):[51]

Ú-dar/da-ar-na-' (OIran. **Vidṛna-*[52]) s. of Ra-hi-mi-il (DINGIR^{meš}) from Nippur, 17.I.432–4.XII.425 BCE,[53] was the only one in his family who bore an Iranian name. His three brothers and his son bore Yahwistic and Aramaic names (one member had an Akkadian name).[54] Ba-ge-e-šú (OIran. **Baga-aiša-* "God-seeking" or a hypocoristicon *Bag(a)iča-*)[55] s. of Ha-na-ni-'-ia-a-ma, gs. of the alphabet scribe Aplâ and master of Gu-uk-ka-' (OIran. **Gau-ka-*, a hypocoristicon based on "bull, beef");[56] is recorded in Bīt-Murānu, 4.VII.417 BCE.[57]

46 See PNA 2/1: 640b, where the name is not interpreted.
47 < OIran. **Kur-ina-* according to Schmitt, *Personennamen in Parthischen*, 119–120:252 (Parth. -<*yn*> can alternatively render *-ēn* < *-aina-*).
48 See Zadok, "Israelites and Judeans," 169:68–72.
49 Radner, *neuassyrischen Texten*, 39, 40.
50 Cf. Zadok "People from Countries."
51 Cf. Zadok, *Jews in Babylonia*, 33–34.
52 Cf. Zadok, *Iranische Personennamen in der neu*, 314–315:580 with lit.
53 Hilprecht and Clay, *Business Documents*, 9, 69, 1.7.8.10.12.l.e. (= Zadok, *The Earliest Diaspora*, 38:74); owner of a cylinder seal (Bregstein *Seal Use*, 362).
54 Cf. Alstola, *Judeans in Babylonia*, 196–200:5.3.3, esp. 197: fig. 10.
55 See Zadok, *Iranische Personennamen in der neu*, 141: 187a–b.
56 See Zadok, *Iranische Personennamen in der neu*, 204:271 with lit.
57 Zadok, *The Earliest Diaspora*, 44:149, cf. Alstola, *Judeans in Babylonia*, 186, 201.

Filiations consisting of an Iranian given name and a West Semitic paternal name are common among West Semites in Babylonia. The inverted filiation, i.e. West Semitic given name and an Iranian paternal name is very rare: Was Ṭāb-šá-lam<<-ma>>-mu son of *Pa-ra-gu-šú* (1st w.,[58] OIran. **Paru-gu-*)[59] born in a mixed marriage?

No Judean filiations with Iranian names are recorded in the rural archives from Yahūdu and its vicinity. The main locus of the Judeans' encounter with proto-Zoroastrianism must have been in Babylon which served as one of the Achaemenid winter capitals. The contact between the elite of the Judean exiles, especially its priests and literati, and the Achaemenid court and officialdom very probably started in the early Achaemenid period. Compare the relationship of Ezra with King Artaxerxes. The presence of magian priests (^{lú}*ma-gu-šá*-A+A) in central Babylonia was also significant. They are recorded in archives from Borsippa and other cities. An anonymous magian priest received 0;1 kor, more than the other recipients. The document[60] belongs to the archive of the Borsippan priest Ardīya s. of Šulâ desc. of Ilīya and is dated to the early Acaemenid period: the archive owner is recorded between 7.XI.4 Nabonidus = 551 and -.-.29 Darius I = 493/2 BCE. An anonymous magian priest, who was in charge of a group of workmen (together with a scribe), is recorded in a letter from Uruk which does not contain a date, but is datable to the early Achaemenid period.[61] Another unnamed magian priest is recorded in Abanu in southeastern Babylonia (where a royal palace was located) at the beginning of the Achaemenid period. He was in charge of the house of the flour millers.[62] Both documents belong to the archive of the Eanna temple of Uruk which was obliged to supply services to the royal sector. Rations consisting of 86 kors of dates were to be distributed among unspecified number of *gardu*-workmen, magian priests (^{lú}*ma-gu-še-e*^{meš}) and palace servants (*mārē ekalli*) of *bīt harê* by the alphabet scribe Bēl-ēṭir s. of Nabû-ahhē-bulliṭ according to a promissory note from Babylon, 7.V.26 Darius I = 496 BCE.[63] The debtor, Bēl-rēmanni s. of Mušebši-Marduk, was obliged to pay within three days. At least two of the five witnesses, viz. Adad-šarra-uṣur s. of Kalbâ and Nabû-zēra-

58 Zadok, *The Earliest Diaspora*, 38:73.

59 Zadok, *Iranische Personennamen in der neu*, 282:425.

60 BM 103669 (see Dandamayev, *Iranians in Achaemenid Babylonia*, 166–167 with lit., and Zadok, "Occupations and Status Categories," xxxiv).

61 Keiser, *Letters and Contracts*, 1, 40 (see Dandamayev, *Iranians in Achaemenid Babylonia*, 166).

62 YOS 3, 66, 5 ff. See Tolini, "repas du Grand Roi," 252 with n. 65 where most of the documentation about Magian priests in Babylonia is discussed.

63 Ungnad, *Vorderasiatische Schriftdenkmäler*, 138/139 = Jursa, *Bēl-rēmanni*, 168 and pl. 25:BM 42383.

(see Dandamayev, *Iranians in Achaemenid Babylonia*, 166 and Jursa, *Bēl-rēmanni*, 168–169).

iddina s. of Sîn-šarra-uṣur (1st and 4th), are linked to the palatial sector. Nabû-kuṣuršu, s. of Rībatu, guaranteed against claims concerning the barley and any other property belonging to Bēl-aḫa-ittannu, s. of Lâbâši, raised by the magian priest (lúma-gu-šú) *A-ti-'-ú-pa-ra-'*, [Babylon?], archive unknown, 12.[x].14 Art. I/II/III = 457/6, 397/6 or 351/0 BCE.[64] The name of the magian priest perhaps originates from OIran. **Aθī-hu-pā-ra* "well-protected from fear" (with *-ra*-extension).[65]

The problem of reconstructing a reliable and fairly comprehensive prosopographical sample of the Judeans in pre-Hellenistic Babylonia was tackled by me in a monograph on this subject from 2002, where I was able to isolate 161 individuals from Babylonia who can be considered Judeans with various degrees of plausibility. Fortunately, their number now is more than double thanks to the new material from Yahudu and other settlements which were linked to this Judean colony (almost 100 additional documents including more than 190 additional individuals). Moreover, the additional material is much more statistically compact as it has an impressive density of attestations. This material is subjected to a thorough socio-economic analysis in a recent monograph of Alstola (2020). However, the task of reaching a definitive statistical pool of the Judean exiles is still a desideratum. In order to reach a reliable statistical pool, it is imperative to compare the enlarged and updated material from Babylonia to that from Judah, the country of origin of the exiles before the deportations, namely the long 7th century (700–586) BCE.

It should be pointed out that no Yahwistic names are recorded in the scanty epigraphic material from Israel and Judah which is datable before 800 BCE (just ten individuals with preserved given names, and partially with paternal names, altogether 14 anthroponyms).

The earliest extra-biblical mention of *Yhw* is his temple in Nebo which is recorded in the Mesha inscription (*c.* 830 BCE). It can be envisaged that the cult of Yhw was transmitted to Nebo in the inheritance of Reuben, traditionally the senior tribe of the Israelite proto-history, who settled northwest of Moab, via the highway ("royal way" *drk hmlk*) which connected northern Hijaz, viz. Midian, the Hisma – and Edom with Moab and the adjacent Reubenite territory.[66] Another way which linked Edom and the north was a westbound one, namely from Eilath to Gaza via Kuntillit ʿAjrūd (ancient Teman), in northeastern Sinai, but still within the orbit of Edom which has become a vassal of Judah while the latter was practically subordinate to the Northern Kingdom. The *Yhw* cult spread to Israelite

64 Hackl, *Materialien*, 1: 240–241:39, 8.
65 Cautiously suggested by Tavernier *apud* Hackl, *Materialien*, 1: 241.
66 See Noth, "Der Wallfahrtsweg," cf. Fleming, *Yahweh before Israel*, but see also Becking. "Review of Fleming."

territory from Edom and Sinai primarily via both Transjordan and the Negev. No wonder that the earliest Yahwistic names are recorded in Kuntillit ʿAjrūd, which was a cultic centre of the local *Yhw* (*Yhw Teman*), where the itinerant merchants of this commercial station worshipped also the *Yhw* of Samaria in *c.* 800 BCE. The percentage of Yahwistic anthroponyms steadily increased towards the end of the 1st temple period; of the 163 individuals from Israel and Judah before 700 BCE – 71 out of 164, that is, 43.29 % – bear Yahwistic names,[67] but during the long 7th century in Judah the percentage became higher: it reached 47.22 % (221 out of 468 individuals). This sample of material which was found mostly *in situ* updates that which was presented by Tigay 36 years ago. In view of the archaeological find, it may be concluded that the pre-exilic Yahwism was practically monolatric and not devoid of idolatrous traits, but I am not going to elaborate on this issue. Since I concentrate on extra-biblical evidence, it should be mentioned that also the religion of the Elephantine Jews, who reached Egypt sometime in the long 7th century, is not a strictly exclusive Yahwism. The relatively rich documentation on the Judean exiles in Babylonia is exclusively socio-economic and does not contain any information about their religious practices. It is not without interest that the Judean Bēl-šarra-uṣur has become the official name of the palatial functionary Yahu-šarra-uṣur in pre-Achaemenid Babylonia. This may hint at an identification of *Yhw* with *Bēl* = *Baʿal*. If this is not just an *interpretatio Babyloniaca*, then it is again an argument against an exclusive Yahwism. In short, there is no extra-biblical evidence that Yahwism evolved to strict monotheism before the Achaemenid period.

Here I shall avoid a discriminate aggregate of an Israelite-Judean prosopographical sample, but aim at a statistical comparison between the percentage of the Yahwistic names in the prosopographical pool from Judah of the long 7th century BCE and that of the Neo- and Late-Babylonian pool between between 572 and 477 BCE: 140 out of 190 individuals = 73.68 % from Yahūdu and its environs bore Yahwistic names. This must be an excessive percentage, due to the fact that the main criterion for defining Judeans in Babylonia is the occurrence of the theophorous element Yhw. No doubt that many crypto-Judeans, probably no less than additional seventy or so, are recorded in the documentation from the Judean colony and its region, but one simply cannot isolate them from the bulk of the pertinent documentation, as they bear common West Semitic and Akkadian an-

67 See Zadok, "Israelites and Judeans," 172 with one modification: to the list of the 70 Yahwistic names (42.94 %) add *Bnyw* in an inked inscription on a jar, 9th–beginning of 8th century BCE from Abel Beth Maacah (Yahalom-Mack *et al.*, "The Iron Age IIA"). Barkay ("Group of Stamped Handles," 122) draws attention that there are fewer Yahwistic names in the 8th century BCE (*c.* 22 % among the Judean royal officials shortly before 700 BCE).

throponyms. I mean that by adding the 70–80 crypto-Judeans from the Yahūdu documentation, wherever it lacks evidence to the contrary,[68] we shall obtain the same percentage as in Judah at the time of the deportation. Yahūdu "Judah", being named after the country or its capital Jerusalem, was a Judean colony, but this does not mean that it was inhabited exclusively by Judeans. They surely were the overwhelming majority there, but one explicit Tyrian is recorded there in 517 BCE together with another two individuals who were perhaps Phoenicians as well.[69] They might have settled in Yahūdu one generation after the Judeans, presumably after the conquest of rebellious Tyre by Nebuchadnezzar II. The Judean settlement was also inhabited by several Arameans and other people indigenous to Babylonia. This is demonstrated by a marriage contract[70] concluded by two parties belonging to the non-urban component of the indigenous Babylonian society who resided in Yahūdu in -.XII.5 Cyrus = 533 BCE. The bride's family was not only of a low social status, but also poor.[71] The contract was concluded between the groom Nabû-bān-ahi son of Kīnâ and ⌜f⌝D/Ṭib?-bi-' daughter of Da-na-a, the mother of the bridegroom Nanâ-kānat. It was issued in the presence of Mu-šá-la-am, the bridegroom's brother thereby indicating his consent[72] in the absence of her father (who is not mentioned at all: both siblings are mentioned without paternal names). No less than seven out of the eight witnesses to the contract were Judeans,[73] very probably neighbours and colleagues of the parties. This is understandable as the settlement had a Judean majority. It stands to reason that when the colony was founded, the authorities settled there at least one or several indigenous families along with the Judean deportees, who formed the majority in order to instruct the deportees who came from rain-fed Judah the basics of the Babylonian irrigation agriculture notably the cultivation of date palms.

Regarding the scenarios and loci of the presumed encounters between Judeans and Iranians, in the first place Persians and Medes, which took place during the Achaemenid period (538–331 BCE), the material is much more limited, scattered and entirely indirect. The basic assumption is that such encounters were limited to the elites of both ethnic groups, namely the Judeans and the Iranians and the main locus must have been Babylon, which served as one of the Achaemenid capitals and was the destination of high-ranking Judean exiles as is proven by the earlier documentation about Jehoiachin and his entourage. At the begin-

68 Like the parties to the marriage contract mentioned below.
69 CUSAS 28, no. 15.
70 Edited with an extensive commentary by Abraham, "West Semitic and Judean Brides."
71 See Abraham, "West Semitic and Judean Brides," 202.
72 The exceptional non-inclusion of the brother in the operative section was noticed by Abraham "West Semitic and Judean Brides," 202a.
73 Abraham "Inheritence Division."

ning of the Achaemenid rule in Babylonia, descendants of Jehoiakin and of the prominent priesthood of the ruined Jerusalem temple resided in Babylon. Direct evidence, namely documentation of Akkadian and other Aramaic indigenous sources for the presence of Judeans in Babylon is very limited. Demographically, most Judeans were settled in the countryside. No more than five Judeans are so far recorded in the capital of Babylon,[74] but this scanty evidence is due to hazards of documentation: palatial archives from Achaemenid Babylon are not recorded and very few foreigners are mentioned in the archive of the main temple of Babylon, Esaggila. Besides, Judeans from the province came to Babylon in 506 BCE in order to settle their affairs: such was the case of Ahiqam's five sons from Yahūdu who divided their inherited business shares according to a deed drafted in Babylon and witnessed by nine individuals, of whom at least four were Judeans.They might have been brought by the parties from Yahūdu or were resident in Babylon (Babylon, 7.VII.16 Darius I = 506 BCE).[75] It is very likely that Judeans who were of a certain standing, like the functionaries of the Achaemenid palatial sector in Babylonia, especially those residing or frequenting the capital of Babylon, had intensive interaction with the Persian authorities. No less than 74 individuals with Iranian names or of Iranian exctraction, predominantly Persians and Medes, resided or were active in Babylon.[76] Some of them intermarried with Babylonians. Several Judeans from Babylonia bore Iranian names. Such names were borne also by at least two of the 19 urban clans of Achaemenid Jerusalem, namely Bigway and Zatu (cf. perhaps Elam). They might have hailed from Teispid or early Achaemenid Babylonia. Their name-giving is compatible with the initial enthusiastic expectations of the descendants of the Judean exiles from Cyrus as well as their gratitude for the fulfillment of his promise to restore the temple of Jerusalem. The fact that the restoration was in all probability demographically relatively insignificant did not basically affect their positive attitude, because all

---

74 1. Né-ri-ia-a-ma s. of Bēl-zēra-ibni, guarantor, was presumably associated with the Egibi firm (Egibi archive), 9.XI.510 BCE (Strassmaier, *Inschriften*, 310, 4), 2. ^{d}Ia-hu-ú-iddina(MU), place not preserved (possibly Babylon), -.-.509/8 BCE, second witness (in a broken context, Stigers, "Neo- and Late Babylonian Documents," 49:44, 19), 3. [^{m}xx(x)] s. of Za-kar-⸢ri?⸣-⸢ia?-ma⸣ ⸤^{lú}se⸣-pir-r[i (alphabet scribe) of? ^{m}?R]a?-man-na, Babylon, 3.X.507 BCE (BM 26553, 7 f., receipt belonging to the archive of the Borsippean clan of Ilīya), 4. Ga-da-la-a-ma s. of Banna-Ea, Babylon, 24.VI.486 BCE (see Alstola, *Judeans in Babylonia*, 223–224), and 5. Ra-hi-im s. of Ba-na-ia-a-ma; Babylon, 8.II.432 BCE, witness (PBS 2/1,5,12.l.e. [impressed with his stamp seal, Bregstein, *Seal Use*, 91). See Alstola, *Judeans in Babylonia*, 223–226.

75 Abraham, "Inheritence Division" = CUSAS 28, 45.

76 Zadok, *Iranische Personennamen in der neu*, 2, 7, 11, 12, 36, 39, 42, 57, 75, 79, 91, 104, 137, 152, 161, 171, 178, 198, 199, 201, 206, 208, 209, 211, 214, 221, 253, 256, 257, 261, 265, 288, 291, 314, 315, 329, 343, 350, 351, 360, 369, 379, 382, 383, 387–389, 400, 415, 417, 430, 437, 448, 451, 473, 480, 487, 524, 528, 539, 542, 559, 564, 565, 575, 589, 614, 615, 621, 623, 627, 631, 639, 653.

the restrictions were within the general policy of the Teispids and Achaemenids towards the conquered population. They did not apply a special policy towards the Judeans (see van der Spek 1982).

About 650 Iranians and bearers of Iranian names are recorded in Achaemenid Babylonia, a very important satrapy of the empire. On the other hand very few Iranians are recorded in Achaemenid Palestine. The governor of the subsatrapy of Judah in 408 BCE, *Bgwhy* (OIran. **Baga-vahya-*), is homonymous with one of the two Judean clans bearing Iranian names. *'wstn* (OIran. **Ava-stāna-*)[77] is mentioned in a petition of the notables of the Elephantinian Jews on 25 November 407 BCE.[78] He is listed after the high priest of Jerusalem and before the nobles of Judea. Therefore it stands to reason that he was a very high official in Judah, presumably a Judean with a Persian name like *Bgwhy*.[79] The Aramaic papyri from the end of the Achaemenid period, which were found in Wādi Dāli contain taxation terms which are recorded in Babylonia, namely *hlk'* = Akkad. *ilku* "corvee" (> "tax"), and *qšt* (Akkad. *qaštu*) "bow-fief".[80] The occurrence of these terms as well as the fact that the Iranian *Wh(w)dt* officiated as judge in the capital of Samaria, may indicate that the taxation terminology and the implementation of the Achaemenid jurisdiction in Samaria and by extension in the rest of Transeuphratene including Judah, were not much different than in Babylonia, the more so since Transeuphratene and Babylonia were one satrapy during the early Achaemenid period. At first glance it seems overbold to draw such a conclusion from isolated references, but one has to bear in mind that unlike the abundant cuneiform evidence from Achaemenid Babylonia, the pertinent documentation from Transuphratene, predominantly in the Aramaic alphabet, was almost entirely recorded on perishable materials.

The encounter between Judeans and Persians impacted early Judaism, but not the Samaritan variety of Yahwistic monotheism: the Pharisees believed in afterlife, a development attributed to Zoroastrian influence, while this fundamental belief did not penetrate the Samaritan religion before the late Roman period. When it did, it was under the influence of the varieties and derivatives of late Judaism, long after the disappearance of the Sadduceans who did not believe in afterlife. It should be remembered that the Samaritans lacked this exilic experience. We may conclude that the sheer presence and political-administrative dominance of the Persians in Palestine did not impact Yahwism, but the initial and decisive impetus was the Teispid conquest of Babylonia followed by the Achaeme-

77 See Tavernier, *Iranica*, 128:4.2.216.

78 TAD A.4.7 = A.4.8, 18.

79 See Porten, *Archives*, 289–290.

80 Not "community" as argued by Lipiński ("Review of Dušek," 232).

nid consolidation of control there which was regarded as salvation after a period of crisis by the Judean elite in Babylon. This was amply expressed in such theological terms by the 2nd and 3rd Isaiah. The latter contains the earliest unmistakable formulation of Yhw as the sole deity. Such influence is discernible in Deutero-Isaiah, Daniel, Esther, Ezra-Nehemiah and in the Qumran "library", especially from the 1st century BCE to 2nd century CE. century CE.[81]

3 Judah

Likewise, very few Jews in Judah bore Iranian names.[82] Only one individual, namely *Wny'* (< **Vanyah-* "victorious")[83] is recorded in the Post-exilic Judah. The name of Another individual, *'wzy* is either OIran. **Uzya-*[84] or Semitic.[85] However, doubt is cast on the textual transmission of this short name.[86] *Ššy* (also Ez. 10, 40) may derive from OPers. **Čiçiya-/*Čiçaya-/*,[87] but the name is too short and there may be other alternatives regarding its origin.

Ḥšbdnh is not Iranian,[88] but a corrupted form of *Ḥšbnh* < *Ḥšbnyh/Ḥšbnyh.*[89] *Mgbyš* is certainly not Iranian,[90] but apparently Semitic.[91]

Two names are recorded in the additions to the Priestly Source (P) of the Pentateuch. Their bearers are attributed to the period of wandering in the Sinai desert, but they must be fictitious as the P source is post-exilic:

Prnk < OIran. **Farnaka-;*[92] *Wpsy* is – if it is the outcome of a graphical metathesis of **Wpys* – presumably OIran. **Vi-paisa-.*[93]

The rich genealogical lists of the Book of Chronicles contain three Iranian names, but two of them may alternatively be Semitic.The only one which is un-

81 See Shaked, "Iranian Influences," 313–314, 324.

82 For Iranian and Iranians in Palestine see in general Schmitt 2017.

83 Hutter, *Iranische Personennamen in der hebräischen Bibel*, 46–47:32 with previous lit.

84 Baumgartner *et al. Hebräisches und Aramäisches*, 20, cf. Zadok, "Die nichthebräischen Namen," 396; for an alternative Iranian etymology see Hutter, *Iranische Personennamen in der hebräischen Bibel*, 29:4.

85 See Zadok, *Pre-Hellenistic Israelite*, 141–142.

86 See Rudolph, *Esra und Nehemia*, 120 *ad* Neh. 3, 25.

87 See Hutter, *Iranische Personennamen in der hebräischen Bibel*, 63–64:63.

88 See Hutter, *Iranische Personennamen in der hebräischen Bibel*, 52:41.

89 Cf. Zadok, *Prosopography of the Israelites*, 759:183:72.

90 See Hutter, *Iranische Personennamen in der hebräischen Bibel*, 54:45 with previous lit.

91 See Zadok, *Pre-Hellenistic Israelite*, 124.

92 See Zadok, *Pre-Hellenistic Israelite*, 176, cf. Hutter, *Iranische Personennamen in der hebräischen Bibel*, 60–61:58.

93 See Zadok 1985: 396 and 1988: 176 (followed by Hutter, *Iranische Personennamen in der hebräischen Bibel*, 47–48:33).

ambiguously Iranian is *Tyry'* (OIran. **Tīriya-*).[94] Regarding *'ḥštry* (OIran. **Xšaθr-iya-*),[95] it may be that the original form was **'šḥwry (>*ḥšwry* with metathesis), a gentilic of his ancestor *'šḥwr.*[96] *Ššn*, which may render OPers. **Čiçina-*[97] (one would expect **Ššyn* as in later, Aramaic sources), may alternatively be Semitic ("byssus-like").[98] *Ssmy* is certainly not Iranian.[99] *Ztm* in the Chronicler's Levitic genealogies is very probably Semitic.[100] It seems that the source of inspiration of the invention of individuals with Iranian names in the Chronicler's imaginary settlement history was the presence of Iranians in southern Palestine in his time, viz. the Achaemenid period (cf. below, 5).

The Census List in the books of Ezra and Nehemiah originates not long before Nehemiah as determined by the occurrence of the Iranian name *Bgwy* (there are more Iranian names in the list) if the headline is an integral part of the list or at least originated not much later than it. A very late date is unacceptable especially since several members of this list recur in relatively early sources.

One has to bear in mind that emigration from Babylonia to another satrapy was against the interests of the rulers. Perhaps the fact that both Babylonia and Judah belonged to the same satrapy well into the late Achaemenid period facilitated such waves of migrations. The pool of returnees probably did not include Judean villagers, who were settled in Babylonian rural areas, since they mostly belonged to the sector of dependent workmen and thus did not enjoy freedom of movement. As is observed by Bloch, the Judean *šušānus* (members of a class of dependent workmen) from Yaḫūdu in central Babylonia were required, probably by a decision of the satrap Uštanu, the satrap of Babylonia and Transeuphratene, to send the horses under their care to Achaemenid military units stationed west of the Euphrates, under Uštanu's command, and perhaps also to join those units when going out for military service. In this way, the Judean *šušānus* at Yahūdu were classified as being "of Across-the-River" (Transeuphratene) and fell under a direct authority of Uštanu, but although they could have served in the satrapy which includes Judah, in all probability they were not allowed to leave their bow-fiefs in Yahūdu and settle in Judah.

The returnees were basically descendants of the temple personnel, namely priests, Levites, oblates, and certain professionals who functioned at the temple,

94 See Hutter, *Iranische Personennamen in der hebräischen Bibel*, 66–67:67.

95 See Hutter, *Iranische Personennamen in der hebräischen Bibel*, 30–31:6.

96 See Zadok, *Prosopography of the Israelites*, 467 with previous lit.

97 See Hutter, *Iranische Personennamen in der hebräischen Bibel*, 64–65:64.

98 See Zadok, *Pre-Hellenistic Israelite*, 138, 159.

99 See Hutter, *Iranische Personennamen in der hebräischen Bibel*, 58:52 with previous lit.

100 The Iranian derivation suggested with all due reserve by Hutter (*Iranische Personennamen in der hebräischen Bibel*, 50:38) is unlikely.

as well as profane members of the elite who resided primarily if not exclusively in the capital of Babylon. They formed urbanite clans.

The numbers of members of each clan in post-exilic Judah are not typological and hence seem reliable, but the lower options should be preferred. The impressive figures presumably result from summing up the numbers of each wave, a process lasting for about 140 years (538 – *c.* 400 BCE). The list of 19 clans is not complete, for there were additional urban kin groups, e.g. the perfumers, goldsmiths and whisperers-magicians who are mentioned in other lists. Thus one obtains over 20 clans. These are basically urban clans, the clans of the free citizens of Jerusalem and Judah. They are analogous to the system of clans which is well-documented in the Babylonian temple cities at that time, and later in Palmyra. *Bgwy* (2056), *ʿylm* (1254) and *Ztwʾ* (845) are among the large profane urban clans. Both *Bgwy* and *Ztwʾ* bear Iranian names and *ʿylm* is homonymous with the land of Elam in southwestern Iran. Two Judeans are recorded at the Elamite capital of Susa which served as the imperial capital in the later winter: they acted as witnesses and were linked to the palatial sector, viz. ^{d}Ia-hu-ú-šarra-uṣur (494 BCE) and Šá-ab-ba-ta-A+A s. of Nabû-šarra-bulliṭ (492 BCE).[101] However, they are recorded in a Babylonian archive and it cannot be ascertained whether they resided in Susa. The same applies to Ta_5-ga-bi-ia-a-ma (26.X.522 BCE)[102] who had to deliver an ass to a Sipparean in Humadēšu in Persis. This implies journey, in which case he might have been a businessman. He is recorded in the archive of the Sipparean Iššar-tarībi (s. of Bunene-ibni) and acted as his agent.[103]

Ten out of these 19 clans are mentioned in the list of people who joined Ezra. This list includes Bgwy and ʿylm (each with 70 members), but not Ztwʾ. The heads of all the three clans were among the signatories of the pact (*ʾamana^{h}*, Neh. 10, 15, 17). Members of *Ztwʾ* clan married alien wives (Ez. 11, 27).

Lipschits (2022) is of the opinion that no more than 300 families (*c.* 1500 people) inhabited Jerusalem(-village), i.e. in the Ophel and adjacent areas between 538 and *c.* 150 BCE. I would suggest that to this minimal estimate one may add few families who might have dwelt in or near unexcavated sections of the Ophel and adjacent areas, as well as in certain spaces of the Temple Mount outside the precincts of the small early post-exilic temple. They certainly consisted of the temple personnel in its broadest sense: it is explicitly stated that the temple oblates (*ntynym*) resided in the Ophel. Basically they lived on donations of Judeans from Judah and outside Judah as well as on support from the Achaemenid government (presumably from the governor of the Transeuphratene satrapy).

101 Zadok, *The Earliest Diaspora*, 46–47.
102 Weszeli "Eseleien," 472–473:2, 17; cf. Zadok, *The Earliest Diaspora*, 31:38.
103 See Pirngruber "Minor Archives," 177 ad 7, rev. 17.

This must be relativized: prior to Nehemiah's governship the clerus did not always receive its rations and therefore had to seek employment in agriculture in the surroundings of Jerusalem. It is reported about "the priests, people of the round district" (*hkhnym 'nšy hkkr*).[104] This refers to the surroundings of Jerusalem in view of the mention of "the sons of the musicians from the *kkr sbybwt Yrwšlm*" (in which case *sbybwt Yrwšlm* "the surroundings of Jerusalem" is a gloss explaining *kkr*), followed by *ḥṣry* Nṭwpty, Byt hglgl as well as the fields of Geba and Azmawet plus explicatory statement: "while the musicians built *ḥṣrym* (enclosures > hamlets) in the surroundings of Jerusalem".[105]

All these locales were within a day walk from the Temple Mount.

The profane clans were basically urban, but after immigrating to Judah it can be envisaged that most of their members had to seek subsistance on their agricultural domains in the Judean countryside, namely in Benjamin, the Shephelah, Bet hak-kerem paradeisos, and perhaps in Engedi which was – at least in the Hellenistic-Roman age – also a royal estate.

The list of Wall Builders has several indications of local builders of the wall, who did not belong to the clerus of the temple.[106] Profane people (excluding administrators) who participated in the building of the wall were members of the clans of Senaah,[107] Harim, Pahath-Moab, Parosh and Zabbay[108] as well as at least three others whose clan is not indicated, but it is reported that they resided opposite the wall (*ngd bytw/bytm*): Jedaiah s. of Harumaph, Azaryah s. of Maaseiah gs. of Ananyah (provided he was not a Levite), Benjamin and Hashub.[109] It is not stated that Palal s. of Uzay and Hanun s. of Zalaph[110] resided there.

Nehemiah[111] was identical[112] with *hTršt'*[113] which is his Iranian alias (<*'tršt* < **Atṛ-šiyāta-*), later misunderstood as a title.[114] Nehemiah's position in the Achae-

104 Neh. 3, 22 (see Rudolph, *Esra und Nehemia*, 120 *ad loc.*).

105 Neh. 12, 28–29.

106 Zadok s. of Baanah and Hananiah s. of Shelemiah (Zadok, *Prosopography of the Israelites*, 775–776:186:13, 39), who were perhaps a priest and a Levite respectively are excluded here. Joiadah s. of Psḥ (Zadok, *Prosopography of the Israelites*, 775:186:14) is also not included here as his paternal name is homonymous with a Nethinim clan.

107 Zadok, *Prosopography of the Israelites*, 756:183:42.

108 Zadok, *Prosopography of the Israelites*, 775:186:23, 24, 31, 36.

109 Zadok, *Prosopography of the Israelites*, 775:186:21, 32–34.

110 Zadok, *Prosopography of the Israelites*, 775–776:186:35, 40.

111 See Zadok, *Prosopography of the Israelites*, 380–393:086.

112 According to Neh. 10, 2.

113 Ez. 2, 63; Neh. 7, 65, 70.

114 According to Benveniste *Titres et noms propres*, 120; cf. Bogolyubov, "Arameyskie Transkripcii," and Greenfield "Tršt'" (rejected by Hutter, *Iranische Personennamen in der hebräischen Bibel*, 69–70:70).

menid court was just that of a royal cupbearer (Heb. *mšqh hmlk*, Aram. *šqh* < *šqy* /**šaqy*/) and not the chief royal cupbearer (Aram. *rb šqh*). His audience with the king took place in the presence of the queen (*šgl* < Akkad. *ša-ekalli*, not a concubine as inexactly rendered in LXX). This implies that the eunuch Nehemiah was her protégé. The news about the destruction of the wall of Jerusalem was reported to Nehemiah by Hanani and other Judeans who came to Susa in the month of Kislev. This indeed falls within period of the king's residence in the winter capital of Susa. It stands to reason that Nehemiah, like the rest of the personnel of the peripatetic royal court and harem, sojourned in Babylon and Ecbatana as well. He came as Artaxerxes' emissary to Judah, but was looked upon by the neighbouring rulers as a little more than an emissary of the court, like other prominent foreigners with a similar upbringing and contacts. Nehemiah expressed his wish to visit the city of his fathers' graves: the Jewish courtier from Susa must have been aware of the popular and spectacular cult of the graves practiced in Elam.

Generally the Achaemenids buried the members of the ruling family in graves hewn in rock, a practice which was abandoned only in post-Achaemenid Iran. It is clear that Nehemiah who became the governor of the sub-satrapy of Judah, reported directly to the supreme authority, i.e. the Achaemenid king and not only to his satrap. The nomination of a governor of local extraction is not exceptional in the late Achaemenid period. More generally, the nomination of a non-Persian (and non-Mede) as a (sub-)satrap is not altogether rare. For instance, Belesys, the satrap of Babylonia in the late-Achaemenid period was a Babylonian and Caria had also an indigenous satrap (Mausolus). A case in point of a satrap who employed his relative is Gubaru of Babylonia: his son Nabūgu was active in the Babylonian administration during his father's lifetime. Having no sons, Nehemiah might have employed his brother Hanani. The latter may be the same person as the homonymous individual who bore the title *śr hbyrh* (Akkad. *rab birti*, OIran. **dizapati-*).

4 Samaria

Several individuals bore Iranian names in Achaemenid Samaria:[115]

The Iranian *Wh(w)dt* (< OIran. **Vahu-dāta-* "Given by the good one"[116] or OPers. "Well-born"[117]) acted as a judge in late Achaemenid Samaria which was

115 Cf. Zadok, "Issues of the deportations," 132.

116 See Dušek, *manuscrits Araméens*, 148 *ad* 2, 10.

117 Tavernier, *Iranica*, 342:4. 2. 1835, cf. Lipiński, "Review of Dušek," 229.

the capital of a sub-satrapy. He is listed alone among the witnesses. Iranian judges are common in Babylonia since Darius I's reign, but unlike Babylonia where these judges were often part of a collegium, all the three occurrences from Samaria are of the same judge alone. The occurrence of an Iranian judge in Samaria strengthens the case of interpreting *dyny'*,[118] which was misunderstood as an ethnonym (cf. LXX Διναῖοι), as Aram. "the judges." It may be that it is just a hazard of documentation, that a judge or even a collegium of judges is not recorded in Achaemenid Judah. A high official bearing the very common Iranian name *Mtrdt* who was based in Samaria, is listed first (or second if *bšlm* is an anthroponym rather than an appellative) in a list of royal officials from there (Ez. 4, 4, 7). It is stated that he acted in the time of Artaxerxes (probably I or rather Xerxes),[119] but his title is not specified. If the order of the list is significant, then he must have been very prominent.

Bgbrt (OIran. **Baga-br̥ta-*),[120] an enslaved person, is mentioned in a papyrus of people from the city of Samaria (probably sometime in the reign of Artaxerxes III 359–338 BCE) which was found in Wādi Dāli.[121] The small corpus of names on coins from Samaria (4th century BCE) has another two Old Iranian names, viz. *Wny* (**Vanya-* "victorious")[122] and probably *Mnpt*.[123] The latter ends in *–pāta-* "protected", possibly by *Manah-* "(good) thought", for the name-type cf. Middle Persian *Mān-dād* "Created by the (good) thought".[124] They are predated by *Mtrdt* and *Štrbwzny* (**Čiθra-baujana-*,[125] both in Ezra). The latter was contemporary with Ttny (< Tattannu) the satrap of Transeuphratene during the reign of Darius I. Additional individuals with Iranian names are *Mtr'* (< OIran. **Miθra-* < **Miθraya-*, early Achaemenid) who is recorded in the Samarian village of Qaddūm.[126] and *Mzdgy* < **Mazdā-gaya-*[127] who is mentioned in an ostracon from the early 4th century BCE found in Yoqneam[128] very close to the northern border of the territory inhabited by Samarians.

---

118 Ez. 4, 9.

119 See Rudolph *Esra und Nehemia*, 33–37 with previous lit.

120 See Butz *apud* Cross "Personal Names," 76–77.

121 Dušek *manuscrits Araméens*, 10, 2: B̊gbr̊t̊, 4: B• gbr• [t], 8: B̊[gbrt], 9.

122 Attested also in Elephantine (see Tavernier, *Iranica*, 338: 4. 2. 1799).

123 Not "Memphite" as rendered by Lipiński ("Review of Dušek," 239, cf. 235, 238).

124 Gignoux *Noms propres sassanides*, 115:560, cf. Zimmer "Zur sprachlichen," 149 *ad* 560.

125 See Hutter, *Iranische Personennamen in der hebräischen Bibel*, 66:66 with previous lit.

126 See Zadok, "On the Prosopography," 664.

127 A *dvandva* compound "Mazda and Gaya" (two theonyms, see Shaked *apud* Naveh, "Published and Unpublished," 116b: 5, 1 = *Studies in West Semitic*, 127 with n. 34). He is listed after *'qbyh* (Judeo-]Samar.) and *'sytwn* (Phoen.).

128 See Zadok "Prosopography of Samaria," 783:5 and 5, 95.

5 Philistia and the Negev

There is good reason for thinking that people from western Media were deported to Philistia, notably to Tall jammi around 716 BCE.[129]

The ostraca:
Ostracon 1: 8 filiations +[x], in which case it would be a decury (at least one generation after the deportation, i.e. not earlier than the 1st half of the 7th century BCE). *Wnnt* is explicable in Iranian terms. Most of the paternal names end in *-š* and are inexplicable in Semitic terms. They may belong to the pre-Iranian substrate of Western Media.

Hrš s. of *K°š* (or *Yhw*[...] ([x]*q*)
Wnnt (s. of)[130] *'dnš* (or *'mnh*/*'gnh*)
Šlm (s. of) *'nš*
Bʿlšm' (s. of) *Šgš* (II *q*)
Rkh (*Hkr* s. of) *Šm'š*
Bʿl' (s. of) *Ḥ°mš*
Ntn (s. of) *Ppš* (*Nnš*)
⸤*Ṭy°*⸥ (s. of) ⸤*Š*l⸥ [...]
Remainder broken away

Ostracon 2: PNN + measures: [x]+ 6 +[x]
[...]*h°* (s. of) *Klyṭbš*
[...](s. of) *Qsryh* (*Qlgryh*)
[...]*y°* (s. of) *Brṣyh* (*Ṣbršyh*)
([...]/)[...]*rwš*.

It was pointed out[131] that no less than five out of the given names are Semitic (1, lines 3, 4, 6–8), i.e. adapted to the local vernacular. This also strongly suggests that the sequence PN_1 PN_2 in lines 2–8 is short for PN_1 (*bn*) PN_2.

Other names from Tall jammi are *Bmlk* (inscribed jar < *'bmlk* with aphaeresis which is common in Phoenician) and *Ddymš* s. of *'lyqm* (seal, possibly Philistine, 8th–7th century BCE), both names are West Semitic.[132]

129 See Naveh "Writing and Scripts," and Na'aman and Zadok, "Sargon II's Deportations"; in brackets are the alternative readings of the names by Misgav, "Ostraca from Tell Jemmeh," 1031.
130 The format PN_1 (s. of) PN_2 has many parallels in the Northwest Semitic epigraphy. The fact that only given names are Semitic strengthens the case that these are filiations and not different individuals.
131 By Na'aman and Zadok, "Sargon II's Deportations," 37.
132 Cf. Avigad and Sass *Corpus of West Semitic*, 493b, s. v. with lit.

Aramaic ostraca:[133] *Ntn*, 4th century BCE (1033b:1948), *Štbr* (wine),[134] 5th century BCE (1033b:1949) < Old Iranian *_Š(iy)āti-bara-_ "Bringing felicity"[135] *Zbydy*, his vineyard and wine (1034–1036:1960: *Zby*[*dy*?], 1962), *Mʿyn* (apparently Arab. *Muʿīn*, Achaemenid period, 1036:1961), *Ḥnn*?, *Bʿlnbw* s. of *Ntn*?, millet (five *qbn*, 1036–1037:1950). Except for the Iranian and Arabian name, all the other anthroponyms are explicable in Aramaic terms.

Dtyn < (OIran. *_Dātaina-_[136]) is recorded in an ostracon from Ashkelon from the 5th century BCE, as well as *Bgz*[*wšt*?] (< *_Baga-zušta-_?) from Tall il-farʿa,[137] very close to the southern border of Philistia. *Bgn* (< *_Bagāna-_) is recorded in Tel Beer-sheba in the 4th century BCE.[138] It cannot be proven that *ʼsp*^{o}*y*^{o} from Achaemenid Arad,[139] whose name is either Semitic (based on ʼ-S-P "to gather" with hypocoristic -*īy*[140]) or Iranian (-*iya*-[pro-]patronymic of *_Aspa-_ "horse"[141]), is a Judean.

6 Elephantine

At most three bearers of Iranian names in Elephantine might have been Jews:

ʼrwrt (OIran. *_Arva-raθa-_ "Having a fast chariot")[142] s. of Yhntn, 6th = penultimate witness in a deed of the Judean Hoshea s. of Hodawyah, 17 Feb. 483 BCE,[143] as well as *Symk* (OIran. *_Syāmaka-_)[144] s. of Mešullam and Ḥwry s. of *Wnh* (OIran. *_Vana-_ "victorious"),[145] both contributors to the Yhw temple in Elephantine, 1 June 400 BCE.[146] *Bgprn* (OIran. *_Baga-farnah-_)[147] s. of *Wšḥy* (OIran. *_Vača-x-aya-_)[148] and

---

133 Misgav, "Ostraca from Tell Jemmeh." (pp. and nos. in brackets).

134 Misgav, "Ostraca from Tell Jemmeh," 1033b:1949 (concerning wine).

135 See Schmitt, "Zu Weiterungen."

136 Differently Cross, "Inscriptions in Phoenician," 357 (contemplating a less likely Semitic origin).

137 Naveh, "Published and Unpublished," 116b = *Studies in West Semitic*, 122 *ad* 5.

138 See Naveh, "Aramaic Ostraca from Tel Beer-sheva," 186 *ad* 33, 4, 43, 4 and 46, 1; cf. Tavernier, *Iranica*, 136: 4.2.269.

139 See Lemaire, "Review of Aharoni," 447 *ad* Aharoni, *Arad Inscriptions*, 23, 1.

140 See Zadok, *Pre-Hellenistic Israelite*, 97.

141 See Zadok, *Pre-Hellenistic Israelite*, 176.

142 See Tavernier, Iranica: 114:4.2.116.

143 TAD D 4.4, 21; cf. Porten, *Archives*, 26 and 144, n. 121.

144 See Tavernier, *Iranica*: 316:4. 2. 1619 with lit.

145 See Tavernier, *Iranica*: 336:4. 2. 1788.

146 TAD C 3.15, 27, 43; cf. Porten, *Archives*, 321:26, 322:37.

147 See Tavernier, *Iranica*: 333:4.2.252 with lit.

148 See Tavernier, *Iranica*: 333:4. 2. 1767.

Wšḥy s. of *Zrmr* (OIran. **Zara-hmāra-* "determined, resolute"),[149] who also contributed to the Yhw temple there,[150] have a purely Iranian three-tier genealogy (their filiations are juxtaposed)[151] and hence may not be originally Jews.

B Sasanian Babylonia

Introduction

A sizable corpus of Iranian names (mostly explicable in Middle Persian terms) is recorded among the clients (beneficiaries) and adversaries of the Magic bowls. Numerous magic bowls were written in sites throughout Babylonia in three Aramaic dialects (each with its own script). Most of the bowls (over 60 %) were written in Jewish Babylonian Aramaic (JBA), about a quarter in Mandaic and 13 % in Old Syriac.[152] It stands to reason that the scribes who wrote the JBA bowls were Jews. Unfortunately, the scribes of all the three categories of the bowls remain anonymous. The clients and adversaries bore a mixture of Semitic (overwhelmingly Aramaic) and Iranian (mostly Middle Persian) names. Few of these customers bear double names, e.g. the female *M'dwkt 'h'ty'* (Persian and Aramaic) in a Mandaic bowl.[153] The findspots of incantation bowls written in JBA can be used as evidence for the presence and the geographical distribution of Jews in Babylonia in addition to the explicit pertinent sources (in the first place the Babylonian Talmud[154] as well as inscriptions from the Dura Europus synagogue) only to a limited extent, since most of the bowls originate from illicit excavations. Few bowls originate, e.g., from Coche,[155] Sippar, Amran, Borsippa, Nippur, Uruk,[156] and possibly Tall Assafa near the Yousifiyyah intake.[157] Many individuals from the corpus of the JBA bowls are included in a section of the prosopography of the

149 See Tavernier, *Iranica*: 369:4. 2. 2044.
150 Cf. Porten, *Archives*, 326:130–131.
151 TAD vol. III, 234:3.15, 136–137.
152 This is a preliminary estimate (see Morony, "Magic and Society," 87, cf. Ford and Abudraham, "Syriac and Mandaic," 75–76 with n. 3).
153 Morgenstern and Schlütter, "Mandaic Amulet," 118, 120, rev. 3.
154 Very few Iranian names in the Babylonian Talmud refer to Jews, e.g. *Drw* < **Dṛva-* "firm" and *Pp'* < **Pāpa-* "protector" or "father". Less likely *Srw* < "cypress" (see Zadok, "Zur Struktur," 245, n. 1).
155 Franco, "Five Aramaic."
156 See Zadok, "On the Arameans," 63.
157 See Hunter, "Two Incantation Bowls," 114 *ad* IM 60494.

Eastern Diaspora from 330 BCE to 650 CE which is compiled by Ilan (2011). However, the lemmatization as well as the linguistic classification and terminology used by her are often inaccurate. Her lack of acquaintance with basic morphological terminology results in wrong definitions of name-components. For example, *B'b-* of *~nwš, kanar* of ~ *Kešwād*[158] are not "prefixes" and *-D'd* (*/dād/* < *dāta*, not "*Dad/Dat*") of *Yzy~*[159] is not a "suffix", *recte* "Vorderglied" and "Hinterglied" (English fore- and hind-component). There is inadequate analysis or lack of parsing of name-components, e.g. *Mhwy*[160]/*M'hwy*[161] where only the base *Māh-* is identified, but not the suffix.

What is presented in the appendix below is not a prosopography, which will hopefully be compiled by J. N. Ford, one of the leading researchers of the magic bowls, but a linguistic classification. In what follows I will concentrate on the morphology and semantics of the names (almost entirely of clients and adversaries)[162] with some remarks on the few identifiable Jews among the customers who unlike the practitioners-scribes were mostly non-Jews.There is some reason to suspect, that not all the names of the customers are real ones, e.g., *Byl* s. of *Nny*,[163] a filiation which consists of two theonyms. For instance, *'wsr'* may be fictitious name.[164]

Names of Jews are a minority; here there are some examples:[165]

Yhwdh s. of *'ḥt*[166] who is mentioned together with *Rbyqw* (< *Rb Y'qwb*), *Šmw'l*, *Ywsy* and *Khn'* (the remaining individuals bore Aramaic names with the exception of one with an Iranian and another with an atypical anthroponym), *Yhwdy* m. of *'ḥwdymmw*,[167] *Rb Mry*, *Ḥnyn'* s. of *Rb Ytm'*,[168] *Rbdymy*, *Rb Dym'*,[169] and *Ḥyṣqyl*[170] (< *Yḥzq'l*). However, *Yhwdh* s. of Nanay is not necessarily a case of

158 Ilan, *Lexicon of Jewish Names*, 185b.

159 Ilan, *Lexicon of Jewish Names*, 184, s. v. *Yazēdād.*

160 Ilan, *Lexicon of Jewish Names*, 190.

161 Bhayro *et al.*, *Aramaic Magic Bowls*, 159.

162 All the Aramaic names in this section are JBA unless otherwise indicated, and the Iranian names and lexemes are Middle Persian unless otherwise stated.

163 Geller, "Four Aramaic," 57–59: D.

164 See Montgomery, *Aramaic Incantation Texts*, 83.

165 For a thorough discussion of Jewish clients and adversaries in the incantation bowls see Shaked, "Rabbis in Incantation Bowls" and Herman "Jewish Identity"; cf. Zadok, "On the Arameans," 62–64.

166 Bhayro *et al.*, *Aramaic Magic Bowls*, 120, 124.

167 Faraj, *Coppe magiche*, 106:10, 5.

168 Segal, *Catalogue*, 024A, 1 and 044A, 7, 10 respectively.

169 Bhayro *et al.*, *Aramaic Magic Bowls*, 26, 29.

170 Shaked *et al.*, *Aramaic Bowl Spells*, 102, 4. 10.

a Jew with a pagan matronym,[171] seeing that *n'n'* is an appellative meaning "mother" in JBA (cf. ↓4). On the whole, most names deriving from the Hebrew Bible can refer to either Jews or Christians,[172] cf., e.g., *Ywhn'n* s. of *'kw'rwy'* and *Ywh'n'n* husband of *Mrym*,[173] clients of Mandaic incantations.[174] The clients mentioned in Isbell 1975, 23–24 may be Jewish or Christian in view of the fact that one of their children is named Abraham.

C Some Conclusions

So far there is no extra-biblical evidence for the presence of Israelites in Media. Iranian presence in Assyria proper recorded from 810 to 618 BCE. Most of the twenty-three individuals with Iranian names (or the gentilic "Median") lived in the urban centres of Assyria proper (Calah, Nineveh and Assur). Some are recorded in the Jazirah. Some Israelite-Judeans dwelled in the same places as the Iranians, but there is no evidence for a cultural or religious encounter. Later on, in the first third of the sixth century BCE, prominent Judeans and some Medes are recorded in an archive from the Southern Fortress of Babylon, but there is no evidence for any encounters. The situation changed radically during the Achaemenid period, when Babylon as one of the Achaemenid capitals became the arena of a Judeo-Iranian interaction.

In Sasanian Babylonia, the symbiosis of Semitic and Iranian cultures is reflected by several double names (↓7.2) and many mixed filiations. Most of the incantation bowls from Babylonia were written by Jewish practitioner-scribes, but among the clients and adversaries Jews (as far as they can be identified as such) are a small minority. The phonology of the Middle Persian names which are recored in Aramaic scripts is still fluid, e.g. names with final voiceless consonants or voiceless uvular stops (e.g., *'dq*, *P'bq*, ↓7.3.1.7) vs the majority which has already undergone the shift from voiceless to voiced (e.g., the names with *-dd*, ↓7.2.1); <*q*> is still exceptionally preserved in medial position (cf. *Yzdnqyrd*, ↓7.2.1). Since the texts are not dated, the phenomenon may not be only indicative of a later date, but also of a dialectal variety, cf., e.g., *Mhdṭ* vs *Mhdd*, *Bdṭ* < *Baga-dāta-* (↓7.2.1). There are typically Zoroastrian theophorous elements, notably of holy

171 As argued by Herman, "Jewish Identity," 137, n. 29.
172 See Shaked, "Rabbis in Incantation Bowls," 100.
173 Segal, *Catalogue*, 097M, 12, 13 and 099M, 12 respectively.
174 For Christians see also Shaked *et al.*, *Aramaic Bowl Spells*, 243.

fires[175] as well as basilophoric[176] and calendar names.[177] Regarding semantics, children named after instruments ("hammer").[178] *Yzy'* is recorded as a client; his co-client is named *Nybryzy'*, which apparently ends in the same component.[179] There is ample evidence of Iranian-Semitic linguistic interference. No less than seven names are either Aramaic or Iranian (↓1.2.1.1.6, 1.2.1.3.4, 1.2.8.2, 1.2.9.1, 1.2.9.2, 1.3.1.4, a, d').

Alphabetic lists of names and appellatives which are discussed above

Anthroponyms

In Aramaic scripts

'bmlk A.5
'dq C
'ḥt B.0
'ḥwdymmw B.0
'kw'rwy' B.0
'rwrt A.6
'sp°y° A.5
'wsr' B.0
'wstn A.2
Bʿlnbw A.5
Bdṭ C
Bgbrt A.4
Bgn A.1, 21, A.5
Bgprn A.6
Bgwhy A.2
Bgz[*wšt?*] A.5
Byl B.0
Ḥnn? A.5
M'dwkt 'h'ty' B, 0
M'hwy B.0
Mʿyn A.5
Mhdd C
Mhdṭ C
Mhwy B.0
Mnpt A.4
Mrym B.0
Mtr' A.4
Mtrdt A.4
Mzdgy A.4 A.4
Nny B.0
Ntn A.5
Nybryzy' C
P'bq C
Pp' B, 0
Rb Dym' B.0
Rbdymy B.0
Rb Mry B.0
Rb Yʿqwb) B.0
Rbyqw B.0
Rb Ytm' B.0
Srw B, 0
Symk A.6
Šmw'l B.0
Štbr A.5
Štrbwzny A.4
Š[*t*]*rkn* A.1, 12
Ttny A.4
Wh(w)dt A.4
Wnh A.6
Wny A.4
Wšḥy A.6
[x]*q* A.5
Yhwdh B.0
Yhwdy B.0
Yḥzq'l B.0
Yṭyhw A.1
Ywhn'n B.0
Ywh'n'n B.0
Ywsy B.0
Yzy' C
Zby[*dy?*) A.5

175 See Zimmer, "Zur sprachlichen," 135:8.1.1; 138–139:8.2.
176 See Zimmer, "Zur sprachlichen," 137:8.1.5.
177 See Zimmer, "Zur sprachlichen," 140–142:8.4.
178 Cf. Lurje, *Personal Names*, 161 *ad* 369.
179 Moriggi, "Two New Incantation Bowls," 45–52, 57:1, 3, 11 and 8 respectively.

In Cuneiform (NB/LB unmarked)

A-bé-eš-ta-am-ba (NA) A.1, 10
Adad-šarra-uṣur (s. of Kalbâ) A.2
Ahiqam A.2
Ardīya (s. of Šulâ desc. of Ilīya) A.2
A-ti-ʾ-ú-pa-ra-ʾ A.2
A-za-ri-iá-u A.1
Ba-ga-a-nu (NA) A.1, 21
Ba-ge-e-šú A.2
Ba-na-ia-a-ma → Ra-hi-im
Banna-Ea → Ga-da-la-a-ma
Barak-ia/iá-u (NA) A.1
Bar-zi-i (NA) A.1, 3, 4, 11, 18
Bar-zi-ia-[*a*] (NA) A.1, 20
Bēl-aḫa-ittannu (s. of Lâbâši) A.2
Bēl-ēṭir (s. of Nabû-ahhē-bulliṭ) A.2
Bēl-rēmanni (s. of Mušebši-Marduk) A.2
Bēl-zēra-ibni → Né-ri-ia-a-ma
Bunene-ibni → Iššar-tarībi
Da-na-a → $^{\ulcorner f \urcorner}$D/Ṭib?-bi-ʾ daughter of Da-na-a A.2
Ga-da-la-a-ma (s. of Banna-Ea) A.2
Gu-uk-ka-ʾ A.2
Ha-na-ni-ʾ-ia-a-ma A.2
Hanani A.3
Handî A.1
Harrānāyu A.1
Hu-ba-na-nu (NA) A.1
^{d}*Ia-hu-ú-iddina* A.2
^{d}*Ia-hu-ú-šarra-uṣur* A.3
Ilīya → Ardīya
Iššar-tarībi (s. of Bunene-ibni) A.3
Kalbâ → Adad-šarra-uṣur
Kīnâ → Nabû-bān-ahi
Ku-re-e-nu (NA) A.1, 23
*Kur-ri-ìl-la-*A+A (NA) A.1
Ku-ta-ki (NA) A.1, 8
Lâbâši → Bēl-aḫa-ittannu

*Mad-*A+A (NA) A.1, 5–7, 11

Mādāyu A.1, 5–7, 11
Ma-du-ki/ku (NA) A.1, 22
Man-nu-kī-Adad A.1, 21
Ma-ri-li-hi (NA) A.1
Mar-lih-ʾ (NA) A.1
Mar-li-hi-ia (NA) A.1
Mar-tú-ʾ (NA) A.1
Mu-šá-la-am A.2
Mušebši-Marduk → Bēl-rēmanni
Nabû-ahhē-bulliṭ → Bēl-ēṭir
Nabû-bān-ahi (s. of Kīnâ) A.2
Nabūgu A.3
Nabû-kuṣuršu (s. of Rībatu) A.2
Nabû-šarra-bulliṭ → *Šá-ab-ba-ta-A+A*
Nabû-zēra-iddina (s. of Sîn-šarra-uṣur) A.2
Nanâ-kānat A.2
Né-ri-ia-a-ma (s. of Bēl-zēra-ibni) A.2
Nūrānu A.1
Pa-ar-nu-u-a (NA) A.1, 16
Pa-ra-ʾ-u (NA) A.1, 9
Pa-ra-an-ša-ka (NA) A.1, 19
Pa-ra-gu-šú A.2
Par-ta-a-ma (NA) A.1, 13
Qar-ha-a (NA) A.1
Ra-hi-im (s. of Ba-na-ia-a-ma) A.2
Ra-hi-mi-il A.2
Rībatu → Nabû-kuṣuršu
Sa-am-bu-uk (NA) A.1, 17
Sili (NA) A.1, 18
Sîn-šarra-uṣur → Nabû-zēra-iddina
⸢*Si*⸣*-ti-ir-ka-a-nu/Si-t*[*i-ir-ka-a-nu*] (NA) A.1, 12
Šá-ab-ba-ta-A+A (s. of Nabû-šarra-bulliṭ) A.3
Šulâ → Ardīya
Ta$_5$*-ga-bi-ia-a-ma* A.3
Tattannu A.4
Ṭāb-šá-lam<<-ma>>-mu A.2
Ú-ar-gi (NA) A.1, 2
Ú-dar/da-ar-na-ʾ A.2
Ú-ma-nu (NA) A.1
Ú-na-ma-a (NA) A.1, 15
Ú-ri-ia-a (NA) A.1, 14
Ur-ru-da (NA) A.1, 1
[xx(x)] (s. of Za-kar-⸢ri?⸣-⸢ia?-ma⸣) A.2
Yahu-šarra-uṣur A.2
Za-kar-⸢ri?⸣-⸢ia?-ma⸣ → [xx(x)]

Arabic

Muʿīn A.5

Biblical Hebrew

ʾḥštry A.3
ʾšḥwr A.3
ʿylm A.3
Bgwy A.3
Bnyw A.2
Ḥšbdnh A.3
Ḥšbnh A.3
Ḥšbnyh/*Ḥšbnyh* A.3
hTršt' A.3
Mgbyš A.3
Prnk A.3
Ssmy A.3
Ššn A.3
Ššy A.3
Tyry' A.3
Wny' A.3
Wpsy A.3
Ztm A.3
Ztw' A.3

Middle Iranian

Kwryn (Parthian) A.1, 22
Mān-dād (Middle Persian) A.4

Philistian

ʾdnš A.5
ʾgnh A.5
ʾlyqm A.5
ʾmnh A.5
ʾnš A.5
Bʿlʾ A.5
Bʿlšmʾ A.5
Bmlk A.5
Brṣyh A.
Ddymš A.5
Dtyn A.5
Hkr A.5
Hrš A.5
Ḥ°mš A.5
Klyṭbš A.5
K°š A.5
Nnš A.5
Ntn A.5
Ppš A.5
Qlgryh A.5
Qsryh A.5
Rkh A.5
Ṣbršyh A.5
Šgš A.5
Šlm A.5
⌞*Šl*⌟ [...] A.5
Šmʾš A.5
⌞*Ṭy*° A.5
Wnnt A.5
Yhw[...] A.5

Reconstructed Old Iranian

**Abi-štamba-* A.1, 10
**Arva-raθa-* A.6
**Aspa-*, *-iya-*(pro-)patronymic of A.5
**Atṛ-šiyāta-* A.3
**Aθī-hu-pā-ra-* A.2
**Ava-stāna-* A.2
**Baga-*, *-āna-*(pro-)patronymic of A.1, 21
**Baga-bṛta-* A.4
Baga-dāta- C
**Baga-aiša-* A.2
**Bag(a)iča-* A.2
**Baga-farnah-* A.6
**Bagāna-* A.5
**Baga-vahya-* A.2
**Baga-zušta-*? A.5
**Bṛziya-* A.1, 3, 4, 20
**Čiθra-baujana-* A.4
**Čiθrakāna-* A.1, 12
**Dātaina-* A.5
**Dṛva-* B, 0
**Far(a)n-saka-* A.1, 19
**Farnah-saka-* A.1, 19
**Farnahvā* A.1, 16
**Farnaka-* A.3
**Farnah-vant-* A.1, 16
**Fratama-* A.1, 13
**Gau-ka-* A.2
**Hu-arga-* A.1, 2
.**Hu-nāma-* A.1, 15
**Kura-*, *-aina-*hypocoristicon of A.1, 22
**Kutaka-* A.1, 8
**Madu-ka-* A.1, 22
**Marta-* A.1
**Mazdā-gaya-* A.4
**Miθra-* A.4
**Miθraya-* A.4
**Pāpa-* B, 0
**Paru-gu-* A.2
**Paruva-* A.1, 9
**Sambu-ka-* A.1, 17
**Syāmaka-* A.6
**Š(iy)āti-bara-* A.5
**Tīriya-* A.3
**Uzya-* A.3
**Vača-x-aya-* A.6
**Vahu-dāta-* A.4
**Vana-* A.6 *
Vanya- A.4
**Vanyah-* A.3
**Varya-* A.1, 14
**Vi-paisa-* A.3
**Xšaθr-iya-* A.3

Reconstructed Old Persian

*Čiçiya-/*Čiçaya- A.3
*Čiçina- A.3

Other reconstructed names

*ḥšwry A.3
*'šḥwry A.3
*Pap(a)hu A.1, 21
*Paphu A.1
*Ššyn A.3
*Wpys – A.3

Royal Achaemenia Elamite

Ú-na-ma A.1, 15

Toponyms and ethnonyms

Abanu A.2
Bīt-Murānu A.2
Byt hglgl A.3
Dūr-Katlimmu A.1, 22
Elamites A.1
ḥṣry Nṭwpty A.3
Kak-mis/š A.1
Kapar-Kuzbi-šarri A.1
kkr sbybwt Yrwšlm A.3
Ma'allānāte A.1
(*Māt-)Paphî* A.1
Pa-pa-ah-hi A.1
Pa-pa-an-hi A.1
kurPa-pa-ha-A+A A.1, 21
Paphi A.1
Qaštu A.1
Tall il-far'a A.5
Tall jammi A.5
Teman A.2
Uruk A.2
Yahūdu A.2
Yhw temple in Nebo A.2

Theonyms

Humban (Elam.) A.1
Yhw Teman A.2
Yhw of Samaria A.2

Appellatives (Aramaic unmarked)

**dizapati-* (OIran.) A.3
dyny' A.4
lúma-gu-šá-A+A (LB) A.2
lúma-gu-še-emeš (LB) A.2
lúma-gu-šú (LB) A.2
mārē ekalli (Akkad.) A.2
bīt hare (Akkad.) A.2
mšqh hmlk (BHeb.) A.3
n'n' B.0
pa-ba-ah-hu-ú (OB Mari) A.1
pabanhi (Hurr.) A.1
papahhu (Hurr.) A.1
pa-ba-ah-hi-im (OB Mari) A.1
rab birti (Akkad.) A.3
rb šqh A.3
ša-ekalli (Akkad.) A.3
šgl (BHeb.) A.3
šqh A.3
šušānus A.3
śr hbyrh (BHeb.) A.3

Subjects

Basilophoric names C
calendar names C
Christians B.0
decury A.5
Eanna temple archive A.2
gardu-workmen A.2
Holy fires as theophorous elements C
identification of *Yhw* with *Bēl* = *Ba'al* A.2
interpretatio Babyloniaca A.2
magian priests A.2
palace servants A.2

Appendix

1 Aramaic names

1.1 Compound names

1.1.1 Verbal sentence

a. With a perfect verb: *Gdbḥr* (of *br* ~, OSyr.)[180] "Gadd has chosen".[181] Mand. *Ywk'b'r*[182]/*Ywkb'r*[183]/*Ywkbr*[184] (an angel with the epithet *zyw'* "splendour, brilliance"[185] and *kwšṭ'* "honesty, truth, justice"[186]) "Y(h)w has dominated, overwhelmed" (G of K-B-R as in Mand.).[187] *Mrymr*[188] "(My) lord has said, commanded; thought".[189] Mand. *Aaštar-bna*[190] "'Aštar has built, fashioned" (B-N-Y, Common Aram.) and *Nḥryb'n'* (fem.)[191] "The (divine) River has built, created". *Qnyh*[192] occurs in the same text as *Ṣrwyh* which strengthens the case that it is a Yahwistic name rather than "reed; idol".

b. With an imperfect verb: *Kynyḥyy*[193] "The just one will live" (K-W/Y-N and Ḥ-W/Y-Y),[194] and perhaps *Bylyḥwy*[195] "Bēl will show, demonstrate" (Ḥ-W/Y-Y, JBA, OSyr., Mand.).

---

180 Moriggi, *Corpus*, 22, 3.
181 See Harviainen, "Aramaic Incantation Bowl," 15 *ad* 3.
182 Yamauchi, *Mandaic Incantation Texts*, 22, 14, 104.
183 Cf. Ford, "Another Look," 260 *ad* 104M, 17.
184 Cf. Shaked *et al.*, *Aramaic Bowl Spells* (2022), 87 with references.
185 Gordon, "Aramaic Magical Bowls," 331–334: E. The same epithet is borne by *Ywsmyr* (/*Yusmir*/, see Ford, "Another Look," 245–246 *ad* 083M, 17).
186 Cf. Ford, "Another Look," 265 *ad* 106M, 10'.
187 Cf. without Tetragramatization Mand. *Kb'r zyw'* (Yamauchi, *Mandaic Incantation Texts*, 22, 63).
188 Ilan, *Lexicon*, 186 with the unacceptable lemmatization *Marmares.*
189 See Nöldeke, "Names," 3283, cf. Zadok, "Zur Struktur," 248:1.1.2.1.
190 Gorea, "Trois nouvelles," 72–78, 90–1, rev. 2–3.
191 Abudraham, "Ancient Mandaic Palimpsest," 2–7, iii, 17, v, 5–6; *Nḥrybn'* (i, 8).
192 Ilan, *Lexicon*, 185–186.
193 Harviainen, "Aramaic Incantation Bowl," 2, 10, 12 (*bis*). *Kylyḥyy* (9) is a secondary form.
194 Differently Shaked, "Rabbis," 114, n. 70.
195 Isbell, *Corpus*, 65, 1.

1.1.2 Nominal sentence

Ḥydmḥdyn (/*Ḥayy-d-mḥadd(i)yān*/) "The living being (epithet > theophorous element)[196] who is the joybringer".[197] Mand. *S'bry' ly'šw* "His hope is in Jesus".[198] *Ḥywtyh* (/*Ḥayyūt-yah*/) "Life is Yah".[199]

1.1.3 Nominal Juxtaposition

Ddgdy' (OSyr.)[200] consists of *Dd* "darling" (elsewhere recorded also as a theophorous element) and *gdy'* "kid".[201] *Mrb'* (referring in all probability to a Christian),[202] Mand. *M'r'b'* (/*Mār-'Abā*/)[203] "Mr. 'Abā" is recorded in Old Syriac as well.[204] Mand. *Mār-sapin*[205] "Mr. S.", whose 2nd component derives from S-P-N "to respect, mind" (JBA, JPA, Targ.), probably a passive participle meaning "respected, worthy". Mand. *Mr'd'*[206] may be of the same type (/*Mār-'Ad(d)ā*/, i.e. "Mr. Ad(d) ā") provided it is not based on a *qatal*-formation of M-R-D. *Mrzwṭr'* denotes "Mr. Little".[207] *Rb M'ry* "Rabbi M." is recorded as an anthroponym.[208] *'(y)m' Slm'* is aptly compared with *'ym' Šlwm*.[209] The 2nd component of fem. *H'w' Sym't* (Mand.) denotes "treasure".[210]

1.1.4 Prepositional clause

Mnmlk' (fem.) "From the King".[211]

196 Cf. Zadok, *West Semites in Babylonia*, 67 and *Pre-Hellenistic Israelite*, 181.

197 The editor (Hunter, "Two Incantation Bowls," 111 *ad* 1, 9, 14) renders it as "Life for gladness", but the last component is a D active participle, not an abstract noun. As for the semantics, the association between "alive, vivid" and "spirited, animated, joyful" is a common phenomenon.

198 See Pognon *Inscriptions mandaïtes*, 103 *ad* 4 and cf. Nöldeke, "Review," 145.

199 See Segal, *Catalogue*, 73b *ad* 034A, 2.

200 Moriggi, *Corpus*, 30, 5 (*Dddgy'*), 14, 22.

201 See Segal, *Catalogue*, 148 *ad* 118ES, 5, 13: 271.

202 Gordon, "Aramaic Magical Bowls," 321–324 and pl. 10:A, 4.

203 Yamauchi, *Mandaic Incantation Texts*, 23, 14.

204 For this name type (< title + PN) see Zadok, "Zur Struktur," 249:1.2.2.2, C.

205 Morgenstern, "Mandaic Magic Bowls," 161: M45 (digest only).

206 Yamauchi, *Mandaic Incantation Texts*, 23, 4.

207 See Segal, *Catalogue*, 80 *ad* 039A, 3.

208 Levene, *Jewish Aramaic Curse Texts*, 024A, 1, 4.

209 By Gordon 1934b: 471 *ad* 467 and pl. 22, 1, 2.

210 Cf. Ford, "Another Look," 264 *ad* DC 14, 183.

211 See Gordon, "Two Aramaic," 235 *ad* I, 1.

1.1.5 Genitive compounds

a. Theophorous names, a'. With passive participle: *Brykyhbyh* "Blessed by Yhw",[212] Mand. *Brikihbh̲,* [213] *Bryk mry'/Bryk mryh*[214] "Blessed by the lord", and presumably *Brkyšmšy* "Blessed by my sun".[215]

b'. With *ʿbd* "servant" and *'mt* "maid": *'bd'yšw*[216]/*'bdyšw*[217] (< *ʿAbd-Īšō*ʾ) "Servant of Jesus" (Christian); Mand. *'bdrhm'n*[218] (< /*ʿAbd-raḥmān*/) "Servant of Raḥmān" ('merciful', cf. *rḥmn'* as an epithet of Yhw in Jewish Aramaic) from Cutha. Aramaic pagan names are *Mšmš* and *Mnbw* mean "Maid of (< *'mt* with aphaeresis and assimilation) of *Šmš* (Sun-god)/*Nbw*".[219] The latter is also recorded without aphaeresis (*'mnbw*).[220] Mand. *'mš'myš* is a variant of *Mšmš* without aphaeresis.[221] With epithets as theophorous elements: *Mmlyk* (fem.)[222] < **'mt-mlyk* and *Mmry'* < **'mt-mry'*, i.e. "Maid of *Mlyk*" ('[divine] king', spelled plene with <y> for /ə/) and "of (the) Lord" (cf. OSyr. *Mmlk'*)[223] respectively. Mand. *'m't-ʿstr'* > *ʿmst'r* originates from Amat-Ištar with < ʿ> for /'/ / "Maid of Ištar".[224]

c'. With *br* "son": *Br'yd'*[225] "son of a feast day" (OSyr., Targ.), i.e. born on a feast, commemorating the time of birth. *Brḥw(')y* "Son of law" (Targ. det. *ḥwyy'/h).*[226] *Br ḥyy'*[227] (Mand.) "Son of life" (his matronym *'nwš'y* means "immortal" in Middle Persian); *Bršbt'/Bršbth*[228] and *Bršpt'*[229] "Sabbath's son" (OSyr. *Bršpt'* and *Bršbt'* refer to the same individual)[230] as well as the homonymous name *Bršb'*.[231]

---

212 See Levene, *Jewish Aramaic Curse Texts*, 97 *ad* SD 27, 11 with lit. (especially Montgomery, *Aramaic Incantation Texts*, 210–211 *ad* 26, 4). Differently Naveh and Shaked, *Amulets and Magic Bowls*, 164–165 *ad* 6, 5.

213 Bhayro *et al.*, *Aramaic Magic Bowls*, 41.

214 Gordon, "Aramaic Incantation Bowls," 127–129:7, 1, 5 and 11 respectively.

215 Cf. Levene, *Jewish Aramaic Curse Texts*, 21.

216 See Shaked *et al.*, *Aramaic Bowl Spells* (2022), 220 *ad* 116, 4.

217 Cf. Morgenstern and Ford, *Aramaic Incantation Bowls*, 56:MS 1927/50, 4 (unpubl.).

218 Segal, *Catalogue*, 078M, 8, cf. Ford, "Another Look," 34, n. 9.

219 See Shaked *et al.*, *Aramaic Bowl Spells* (2022), 8b (cf. Shaked *et al.*, *Aramaic Bowl Spells* [2013], 100); cf. Morgenstern and Abudraham, "A Mandaean Lamella," 231 *ad* 158.

220 See Shaked *et al.*, *Aramaic Bowl Spells* (2022), 209.

221 See Morgenstern, "Five Mandaic," 112 *ad* 24, 10.

222 Müller-Kessler, *Zauberschalentexte*, 12, 4.

223 See Morgenstern and Ford, *Aramaic Incantation Bowls*, 102, n. 380 *ad* 3034, 4.

224 See Morgenstern, "Five Mandaic," 112 *ad* 25, 10.

225 Ilan, *Lexicon*, 171–172.

226 Differently Segal, *Catalogue*, 73 *ad* 034A, 1, 3.

227 Yamauchi, Mandaic Incantation Texts, 22, 72, 105.

228 Morgenstern and Ford, *Aramaic Incantation Bowls* 3026, 4, 8 and 3023, 4, 5, 3064, 2 respectively; cf. 72, n. 244 where more "calendar names" are discussed.

229 See Naveh and Shaked, *Amulets and Magic Bowls*, 183 *ad* 10, 7.

230 Moriggi, *Corpus*, 24, 7, 11 and 13 respectively.

231 Gordon, "Aramaic Incantation Bowls," 350–351:IM 11113.

Interestingly, Talm. *Br-šbty* is described as a distinctive non-Jewish name.[232] *Brgll* "Son of *G.*"[233] (G-L-L "to exalt", CPA, SA). Perhaps *Bršwty*[234] is also of this type. *Bršybby* apparently means "Son of the neighbouring".[235] Mand. *Brb'by'*[236] "Son of *B'by*'" (cf. *B'b'y* ↓4), *Brm'm'y*[237] "Son of *M'm'y*" and *Br'ḥ'y* "Son of *'ḥ'y*"[238] (cf. ↓1.2.7.1). For *Br Gdbḥr* see ↑1.1.1. *Br'm'* (Mand.)[239] "Son of the paternal uncle". *Brb'mh* was interpreted as "Son of his paternal uncle"[240] which leaves the *-b-* unaccounted for. Cf. Talm. *Br Qydry* (a distinctive non-Jewish name),[241] whose 2nd componenent may derive from Q-D-R "to be dark" (Aram.) or be an archaic gentilic "Qedarite's son". *Brshdy* (OSyr. *Br shd'*)[242] "Martyrs' son" is a Christian name.[243]

d'. With *bt* "daughter": *Btgd'*[244] "Daughter of Fortune",[245] *Btḥyy*[246] "Daughter of life"; *Btqnh*[247] "Daughter of *Qnh*" (*qatal*-formation of Q-N-Y "create, purchase"); *Btlylyt'*[248] "Daughter of Lilith"; *Btn'ny*[249] "d. of Nanay" (a goddess). *Btšbty (*with assimilation *Bšbty (/Baš-šabbatay/)*,[250] *Btšptyy*[251] *"Šabbatay*'s daughter", cf. Mand. *Pt špt(')*[252] "Sabbath's daughter". Mand. *B't 'sy'*[253] denotes "The Physician's daughter"; *Bt gyl'*[254] "Daughter of the (same) age"; *Bt'nb'* (*/Bat-'inbā/*, OSyr.) "daughter of the fruit".[255] *Btšyty* interchanges with *Btšytwn*[256] (< *Btšytyn, lit.* "Daughter of

232 BT Gittin 11a, cf. Kiperwasser and Shapira, "Encounters," 300.
233 Cf. Montgomery, *Aramaic Incantation Texts*, 186 *ad* 15, 3.
234 Ilan, *Lexicon*, 172a. For the type *br* + PN/appelative cf. Zadok, "Zur Struktur," 250:1.4, C.
235 Differently Montgomery, *Aramaic Incantation Texts*, 186 *ad* 2.
236 Pognon, *Inscriptions mandaïtes*, 19.
237 Segal, *Catalogue*, 103M, 2.
238 See Segal, *Catalogue*, 127 *ad* 096M, 45.
239 Jursa, "Eine Mandäische," 146, 3, cf. Abudraham, "Three Mandaic," 82.
240 By Segal, *Catalogue*, 66 *ad* 024A, 6.
241 BT Gittin 11a, cf. Kiperwasser and Shapira, "Encounters," 300.
242 Moriggi, *Corpus*, 13, 9–10.
243 See Shaked *et al.*, *Aramaic Bowl Spells* (2013), 100.
244 Shaked *et al.*, *Aramaic Bowl Spells* (2013), 58a, 3, 5.
245 Cf. the male's name *Bryg[d']* (*/Bar-giddā/*) "Son of Fortune", which is extant in a Parthian inscription from Dura-Europos (the 2nd component with *qall* > *qill*, not **Bar-gad-ā* as normalized by Schmitt, *Personennamen* 79:136).
246 Shaked *et al.*, *Aramaic Bowl Spells* (2022), 105, 4; 106, 4.
247 Bhayro *et al.*, *Aramaic Magic Bowls*, 40.
248 Bhayro *et al.*, *Aramaic Magic Bowls*, 24.
249 Shaked *et al.*, *Aramaic Bowl Spells* (2013), 44, 4 [*ny*], 9 (*n* ∘ *y* ∘).
250 Bhayro *et al.*, *Aramaic Magic Bowls*, 40.
251 Shaked *et al.*, *Aramaic Bowl Spells* (2013), 17, 4, 7.
252 Yamauchi, *Mandaic Incantation Texts*, 1, 5, 8.
253 Yamauchi, *Mandaic Incantation Texts*, 3, 6, 9.
254 See Müller-Kessler, "Die Zauberschalensammlung," 123 *ad* 036A, 3.
255 See Segal, *Catalogue*, 148 *ad* 117ES, 10.
256 Levene, *Jewish Aramaic Curse Texts*, 041A, 15, 19 and 1, 18 respectively.

sixty", presumably "A lady of sixty years"[257]). Christian names[258] are *Btšhdy*[259] (OSyr. *Btshd'*)[260] "Martyrs' daughter" as well as *Btḥdšbh*,[261] *Btḥpšb'*[262] (< *Btḥdšb'*) "daughter of Sunday".

e'. With *'b* "father": *'bwsmk'*[263] (/*Abū-samkā*/) looks hybrid (Arameo-Arabic): it apparently consists of *'bw* "father of" (Arab.) and *smk'* "support" (Aram.), a *kunya*.

f'. Other: Mand. *D'dmnd'*[264] may denote "Beloved of Manda". Alternatively "Given by Manda", a hybrid (MPers.-Aram.) name like *Dād-Īšōʿ* "Given by Jesus".[265] *Manda* < *Mandaʿ* denotes "knowledge, γνῶσις"; *Manda ḏ-hiia* is the outstanding saviour spirit of the Mandaic religion; *'ylyšbḥ* "Praise of my god".[266]

b. Substitute names: *'b'b'y*[267] "My father's father"; *'ḥdbwy* "His father's brother"[268] *'ḥdb'y*,[269] possibly "My father's brother", *'bymy* "My mother's father" (same meaning as *'bdymy*[270]/*'bwd(y)my*[271] and with aphaeresis *Bwdymy*[272] and *Bydymy'*[273]), *'ym' dymh*[274]/*'ymh d'ymh*[275] "Her mother's mother"[276]; *'ym(y)d'bw*[277]/*'ymydbw*[278]/*'ymdbw*[279] /*(')ymṭbw*[280]/*'ym'ṭbw*[281] (Εμμεδαβος[282]), OSyr. *ym'd'bwhy*[283]/

257 See Segal, *Catalogue*, 65 *ad* 024A, 5.
258 See Shaked *et al.*, *Aramaic Bowl Spells* (2013), 100.
259 Shaked *et al.*, *Aramaic Bowl Spells* (2022), 98, 7, 14, 17.
260 Moriggi, *Corpus*, 6, 12, 14.
261 Gordon, "Aramaic Magical Bowls," 321–324 and pl. 10:A, 4.
262 Shaked *et al.*, *Aramaic Bowl Spells* (2022), 99, 2, 5, 19, 22.
263 Shaked *et al.*, *Aramaic Bowl Spells* (2013), 13, 3, 7.
264 Morgenstern, "Five Mandaic," 109–11112:24, 4, 8, 11, 15.
265 Cf. Gignoux, Jullien and Jullien, *Noms propres*, 63–64.
266 See Levene, *Jewish Aramaic Curse Texts*, 95 *ad* SD 27, 4.
267 Levene, *Jewish Aramaic Curse Texts*, B7, 1.
268 See Ford, "Phonetic Spellings," 237 (erroneously listed as an Arabic name by Ilan, *Lexicon*, 257).
269 See Ford, "Phonetic Spellings," 237–238.
270 Bhayro *et al.*, *Aramaic Magic Bowls*, 120, 124 (see Ford, "Phonetic Spellings," 236, n. 56).
271 Shaked *et al.*, *Aramaic Bowl Spells* (2013), 345, index, s. v. with references.
272 Morgenstern and Ford, *Aramaic Incantation Bowls* 3058, 8.
273 Gordon, "Magic Bowls," 238:ii, 4.
274 Harviainen, "Aramaic Incantation Bowl," 5, 8.
275 Geller, "More magic spells," 331–335:B, 8 f., 23, cf. Shaked, "Rabbis," 115.
276 See Ford, "Phonetic Spellings," 237.
277 Bhayro *et al.*, *Aramaic Magic Bowls*, 55, 75.
278 See Ford, "Phonetic Spellings," 237, n. 59.
279 Bhayro *et al.*, *Aramaic Magic Bowls*, 63 (see Ford, "Phonetic Spellings," 237, n. 60).
280 Bhayro *et al.*, *Aramaic Magic Bowls*, 25. For the spelling of the subordinating particle with *ṭ* instead of *d* see Ford, "Phonetic Spellings," 229.
281 Ford, "Phonetic Spellings," 238.
282 Jarry, "Inscriptions arabes," 208:153.
283 Not Iranian as suggested by Müller-Kessler, "A Mandaic Gold Amulet," 336 *ad* 334–336, 2.

Mand. *ʿmadabu* "Her father's mother";[284] *'mdbn* "The father's mother";[285] *'ḥwdymw (si vera lectio)*[286] "His mother's brother"; *'ḥt'd'b(w)h*[287]/*ḥt'd'bh*[288] (with aphaeresis)/*'ḥtbw*[289]/*'ḥt'ṭ'bwh,*[290] *'ḥt'bw,*[291] *'ḥ'dbh,*[292] *Ḥtdbw*[293] (with aphaeresis), Mand. *'ḥṭṭbw*[294] (with aphaeresis Mand. *Ḥ'tṭ'bw*)[295] "Her father's sister", *'ḥtby*[296] "My father's sister", Mand. *Ahtaṭbun* "Our father's sister".[297] *'ḥtym'*/Mand. *Ahat 'ma* "(Her) mother's sister";[298] *'<ḥ>thdmh*[299]/*'ḥt'ṭym'/h*[300] "Her mother's sister" (with aphaeresis Mand. *Ḥtṭym'*[301] and with assimilation of *t* to the following dental Mand. *Ḥṭym'*[302]), and *'ḥtmy*[303] "My mother's sister", Mand. *'h't'm'* "The mother's sister".[304] Mand. *'ḥt'ṭbwn*[305] "Our father's sister" (all substitute names).[306] *Br'ḥw*[307] "His brother's son", *Br(')ym'*[308] (OSyr. *Brym'*)[309] "the mother's son" and

---

284 Ford, "Phonetic Spellings," 237 with n. 60.
285 See Ford, "Phonetic Spellings," 237, n. 59.
286 Faraj, *Coppe magiche*, 10, 5.
287 Bhayro *et al.*, *Aramaic Magic Bowls*, 220, index, s.v. with references (see Ford, "Phonetic Spellings," 237).
288 Wohlstein, "Über einige aramäische," 9, 30–34:[VA] 2414, 5 = *'ḥt'd'bwh*, 9.
289 See Ford, "Phonetic Spellings," 237.
290 For the spelling of the subordinating particle with *ṭ* instead of *d* see Ford, "Phonetic Spellings," 229 and cf. Levene, *Jewish Aramaic Curse Texts*, 96 *ad* SD 27, 7.
291 See Ford, "Phonetic Spellings," 237, n. 58 *ad* Segal, *Catalogue*, 61: 019A, 2.
292 With assimilation of *t* to the following *d* (cf. Wohlstein, "Über einige aramäische," 9, 29–30 *ad* [VA] 2426, 2).
293 Ford, "Phonetic Spellings," 237, n. 57.
294 Ford, "Phonetic Spellings," 238.
295 See Abudraham, "Three Mandaic," 92–93 *ad* 3, 15.
296 Gordon, "Aramaic Incantation Bowls," 349:IM 9726.
297 See Ford, "Phonetic Spellings," 239 with n. 68.
298 See Ford, "Phonetic Spellings," 237 with n. 61.
299 Bhayro *et al.*, *Aramaic Magic Bowls*, 108.
300 See Levene, *Jewish Aramaic Curse Texts*, 97 *ad* SD 27, 11. For the spelling of the subordinating particle with *ṭ* instead of *d* see Ford, "Phonetic Spellings," 229, 238.
301 See Abudraham, "Three Mandaic," 93.
302 Yamauchi, *Mandaic Incantation Texts*, 5, 2, 21. For the spelling of the subordinating particle with *ṭ* instead of *d* see Ford, "Phonetic Spellings," 229, 238.
303 Bhayro *et al.*, *Aramaic Magic Bowls*, 29. For the spelling of the subordinating particle with *ṭ* instead of *d* see Ford, "Phonetic Spellings," 229.
304 See Nöldeke, "Review," 143 *ad* Pognon, *Inscriptions mandaïtes*, 12.
305 Yamauchi, *Mandaic Incantation Texts*, 9, 22, 25. For the spelling of the subordinating particle with *ṭ* instead of *d* see Ford, "Phonetic Spellings," 229.
306 See Zadok, "Zur Struktur," 250:1.4, E.
307 Bhayro *et al.*, *Aramaic Magic Bowls*, 157.
308 Bhayro *et al.*, *Aramaic Magic Bowls*, 73 (cf. Naveh and Shaked, *Amulets and Magic Bowls*, 182 *ad* 10, 5.
309 Moriggi, *Corpus*, 24, 4, 8.

probably *'h't rbt'* (fem.)[310] "the big sister" (presumably referring to the firstborn sister). It is noteworthy that *'ḥdbwy* was son of *'ḥtbw.*[311] *Brdwd*[312] may denote "cousin" (Hebraism in JPA and Targ.), or it contained a dialectal form of *dd* "paternal uncle" (OSyr., Palm., Nab., cf. QA *br ddy* "My uncle's son"). Mand. *Ptp'p'* (< /*Bat-Pāpā*/) "daughter of the father".[313]

1.2 Simplex names

1.2.1 *qVtl*

'rḥ' (fem., + – *ā*, ↓1.3.3.1.1) "traveller, guest" (JBA, OSyr., JPA, Targ.).[314]

1.2.1.1 *qatl*

1.2.1.1.1 With stable consonants

Kspy[315] (+ – *āy*, ↓1.3.1.4) and Mand. *Kspwnt'*[316] (fem., + -*ōn-tā*, ↓1.3.3.2.12) are based on *ksp* "silver".

1.2.1.1.2 With resonant consonants

C_1 = resonant: *Mšk'y*[317] (+ – *āy*, ↓1.3.1.4) may be based on M-Š-K "to pull, draw out, attract".[318] *Rqd't'*[319] (+ -*ā-tā*, ↓1.3.3.2.2) is based on R-Q-D "to dance" (Aram.).

$C_{1,\ 2}$ = resonants: *Mlky*[320] and *Mlkwn'y*[321] are based on *mlk* "king" (cf. *Mlkwn*[y]). The former ends in -*āy* (↓1.3.1.4) and the latter is based on *mlkwn* "kinglet, chieftain" (det. *Mlkwn'*[322] (with diminutive -*ōn*) and -*āy* (↓1.3.2.4), which

310 Pognon, *Inscriptions mandaïtes*, 26.
311 Wohlstein "Über einige aramäische," 8, 328–340:[VA] 2422, 2, 27–28, 31–32, 40–41.
312 Moriggi, "Two New," 45–52, 57:1, 11.
313 See Müller-Kessler, "A Mandaic Lead Roll," 482 *ad* A, 5, B, 4.
314 Cf. Montgomery, *Aramaic Incantation Texts*, 222 *ad* 30, 1.
315 Bhayro *et al.*, *Aramaic Magic Bowls*, 93, 94.
316 See Müller-Kessler, "Die Zauberschalensammlung," 134 *ad* 088M, 5.
317 Ilan, *Lexicon*, 193a (with a wrong lemmatization). Such wrong lemmatizations are also Mihrdan (193–194), *Sāpōr* (201, *recte* < *Šāh-puhr*), *Aštād-Maha-Dūxt* (210–211, *recte Aštād-Māh-duxt*, 210–211)
318 Cf. Zadok, "Zur Struktur," 252:A.2.
319 Yamauchi, *Mandaic Incantation Texts*, 11, 51.
320 Gordon, "Aramaic Magical Bowls," 324–326 and pl. 11:B, 2.
321 Ilan, *Lexicon*, 190–191.
322 See Morgenstern and Ford, *Aramaic Incantation Bowls*, 120, n. 451 *ad* 3042, 10–11.

is adjectival (kinglet/chieftain-like"). However, *Mlkwn'y* is an emendation as the text has *Mlbwn'y*. The name may be alternatively be based on **mlb*, cf. OSyr. *mlb'* "perfume" (a loanword), in which case it is not originally of the *qatl*-formation.

$C_{1,3}$ = resonant: *Nṭrwy*[323] (+ *-ōy*, ↓1.3.1.6) is based on N-Ṭ-R "to guard".[324]

C_2 = resonant: *Brkyt'* consists of B-R-K "to bless"[325] and *-ay-t-ā* (↓1.3.3.2.19). *Krkwy (/Karkōy/* (> */Krakōy/* in view of *'krkwy*[326]), with *k* > *q* due to */r/ Qrqwy*,[327] fem.) is based on Aram. *krk* "town" (like MPers. *šahrestān*)[328] thereby denoting "urban". *Šrkh*[329] (+ *-ā*, ↓1.3.1.1), may denote "remnant" (OSyr., CPA, Targ.). *Ṭrdy* (fem.) may consist of Ṭ-R-D "to drive out; confine" (Common Aram., cf. Neo-Babylonian < Aram. *Ṭa-ra-da-ni*[330]) and *-īy* or *-āy* (↓1.3.3.1.3).

$C_{2,3}$ = resonants: The female's name *Qrnnyt'* is based on *qrn* "horn" and ends with adjectival *-ān* plus fem. *-īt-ā* (↓1.3.3.2.20) thereby denoting "horned".[331] *Šlm'* (fem.,[332] + *-ā*, ↓1.3.3.1.1) is based on Š-L-M "to be whole, complete, perfect" (Common Aram.).

C_3 = resonant: *Bgrn* cannot render Iran. *Bagarat*,[333] but may consist of B-G-R and adjectival *-ān* (↓1.3.1.7), thereby meaning "mature" (cf. *bgyr*). *Kpn(')y*[334] (+ – *āy*, ↓1.3.1.4) is apparently based on *kpn* "hunger,"[335] i.e. "related to hunger" (perhaps an *Ereignisname*), provided that it is not an Iranian name.[336] *Spr'y*[337] (> *Spr'*,[338] + *-āy* and *–ā* respectively, ↓1.3.1.1, 1.3.1.4) is based on *spr* "document,

323 Moriggi, *Corpus*, 24, 11.

324 Cf. Naveh and Shaked, *Amulets and Magic Bowls*, 183 *ad* 11,

325 See Levene, *Jewish Aramaic Curse Texts*, 36 *ad* VA 2423, 5, 11 who transcribes the suffix as *-īta*.

326 Gordon, "Aramaic Incantation Bowls," 131:10, 3.

327 Gordon, "Aramaic Magical Bowls," 324–326 and pl. 11:B, 3.

328 See Shaked, "Peace Be upon You," 214.

329 Ilan, *Lexicon*, 202a (with a wrong lemmatization).

330 Cf. Zadok "People from Countries," 123.

331 Cf. Levene, *Jewish Aramaic Curse Texts*, 96 *ad* SD 27, 8.

332 Schwab "Les coupes magiques," 331–334: I.

333 Despite Ilan, *Lexicon*, 170b.

334 Morgenstern and Ford, *Aramaic Incantation Bowls* 3016, 1.

335 Montgomery, *Aramaic Incantation Texts*, 166 *ad* 10, 1 and Levene, *Jewish Aramaic Curse Texts*, 53 *ad* VA 2434, 4 render *Kpny* and *Kpn'y* "the hungry one" which is not far off the mark; "hungry" in Aramaic is *kpyn*.

336 As cautiously suggested by Naveh and Shaked, *Amulets and Magic Bowls*, 159 *ad Q(bn)y* (4, 7).

337 Shaked *et al.*, *Aramaic Bowl Spells* (2013), 63, 2, 4.

338 This shift is apparently extant also in Mand. *B(')šnyr'y* (fem.,unexpl., cf. Ford, "Another Look," 241 *ad* 078M, 10 and 244 *ad* 083M,8–9) > *Bšnyr'* (cf. Müller-Kessler, "Die Zauberschalensammlung,"130 *ad* Segal, *Catalogue*, 077M, 8). Is it based on MPers. *bašn* "top, peak; stature; mane" (with a Parthian cognate, cf. Durkin-Meisterernst, *Grammatik*, 162–163: 4.1.3.5, 2, i)? It is apparently the 1st component of MPers. *bšnbyd* (*/bašnbed/*) "pagan priest". Cf. Parth. *Bšnyn* (with

letter, book".[339] *Šgly* (fem.,[340] + *-āy* or *-īy*, ↓1.3.3.1.), Mand. *Šgl'* (fem.,[341] + *-ā*, ↓1.3.3.1.1), cf. BAram. and Hatran *šglh* (det. *šglt'*), whose feminine marker is secondary in view of late BHeb. *šgl* < Akkad. *ša-ekalli* "queen" > "consort" in non-royal milieu as is the case here.

1.2.1.1.3 With (proto-)gutturals

'bd'[342] may either originally be *'bd'* "servant"[343] (+ *-ā*, ↓1.3.1.1) or based on MPers. *abd* "wonderful". *Shdwy*[344] and OSyr. *Shd'*[345] are based on *shd* "martyr" plus *-ōy* and *-ā* respectively (↓1.3.1.1, 1.3.1.6).

1.2.1.1.4 With resonants and (proto-)gutturals

Nḥlt (fem., + *-at*, ↓1.3.3.1.2)[346] "inheritance".

1.2.1.1.5 With *y-* and a resonant

Ytm'[347] "orphan" (+ *-ā*, ↓1.3.1.1).

1.2.1.1.6 With other unstable consonants

a. *qat'*: *Mr, Mry, Mry'* (+ *-īy* and *-yā*, ↓1.3.1.3, 1.3.1.5) "master, lord"[348] and its feminine counterpart *M'rt* (*Mārat*,[349] "lady", *qat'* > *qāt*) and in the (originally) determinate state *Mrt'*.[350] *M'r'y*[351] (+ *-āy*, ↓1.3.1.4) and *M'rwy*[352] (+ *-ōy*, ↓1.3.1.6) are also

-in; a Semitic derivation, which is cautiously considered by Schmitt, *Personennamen* 82:146, is unlikely despite of the possibility that his son bears a Semitic name; mixed filiations are not rare).

339 Cf. Fain *et al.*, "Aramaic Incantation Bowls," 294 *ad* S-445, 1.
340 Geller, "Eight Incantation Bowls," 115–116:Aaron F, 1.
341 Abudraham, "Three Mandaic," 88–93:3, 15.
342 Ilan, *Lexicon*, 163.
343 See Segal, *Catalogue*, 64 *ad* 023A, 2, 10.
344 Shaked *et al.*, *Aramaic Bowl Spells* (2022), 87, 6.
345 Moriggi, *Corpus*, 13, 10.
346 Segal, *Catalogue*, 024A, 7.
347 Segal, *Catalogue*, 044A, 7, 10.
348 See Levene, *Jewish Aramaic Curse Texts*, 36 *ad* VA 2423, 3; *Mry* is recorded in Shaked *et al.*, *Aramaic Bowl Spells* (2022), 69, 1; 79, 2 and *Mry'* in Gordon, "Aramaic Incantation Bowls," 123–124:5, 5, 11, 13.
349 Bhayro *et al.*, *Aramaic Magic Bowls*, 96.
350 Cf. Montgomery, *Aramaic Incantation Texts*, 158 *ad* 8, 5.
351 Gordon, "Aramaic Incantation Bowls," 273–276 and pls. 2–3 on 283, 6.
352 Naveh and Shaked, *Amulets and Magic Bowls*, 7, 1; not Iranian as erroneously claimed by Ilan, *Lexicon*, 192–193.

based on *mr'* "lord".[353] *Mrt'y* (+ *-āy*, ↓1.3.3.1.4) is the same woman as *Mrt'*[354] which like *Mrty*[355] is based on *mrt* "lady". Likewise, Mand. *Mr't'y*[356] is based on *Mr't* "lady".

b. *qaty*: *Dky'*[357] (+ *-ā*, ↓1.3.1.1) "pure, clean"; *Zkwt* (if this is the original form) derives from Z-K-Y (+ *-ūt*, ↓1.3.1.10) thereby denoting "merit, benefit".[358] It is with elision of *-y* like Mand. *Z'kwy'*[359] which probably means "innocent". *Rby*[360] means "young girl" (det. *rbyt'*,[361] JBA, Mand., JPA, SA, Targ., OSyr.[362]).

c. *qawy*: *Rwy'*[363] (+ *-ā*, ↓1.3.1.1) may denote "saturated" (to R-W/Y-Y, common Aram.). *N'w'* (fem.) may originate from *nw'y* "beauty" (Targ., hapax), provided it is not a Hebraism.[364] Alternatively Iranian (↓7.3.1).

d. *qa'y: Gyyt* (fem., + *-at*, ↓1.3.3.1.2)[365] may be the feminine equivalent of *g'y* "proud, sumptuous; pleasant, splendid" (OSyr., QA, Targ.). *G'ywt*[366] > *Gywt* (fem.,[367] +*-ūt*, ↓1.3.3.1.6) means "magnificence, splendour, pride" (to G-ʾ-Y, JBA, Mand., OSyr., Targ.). *Gywnyy* (fem.)[368] may be based on **ga'y-ōn* > *g'wn*, originally "proud; high" > JBA *g'wn* "head of an Academy" and the OT hapax *g'ywnym* pl. of **g'ywn*.[369]

353 See Gignoux, Jullien and Jullien, *Noms propres*, 97:279a.
354 Franco, "Five Aramaic," 242 and fig. 3 on 241:C_{10}-118, 13; 242–245 and fig. 4; 245–249 and fig. 5:C_{11}-3, 2;
355 Levene, *Jewish Aramaic Curse Texts*, 024, 6.
356 Yamauchi, *Mandaic Incantation Texts*, 25, 16.
357 Naveh and Shaked, *Amulets and Magic Bowls*, 134 and pls. 16–17:2, 10.
358 See McCullough, *Jewish and Mandean*, 8 *ad* 4 who calls attention to the spelling *Zkwš* and *Zḥwt* in the same text.
359 Gordon, "Two Magic Bowls," 309–310, 6.
360 Not /*Rabbē*/ as normalized by J. N. Epstein *apud* Gordon, "Aramaic Magical Bowls," 334 *ad* B, 2.
361 Ilan, *Lexicon*, 247b.
362 Moriggi, *Corpus*, 24, 11, 14.
363 Moriggi, "Two New," 45–52, 57:1, 11.
364 See Segal, *Catalogue*, 84b *ad* 041A, 12.
365 Isbell, *Corpus*, 62, 4 (*bis*). Ilan (*Lexicon*, 219) erroneously lists it together with *Gywt* with a wrong lemmatization and an unfounded comparison with an Iranian compound name.
366 Levene, *Jewish Aramaic Curse Texts*, 043A, 2, 3.
367 Geller, "Eight Incantation Bowls," 106–107:Aaron A, 3.
368 Shaked *et al.*, *Aramaic Bowl Spells* (2013), 56, 3, 5, 9.
369 Cf. Montgomery, *Aramaic Incantation Texts*, 156 *ad* 8, 1, with other attempts at an interpretation.

1.2.1.2 *qitl*

1.2.1.2.1 With stable consonants

Zypty[370] (+ – *āy*, ↓1.3.1.4) is based on *zpt* "pitch".

1.2.1.2.2 With resonant consonants

Nybryt'[371] (+ *-īt-ā*, ↓1.3.3.2.3) apparently derives from N-B-R, cf. OSyr. *nbr'* "claw" > "a device for fastening clothing". *Tyql'*[372] (Θεκλα, fem., with *-ā*, ↓1.3.3.1.1) derives from T-Q-L (< Ṯ-Q-L) ""to weigh, balance".

1.2.1.2.3 With (proto-)gutturals

Ḥylpy (fem.)[373] is based on Ḥ-L-P (see ↓1.2.12.2.1, + *-āy*, ↓1.3.3.1.4). *Ḥysdy*[374] consists of *ḥsd* "devotion, devout love, grace"[375] and *-āy* (↓1.3.1.4).

qi'l > *qayl:* Mand. *R'm'y* (fem., + *-āy*, ↓1.3.3.1.4)[376] is based on *r'm* "buffalo, aurochs" (JBA, OSyr., SA, QA, Targ.), "unicorn" (OSyr.). Mand. *Gyrby* (fem., + – *āy*, ↓1.3.3.1.4) "northerner".[377]

1.2.1.2.4 With unstable consonants

a. *qity: Ḥylywn (> Hylywn*[378], fem., + *-ōn*, ↓1.3.3.1.9) may be based on Ḥ-L-Y "to be sweet, pleasant" (common Aram.).

b. *qi'y: Gwt*[379] denotes "pride" (Mand., BAram., QA, Targ.); it derives from G-'-Y with elision of *-y* (+ *-ūt*, ↓1.3.3.1.6).[380]

---

370 Bhayro *et al., Aramaic Magic Bowls*, 42, 55.
371 Segal, *Catalogue*, 035A, 3.
372 Shaked *et al., Aramaic Bowl Spells* (2013), 20, 2, 5.
373 Bhayro *et al., Aramaic Magic Bowls*, 26.
374 Isbell, *Corpus*, 64, 3.
375 See Zadok, "Zur Struktur," 263:2.1.1.2.
376 Cf. Ford, "Another Look," 264 *ad* 106M, 6.
377 See Segal, *Catalogue*, 135 *ad* 103M, 6.
378 Ilan, *Lexicon*, 222.
379 Geller, "Eight Incantation Bowls," 115–116:Aaron F, 1.
380 For a futile attempt at an Iranian etymology cf. Ilan, *Lexicon*, 177b.

1.2.1.3 *qutl*

1.2.1.3.1 With stable consonants

Pwšky[381] "handbreadth" (Aram., plus adjectival *-āy*, ↓1.3.3.1.4).

1.2.1.3.2 With resonant consonants

Dwkry[382] "masculine" (cf. OSyr. *dkry*, *qetl* < *qutl* +-*āy*, ↓1.3.1.4), *Kwpry* (fem., + *-āy*, ↓1.3.3.1.4)[383] is based on *kwpr* "henna" (JBA, OSyr.). *Šwrš'*,[384] *Šršw(m)*[385] and *Šršy*[386]/*Šršyy*[387] (fem.) are based on *šrš* "root" > "radical, original, offspring"[388] (+ *-ō* < *-ōm* ~ adjectival *-ōn* and *-āy* respectively, ↓1.3.1.4, 1.3.1.9).

1.2.1.3.3 With resonants and (proto-)gutturals

Mand. *Hwlpwn'* (fem., plus *-ōn-ā*, ↓1.3.3.2.10)[389] is based on Ḥ-L-P (see ↓1.2.12.2.1).

1.2.1.3.4 > *qitl*

Dwpš'y (fem.) < *Dwbš'y* consists of Aram. *dwbš* "honey"[390] (with attenuation *u* > *i* *Dypšy*, male)[391] and *-āy* (↓1.3.3.1.4). *Dybš't'* (fem., a demonic authority)[392] has the same base with *-at-ā* (↓1.3.3.2.2). *Symkwy* (fem., + *-ōy*, ↓1.3.3.1.5) is perhaps based on *swmk* "thickness" (extant in JBA, Mand., Targ. *swmk'*), i.e. "thick" (with attenuation *u* > *i*); alternatively Iranian (↓7.3.2.13). *Byrl'* (defective *Brl'*)[393] "beryl, cristal-like" (JBA, Targ. *bwrl'*, OSyr. *brwl'*, *blwr'*). It is an Iranian (< Pali < Old Indian *verluriya*) loanword in Aramaic.[394]

---

381 Ilan, *Lexicon*, 199b.
382 Ilan, *Lexicon*, 218a.
383 Bhayro *et al.*, *Aramaic Magic Bowls*, 38.
384 See Segal, *Catalogue*, 45b *ad* 004A, 4.
385 Ilan, *Lexicon*, 201–202 (with a wrong lemmatization).
386 It cannot render *Srōšay* as claimed by Faraj, "Remarks," 92 *ad* 90–95, 1.
387 Ilan, *Lexicon*, 251b.
388 Cf. Zadok, *Pre-Hellenistic Israelite*, 69 and Mand. *šyrš'* "tribe" (cf. Ford, "Another Look," 269 *ad* 107M).
389 Cf. Ford, "Another Look," 272 *ad* 112M, 6.
390 See Morgenstern and Ford, *Aramaic Incantation Bowls*, 48 with n. 144.
391 Gordon, "Aramaic Magical Bowls," 324–326 and pl. 11:B, 2.
392 Shaked *et al.*, *Aramaic Bowl Spells* (2013), 26, 4.
393 Gordon 1934b: 467 and pl. 22, 1, 2.
394 See Ciancaglini, *Iranian Loanwords*, 128–129.

1.2.1.3.5 *quty*

Bws'[395] and *Bws(')y*[396] perhaps derive from B-S-Y "to despise, neglect" (JBA, Mand., OSyr., CPA), cf. *bwsy'* "willful negligence" (JBA, JPA, Targ.), in which case the names may be apotropaic.

1.2.2 *qVtVl*

Ktšytwn (fem.)[397] is apparently based on K-T-Š "crush; be excited" (cf. Χθουσιων/*Ktwšyn*[398]), in this case and in view of the combination of the adjectival suffixes *-īt-ōn* (↓1.3.3.2.8) it possibly has the meaning "smitten (with skin disease)".[399]

1.2.2.1 *qatal*

Dhb'y (based on *dhb* "gold") denotes "goldsmith".[400] *Nṭr* and *Nṭrty* (fem., + *-t-īy*, ↓1.3.3.2.5) are based on N-Ṭ-R "to guard, protect".[401] If *Mṭry'* is based on *mṭr* "rain" (extant in the Semitic onomastica), then it apparently ends with *-īy-ā* (↓1.3.2.1, an Iranian derivation is less likely).[402] *Ḥp'y*[403] may derive from Ḥ-P-Y "to cover, hide" (common Aram.).

1.2.2.2 *qutul*

For *Bwlwq'*[404] (+ *-ā*, ↓1.3.1.1) compare OSyr. *bwlq(')* (*quttāl*) "noteworthy appearance".

1.2.3 *qātil*

Khn'[405] (+ *-ā*, ↓1.3.1.1) "priest". *Ywyt'*,[406] *Ywyt'y* (fem., + *-t-āy*, ↓1.3.3.2.4) may have the same base as *Y'yt'* "beautiful, handsome, fitting".[407]

---

395 Ford, "Phonetic Spellings," 233:MS 2053/252, 5 (unpubl.).

396 Ilan, *Lexicon*, 173–174.

397 Ilan, *Lexicon*, 230a.

398 See Zadok, "Zur Struktur," 269:2.1.5.3.

399 Cf. Morgenstern and Abudraham, "A Mandaean Lamella," 233 *ad* 204.

400 See Montgomery, *Aramaic Incantation Texts*, 198 *ad* 19, 4.

401 Cf. Faraj and Moriggi, "Two New," 77–80:IM 62265, 2, 6;Levene, *Jewish Aramaic Curse Texts*, 96 *ad* SD 37, 7.

402 Cautiously suggested by Naveh and Shaked, *Amulets and Magic Bowls*, 183 *ad* 10, 7.

403 Cf. Morgenstern and Ford, *Aramaic Incantation Bowls*, 187, n. 613 *ad* Faraj, *Coppe magiche*, 6, 4.

404 Ilan *Lexicon*, 171b.

405 Bhayro *et al.*, *Aramaic Magic Bowls*, 120, 124.

406 Geller, "Eight Incantation Bowls," 111–112: Aaron C, 2.

407 See Zadok, "Zur Struktur," 266: 2.1.3; Naveh and Shaked, *Amulets and Magic Bowls*, 204 *ad* 13, 1.

1.2.4 *qatV:l*

1.2.4.1 *qatāl*

Db'rh[408] may consist of D-B-R "to lead" and *-ā* (↓1.3.1.1). Mand. *Kz'by't*[409] (+ fem. *-y-āt*, ↓1.3.3.2.13) is apparently based on K-Z-B, which is the Canaanite-Hebrew cognate of common Aram. K-D-B "to lie" whose *qatāl*-formation denotes "lie, fiction" (Official Aram., JBA, Mand., SA, QA, Targ.), a form with z- is extant only in JPA *kzbn* "deceiver" which may be a Hebraism. Perhaps it is an apotropaic name.

1.2.4.2 *qatīl*

1.2.4.2.1 With resonant consonants

Brykh (fem., + *-ā*, ↓1.3.3.1.1)[410] "blessed"; *Gnyb'*[411] (+ *-ā*, ↓1.3.1.1) denotes either "tail" (JAram.),[412] or "unclean" (OSyr., Mand.) or "stolen" (OSyr., Targ.); *Grybt'* (fem., + *-t-ā*, ↓1.3.3.2.1) "scabby";[413] *Ktym'*[414] (+ *-ā*, ↓1.3.1.1) "stained" (Targ. *ktym*); *Mlyk'* (fem.,[415] + *-ā*, ↓1.3.3.1.1), presumably for *mlykh* "promised" (OSyr.). *Qrysty'* (fem.) ends with a feminine suffix (*-yā*) preceded by the feminine marker *-t* (↓1.3.3.2.6). It may be based on Q-R-S "to become dry" (OSyr., JBA, Targ.), thereby meaning "the dry/hard one".[416] *Zbyn'*[417] (+ *-ā*, ↓1.3.1.1), *Zbynt'* (fem., + *-t-ā*, ↓1.3.3.2.1) "sold".[418]

1.2.4.2.2 With (proto-)gutturals or *h-*

'qyb'[419] (+ *-ā*, ↓1.3.1.1) derives from '-Q-B "to seek, look for; fulfill". *Hdyst'*[420] (fem.) may be based on H-D-S "to contemplate, ponder" (OSyr., + *-t-ā*, ↓1.3.3.2.1).

---

408 Naveh and Shaked, *Magic Spells* 123–124: 14, 2.
409 Yamauchi, *Mandaic Incantation Texts*, 11, 4, 51.
410 Bhayro *et al.*, *Aramaic Magic Bowls*, 60.
411 Moriggi, *Corpus*, 1, 9, 10 (*bis*).
412 See Zadok, "Zur Struktur," 267:2.1.5.2.
413 See Montgomery, *Aramaic Incantation Texts*, 124 *ad* 2, 3.
414 Schwab, L. (quoted by Montgomery, *Aramaic Incantation Texts*, 278a, index, s. v.).
415 Moriggi, *Corpus*, 29, 7. [ex Segal 118ES; cf. Zadok, "Zur Struktur," 268:2.1.5.2]
416 Cf. McCullough, *Jewish and Mandean*, 5 *ad* A, 3.
417 Segal, *Catalogue*, 023A, 2, 11.
418 See Gordon, "Aramaic Magical Bowls," 329 *ad* D, 6;
419 Hunter, "Two Incantation Bowls," 111:1, 9.
420 Ilan, *Lexicon*, 221–222.

1.2.4.2.3 With resonants and (proto-)gutturals

Rḥym'[421] (+ *-ā*, ↓1.3.1.1) "beloved, loving" (to R-Ḥ-M, Common Aram.); alternatively to *qattīl* (↓1.2.6.1.1). (*Š'ylt'*[422]/*Šylt'*/*Šlt'*[423] + *-t-ā*, ↓1.3.3.2.1)/*Š'ylt'y* (fem.),[424] *Šylty*[425] (-+ *-t-āy*, ↓1.3.3.2.4) *Šyly*,[426] *Š'ly*[427] (if defective for **Š'yly*, + *-īy*, ↓1.3.1.5), OSyr. *Šyl'y*[428] (+ *-āy*, ↓1.3.1.4), Mand. *Šyl*[429]/*Šl*[430] and *Šylwy'* (fem., + *-t-ā*, ↓1.3.3.2.1)[431] "borrowed, requested"[432] (to Š-'-L, partially with contraction of /'/); fem. *'wyrty* (> *'wyrty*,[433] + *-t-īy*, ↓1.3.3.2.5) "one-eyed female" (Aram.);[434] *'wr'/h* (fem., if it is defective for *'wyr'*) may be the masculine equivalent thereof.[435] *Ḥlyp'y* (fem.,[436] + *-āy*, ↓1.3.3.1.4) is based on Ḥ-L-P (see ↓1.2.12.2.1). *'pyl'*[437] (+ *-ā*, ↓1.3.1.1) derives from '-P-L "to become dark" (SA), cf. *'pl* "late appearing" and MHeb. *'pylh* (fem. adj.) "dark".

1.2.4.3 *qatūl*

Mand. *Hlwp'*[438] (+ *-ā*, ↓1.3.1.1) is based on Ḥ-L-P (see ↓1.2.12.2.1). *Nqwbt'* (fem., + *-t-ā*, ↓1.3.3.2.1) is based on N-Q-B "to perforate".[439] Mand. *Q'ywm* (fem.),[440] *Qywm'*[441] (+ *-ā*, ↓1.3.1.1), fem. *Qywmt'* (JBA, OSyr.; > *Qyymt'*/*Qymt'*[442])/Mand. *Q'ywmt'*[443] (+ *-t-ā*, ↓1.3.3.2.1) "enduring, permanent"[444] (Mand., OSyr., Palm., JPA, SA, CPA).

---

421 Isbell 1978, 8.
422 Bhayro *et al.*, *Aramaic Magic Bowls*, 69.
423 Bhayro *et al.*, *Aramaic Magic Bowls*, 55, 75.
424 Levene, *Jewish Aramaic Curse Texts*, 132, 3.
425 Levene, *Jewish Aramaic Curse Texts*, 024A, 6.
426 See Montgomery, *Aramaic Incantation Texts*, 177 *ad* 12, 11.
427 Isbell, "Two New," 20–23:N-IV, 3.
428 Müller-Kessler, "A Mandaic Gold Amulet," 334–337, 2.
429 Abudraham, "Three Mandaic," 83–85: 2, 6, 57, 65.
430 Abudraham, "Three Mandaic," 82:MS 2054/81, 11 (unpubl.).
431 See Segal, *Catalogue*, 121 *ad* 092M, 13 and 095M, 1; *Šīlī* (Justi, *Iranisches Namenbuch* 301a) is Aramaic *Šyly*.
432 See Zadok, "Zur Struktur," 268:2.1.5.2.
433 Ilan, *Lexicon*, 211.
434 See Gordon, "Aramaic Incantation Bowls," 122 *ad* 4, 2. For the form and the fem. suff. *-ty* see M. Morgenstern in Shaked *et al.*, *Aramaic Bowl Spells* (2013), 48–49.
435 See Morgenstern and Ford, *Aramaic Incantation Bowls*, 114 with n. 441 *ad* 3041+3070x, 2, 7.
436 See Ford, "Another Look," 269 *ad* 107M, 3'.
437 Gordon, "Aramaic Incantation Bowls," 117–119 and pl. 1 on 132:1, 2.
438 See Montgomery, *Aramaic Incantation Texts*, 219 *ad* 29, 8.
439 See Levene, *Jewish Aramaic Curse Texts*, 96 *ad* SD 27, 8.
440 See Ford, "Another Look," 260 *ad* 103M, 14.
441 Yamauchi, *Mandaic Incantation Texts*, 10, 2.
442 Ilan, *Lexicon*, 228.
443 Cf. Ford, "Another Look," 272 *ad* 112M, 8.
444 See Segal, *Catalogue*, 149 *ad* 120Sy, 3.

1.2.4.4 *qitūl*

Qywmt' "patroness" (OSyr.); *Ḥdwy* is not Iranian,[445] but derives from Ḥ-D-Y "rejoice"; *Tylwl'*[446] (fem., + *-ā*, ↓1.3.3.1.1) "fortress" (Old Aram., JPA *tlwl*).

1.2.4.5 *qutīl*

Mand. *Hwmymy'*[447] (fem., + *-yā*, ↓1.3.3.1.7) is apparently based on Ḥ-M-M "to be warm".

1.2.5 *qV:tV:l*

1.2.5.1 *qātūl*

Sḥwr' (*Rb* ~) "merchant" (JPA) or "beggar" (OSyr.).

1.2.5.2 *qītāl*

'ylw[448] (fem.), det. *'ylwt'* (+ *-t-ā*, ↓1.3.3.2.1) "aid" (OSyr.).

1.2.6 *qVttVl*

qittal

Mand. *Ṣp'r* (fem.) "bird" (common Aram.).

1.2.6.1 *qVttV:l*

1.2.6.1.1 *qattīl*

Smynt' (fem.)[449] denotes "pomace" (OSyr. < Akkad.). *Šḥyn*[450] "hot" (OSyr., JPA), presumably "hot(-tempered", OSyr.); *Špyr*[451] "beautiful, good"; *Šlym'* (OSyr., +-*ā*, ↓1.3.1.1, probably Christian)[452] "perfect; allied, at peace with" (Mand., CPA, Targ.; Š-L-M is common Aram.). *Rḥym'* may belong here ("lovable, pleasant", OSyr.) or to *qatīl* (↑1.2.4.2.2).

---

445 As erroneously implied by Ilan, *Lexicon*, 187.
446 Ilan, *Lexicon*, 254b.
447 See Segal, *Catalogue*, 135 *ad* 103M, 15.
448 Shaked *et al.*, *Aramaic Bowl Spells* (2022), 65, 8.
449 Bhayro *et al. Aramaic Magic Bowls*, 24.
450 Isbell, *Corpus*, 61, 3.
451 Gordon, "Aramaic Incantation Bowls," 277:Ashmolean 1931.177.
452 See Ford [and Abudraham] "Syriac and Mandaic," 92 *ad* 4, 4.

1.2.6.1.2 *qittāl*

*ʿlʾh*ʾ[453] "supreme, high, exalted" (common Aram., + *-ā*, ↓1.3.1.1) derives from ʿ-L-Y with *-y-* > *-ʾ*.

1.2.6.1.3 *quttāl*

Dwbr[454] "behaviour; (divine) governance" (OSyr., SA, to D-B-R "to lead, drive"); Mand. *Swm(ʾ)qʾ*[455] (+ *-ā*, ↓1.3.1.1) "red". Mand. *Dwmʾy* (fem.)[456] may denote "likening" (*dwmy*(ʾ), OSyr.).

1.2.6.1.4 *quttūl* > *qittūl*

ʾwkmy (> *ʾwkmw, ʾykwmh/y*[457]) is based on *ʾwkm* "black" (+ *-ā, -īy, -ō*, ↓1.3.1.1, 1.3.1.2, 1.3.1.5).

1.2.6.2 *qrtwl* (with dissimilatory *-r-)*

Perhaps *Grdwštʾ* (fem.,[458] + *-t-ā*, ↓1.3.3.2.1) if it derives from G-R-D-Š "to gnaw, erode, be broken, wounded" (JBA, OSyr.).

1.2.7 *qVl*

1.2.7.1 *qal*

ʾbʾ[459] (+ *-ā*, ↓1.3.1.1), *ʾbʾy* (with *a-* > *i-* *ʾybʾ, ʾybʾy*,[460] + *-ā, -āy*, and *-ōy*, ↓1.3.1.1, 1.3.1.4, 1.3.1.6), *ʾbyy*[461] (+ *-āy*, ↓1.3.1.4), *ʾbwy*,[462] and *ʾbwyʾ* (Mand., fem.)[463] *ʾḥwy*[464] (+ *-ōy*, ↓1.3.1.6), *ʾḥy*[465] (with *a-* > *i-* *ʾyḥy*,[466] + – *īy*, ↓1.3.1.4), Mand. *ʿhʾy*[467] (with aphaeresis

---

453 Gordon, "Aramaic Incantation Bowls," 344–345: Fitzwilliam, 12.
454 Gordon, "Aramaic and Mandaic," 86–90 and pls. 2–4:H, 1.
455 Pognon, *Inscriptions mandaïtes*, 25.
456 Segal, *Catalogue*, 087M, 7.
457 Ilan, *Lexicon*, 166 (with a wrong lemmatization).
458 Segal, *Catalogue*, 44b *ad* 002A, 2 cautiously suggests an Iranian etymology which is phonologically incompatible.
459 Wohlstein, "Über einige aramäische," 9, 12–27:[VA] 2416, 3, 18.
460 Gordon, "Aramaic and Mandaic," 90–92 and pl.6:J, 5.
461 See Ford, "Phonetic Spellings," 219–220 *ad* Gorea, "Trois nouvelles," 85–89 and 92–93:3, 3.
462 Shaked *et al.*, *Aramaic Bowl Spells* (2022), 108, 2.
463 Morgenstern, "Five Mandaic," 109–111:24, 4, 13, 15.
464 See Fain *et al.*, "Aramaic Incantation Bowls," 290 *ad* S-443, 1.
465 Shaked *et al.*, *Aramaic Bowl Spells* (2013), 58, 3, 5.
466 Shaked *et al.*, *Aramaic Bowl Spells* (2013), 40, 4.
467 Müller-Kessler, "A Mandaic Lead Roll," 489, rev. 3ʾ. With an epithet *rbʾ* "bigger, older" in Mand. *ʾḥʾyrbʾ* (Abudraham, "Three Mandaic," 88–93:3, 15).

Ḥ'y,[468] cf. Geonic *H'y*, + *-āy*, ↓1.3.1.4), are based on *'b* "father"[469] and *'ḥ* "brother" respectively. OSyr. *Ḥwn'* > *Hwn'*[470] is based on *'ḥ* with aphaeresis (with diminutive *-ōn-ā* thereby meaning "little brother", ↓1.3.2.3). It is noteworthy that females bore the names *'bh*,[471] *'by*[472] and (Mand.) *'by'*.[473] *'ḥt*,[474] *'ḥt'*,[475] *'ḥ't'*[476] (+ *-ā*, ↓1.3.3.1.1), *'ḥ'ty'*[477] (+ *-āy*, ↓1.3.3.1.4), are based on *'ḥ't* "sister" (*'ḥt*[478]/Mand. *'h't*[479] without suffix is also recorded as an anthroponym), Mand. *'h'ty'*[480] (+ *-yā*, ↓1.3.3.1.7). *Ḥ'twy* (/*Ḥātōy*/) and *Ḥātōnāy* (OSyr., fem.) have the same base[481] with aphaeresis. The latter ends with a suffix combination (*-ōn-āy*, ↓1.3.3.2.11). Her daughter's name, *'Aḥātāy*, has the same base[482] without aphaeresis (+ – *āy*,↓1.3.3.1.4). *'ḥtwnty*[483] (+ – *ōn-t-āy*, ↓1.3.3.2.14), has the same base, but *Ḥty*[484]/*Ḥt'y*[485] (+ – *āy*, ↓1.3.3.1.4) is with aphaeresis. Has *Ḥwty*[486] (+ *āy* or *-īy*, ↓1.3.3.1.3) the same base with aphaeresis and *ā* > *ō* (as in Canaanite)? Regarding *'bw*,[487] it cammot be excluded, that it originates from abstract nouns, viz. *'bw*, det. *'bwt'* "defense, advocacy" (OSyr., QA < Akkad. *abbūtu*). The distinctive non-Jewish name *Bty*[488] may be based on *bt* < *brt* "daughter". Perhaps Šbwn,[489] which may denote "splinter" (Mand.), belongs here as well. OSyr. *'nty* (fem.)[490] may be based on the name of the goddess Anat, cf. also the Mandaic numen *'nt ḥy'*.

---

468 Abudraham, "Three Mandaic," 61, 62, 93–94:1, 2.
469 See Morgenstern and Ford, *Aramaic Incantation Bowls*, 19, n. 40 *ad* 3005, 5, 3019, 4.
470 Moriggi, *Corpus*, 23, 10, 12 and 2 respectively.
471 Faraj, "Remarks," 90–95, 1.
472 Gordon, "Aramaic Incantation Bowls," 350–351:IM 11113.
473 Gordon, "Aramaic and Mandaic," 95=100 and pl. 10:M, 3.
474 Shaked *et al.*, *Aramaic Bowl Spells* (2013), 8, 7.
475 Shaked *et al.*, *Aramaic Bowl Spells* (2013), 63, 5.
476 Yamauchi, *Mandaic Incantation Texts*, 21, 4, 9, 13, 16, 23.
477 Cf. Morgenstern and Schlütter, "A Mandaic Amulet," 122 *ad* rev. 3, 17.
478 Shaked *et al.*, *Aramaic Bowl Spells* (2013), 8, 7.
479 Yamauchi, *Mandaic Incantation Texts*, 19, 2, 21; 27, 3, 4, 16.
480 Morgenstern and Schlütter, "A Mandaic Amulet," 118, 120, rev. 3.
481 See Montgomery, *Aramaic Incantation Texts*, 143 *ad* 6, 3.
482 For both names see Morgenstern and Ford, *Aramaic Incantation Bowls*, 177, n. 591 *ad* 3056, 3, 3066, 3.
483 See Morgenstern and Ford, *Aramaic Incantation Bowls*, 177, n. 591 *ad* Segal, *Catalogue*, 020A, 4.
484 Shaked *et al.*, *Aramaic Bowl Spells* (2013), 36, 2, 3.
485 Shaked *et al.*, *Aramaic Bowl Spells* (2022), 101, 14, 17.
486 Bhayro *et al.*, *Aramaic Magic Bowls*, 120, 124.
487 Shaked *et al.*, *Aramaic Bowl Spells* (2013), 40, 3, 4 (*bis*).
488 BT Gittin 11a, cf. Kiperwasser and Shapira, "Encounters," 300.
489 Isbell, *Corpus*, 63, 2.
490 Moriggi, *Corpus*, 18, 2, 11.

1.2.7.2 *qul*

Šwmwny (fem.), which ends in *-ōn-īy* (↓1.3.3.2.10), is apparently based on *šm* "name".[491]

1.2.8 With diphthongs

1.2.8.1 *qawl*

Ḥwrn,[492] which consists of Ḥ-W/Y-R and adjectival *-ān* (↓1.3.1.7) may denote "whitish, grey", like OSyr. *ḥwrny* with a combination of suffixes (*-ān-āy*). The latter may alternatively denote "love incited" (JBA *ḥwrn'h*, to Ḥ-R-R).[493] *Nwpy'*[494] may either render OSyr. *nwpy'* (+ *-yā*, ↓1.3.1.3) "the boundless" or based on N-W/Y-P (Sab. "to bestow"), cf. Sab. *Nwfm* (3 ×), *Nwfn* (3 ×, also Hadrami, 1 ×)[495] and *-(ā)yā*. Perhaps *'wny* (defective *'ny*) and *'wn'* (both fem.)[496] are based on *'wn* "power, natural urge" (Official Aram.; the Biblical Hebrew cognate *'wn* "vigour" is onomastically productive).[497]

1.2.8.2 *qayl*

Byt'[498] "house, clan"; *Ḥyl* (fem.)[499] "power, strength; preciousness, wealth, abundance" (Aram.), cf. BHeb. *'št ḥyl* "woman of valour". *'ynh*[500] and *'ynwy*[501] are perhaps originally *ʿynh* and *ʿynwy*, in which case they are based on *ʿyn* "eye"; cf. *ʿyn'*,[502] i.e. consisting of *ʿyn* "eye" and *-ā* (↓1.3.1.1) or *-ōy* (↓1.3.1.6). Alternatively, the forms based on *'yn* may originate from Persian "mirror".[503] *Qyny* (alias[504]) may be based on *qyn(')* "crossbeam" (OSyr., + *-āy*, ↓1.3.1.4).

---

491 Differently Levene, *Jewish Aramaic Curse Texts*, 95 *ad* SD 27, 5.
492 Ilan, *Lexicon*, 232.
493 Cf. Müller-Kessler, "Beiträge zum Babylonisch," 231 *ad* 443a.
494 Oelsner "Review," 39–41, i, 2.
495 Harding, *Index and Concordance*, 604.
496 For references see Ilan, *Lexicon*, 243–244.
497 See Zadok, *Pre-Hellenistic Israelite*, 144.
498 Ilan, *Lexicon*, 214 (with a wrong lemmatization).
499 Isbell, *Corpus*, 70, 3.
500 Ilan, *Lexicon*, 211.
501 Shaked *et al.*, *Aramaic Bowl Spells* (2013), 40, 3, 4 (*bis*).
502 See Segal, *Catalogue*, 60 *ad* 019A, 1. For the /ʿ/ in JBA see Juusola, *Linguistic Pecularities*, 37–38 and M. Morgenstern in Shaked *et al.*, *Aramaic Bowl Spells* (2013), 40.
503 See Shaked, "Rabbis," 108.
504 Ilan, *Lexicon*, 227–228.

1.2.9 *qV:l*

1.2.9.1 *qāl*

Ḥlyy consists of *ḥl* "maternal uncle"[505] and *-āy* (↓1.3.1.4). *Ṭb'* (fem.)[506] (+ *-ā*, ↓1.3.3.1.1) "good". Mand. *D'r'* (fem.)[507] (+ *-ā*, ↓1.3.3.1.1) may denote "age, generation; rank" (common Aram.).

< *qa'l*: *R'šn* (fem.) may denote "chief, ruler" (OSyr. and Targ., *ryšn, r'šn'*)[508] (+ *-ān*, ↓1.3.3.8); alternatively Middle Persian (↓7.1).

1.2.9.2 *qīl*

Gyst' (fem.)[509] perhaps denotes "sister-in-law", the hypothetical female counterpart (+ *-t-ā*, ↓1.3.3.2.1) of *gys'* "brother-in-law" (JBA; OSyr. (')*gys'*, JPA *'gys*), in which case it would be a substitute name. *Sysnwy* (male[510] and female[511]) is perhaps based on *sysn* (OSyr., name of an unidentified bird, + *-ōy*, ↓1.3.1.6). Regarding *Sys'* (+ *-ā*, ↓1.3.1.1) and *Sysyn*[512] (+ *-īn*, ↓1.3.1.8), the former is based on *sys* "tuft" (JBA, Targ. with an Old Syriac cognate), "coil of threads" (OSyr., MHeb.) and the latter ("chamomile") is an Akkadian loanword in JBA like sysyn "fruited branch of a date-palm"[513]. *Zywn* (fem.)[514] (+ *-ān*, ↓1.3.3.1.8) "splendid" (Mand., OSyr., where it is also a designation of a Manichean sacral being) is based on *zyw* "splendour" (< Akkad. *zīmu*). *Zyywy* (fem.)[515] has the same base (+ *-āy*, ↓1.3.3.1.4). However, both names are alternatively explicable in Persian terms (↓7.3.1.1, b, a', 7.3.1.4). *Gīlāy* (fem.,[516] + *-āy*, ↓1.3.3.1.4) may be based on either *gyl* "age" (Aram.) or MPers. *gil* "clay". The female's name *Nyry*[517] (+ *-āy*, ↓1.3.3.1.4) may also be Hebrew unless it is based on the star's name *nyr* (OSyr.).

---

505 See Morgenstern and Ford, *Aramaic Incantation Bowls*, 60 with n. 258 *ad* 3016, 1.
506 Müller-Kessler, *Zauberschalentexte*, 33b, 15.
507 Cf. Ford, "Another Look," 264 *ad* 106M, 6.
508 See Montgomery, *Aramaic Incantation Texts*, 219 *ad* 29, 5.
509 Shaked *et al.*, *Aramaic Bowl Spells* (2013), 64, 8.
510 Moriggi, "Two New," 52–56, 58:2, 5.
511 Bhayro *et al.*, *Aramaic Magic Bowls*, 1.
512 Ilan, *Lexicon*, 202–203 (with a wrong lemmatization).
513 See Schwartz "Sasm," 255, cf. Sims-Williams, *Bactrian Personal Names*, 129:435.
514 Moriggi, "Two New," 45 and 57:1, 11.
515 Gordon, "Aramaic Incantation Bowls," 342–344:BM 91776, 5, 7.
516 MS 2053/220 (unpubl., quoted by Shaked, "Rabbis," 105 with n. 26).
517 Moriggi, "Two New," 45–52, 57:1, 8.

1.2.9.3 *qūl*

Gwr'[518] (+ -*ā*, ↓1.3.1.1), *Gwry'/h*[519] (+ -*yā*, ↓1.3.1.3), and *Gwryt'* (fem., + -*īt-ā*, ↓1.3.3.2.3) are based on *gwr* (cf. Palm. ~) "young lion".[520] *Gwryy* (+ -*āy*, ↓1.3.1.4) is either Semitic (to *gwr* "whelp") or Iranian (*gōr* "onager, wild ass").[521] The same applies to *Gwrwy*[522] (+ -*ōy*, ↓1.3.1.6). *Gwsy*[523] (+ -*āy*, ↓1.3.1.4, cf. NB/LB *Gu-sa*-A+A);[524] *Kwpyt(')y* (fem.) apparently consists of *kwpyt'* (OSyr.) and -*āy* (↓1.3.3.1.4) thereby denoting "water-pitcher-like".[525] Mand. *Nwnt'(y)*[526] (fem., + -*ā* or -*āy*, ↓1.3.3.1.1, 1.3.3.1.4) is perhaps based on *nwn* "fish" (common Aram.). OSyr. *Zwṭy*[527] (+ -*āy*, ↓1.3.1.4) denotes "the younger (one)". *Pwrty* (fem.), which is possibly based on *pwrt* "portion, small amount" (JBA, Mand., Hatran, Targ.), apparently ends with the fem. suff. -*āy* or -*īy* (↓1.3.3.1.3) in which case it may denote "fractured, minute".[528]

1.2.10 *qVll*

1.2.10.1 *qall*

1.2.10.1.1 With stable consonants

The base of *Gdn'*,[529] viz. *gd* "fortune", is followed by adjectival -*ān* plus -*ā* (↓1.3.2.2) thereby denoting "fortunate". *Gdyy*,[530] Mand. *Gd'y* (2 ×)[531] and OSyr. *gdy* have the same base (with -*āy*, ↓1.3.1.4) and meaning. The variant *Gwd'y* in the same text (1 ×)[532] may be compared to the variant *gyd'* (JBA, Targ.) "fortune; coriander". *Kdy*[533]

---

518 Ilan, *Lexicon*, 220.
519 Shaked *et al.*, *Aramaic Bowl Spells* (2022), 113, 1, 10.
520 See Stark *Personal Names*, 81b.
521 See Naveh and Shaked, *Magic Spells* 116 *ad* 15, 3.
522 See Montgomery, *Aramaic Incantation Texts*, 208 *ad* 25, 1.
523 Ilan, *Lexicon*, 220b.
524 Cf. Zadok, *West Semites in Babylonia*, 63, 164.
525 See Montgomery, *Aramaic Incantation Texts*, 122 *ad* 2, 1; 12, 11.
526 See Müller-Kessler, "Die Zauberschalensammlung," 139b *ad* Segal, *Catalogue*, 090M, 3.
527 Ford [and Abudraham] "Syriac and Mandaic," 96–98:6, 10, 12, 13.
528 See Segal, *Catalogue*, 47a *ad* 005A, 2.
529 Shaked *et al.*, *Aramaic Bowl Spells* (2022), 100, 4, 7, 8.
530 Differently Segal, *Catalogue*, 91 *ad* 048A, 7 (to *gdy* "kid").
531 Müller-Kessler, *Zauberschalentexte*, 2A, 6, 11.
532 Müller-Kessler, *Zauberschalentexte*, 2A, 5.
533 Not identical with the Iranian name *Kwd(')y* (/*Xwadāy*/) "lord" (see Naveh and Shaked, *Amulets and Magic Bowls*, 175 *ad* 8, ii, 4, iii, 5) despite Ilan, *Lexicon*, 188a.

is apparently based on *kd* with adjectival *-āy* (↓1.3.1.4), i.e. "pot-like", cf. *Kdh*[534] (+ *-ā*, ↓1.3.1.1). *Klt'* "bride".[535]

1.2.10.1.2 With resonant consonants

R'bh[536] and *Rby'*[537] are based on *rb* "master" plus *-ā* (↓1.3.1.1) and *-yā* (↓1.3.1.3) respectively.

1.2.10.1.3 With (proto-)gutturals

Mand. *'zy'* (/*Azia*/, fem.)[538] may originate from *ʿzy'* which is based on *ʿz* "strong" (to ʿ-Z-Z, + *-yā*, ↓1.3.3.1.7). *Ḥyy'*[539] consists of *ḥy* "living" *(qall > qill)* and *-ā* (↓1.3.1.1). *Ḥyyn* has the same base[540] with hypocoristic *-ān* (↓1.3.1.7).

1.2.10.1.4 With unstable consonants

'd' and *'dy* (the latter refers to male and female) are based on *Addu*[541] (the storm god worshipped by the Arameans). They end in hypocoristic *-ā* and *-āy* respectively (↓1.3.1.1, 1.3.3.1.4).

1.2.10.2 *qill*

ʿm'[542]/ʿmh[543] (+ *-ā*, ↓1.3.3.1.1) "mother", *ʿym'*[544] (+ *-ā*, ↓1.3.3.1.1), *ʿymʿy* (fem.)[545]/ *ʿymy*[546]/*ʿymyy*[547] (+ *-āy*, ↓1.3.3.1.4), Mand. *ʿmy'*[548] (+ *-yā*, ↓1.3.3.1.7), *ʿmʿy* and with aphaeresis *Mʿy*[549] are based on the same lexeme (+ *-āy*, ↓1.3.3.1.4). *Ṣdh* (in Jewish

534 See Zadok, "Zur Struktur," 281: 2.1.10.4.1.
535 See Montgomery (and A. T. Clay *apud* Montgomery) *Aramaic Incantation Texts*, 191 *ad* 17, 7.
536 Bhayro *et al.*, *Aramaic Magic Bowls*, 73.
537 Bhayro *et al.*, *Aramaic Magic Bowls*, 120, 124.
538 Lidzbarski, *Ephemeris*, 98–99:3 = Bhayro *et al.*, *Aramaic Magic Bowls*, 31, 35 (VA 2435).
539 Shaked *et al.*, *Aramaic Bowl Spells* (2013), 57, 4 (*bis*).
540 Cf. Levene, *Jewish Aramaic Curse Texts*, 96 *ad* SD 27, 9.
541 See Morgenstern and Ford, *Aramaic Incantation Bowls*, 68, n. 232.
542 Faraj, "Remarks," 90–95, 9.
543 Isbell, *Corpus*, 64, 4.
544 Shaked *et al.*, *Aramaic Bowl Spells* (2013), 19, 2, 7, 13; 2022, 79, 1–2, 8.
545 Bhayro *et al.*, *Aramaic Magic Bowls*, 24.
546 Shaked *et al.*, *Aramaic Bowl Spells* (2013), 50, 1, 8, 9; 51, 1, 6, 7; 52, 2, 9, 10; 53, 6, 7; 54, 7.
547 Geller, "Eight Incantation Bowls," 114:Aaron E, 9.
548 Pognon, *Inscriptions mandaïtes*, 19.
549 See Ford, "Another Look," 259 *ad* 103M, 9.

script)/*Ṣdn* (in Proto-Syriac script)[550] is presumably based on Ṣ-D-D.[551] *Ryby* (*Rb* ~)[552] may consist of R-B-Y or R-B-B "to grow" and *–āy* (↓1.3.1.3).

1.2.10.3 *qull*

ʿwlh[553] (+ *-ā*, ↓1.3.1.1) may be a plene spelling of a form deriving from Ġ-L-L "to enter".[554] *Ḥwb'*,[555] OSyr. *Ḥwb(')y* (both fem.)[556] are based on *ḥwb* "love" (+ *-ā*, *-āy*, ↓1.3.3.1.1, 1.3.3.1.4).

1.2.11 *qlql*

Ṣwṣl' (fem., + *-ā*, ↓1.3.3.1.1),[557] cf. JBA and OSyr. *ṣwṣl'* "small dove" (perhaps "ring-dove"), fem. *ṣwṣylt'*, cf. JBA and OSyr. *ṣylṣwl'* "a bird that catches fish". *Kkr* (< **Krkr*), *Kkry* (fem.)[558] (+ *-āy* or *-īy*, 1.3.3.1.3) denotes either "talent; loaf" or "honeycomb" in view of OSyr. and Targ. *kkryt'*.[559]

1.2.12 With preformatives

1.2.12.1 *'-*

1.2.12.1.1 *aqtVl*

'brq'[560] is based on B-R-Q and ends in *-ā* (↓1.3.1.1). *'gblth*[561] apparently derives from G-B-L "to knead, form, fabricate" (JBA, Mand., OSyr., JPA, CPA, SA) plus *-t-ā* (↓1.3.2.8), cf. JAram. *Gbylh*.[562] *'gzr* (with the title *rb*, a demonic authority)[563] derives from G-Z-R "to shear, cut off fruit, be circumcised; decree" (JBA, OSyr., Mand., JPA), cf. Mand. *agzara* "being cut-off, exile, banishment". *'nbyh* (fem.) is not a

550 For the scripts see Naveh, "Some New Jewish," 236. Both spellings refer to the same lady.
551 Cf. Zadok, "Zur Struktur," 282:2.1.10.4.2.
552 Segal, *Catalogue*, 024A, 6, cf. Shaked, "Rabbis," 107.
553 Isbell, "Two New," 20–23:N-IV, 3.
554 Cf. Zadok, *Pre-Hellenistic Israelite*, 151.
555 Martinez Borobio "A Magical Bowl," 324–325, 335, 9.
556 Shaked *et al.*, *Aramaic Bowl Spells* (2022), 98, 5 (*Ḥ[w]b'[y]*), 14, 17 (both *Ḥwby*).
557 Müller-Kessler, "Syrische Zauberschalen," 119–121 = Moriggi, *Corpus*, 18, 3.
558 JNF 247, 2 (unpubl., quoted by Morgenstern and Ford, *Aramaic Incantation Bowls*, 48a).
559 See Morgenstern and Ford, *Aramaic Incantation Bowls*, 47–48 *ad* 3012, 2.
560 Moriggi, *Corpus*, 18, 2, 4.
561 Ilan, *Lexicon*, 165b.
562 See Zadok, "Zur Struktur," 267:2.1.5.2.
563 See Shaked *et al.*, *Aramaic Bowl Spells* (2013), 151 *ad* 26, 3.

straightforward Yahwistic name,[564] but perhaps derives from N-B-Y "to prophesy" (JBA, OSyr., Mand., like *Nby*°'°), (*si vera lectio*, fem.).[565]

1.2.12.1.2 *aqtul*

Mand. *Amkur*[566] perhaps derives from M-K-R "to acquire property; to betroth" (Official Aram., OSyr., Mand.; C "to give in marriage", OSyr.).

1.2.12.2 *m-*

1.2.12.2.1 *maqtal*

Mḥlp' (male, + *-ā*, ↓1.3.1.1), *Mḥlpt'*[567]/*Mḥlpth*,[568] (female, +*-t-ā*, ↓1.3.3.2.1), as well as *Mḥlpn'* (+ *-ān-ā*, ↓1.3.2.2) are based on a *maqtal*-formation of Ḥ-L-P (< Ḫ-L-P) "to be changed, substitute one thing for another", thereby denoting "substitute".[569] *Mšršyh*[570] (+ *-yā*, ↓1.3.1.3) and its feminine counterpart *Mšršyt'*[571] (+ *-īt-ā*, ↓1.3.3.2.3) as well as *Mšrštn'*[572] (with an adjectival suffix *-t-ān*, ↓1.3.2.8) derive from Š-R-Š (↑1.2.1.3.2). Mand. *Mnd'y* (fem., + *-āy*, ↓1.3.3.1.4) is based on *mnd'* (< *mnd'*), cf. *mnd'' dhyy'*, the supreme saviour spirit of the Mandeans.[573]

1.2.12.2.2 *mqtl*

Msnq'[574] (+ *-ā-*, ↓1.3.1.1) is an active participle of S-N-Q C: "to compel, force to require" (OSyr.), cf. perhaps JBA *msnqy* (an adjective of an unclear meaning according to CAL).

---

564 As wrongly implied by Ilan, *Lexicon*, 208a.
565 Shaked *et al.*, *Aramaic Bowl Spells* (2013), 21, 6, 10.
566 Gorea, "Trois nouvelles," 72–78, 90–91:1, rev, 2–3.
567 Shaked *et al.*, *Aramaic Bowl Spells* (2013), 62, 4, 5 and 16, 4; 17, 2, 4, 7 respectively.
568 Shaked *et al.*, *Aramaic Bowl Spells* (2022), 66, 1.
569 See Fain *et al.*, "Aramaic Incantation Bowls," 287 *ad* S-442, 2: *Mḥlpn'*; cf. Morgenstern and Ford, *Aramaic Incantation Bowls*, 11.
570 Cf. Montgomery, *Aramaic Incantation Texts*, 198 *ad* 19, 3.
571 Bhayro *et al.*, *Aramaic Magic Bowls*, 40, 79, 120, 124 and 111, 140 respectively; Geller, "Eight Incantation Bowls," 114: Aaron E, 9.
572 Levene, *Jewish Aramaic Curse Texts*, 024A, 6.
573 See Segal, *Catalogue*, 136a *ad* 103M, 15.
574 Shaked *et al.*, *Aramaic Bowl Spells* (2013), 20, 2.

1.2.12.2.3 *mVqīl*

Mqym "constant" (OSyr.) or "He who causes to arise" (Arab.).[575]

1.2.12.3 *t-*

1.2.12.3.1 *tyqtl*

Mand. *Tyrmy'*[576] (fem., +-*ā*, ↓1.3.3.1.1), cf. *trmy* "foundation" (from R-M-Y C "to install, set up", OSyr.).

1.3 Suffixed names

1.3.1 Non-combined

1.3.1.1 *-ā* (<-'/-*h*>)[577]

a. With -': *'b'* (↑1.2.7.1),*'bd'* (↑1.2.1.1), *'brq'* (↑1.2.12.1.1), *'d'* (↑1.2.10.1.4), *'pyl'* (↑1.2.4.2), *ʿyb'* (↑1.2.7.1),*ʿqyb'*, *Gnyb'* (↑1.2.4.2), *Byrl'* (↑1.2.1.3), *Byt'* (↑1.2.8.2), *Bwlwq'* (↑1.2.2.2), *Dky'* (↑1.2.1.1), *Gwr'* (↑1.2.9.3), *Hlwp'* (↑1.2.4.3), *Ḥyy'* (↑1.2.10.1), *Khn'* (↑1.2.3), *Ktym'* (↑1.2.4.2), *Mḥlp'* (↑1.2.12.2.1), *Msnq'* (↑1.2.12.2.2), *Qywm'* (↑1.2.4.3), *R'bh* (↑1.2.10.1), *Shd'* (↑1.2.1.1), *Sḥwr'* (↑1.2.5.1), *Spr'* (↑1.2.1.1), *Sys'* (↑1.2.9.2), *Šlm'* (↑1.2.1.1), *ʿyn'* (↑1.2.8.2), *Mḥlp'* (↑1.2.12.2.1), *Rwy'* (↑1.2.1.1), *Šlym'* (↑1.2.6.1.1), *Šwrš'* (↑1.2.1.3), *Zbyn'* (↑1.2.4.2).

b. With -*h*: *ʾl'h'* (↑1.2.6.1.2), *ʿykwmh* (↑1.2.6.1.4), *ʿynh* (↑1.2.8.2), *ʿwlh* (↑1.2.10.3), *Db'rh* (↑1.2.4.1), *Kdh* (↑1.2.10.1), *Šrkh* (↑1.2.1.1).

1.3.1.2 *-ō*

'wkmw (↑1.2.6.1.4).

1.3.1.3. *-yā*

Mry' (↑1.2.1.1), *Mšršršyh* (↑1.2.12.2.1); *Azia* (Mand., ↑1.2.10.1) and possibly *Nwpy'* (↑1.2.8.1).

1.3.1.4 *-āy*

a. Adjectival: a'. With -ʾy: *'b'y* (with *a-* > *i-* *ʿyb'y*, ↑1.2.7.1), *Dypšy* (↑1.2.1.3), *M'r'y* (↑1.2.1.1), *Dhb'y* (↑1.2.2.1), *Mšk'y* (↑1.2.1.1); *Nhyl'y*,[578] OSyr. *Šyl'y* (↑1.2.4.2) and Mand.

575 Cf. Segal, *Catalogue*, 86a *ad* 044A, 13 who refers to Stark 1971: 96b.

576 Yamauchi, *Mandaic Incantation Texts*, 24, 8.

577 For this graphemic interchange in JBA incantation bowls see Juusola, *Linguistic Peculiarities*, 30.

578 Ilan, *Lexicon*, 195a (see Zadok, "Zur Struktur," 268).

'h'y (↑1.2.7.1). *-āy* is abbreviated to *–ā* in *Kpn(')y, Spr'y* (> *Spr'*, ↑1.2.1.1) and *Ḥwb(')y* (OSyr., ↑1.2.10.3).

b'. With *-yy*: *Gwryy* (↑1.2.9.3).

c'. With *-y*: *'ḥy* (with *a-* > *i-* *'yḥy*, ↑1.2.7.1), *Dwkry* (*qetl* < *qutl*, ↑1.2.1.3), *Kdy* (↑1.2.10.1.1), *Kspy* (↑1.2.1.1), *Pwšky* (↑1.2.1.3.1), *Qyny* (↑1.2.8.2), *Ryby* (↑1.2.10.2), *Zypty* (↑1.2.1.2), *Zyywy* (↑1.2.9.2); OSyr. *Zwṭy* (↑1.2.9.3).

d'. Gentilics: *Prs'*[579] may originate from **Prs'y* "Persian" (gentilic), cf. *Nwkr'*[580] which is presumably short for *Nwkr'y'* below. *Nypr'* is defective for **Nypr'y*, cf. Mand. *Niprai* "Nippurean."[581] *Mbwg*[582] is short for the gentilic *Mbwg(')y*, a common anthroponym of Arameophone pagans referring to Hierapolis, where the main temple of Dea Syria was located. Mand. *Gwk'yy'* (of the double name G. *'dwr yzd'n*, MPers. /*Ādur-yazdān*/)[583] may be a gentilic of *Gwk'*, the forerunner of Arab. *Jūḫā* (Geonic *Gwky*) referring to a region in eastern Babylonia.[584] Alternatively it may be a hypocoristicon based on **Gaw* "ox, bull, cow" with the combined suffix *-ak-āy-a* (↓7.3.2.14). Cf. Mand. (*Pīr*) *Nwkr'y'*[585] (gentilic masc. *-āy-ā*).

b. Hypocoristic: a'. With *-'y*: *Gd'y* (↑1.2.10.1).

b'. With -yy: *Gdyy* (↑1.2.10.1), *Ḥlyy* (↑1.2.9.1).

c'. With *-y*: *Ḥysdy* (↑1.2.1.2) may be a hypocoristicon of a compound like *Ḥsdyh*, seeing that the adjective of *ḥsd* (JBA *ḥsdn* "gracious") ends in *-ān*. Besides, adjectives of the same root are extant (*ḥsy/wd*).

1.3.1.5 -*īy*

Mry (↑1.2.1.1).

1.3.1.6 -*ōy* (adjectival)[586]

'ynwy (↑1.2.8.2), *'bwy*, *'ḥwy* (↑1.2.7.1), *M'rwy*, *Nṭrwy*, *Shdwy* (↑1.2.1.1). *Sysnwy* (male and female, ↑1.2.9.2).

---

579 Gordon, "Aramaic Incantation Bowls," 121, 3.

580 Faraj, "Aramaico orientale," 272–273:IM 2929, 3.

581 See Müller-Kessler, "The Story of Bguzan-Lilit," 197 and Morgenstern and Ford, *Aramaic Incantation Bowls*, 14, n. 14 *ad* 3003, 2, 9 and 3021, 3.

582 Ilan, *Lexicon*, 189b.

583 Yamauchi, *Mandaic Incantation Texts*, 11, 50.

584 For this region see Gil "'The Rādhānite Merchants," 317–319.

585 Yamauchi, *Mandaic Incantation Texts*, 22, 9–10 and *passim* in this incantation.

586 A vocalization *-u/ūy* relies on the New Persian rendering, but the Arabic script has no sign for *ō*. [cf. Akboes]. The suffix is thought to be due to Iranian linguistic interference (see Fain *et al.*, "Aramaic Incantation Bowls," 290). However, It is recorded also in a transcription of an Aramaic name from Syria (Ακβοεος, cf. Zadok "Post-Biblical," xix:2.2.2.2) and possibly in NB *A-ṣ/za-al-lu-⌞ia⌟* (CT 56, 87, rev. ii, 28, based on ' '-Z-L "to go"), NA *Ha-an-nu-ia* (based on Ḥ-N-N "to

1.3.1.7 *-ān*

a. **Adjectival**: *Bgrn* (↑1.2.1.1), *Ḥwrn* (↑1.2.8.1).

b. **Hypocoristic**: *Ḥyyn* (1.2.10.1). It becomes *-ā* in the female's name *Ṣdh/n* (↑1.2.10.2).

1.3.1.8 *-īn*

Sysyn (↑1.2.9.2).

1.3.1.9 *-ōm*

Šršw(m, ↑1.2.1.3).

1.3.1.10 *-ū(t)*

Zkwt (↑1.2.1.1).

1.3.2 Combined suffixes

1.3.2.1 *-īy-ā*

Possibly *Mṭry'* (↑1.2.2.1).

1.3.2.2 *-ān-ā*

Gdn' (↑1.2.10.1), *Mḥlpn'* (↑1.2.12.2.1).

1.3.2.3 *-ōn-ā*

'bwn' (↑1.2.7.1), *Ḥwn'* > *Hwn'* (both diminutive, ↑1.2.7.1); *Mlkwn'* (↑1.2.1.1.2). The distinctive non-Jewish name *Nqym-'wn',*[587] the accuracy of its transmission is not beyond doubt, may be based on the onomastically productive root N-Q-M "to avenge" (Aram., Heb., Arab., Eth.).

1.3.2.4 *-ōn-āy*

Gywnyy and *Mlkwn'y*/*Mlkwn*[*y*] (↑1.2.1.1).

1.3.2.5 *-āy-ā*

Mand. *'my'* (↑1.2.10.2).

---

be merciful", see [G. Van Buylaere and] R. Zadok, PNA 2: 455a, s. v.), and NA *Ig-ru-ia* (based on '-G-R "to hire", see [K. Kessler and] R. Zadok, PNA 2: 508b, s. v.), all explicable in Aramaic terms.

587 BT Gittin 11a, cf. Kipperwasser and Shapira 2014: 300.

1.3.2.6 *-ōy-ā*

Mand. *Šylwy'* (↑1.2.4.2) and *Z'kwy'* (↑1.2.1.1).

1.3.2.7 *-t-ā*

'gblth (↑1.2.12.1.1).

1.3.2.8 *-t-ān-ā*

An adjectival suffix: *Mšrštn'* (↑1.2.12.2.1).

1.3.3 Feminine suffixes

1.3.3.1 Non-combined

1.3.3.1.1 *-ā*

a. With –': *'(y)m'* (↑1.2.10.2), *'rḥ'* (↑1.2.1), *'wn'* (↑1.2.8.1), *D'r'* (↑1.2.9.1), *Ḥwb'* (↑1.2.10.3), *Mlyk'* (↑1.2.4.2), *Ṣwṣl'* (↑1.2.11), *Šgl'* (↑1.2.1.1), *Šlm'* (↑1.2.1 1); *Tylwl'* (↑1.2.4.4), *Tyql'* (↑1.2.1.2), *Ṭb'*,

b. With *-h*: *'mh* (↑1.2.10.2), *Brykh* (↑1.24.2), *Ṣdh/n* (↑1.2.10.2).

1.3.3.1.2 *-at*

Gyyt (↑1.2.1.1), *Nḥlt* (↑1.2.1.1).

1.3.3.1.3 *-āy* or *-īy*

Ḥwty (↑1.2.7.1), *Ḥylpy* (↑1.2.1.2), *Kkry* (↑1.2.11), *Šgly* (↑1.2.1.1), *Ṭrdy* (↑1.2.1.1), *Pwrty* (↑1.2.9.3).

1.3.3.1.4 *-āy*

a. Hypocoristic: *'dy* (↑1.2.10.1.4).

b. Adjectival: a'. With *-'y*: *'ym'y* (↑1.2.10.2), *Dwpš'y* < *Dwbš'y* (↑1.2.1.3), *Kwpyt(')y* (↑1.2.9.3), *Nwnt'y* (↑1.2.9.3); *'Aḥātāy* (OSyr., ↑1.2.7.1), *Ḥt'y* (↑1.2.7.1), Mand. *Mr't'y/Mrt'y* (↑1.2.1.1), *Mnd'y* (↑1.2.12.2.1) and possibly *Nyry* (↑1.2.9.2).

b'. With *-yy*: *'ymyy* (↑1.2.10.2).

c'. With *-y*: *'ymy* (↑1.2.10.2), *Gyrby* (Mand., ↑1.2.1.2), *Ḥty* (↑1.2.7.1), *Kwpry* (↑1.2.1.3).

1.3.3.1.5 *-ōy*

Krkwy/'krkwy ,Qrqwy (↑1.2.1.1), *Ḥ'twy* (↑1.2.7.1), *Symkwy* (↑1.2.1.3.4); *Sysnwy* (male and female, ↑1.2.9.2); *Dydwy* (↓4).

1.3.3.1.6 *-ūt* (suffix of abstract nouns)

G(')ywt[588] (↑1.2.1.1)/*Gwt* (↑1.2.1.2),

1.3.3.1.7 *-yā*

Mand. *'h'ty'* (↑1.2.7.1), *Dwdy'* (↓4) and Mand. *'my'* (↑1.2.10.2), *'zy'* (↑1.2.10.1), and *Hwmymy'* (↑1.2.4.5).

1.3.3.1.8 *-ān*

R'šn (↑1.2.9.1) and *Zywn* (↑1.2.9.2); both are alternatively Middle Persian (↓7.1, 7.3.1.4).

1.3.3.1.9 *-ōn*

Ḥylywn (> Hylywn, ↑1.2.1.2), presumably a diminutive.

1.3.3.1.10 *-ū(t)*

Attached to *'b* in *'bw* (↑1.2.7.1) and to *'yl in 'ylw* (↑1.2.5.2, both females).

1.3.3.2 Combined

1.3.3.2.1 *-t-ā (-t')*

Grdwšt' (↑1.2.6.2), *Grybt'* (↑1.2.4.2), *Mḥlpt'* (also *Mḥlpth,* ↑1.2.12.2.1), *Nqwbt'* (↑1.2.4.3), *Qywmt' (> Qyymt'/Qymt'*, OSyr., ↑1.2.4.3); *Š'ylt'/Šylt'/Šlt'* (↑1.2.4.2), *Nrt'*[589] apparently ends in the same suffix. Mand. *Mrt'* (↑1.2.1.1). *Hdyst'* (↑1.2.4.2.2).

Hybrid: *K°wrht°'°* (/*Xwarrahtā*/)[590] is based on MPers. *xwarrah* "fortune, glory, splendour, happy shine", thereby being a hypocoristic.

1.3.3.2.2 *-at-ā* (-'t')

Dybš't' (↑1.2.1.3), Mand. *Rqd't'* (↑1.2.1.1).

1.3.3.2.3 *-īt-ā*

Gwryt' (↑1.2.9.3), *Mšršyt'* (↑1.2.12.2.1); is *Mrwšyt'*[591] based on JPA *mrwš* (perhaps "vessel")? *Nybryt'* (↑1.2.1.2.2); *'qryt'*[592] presumably mean "accidental, incidental" (JBA).

---

588 Levene, *Jewish Aramaic Curse Texts,* 043A, 2, 3.

589 Levene, *Jewish Aramaic Curse Texts,* 97 *ad* SD 27, 10 (unexpl.).

590 Shaked *et al., Aramaic Bowl Spells* (2013),

591 Ilan, *Lexicon,* 238b.

592 Shaked *et al., Aramaic Bowl Spells* (2013), 31, 8.

1.3.3.2.4 *-t-āy*

Š'ylt'y (↑1.2.4.2). *Ywyt'*, *Ywyt'y* is based on an adjective (↑1.2.4.2), in which case the suffix would be hypocoristic. This suffix is attached to Iranian forms in the female names *'nwšt'y* (also *'nwšt'*,[593] to *anōš*), *Bzwrgwn't'y* (Mand.) whose initial component is MPers. *vuzurg* > *buzurg* "big, great"[594] as well as Mand. *Kwšynt'y* (*/Xwašin-tāy/*,[595] based on an *-in*-hypocoristic of MPers. *xwaš*) and *Gwšn'ṣt'y*[596] (*/Gušn-aṣ-tāy/*), a two-stem hypocoristicon ("*Zweistämmiger Kosename*") being based on the compound *Gwšnsp.*[597] Less transparent is *Bwpt'y*,[598] which is apparently based on a lallative form or on MPers. *būf* "owl"; cf. ↑1.1.5, a, f'. This linguistic interference is extant also in Iranian loanwords in Aramaic: the Aramaic feminine marker is attached also to Persian appellatives, e.g., *ptkrt'* "(female) idol" (JBA, OSyr. vs masc. *ptkr'* etc.).[599] *'wšpyzknt'* (JBA) "landlady", the feminine counterpart of *'špyzkn(')* "host, innkeeper" (JBA, OSyr., Hatran). Another example may be the female name *Mrqwnt'*[600] which may be the feminine counterpart of the Grecized Latin name *Mrqywn* (with elision of *-y-*). *Mrqywn* is recorded as a client in an Old Syriac magic bowl.[601]

1.3.3.2.5 *-ty* (*-t-īy* or *-t-āy*)

It appears sporadically alongside the regular fem. sg. emphatic state *-t'/h*[602]) in *Nṭrty* (↑1.2.2.1), *Mrty* (↑1.2.1.1.6) and *Šylty* (↑1.2.4.2).

1.3.3.2.6 *-t-yā*

Qrysty' (↑1.2.4.2).

1.3.3.2.7 *-at-āy*

Bys't'y.[603]

---

593 Cf. McCullough, *Jewish and Mandean*, 52 *ad* E, 4.

594 Cf. McCullough, *Jewish and Mandean*, 16–17 *ad* C, 3.

595 MS 2054/52, 13 (unpubl., quoted by Abudraham and Morgenstern, "Mandaic Incantation(s)," 754).

596 Abudraham, "Three Mandaic," 83–85:2, 8, 60.

597 For a possible occurrence of this name type in Middle Iranian, viz. Bactrian, see Sims-Williams, *Bactrian Personal Names*, 10.

598 Shaked *et al.*, *Aramaic Bowl Spells* (2013), 63, 5.

599 Cf. Ciancaglini, *Iranian Loanwords*, 243.

600 Shaked *et al.*, *Aramaic Bowl Spells* (2022), 107, 3.

601 Moriggi, *Corpus*, 45, 3a, 4a.

602 See Juusola, *Linguistic Pecularities*, 142–143.

603 Abudraham, "Three Mandaic," 60–82, 93–94:1, 7.

1.3.3.2.8 *-īt-ōn*

Ktšytwn (↑1.2.2).

1.3.3.2.9 *-ōn-ā*

Hwlpwn' (↑1.2.1.3.3).

1.3.3.2.10 *-ōn-īy*

Šwmwny (↑1.2.9.3).

1.3.3.2.11 *-ōn-āy*

Ḥātōnāy (OSyr., ↑1.2.7.1).

1.3.3.2.12 *-ūt-ā*

Mrwt' "control, subjugation" (JPA, Targ.).

1.3.3.2.13 *-ōn-t-ā*

Kspwnt' (Mand., ↑1.2.1.1).

1.3.3.2.14 *-y-āt*

Mand. *Kz'by't* (↑1.2.4.1).

1.3.3.2.15 *-ōn-t-āy*

'ḥtwnty (↑1.2.7.1).

1.3.3.2.16 - *āy-ā*

B'b'y'[604] (↓4, with *b* > *v* OSyr. *B'w'y*).[605]

1.3.3.2.17 *-ōy-ā*

'bwy' (↑1.2.7.1).

---

604 Segal, *Catalogue*, 103M, 8.

605 See Harviainen, "Aramaic Incantation Bowl," 14–15 *ad* 2.

1.3.3.2.18 *-t-ōy*

Possibly Mand. *Kwštwy*[606]*(/Xwaštōy/).*

1.3.3.2.19 *-t-ōy-a*

Mand. *Bḥrtwy'*[607] is apparently based on MPers. *bahr* "lot, share"(↓7.3.2.9).

1.3.3.2.20 *-āy-t-ā* (gentilic)

Bblyt'[608] "Babylonian", *Brkyt'* (↑1.2.1.1), *Nwkryyt'*[609]*/Nwkryt'* "stranger" (↑1.2.1.3),[610] and apparently in Mand. *'wg'yt'.*[611]

1.3.3.2.21 *-ān-īt-ā*

Qrnnyt' (↑1.2.1.1).

1.3.4 Two-stem hypocoristicon

If *Yynyy*[612] originates from *Yn'y* (with *ya-* > *yi-*) it may be a two-stem hypocoristicon (*y-n-*).[613]

2 Originally Hebrew-Canaanite

'dwn[614] "master, guardian" (SA, Targ., Nabatean referring to Jews).

3 Arabian and Arabic

'dyb "polite, honest, learned"[615] (cf. LB *A-di-ba-'* and Saf. *'db* [2 ×]).[616] *Prd Bwryḥmn* perhaps originates from *Farīd* and *Abū raḥmān*[617] (*kunya*) with aphaeresis. *'wm*

---

606 Segal, *Catalogue*, 096M, 46.
607 Morgenstern, "Five Mandaic," 112–114:26, 4 (<w>), 8.
608 See Morgenstern and Ford, *Aramaic Incantation Bowls*, 14, n. 14.
609 Gordon, "Aramaic Incantation Bowls," 121, 2.
610 Bhayro *et al.*, *Aramaic Magic Bowls*, 57.
611 Segal, *Catalogue*, 103M, 7.
612 See McCullough, *Jewish and Mandean*, 8 *ad* B, 2.
613 See Zadok, "Zur Struktur," 308:3.2.
614 Ilan, *Lexicon*, 164a (wrongly listed s. v. Ādhur, 1).
615 Cf. Shaked, "Form and Purpose," 6.
616 See Zadok, *West Semites in Babylonia*, 232 and Harding, *Index and Concordance*, 31.
617 Segal, *Catalogue*, 78 *ad* 037A, 7 suggested [A]bu [Abd]raḥman which is unnecessary.

'lḥwb'b (fem.) d. of *Rwmn'*.[618] The latter is based on Arab. *rummān* "pommegranate". *Pḥd'*[619] may denote "the tribe, clan" (Palm. *pḥd* < Arab. *fāḫiḏ*). *'ynqdw*[620] (apparently with wawation) perhaps derives from N-Q-D, cf. Saf. *Nqd* (2 ×) and Arab. *Nuqayd.*[621] *Kwmyš*[622] may be a *qutayl*-diminutive of *Kmš* (Saf., 5 ×, Arab. *kamš* "quick, alert").[623] Mand. *'wl'ym'* (fem.) can be of the same pattern thereby meaning "clever little girl".[624] *'bwsmk' (/Abū-samkā)* looks hybrid: it apparently consists of *'bw* "father of" (Arab.) and *smk'* "support" (Aram.), i.e. a *kunya*. *Ḥbyby* "beloved, darling"[625] (*qatīl*-formation of *Ḥ-B-B* plus -*īy*).

4 Atypical names

Names with repetitive (mostly reduplicative) syllables look atypical,[626] but many of them are based on lallative forms which denote informal kinship terms:

B'by,[627] *B'b'y,*[628] *B'bwy,*[629] *B'bw,*[630] *P(')p'/y*[631] "dad". *Bptwy* (fem.) may have the same base (with *b* > *ḇ* > *f*).[632] with the feminine marker (+ -*ōy*, ↑1.3.3.2.17). A derivation from *bāft* "woven" (NPers.)[633] is less likely seeing that its MPers. forerunner is begins with *w*-. *M'mh*[634]/*M'my*/*M(')m'*/*M(')my*[635]/*M'm'y*[636] (*M.* wife of

618 For the reading and transcription see Bhayro *et al., Aramaic Magic Bowls,* 134–136:98–99 (correct Ilan, *Lexicon,* 211b, s. v. Aysalhubab).

619 Ilan, *Lexicon,* 196.

620 Isbell, *Corpus,* 61, 2.

621 Harding, *Index and Concordance,* 597.

622 It is not related to the Pontic Iranian name in Justi, *Iranisches Namenbuch* 165b, top, which is quoted by Montgomery, *Aramaic Incantation Texts,* 191 *ad* 17, 2. Semitic without further specification according to D. Shapira *apud* Ilan, *Lexicon,* 231a.

623 Harding, *Index and Concordance,* 505.

624 See Segal, *Catalogue,* 136 *ad* 103M, 13.

625 See Naveh, "Some New Jewish," 236.

626 They are recorded in Middle Iranian onomastica such as the Bactrian one (see Sims-Williams, *Bactrian Personal Names,* 10).

627 See McCullough, *Jewish and Mandean,* 4 *ad* A, 3, 4.

628 Morgenstern and Schlütter, "A Mandaic Amulet," 118, 120, 47; cf. Sims-Williams, *Bactrian Personal Names,* 38:40. Extant in Mand. *B'b'ydwkt* (↓7.2.1, i).

629 See Segal, *Catalogue,* 64 *ad* 023A, 2 f.

630 Wohlstein, "Über einige aramäische," 9, 34–41: [VA] 2417, 15.

631 Ilan, *Lexicon,* 196–199.

632 See Naveh and Shaked, *Magic Spells* 124 *ad* 18, 4. For this shift see Juusola, *Linguistic Peculiarities,* 42 with n. 109 (who does not include this case in his selective list of examples).

633 As implied by Ilan (2011: 212) who erroneously rienders the suffix as "well".

634 Shaked *et al., Aramaic Bowl Spells* (2013), 56, 2, 8.

635 Ilan, *Lexicon,* 236–238.

636 Segal, *Catalogue,* 208b, s. v. with references.

Brṣwm' was in all probability Christian) "mum". *D'd'*[637]/*D'dh,*[638] *Ddy*[639]/*D'dy'* (all fem.)[640] may be based on *dd* "beloved" (OSyr., Palm., Nab.); alternatively, the forms with –(')*y* may denote "mother" or "grandmother" (JBA *d'dy*). *Yy'* refers to both a male and a female.[641] As a male's name it means "brother" (Mand. *iaia*) while Mand. *dadia* denotes "older brother". Noteworthy filiations are *D'dy* s. of *Dydwy,*[642] *Ddy* d. of *Dwdy*[643] and Mand. *D'dwy'* s. of *D'dy'.*[644] *Q'qy* (fem.) apparently ends in -*î* < -*īy* and *Q'q'y* (fem.) in -*āy*, the transcriptions *Kākūī* and *Kākōē*[645] are incorrect; cf. Mand. *Q'q'y*[646]/*Q'q'y'*[647] (fem.). These forms may be based on an Iranian dialectal endearing term for "uncle" or possibly on OSyr. *qq'* "pelican",[648] cf. *Q'qh* (fem.).[649] Mand. *Qwq'y,*[650] *Qwqy*[651] may denote a species of bird in view of JBA *qwqy, qwq'h* (onomatopoeic). *L'ly*/*L'lw* (fem.)[652] may be based on a forerunner of NPers. *lāl* "ruby"[653] or "tulip" (cf. *Lāleh*);[654] *L'lh*[655] and *Lyly*[656] are with a reduplicated syllable. *N'nh,*[657] *N'n'* , *Nn'y*[658] and *N'n'y* (fem.)[659] denote "mother" in JBA and OSyr. *nānā*;[660] *Nny* and *Nnyh*[661] may be based on the same lexeme.

637 Isbell, *Corpus*, 4, 2.
638 See Montgomery, *Aramaic Incantation Texts*, 175 *ad* 12, 11.
639 Faraj, "Aramaico orientale," 272–273:IM 2929, 4.
640 Gordon, "Aramaic and Mandaic," 95–100 and pls. 10–13:M, 2nd panel.
641 Cook "An Aramaic Incantation," 79–80, 4; Shaked *et al., Aramaic Bowl Spells* (2013), 108.
642 Ford, "Phonetic Spellings," 243, n. 80.
643 Faraj, "Remarks," 90–94, 15.
644 Gordon, "Aramaic and Mandaic," 95–100 and pls. 10–13:M, 2nd panel.
645 Ilan, *Lexicon*, 185a, 228–229.
646 Yamauchi, *Mandaic Incantation Texts*, 28, 5.
647 Segal, *Catalogue*, 098M, 8.
648 For the Old Syriac derivation of *Q'qy* see Montgomery, *Aramaic Incantation Texts*, 206 *ad* 24, 3.
649 Shaked *et al., Aramaic Bowl Spells* (2022), 108, 1, 2.
650 Yamauchi, *Mandaic Incantation Texts*, 26, 3, 18, 19, 21, 22, 23, 24, 26.
651 Gordon, "Aramaic and Mandaic," 95–100 and pls. 10–13:M, 3.
652 Ilan, *Lexicon*, 233.
653 See Morgenstern and Ford, *Aramaic Incantation Bowls*, 53.
654 Justi, *Iranisches Namenbuch* 182b.
655 Isbell, *Corpus*, 65, 2.
656 Ilan, *Lexicon*, 233.
657 Bhayro *et al., Aramaic Magic Bowls*, 96.
658 Segal, *Catalogue*, 103M, 9.
659 Gordon, "Aramaic and Mandaic," 95–100 and pls. 10–13:M, 4, 11.
660 See Sokoloff *Dictionary*, 688a.
661 Ilan, *Lexicon*, 242.

Other onomatopoeic names are *T'ṭ'*[662](Mand., fem.), *Tyty,*[663] *Ṭ'ṭ',*[664] *Ṭwṭ'y,*[665] *Ṭ'ṭy*[666], *Ṭ'ṭ'y,*[667] *Ṭ'ṭy'* (both Mand.),[668] *Ṭ'/wṭ'*[669] as well as *Dwd'y,*[670] *Dwd'y'*[671]/*Dwdy',*[672] *Dwdw,*[673] *Dwd',*[674] *Dwdyy*[675] and *Dydwy* (all fem.).[676] OSyr. *Dwt'y* (fem.)[677] may be the same name as *Dwdyy* with dissimilation. *'ydy* (fem.),[678] *Gwy,*[679] and *Gy'*[680]/*Gyy(y)*[681] (fem.) have only one stable consonant each. The base of *Y'y'* (fem. and masc.),[682] *'yy,*[683] *'yy', 'yw'/'ywy/'yyw(')y,*[684] *Ywy'y/Yw'yy*[685] (all fem.) is devoid of stable consonants; cf. *'yhy.*[686]

Non-suffixed names arranged by prosody

Ca-Ca: *D'd' /D'dh, L'lh, M'mh/M(')m', N'n'/N'nh; P(')p', Q'qh, T't', Ṭ'ṭ', Y(')y' , Y'y';*
Ci-Ci: *Lyly, Tyty;*
Cu-Cu: *Dwdw.*

662 Montgomery, *Aramaic Incantation Texts,* 39, 9.
663 Shaked *et al., Aramaic Bowl Spells* (2013), 16, 4, 9.
664 Isbell, *Corpus,* 70, 1,
665 Shaked *et al., Aramaic Bowl Spells* (2013), 19, 2, 7.
666 Bhayro *et al., Aramaic Magic Bowls,* 120, 124.
667 Abudraham, "Three Mandaic," 89–93:3, 15.
668 Segal, *Catalogue,* 103M, 9.
669 Ilan, *Lexicon,* 254a.
670 Geller, "More magic spells," 331–335:B, 8, 23.
671 Gordon, "Aramaic and Mandaic," 100–103 and pl. 14:N, 3.
672 Gorea, "Trois nouvelles," 85–89 and 92–93:3, 3.
673 Isbell, *Corpus,* 63, 2.
674 Gordon, "Aramaic Incantation Bowls," 127–129:7, 11.
675 Gordon, "Aramaic Incantation Bowls," 127–129:7, 2.
676 Franco, "Five Aramaic," 236–240 and fig. 1 on 235:C_{10}-116, 2, 5, 8; 242–245 and fig. 4; 245–249 and fig. 5:C_{11}-3, 2.
677 Moriggi, *Corpus,* 41, 3, 13.
678 Cf. Fain *et al.*, "Aramaic Incantation Bowls," 302 with n. 32 *ad* S-448, 2.
679 Isbel 1975, 4, 1, 5, 9.
680 Shaked *et al., Aramaic Bowl Spells* (2022), 69, 1.
681 Shaked *et al., Aramaic Bowl Spells* (2022), 76, 7; 105, 4; 106, 3.
682 Bhayro *et al., Aramaic Magic Bowls,* 108.
683 Cf. Faraj and Moriggi, "Two New," 75–76 *ad* IM 71180, 2.
684 Shaked *et al., Aramaic Bowl Spells* (2013), 345, index, s.vv. with references.
685 Shaked *et al., Aramaic Bowl Spells* (2022), 88, 1, 3.
686 Montgomery, *Aramaic Incantation Texts,* 18, 1.

Arranged by suffixes

-ā: *Dwd', Gy', Ṭwṭ';*
-ō: *B'bw, L'lw;*
-āy, a. With –'y: *'yyw'y, B'b'y, Dwd'y, Dwt'y, M'm'y, N(')n'y, P(')p'y,Q'q'y, Qwq'y, Ṭ'ṭ'y, Ṭwṭ'y, Ywy'y;*
b. With -*yy*: *Dwdyy, Gyy(y), Yw'yy;*
-āy or -īy: *'ydy, 'yhy, B'by, D(')dy, Dwdy, Gwy, L'ly, M(')my, Nny, Q'qy, Qwqy, Ṭ'ṭy;*
-ōy: *B'bwy, Dydwy;*
-yā: *D'dy', Dwdy', Nnyh, Ṭ'ṭy';*
-āy-ā: *Dwd'y', Q'q'y';*
-ōy-ā: *D'dwy'.*

5 Semitic or Iranian names

B'n'y (fem.)[687] is either Semitic (to B-N-Y "to build") or Iranian (hypocoristic of a compound with **bānu-* "light, splendour", cf. MPers. *Bānag*[688]). The same applies to *Dwdy* and most of the names listed s. v. *Daδī.*[689]

6 Originally Iranian, but borrowed in Aramaic

Mand. *Šrwl'/Šrwlh̲*[690] apparently renders Mand. *šaruala* "trouser" (< *šrbl*, an Iranian loanword, MPers. with metathesis *šalwar*), for the semantics cf. the Arabic anthroponym *Quftān* "mantle"). Mand. *'ṭrwg'* (fem.)[691] *"citrus medica"*[692] may be (like many phytonyms) a cultural word, a *Wanderwort. Mgyt'* (fem.)[693] is apparently based on **mg.* which ultimately may originate from *mgwš* (> *'mgwš*) > MPers. *moγ* "Magian priest".[694]

---

687 Ilan, *Lexicon*, 213–214.
688 Gignoux, *Noms propres*, 54:183; for more comparanda cf., e.g., Sims-Williams, *Bactrian Personal Names*, 45:71; Schmitt, *Personennamen* 53:61, 140:303 and Martirosyan, *Iranian Personal Names*, 144–158.
689 Ilan, *Lexicon*, 215–217.
690 Cf. Müller-Kessler, "Die Zauberschalensammlung," 134 *ad* 088M and 089M.
691 Pognon, *Inscriptions mandaïtes*, 17.
692 Cf. Nöldeke, "Review," 144; Ciancaglini, *Iranian Loanwords*, 105.
693 Shaked *et al.*, *Aramaic Bowl Spells* (2013), 25, 9.
694 Cf. Ciancaglini, *Iranian Loanwords*, 201–202.

7 Iranian

Some individuals bore more than one name,[695] e.g. *M'hdwkt* (MPers., ↓7.2.1, i) alias *'h'ty'* (Aram., ↑1.3.3.1.7).[696]

7.1 Simplex names

Several such names are inherited from Old Iranian:

'rw < OIran. **Arva-* "swift, brave";[697] *'ry'*[698] < OIran. **Ariya-* "Aryan, Iranian"[699] (both may originate from compound names with these components). *'ṭš*[700] < MPers. *Ātaxš* "fire". Mand. *Šyryn* (fem.)[701] renders MPers. *šīrēn* "sweet". *'brs'm* (a scribe according to an inscription from the synagogue of Dura Europos)[702] – with the normalization */Abursām/* it is at least homophonous with the Middle Persian appellative "balm, balsam".[703] *'ysprm* (< */Sparham/*, fem.) "basil";[704] *Ysmyn* "jasmine"[705] > *'smyn* > *Smyn*[706] (fem., with *ya* – > *a-* > *ø-*); *Škr*[707] (*/Šakar/*, fem.) "sugar" (for the semantics cf. the Aramaic female names meaning "honey", ↑1.2.1.3.4). *'bn*[708] (*/Ābān/*) is plural of *āb* "water" and the name of the 10th day of the Mazdean calendar.[709] *'spnz*[710] can render MPers. *aspinj* "hospitality". It is related to *'yšpyz'* which is compared to OSyr. *'špz'*, JBA *'wšpyz'* "lodging"[711] with a

695 All the names and appellatives in this section are Middle Persian unless otherwise indicated.
696 For this phenomenon in Middle Persian see Zimmer, "Zur sprachlichen," 145–146:9.2.
697 It cannot render Ἀρύνις as claimed by Ilan, *Lexicon*, 209. Cf., e.g. NA *A-ru-a* (Schmitt, *Iranische Personennamen in der neuassyrischen*, 50:20) and the initial component of Sogd. *'rwmyw*, *'rwprmyn* (Lurje, *Personal Names*, 103:143, 144).
698 Müller-Kessler, *Zauberschalentexte*, 14, 5, 6.
699 Cf., e.g., Schmitt *Die Iranischen und Iranier-Namen*, 42; 2009: 47:15.
700 Shaked *et al.*, *Aramaic Bowl Spells* (2013), 63, 5.
701 Yamauchi, *Mandaic Incantation Texts*, 29, 9, 41, 46.
702 Ilan, *Lexicon*, 163a.
703 See Schmitt, *Personennamen* 41–42:31 and Martirosyan, *Iranian Personal Names*, 95–96:42 with previous lit.; cf. Ciancaglini, *Iranian Loanwords*, 114, s. v. *'pwrsm'*.
704 See Segal, *Catalogue*, 62 *ad* 020A, 4.
705 See Montgomery, *Aramaic Incantation Texts*, 117 *ad* 12, 11.
706 Wohlstein, "Über einige aramäische," 9, 34–41: [VA] 2417, 16, 20.
707 JNF 291 (unpubl., quoted by Shaked *et al.*, *Aramaic Bowl Spells* [2022], 209).
708 Gordon, "Aramaic Incantation Bowls," 121:4, 1 (cf. Shaked *apud* Greenfield and Naveh 1985a: 106).
709 See Gignoux *et al.* 2009: 29:1.
710 Montgomery, *Aramaic Incantation Texts*, 7, 4.
711 By Montgomery, *Aramaic Incantation Texts*, 221–222 *ad* 30, 1 (cf. Sogd. *Sp'nc /Səpanj/* "inn", Lurje, *Personal Names*, 348:1088).

distant assimilation *s* > *š*[712] due to the presence of */j/*. *'yšpyz'*, was the son of *'rḥ'* "guest", in which case both members of the filiation while deriving from two unrelated languages belong to the same semantic field. Therefore one may suspect that the actual name and matronym of the client with this filiation were disguised under an invented combination. *R'šn* (fem.) may render MPers. *rōšn* "light; bright" (alternatively Aram., ↑1.2.9.1). OSyr. *Kwrh*[713] (fem.) renders *Xwarrah* < **Xvarnah-*. *Kwd'y* (*Xwadāy/*) denotes "lord".[714] *D'nyš* may be compared to the New Persian anthroponym *Dāniš* "knowledge" (< MPers. *dānišn*).[715] For *S'm* (of the double name Mand. ~ *Ywh'n'*)[716] cf. Av. *Sāma-*,[717] MPers. and NPers. *Sām* "black",[718] as well as Sogd. *S'm* and Bact. Σαμο.[719] *Kwsty* (fem.)[720] may render MPers. *xwastīh* "confession, belief, faith". *B'my* (fem.)[721] goes back to OIran. **Bāmyā-*, Av. *bāmyā* "bright, radiant, glittering", cf. the males' names RAE *Ba-mi-ia* < **Bāmya-*[722] and MPers. *Bām*;[723] alternatively with adjectivizing *-ay* (*Bāmay* "related to brilliance", "brilliant").[724] Theonyms used as an anthroponyms are *Hwrmyz*[725] (also Mand.)[726]/OSyr. *Ḥwrmyz*[727] and *'štd* < Av. *Arštat-* "(Goddess of) rectitude."[728] A traditional name is, e.g., *'prydwn*[729] (< MPers. */Frēdōn/*[730] < Av. *Θraētaona-*).

---

712 See Ciancaglini, *Iranian Loanwords*, 118–119.
713 Müller-Kessler "Review," 271 *ad* 35.
714 See Naveh and Shaked, *Amulets and Magic Bowls*, 175 *ad* 8, ii, 4, iii, 5; cf. Gignoux, *Noms propres*, 186:1024.
715 *Dāniš* is recorded as an anthroponym in New Persian. Hunter ("Two Mandaic," 612 *ad* 609 and pl. 25 after 619:18N19, segment 3, 27) compares a New Persian compound name beginning with *Dāniš*, viz. *Dānišwer* (Justi, *Iranisches Namenbuch* 77 where all the three anthroponyms are registered as well as *Dānišmend* < MPers. *dānišnōmand* "knowing", cf. Morgenstern and Ford, *Aramaic Incantation Bowls*, 191, n. 617 who compare also NPers. *Dānūyeh*).
716 Cf. Ford, "Another Look," 264 *ad* DC 14, 183.
717 Cf. Zimmer, "Zur sprachlichen," 124 *ad* 823.
718 See Gignoux, *Noms propres*, 156:823.
719 See Lurje, *Personal Names*, 341, 1061; Sims-Williams, *Bactrian Personal Names*, 123:409.
720 Ilan, *Lexicon*, 221b with a wrong lemmatization (*Gusti*) and interpretation.
721 Ilan, *Lexicon*, 213b.
722 See Hinz *Altiranisches Sprachgut*, 62, s. v.; alternatively an *-iya*-hypocoristic to **bāma-* (or *bāma*-containing compounds) according to Mayrhofer, *Onomastica Persepolitana*, 8.248.
723 See Gignoux, *Noms propres*, 54:181.
724 See Shaked, "Peace Be upon You," 214.
725 Segal, *Catalogue*, 023A, 3, 11.
726 Segal, *Catalogue*, 083M, 7.
727 Moriggi, *Corpus*, 13, 9 (*bis*).
728 See Segal, *Catalogue*, 67 *ad* 026A, 2–3 (cf. Ford, "Phonetic Spellings," 218; differently Müller-Kessler, "Die Zauberschalensammlung," 103).
729 Müller-Kessler, *Zauberschalentexte*, 11d, 2, 11.
730 Cf. Martirosyan, *Iranian Personal Names*, 229–230:406 with lit.

7.2 Compound names

They generally consist of two components. An individual bearing three names (or a tripartite compound?) is Mand. *'zy'zd'n kw'st B'nd'd.*[731]

7.2.1 Determinative compound names

a. With *-dād* "was given":[732] The 1st component of the name (*Yzydd,*[733] *Yzyd'd,*[734] OSyr. *Yzydd'd*[735] > *'zd'd,* cf. the simplex *Yzyd*[736]) is a plene spelling rendering the Middle Persian outcome of OIran. **Yazata-dāta-* "Given by the gods".[737] It is also extant in *Hwrmzdd*[738] and *Zwrwndd*[739] (MPers. *Zurvān-dād*)[740] "Given by Ahura-Mazdah" and "Given by Zurvān", *Byzdd* (*/Bay-yaz(a)d-dād/*)[741] "Given by the god *Bay* (< *Baga-*)",[742] *Bdṭ* (< *Baga-dāta-*[743]), *Mhdṭ*[744]/*Mhdd,*[745] OSyr. *M'ḥdṭ*[746] < MPers. *Māh-dād* "Given by the Moon-god"[747] and *Yzyd Mḥdṭ* (*/Yazad-Māh-dāt/*) "Given by the deity Moon".[748] *Bhmndd* (*/Bahmān-dād/*) "Given by *Bahmān*". *Prwkdd* (*/Farrox-dād/*),[749] OSyr. *Prwkd'd*[750] means "Given by the fortunate, happy (one)".[751]

731 Morgenstern, "Five Mandaic," 118–121:154, 3, 12.

732 See Zimmer, "Zur sprachlichen," 128 with n. 93 and Schmitt, *Personennamen* 9; cf. MPers. and NPers. *Xudāidādh* (Justi, *Iranisches Namenbuch* 177a, the Judeo-Persian equivalent of Heb. *Yhwntn*).

733 Bhayro *et al., Aramaic Magic Bowls,* 46.

734 Montgomery, *Aramaic Incantation Texts,* 27, 7, 10.

735 Moriggi, *Corpus,* 36, 2, cf. Montgomery, *Aramaic Incantation Texts,* 150 *ad* 7, 3.

736 See Naveh and Shaked, *Amulets and Magic Bowls,* 157–158 (cf. Morgenstern and Ford, *Aramaic Incantation Bowls* 3062, 2).

737 For MPers. *yazd* < *yazad* < OIran. *yazata-* see Durkin-Meisterernst, *Grammatik,* 200 and Gignoux, Julien, and Julien, *Noms propres,* 147.

738 Gordon, "Aramaic Incantation Bowls," 272–273 and 281, pl. 1:10, 2.

739 Cf. Morgenstern and Ford, *Aramaic Incantation Bowls,* 95, n. 360 *ad* 18 = HS 3032, 1, 2.

740 Gignoux, *Noms propres,* 196:1091 (also Parth., Schmitt, *Personennamen* 251:618).

741 See Shaked *et al., Aramaic Bowl Spells* (2022), 17 *ad* 66, 1.

742 See Shaked in Shaked *et al., Aramaic Bowl Spells* (2022), 8a, 17b *ad* 70a, 8; 95, 4, 8, 13; 110, 5.

743 Ilan, *Lexicon,* 212b.

744 Isbell, *Corpus,* 67, 6.

745 See Segal, *Catalogue,* 55 *ad* 013A, 3.

746 Moriggi, *Corpus,* 12, 3, 5, 10.

747 See Gignoux, *Noms propres,* 111:529 (borrowed in Sogdian, Lurje, *Personal Names,* 233, 646, cf. Parth. *Mhdt, Mhdtk,* Schmitt, *Personennamen,* 124–125:267–268).

748 See Naveh and Shaked, *Magic Spells,* 133 *ad* 23, 5.

749 Cf. Gordon, "An Aramaic Exorcism," 328 *ad* D, 5 who aptly refers to Justi, *Iranisches Namenbuch* 96a, s. v. *Farux*^{w}*dādh*; Shaked, "Form and Purpose," 22: 9, 1.

750 Moriggi, *Corpus,* 28, 6, 7, 11.

751 For the semantics see Zimmer, "Zur sprachlichen," 136:8.1.3. Not "created by F." as understood by Gignoux, *Noms propres,* 84:358.

Mhyndd[752] (apparently to *Māhin-*[753]) begins with *Māh* "Moon-god" (for the suffix of the 1st component compare that of MPers. *Gušnēn-dād*[754]). *'bndd*[755] is perhaps a calendar name, presumably "Given by the 8th month" or "Given by the 10th day". *Gwšnzd(')d* "Given by *Gušnasp*" (short for *Ādur-Gušnasp*, a numen in Zoroastrianism).[756] *Bwzmndd*[757] – a numen *Bwzmn* is not recorded. It apparently consists of MPers. *bōz* "redemption" and *-man*. The latter is a rare suffix (or final component).[758] Mand. *'smnd'r*[759] ends in *-d'r*, which for semantic reasons cannot be the comparative suffix. Perhaps it is a scribal error for and *'smnd'd* "Given by Heaven". *Dd'pry*[760] apparently consists of *dād* "law, justice" and *'pry* (< *āfrīn* "praise, blessing"?) or it denotes "Friend of the law".

b. With *-dōst* "beloved": *Pdrdst* > *Pddws*, Mand. *Pidardōst* (both fem.)[761] denote "Beloved by her father".[762] *Srdwst* (fem.) apparently consists of *sar* "head"[763] and *-dōst*, MPers. "friend, beloved", perhaps "Chief friend",[764] cf. MPers. *Xwadāy-dōst*[765] on the one hand and the New Persian female name *Sarjihān* "Chief of the world"[766] on the other. Mand. *B'wydws*[767] apparently consists of *B'wy* and *dws* < *dwst*.

c. With *pryd* (< /*āfrīd* < OIran. **ā-frīta-*) "blessed; created": *Yzdnpryd* (fem., /*Yazdān-āfrīd*/) "Blessed/Created by the gods",[768] *'nwš(')pryt* (< /*Anōš-āfrīd*/) "Bless-

---

752 Gordon, "Two Aramaic," 233–236 and pls. 1–5 on 238–242:i, 2.

753 Cf. Parth. *Mhyn* (Schmitt, *Personennamen* 125–126:270, cf. also 271).

754 See Gignoux *Noms propres sassanides*, 94:419, 421.

755 Ilan, *Lexicon*, 163b.

756 Morgenstern and Ford, *Aramaic Incantation Bowls*, 131, n. 462 *ad* 3046+3069, 2, 5, 6, 7 (see Shaked, "Form and Purpose," 10).

757 The name is wrongly lemmatized and interpreted by Ilan (*Lexicon*, 14, 173b).

758 See Durkin-Meisterernst, *Grammatik*, 188:4.1.3.47.11 (the only registered example is *istaw-man*).

759 Müller-Kessler, *Zauberschalentexte*, 39, 7.

760 Levene, *Jewish Aramaic Curse Texts*, 043A, 2, 16.

761 Morgenstern, "Mandaic Magic Bowls," 162: unnumbered A (digest only). *Pddws* (fem., Shaked 2022, 82, 12, 17, 18,) may originally be the same name.

762 See Shaked *et al.*, *Aramaic Bowl Spells* (2022), 66 *ad* 82, 12, 17, 18, 20.

763 Cf. Ilan, *Lexicon*, 250a.

764 It does not originate from Zaraθuštra as suggested by Montgomery, *Aramaic Incantation Texts*, 163 *ad* 9, 4.

765 Gignoux, *Noms propres*, 186:1026, cf. the Bactrian and Sogdian semantic comparanda discussed by Sims-Williams, *Bactrian Personal Names*, 144:501.

766 See Justi, *Iranisches Namenbuch* 288b.

767 Cf. Müller-Kessler, "Die Zauberschalensammlung," 135 *ad* 098M, 8, 10, 11.

768 See Levene, *Jewish Aramaic Curse Texts*, 96 with n. 121 *ad* SD 27, 10.

ed/Created by the immortal, eternal";[769] and *Š'h'pryd*[770]/*Š'hpryd*[771]/*Šhpryd*[772] (fem., /*Šāh-āfrīd*/) "Blessed/Created by the king".[773] It is the initial component (with aphaeresis) of Mand. *Prydrmyṣ*[774] (< *Āfrīd-Hormizd*/).

d. With < OIran. *hu-:[775] *K(w)srw* (/*Xusrō*/ or /*Xusraw*/),[776] Mand. *Ksrw'*[777] < MPers. *Husrav* < OIran. **Hu-sravah-* "of good reputation, renown".[778]

e. Other: The 2nd component of *Mhmd* (fem.)[779] may go back to OIran. **mata-*, i.e. "Thought (> 'planned') by the Moon-god". *Sēbuxt*,[780] Mand. *Dṣh'rbwkt*[781] (/*Čahārbuxt*/) "Saved, delivered by the three/four",[782] cf. *Yazdānbuxt* "Saved, delivered by the gods"[783] and *Yazdānxvast* "Desired by the gods";[784] *Yzdn* (/*Yazdān*/),[785] which is a *pluralis maiestatis* (presumably referring to the main god Ahura-Mazdah)[786] is extant, e.g., in *Yzdnqyrd* (/*Yazdān-qerd*/ > *Yazdān-gerd*)[787] "Made by the gods".[788] *Ddb[y]h*[789]/*D'dbh*[790]/*Ddbh*[791] (/*Dād-beh*/ < ~-*veh*)[792] and Mand. *Z'dbh*[793] (/*Zād-beh*/) "Born better" have an Old Iranian precursor, viz. **Zāta-vahya-*[794] and its Old Persian counterpart. *Mhpyrwz*[795] whose 2nd component (MPers. *pērōz*)

769 See Segal, *Catalogue*, 157 *ad* 015A, 2 quoting Gignoux, *Noms propres*, 42:101, 48:140, 126:628, 139:704 (cf. Ilan, *Lexicon*, 208b: "Created immortally").
770 Segal, *Catalogue*, 077M, 8.
771 Cf. Ford, "Another Look," 241 *ad* 078M, 11.
772 Cf. Müller-Kessler, "Die Zauberschalensammlung," 132b *ad* 084M, 3.
773 See Segal, *Catalogue*, 104 *ad* 077M, 8.
774 Müller-Kessler, "A Mandaic Gold Amulet," a, 5, 61, 67; b,3, 27–28.
775 Cf. Zimmer, "Zur sprachlichen," 133–134:7.5.
776 Bhayro *et al.*, *Aramaic Magic Bowls*, 224–225, index, s.vv. with references. See Schmitt, *Personennamen*, 112:232 with previous lit.
777 Yamauchi, *Mandaic Incantation Texts*, 27, 2, 6, 9, 10, 12, 15, 16, 17.
778 See Gignoux, *Noms propres*, 100:465.
779 Ilan, *Lexicon*, 236a.
780 Ilan, *Lexicon*, 202a.
781 Cf. Müller-Kessler, "Die Zauberschalensammlung," 135 *ad* 096M, 37–39.
782 See Shaked, "Peace Be upon You," 214, cf. Gignoux, Jullien and Jullien, *Noms propres*, 61:142.
783 For the names consisting of number+*buxt* see Zimmer, "Zur sprachlichen," 123 *ad* 833, 874a.
784 See Shaked, "Peace Be upon You," 214.
785 Bhayro *et al.*, *Aramaic Magic Bowls*, 46.
786 See Zimmer, "Zur sprachlichen," 119 with n. 45.
787 Shaked *et al.*, *Aramaic Bowl Spells* (2022), 219, 305, top, s. v.
788 See Gignoux, *Noms propres*, 192:1065.
789 Moriggi, *Corpus*, 3, 2; cf. perhaps NPers. *Dādbūyeh* (Justi, *Iranisches Namenbuch*, 75).
790 Moriggi, *Corpus*, 3, 6; 5, 5, 10.
791 Isbell, *Corpus*, 4, 1, 12.
792 Gignoux, *Noms propres*, 119:581 (cf. 211 for other names ending in *-veh*).
793 Yamauchi, *Mandaic Incantation Texts*, 8, 15, 23, 26, 46, 52; 12, 7, 12, 22.
794 Cf. Zadok, *Iranische Personennamen in der neu*, 327:637.
795 Isbell, *Corpus*, 58, 8 (*M<h>pyrwz*, 3, 11, *Mhp<y>rwz*, 2).

means "victorious" (< OIran. **Pary-auǰah-* "Having strength all around", i.e. a *bahuvrīhi*).[796] The name with an inverted order (**Pyrwzmh*, like *Pērōz-Ohrmazd*) would mean "Victorious Moon-god" or "Victorious through the Moon-God",[797] in which case this compound can be regarded as a determinative one. *Kyrbg'rzn* (fem.)[798] consists of *kirbag* "virtue, good deed" and *arzān* "valuable, worthy", i.e. "Worthy for her virtue".

f. *Zād* < **zāta-* "born": *Ztzd*[799] apparently ends in -**zāta-* "born" which is used as a (pro-)patronymic, in this case of it is attached to *Zt* < **Zāta-*, the whole compound is with dissimilation of dentals. This name-type is extant, e.g., in *Zrmzd* (*/Zarm-zād/*),[800] OSyr. *Prwkz'd*, Mand. *Pr(w)kz'd* (*/Farrox-zād/*)[801] and *Šyrz'd*[802] (*/Šērzād/*) "lion's son" (< "born to a lion").[803] However, the former may be a variant of Mand. *Prwk'z'd*.[804] Another compound with *Prwk* is *Zd'n Prwk* (= OSyr. ~, Mand. *Z'd'nprwk*,[805] i.e. */Zādān-Farrox/*);[806] cf. *Zydyn Šbwr*.[807] Is Mand. *B'z'd'n*[808] a defective spelling of **B'yz'd'n*, i.e. consisting of *Bāy* "god" and *zādān*? Its gender cannot be determined since the name-bearer is a member of a group of children who are subsumed as "sons and daughters". Mand. *Z'dn'hwg*[809] apparently begins with *zādān*. Does *Zyzt'q*[810] end with a forerunner of -*zādāg*?

g. *pūr* < *puhr* "son": *Bwrzpwry* (*/Burz-pūri/*)[811] is based on *Burz-pūr* (< **Burz-puhr*) "son of the exalted (one)" > OSyr. *Bwṣpḥry*.[812] -*pwhr'q'* of Mand.

---

796 See Schmitt, *Personennamen* 158–159:351 *in fine*.

797 Gignoux, *Noms propres*, 148:765. Segal, *Catalogue*, 48b *ad* 006A, 34 renders *Mhpyrwz* as "Victorious through the Moon-God", but this requires an inverted order.

798 Ford, "Phonetic Spellings," 238, n. 66 (unpubl.).

799 Moriggi, *Corpus*, 15, 17, 30.

800 Gordon, "Two Aramaic," 233–236 and pls. 1–5 on 238–242:I, 2.

801 Moriggi, *Corpus*, 48, 1, 4 and Yamauchi, *Mandaic Incantation Texts*, 33, 3, 22, 25, 26, 27.

802 McCullough, *Jewish and Mandean*, E, 4.

803 See Gignoux, Jullien and Jullien, *Noms propres*, 131:406.

804 See Abu Samra "A New Mandaic," 59 *ad* 13, exterior 1.

805 Abudraham, "Three Mandaic," 83–85:2, 61.

806 See Gignoux, Jullien and Jullien, *Noms propres*, 148:462ab. *Z'd'nprwk* is recorded twice in a bowl published by Hyvernant. The variant *Zdynprwk* occurs only once there, but it may be a misreading since the only published photograph is not clear (see Gordon, "Aramaic Magical Bowls," 331, n. 1).

807 Compared by Gordon, "Aramaic Magical Bowls," 331–334 and pls. 14, 15, F, 1.

808 Abudraham, "Three Mandaic," 83–85:2, 9, 61.

809 Müller-Kessler, "Die Zauberschalensammlung," 134: 087M, 7 (*bis*), cf. Müller-Kessler, "The Story of Bguzan-Lilit," 191 (unpubl.). It is read *Z'rn'hwg* by Ford (2002a: 250 *ad loc.*) but <*d*> and <*r*> are indistinguishable in Mandaic.

810 Gordon, "Aramaic Incantation Bowls," 354–355 (Malmö).

811 Bhayro *et al.*, *Aramaic Magic Bowls*, 95.

812 Moriggi, *Corpus*, 18, 4.

Gwspwhr'q'[813] seems to be based on *-puhr* "son" (-/*puhrak*/[814]), like *-duxtag* (of MPers. *Ohrmazd-, Panāh-, Šābuhr-duxtag*)[815] which is based on *duxt* "daughter".

h. *Āzād* "free-born, noble"

Mand. *Zadbḫ* is the outcome of MPers. *Āzād-beh* with aphaeresis.[816] *Āzād* is the 2nd component of *'mwl'zd* (fem.),[817] whose initial component denotes "immortal"[818] (cf. the names with *anōš*, ↓7.2.4, b). Mand. *Dwkt'z'd* (/*Duxt-āzād*/) and *Xwš'z'd* (/*Xwaš -āzād* /[819]) where it is attached to *duxt* "daughter"[820] and *xwaš* "pleasant, sweet, nice". *Mwšk'zd* (/*Muškāzād*/,[821] fem., to *mušk* "musk"). It is the 1st component of *'z'dw'r* (fem.) if the reading is correct.[822] *Ṭšyḥr'zd* (/*Čihr-āzād*/) means "of noble extraction".[823]

i. Female names with *duxt* (> *dux* > *du*) "daughter"

The full form is spelled *dwkt* and *d'kt*. The rare spelling *-dwkty* is extant only in Old Syriac. Compounds with this component in initial position always begin with *dwkt-*, while *-dwk* is the commonest form in final position (*-dwg* is a hapax); *-du* is almost exclusively recorded in Mandaic; *-ag* < *-ak* is attached only to *dwkt*.

a'. As a final component

a''. Attached to theonyms and numina: *Myrdwk* (/*Mi(h)r-dux*/, to *Mihr* < *Miθra-*);[824]

Ršndwk denotes "*Rašn*'s daughter"[825] *'b'ndwkt* (Mand.)[826] (/*Ābānduxt*/)[827] > *'bndwk, b'ndwk,*[828] Mand. *Abandu* (/*Ābāndu*/)[829] "Daughter of Waters" as a numen.

---

813 Gordon, "Aramaic Incantation Bowls," 344–345: Fitzwilliam, 10, 12.

814 Cf. Zimmer, "Zur sprachlichen," 132 *ad* 777.

815 Gignoux, *Noms propres*, 140:711, 145:745, 162:859.

816 See Nöldeke, "Review," 144 as well as Morgenstern and Ford, *Aramaic Incantation Bowls*, 200, n. 630 *ad* 3025, 2, 8 (The form with and without aphaeresis is extant in Middle Persian, see Justi, *Iranisches Namenbuch*, 53: "edle Gute").

817 Isbell, *Corpus*, 4, 6.

818 Cf. Ilan, *Lexicon*, 208a who compares NPers. *Āmuleh* (fem.) "immortal" (Justi, *Iranisches Namenbuch* 15a).

819 Abudraham and Morgenstern, "Mandaic Incantation(s)," 754: SD 63, 4.

820 Inversion of **Āzād-duxt* meaning "noble, free daughter" (cf. Segal, *Catalogue*, 135 *ad* 105M, 5 and Sogd. *''z'd dwxt*, Lurje, *Personal Names*, 77:40).

821 Bhayro *et al.*, *Aramaic Magic Bowls*, 88.

822 Bhayro *et al.*, *Aramaic Magic Bowls*, 1.

823 See Montgomery, *Aramaic Incantation Texts*, 186 *ad* 15, 2 who refers to Justi, *Iranisches Namenbuch* 163a.

824 See Shaked, "Form and Purpose," 10 *ad* 3, 4 and "Rabbis," 115–116, n. 74.

825 Cf. Ilan, *Lexicon*, 246–247.

826 Müller-Kessler, "The Story of Bguzan-Lilit," 187, 195, 30–31.

827 Cf. Justi, *Iranisches Namenbuch*, 1a.

828 Montgomery, *Aramaic Incantation Texts*, 5, 1.

829 Bhayro *et al.*, *Aramaic Magic Bowls*, 97.

Ādur-: *'drdwk* (>*'drdwg*[830]), Mand. *'drdwkt* >*'drdw* (/*Ādur- du(xt)*/) "Daughter of the (holy) Fire";[831] *Y'zd'ndwkt*[832] > *'yzdndwk*[833] > *'zdndwk* (also with ʿ-),[834] Mand. *Y'zd'ndwk* (/*Yazdān-dux*/)[835] > *Yzd'ndw* (/*Yazdān-du*/)[836] "Daughter of the gods". *Mh'dwk*/*M(h)dwk*[837]/ *Mhdwk*[838] (/*Māh-dux*/), Mand. *M'dwkt*[839] (< /*Māh-duxt*/)/*Mad-uk*,[840] "Daughter of the Moon-god". *Mḥzydwk* (/*Māh-yazad-dux*/)[841] has the same denotation. *Xwardux* "Daughter of the Sun-god".[842] *Kwršd* (/*Xwar-xšēd*/ > /*Xwar-šēd*/)[843] MPers. "Sun" (< "brilliant Sun"), a divine epithet, is extant in *Kwrkšydwk* (/*Xwar-xšēd-dux*/) > *Kw[r]šdwk*[844] (/*Xwar-šēd-dux*/, same text and person).[845] *Gwšnzdwk* (< /*Gušnasp-dux*/),[846] *Gwšnzdwkt* (> *Gwšndwkt*) > Mand. *Gwšnzdw* (/*Gušnaz-du*/)[847] "Gušnasp's daughter";[848] *Bhmn* (of ~-*dwk*,[849] ~-*duxt*[850]) "Daughter of < **Vahu-manah-*". *Hwrmyzdwk*,[851] (/*Hormizd-dux*/) > *Hwrmsdwk*,[852] cf. OSyr.

---

830 Cf. Morgenstern and Ford, *Aramaic Incantation Bowls*, 133:IMJ 69.20.265, 24 (unpubl.).

831 Morgenstern and Ford, *Aramaic Incantation Bowls*, 3046+3069, 2–3, 5; Müller-Kessler, "A Mandaic Gold Amulet," 84, 4–5 and MS 2054/105, 3–4 (unpubl., quoted by Abudraham and Morgenstern, "Mandaic Incantation(s)," 754)

832 Schøyen 2054/99, 10 (unpubl., quoted by Morgenstern and Schlütter, 2018: 123 *ad* rev. 20).

833 Cf. Montgomery, *Aramaic Incantation Texts*, 150 *ad* 7, 4 who refers to Justi, *Iranisches Namenbuch*, 146b.

834 Cf. Naveh and Shaked, *Amulets and Magic Bowls*, 182 *ad* 10.

835 Ford, "Another Look," 250 *ad* 087M, 5.

836 MS 2054/76, 47 (unpubl., quoted by Abudraham and Morgenstern, "Mandaic Incantation(s)," 754).

837 Cf. Ilan, *Lexicon*, 234–235.

838 Cook "An Aramaic Incantation," 79–80, 1, 4.

839 See Morgenstern and Schlütter, "A Mandaic Amulet," 122 *ad* 118, 120, rev. 3.

840 Morgenstern and Ford, *Aramaic Incantation Bowls*, 3021, 2, 8 (see Shaked in Shaked *et al.*, *Aramaic Bowl Spells* [2022], 8a).

841 See Naveh and Shaked, *Amulets and Magic Bowls*, 157–158 *ad* 4, 7.

842 Cf. Shaked, "Rabbis," 108:MS 2053/222 (unpubl.).

843 Bhayro *et al.*, *Aramaic Magic Bowls*, 105.

844 See Shaked *et al.*, *Aramaic Bowl Spells* (2022), 219 *ad* 118, 1.

845 Shaked *et al.*, *Aramaic Bowl Spells* (2022), 76, 3, 7.

846 See Shaked, "Form and Purpose," 10 *ad* 3, 4.

847 MS 2054/72, 3–4 (unpubl., quoted by Abudraham and Morgenstern, "Mandaic Incantation(s)," 754).

848 Müller-Kessler and Kwasman "A Unique Talmudic," 160–162, 1, 2 and E.

849 Montgomery, *Aramaic Incantation Texts*, 13, 4, 10, 12 (also *Bhmnydwk*, Bhayro *et al.*, *Aramaic Magic Bowls*, 117 with -<y-> for /ə/).

850 Ilan, *Lexicon*, 212–213.

851 Montgomery, *Aramaic Incantation Texts*, 14, 1; Shaked *et al.*, *Aramaic Bowl Spells* (2013), 348 with references.

852 Gordon, "Aramaic and Mandaic," 93–95 and pls. 8–9:i, 10.

Hwrmyzdwkty[853] and Arm. < MPers. *Orm(i)zduxt*[854] " Daughter of Ahura-Mazdah". *Myzdwk* renders either **Mizd-uk* (↓7.3.1.10) or */Mizd-dux/*, i.e. either "Daughter of *Mizd*" (MPers. "reward") or "Daughter of Mazdah". MPers. *Srōš* < Av. *Sraoša-* (god of obedience) is the initial component of *Šrwšdwk*[855] (< */Srōš-dux/* with *s*> *š* distant assimilation) "*Sraoša*'s daughter". *Zwrwndwk* (*/Zurvān-dux/*) "Zurvān's daughter";[856] *Bhrndwk* (< */Bahrām-dux/*), Mand. *Bḥrndw*/*Wḥrndw*[857] "Bahrām's daughter";[858] *'drbhrm*[859] (< MPers. */Ādur-wahrām/*) is named after the holy fire of a deity or a homonymous king.[860] *'smndwk*[861] (var. *'ysmndwk*), OSyr. *'smndwkt*[862] (*/Asmān-duxt/*) is "Daughter of Heaven" (as a numen).[863] *Dyndwk* (with assimilation *Dydwk*),[864] Mand. ~[865] (> *Dndwk*[866]/Mand. *D'ndwk*,[867] cf. OSyr. *Dnd'kt*[868] means "Daughter of *daēna-* (religion)". The spelling *d'kt*[869] is recorded in OSyr. *Prd'kt*[870] (*/Farr-duxt/* < */Farrah-duxt/*) "Xvarnah's daughter"; *Mhgwšnzd'kt*[871] "Daughter of Māh-Gušnasp".

b". Attached to royal names: *D'rydwk (/Dārāy-dux/)* "daughter of Darius"[872] (defective *Drydwk*);[873] *Šb(w)rdwk*[874] *(< /Šābuhr-dux/)* > Mand. *Š'bwrdw* (*Šābur-du/*),[875] *Nrsydwk* (*/Narsay-dux/*)"d. of *Narseh*", cf. Mand. *Nrs'ydwkt*[876] (*/Narsay-*

853 Moriggi, *Corpus*, 41, 13.
854 See Martirosyan, *Iranian Personal Names*, 290–291:587 where also Middle Persian and Parthian extended forms (with *-duxtag*) are discussed.
855 Puškin (Museum) 370 (unpubl.) quoted by J. N. Ford *apud* Faraj, "Remarks," 92 with n. 13.
856 See Morgenstern and Ford, *Aramaic Incantation Bowls*, 96 *ad* 3032, 1–2, 2–3, 3.
857 See Abudraham, "Ancient Mandaic Palimpsest," 9 *ad* 2–4, i, 7.
858 See Segal, *Catalogue*, 55 *ad* 013A, 6, cf. Fain *et al.*, "Aramaic Incantation Bowls," 301–302 *ad* S-448, 2 who refer to Gignoux, *Noms propres* (Supp.), 65:342.
859 Morgenstern and Ford, *Aramaic Incantation Bowls* 3042, 10.
860 See Gignoux, *Noms propres*, 39:80.
861 Cf. Montgomery, *Aramaic Incantation Texts*, 175 *ad* 12, 1.
862 Moriggi, *Corpus*, 3, 2, 6, 9; 5, 5, 10.
863 See Levene, *Jewish Aramaic Curse Texts*, 21.
864 Cf. Levene, *Jewish Aramaic Curse Texts*, 75.
865 Yamauchi, *Mandaic Incantation Texts*, 16, 15.
866 Bhayro *et al.*, *Aramaic Magic Bowls*, 1 and 66, 83.
867 Yamauchi, *Mandaic Incantation Texts*, 14, 1.
868 Moriggi, *Corpus*, 18, 4.
869 On the spelling *d'kt* for */duxt/* see Müller-Kessler, "Syrische Zauberschalen," 120 *ad* 2.
870 Moriggi, *Corpus*, 18, 1, 11.
871 Moriggi, *Corpus*, 18, 3, 11.
872 See Segal, *Catalogue*, 59 *ad* 017A, 3.
873 Shaked *et al.*, *Aramaic Bowl Spells* (2022), 77, 1.
874 See Morgenstern and Ford, *Aramaic Incantation Bowls*, 33, n. 85.
875 MS 2054/104, 7–8 (unpubl., quoted by Abudraham and Morgenstern, "Mandaic Incantation(s)," 754).
876 McCullough, *Jewish and Mandean*, E, 3, 14, 18.

duxt/ > *N'rsyd[wk]*[877]) < MPers. *Narseh-duxt.*[878] *Narseh* (*Nrsy*) and *Šābuhr* are names of Sasanian kings;[879] cf. Mand. *Ksrydwk*[880] "daughter of Xusro"; *Šhd'kt*[881] (< */Šāh-duxt/)* "King's daughter".

c". Attached to other anthroponyms: *Brndwk* (*/Barān-dux/*) "daughter of *Barān*".[882] The latter is recorded as a male's name (*Br'n*).[883] It is an *-ān* (pro-) patronymic of **Bara-* (to a compound with *bar-* "to bear").[884] The initial component of *Mhndwk (/Māhēn-dux*[885]/Mand. *Mḥyndwkt*[886] ends in *-ēn* (< *-aina-*)[887] like those of *Bwrzyndwk* (*/Burzēn-dux/*,[888] cf. MPers. *Burzēnmihr*, the 3rd major Fire of Sasanian Iran) and *Šhryndwk* (*/Šahrēn-dux/*).[889] They are based on *Māh* "Moon-god", *Burz* (the god of agriculture) and *šahr* "land, country; city". *Sysyndwk*[890] is based on an anthroponym. OSyr. *Pnhqdwk* (*/Panāhak-dux/*) "daughter of *Panāhak*". The latter is based on *panāh* "protector; refuge" plus *-k* < OIran. *-ka-*.[891] *Prṭdwk* (*/Frād-dux/*)[892] and Mand. *B'b'ydwkt*[893] begin with *Frāda* and *Bābāy*[894] respectively and *Gwlndwk*[895] (*/Gulān-dux/*) with an *-ān*-(pro-)patronymic of **Gul* (MPers. *gul* "rose"); *N(y)wndwk*[896] (OSyr. *Nywndwkt*[897]) (*/Nēwān-duxt/*) "Daughter of *Nēwān*". The latter is an *-ān* (pro-)patronymic of MPers. *nēw* "good, brave,

---

877 Müller-Kessler, *Zauberschalentexte*, 41, 2, 7.
878 Gignoux, *Noms propres*, 134:679.
879 See Gignoux, *Noms propres*, 134:678, s. v. *Narseh*; *Nrsy* is recorded in Shaked *et al.*, *Aramaic Bowl Spells* (2013), 48, 3, 8; 61, 3 (*bis*).
880 Yamauchi, *Mandaic Incantation Texts*, 14, 1; 16, 15, 18.
881 Moriggi, *Corpus*, 2, 4.
882 Bhayro *et al.*, *Aramaic Magic Bowls*, 88.
883 Levene, *Jewish Aramaic Curse Texts*, M163, 8.
884 OSyr. *Brny*, which is lemmatized as *Barān* by Gignoux, Jullien and Jullien, *Noms propres*, 52:96a, is in fact an Aramaic two-stem hypocoristicon, viz. *br* + *n* < *Nbw* (cf. Zadok, "Zur Struktur," 255:F.1).
885 See Shaked, "Peace Be upon You," 214.
886 Yamauchi, *Mandaic Incantation Texts*, 4, 7.
887 Therefore the alternative transcription *Māhān~* is less likely.
888 Morgenstern and Ford, *Aramaic Incantation Bowls*, 77:SD 2, 3 (unpubl.).
889 Bhayro *et al.*, *Aramaic Magic Bowls*, 5.
890 Müller-Kessler, *Zauberschalentexte*, 40c, 3.
891 See Naveh and Shaked, *Amulets and Magic Bowls*, 183 *ad* 11; Gignoux, Jullien and Jullien, *Noms propres*, 112:332.
892 See Naveh and Shaked, *Amulets and Magic Bowls*, 156 *ad* 4, 6.
893 Segal, *Catalogue*, 112M, 8.
894 For related names cf. Gignoux, *Noms propres*, 52–54:141 f.
895 Morgenstern and Ford 2020: 53, n. 166:DS 31, 12–13 (unpubl.).
896 Ilan, *Lexicon*, 242–243.
897 Moriggi, *Corpus*, 41, 6, 11.

virtuous".[898] Alternatively "Daughter of good, brave, virtuous ones"; cf. Sogd. < MIran. *Nyw'nz'dg* /*Nēwān-zādāg*/ "Son of good, brave, virtuous ones".[899] OSyr. *Ršnyndwk*[900] is attached to an anthroponym which consists of *Ršn* and the suffix *-ēn*.[901] *R(y)šyndwk* may be a scribal error for *Ršywndwk* (/*Rašewan-dux*/),[902] < *Ršwndwkt*.[903]

d". Attached to toponyms: *Mrwdwk*[904] may render **Marv-dux(t)*, *lit.* "daughter of Marv" (< *Margu-*), "Margianite" (for the pattern GN + *duxt*, cf. *Armin-*, *Ērān-duxt*).[905]

e". Attached to appellatives: *Šhdwk*[906]/Mand. *Š'hdwk*[907] "King's daughter"; *'zrmydwk*[908] < MPers. /*Azarmīg-duxt*/. The latter is recorded in Mand. *Azarmidukt* together with the shortest form *Azarmidu*[909] "Honoured, respected daughter".[910] *Br'zdwk*[911]/*Brzdwk* (/*Varāz-dux*/, to *warāz* "boar").[912] The initial component of *Nwdwk* renders either MPers. *nēw-* "good, brave" or *now-* "new".[913] Mand. *Kwšdwk* (/*Xwaš-dux*/) denotes "Daughter of the happy, pleasant one".[914] *Nygrydwk*[915] possibly denotes "The daughter of the picture, image" (MPers. *nigār*). The initial component (*Qwdq'*) of *Qwdq'dwk* "Q.'s daughter", cannot render *Kurūxān*,[916] but may go back to OIran. **Kauta-ka-* > MPers. *kōdak* "young, small; child,

---

898 See Segal, *Catalogue*, 55 *ad* 013A, 3 and Shaked, "Form and Purpose," 10 (cf. Justi, *Iranisches Namenbuch* 228–229).

899 See Lurje, *Personal Names*, 287:857.

900 Moriggi, *Corpus*, 25, 2; 27, 2, 3, 4 (*bis*).

901 Cf. Naveh and Shaked, *Magic Spells* 119 *ad* 16, 2 and 121–122:17, 4.

902 Cf., e.g., Shaked *et al.*, *Aramaic Bowl Spells* (2013), 15, 2; 29, 4 (*Ršwdwk* in 29, 2 is with assimilation if not a scribal error); 30, 9, 11, 12; 37, 8; 47, 4.

903 Shaked *et al.*, *Aramaic Bowl Spells* (2022), 72, 5 ([*Ršwn*]*dwkt* in line 1; the name of the same individual is elsewhere spelled without *-t*).

904 Ilan, *Lexicon*, 238b.

905 Gignoux, *Noms propres*, 48:138; 79:334; cf. Zimmer, "Zur sprachlichen," 142 *ad* 138, 334.

906 Isbell, *Corpus*, 61, 2 (not *Šāhān-Dūxt* as erroneously lemmatized by Ilan, *Lexicon*, 249a).

907 Yamauchi, *Mandaic Incantation Texts*, 18a, 3; 18b, 8; 18c, 5, 14.

908 Ilan, *Lexicon*, 212a.

909 Morgenstern and Ford, *Aramaic Incantation Bowls*, 17 with n. 31: JNF 40, 5, 10 and 14, 16 respectively.

910 See Zimmer, "Zur sprachlichen," 118–119 *ad* 167; cf. Gignoux, Jullien and Jullien, *Noms propres*, 46:75, Martirosyan, *Iranian Personal Names*, 78:4 and Justi, *Iranisches Namenbuch* 54a.

911 Morgenstern and Ford, *Aramaic Incantation Bowls*, 36, n. 105:VA 2180, 7–8.

912 See Naveh and Shaked, *Amulets and Magic Bowls*, 157 *ad* 4, 7; cf. Zimmer, "Zur sprachlichen," 125 *ad* 940.

913 This is implied by Shaked *et al.*, *Aramaic Bowl Spells* (2022), 194 *ad* 109, 2.

914 See Segal, *Catalogue*, 127 *ad* 095M, 45.

915 Segal, *Catalogue*, 048A, 8.

916 As erroneously stated by Ilan, *Lexicon*, 231b, s. v. *Kurūxān-Dūxt*.

youngster".[917] *Mydwkt*,[918] OSyr. *M'ydwkt*[919]/Mand. *Myhdwkt*[920] (/*Māy-duxt*/), means perhaps "The female's daughter", cf. Parth. *Myk* (/*Māyak*/),[921] which is based on OIran. **māy* "woman".[922]

b'. As an initial component: *Dwktbyh* (/*Duxt-beh*/)[923] (> *Dwktby*),[924] OSyr. *Dwktʿyb'*[925] consists of *duxt* "daughter" and *beh* (< *veh*[926] < OIran. **vahyah-*) "better". On the face of it, Mand. *Dwkt'nwbh̠*[927] has *duxt* and *beh* as an initial and final components respectively, but this leaves <'*nw*> unaccounted for. The female's name *Dwktnšh*, Mand. *Duktanša* (/*Duxtān-šāh*/)[928] lacks gender congruency. It is rendered (rather *ad sensum*) "König(in) der Mädchen".[929] On the face of it, it is a juxtaposition, cf. Arm. < MIran. *Šahanduxt*.[930] Or is it a corruption of *Dwkt'nwš* (Mand.)[931] < MPers. *Duxt-anōš*[932]? Mand. *Dwktnprwk* (fem.) has the same 1st component which is followed by *farrox*[933] "happy, fortunate".

7.2.2 Possessive compounds (*bahuvrihi*)[934]

a. With *(Ādur-)Gušnasp* (one of the Sasanid sacred fires): *Gwšnsp* (/*Gušn-asp*/)[935] > *Gwšns*[936] originates from OIran. **Vṛšna-aspa-* "Having male/strong horses".[937] It is contained in *'rgwšnsp*[938] (perhaps < /**Arg-Gušnasp*/ "valuable G.") and juxta-

917 See Zadok 2002: 36 and Schmitt, *Iranische Personennamen in der neuassyrischen*, 105:83.
918 Müller-Kessler, *Zauberschalentexte*, 38a, 4, 14.
919 Moriggi, *Corpus*, 7, 2, 6, 10, 11.
920 See Müller-Kessler, "Die Zauberschalensammlung," 135a *ad* 095M, 2.
921 Schmitt, *Personennamen* 142:307.
922 Bailey "Armeno-indoiranica," 95, 111–112; 1979: 110b.
923 Shaked, "Form and Purpose," 22, 28:8, 1:
924 Shaked *et al.*, *Aramaic Bowl Spells* (2022), 72, 2, 6.
925 Moriggi, *Corpus*, 10, 10.
926 <*b*> was apparently pronounced [*w*] in JBA according to Juusola, *Linguistic Pecularities*, 42 with n. 104.
927 Cf. Müller-Kessler, "Die Zauberschalensammlung," 134b *ad* 088M, 4.
928 Cf. Shaked *et al.*, *Aramaic Bowl Spells* (2022), 166.
929 Justi, *Iranisches Namenbuch* 86b (one would expect *bāmbišn* "queen" instead of *šāh*).
930 Martirosyan, *Iranian Personal Names*, 275:539.
931 Yamauchi, *Mandaic Incantation Texts*, 20, 2 (<'>), 8 (<'>), 10, 14, 20, 22; 26, 31 (see Gordon, "Aramaic and Mandaic," 100 *ad* 95–100 and pls. 11–13:M, 15, 17).
932 Gignoux, *Noms propres*, 78:326.
933 Cf. McCullough, *Jewish and Mandean*, 16 *ad* C, 2.
934 Including cases of inverted *bahuvrihi* (cf. Thordarson, *Ossetic Grammatical Studies*, 94–104).
935 See Segal, *Catalogue*, 57 *ad* 015A, 1; for the Old Syriac occurrence cf. Moriggi, *Corpus*, 24, 14.
936 Gordon, "Aramaic Incantation Bowls," 342–344:BM 91776, 1.
937 See Gignoux, *Noms propres*, 91–92:408 (cf. Martirosyan, *Iranian Personal Names*, 366–367:806).
938 Gordon, "Aramaic and Mandaic," 93–95 and pls. 8–9:L, 4, 10, 12.

posed with *Mihr* in Mand. *Myr' Gwšn'sp*; the same text has *Br'n Gwšnsp*[939] (> *Br'ngwšnsnz*[940] > *Br'gwšnsnz*[941]). Other juxtapositions are *Bhrm Gwšnsp*,[942] *'b'ngwšmys* (< /*Ābān-Gušnasp*/[943]) and *Mh'dwr Gwšnsp* (OSyr.)[944] (MPers. *Māh-Ādur-Gušnasp*)[945] > Mand. *Māh-Ādur-Gušnaṣ*[946] and the three-tier name Mand. *M'bḥr'ngwšnṣ*[947] (< /**Māh-Bahrān-Gušnasp*/).

b. With *xwarrah* (< Av. *Xvarnah-*) "Fortune, glory, splendour, happy shine":[948]

'dynkwryh (/*Ādīn-xwarrih*/),[949] whose 2nd component is based on *xwarrah*, begins with *'dyn*, presumably < OIran. **Āt-ina-*,[950] which is extant also in *'dyngwšns*[951]/*'dyngwšnṣ*[952] (< /*Ādīn-Gušnasp*/). Mand. *'ran kurh̲* (/*Ērān-xwarrah*/) denotes "Fortune, glory, splendour of Iran".[953] and Mand. *Bwrz-kwrh* (/*Burz-xwarrah*/) (fem.)[954] means "The exalted xvarnah", a compound name consisting of *burz* and a numen, like MPers. *Burz-ātaxš* and *Burz-Ādur-Gušnasp*[955] as well as *burz* +DN.[956]

c. Other: *Gwlšr* (< /*Gul-šahr*/) "city, land of roses"[957] > Arm. *Gulšar*.[958]

---

939 See Müller-Kessler, "A Mandaic Gold Amulet," 341 *ad* 337–341, 2–4, 26–27.
940 Bhayro *et al.*, *Aramaic Magic Bowls*, 145.
941 Bhayro *et al.*, *Aramaic Magic Bowls*, 117.
942 Gordon, "Two Magic Bowls," 306–309, 5, cf. Müller-Kessler, "Die Zauberschalensammlung," 99 *ad* 068A, 5.
943 See Shaked *apud* Greenfield and Naveh 1985: 106; cf. Ford, "Another Look," 240 *ad* 079M, 3.
944 Moriggi, *Corpus*, 22, 3.
945 See Gignoux, *Noms propres*, 109:517.
946 [Ford and] Abudraham "Syriac and Mandaic," 103–105: 8, 13, 17.
947 MS 2087/05 (unpubl., quoted by Abudraham, "Ancient Mandaic Palimpsest," 9 *ad* 7–8).
948 For the originally Avestan form and the originally Median equivalent *farr* (< **farnah-*) see Zimmer, "Zur sprachlichen," 131–132. For the probable classification of compounds cf. Sims-Williams, *Bactrian Personal Names*, 9 *ad* Bact. -φαρο.
949 Shaked *et al.*, *Aramaic Bowl Spells* (2013), 11, 9, 12, 14, 17, 18.
950 See Morgenstern and Ford, *Aramaic Incantation Bowls*, 43 with n. 123 *ad* 3010, 3 (cf. Gignoux, Jullien and Jullien, *Noms propres*, 31:12).
951 Bhayro *et al.*, *Aramaic Magic Bowls*, 1.
952 See Morgenstern and Ford, *Aramaic Incantation Bowls*, 44 with n. 130 (also Mand.).
953 See P. Lurje *apud* Fain *et al.*, "Aramaic Incantation Bowls," 306 *ad* S-449, 3.
954 Morgenstern "Five Mandaic," 112–114:26, 8.
955 Gignoux, *Noms propres*, 61:229, 62:235.
956 Cf. Gignoux, *Noms propres*, 62:234, 64:244; Gignoux, Jullien and Jullien, *Noms propres*, 28:75.
957 See Morgenstern and Ford, *Aramaic Incantation Bowls*, 53:SD 22AL, 6 (unpubl.) who refer to Justi, *Iranisches Namenbuch* 120a.
958 See Martirosyan, *Iranian Personal Names*, 165–166:226.

Mand. *Mhrbn*[959] renders MPers. *Mihr-bān* < OIran. **Miθra-bānu-* "Having Mithra's splendour"[960], cf. Parth. *Mtrybn*[961] and Lat. *Meribanes*.[962] Mand. *Y'z'dp'n'h*[963] (*/Yazad-panāh/* > */Yazd-panāh/*) means "Having the protection of god".[964] Mand. *M'pn'*[965] presumably originates from */*Māh-panāh/* "Having the protection of the Moon-god". Its gender cannot be determined since the name-bearer is a member of a group of children who are subsumed as "sons and daughters". The same component with inverted order is extant in *Pn'ḥwrmyz*[966] (< */Panāh-Hormiz/*).[967] If it is not a mere juxtaposition, it may mean originally "Having the protection of Ahura-Mazdah". OSyr. *Mḥbwd*[968] < MPers. *Māh-būd* means "Having the awareness of the Moon-god".[969] *Zrnkš* (*/Zarīn-kaš/*, fem.) denotes "Having golden armpit".[970] *Nwrd*[971] may originate from OIran. **Nava-vṛdā-* "New rose" (or "New growth"), cf. Arm. *Nuard* (fem.); an alternative derivation, viz. a survival of OIran. **Naiba-vṛdā* "Good, beautiful rose"[972] (or rather "Of beautiful growth")[973] cannot be excluded, but in this case one would expect a spelling <*nywrd*> seeing that the Middle Persian outcome of OIran. **naiba-* is *nēw*. *Kykwš* (*/Kay-xwaš/*) and her father-in-law *Dynkwš* (*/Dēn-xwaš/*)[974] share a common 2nd component, viz. *xwaš* "pleasant, sweet, nice", which is attached to *kay* (< OIran. **kavi-*), the eponym of the legendary dynasty of the Kayanids, and to *dēn* "religion"[975] ("Having a pleasant religion"). Cf. Arm. *Xošnam* (also *Namxoš*) < early

---

959 Pognon, *Inscriptions mandaïtes*, 12 and 17.
960 See Gignoux, *Noms propres*, 127:636.
961 Schmitt, *Personennamen* 140:303 with comparanda,
962 Cf. Montgomery, *Aramaic Incantation Texts*, 278a, index, s. v. *Mhrbn* who refers to Justi, *Iranisches Namenbuch* 208, s. v. *Mitnāpān*, 3.
963 Pognon, *Inscriptions mandaïtes*, 4.
964 See Gignoux, Jullien and Jullien, *Noms propres*, 145–146:455a–g.
965 Abudraham, "Three Mandaic," 83–85:2, 8, 60.
966 Geller, "Eight Incantation Bowls," 106–107:Aaron A, 3.
967 The graphemes <*h*> and <*ḥ*> are identical in the script of the JBA incantation bowls (see Juusola, *Linguistic Pecularities*, 34–35).
968 Moriggi, *Corpus*, 22, 3.
969 Cf. Harviainen, "Aramaic Incantation Bowl," 15 *ad* 3 who refers to Justi, *Iranisches Namenbuch* 185.
970 Cf. Montgomery, *Aramaic Incantation Texts*, 205 *ad* 24, 5 (*bis*) who refers to Justi, *Iranisches Namenbuch* 382b.
971 Shaked *et al.*, *Aramaic Bowl Spells* (2013), 21, 6, 10.
972 Both alternatives are considered for the name in the Armenian collateral tradition by Martirosyan, *Iranian Personal Names*, 272:532.
973 Extant in LB *Né-ba-'-mar-du-'* (see Zadok, *Iranische Personennamen in der neu*, 275:393).
974 Shaked *et al.*, *Aramaic Bowl Spells* (2013), 63, 6, 7.
975 For the semantics of this term cf. Zimmer, "Zur sprachlichen," 130:6.7.

NPers. *Xōšnām* "Having a pleasant name".[976] The same component is extant in OSyr. *Bwrzkwš*[977] (/*Burz-xwaš*/). *Gwnkwš* (/*Gōn-xwaš*/,[978] fem.) may denote "(Having a) nice colour". OSyr. *Prw<k>rwy*[979] (/*Farrox-rōy*/) > *Prwkyrw*[980] denotes "Fortunate by (= thanks to) his appearance".[981]

7.2.3 *"Verbale Rektion"* compounds

E.g., *Gwndsp* (> *Gwnds, Gwnd's, 'wnd's*)[982] < OIran. **Vinda-aspa-* "who finds the horses".

7.2.4 With other frequent components

Some compound names are of the *Karmadhāraya* type, e.g., *Māh-anōš, Xwarrah*/*Farr* (below, b) and *Prwk-Kwsrw*,[983] Mand. *Prwksr(')w'*[984] "Happy, fortunate Xusro"[985] (with assimilation of *-x* to the following *x* in Mandaic). *Byhr'm* (of *Yhy'* ~)[986] may render /*Beh-rām*/ "*Rām* (< OIran. DN **Rāman-* "rest, peace, tranquility") is good" or "Good *Rām*". The type *veh* (> *beh*) + numen (cf., e.g. Mand. *B(y)ḥ(')dwr*/*Pyḥ'dwr*[987] < MPers. *Weh-Ādur*[988]) is common in the Middle Persian onomasticon.[989] Mand. *Byḥksr'*[990] is of the same type as MPers. *Wēh-Šābuhr*,[991] i.e. "Sage Xusro".

a. With *friy* "friend, dear":[992] *'nwšpry*[993] "Friend of the immortal", *Mhpry*[994] "Friend of the Moon-god", and *Šdnpry* "Friend of *Šādān*".[995] The latter is an *-ān*

976 For the latter see Martirosyan, *Iranian Personal Names*, 202:327.
977 Moriggi, *Corpus*, 11, 8, 9.
978 Bhayro *et al.*, *Aramaic Magic Bowls*, 143, 148.
979 This emendation is implied by Nöldeke, *Persische Studien*, 15, n.1.
980 Pognon, *Inscriptions mandaïtes*, 26.
981 Cf. Montgomery, *Aramaic Incantation Texts*, 279b, index, s. v. who refers to Justi, *Iranisches Namenbuch* 96b, s. v. **Farruxrūī*.
982 Shaked *et al.*, *Aramaic Bowl Spells* (2013), 346, index, s.vv. with references.
983 Isbell, *Corpus*, 61, 2, 5.
984 Yamauchi, *Mandaic Incantation Texts*, 20, 2, 8, 10.
985 See F. C. Andreas *apud* Lidzbarski, *Ephemeris*, 100, n. 1.
986 Müller-Kessler, *Zauberschalentexte*, 41f, 34, 62, 65.
987 See Abudraham, "Ancient Mandaic Palimpsest," 11 *ad* vii, 9; cf. Ford, "Another Look," 265 *ad* 106M, 6: *Pyh'dwr'*.
988 Gignoux, *Noms propres*, 177:967.
989 Cf. Gignoux, *Noms propres*, 177–180:967, 981, 983, 985, 986.
990 Morgenstern, "Five Mandaic," 112–114:26, 4, 8.
991 See Gignoux, *Noms propres*, 181:990.
992 Cf. Zimmer, "Zur sprachlichen," 148 *ad* 383.
993 Shaked *et al.*, *Aramaic Bowl Spells* (2013), 12, 2, 11, 18.
994 Levene, *Jewish Aramaic Curse Texts*, 043A, 3.
995 Cf. Levene, *Jewish Aramaic Curse Texts*, 95 *ad* SD 27, 7.

(pro-)patronymic of *šād* "The happy (one)". *Gwšnṣppry*[996] "Friend of *Gušnasp*". *M'd'r* (/*mādar*/) *'pry* (fem.) "love of (her) mother", if the 2nd component is MPers. *friy*,[997] cf. MPers. *Friy-Ohrmazd* (same name as fem. *'ypr' Hwrmyz)*;[998] *Prybrd* (/*Friya-bard*/).[999]

b. With *anōš* "immortal"

OSyr. *M'h'nw*[*š*][1000] (Mand. *Mḥ(')nwš*)[1001] renders MPers. *Māh-anōš* "The immortal Moon-god".[1002] *B(')bnwš*[1003]/Mand. *B'b(')nwš*/*Bb'nwš*[1004] (/*Bāb-anōš*/ son of *Mḥnwš*) literally denotes "immortal father" (short for his paternal name *Māh-anōš*) and Mand. *M'd'nwš* (/*Mād-anōš*/, fem.)[1005] may denote "The immortal mother" in view of Mand. *Z'd'nwš* (/*Zād-anōš*/) "born to *Anōš*" whose mother was indeed named *'nwš*.[1006] The unexplained compound names *'rznyš*[1007] and *Mt'nyš* (both fem.)[1008] may be read *'rznwš* and *Mt'nwš* respectively seeing that the graphemes <*w*> and <*y*> are indistinguishable in the script of the JBA incantation bowls.[1009] The former begins with MPers. *arz* "worth, value". The second component of both names, viz. –(')*nwš*, may render *-anōš*. The 1st component of the latter (<*mt*>) may be a defective spelling of /*mād*/ "mother" (cf. Mand. *M'd'nwš* just above). *Bhr'nwš* (/*Bahr-anōš*/, fem.) "Whose lot is immortality".[1010] *N'm'nš*[1011] may be a defective spelling of /*Nām-anōš*/ "Whose name, reputation is immortal, eternal". Mand. *Kw'r'nwš* (/*Xwarrah-anōš*/[1012]) "Immortal *Xvarnah*", cf. OSyr. *Prnwš* < MPers. *Farr-anōš* < *Farrah-anōš*[1013] with the same meaning.

---

996 Shaked *et al.*, *Aramaic Bowl Spells* (2013), 23, 5; 37, 2; 59, 5, 7.

997 See Naveh and Shaked, *Amulets and Magic Bowls*, 146–148 *ad* 3, 1, where an alternative interpretation is also considered but it implies that the last component is the result of omission of a final consonant (*-n*).

998 See Goodblatt 1976.

999 See Naveh and Shaked, *Magic Spells* 130 *ad* 21, 3.

1000 Moriggi, *Corpus*, 19, 2.

1001 Yamauchi, *Mandaic Incantation Texts*, 370, index, s. v. with references.

1002 See Gignoux, *Noms propres*, 110:524.

1003 Cf. Montgomery, *Aramaic Incantation Texts*, 162 *ad* 9, 4.

1004 Yamauchi, *Mandaic Incantation Texts*, 368, index, s. v. with references.

1005 Cf. Müller-Kessler 2001–2002: 136 *ad* 099M, 14.

1006 See the filiation in Yamauchi, *Mandaic Incantation Texts*, 8, 14–15, 24–25, 26–27, 53–55; 12, 37, 39. *'z'd'nwš* in 8, 46–47 is an error caused by the appearance of *'z'd'y* at the beginning of the following line.

1007 Gordon, "Aramaic Magical Bowls," 321–324 and pl. 10: A. 1.

1008 Montgomery, *Aramaic Incantation Texts*, 29, 5.

1009 See Juusola, *Linguistic Pecularities*, 35.

1010 See M. Macuch *apud* Müller-Kessler 1994: 7–8.The other two alternatives, viz. "Immortal spring" (*bahār* < *wahār*) or "pleasant, sweet spring" considered by Macuch seem less likely.

1011 Isbell, "Two New," 16–18:De Menil, i, 12; iii, 1; iv, 3.

1012 Cf. Nöldeke, "Review," 144 *ad* Pognon, *Inscriptions mandaïtes*, B.

1013 See Gignoux, Jullien and Jullien, *Noms propres*, 69–70:176.

7.2.5 Originally professional designations and titles[1014]

Zwn'wr < **zyn'wr*[1015] (/*Zēnawar*/) < OIran. **zaina-bara-* "weapon bearer". *'dwrbyṭ* (> *'dwrbyṭ* > *'dwbṭ*,[1016] < MPers. *Ādur-bed* < OIran. **āṭr-pati-* "chief of fire"[1017] and *Gwlbyt*[1018] < MPers. *Gul-bed* < OIran. **vṛda-pati-* "chief of florists" (Parth. Wrdpt /*Vardbed*/,[1019] Arm. < Iran. *Vardapet*).[1020]

7.2.6 Originally toponyms

Mand. fem. *Kwr'sn*[1021] (/*Xwar-āsān*/) "sunrise" (> "east").[1022]

7.2.7 Other compound names

The Moon-god (*Māh*) is the initial component of *Mhyzyd*[1023] "*Māh* is god". Mand. *Mzd'n'sp's*[1024] begins with an *ān*-(pro-)patronymic of *Mazdah*, and ends with MPers. *spās* "service, gratitude".[1025] *Kwdbwd* (/*Xwad-būd*/),[1026] "self-awarness", *Zn bwd* (/*Zan-būd*/, fem.)[1027] "Becoming a wife". *M'bwndr* "The Moon-god is firm"[1028] (cf. NPers. *bundar*). *Hrmsdr* perhaps originates from **Hormazd-dyār*.[1029] Alternatively it may be a two stem hypocoristicon < **Hormazd-d-ar*.[1030] *'rtšryh* is considered a form of Artaxerxes by Montgomery[1031] who quoted *Αρτασηριος*[1032] – unde-

---

1014 Occupational terms and titles are recorded as anthroponyms also in Bactrian (see Sims-Williams, *Bactrian Personal Names*, 10).

1015 Cf. Ilan, *Lexicon*, 206b with reference to Justi, *Iranisches Namenbuch* 386a, but with an inaccurate lemmatization.

1016 See Morgenstern and Ford, *Aramaic Incantation Bowls*, 138 *ad* 3047, 1.

1017 See Gignoux, *Noms propres*, 32:39.

1018 Bhayro *et al.*, *Aramaic Magic Bowls*, 136.

1019 Schmitt, *Personennamen* 228:551.

1020 See Martirosyan, *Iranian Personal Names*, 352–353:774; cf. Zimmer, "Zur sprachlichen," 129 *ad* 398.

1021 Yamauchi, *Mandaic Incantation Texts*, 15, 18.

1022 Cf. NPers. *Xurāsān* which was borne by males (Justi, *Iranisches Namenbuch* 178b).

1023 Cf. Shaked *et al.*, *Aramaic Bowl Spells* (2022), 209.

1024 Yamauchi, *Mandaic Incantation Texts*, 20, 3.

1025 Cf. F. C. Andreas *apud* Lidzbarski, *Ephemeris*, 100, n. 5.

1026 Bhayro *et al.*, *Aramaic Magic Bowls*, 93, 94.

1027 Bhayro *et al.*, *Aramaic Magic Bowls*, 103.

1028 Müller-Kessler 1994: 8 renders *bwndr* as "Beschützer" referring to Justi, *Iranisches Namenbuch* 72–73, s. v. *Bundār* who renders it as "reicher Mann".

1029 See Montgomery, *Aramaic Incantation Texts*, 201 *ad* 20, 2 who refers to MPers. *Ōrmaz(d)yār* (Justi, *Iranisches Namenbuch* 10a).

1030 For the pattern cf., e.g., MPers. *Ādur-dār* < **Ādur-d-ara* (Gignoux, *Noms propres*, 33:48).

1031 1913: 191 *ad* 17, 7.

1032 Justi, *Iranisches Namenbuch* 35, s. v. *Artaxšaθrā*.

niably a form based on *'rtšyr* < **Rta-xš-ira-*,[1033] cf. Arm. *Artašir*.[1034] On the face of it, the additional *-y-* resembles the additional *-ι-* of the Greek form. However, it should be borne in mind that the bowl was inscribed by a Jewish practitioner-scribe. Did he intentionally add *-yh* to the originally royal name, thereby "Tetragrammatizing" it?[1035] The practice of Tetragrammatization of anthroponyms was not alien to Jewish scribes.[1036] This tendency is analogous to adding the Aramaic word *'l (<-'yl>)* "god" to angels with Iranian names, e.g. Mand. *Sḥṭ'yl*[1037] to MPers. *saxt* "strong, hard". Unexplained (or partally explained) compounds are, e.g., *M'h'y 'z'yd*,[1038] whose initial component is based on *Māh* "Moon-god". It seems that his matronym, *M'k'š*,[1039] begins with the same theophorous element. *Hdrbdw*.[1040] Its initial component may be compared to the base of MPers. *Hadarān*, the 1st component of a chain, and what follows to MPers. *Bādug* (with omission of *-g*),[1041] but both are unexplained. *'šrḥy* and *'šrqwm* (both females) are hitherto unexplained.[1042] The former is recorded twice in Hebrew epigraphy, but on unprovenanced artefacts whose authenticity is dubious.[1043]

7.2.8 Compound divine names and divine epithets used as anthroponyms

'yspndrmyd[1044] (> *'yṣpndrmyd*, fem.)[1045] < MPers. *Spandarmad*[1046]< Av. *Spəntā Ārmaiti-* "Holy devotion" is a divine name used as an anthroponym. Similarly, *Kwrkšyd*[1047]/Mand. *K[u]rkšid*[1048] (/*Xwar-xšēd*/) > *Kwršd* (/*Xwar-šēd*/),[1049] i.e. MPers.

1033 See Schmitt 1979 [1980] and Huyse 1999: 12–13.
1034 Martirosyan, *Iranian Personal Names*, 126–127:119 with lit.
1035 Cf. Ilan, *Lexicon*, 168b.
1036 Cf. Zadok 2018a: 434:0952.
1037 Cf. Yamauchi, *Mandaic Incantation Texts*, 366, index, s. v. (with variants).
1038 Cf. Müller-Kessler, "Die Zauberschalensammlung," 135, n. 20 *ad* Hunter, "Two Incantation Bowls," 117:2, 13.
1039 Hunter, "Two Incantation Bowls," 117: 2, 3, 17.
1040 Montgomery, *Aramaic Incantation Texts*, 25, 2.
1041 Gignoux, *Noms propres*, 95:425 and 54:179 respectively.
1042 Levene, *Jewish Aramaic Curse Texts*, 95, SD 27, 7 and 97, SD 27, 11.
1043 Avigad 1986: 84–85:126 (the name of the 2nd individual is damaged). *'mṭwr*, *'yswr*/*'ysr' 'ṭywn'*, *Mkst*, and *'yš'* do not match the Iranian etymologies (despite Ilan, *Lexicon*, 169–170, 181–182, 207b, 240b, s.vv.).
1044 Morgenstern and Ford, *Aramaic Incantation Bowls* 3046+3069, 2, 5, 6, 7.
1045 Montgomery, *Aramaic Incantation Texts*, 26, 4.
1046 Gignoux, *Noms propres*, 159:843; 2003: 59:305.
1047 Gordon, "Aramaic Incantation Bowls," 342–344:BM 91776, 1.
1048 Bhayro *et al.*, *Aramaic Magic Bowls*, 41.
1049 Bhayro *et al.*, *Aramaic Magic Bowls*, 105. The spelling *-xšēd* is historical according to Shaked *et al.*, *Aramaic Bowl Spells* (2022), 219b.

“Sun” (< “brilliant Sun”)[1050] is a divine epithet used as an anthroponym (> Sogd. PN *Xwrxšyδ*).[1051] *Bhmn* is also recorded as an anthroponym.[1052]

7.2.9 Juxtaposition (mechanical contraction, *Schein-dvandva*)[1053]

a. Anthroponyms formed by combination of two divine names (both fem.): *Hwrmyzd’nhyh* (/*Hormizd-Anāhīh*/),[1054] i.e. Ahura-Mazdah and Anahita, *M’n’hyd*,[1055] i.e. “Māh and Anahita”, *Myhrnhyd*,[1056] i.e. “Mithra and Anahita”, as well as OSyr. *’zdn’nyt*[1057] (“the gods” and Anahita), *Myḥrḥwrmyzd*[1058] (/*Myr’ḥrmyz*[1059]), i.e. Mithra and Ahura-Mazdah and *M’dwr* which consists of *Māh* “Moon-god” and *Ādur* “Holy fire”.[1060] They can perhaps be interpreted as exocentric compounds meaning “dedicated/belonging to DN$_1$ and DN$_2$”.[1061] A hybrid name consisting of two theonyms is *’štr’ Nhyd* (alias-name of a client)[1062] “The goddess (Palm., Hatr.) Anahita”.

b. Anthroponyms formed by combination of a theonym and a personal name: *’štd* (/*Aštād*/) [2]*Mh’d<<y>>wk*[1063] (/*Māh-dux*/); MPers. *Mihr-Šābuhr*[1064]/Mand. *Mršbwr*[1065] consists of *Mihr* > *Mr* and *Šābuhr* (royal name, a plene spelling of the RN is *Š’bwr*[1066]). *M’kwsrw* (/*Māxusrō*/)[1067] is of the same type, viz. *Māh* and a royal name (his matronym also contains *Māh*). The same divine name is juxtaposed with another anthroponym in *M’brzyn*, viz./*Mā(h)-burzin*/,[1068] and perhaps in

---

1050 Cf. Zimmer, “Zur sprachlichen,” 127 *ad* 1039.
1051 See Lurje, *Personal Names*, 444:1449.
1052 Shaked *et al.*, *Aramaic Bowl Spells* (2022), 69, 1.
1053 For this category see Schmitt 1995.
1054 Bhayro *et al.*, *Aramaic Magic Bowls*, 103.
1055 Gordon, “Aramaic Incantation Bowls,” 278: (Ashmolean) 1931.473, 10, 13.
1056 Shaked *et al.*, *Aramaic Bowl Spells* (2013), 349, s. v. with references.
1057 Moriggi, *Corpus*, 18, 4.
1058 Moriggi, *Corpus*, 6, 1, 3, 7, 11.
1059 Moriggi, *Corpus*, 45, 3b.
1060 See Müller-Kessler, “A Mandaic Gold Amulet,” 84–85 *ad* 5, 16, 30.
1061 See Sims-Williams, *Bactrian Personal Names*, 9 regarding the Bactrian analogous combinations.
1062 Gordon, “Two Magic Bowls,” 306–309, 5, cf. Müller-Kessler, “Die Zauberschalensammlung,” 130 *ad* 068A.
1063 Isbell, *Corpus*, 66, 1 f.
1064 Gignoux, *Noms propres*, 130:656.
1065 Yamauchi, *Mandaic Incantation Texts*, 10, 3.
1066 Gordon, “Aramaic Incantation Bowls,” 356–357:Ex 4283, 43 (cf. *Š’b’wr*, 2).
1067 Shaked *et al.*, *Aramaic Bowl Spells* (2022), 73, 1, 5, 9.
1068 Misundersood by McCullough, *Jewish and Mandean*, 5 *ad* A, 2. For interpretation (also with the defective spelling *Mhbwrzn*) see Gignoux, Jullien and Jullien, *Noms propres*, 94:266.

Mhgw'n (/*Māh-gāwān* /)[1069] whose 2nd component may be an -*ān*-(pro-)patronymic of **Gāw* "ox, bull, cow".[1070] Juxtaposition of an anthroponym and a theonym, i.e. with an inverted order is *Sysyn 'n'hyd*[1071] (/*Sīsin-Anāhīd*/, fem.) > Mand. *Sysyn'yd.*[1072]

7.3 Suffixed names

It is explicitly stated that the same individual had both a compound name and a hypocoristicon thereof, viz. *Myrdbwk* and *Myrd'*.[1073] The former apparently ends with -*bux* < *buxt* "saved" (for the omission of -*t* cf. the numerous occurrences of -*dux* < -*duxt* above). It is apparently juxtaposed to /*merd*-/, a variant of *mard* "man" (like the base of Mand. < MPers. *Merdānōy,* ↓7.3.1.2, a, b'). *Myrd'* ends with -<'> = -/*ā*/ which is a very common hypocoristic suffix in Aramaic, thereby being another example of Iranian-Aramaic linguistic interference.

7.3.1 Non-combined suffixes

Skt' (mentioned together with *Sktš*, *Sktwš* and *Sktt* which apparently have the same base[1074]) from Susa is perhaps based on MPers. *saxt* "strong, hard"[1075] like Sogd. (< MPers.) *Sxtwy* (/*Saxtōy*/).[1076] It apparently ends with a non-combined suffix. *Gyrw*[1077] may originate from **Gyrwy.* It is perhaps based on **gar*, cf. MPers. *garān* "heavy, serious" > NPers. *girān. N'w'* (fem.) may be based on *naw*- "new", which is extant in MPers. *nawrūz*, Arm. *Nawasard* < OIran. **Nava-sarda*- (cf. Choresm. *N'wsrdyk*)[1078] and Sogd. *n'w*;[1079] Alternatively Aramaic (↑1.2.1.1.6).

1069 Bhayro *et al.*, *Aramaic Magic Bowls,* 1.
1070 Cf. MPers. *Gōzan* (Gignoux, *Noms propres*, 90:396), Martirosyan, *Iranian Personal Names*, 209, 227, as well as, Perhaps, Parth. *Gwdt, Gwdtyt, Gwk* (Schmitt, *Personennamen* 97–98:190–192).
1071 Müller-Kessler, *Zauberschalentexte*, 41e, 4, 34, 40.
1072 See Abudraham 2023: 16–17 *ad* 3.
1073 Yamauchi, "Aramaic Magic Bowls," 514–518: B, 3, 10, 14.
1074 S. A. Kaufman *apud* Isbell, "Two New," 15 cautiously suggests that all these forms refer to the same individual.
1075 Cf. Ilan, *Lexicon*, 201a.
1076 See Lurje, *Personal Names*, 359:1127.
1077 Morgenstern and Ford, *Aramaic Incantation Bowls*, 533, n. 166:SD 40A, 2 (unpubl.).
1078 See Martirosyan, *Iranian Personal Names*, 267–268:518–520.
1079 See Lurje, *Personal Names*, 265:765.

7.3.1.1 *-āy* (<-'y, yy, y>)[1080]

a Males

a'. Adjectives: For *Rsy*[1081] cf. perhaps NPers. *Rasā* "skillful, capable, clever".[1082]

b'. Hypocoristic:[1083] *'rdy*[1084] is based on the theophorous element *Arda* < **Ṛta-*. For *M'h'y* see ↑7.2.7.

With *-āy* > *-ā* (presumably due to the Aramaic-speaking milieu, the more so since *-ā* is the most frequent suffix of Aramaic names): *'ṣp'*[1085] perhaps originates from *'sp'* with *s* > *ṣ* (cf. with the same consonantal cluster *'yṣpndwy*, ↓7.3.1.2, b, b'), in which case it would be based on MPers. *asp* "horse".[1086]

b Females

a'. Adjectival: *Gwn'y* (/*Gōnāy*/),[1087] and *Bwsty* (/*Bōstāy*/) are based on MPers. *gōn* "colour, complexion" and *bōstān* "garden"[1088] respectively (the latter with omission of *-n*). Another such form with omission of *-n* is *'smyy* (/*Asmāy*/) which is based on *asmān* "Heaven".[1089] It may be a hypocoristicon of compounds like MPers. *Asm-bād.*[1090] *Myryy* is based on *Mihr.*[1091] Mand. *'yspynd'rmyd'y* is based on the theonym *Spəṇtā-Ārmaiti-.*[1092] *Prwrd'y*[1093]/*Prwrdy*[1094] (/*Fravardāy*/) is based on MPers. *fraward* (*frawahr*) "Man's immortal soul, guardian angel during his lifetime". On the face of it, *Byryy* and *Byrwy*, which end in *-āy* and –ōy respectively, are perhaps based on a late form of *wīr* "male, man" (cf. *Wīrōy*[1095]), but this is semantically unlikely for females' names. Perhaps they are based on a late form

---

1080 See Nöldeke, *Persische Studien*, 29–31; cf., e.g., Manichean Parth. *žīwāy* "alive" (Durkin-Meisterernst, *Dictionary*, 200, 388a); cf. Durkin-Meisterernst, *Dictionary*, 364:315 and the related suffix *-aya-* (Martirosyan, *Iranian Personal Names*, 20–21 with lit.).
1081 Shaked *et al.*, *Aramaic Bowl Spells* (2022), 109, 2.
1082 Justi, *Iranisches Namenbuch* 259a.
1083 Cf. Martirosyan, *Iranian Personal Names*, 308:639 *in fine*.
1084 Shaked *et al.*, *Aramaic Bowl Spells* (2022), 98, 5, 7, 12, 14, 17.
1085 Martinez Borobio "A Magical Bowl," 324–325, 335, 9.
1086 Cf., e.g., LB *As-pa-'* (see Zadok, *Iranische Personennamen in der neu*, 119: 106).
1087 Bhayro *et al.*, *Aramaic Magic Bowls*, 146.
1088 See Shaked, "Form and Purpose," 10 *ad* 3, 4.
1089 See Levene, *Jewish Aramaic Curse Texts*, 90.
1090 See Gignoux, *Noms propres* (Supp.), 24:40.
1091 Differently Levene, *Jewish Aramaic Curse Texts*, 96 *ad* SD 27, 9.
1092 See Abudraham, "Three Mandaic," 71.
1093 See Segal, *Catalogue*, 121 *ad* 092M.
1094 Bhayro *et al.*, *Aramaic Magic Bowls*, 96.
1095 See Martirosyan, *Iranian Personal Names*, 148:168, 365:802 and Gignoux, *Noms propres*, 183:1008; Gignoux, Jullien and Jullien, *Noms propres*, 55:112.

of the Akkadian theonym *Bēl*.[1096] *Dwst'y* > *Dwst'*[1097] is based on *dōst* "friend".[1098] Is Mand. *Kwm'y*[1099] based on the outcome of MPers. *xwamn* "dream"? *Rw'y* (4 ×)[1100] (/*Rawāy*/, cf. Mand. *Ruai*[1101]) may be the same name as NPers. *Rawāī*[1102] if the variant *Rʿw'y* (1 ×)[1103] is merely orthographic. *Sm'y* is the same female as *Sm'* and *Smw*;[1104] cf. Mand. *S'm'y*.[1105] These forms are probably based on *sām* < OIran. **sāma-* "black" (cf. Av. *Sāma-*);[1106] alternatively to Aramaic *smy'* "blind" (with elision of *-y-*).[1107] *Zyywy* may be based on MPers. *zīw*, cf. Parth. *žīwāy* "alive, lively"; alternatively Aramaic (↑1.2.9.2).

b'. Hypocoristic: *Dwkt'y*[1108]/*Dwkty*[1109] (/*Duxtāy*/) is based on *duxt* "daughter". It may originate from a compound name with *duxt* (↑7.2.1, i). *Gwšny*[1110] (also OSyr.)[1111]/Mand. *Gwšn'y*[1112] is a hypocoristicon of *Gwšnsp*. *Myry*,[1113] is based on *Mihr*, provided that it is not an abbreviation of Heb. *Mrym*. *'wdyy* (/*Awdāy*/),[1114] *Bwrz'y* (/*Burzāy*/)[1115] and Mand. *Kwš'y*[1116] (/*Xwašāy*/) are also hypocoristica as they are based on the Middle Persian adjectives *awd* < *abd* "wonderful", *burz* "exalted" and *xwaš* "pleasant, sweet, nice" respectively. *Nywy* (/*Nēwāy*)[1117] is attached to *nēw* "good".*'nwš'y* denotes "immortal" or "sweet, pleas-

1096 Cf. Gignoux, *Noms propres*, 58:207 and Levene, *Jewish Aramaic Curse Texts*, 90.
1097 Gordon, "Aramaic Incantation Bowls," 127–129:7, 2 and 7 respectively.
1098 Cf. MPers. *Dōstag* (Gignoux, *Noms propres*, 77:320).
1099 Yamauchi, *Mandaic Incantation Texts*, 33, 3, 22, 25, 26, 27.
1100 Müller-Kessler, *Zauberschalentexte*, 38, 3, 17, 40; 38a, 5.
1101 See Morgenstern and Ford 2020: 191, n. 618 *ad* 3011, 3–4, 17, 40–42 who refer to Justi, *Iranisches Namenbuch* 260.
1102 Justi, *Iranisches Namenbuch* 260a.
1103 Müller-Kessler, *Zauberschalentexte*, 38, 4.
1104 Franco, "Five Aramaic," 236–240 and fig. 1 on 235:C_{10}-116, 2, 5, 8; 242 and fig. 3 on 241:C_{10}-119, 13; 242–245 and fig. 4; 245–249 and fig. 5: C_{11}-113, 2.
1105 Abudraham, "Three Mandaic," 83–85:2, 7.
1106 Cf. Gignoux, *Noms propres*, 156:823.
1107 Cf. Montgomery, *Aramaic Incantation Texts*, 118–119 *ad* 1, 7 and 13, 2.
1108 Bhayro *et al.*, *Aramaic Magic Bowls*, 1.
1109 Shaked *et al.*, *Aramaic Bowl Spells* (2013), 35, 7, 10.
1110 Bhayro *et al.*, *Aramaic Magic Bowls*, 96.
1111 Moriggi, *Corpus*, 14, 13; 28, 4, 6, 7, 11.
1112 Gordon, "Aramaic and Mandaic," 95–100 and pls. 10–13:M, 3.
1113 Shaked *et al.*, *Aramaic Bowl Spells* (2013), 36, 3.
1114 Levene, *Jewish Aramaic Curse Texts*, 90–94:VA 2417, 11.
1115 Bhayro *et al.*, *Aramaic Magic Bowls*, 66, 83.
1116 McCullough, *Jewish and Mandean*, D, 3, 11, 18.
1117 Bhayro *et al.*, *Aramaic Magic Bowls*, 100, 143, 148, 169.

ant"[1118] (Mand. ~,[1119] cf. without a suffix *'nwš*,[1120] which is also used as nickname.[1121] It is also extant in Mandaic.[1122] *P'ly* may originate from *Pāhrāy*,[1123] which is based on *pāhr* < OIran. **pāθra-* "guard, defence" (with *r* > *l*). Hence it can be a hypocoristicon of Middle Persian compound names with *pāhr*.[1124]

7.3.1.2 -*ōy*[1125] (<-*wy*, <-*why*> is recorded once in Mandaic)

a. Males, a'. Adjectival: *D'štwy*[1126] (/*Daštōy*/) and *Dynwy* (OSyr.,[1127] /*Dēnōy*/) are based on *dašt* "plain" and *dēn* "religion". *N'mwy*[1128] renders MPers. *Nāmōy* which is based on *nām* "name, reputation".[1129] *Šyrwy* is based on either *šēr* "lion"[1130] or *šīr* "milk" ("milk-like" > "sweet"[1131]). *Z'rwy* (OSyr.,[1132] /*Zārōy*/) is possibly based on *zār* "field".[1133] OSyr. *Ṭšyḥrw(h)y* (/*Čihrōy*/) is based on the Middle Persian outcome of OIran. **čiθra-* "seed, lineage, origin" or "visible form, appearance, face".[1134] *Š'bwy*[1135]/Mand. *Š'bwy*[1136] is based on *šab* "night" (var. *Š'bh'*[1137]), cf. MPers. *Šabānag* "nocturnal".[1138]

1118 See Naveh and Shaked, *Amulets and Magic Bowls*, 148–149 *ad* 3, 2.
1119 Yamauchi, *Mandaic Incantation Texts*, 4, 7.
1120 Gordon, "Two Aramaic," 233–236 and pls. 1–5 on 238–242:I, 2.
1121 Shaked *et al.*, *Aramaic Bowl Spells* (2013), 11, 9, 17.
1122 Yamauchi, *Mandaic Incantation Texts*, 368, index, s. v. with references.
1123 See Naveh and Shaked, *Amulets and Magic Bowls*, 175 *ad* 8, ii, 5, iii, 6.
1124 Cf. Gignoux, *Noms propres*, 143:734–736 and for hypothetical Old Iranian forerunners and their Middle Iranian outcome Martirosyan, *Iranian Personal Names*, 297–300:608, 613.
1125 Thoroughly discussed by Nöldeke, *Persische Studien*, 4–11 where many such names are explained (cf. Martirosyan, *Iranian Personal Names*, 19–20:5.8). See Bailey "Armeno-indoiranica," 90–94 and Benveniste 1966: 45–48. Cf. the reverse indexes of Gignoux, *Noms propres*, 218, 2003: 77b, Gignoux, Jullien and Jullien, *Noms propres*, 179–180 as well as, e.g., Sogd. *Sxtwy* (< /*Saxtōy*/, < MPers., to *saxt* "strong", see Lurje, *Personal Names*, 359:1127).
1126 Shaked *et al.*, *Aramaic Bowl Spells* (2013), 63, 6.
1127 Moriggi, *Corpus*, 4, 2, 5, 9, 11; 7, 12; 43, 23.
1128 Ilan, *Lexicon*, 195, s. v. *Nāmēō* (inaccurate lemmatization).
1129 Gignoux, *Noms propres*, 133:673.
1130 See Segal, *Catalogue*, 79 *ad* 038A, 3 (not "good lion" as understood by Ilan, *Lexicon*, 202).
1131 See Shaked, "Peace Be upon You," 214.
1132 Moriggi, *Corpus*, 9, 3,
1133 See Gignoux, Jullien and Jullien, *Noms propres*, 151:471 (cf. Martirosyan, *Iranian Personal Names*, 192:295).
1134 See Müller-Kessler, "Die Zauberschalensammlung," 139a *ad* 120Sy, 2.
1135 Bhayro *et al.*, *Aramaic Magic Bowls*, 56.
1136 Gordon, "Aramaic Incantation Bowls," 344–345, 41.
1137 Gordon, "Aramaic Incantation Bowls," 344–345, 8.
1138 See Shaked, "Peace Be upon You," 214.

b'. Hypocoristic: The suffix *-ōy* is hypocoristic when it is attached to theophorous elements and numina:

'rdwy[1139] (to **Ṛta*); *Pnwy* (*/Pānōy/* > Arab. < NPers. *Fannuyeh*)[1140] is based on *pān* "protector, guard" (a theophorous element < epithet of MPers. *Pān-dād* "Given by the guard, protector").[1141] *Mirdanuia* (Mand.) renders *Merdānōy* < *Mardānōy*,[1142] which may be based on either MPers. *mardān* "men" or (seeing that bases with a plural form are very rare) on a form which originates from OIran. **martan-* (extant in Av. *marətan-*) "mortal, man". Is Mand. *'p'rwy*[1143] based on a forerunner of MPers. *abar* "higher"?

b. Females, a'. Adjectival: *Symwy*[1144] (*/Sēmōy/*) is based on *(a)sēm* "silver", thereby meaning "silvern", cf. OSyr. *Symy* < MPers. *Sēmiy*.[1145] *Q'mwy/Qmwy* is based on MPers. *kām* < OIran. **kāma-* "will, desire".[1146] Mand. <*Maduih̲*> (*/Mādōy/*),[1147] OSyr. *M'dwyy* and *Bḥrwy*[1148] are based on *mād* "wine"[1149] and *bahār* "spring".[1150] The latter is recorded as an anthroponym (Mand. *Bh'r*).[1151] *Dwktwy*[1152] is based on *duxt-* "daughter" and Mand. *Nazuia* (*/Nāzōy/*)[1153] on MPers. *nāz* "grace, charm; pleasure, delight".[1154] *Šhrwy*[1155] and *Škrwy* (*/Šakarōy/*)[1156] are based on *šahr* (< OIran. **xšaθra-* "region" > "town") and *šakar* "sugar" respectively. *Kwmbwy* (*/Xumbōy/*) "pitcher-like" (to *xumb*)[1157] apparently refers to a physical trait like obesity. Since this is a female name, a denotation "fragrant" is attractive, but the appellative *xwmbwy* with this meaning is recorded in Parthian, not in

---

1139 Ilan, *Lexicon*, 168.

1140 See Montgomery, *Aramaic Incantation Texts*, 177 *ad* 12, 11, cf. Nöldeke, *Persische Studien*, 21.

1141 See Segal, *Catalogue*, 51b *ad* 009A, 11 who refers to Gignoux, *Noms propres*, 145:749.

1142 See Morgenstern and Ford, *Aramaic Incantation Bowls*, 260, n. 633 *ad* 3025, 4.

1143 Yamauchi, *Mandaic Incantation Texts*, 15, 8.

1144 Myhrman 1909.

1145 See Gignoux, Jullien and Jullien, *Noms propres*, 123:376; cf. Arm. < MIran. *Seme/ik* (Martirosyan, *Iranian Personal Names*, 321:679).

1146 See Gordon, "Aramaic Magical Bowls," 329 *ad* D, 6, 14, 15 and 11 respectively (not "good desire" as rendered by Ilan, *Lexicon*, 229b).

1147 Morgenstern and Ford, *Aramaic Incantation Bowls*, 197 *ad* HS 3021, 3.

1148 Moriggi, *Corpus*, 6, 12, 14.

1149 Not "good wine" as rendered by Ilan 2011: 233–234.

1150 "Related to spring time" (see Shaked, "Peace Be upon You," 214).

1151 See McCullough, *Jewish and Mandean*, 52 *ad* E, 4.

1152 Shaked *et al.*, *Aramaic Bowl Spells* (2013), 34, 1–2, 5–6, 8, 10, 12.

1153 Bhayro *et al.*, *Aramaic Magic Bowls*, 41.

1154 Cf. Martirosyan, *Iranian Personal Names*, 265–266:510, 512, 513.

1155 Bhayro *et al.*, *Aramaic Magic Bowls*, 147–148:120: *Šāhrōy (recte Šahrōy)*.

1156 Shaked *et al.*, *Aramaic Bowl Spells* (2022), 85, 14, 17; 97, 2.

1157 See Gignoux, Jullien and Jullien, *Noms propres*, 138:433 *ad* Moriggi, *Corpus*, 7, 3, 7, 10.

Middle Persian. *M(w)škwy* is based on MPers. *mušk* "musk";[1158] female names deriving from perfumes are a universal phenomenon. *'brwy*[1159] may be based on **'br* < OIran. **abra-* "dark colour" (cf. RAE *Ap-pír-mar-ša* < OIran. **Abra-varsa-* "Having dark-coloured hair"[1160]). *Ḥz'rwy* is based on *hazār* "thousand".[1161]

Gylwy[1162] may be based on MPers. *gil* "clay", in which case it would be a plene spelling like Arab. (< NPers.) *Jīlūyeh.*[1163] *Dynrwy* (*/Dēnārōy/*, OSyr.)[1164] is based on *dēnār* "(gold) dinar"[1165] (< Latin).

b'. Hypocoristic, α. Based on Adjectives: *Bwrzwy* (*/Burzōy/*)[1166] is based on MPers. *burz* "high, lofty, exalted",[1167] *Swrwy*[1168] on MPers. *sūr* < OIran. **sūra-* "strong" and *Zyqwy* may be based on *zīk*, Gk. Ζηκ, which refers to a Persian (> Arm. *Zik*) and means "lively, vivid".[1169] *Prkwy* (*/Farroxōy/*)[1170] is based on *farrox* "fortunate, happy". *Prwk* (*/Farrox/*) "fotunate, blessed, happy" by itself is also recorded as an anthroponym.[1171] *'šwy*[1172] perhaps goes back to MPers. *ašō* < Av. *ašava-* "righteous". The suffix of *Hyndwy* "Indian"[1173] is synonymous with MPers. *Hindūg*, whose base originates from Old Persian *Hindu-*, an *-u* stem. *Hndw* is also recorded as a female's name.[1174] *Ḥyndw* and *Ḥyndwyt'* (the latter with the feminine gentilic suffix) are recorded as anthroponyms in Mandaic.[1175]

β. Based on theophorous elements: *Mzdw'y*[1176] is based on the Middle Iranian descendant of *Mazdah*. *'yṣpndwy* is based on the Middle Iranian outcome of

---

1158 See Ilan, *Lexicon*, 241a (cf. Ciancaglini, *Iranian Loanwords*, 204).
1159 Ilan, *Lexicon*, 207a.
1160 See Gershevitch 1969: 179, cf. Tavernier 2007: 101:4.2.19.
1161 See Ilan, *Lexicon*, 222a.
1162 Moriggi, *Corpus*, 2, 3.
1163 Justi, *Iranisches Namenbuch* 115b, cf. Nöldeke, *Persische Studien*, 17, 22, top.
1164 Müller-Kessler 2004: 271 *ad* 35.
1165 Cf. Lecoq 1993: 130 *ad* 313.
1166 Bhayro *et al.*, *Aramaic Magic Bowls*, 62.
1167 See Segal, *Catalogue*, 79 *ad* 038A, 3, cf. Martirosyan, *Iranian Personal Names*, 365:802.
1168 Faraj and Moriggi, "Two New," 77–80:IM 62265, 2, 6 (to compounds like, e.g., Av. *Sūrō.yazata-*, Mayrhofer 1977: 79).
1169 For the Middle Iranian and Armenian documentation see Martirosyan, *Iranian Personal Names*, 194–195:302 with lit.
1170 Shaked *et al* 2013, 36, 3.
1171 Cf., e.g., Shaked *et al.*, *Aramaic Bowl Spells* (2013), 350, s. v.
1172 Geller, "Eight Incantation Bowls," 115 and pl. 10:Aaron F, 1.
1173 Ilan, *Lexicon*, 222–223.
1174 See Montgomery, *Aramaic Incantation Texts*, 205 *ad* 24, 1.
1175 Yamauchi, *Mandaic Incantation Texts*, 25, 16 and 23, 3, 9, 12, 13 respectively.
1176 See Gordon 1934b: 471 *ad* 467 and pl. 22, 1, 2; cf. Juusola, *Linguistic Pecularities*, 54 with n. 214.

OIran. **Spanta-* (Av. *Spəṇtā-[Ārmaiti-]*) "Holy devotion"[1177] (with an additional initial vowel in order to avoid the consonant cluster *sp-* and *s* > *ṣ*). It is a hypocoristic of either the compound theonym *'yspndrmyd* (↑7.2.8) or a compound anthroponym with **Spanta.*[1178] *Ršnwy* is based on the theophorous element ("mythological" is inaccurate) *Rašn* < Av. *Rašnu*[1179] (god of justice; or the 18th day as a calendar name), and probably *'drwy*[1180] (to *ādur* "fire").

γ. Deriving from compound anthroponyms: *Nrswy*[1181] is based on the common anthroponym *Narseh* (also a royal name). *Gwšny, Gwšnwy*[1182] are hypocoristica of *Gwšnsp* (↑7.2.2, a).

δ. Unexplained bases: The base of *Šīšōy* and *Šyšyn (/Šīšēn/)*,[1183] *Šyš'y*[1184] (also Mand.[1185]) derives perhaps from OPers. *Čiç-* < *Čiθr-* (cf. *ad Ššy and Šyšn*, ↑A, 3).[1186]

c. Referring to both males and females: *'smwy* (*/Asmōy/*, fem.[1187] and male[1188]) is based on *asmān* "Heaven". *M'hwy*[1189]/*Mhwy*[1190] (to *Māh*), *Myhrwy*[1191] (to *Miθra*).[1192] *Zdwy*[1193] (cf. Mand. *Z'dwy'*)[1194] is based on MPers. *zād* (< OIran. **zāta-*) "born"[1195] (a passive participle). *Grygwy*[1196] is perhaps based on **garīg* "mountainous" (to MPers. *gar* "mountain").

1177 See Montgomery, *Aramaic Incantation Texts*, 193 *ad* 18, 2, 10.

1178 Cf., e.g. the Middle Persian names listed in Gignoux, *Noms propres*, 159:843–845, Gignoux, Jullien and Jullien, *Noms propres*, 123–124:379, Parth. *Spndtk* (Schmitt, *Personennamen* 193:445 with Bactrian and Sogdian comparanda) and the Armenian < Middle Iranian anthroponyms listed by Martirosyan, *Iranian Personal Names*, 329–330: 707–709.

1179 See Montgomery, *Aramaic Incantation Texts*, 158 *ad* 8, 4.

1180 Shaked *et al* 2022, 73, 2, 6.

1181 Shaked *et al.*, *Aramaic Bowl Spells* (2022), 73, 2, 5.

1182 Bhayro *et al.*, *Aramaic Magic Bowls*, 96 and 111, 140 respectively.

1183 Cf. Shaked, "Peace Be upon You," 214 and for the latter Montgomery, *Aramaic Incantation Texts*, 219–220 *ad* 29, 8.

1184 Isbell, *Corpus*, 61, 2.

1185 Yamauchi, *Mandaic Incantation Texts*, 3, 10.

1186 For more names whose base is the same cf. Levene, *Jewish Aramaic Curse Texts*, 21.

1187 Bhayro *et al.*, *Aramaic Magic Bowls*, 13.

1188 Wolfe 1, 5 (unpubl., quoted by Morgenstern and Ford, *Aramaic Incantation Bowls*, 53, n. 165).

1189 Bhayro *et al.*, *Aramaic Magic Bowls*, 150.

1190 Ilan, *Lexicon*, 190 with references.

1191 Ilan, *Lexicon*, 194a; Bhayro *et al.*, *Aramaic Magic Bowls*, 1.

1192 Cf. Gignoux, *Noms propres*, 130:652.

1193 Gordon, "Aramaic and Mandaic," 92–93 and pl. 7:K, 1, 5.

1194 Yamauchi, *Mandaic Incantation Texts*, 23, 9, 12, 14.

1195 Cf. Morgenstern and Ford, *Aramaic Incantation Bowls*, 59, n. 197 *ad* 3016, 1.5 and Martirosyan, *Iranian Personal Names*, 189:287.

1196 Cf. Morgenstern and Ford, *Aramaic Incantation Bowls*, 15.

7.3.1.3 ***-āt*** (> MPers. *-ād* < OIran. *–āta-*)[1197]

It is spelled with < *ṭ*> in *Myhrṭ*,[1198] OSyr. *Myḥrṭ*,[1199] Mand. *Mihraṭ*,[1200] (MPers. *Mihrād* < OIran. **Miθrāta-*;[1201] *Myhl'd* is a later form thereof[1202]), and *B'nd'd* (↑7.2, MPers. *Windād*[1203]), cf. *Mzdhṭ* (not a customer)[1204] which is based on *Mazdah*.

7.3.1.4 ***-ān*** (< OIran. *-āna-* (pro-)patronymic)[1205]

M'ḥ'n (Mand.)[1206] < MPers. *Māhān* is based on *Māh*.[1207] *Pryn* (/*Friyān*/)[1208] is based on **friya-* "dear, friend", cf. the Avestan family name *Friiāna-*, Pontic Iran. Φλιανος, RAE < OIran. **Fryāna-*[1209] and the Manichean Parthian appellative *fry'n* "friend, beloved". *Wrtn*[1210] < OIran. **Vartana-* "chariot" (cf. Parth. *Wrtn*[1211]). *Zd'n*[1212] and fem. *Zdn*[1213] are based on *zād* "born" and Mand. *Prwk'n*[1214] (/*Farroxān*/ < MPers. ~[1215] > Sogd. *Frwx'n*[1216]) on *farrox* "fortunate". *Zywn* may be based on MPers. *zīw* "alive" (alternatively Aram., ↑1.2.9.2). Cf. *Mzd'n* of Mand. *Mzd'n'sp's* (↑7.2.7), *Br'n* of *Br'ndwk*, *Gwln* of *Gwlndwk* and *N(y)wn* of *N(y)wndwk* (↑7.2.1, i).

1197 Cf. the examples in Schmitt, *Personennamen* 61:84 *in fine* and in Martirosyan, *Iranian Personal Names*, 19:5.7.

1198 Cf. Morgenstern and Ford, *Aramaic Incantation Bowls*, 33 with n. 84 *ad* 3008, 2, 5.

1199 Moriggi, *Corpus*, 17, 1, 7 (*Myḥr*<*ṭ*>).

1200 Morgenstern and Abudraham, "A Mandaean Lamella," 220, 176.

1201 See Gignoux, *Noms propres sassanides*, 124:615.

1202 Differently Shaked, "Rabbis," 116, n. 74.

1203 Gignoux, *Noms propres sassanides*, 182:998.

1204 Cf. Shaked, "Rabbis," 113:1.2, 8.

1205 Cf. Durkin-Meisterernst, *Grammatik*, 162:312 as well as Sims-Williams, *Bactrian Personal Names*, 11 (-ανο) and Martirosyan, *Iranian Personal Names*, 17–19:5.5.

1206 Morgenstern, "Five Mandaic," 114–115:139, 10, 13, 14.

1207 Cf. Gignoux, *Noms propres*, 110:522.

1208 Moriggi, "Two New," 52–56, 58:2, 5.

1209 See Tavernier, *Iranica*, 184:612, Lurje, *Personal Names*, 304:927 with lit.; cf. Schmitt, *Personennamen* 171: 384.

1210 Ilan, *Lexicon*, 204b, s. v. *Wardān*.

1211 See Schmitt, *Personennamen*, 230:560. Differently Gignoux, Jullien and Jullien, *Noms propres*, 137:429 who are of the opinion that it is based on **varta/i* "valor".

1212 Gordon, "Aramaic Magical Bowls," 331–334: E and F.

1213 Bhayro *et al.*, *Aramaic Magic Bowls*, 123..

1214 Yamauchi, *Mandaic Incantation Texts*, 18a, 2; 18b, 8; 18c, 4, 8, 13.

1215 Gignoux, *Noms propres*, 83:354.

1216 See Lurje, *Personal Names*, 145:309.

7.3.1.5 *-in* (< OIran. *-ina-*, hypocoristic[1217])

Bwrzyn (fem., *bwrz* /*burz*/ "lofty"[1218] + *-in* like in *Wrzyn* (fem.[1219] < MPers. *Wārzin*. The latter may be based on *warz-* "to work, act, practice".[1220] Perhaps *'myn* (fem., OSyr.)[1221] goes back to OIran. **Am-ina-*, which is based on **Ama-* "strong".[1222] *Gwšnyn* (of *'dyn* ~) is a presumably a misreading of *Gwšnṣ;*[1223] *'dyn* < OIran. **Āt-ina-* (↑7.2.2, b).

7.3.1.6 *-ēn* (< OIran. *-aina-*)

a. "Stoffadjektiv": *Zryn* (/*Zarrēn*/) "golden".[1224]

b. Hypocoristic:[1225] *-dwk(t)* is attached to *Burzēn-*, *Māhēn-*, *Rašnēn-* and *Šahrēn-* (↑7.2.1, i).

7.3.1.7 *-ak* > *-ag* <(')*g*/*q*> (< OIran. *-(a)ka-*)[1226]

a. Adjectives: Mand. *Ṭṣšmag* (/*Čašmag*/)[1227] "renowned" (MPers.).[1228] *'dq* (*Adaces*)[1229] < OIran. **Ādāka-* which is based on the Old Iranian equivalent of Av. *ā-dā-* "reward".[1230] *Drktq* (/*Draxtaq*/)[1231] is based on *draxt* "tree". *P'bq*[1232] (/*Pābak*/ < /*Pāpak*/) is based on **pāpa-* "father, dad".[1233] *Z'rq*[1234] may be a plene

---

1217 Cf., e.g., Martirosyan, *Iranian Personal Names,* 22:5.1.1

1218 Cf. Ilan, *Lexicon,* 214–215.

1219 Cf. Ilan, *Lexicon,* 255b.

1220 See Martirosyan, *Iranian Personal Names,* 359:786.

1221 Moriggi, *Corpus,* 13, 10.

1222 A Semitic derivation, e.g. "constant, trustworthy" (Mand., OSyr.) is incompatible with a female's name.

1223 See Morgenstern and Ford, *Aramaic Incantation Bowls,* 44, n. 130 *ad* Gordon, "Aramaic Incantation Bowls," 350:IM 9736.

1224 Cf. Hunter 1996: 228–229 and fig. 2, 2 who quotes Justi, *Iranisches Namenbuch* 382.

1225 Cf., e.g., the long list in Martirosyan, *Iranian Personal Names,* 13–15.

1226 See Nöldeke, *Persische Studien,* 31–33, cf. Durkin-Meisterernst, *Grammatik,* 155–158: 295–300 and Sims-Williams, *Bactrian Personal Names,* 11 as well as the long list in Martirosyan, *Iranian Personal Names,* 15–17:5.3.

1227 Bhayro *et al., Aramaic Magic Bowls,* 31.

1228 See W. Sundermann *apud* Zimmer, "Zur sprachlichen," 120 *ad* 266.

1229 Cf. Montgomery, *Aramaic Incantation Texts,* 143 *ad* 6, 3 who refers to Justi, *Iranisches Namenbuch* 2b and Nöldeke, *Persische Studien,* 33 (the variant Δάκης is probably secondary).

1230 See Zadok 1976b: 247, n. 4 = Zadok, *Iranische Personennamen in der neu,* 73:5 (cf. Tavernier, *Iranica,* 102:4.2.28 and Lurje, *Personal Names,* 66:5).

1231 Shaked *et al., Aramaic Bowl Spells* (2013), 24, 10; 46, 4.

1232 Cf. Montgomery, *Aramaic Incantation Texts,* 122 *ad* 2, 1.

1233 See Gignoux, *Noms propres,* 141–142:723; Schmitt, *Personennamen* 146–147:320 with previous lit.

1234 Gordon, "Aramaic Magical Bowls," 328–331 and pl. 13:D, 6, 11.

spelling for /*Zarak*/ or /*Zarrak*/ > *Zarag* (to either *zari-* "yellow" or *zar* < **zarant-* "old")[1235] or *Zarrag* (based on *zarr* "gold").[1236]

b. Hypocoristic, a'. Based on nouns: *Nb'zk* (fem.)[1237] is based on the hypothetical Middle Iranian descendant of OIran. **Navāza-* "boatman, skipper" (Av. *navāza-*), cf. the Armenian loanword *navaz* on the one hand and Νάβαζος[1238] in a Pontic Iranian milieu on the other;[1239] OSyr. *Pnhq* (of /*Panāhak-dux*/, ↑7.2.1, i).

b'. Based on adjectives: *Bwrzq* is based on *burz* "high, lofty, exalted"[1240] and *Burzidag* on a participle meaning "exalted, honoured".[1241] Mand. *'nwš'g*[1242] is based on *anōš* "immortal" or "sweet, pleasant" (cf. ↑7.2.4, b). *Przq*[1243] is defective for **Prwzq* (/*Pērōzag*/) which is based on *Pērōz* "victorious".[1244]

7.3.1.8 *-āk* > *-āg*

Mand. *Ruzag* (fem.) < MPers. *Rōzāg* "lightning"[1245] and *Ḥwnyq* which may render the forerunner of MPers. *Huniyāg*[1246] "delightful"[1247] (alternatively to ↓7.3.1.9).

7.3.1.9 *īk* > *-īg* (< OIran. *-ika-*, *adjectival*)[1248]

Kwryg[1249] is based on *Xvar* "Sun"[1250] (cf. the following name). *Ḥwnyq* may be same name as Parth. *Hwnyk* (/*Xwanik*/), whose base may originate from OIran. **xvan-* "sun".[1251] In this case it would be homonymous with the preceding name (alternatively to ↑7.3.1.8). *Kwsyg* (fem.)[1252] is apparently based on *Xvās* of unclear

---

1235 Gignoux, *Noms propres*, 194: 1076.
1236 Gignoux, *Noms propres* (Supp.), 70:381.
1237 Montgomery, *Aramaic Incantation Texts*, 28, 2.
1238 Justi, *Iranisches Namenbuch* 218b.
1239 The latter is compared by Ilan, *Lexicon*, 241b.
1240 Shaked *et al.*, *Aramaic Bowl Spells* (2022), 83, 2.
1241 See Gignoux, *Noms propres* (Supp.), 28:72.
1242 Yamauchi, *Mandaic Incantation Texts*, 22, 14, 105.
1243 Ilan, *Lexicon*, 199.
1244 Cf. Ilan, *Lexicon*, 199 with 245.
1245 See C. Ciancaglini *apud* Fain *et al.*, "Aramaic Incantation Bowls," 306 *ad* S-449, 2.
1246 See Morgenstern and Ford, *Aramaic Incantation Bowls*, 185 with n. 609.
1247 See Gignoux, *Noms propres*, 100:461.
1248 Cf. Durkin-Meisterernst, *Grammatik*, 160:306; 174–175:344 and Martirosyan, *Iranian Personal Names*,20–21:5.10 with lit.
1249 Bhayro *et al.*, *Aramaic Magic Bowls*, 60.
1250 Gignoux, *Noms propres*, 187:1033.
1251 See Schmitt, *Personennamen* 109:223 (cf. 108–109:221).
1252 Yamauchi, "Aramaic Magic Bowls," 514:B, 3.

etymology.[1253] *Dwdyq*[1254] and *Pbyg*[1255] have the same bases as *Dwdy* and *P'bq* (↑4, 7.3.1.7).

7.3.1.10 -*uk* < -*uka*-[1256]

'rdwk[1257] may begin with *Arda* < **Ṛta-*, provided that this female's name is not a defective spelling of a compound with *-dwk* "daughter". *Kwrwq* ∘ [1258] (/*Xwaruk*/) < OIran. **Xvaruka-*, i.e. based on *Xvar-* "Sun(-god)". *Myzdwk* < **Mizd-ukā-* may be based on MPers. *mizd* "reward"[1259] (alternatively a compound with *-dux*, ↑7.2.1, i). A compound name with *-uk* may be Mand. *Z'dn'hwg* (↑7.2.1, f).

7.3.1.11 -*ōn*

Zdwn[1260] is based on *zād* "born".

7.3.1.12 -*ya* (< -*y'* >)

Apparently a feminine hypocoristic suffix if the base of *Myryh*[1261] (referring to a female) originates from *Myhr. Bṭy'* (fem.)[1262] is perhaps derived from *bṭy* "a kind of jar" < OIran. **bāta-*.[1263]

1253 Cf. Schmitt, *Personennamen* 111:229 and Martirosyan, *Iranian Personal Names*, 204:335 *ad* Arm. < Iran. **Xostik*.

1254 Quoted from an unpublished document by Morgenstern and Ford, *Aramaic Incantation Bowls*, 82b *ad* 4–5.

1255 Bhayro *et al.*, *Aramaic Magic Bowls*, 120, 124.

1256 Cf. Martirosyan, *Iranian Personal Names*, 24–25:5.17 with lit.

1257 Shaked *et al.*, *Aramaic Bowl Spells* (2022), 119, 3, 4.

1258 Shaked *et al.*, *Aramaic Bowl Spells* (2013), 38, 4.

1259 See Segal, *Catalogue*, 95a *ad* 056A, 6.

1260 Bhayro *et al.*, *Aramaic Magic Bowls*, 150.

1261 Shaked *et al.*, *Aramaic Bowl Spells* (2022), 90, 2.

1262 Levene, *Jewish Aramaic Curse Texts*, 52 *ad* VA 2434, 3, 5 (unexpl.).

1263 Ciancaglini, *Iranian Loanwords*, 125–126, s. v. *bṭyt'*.

7.3.2 Combined suffixes

7.3.2.1 ***-ak-ān*** > *-ag-ān* (pro-)patronymic[1264]
Myhrqn (to *Myhr*[1265]), cf. Parth. *Mtrkn*;[1266] *Nwkwrgn*/*Nykrygn*[1267]/*Nykwrgn*[1268] (> Arm. *Nixorakan*)[1269] is based on a forerunner of NPers. *Naxvār* > OSyr. *Naxvār*, Arab. *nixwār* "prince", Arm. *Nixor*.[1270]

7.3.2.2 ***-ak-āy*** (hypocoristic)
Mand. *M'ḥrq'y*[1271] (to *Mihr*, cf. MPers. *Mihrag*,[1272] and Parth. *Mtrk* /*Mihrak*/[1273]) and Mand. *Kwš'q'y* (/*Xwašakāy*/, fem.,[1274] to *xwaš*, ↑7.2.2, c, cf. MPers. *Xwašag*[1275]) and possibly Mand. *Qyš'gy*.[1276] The latter is based on MPers. *kēš* "dogma, faith"[1277] with an adjectival *-ag* < *-ak* plus hypocoristic *-āy*.

7.3.2.3 ***-an-āy***
Bwrzny is based on *burz* "high, elevated",[1278] in which case the suffixes are hypocoristic.

1264 Cf. Durkin-Meisterernst, *Grammatik*, 158–159:302–303, Sims-Williams, *Bactrian Personal Names*, 11 (-γ/κανο) and Martirosyan, *Iranian Personal Names*, 17:5.4.
1265 See Shaked *et al.*, *Aramaic Bowl Spells* (2022), 209 *ad* 114, 8; cf. Schmitt, *Personennamen* 134:289 and Martirosyan, *Iranian Personal Names*, 250:459.
1266 See Schmitt, *Personennamen* 139:302m–o.
1267 Cf. Levene, *Jewish Aramaic Curse Texts*, 75.
1268 Bhayro *et al.*, *Aramaic Magic Bowls*, 94.
1269 Martirosyan, *Iranian Personal Names*, 270:527. Cf. the Old Syriac title *nkwrgn* (Ciancaglini, *Iranian Loanwords*, 215).
1270 See Martirosyan, *Iranian Personal Names*, 270:526.
1271 Yamauchi, *Mandaic Incantation Texts*, 17, 4 (<y>), 17; 20, 28.
1272 Gignoux, *Noms propres*, 126:629.
1273 See Schmitt, *Personennamen* 134: 289 with comparanda.
1274 Abudraham and Morgenstern, "Mandaic Incantation(s)," 746, i, 4, 750–752, iii, 27–28, 42–43, iv, 13–14, 37–38.
1275 Gignoux, *Noms propres*, 189:1043, cf. Martirosyan, *Iranian Personal Names*, 201–202:326.
1276 McCullough, *Jewish and Mandean*, E, 4.
1277 Presumably contained in Arm. < Iran. *Kiškēn* according to Martirosyan, *Iranian Personal Names*, 217:371.
1278 See Shaked, "Form and Purpose," 10 *ad* 3, 12.

7.3.2.4 *-īn-īk*

Kuriniq (/*Xvarīnīk*/, Mand., fem.)[1279] is based on *Xwar* "Sun", cf. MPers. *Xwarīn* (hypocoristc).[1280]

7.3.2.5 *-īg-āy*

Zwryg'y (/*Zōrīg-āy*/) is based on MPers. *zōrīg* "powerful, strong",[1281] cf. *Zōrag.*[1282]

7.3.2.6 *-īk-ān*

Kmykn[1283] is apparently based on *kām* "will, desire".

7.3.2.7 *-in-āy* (hypocoristic)

Rdyny[1284] is perhaps based on *Rād* "generous, liberal".[1285]

7.3.2.8 *-it-āy*

Zwyt'y may be based on **zīw* "alive, lively",[1286] cf. Arm. < Iran. *Zuit'ay.*[1287] It is possibly hypocoristic.

7.3.2.9 *-iz-ag* (< *ič-ak-*, diminutive)

Mand. <<w>>*B'ḥrʿz'g*[1288] (fem., based on MPers. *bahr* "portion, share, lot"), Mand. *Kw(')šyz'g*[1289]/*Kwšyz'g*[1290]/*Kw'šʿz'g*[1291] is based on *xwaš* "pleasant, sweet, nice"; cf. MPers. *Bārīzag.*[1292]

1279 Bhayro *et al., Aramaic Magic Bowls,* 87.
1280 Gignoux, *Noms propres,* 187:1034, s. v. *Xvarin* <*Ḥwln(y)*>, presumably a defective spelling of **Ḥwlyn*.
1281 Cf. Naveh and Shaked, *Amulets and Magic Bowls,* 208 *ad* 13, 8.
1282 Gignoux, Jullien and Jullien, *Noms propres,* 151:474ab.
1283 Cf. Müller-Kessler, "Die Zauberschalensammlung," 124 *ad* 036A, 2–3.
1284 Ilan, *Lexicon,* 199–200.
1285 Cf. Gignoux, *Noms propres,* 151: 787 and Martirosyan, *Iranian Personal Names,* 308–309:642.
1286 Not Aramaic as understood by Montgomery, *Aramaic Incantation Texts,* 124 *ad* 2, 3.
1287 See Martirosyan, *Iranian Personal Names,* 198:313 (cf. 197–198:312).
1288 Morgenstern, "Five Mandaic," 114–117:139, 10, 13, 14, 17, 19, 21.
1289 Yamauchi, *Mandaic Incantation Texts,* 17, 4, 17, 20.
1290 Yamauchi, *Mandaic Incantation Texts,* 20, 2, 3, 5, 11.
1291 Cf. Müller-Kessler, "Die Zauberschalensammlung," 135, n. 20 *ad* Hunter 1997–1998.
1292 See Gignoux, *Noms propres,* 55:188.

7.3.2.10 *-i-ag*

Apparently attached to *xwaš* "pleasant, sweet, nice" in *Kwšy'g*.[1293]

7.3.2.11 *-ōy-a*

(<*wy'/h*>, cf. Arab. < early NPers. <*-wyh*> with a secondary vocalization[1294]). The suffix is recorded only in Mandaic; it seems to be closely related to *-ōy*.

a. Males, a'. Adjectival: *Pprwyh*[1295] > Arab. *Babruye*, which is probably based on MPers. *babr* "tiger".[1296] *Šhrwy.'*[1297] is based on MPers. *šahr* "kingdom, city". *Mwškwy'*[1298] is based on either *mušk* "musk" or belongs to ↓7.3.2.15.

b'. Hypocoristic: *Bwktwy'* (of a name containing *buxt* "saved, delivered"[1299]) and *Bynd'dwy'*[1300] which is based on a late form of the passive participle *windād* "found, obtained, gained",[1301] and *Z'dwy'*[1302] (↑7.3.1.2). *Dz'wnwy'*[1303] is perhaps based on MPers. *juwān* > NPers. *jawān* "young" with –'- which was added in order to indicate a pronunciation of late Middle Persian resembling that of New Persian. *Ršnwyh*[1304] and *Yzdwyh*[1305] are based on *Rašn* and *yazd* < *yazata-* (cf. *Yazdōy*[1306]) respectively.

b. Females, a'. Adjectival: For *Gyl'wy'*[1307] cf. *Gylwy* (↑7.3.1.2). *Myšwy'*(fem.) is based on MPers. *mēš* "sheep, ewe".[1308] *Y'qwndwy'* is based on MPers. *yākand*

1293 Isbell, *Corpus*, 61, 2. Cf. the New Persian etymology suggested by F. C. Andreas *apud* Lidzbarski, *Ephemeris*, 100, n. 3.

1294 Thoroughly discussed by Nöldeke, *Persische Studien*, 4–9, 11–29 where numerous such names are explained.

1295 Pognon, *Inscriptions mandaïtes*, 12 and 17.

1296 According to Montgomery, *Aramaic Incantation Texts*, 279b, index, s. v., who refers to Nöldeke, *Persische Studien*, 10.

1297 See Segal, *Catalogue*, 123 *ad* 093M, 13.

1298 Cf. Abudraham, "Three Mandaic," 82 with n. 108.

1299 Cf. McCullough, *Jewish and Mandean*, 33 *ad* D, 3, 11.

1300 Gordon, "Aramaic and Mandaic," 95–100 and pls. 10–13:M, 3.

1301 Cf. Gignoux, *Noms propres*, 182:998; hypocoristic of compound names with *windād* (cf. Gignoux, *Noms propres*, 85:370, 114:551; 182:999–1001; cf. also Schmitt, *Personennamen* 225:543 and Martirosyan, *Iranian Personal Names*, 366:804).

1302 Yamauchi, *Mandaic Incantation Texts*, 23, 9, 12, 14.

1303 Montgomery, *Aramaic Incantation Texts*, 38, 9.

1304 Pognon, *Inscriptions mandaïtes*, 12, 17 and 30.

1305 Pognon, *Inscriptions mandaïtes*, 12.

1306 See Gignoux, Jullien and Jullien 2009: 145:454a–b and cf. Montgomery, *Aramaic Incantation Texts*, 277b, index, s. v.

1307 See Ford, "Another Look," 260 *ad* 104M, 12, 14.

1308 See Segal, *Catalogue*, 103 *ad* 076M, 8. For the reading cf. Ford, "Another Look," 239 *ad* 076M, 5 and 241 *ad* 080M, 2. It has a variant *Myšwy'* (see Ford, "Another Look," 243 *ad* 081M, 18).

(*yākund) "ruby"[1309] *Šyštwyh̲*[1310] perhaps originates from OIran. **čisti-* (Av. *čistay-*) "knowledge, insight; doctrine" with assimilation.

b'. Hypocoristic: *'prydwy'/Apriduia* (/*Āfrīdōy*/[1311]) is based on MPers. *āfrīd* "blessed; created" (↑7.2.1, c) and *Dwktwyh̲*[1312] and *Dwstwy'*[1313] are based on *duxt* and *dōst* (↑7.3.1.1, b, a') respectively.

7.3.2.12 *-ēn-ā*

Perhaps Mand. *W'dmynh'*[1314] if it is based on MPers. *Wādām* "almond"[1315] and followed by *-ēn* (< OIran. "*Stoffadjektiv*" *-aina-*),[1316] i.e. "made, prepared from almonds", in which case the final suffix would be due to Mandaic linguistic interference.

7.3.2.13 *-ak-ōy*

Symkwy may be based on MPers. *sēm* "silver";[1317]aternatively Semitic (↑1.2.1.3.4). Regarding *Šrqwy*, an identification with NPers. *Šērkōh* "lion of the mountain"[1318] is incompatible with its orthography and gender. Cf. perhaps Sogd. *Šyr'k(k)*, i.e. /*Širak*/ which is based on *šir* "good" (with Parthian and possibly Scythian comparanda).[1319]

7.3.2.14 *-ak-āy-a*

Gwk'yy' (Mand., cf. Parth. *Gwk*[1320]); alternatively a gentilic (↑1.3.1.4, a, d').

7.3.2.15 *-k-ōy-a*

Mand. *Mwškwy'* (to **mūš* "mouse",[1321] alternatively to ↑7.3.2.11).

1309 See Segal, *Catalogue*, 124 *ad* 094M, 1.

1310 Müller-Kessler, "Die Zauberschalensammlung," 137b *ad* 105M, 11, 12, 13.

1311 Bhayro *et al.*, *Aramaic Magic Bowls*, 41.

1312 Jursa, "Eine Mandäische," 146, 3.

1313 Cf. Ford, "Another Look," 270 *ad* 109M, 28.

1314 Cf. Müller-Kessler "Die Zauberschalensammlung," 136 *ad* 101M, 9.

1315 Gignoux, *Noms propres*, 169:914.

1316 Cf. Durkin-Meisterernst, *Grammatik*, 167:4.1.3.18, C.

1317 See Montgomery, *Aramaic Incantation Texts*, 222 *ad* 30, 2 who refers to Σείμεικος from Tanais (Justi, *Iranisches Namenbuch* 294a); for comparanda cf. Martirosyan, *Iranian Personal Names*, 321:679 and Ciancaglini, *Iranian Loanwords*, 218.

1318 Justi, *Iranisches Namenbuch*, 296a.

1319 See Lurje, *Personal Names*, 376–377:1191.

1320 See Schmitt, *Personennamen*, 98:192.

1321 Cf. Parth. *Mwšk* (/*Mušk*/, see Schmitt, *Personennamen* 142:306, cf. Martirosyan, *Iranian Personal Names*, 261: 497)..

7.3.2.16 *-ak-ōy-a*

Mand. *Xwašakōya*[1322] is based on *xwaš* (↑7,2,2, c). Mand. *Myškwy'*[1323] is based on MPers. *mēš* "sheep, ewe".

7.4 Two-stem hypocoristicon

'rdbyštwyh[1324] – its base originates from MPers. *Ard-vahišt* (with contraction of the 2nd component) < OIran. **Ṛtā-vahišta-* "Best through Arta".[1325]

7.5 Compound names with suffixal extensions

-ak: *M'bwrz'q* (Mand., fem.)[1326] is based on *Māh-burz* (MPers.) "exalted by the Moon-god."[1327]

-in: *Spdrmyn* (*'yspdrmyn*, fem.) > *Smdrmyn*[1328] (with assimilation) is based on **spāda-* and -**arma-*, thereby meaning "The arm of the army".[1329] Mand. *Pq' mznd'* (fem.),[1330] consists of two adjectives, viz. MPers. *pāk* "clean, pure, holy" and a continuant of Av. *mazant-* "great, spacious; enormous, comprehensive" (cf. *Mazend*).[1331] Both components end with *-ā*. The compound apparently denotes "Pure M.". *-ōy* is perhaps attached to Mand. *Kwz'ḥrwy*[1332] whose initial component perhaps originates from OIran. **Hu-vazar-* "Having good force, might".

1322 MS 2087/37–38 (unpubl., quoted by Abudraham and Morgenstern, "Mandaic Incantation(s)," 754).

1323 Abudraham, "Three Mandaic," 83–85:2, 7, 58.

1324 Abudraham, "Three Mandaic," 83–85:2, 9.

1325 Cf. Gignoux, *Noms propres*, 48: 136.

1326 Morgenstern, "Five Mandaic," 114–115:139, 10, 13, 14.

1327 Cf. Gignoux, *Noms propres*, 110: 527.

1328 Morgenstern and Ford, *Aramaic Incantation Bowls*, 3012, 2.

1329 Therefore the secondary form *Smdrmyn* cannot be compared (as is cautiously suggested by Morgenstern and Ford, *Aramaic Incantation Bowls*, 47 *ad loc.*) with Σμερδομένης in Herodotos, which renders OPers. **Bṛdi-manah-/-maniš* (see Schmitt, *Iranische Personennamen in der griechischen*, 336–337:304 with lit.). For compound names with **spāda-* cf., e.g., Schmitt, *Personennamen* 192–193:442 and Lurje, *Personal Names*, 347–348:1086–1087.

1330 Morgenstern, "Five Mandaic," 112–114:26, 8.

1331 Justi, *Iranisches Namenbuch* 201b.

1332 Yamauchi, *Mandaic Incantation Texts*, 15 [= Pognon, *Inscriptions mandaïtes*, 29], 9), *Kwz'ḥrw* (Yamauchi, *Mandaic Incantation Texts*, 15, 17), *Kz'ḥrw* (Yamauchi, *Mandaic Incantation Texts*, 15, 25), *Kwzḥwrwy* (Yamauchi, *Mandaic Incantation Texts*, 3 [= Pognon, *Inscriptions mandaïtes*, 3], 11).

Bibliography

Abraham, Kathleen, "West Semitic and Judean Brides in Cuneiform Sources from the Sixth Century BCE: New Evidence from a Marriage Contract from Āl-Yahudu," *AfO* 51 (2005–2006): 198–219.

Abraham, Kathleen, "An Inheritence Division among Judeans in Babylonia from the Early Persian Period," pages 206–221 in Lubetski, M. (ed.), *New Seals and Inscriptions, Hebrew, Idumean and Cuneiform*. Hebrew Bible Monographs 8. Sheffield: Sheffield Phoenix Press, 2007.

Abudraham, Ohad, "Three Mandaic Incantation Bowls from the Yosef Matisyahu Collection," *Lešonénu* 77 (2014): 59–98.

Abudraham, Ohad, "An Ancient Mandaic Palimpsest Amulet: An Examination of Three Magic Lamellae from the Schøyen Collection," *ErIs* 34 (2021): 1–12.

Abudraham, Ohad, "A New Reading of a Mandaic Incantation Bowl in the Miami University Art Museum," pages 13–29 in Breuer, Y., Fassberg, S. and Stadel, Ch. (eds.), *David Talshir Memorial Volume*, Mḥqrym bLšwn 20. Jerusalem: Magnes Press, 2023.

Abudraham, Ohad and Morgenstern, Matthew, "Mandaic Incantation(s) on Lead Scrolls from the Schøyen Collection," *JAOS* 137 (2017): 737–765.

Abu Samra, Gaby, "A New Mandaic Magical Bowl," pages 55–69 in Voigt, R. (ed.), *«Durch dein Wort jegliches Ding!»/«Through Thy Word All Things Were Made!». Zum Gedenken an Rudolph Macuch (1919–1993). 2. Mandäistische und samaritanistische Tagung/2. International Conference of Mandaic and Samaritan Studies*. Wiesbaden: Harrassowitz, 2013.

Aharoni, Yohanan, *et al.*, *Arad Inscriptions*. Jerusalem: IES, 1981.

Alstola, Tero, *Judeans in Babylonia: A Study of the Deportees in the Sixth and Fifth Centuries BCE*. CHANE 109. Leiden: Brill, 2020.

Avigad, Nahman, *Hebrew Bullae from the Time of Jeremiah*. Jerusalem: IES, 1986.

Avigad, Nahman and Sass, Benjaim, *Corpus of West Semitic Stamp Seals*. Publications of the Israel Academy of Sciences and Humanities. Jerusalem: IES, 1997.

Bagg, Ariel M., *Die Orts- und Gewässernamen der neuassyrischen Zeit*, (= Répertoire Géographique des Textes Cunéiformes 6, 7). Wiesbaden: Reichert, 2007, 2020.

Bailey, Harold W., "Armeno-indoiranica," TPS 55.1 (1956): 88–126.

Bailey, Harold W., *Dictionary of Khotan Saka*. Cambridge: Cambridge University Press, 1979.

Baker, Heather D., and Parpola, Simo (eds.), *Prosopography of the Neo-Assyrian Empire* 2. Helsinki: The Neo-Assyrian Text Corpus Project, 2000–2001.

Barkay, Gabriel, A Group of Stamped Handles from Judah. ErIs 23 (1992): 113–128 (in Hebrew).

Baumgartner, Walter, Stamm, Johann J., and Hartmann, Benedikt, *Hebräisches und Aramäisches Lexikon zum Alten Testament*. 3rd ed. Leiden: Brill, 1967–1995.

Becking, Bob, "Review of Fleming 2021," *Bibliotheca Orientalis* 79 (2022.): 160–162.

Benveniste, Émile, *Titres et noms propres en iranien ancient*. Travaux de l'Institut d'Études *Iranienne* de l'Université de Paris, 1. Paris: Librairie C. Klincksieck, 1966.

Bhayro, Siam, Ford, James N., Levene, Dan, and -Paz Saar, Ortal, *Aramaic Magic Bowls in the Vorderasiatisches Museum in Berlin: Descriptive List and Edition of Selected Texts*. Magical and Religious Literature of Late Antiquity 7. Leiden: Brill, 2018.

Bloch, Yigal, "Judeans in Sippar and Susa during the First Century of the Babylonian Exile: Assimilation and Perseverance under Neo-Babylonian and Achaemenid Rule," *Journal of the Ancient Near Eastern History* 1 (2014): 119–172.

Bloch, Yigal, "From Horse Trainers to Dependent Workers: The Šušānu Class in the Late Babylonian Period, with a Special Focus on Āl-Yāḫudu Tablets," *KASKAL* 14 (2017): 91–118.

Bogolyubov, Mikhail N., "Arameyskie Transkripcii Iranskix Ličnix Imen v Elamskix Dokumentax iz Krepostnoy Sten'i Persepol'ya," *Philologia Orientalis* (Tbilisi) 4 (1976): 210–214.

Bregstein, Linda, *Seal Use in Fifth Century B.C. Nippur, Iraq: A Study of Seal Selection and Sealing Practices in the Murašû Archive*, doctoral dissertation, University of Pennsylvania, 1993.

Ciancaglini, Claudia A., *Iranian Loanwords in Syriac*, Beiträge zur Iranistik 28. Wiesbaden: Reichert Verlag.

Cook, Edward M., "An Aramaic Incantation Bowl from Khafaje," *BASOR* 285 (1992): 79–81.

Cross, Frank M., "Personal Names in the Samaria Papyri," *BASOR* 344 (2006): 75–90.

Cross, Frank M., "Inscriptions in Phoenician and Other Scripts," pages 333–365 in Stager, L.E., Schloen, J.D. and Master, D.M. (eds.), *Ashkelon 1: Introduction and Overview (1985–2006).* Final Reports of the Leon Levy Expedition to Ashkelon 1. Harvard Semitic Museum Publications. Winona Lake: Eisenbrauns, 2008.

Dandamayev, Muhammad A., *Iranians in Achaemenid Babylonia*. Columbia Lectures on Iranian Studies 6. Costa Mesa: Mazda. Publishers, 1992.

Durand, J.-M., "Review of : Arnaud, D. 1986. *Recherches au Pays d'Aštata*. Emar 6: Textes sumériens et accadiens, 1–3." *RA* 83 (1989): 163–191.

Durkin-Meisterernst, D., *Dictionary of Manichaean Middle Persian and Parthian*. Corpus Fontium Manichaecorum 3.1. Turnhout, 2004.

Durkin-Meisterernst, D., *Grammatik des Westmitteliranischen (Parthisch und Mittelpersisch)*. Grammatica Iranica 1. Veröffentlichungen zur Iranistik 73. Sitzungsberichte der Österreichischen Akademie der Wissenschaften, Philosophisch-Historische Klasse 850, Wien: ÖAW, 2014.

Dušek, Jan, *Les manuscrits Araméens du Wadi Daliyeh et la Samarie vers 450–332 av, J.-C.* CHANE 30. Leiden: Brill, 2007.

Fain, Tatyana, Ford, James N., and Lyavdansky, Alexey, "Aramaic Incantation Bowls at the State Hermitage Museum, St. Petersburg," pages 283–311 in Kogan L. *et al.* (eds.), *Babel und Bibel 9: Proceedings of the 6th Biennial Meeting of the International Association for Comparative Semitics and Other Studies*. Bibel und Babel 9. Winona Lake, Eisenbrauns, 2016.

Faraj, Ali H., "Aramaico orientale e coppe magiche mesopotamiche: riflessioni e definizioni," *Mesopotamia* 42 (2007): 269–275.

Faraj, Ali H., *Coppe magiche dall'antico Iraq*. Milano: Lampi Di Stampa, 2010.

Faraj, Ali H., "Remarks on a New Aramaic Incantation Bowl IM 77781," *JSS* 68 (2023): 90–95.

Faraj, Ali H. and Moriggi, Marco, "Two Incantation Bowls from the Iraq Museum (Baghdad)," *OrNS* 74 (2005): 71–82.

Fleming, Daniel E., *Yahweh before Israel: Glimpses of History in a Divine Name*. Cambridge: Cambridge University Press, 2021.

Ford, James N., "Review of Segal 2000," *JSAI* 26 (2002): 237–272.

Ford, James N., "Another Look at the Mandaic Incantation BM 91715," *JANES* 29 (2002): 31–47.

Ford, James N., "Phonetic Spellings of the Subordinating Particle *d(y)* in the Jewish Babylonian Aramaic Magic Bowls," *Aramaic Studies* 10 (2012): 215–247.

Ford, James N., and Abudraham, Ohad, "Syriac and Mandaic Incantation Bowls," pages 75–111 in Regev, D. and Hizmi, H. (eds.), *Finds Gone Astray: ADCA Confiscated Items*. Publications of the Antiquities Department of the Civil Administration. Jerusalem: ADCA, 2018.

Franco, Fulvio, Five Aramaic Incantation Bowls from Tel Baruda (Coche). *Mesopotamia* 13–14 (1978–1979): 233–249.

Galil, Gershon, Israelite Exiles in Media: A New Look at ND 2443+. *Vetus Testamentum* 59 (2009): 71–79.

Geller, Mark J., "Two Incantation Bowls Inscribed in Syriac and Aramaic," *BSOAS* 39 (1976): 422–427.

Geller, Mark J., "Four Aramaic Incantation Bowls," pages 47–60 in Rendsburg, G. *et al.* (eds.), *The Bible World: Essays in Honor of Cyrus H. Gordon*. New York: Ktav, 1980.

Geller, Mark J., "Eight Incantation Bowls," *OLP* 17 (1986): 101–116.
Geller, Mark J., "More Magic Spells and Formulae," *BSOAS* 60 (1997): 327–335.
Gershevitch, Ilya, "Amber at Persepolis," pages 167–251 in *Studia Classica et Orientalia Antonino Pagliaro Oblata*, 2. Roma: Tip. Eredi Dott. G. Bardi, 1969.
Gignoux, Philippe, *Noms propres sassanides en moyen-perse épigraphique*. IPNB 2/3. SbÖAW Phil-hist. Kl., Sonderpublikation des Instituts für Iranistik. Wien: ÖAW, 1986.
Gignoux, Philippe, *Noms propres sassanides en moyen-perse épigraphique. Supplément (1986–2001)*. IPNB 2/3. ÖAW Phil-hist. Kl., Sonderpublikation des Instituts für Iranistik. Wien: ÖAW, 2003.
Gignoux, Philippe, Jullien, Christelle, and Jullien, Florence, *Noms propres syriaques d'origine iranienne*. IPNB 7/5. Iranische Onomastik 5. SÖAW Phil-hist. Kl. 789. Wien: ÖAW, 2009.
Gil, Moshe, "'The Rādhānite Merchants and the Land of Rādhān," *JESHO* 17 (1974): 299–328.
Goodblatt, David, "'ypr' hwrmyz Mother of King Shapur and 'pr' hwrmyz Mother of Khusro: A Note on the Name 'ypr'/'pr' hwrmyz," *JAOS* 96 (1976): 135–136.
Gordon, Cyrus H., "Aramaic Magical Bowls in the Istanbul and Baghdad Museum," *ArOr* 6 (1934): 319–334 and pls. 10–15.
Gordon, Cyrus H., "An Aramaic Exorcism," *ArOr* 6 (1934): 466–474 and pls. 22–25.
Gordon, Cyrus H., "Aramaic and Mandaic Magic Bowls," *ArOr* 9 (1937): 84–106.
Gordon, Cyrus H., "Aramaic Incantation Bowls," *OrNS* 10 (1941): 116–141; 272–284; 339–360.
Gordon, Cyrus H., "Two Magic Bowls in Teheran," *OrNS* 20 (1951): 306–315.
Gordon, Cyrus H., "Two Aramaic Incantations," pages 231–244 in Tuttle, G.A. (ed.), *Biblical and Near Eastern Essays in Honor of William S. LaSor.* Grand Rapids: Eerdmans, 1978.
Gordon, Cyrus H., "Magic Bowls in the Moriah Collection," *OrNS* 53 (1984): 220–239.
Gorea, Maria, "Trois nouvelles coupes magiques araméennes," *Semitica* 51 (2003): 73–93.
Greenfield, Jonas C., "Tršt'," pages 8: 946 in *Encyclopadia Biblica* Jerusalem: Mossad Bialik, 1982 (in Hebrew).
Greenfield, Jonas C. and Naveh, Joseph "A Mandaic Lead Amulet with Four Incantations," *ErIs* 18 (1985): 97–107.
Hackl, Johannes, *Materialien zur Urkundenlehre und Archivkunde der spätzeitlichen Texte aus Nordbabylonien 1, 2*. Dissertation, University of Vienna. Vienna, 2013.
Harding, G. Lankester, *An Index and Concordance of Pre-Islamic Arabian Names and Inscriptions*. Near and Middle East Series 9. Toronto: University of Toronto Press, 1971.
Harviainen, Tapani, "A Syriac Incantation Bowl in the Finnish National Museum, Helsinki: A Specimen of Eastern Aramaic 'koine'," *StOr* 51/1 (1978).
Harviainen, Tapani, "An Aramaic Incantation Bowl from Borsippa: Another specimen of Eastern Aramaic 'koiné'," *StOr* 51/14 (1981): 1–15.
Herman, Geoffrey, "Jewish Identity in Babylonia in the Period of the Incantation Bowls," pages 131–152 in Rivlin-Katz, D., Hacham, N., Herman, G. and Sagiv, L. (eds), *A Question of Identity: Social, Political and Historical Aspects of Identity Dynamics in Jewish and Other Contexts*. Berlin: de Gruyter, 2019.
Hilprecht, Hermann V. and Clay, Albert T., *Business Documents of the Murashû Sons of Nippur Dated in the Reign of Artaxerxes I. (464–424 B.C.)*. The Babylonian Expedition of the University of Pennsylvania 9. Philadelphia, 1898.
Hinz, Walther, *Altiranisches Sprachgut der Nebenüberlieferungen*. Göttinger Orientforschungen, 3/3. Wiesbaden: Harrassowitz, 1975.
Homès-Fredericq, Denyse, Garelli, Paul, et al. *Ma'allānāte, archives d'un centre provincial de l'empire assyrien*. Akkadica Supplementum 13. Greater Mesopotamia Studies 2. Brussels: Centre Assyriologique Georges Dossin, 2018.

Hunter, Erica C. D., "Two Mandaic Incantation Bowls from Nippur," *BaM* 25 (1994): 605–618 and pl. 25 after 619.

Hunter, Erica C. D., "Incantation Bowls: A Mesopotamian Phenomenon?," *OrNS* 65 (1996): 220–233.

Hunter, Erica C. D., "Two Incantation Bowls from the Collection of the Iraq Museum," *Sumer* 49 (1997–1998): 107–126.

Hutter, Manfred, *Iranische Personennamen in der hebräischen Bibel. Iranisches Personennamenbuch*, 7, Iranische Namen in semitischen Nebenüberlieferungen, Fasz. 2. Iranische Onomastik 14. SbÖAW, Phil-hist. Kl. 860. Wien: ÖAW, 2015.

Huyse, Philip, *Die dreisprachige Inschrift Šābuhrs I. an der Ka`ba-i Zaradušt (SKZ)*. Corpus Inscriptionum Iranicarum 3/1/1. London: School of Oriental and African Studies, 1999.

Ilan, Tal, (with the collaboration of K. Hünefeld) *Lexicon of Jewish Names in Late Antiquity. Part 4: The Eastern Diaspora 330 BCE–650 CE*. Texts and Studies in Ancient Judaism 141. Tübingen: Mohr Siebeck, 2011.

Isbell, Charles D., *Corpus of the Aramaic Incantation Bowls*. SBL Dissertation Series 17. Missoula: Scholars Press, 1975.

Isbell, Charles D., "Two New Aramaic Incantation Bowls," *BASOR* 223 (1976): 15–23.

Jarry, Jacques, "Inscriptions arabes, syriaques et grecques du massif du Belus en Syrie du Nord," *Annales Islamologiques* 7 (1967): 139–220.

Jursa, Michael, "Eine Mandäische Zauberschale in Schweizer Privatbesitz," AfO 48–49 (2001–2002): 146.

Justi, Ferdinand, *Iranisches Namenbuch*. Marburg: N. G. Elwert (repr. Hildesheim 1963), 1895.

Juusola, Hannu, *Linguistic Pecularities in the Aramaic Magic Bowl Texts*. StOr 86. Helsinki: Finnish Oriental Society, 1999.

Keiser, Clarence E.. *Letters and Contracts from Erech, Written in the Neo-Babylonian Period.* Babylonian Inscriptions in the Collection of J. B. Nies 1. New Haven: Yale University Press, 1917.

Kiperwasser, Reuven and Shapira, Dan, "Encounters between Iranian Myth and Rabbinic Mythmakers in the Babylonian Talmud," pages 285–304 in Gabbay, U. and Secunda, Sh. (eds.), *Encounters by the Rivers of Babylon: Scholarly Conversations between Jews, Iranians and Babylonians in Antiquity*. Texts and Studies in Ancient Judaism 160. Tübingen: Mohr Siebeck, 2014.

Kupper, Jean-Robert, *Lettres royales du temps de Zimri-Lim*. Archives Royales de Mari 28. Paris: Études et Recherche sur les Civilisations, 1998.

Lecoq, Pierre. "Review of Gignoux 1986," StIr 22 (1993): 127–133.

Lemaire, André, "Review of Aharoni 1981," OrNS 52 (1983): 444–447.

Levene, Dan, *Jewish Aramaic Curse Texts from Late-Antique Mesopotamia*. Magical and Religious Literature of Late Antiquity 2. Leiden: Brill, 2013.

Lidzbarski, Mark, *Ephemeris für Semitische Epigraphik, 1, 1900–1902*. Giessen: Alfred Töpelmann, 1902.

Lipiński, Edward, "Review of Dušek 2007," *Palamedes* 3 (2008): 227–246.

Lipiński Edward, *Studies in Aramaic Inscriptions and Onomastics* 3: Maʿlānā. Orientalia Lovaniensia Analecta 200. Leuven: Leuven University Press, 2010.

Lipschits, Oded, "'Those who live in these ruins in the land of Israel' (Ez. 33:24): Some Thoughts on Living in the Shadow of Ruins in Persian-period Judah." pages 279–304 in Yahwism under the Achaemenid Empire, Prof. Shaul Shaked in memoriam. Gad Barnea and Reinhard Kratz, eds. (BZAW; Berlin: de Gruyter, forthcoming 2024).

Lurje, Pavel B. 2010. *Personal Names in Sogdian Texts*. IPNB 2/8. Iranische
Onomastik 8. SbÖAW Phil-hist. Kl. 808. Vienna.

Martinez Borobio, E., "A Magical Bowl in Judaeo-Aramaic," *Isimu* 6 (2003): 323–336.

Martirosyan, Hrach, *Iranian Personal Names in Armenian Collateral Tradition*. IPNB 5/3. Iranische Onomastik 17. SbÖAW Phil-hist. Kl. 912. Wien: ÖAW, 2021.
Mayrhofer, Manfred, *Onomastica Persepolitana: Das altiranische Namengut der Persepolis-Täfelchen*. SbÖAW Phil-hist. Kl. 286. Wien: ÖAW, 1973.
Mayrhofer, Manfred, *Die avestischen Namen*, IPNB 1/1. ÖAW Phil-hist. Kl., Sonderpublikation der iranischen Kommission. Wien: ÖAW, 1977.
McCullough, William S., *Jewish and Mandean Incantation Bowls in the Royal Ontario Museum*. Near and Middle East Series 5. Toronto: University of Toronto Press, 1967.
Misgav, Haggai, "Ostraca from Tell Jemmeh," pages 1031–1037 in Ben-Shlomo, D. and Van Beek, G. (eds.), *The Smithsonian Institute Excavation at Tell Jemmeh, Israel, 1970–1990*. Smithsonian Contributions to Anthropology 50. Washington: Smithsonian Institute Scholarly Press, 2014.
Montgomery, James A., *Aramaic Incantation Texts from Nippur*. PBS 3. Philadelphia: University Museum, 1913.
Moriggi, Marco, "Two New Incantation Bowls from Rome (Italy)," *Aramaic Studies* 3 (2005): 43–58.
Moriggi, Marco, *A Corpus of Syriac Incantation Bowls: Syriac Magical Texts from Late-Antique Mesopotamia*. Magical and Religious Literature of Late Antiquity 3. Leiden: Brill, 2014.
Morgenstern, Matthew, "Mandaic Magic Bowls in the Moussaieff Collection: A Preliminary Survey," pages 157–170 in Lubetski, M. and E. (eds.), *New Inscriptions and Seals Relating to the Biblical World*. SBL Archaeology and Biblical Studies 19. Atlanta: SBL, 2012.
Morgenstern, Matthew, "Five Mandaic Magic Bowls from the Moussaieff Collection," *ErIs* 34 (2021): 106–122.
Morgenstern, Matthew, and Abudraham, Ohad, "A Mandaean Lamella and Its Parallels: BM 132957+ BM 132947+ BM 132954," pages 202–240 in Moriggi, M. and Bhayro, S. (eds.), *Studies in the Syriac Magical Traditions*. Magical and Religious Literature of Late Antiquity 9. Leiden: Brill, 2022.
Morgenstern, Matthew, and Ford, James N., *Aramaic Incantation Bowls in Museum Collections, 1: The Frau Professor Hilprecht Collection of Babylonian Antiquities, Jena*. Magical and Religious Literature of Late Antiquity 8. Leiden: Brill, 2019.
Morgenstern, Matthew, and Schlütter, Maleen, "A Mandaic Amulet on Lead – MS 2087/1." *ErIs* 32 (2016): 115–134 (in Hebrew).
Morony, Michael G., "Magic and Society in Late Sasanian Iran," pages 83–107 in Noegel, S., Walker, J. and Wheeler, B. (eds.), *Prayer, Magic and the Stars in the Ancient and Late Antique World*. University Park: The Pennsylvania State University Press, 2003.
Müller-Kessler, Christa, "Eine Mandäische Zauberschale im Museum für Vor- und Frühgeschichte zu Berlin," *OrNS* 63 (1994): 5–9.
Müller-Kessler, Christa, "The Story of Bguzan-Lilit, Daughter of Zanay-Lilit," *JAOS* 116 (1996): 185–195.
Müller-Kessler, Christa, "A Mandaic Gold Amulet in the British Museum," *BASOR* 311 (1998): 83–88.
Müller-Kessler, Christa, "Die Zauberschalensammlung des British Museum," *AfO* 48–49 (2001–2002): 115–145.
Müller-Kessler, Christa, *Die Zauberschalentexte in der Hilprecht-Sammlung, Jena, und weitere Nippur-Texte anderer Sammlungen*. Texte und Materialen der Hilprecht Collection, 7. Wiesbaden: Harrassowitz, 2005.
Müller-Kessler, Christa, "Syrische Zauberschalen – Korrekturen und Nachträge," *WO* 36 (2006): 116–130.
Müller-Kessler, Christa, "Review of Moriggi, M. 2004," *La Lingua delle coppe magiche siriache*. Quaderni di Semitistica 21. Florence. WO 36 (2006): 265–272.
Müller-Kessler, Christa, "A Mandaic Lead Roll in the Collections of the Kelsey Museum, Michigan" Fighting Evil Entities of Death," ARAM 22 (2010): 477–493.

Müller-Kessler, Christa, "Beiträge zum Babylonisch-Talmudisch-Aramäischen Wörterbuch," OrNS 80 (2011): 214–251.
Müller-Kessler, Christa, and Kwasman, Theodore, "A Unique Talmudic Aramaic Incantation Bowl," *JAOS* 120 (2000): 159–165.
Myhrman, David W., "An Aramaic Incantation Text," pages 342–351 in *Hilprecht Anniversary Volume*. Leipzig: J. C. Hinrichs, 1909.
Na'aman, Nadav and Zadok, Ran, "Sargon II's Deportations to Israel and Philistia (716–708 B.C.)," *JCS* 40 (1988): 36–46.
Nashef, Khaled, *Die Orts- und Gewässernamen der mittelbabylonischen und mittelassyrischen Zeit*, (= Répertoire Géographique des Textes Cunéiformes 5). Wiesbaden: Reichert, 1982.
Naveh, Joseph, "The Aramaic Ostraca from Tel Beer-sheva (Seasons 1971–1976)," *Tel Aviv* 6 (1979): 182–198.
Naveh, Joseph, "Published and Unpublished Aramaic Ostraca," *'Atiqot* 17 (1985): 114–121 = Naveh 2009: 117–131.
Naveh, Joseph, "Writing and Scripts in Seventh-Century B. C. E. Palestine: The New Evidence from Tell Jemmeh," *IEJ* 35 (1985): 11–15.
Naveh, Joseph, "Some New Jewish Palestinian Aramaic Amulets," *JSAI* 26 (2002): 231–236.
Naveh, Joseph, *Studies in West Semitic Epigraphy: Selected Papers*. Jerusalem: Magnes Press, 2009.
Naveh, Joseph and Shaked, Shaul, *Magic Spells and Formulae: Aramaic Incantations of Late Antiquity*. Jerusalem: Magnes Press, 1993.
Naveh, Joseph and Shaked, Shaul, *Amulets and Magic Bowls: Aramaic Incantations of Late Antiquity*, 3rd ed. Jerusalem: Magnes Press, 1998.
Nöldeke, Theodor, *Persische Studien* 1–2. SbÖAW Phil-hist. Kl. 116/1/8, 126/12. Wien: ÖAW, 1888, 1892.
Nöldeke, Theodor, "Review of Pognon 1898," WZKM 12 (1898): 141–147; 353–361.
Nöldeke, Theodor, "Names," pages 3271–3331 in Cheyne, T.K. and Black, J.S. (eds.), *Encyclopaedia Biblica: A Critical Dictionary of the Literary, Political and Religious History, the Archaeology, Geography and Natural History of the Bible* 3. London: Adam and Charles Black, 1902.
Noth, Martin, "Der Wallfahrtsweg zum Sinai (Nu 33)," *Palästinajahrbuch* 36 (1940): 5–28 (reprinted in Noth 1971: 55–74).
Noth, Martin, *Aufsätze zur biblischen Landes- und Altertumskunde. 1: Archäologische, exegetiche und topographische Untersuchungen zur Geschichte Israels*. Neukirchen-Vluyn: Neukirchener Verlag, 1971.
Oelsner, Joachim, "Review of Naveh and Shaked 1985," OLZ 84 (1989): 38–41.
Pirngruber, Reinhard, "Minor Archives from First-Millennium BCE Babylonia: The Archive of Iššar-tarībi from Sippar," *JCS* 72 (2020): 165–198.
Pognon, Henri, "Une incantation contre les génies malfaisants en mandaïte," *Mémoires de la Societé Linguistique du Paris* 8 (1892): 193–234.
Pognon, Henri, *Inscriptions mandaïtes des coupes de Khouabir*, Paris: Impr. Nationale, 1898.
Porten, Bezalel, *Archives from Elephantine: The Life of an Ancient Jewish Military Colony*. Berkeley: University of California Press, 1968.
Porten, Bezalel and Yardeni, Ada, *Textbook of Aramaic Documents from Ancient Egypt, newly Copied, Edited and Translated into Hebrew and English*, 1: *Letters*; 3: *Literature, Accounts, Lists*; 4: *Ostraca and Assorted Inscriptions*. Jerusalem: Magness Press, 1986, 1993, 1999.
Radner, Karen, *Die neuassyrischen Texten von Dūr-Katlimmu*. Berichte der Ausgrabungen aus Tell Šēḫ Ḥamad 6, Berlin: Dietrich Reimer Verlag, 2002.
Radner, Karen, "The 'Lost Tribes of Israel' in the Context of the Resettlement Programme of the Assyrian Empire," pages 101–123 in Hasegawa, Sh., Levin, Ch. and Radner, K. (eds.) *The Last Days of the Kingdom of Israel*. BZAW 511. Berlin: De Gruyter, 2019.

Radner, Karen and Parpola, Simo (eds.), *Prosopography of the Neo-Assyrian Empire* 1. Helsinki: The Neo-Assyrian Text Corpus Project, 1998–1999.
Richter, Thomas, *Bibliographisches Glossar des Hurritischen*. Wiesbaden: Harrassowitz, 2012.
Rudolph, Wilhelm, *Esra und Nehemia samt 3. Esra*. HAT 1/20. Tübingen: J. C. B. Mohr, 1949.
Schmitt, Rüdiger, "Artaxerxes, Ardašīr und Verwandte," *Incontri Linguistici* 5 (1979 [1980]): 61–72.
Schmitt, Rüdiger, "Iranische Namen," pages 678–690 in *Namenforschung. Ein Internationales Handbuch zur Onomastik*, 1. Teilband. Berlin: De Gruyter, 1995.
Schmitt, Rüdiger, "Zu Weiterungen rund um den Namen iran. *Š(iy)ātibara," *Archiv für Bulgarische Philologie* 3 (1999): 169–172.
Schmitt, Rüdiger, *Die Iranischen und Iranier-Namen in den Schriften Xenophons (Iranica Graeca Vetustiora 2)*. Veröffentlichungen der Kommission für Iranistik 29. SbÖAW Phil-hist. Kl. 692. Wien: ÖAW, 2002.
Schmitt, Rüdiger, *Iranische Personennamen in der neuassyrischen Nebenüberlieferung*. IPNB 7/1A. Iranische Onomastik 6. SbÖAW Phil-hist. Kl. 792. Wien: ÖAW, 2009.
Schmitt, Rüdiger, *Iranische Personennamen in der griechischen Literatur vor Alexander d. Gr.* IPNB 5/5A. Iranische Onomastik 9. SbÖAW Phil-hist. Kl. 823. Wien: ÖAW, 2011.
Schmitt, Rüdiger, *Personennamen in Parthischen Epigraphischen Quellen*. IPNB 2/5. Iranische Onomastik 15. SbÖAW Phil-hist. Kl. 881. Wien: ÖAW, 2016.
Schmitt, Rüdiger, "Die Rolle des Altpersischen im achaimenidischen Palästina," pages 321–342 in Hübner, U. and Niehr, H. (eds.), *Sprachen in Palästina im 2. Und 1. Jahrtausend v. Chr.* ADPV 43. Wiesbaden: Harrassowitz, 2017.
Schwab, Moïse, "Les coupes magiques et l'hydromancie dans l'antiquité orientale," *Proceedings of the Society of Biblical Archaeology* 12 (1890): 292–342.
Schwartz, Martin, "Sasm, Sesen, St. Sisinnios, Sesengen Barpharangēs, and ... 'Semanglof'," *Bulletin of the Asia Institute* 10 (1996 [1998]): 253–257.
Segal, Judah B., *Catalogue of the Aramaic and Mandaic Incantation Bowls in the British Museum*. London: British Museum Press, 2000.
Shaked, Shaul, "Iranian Influences on Judaism First Century B.C.E. to Second Century C.E.," pages 308–324, 441–442 in Davies, W.D. and Finkelstein, L. (eds.), *The Cambridge History of Judaism* 1. Cambridge: Cambridge University Press 2024, 1984.
Shaked, Shaul, "'Peace Be upon You, Exalted Angels': On Hekhalot, Liturgy and Incantation Bowls," *Jewish Studies Quaterly* 2 (1995): 197–219.
Shaked, Shaul, "Jesus in the Magic Bowl: Apropos Dan Levene's '... and by the Names of Jesus ...'," *Jewish Studies Quaterly* 6 (1999): 309–319.
Shaked, Shaul, "Form and Purpose in Aramaic Spells: Some Jewish Themes (The Poetic of Magic Spells)," pages 1–30 in Shaul Shaked (ed.), *Officina Magica: Essays on the Practice of Magic in Antiquity. Conference Proceedings of the Institute of Jewish Studies, University of London.* IJS Studies in Judaica 4. Leiden: Brill 1–30, 2005.
Shaked, Shaul, "Rabbis in Incantation Bowls," pages 97–119 in Geller, M.J. (ed.), *The Archaeology and Material Culture of the Babylonian Talmud*. Leiden: Brill, 2015.
Shaked, Shaul, *et al.*, *Aramaic Bowl Spells: Jewish Babylonian Aramaic Bowls* 1. Magical and Religious Literature of Late Antiquity 1. Manuscripts in the Schøyen Collection 20. Leiden: Brill, 2013.
Shaked, Shaul, *et al.*, *Aramaic Bowl Spells: Jewish Babylonian Aramaic Bowls* 2. Magical and Religious Literature of Late Antiquity 10. Manuscripts in the Schøyen Collection 41. Leiden: Brill, 2022.
Sims-Williams, Nicholas, *Bactrian Personal Names*. IPNB 2/7. Iranische Onomastik 7. SbÖAW Phil-hist. Kl. 806. Wien: ÖAW, 2010.
Smith, Mark S., *The Early History of God: Yahweh and the Other Deities of Ancient Israel.* San Francisco: Harper & Row, 1990.

Sokoloff, M., *A Dictionary of Jewish Babylonian Aramaic of the Talmudic and Geonic Periods*. 2nd revised and expanded ed. Ramat Gan: Bar Ilan University Press, 2020.
Spek, Robartus J. van der, "Did Cyrus the Great Introduce a New Policy Towards Subdued Nations? Cyrus in Assyrian Perspective," *Persica* 10 (1982): 278–283.
Stamm, Johann J., "Hebräische Frauennamen," pages 301–339 in B. Hartmann *et al.* (eds.), *Hebräische Wortforschung. Festschrift zum 80. Geburtstag von Walter Baumgartner.* Supplement to Vetus Testamentum 16. Leiden: Brill, 1967.
Stamm, Johann J., *Beiträge zur Hebräischen und Altorientalischen Namenkunde.* Jenni, E. and Klopfenstein, M.A., eds. OBO 30. Freibug and Göttingen: Vandenhoeck Ruprecht, 1980.
Stark, Jürgen K. *Personal Names in Palmyrene Inscriptions*. Oxford: Clarendon Press, 1971.
Stigers, Harold G., "Neo- and Late Babylonian Documents from the John Frederick Lewis Collection," *JCS* 28 (1976): 3–59.
Strassmaier, Johann N., *Inschriften von Darius, König von Babylon*. Leipzig, 1892.
Tavernier, Jan, *Iranica in the Achaemenid Period (ca. 550–330 B.C.): Lexicon of Old Iranian Proper Names and Loanwords, Attested in Non-Iranian Texts*. Orientalia Lovaniensia Analecta 158. Leuven: Peeters, 2007.
Thordarson, Fridrik, *Ossetic Grammatical Studies*. Veröffentlichungen zur Iranistik 48. SbÖAW Phil-hist. Kl. 788. The Institute for Comparative Research in Human Culture B/131. Wien: ÖAW, 2009.
Tigay, Jeffrey H., *You Shall Have no Other Gods: Israelite Religion in the Light of Hebrew Inscriptions*. HSS 12. Atlanta: Scholars Press, 1986.
Tolini, Gauthier, "Les repas du Grand Roi en Babylonie: Cambyse et le palais d'Abanu," pages 237–254 in Faivre, X., Lion, B. and Michel, C. (eds.), *Et il y eut un esprit dans l'homme. Jean Bottéro et la Mésopotamie.* Travaux de la Maison René-Ginovès. Paris: De Boccard, 2009.
Ungnad, Arthur, *Vorderasiatische Schriftdenkmäler* der *königlichen Museen zu Berlin* 3. Leipzig: J. C. Hinrich'sche Buchhandlung, 1907.
Waerzeggers, Caroline, "Locating Contact in the Babylonian Exile: Some Reflections on Tracing Judean-Babylonian Encounters in Cuneiform Texts," pages 131–146 in Gabbay, U. and Secunda, Sh. (eds.), *Encounters by the Rivers of Babylon: Scholarly Conversations between Jews, Iranians and Babylonians in Antiquity.* Texts and Studies in Ancient Judaism 160. Tübingen: Mohr Siebeck, 2014.
Weszeli, Michaela, "Eseleien," *WZKM* 86 (1996): 461–478.
Wohlstein, Josef, "Über einige aramäische Inschriften auf Thongefässen des Königlichen Museums zu Berlin," *ZA* 8 (1893): 313–340; 9 (1894): 11–41.
Yahalom-Mack, Naama, Panitz-Cohen, Nava, Rollston, Christopher A. *et al.*, "The Iron Age IIA 'Benyaw Inscription' on a Jar from Tel Abel Beth Maacah," *PEQ* 155: 68–90, 2021.
Yamauchi, Edwin M., "Aramaic Magic Bowls," *JAOS* 85 (1965): 511–523.
Yamauchi, Edwin M., *Mandaic Incantation Texts*. AOS 49. New Haven: American Oriental Society, 1967.
Zadok, Ran, "Review of Hinz 1975," *Bibliotheca Orientalis* 33 (1976): 213–219.
Zadok, Ran, "On Five Iranian Names in the Old Testament," *VT* 26 (1976): 246–247.
Zadok, Ran, *On West Semites in Babylonia during the Chaldean and Achaemenian Periods: An Onomastic Study*. Jerusalem : Wanaarta, 1978.
Zadok, Ran, *The Jews in Babylonia during the Chaldean and Achaemenian Periods according to Babylonian Sources*. Studies in the History of the Jewish People and the Land of Israel. Monograph Series 3. Haifa, 1979.
Zadok, Ran, "Die nichthebräischen Namen der Israeliten vor dem hellenistischen Zeitalter," UF 17 (1985): 387–398.
Zadok, Ran, "Zur Struktur der nachbiblischen jüdischen Personennamen semitischen Ursprungs," *Trumah* (Jahrbuch der Hochschule für jüdische Studien, Heidelberg) 1 (1987): 243–343.

Zadok, Ran, *The Pre-Hellenistic Israelite Anthroponymy and Prosopography*. Orientalia Lovaniensia Analecta 28. Leuven: Peeters, 1988.

Zadok, Ran, "Some Kassite and Iranian Names from Mesopotamia," NABU 1990/72.

Zadok, Ran, "On the Post-Biblical Jewish Onomasticon and Its Background," pages v–xxviii in Kasher, A. and Oppenheimer, A. (eds.), *Dor le-Dor. From the End of the Biblical Times up to the Redaction of the Talmud*. Studies in Honor of Joshua Efron. Jerusalem: Mossad Bialik, 1995.

Zadok, Ran, "Some Iranians in Cuneiform Documents," NABU 1997/149.

Zadok, Ran, "A Prosopography of Samaria and Edom/Idumea," *Ugarit Forschungen* 30 (1998): 781–828.

Zadok, Ran, "On the Prosopography and Onomastics of Syria-Palestine and Adjacent Regions," *Ugarit Forschungen* 32 (2000), 599–674.

Zadok, Ran, *The Earliest Diaspora: Israelites and Judeans in Pre-Hellenistic Mesopotamia*. Publications of the Diaspora Research Institute, 151. Tel Aviv: Diaspora Research Institute, 2002.

Zadok, Ran, "Two Old Iranian Anthroponyms," NABU 2002/45.

Zadok, Ran, "Israelites, Judeans and Iranians in Mesopotamia and Adjacent Regions," pages 2: 98–127 in Ellens, J.H., Ellens, D., Knierim, R.P and Kalimi, I. (eds.), *God's Word for Our World. Theological and Cultural Studies in Honor of Simon John De Vries*. London: T & T Clark, 2004.

Zadok, Ran, *Iranische Personennamen in der neu- und spätbabylonischen Nebenüberlieferung*. IPNB 7/1B. Iranische Onomastik 4. SbÖAW Phil-hist. Kl. 777. Wien: ÖAW, 2009.

Zadok, Ran, "Occupations and Status Categories (Classes) in Borsippa," pages xxxi–lxiii in Shahar, Y., Oppenheimer, A. and Mustigman, R. (eds.), *Israel and the Diaspora in the Time of the Second Temple and the Mishna. Arieh Kasher Memorial Volume*. Teudah 25. Tel Aviv: Tel-Aviv University Press, 2012.

Zadok, Ran, "Israelites and Judeans in the Neo-Assyrian Documentation (732–602 BCE): An Overview of the Sources and a Socio-Historical Assessment," *BASOR* 374 (2015): 159–189.

Zadok, Ran, A *Prosopography of the Israelites in Old Testament Traditions: A Contextualized Handbook*. Tel Aviv: Archaeological Center Publications, 2018.

Zadok, Ran, "People from Countries West and North of Babylonia in Babylon during the Reign of Nebuchadnezzar," *HeBAI* 7 (2018): 112–129.

Zadok, Ran, "Onomastics as a Historical Source: How to Use and to Deal with It," pages 399–488 in Lanfranchi, G.B., Mattila, R. and Rollinger, R. (eds.), *Writing Neo-Assyrian History: Sources, Problems and Approaches. Proceedings of the International Meeting, University of Helsinki, September 22nd–25th, 2014*. Publications of the Foundation for Finish Assyriological Research 24. State Archives of Assyria Studies 29. Helsinki: Neo-Assyrian Text Corpus Project, 2019.

Zadok, Ran, "On the Arameans and the Indigenous Population in Babylonia from the Period of the Neo-Babylonian Empire down to the End of the Sasanian Empire," pages 34–68 in Maeir, A., Berlejung, A., Eshel, E. and Oshima, T. (eds.), *New Perspectives on Aramaic Epigraphy in Mesopotamia, Qumran, Egypt and Idumea. Proceedings of the Joint RIAB Minerva Center and the Jeselsohn Epigraphic Center of Jewish History Conference Held on March 1–3, 2017 in Ramat-Gan/Jerusalem and a RIAB Minerva Center Workshop Held on 4: May 18, 2018 in Leipzig*. Orientalische Religionen in der Antike 40. Tubingen: Mohr Siebeck, 2021.

Zadok, Ran, "Issues of the Deportations of the Israelites-Judeans and Their Aftermath," H*e*BAI 11 (2022): 113–147.

Zehnder, Markus, P., *Umgang mit Fremden in Israel und Assyrien. Ein Beitrag zur Anthropologie des "Fremden" in Licht antiker Quellen*. Beiträge zur Wissenschaft vom Alten und Neuen Testament. NF 8 (= 168). Stuttgart: Kohlhammer, 2005.

Zimmer, Stefan, "Zur sprachlichen Deutung sasanidischer Personennamen," A*o*F 18 (1991): 109–150.

Abbreviations

AB	The Anchor Bible
ADPV	Abhandlungen des Deutschen Palästina-Vereins
AGAJU	Arbeiten zur Geschichte des antiken Judentums und des Urchristentums
AIA	Stephen A. Kaufman. *The Akkadian Influences on Aramaic.* Assyriological Studies 19. Chicago: University of Chicago Press, 1974
AIAL	Ancient Israel and Its Literature
AJS>	*Association for Jewish Studies*
AJSL	*American Journal of Semitic Languages and Literature*
AL	Andrè Lemaire
ART	Bowman, Raymond A. *Aramaic Ritual Texts from Persepolis.* University of Chicago Oriental Institute publications. Chicago: University of Chicago Press, 1970
ASN	Hinz, W. *Altiranisches Sprachgut der Nebenüberlieferungen.* Wiesbaden: Harrassowitz, 1975
ASOR	American Schools of Oriental Research
BA	*Biblical Archaeologist*
BaAr	Babylonische Archive
BASOR	*Bulletin of the American Schools of Oriental Research*
BM	British Museum
BMA	Roth, Martha T. *Babylonian Marriage Agreements: 7th–3rd Centuries B.C.* AOAT 222. Neukirchen: Neukirchener Verlag, 1989
BO	*Bibliotheca Orientalis*
BSOAS	*Bulletin of the School of Oriental and African Studies*
C	Cowley, Arthur E. *Aramaic Papyri of the Fifth Century B.C.* Oxford: Clarendon Press, 1923
CAL	Kaufman, Stephen A., n. d. "Comprehensive Aramaic Lexicon Project." http://cal.huc.edu
CBQ	*Catholic Biblical Quarterly*
CD	Walter E. Crum, *A Coptic Dictionary.* Oxford: Clarendon Press, 1939
CDD	Chicago Demotic Dictionary (online access: https://isac.uchicago.edu/research/publications/chicago-demotic-dictionary)
CHANE	Culture and History of the Ancient Near East
CG	H. Lozachmeur. *La collection Clermont-Ganneau: Ostraca, épigraphes sur jarre, étiquettes de bois.* 2 vols. MPAIBL N.S. 35. Paris: Boccard, 2006
CIS	Copenhagen
CUSAS 28	Pearce, Laurie, and Cornelia Wunsch. 2014. *Documents of Judean Exiles and West Semites in Babylonia in the Collection of David Sofer.* CUSAS 28. Bethesda: CDL Press
DAÉ	Grelot, Pierre. *Documents araméens d'Égypte*. Paris: Éditions du Cerf, 1972
DJA	Michael Sokoloff. *A Dictionary of Judean Aramaic.* Ramat-Gan: Bar Ilan University Press, 2003
DJPA^3	Michael Sokoloff. *A Dictionary of Jewish Palestinian Aramaic.* 3rd rev. and expanded edition. Ramat-Gan: Bar Ilan University Press, 2017
DJD	Discoveries in the Judaean Desert

https://doi.org/10.1515/9783111018638-020

DNWSI	Hoftijzer, J., K. Jongeling, Richard C. Steiner, Bezalel Porten, A. Mosak Moshavi, and Charles-F. Jean. *Dictionary of the North-west Semitic inscriptions*. 2 vols. Leiden: Brill, 1995
EI	*Eretz Israel*
EPE	Bezalel Porten, Joel J. Farber, Cary J. Martin, Günther Vittmann, Leslie S. B. MacCoull, Sarah Clackson, Simon Hopkins, and Ramon Katzoff. *The Elephantine Papyri in English: Three Millennia of Cross-Cultural Continuity and Change*. DMOA 22. 2nd rev. ed. Leiden: Brill, 2011
EstBib	*Estudios biblicos*
FAT	Forschungen zum Alten Testaments
GEA	Takamitsu Muraoka and Bezalel Porten. *A Grammar of Egyptian Aramaic*. HdO 32. 2nd rev. ed. Leiden: Brill, 2003
HALOT	Ludwig Koehler and Walter Baumgartner. *The Hebrew and Aramaic Lexicon of the Old Testament*, trans. Mervyn E. J. Richardson. 5 vols. Rev. ed. by W. Baumgartner and J. J. Stamm. Leiden: Brill, 1994–2000
HAT	Handbuch zum Alten Testament
HKAT	Göttinger Handkommentar zum Alten Testament
HSS	Harvard Semitic Studies
HTR	*Harvard Theological Review*
IA	*Institute of Archaeology*
ICC	The International Critical Commentary
IEJ	*Israel Exploration Journal*
IM	Tablets in the Iraq Museum, Baghdad
ISAP	Institute for the Study of Aramaic Papyri
JSOTSup	*Journal for the Study of the Old Testament*, Supplement Series
JAAJ	*Judaïsme Ancien – Ancient Judaism*
JANER	*Journal of Ancient Near Eastern Religions*
JANES	*Journal of the Ancient Near Eastern Society*
JAOS	*Journal of the American Oriental Society*
JEMAHS	*Journal of Eastern Mediterranean Archaeology Heritage Studies*
JNES	*Journal of Near Eastern Studies*
JPS	Jewish Publication Society
JQR	*Jewish Quarterly Review*
JSJ	*Journal for the Study of Judaism in the Persian, Hellenistic, and Roman Period*
JSP	Judea and Samaria Publications
KAI	Herbert Donner, and Wolfgang Röllig. *Kanaanäische und aramäische Inschriften*, vol. 2: Kommentar. Wiesbaden: Harrassowitz, 1973
KHC	Kurzer Hand-Commentar zum Alten Testament
MdB	*Le Monde de la Bible*
NAP	*Moore, James D. 2022. New Aramaic Papyri from Elephantine in Berlin. Studies on Elephantine 1. Leiden: Brill. https://brill.com/view/title/61396.*
Nbn	Strassmaier, J. N., and Basil Thomas Alfred Evetts. 1889. *Babylonische Texte: von den Thontafeln des Britischen Museums*. 13 vols. Leipzig: E. Pfeiffer
NICOT	New International Commentary on the Old Testament
NSR	Numismatic Studies and Researches
NTOA	Novum Testamenturn et Orbis Antiquus

OBO	Orbis Biblicus et Orientalis
OECT 9	McEwan, Gilbert J. P. 1984. *Late Babylonian texts in the Ashmolean Museum*, Oxford: Oxford University Press
ORA	Orientalische Religionen in der Antike/Oriental Religions in Antiquity
OTL	Old Testament Library
PEQ	*Palestine Exploration Quarterly*
PJ	*Palästina-Jahrbuch*
PNA 1	Parpola, S. and Radner, K. (eds.) 1998–1999. *The Prosopography of the Neo-Assyrian Empire* 1. Helsinki
PNA 2–3	S. Parpola and Baker, H.D. (eds.) 2000–2001 and 2002–2011 respectively. *The Prosopography of the Neo-Assyrian Empire* 2–3. Helsinki
RG	Zadok, Ran. 1985. *Geographical Names According to New- and Late-Babylonian Texts*. RGTC 8 Wiesbaden: L. Reichert
RVV	Religionsgeschichtliche Versuche und Vorarbeiten
SBL	Society of Biblical Literature
SCS	Septuagint and cognate studies series
SJ	Studia Judaica
TA	*Tel Aviv*
TAD	Porten, Bezalel and Yardeni, Ada, *Textbook of Aramaic Documents from Ancient Egypt: Newly Copied, Edited and Translated in English I–IV.* Jerusalem, 1986–1999
Transeu	Transeuphratène
TAO	Porten, Bezalel and Yardeni, Ada, *Textbook of Aramaic Ostraca from Idumea*, Volumes 1–5. University Park, Eisenbrauns, 2014–2023
TSAJ	Texts and Studies in Ancient Judaism
VAS 3	Ungnad, *Neubabylonische Urkunden* (Sanherib, Asarhaddon, Assurbanipal, Šamaššumukīn, Kandalanu, Sin šarriškun und die Herrscher des neubabylonisches Reiches) und achämenidische Urkunden. Vorderasiatische Schriftdenkmaler 3
VT	*Vetus Testamentun*
VTSup	*Vetus Testamentum*, Supplements
WBC	Word Biblical Commentary
WUNT	Wissenschaftliche Untersuchungen zum Neuen Testament
YOS	Yale Oriental Series
ZAW	*Zeitschrift für die alttestamentliche Wissenschaft*
ZDMG	*Zeitschrift der Deutschen Morgenländischen Gesellschaft*
ZDPV	*Zeitschrift des Deutschen Palästina-Vereins*

LH	Laws of Laws of Hammurabi
Aram.	Aramaic
Arm.	Armenian
Av.	Avestan
Bact.	Bactrian
Baram.	Biblical Aramaic
BHeb.	Biblical Hebrew
CA	Classical Arabic
Choresm.	Choresmian
CPA	Christian Palesinian Aramaic

cstr. st.	construct state
d.	daughter
desc.	descendent
det.	determinate state
f.	father
gent.	gentilic
gs.	grandson
JAram.	Jewish Aramaic
JBA	Jewish Babylonian Aramaic
JPA	Jewish Palestinian Aramaic
m.	mother
Mand.	Mandaic
MPers.	Middle Persian
Nab.	Nabatean
NPers.	New Persian
OIran.	Old Iranian
OSyr.	Old Syriac
Palm.	Palmyrene
Parth.	Parthian
QA	Qumran Aramaic
s.	son
SA	Samaritan Aramaic
Sab.	Sabaic
Saf.	Safaitic
Sem.	Semitic
Sogd.	Sogdian
Targ.	a cover name for the various Jewish Aramaic translations of the scripture
w.	witness

Index

https://doi.org/10.1515/9783111018638-021